American Sp

e

David B. Biesel

1. *Effa Manley and the Newark Eagles* by James Overmyer, 1993.
2. *The United States and World Cup Competition: An Encyclopedic History of the United States in International Competition* by Colin Jose, 1994.
3. *Slide, Kelly, Slide: The Wild Life and Times of Mike "King" Kelly, Baseball's First Superstar* by Marty Appel, 1996.
4. *Baseball by the Numbers* by Mark Stang and Linda Harkness, 1997.
5. *Roller Skating for Gold* by David H. Lewis, 1997.
6. *Baseball's Biggest Blunder: The Bonus Rule of 1953–1957* by Brent Kelley, 1997.
7. *Lights On! The Wild Century-Long Saga of Night Baseball* by David Pietrusza, 1997.
8. *Windy City Wars: Labor, Leisure, and Sport in the Making of Chicago* by Gerald R. Gems, 1997.
9. *The American Soccer League 1921–1931: The Golden Years of American Soccer* by Colin Jose, 1998.
10. *The League That Failed* by David Quentin Voigt, 1998.
11. *Jimmie Foxx: The Pride of Sudlersville* by Mark R. Millikin, 1998.
12. *Baseball's Radical for All Seasons: A Biography of John Montgomery Ward* by David Stevens, 1998.
13. *College Basketball's National Championships: The Complete Record of Every Tournament Ever Played* by Morgan G. Brenner, 1998.
14. *Chris Von der Ahe and the St. Louis Browns* by J. Thomas Hetrick, 1999.
15. *Before the Glory: The Best Players in the Pre-NBA Days of Pro Basketball* by William F. Himmelman and Karel de Veer, 1999.
16. *For Pride, Profit, and Patriarchy: Football and the Incorporation of American Cultural Values* by Gerald R. Gems, 2000.
17. *Sunday at the Ballpark: Billy Sunday's Professional Baseball Career, 1883–1890* by Wendy Knickerbocker, 2000.
18. *Major Leagues* by Thomas W. Brucato, 2001.
19. *Whose Baseball? The National Pastime and Cultural Diversity in California, 1859–1941* by Joel S. Franks, 2001.
20. *The Encyclopedia of American Soccer History* by Roger Allaway, Colin Jose, David Litterer, 2001.

21. *Football's Stars of Summer: A History of the College All-Star Football Game Series of 1934–1976* by Raymond Schmidt, 2001.
22. *Major League Champions 1871-2001* by Thomas W. Brucato, 2002.
23. *Biographical Directory of Professional Basketball Coaches* by Jeff Marcus, 2003.
24. *Mel Ott: The Gentle Giant* by Alfred M. Martin, 2003.
25. *The Fierce Fun of Ducky Medwick* by Tom Barthel, 2003.
26. *History of the Junior World Series* by Bob Bailey, 2004.
27. *Border Wars: The First Fifty Years of Atlantic Coast Conference Football* by K. Adam Powell

A related title by the series editor:

Can You Name That Team? A Guide to Professional Baseball, Football, Soccer, Hockey, and Basketball Teams and Leagues by David B. Biesel, 1991.

Border Wars

The First Fifty Years of Atlantic Coast Conference Football

K. Adam Powell

American Sports History Series, No. 27

The Scarecrow Press, Inc.
Lanham, Maryland • Toronto • Oxford
2004

SCARECROW PRESS, INC.

Published in the United States of America
by Scarecrow Press, Inc.
A wholly owned subsidiary of
The Rowman & Littlefield Publishing Group, Inc.
4501 Forbes Boulevard, Suite 200, Lanham, Maryland 20706
www.scarecrowpress.com

PO Box 317, Oxford, OX2 9RU, UK

British Library Cataloguing in Publication Information Available

Library of Congress Cataloging-in-Publication Data

Powell, K. Adam, 1979–
    Border wars : the first fifty years of Atlantic Coast Conference football / K.
Adam Powell.
        p. cm.—(American sports history ; no.27)
    Includes bibliographical references and index.
    ISBN 0-8108-4839-2 (alk. paper)
    1. Atlantic Coast Conference. 2. Football—South Atlantic States. I. Title. II.
Series.
GV958.5.A75 P69 2004
796.332/0975 22   2004041460

♾™ The paper used in this publication meets the minimum requirements of
American National Standard for Information Sciences—Permanence of
Paper for Printed Library Materials, ANSI/NISO Z39.48-1992.
Manufactured in the United States of America.

For my Mom and Dad, who always instilled in me the belief that I could do something like this.

Contents

Acknowledgments   ix
Foreword   xi
Introduction   xv

1	A New League, a New Champion (1953)	1
2	Breaking Ground (1954-1959)	9
3	A Devil of a Dynasty (1960-1962)	37
4	An Era of Change (1963-1968)	51
5	One-Hit Wonders (1969-1970)	83
6	Blue Heaven (1971-1972)	95
7	Red Tide (1973-1976)	109
8	Running Wild (1977-1980)	135
9	Orange Crush (1981)	163
10	A Two-Team League (1982-1988)	175
11	Breaking Through (1989)	217
12	Wrecking Crew (1990)	229
13	A New Arrival (1991-2000)	241
14	A Half Century Comes to an End (2001-2002)	323
15	The Future of Atlantic Coast Conference Football	347

Appendix A: Coaching Records   361
Appendix B: Season Records   365
Bibliography   383
Index   393
About the Author   420

Acknowledgments

In this, my first probe into the world of nonfiction sportswriting, there are a great number of people to whom I owe thanks. It has taken the hard work of a lot of people for this project to become a reality, and it would be both naive and irresponsible of me to deny these individuals the credit they deserve.

A very special "Thank You" goes to Woody Durham, who has written the foreword to my book. As the voice of the University of North Carolina football team for more than three decades, Mr. Durham has experienced many of the great moments in this book on a personal level. Woody was my first choice all along for the foreword, and his contribution brings credibility and wisdom the likes of which few others could have provided.

Another special thanks goes to Dr. Jerry Punch, who provided me with personal reflections from his experiences as a member of the North Carolina State football team in the early 1970s and as a college football analyst for ABC and ESPN. Dr. Punch's stories about Bobby Bowden, Lou Holtz, Chuck Amato, and Ralph Friedgen are the kind of insightful, thought-provoking material that I craved to include in this book. I won't soon forget our softball victory in Kentucky over the Craftsman Truck drivers, Doc! No mercy!

I must also acknowledge the nine member institutions of the Atlantic Coast Conference and the Sports Information Offices of each school. In addition, there are a number of individuals that I would like to thank singularly. Clemson University; Stephanie Adams and Mike Kohl; Duke University; Thomas Harkins; Florida State University; Beverly McNeil; Georgia Institute of Technology; Allison George; North Carolina State University; Hermann Trojanowski and Bernard McTigue; University of Maryland; Anne Turkos; University of North Carolina; Steve Kirschner and Kevin Best; Wake Forest University; Lisa Persinger; University Photo Services of Chapel Hill, NC.

Foreword

In its first fifty years, the Atlantic Coast Conference won nearly ninety national championships. The most were earned by women's soccer at North Carolina, but more attention was given to the nine titles in basketball captured by North Carolina, Duke, N.C. State, and Maryland. They certainly got more headlines than the five top spots in football occupied through the years by Maryland, Clemson, Georgia Tech, and Florida State.

In fact, the league's first national championship in its very first year of 1953 was won by Jim Tatum's football Terrapins at Maryland. He was one of the ACC's four Hall of Fame coaches, along with Clemson's Frank Howard, Bill Murray of Duke, and Jerry Claiborne from Maryland. Tatum guided the Terps to a top-three finish for three straight years before returning to North Carolina, his alma mater. Three other coaches also worked at different conference schools.

Bill Dooley, the third winningest coach in league history, spent eleven years at North Carolina before going to Virginia Tech for nine years and then spending his last six years at Wake Forest. Bobby Ross was at Maryland for five years, but spent the next five years at Georgia Tech. It was there he guided the Yellow Jackets to a share of the national championship in 1990, just eight years after the Atlanta school came into the loop. Al Groh got his first head coaching position at Wake Forest in the early 1980s, but he has now found his way back to Virginia, his alma mater.

Overall, counting South Carolina, which dropped out following the 1970-1971 season, there have been eighty head football coaches in the ACC, but only one at Florida State. Bobby Bowden was there when the Seminoles helped expand the conference in 1992. During the school's first eleven years in the league, his teams went 83-5 against ACC opponents, won eight league titles outright, shared two others, and captured two national championships in 1993 and 1999. Since joining the conference, Florida State has produced twenty of the sixty-nine All-Americans from the ACC, as well as two Heisman Trophy winners. Quarterback Charlie Ward won the honor in 1993, and Chris Weinke, another signal caller, was the winner in 2000.

Florida State's entry into the league was certainly one of the milestones in the development of ACC football. The first came in 1956, when TV producer Castleman D. Chesley put together a four-game package on Saturday afternoons. He would later bring regional and national exposure to ACC basketball. In 1960, the conference adopted a minimum SAT score of 750 for incoming student-athletes. By 1964, the bar had been raised to 800, which was higher than the national standard adopted by the NCAA. The higher SAT score had a negative effect on recruiting, and in 1971 it forced the withdrawal of South Carolina. Both athletic director and head football coach Paul Dietzel and head basketball coach Frank McGuire later blamed each other for the move, which turned out to be a big mistake for the Gamecocks.

In the mid-1960s, Maryland broke the ACC color barrier when Navy transfer Darryl Hill was accepted for admission in College Park. The six-foot wingback was a good player for Tom Nugent, with forty-three catches in 1963 for 516 yards and seven touchdowns. A short time later, Bill Tate, a former Illinois assistant, was recruiting African Americans as the new head coach at Wake Forest. Freddie Summers, a junior college transfer, was Tate's starting quarterback, and no other predominantly white university in the South had a black in that position prior to 1967.

Clemson was a big surprise in 1981. Coming off a 6-5 season in Danny Ford's third season as head coach, the Tigers knocked off defending national champion Georgia, 13-3, in the third game of the season, snapping the Dawgs' fifteen-game winning streak. Ninth-ranked North Carolina, the league's other Top Ten entry, was the eighth victim, 10-8, on national television. Consecutive victories over Maryland and South Carolina followed.

Then, when Penn State beat Pittsburgh, the Tigers moved into No. 1 as the nation's only undefeated squad. Clemson wrapped up the national championship with a 22-15 decision against Nebraska in the Orange Bowl. However, the celebration was tainted by a two-year probation imposed by the NCAA and a three-year ban of postseason bowl participation levied by the Atlantic Coast Conference. It was one of the circuit's darkest moments, and certainly the blackest in its football history.

A number of books have documented various stages of the ACC's first fifty years, but only a few have been written about the exploits in football, and three of those have dealt specifically with South Carolina, Georgia Tech, and Florida State. Now K. Adam Powell, who describes himself simply as a young fan, has undertaken the chore of detailing the last half century of ACC football.

Many of the events unfolded and games were played before he was born, but he has spent the past two years doing extensive research for *Border Wars* from the very beginning until the present. The familiarity he has gained with this subject even allows him the luxury of looking into the future. None of us really know what the future holds for ACC football, but it could be an even more exciting time with new teams and new thrills over the next fifty years.

Woody Durham
Tar Heel Sports Network

Introduction

In October 1888, football was introduced to the Southern United States when Wake Forest College and the University of North Carolina challenged each other to a game at the Raleigh Fairgrounds. Wake Forest won that day by a score of 6-4, and a month later Trinity College, the predecessor to Duke University, also triumphed against UNC, taking a 16-0 score on Thanksgiving Day in front of 600 spectators. These were the first intercollegiate football contests played south of the Mason-Dixon Line. Although history disputes which game actually came first, the round-robin series of games played between the three schools that autumn and the following autumn helped form the North Carolina Intercollegiate Football Association (NCIFA), the first alliance of football-playing institutions in the South.

The Americanized version of gridiron football, derived from the European games of soccer and rugby, spread quickly through the growing United States in the years following the Civil War and Reconstruction. By the turn of the century, several major universities had aligned with other schools to form athletic conferences. In 1922, the Southern Conference (SC) was formed as a result of discord between the members of the Southern Intercollegiate Athletic Association (SIAA). The SIAA had grown to twenty-nine members by 1920, and the disparity between the larger and smaller schools necessitated the formation of the new league.

For three decades, the Southern Conference showcased some of the best amateur football in America, and throughout much of the early part of the twentieth century, the league stood supreme in that region of the country. That changed somewhat in 1933, when thirteen schools left to create the Southeastern Conference, leaving ten schools in the old league. Nonetheless, the SC continued to expand, adding six schools in 1936 and George Washington and West Virginia in the

1940s.

By the end of the 1940s, the Southern Conference was back up to seventeen schools. In the coming years, many schools grew tired of policies instituted by the league's governing body. The larger schools, many of which had stadiums that held 30,000 or more, could not justify scheduling road games against the smaller schools, which had stadiums that held 10,000 or less. In addition, Southern Conference officials voted in 1951 to eliminate bowl participation from its teams. If a team in the conference went on to play in a postseason game, as the University of Maryland did following the 1951 season, that school would face a one-year probation, in which they were disallowed to play other teams in the conference.

In the early morning hours of May 8, 1953, at the annual Southern Conference spring meeting, seven institutions elected to break away and form a new league. After eight hours of deliberation at the Sedgfield Inn in Greensboro, N.C., Clemson University, Duke University, the University of Maryland, the University of North Carolina, North Carolina State University, Wake Forest University, and the University of South Carolina voted to pull out. Five weeks later, the schools met again in Raleigh and agreed on a set of bylaws and a new name. Due to the geographical locations of the respective schools, it was agreed that the new league would be named the Atlantic Coast Conference (ACC).

In December of that year, the University of Virginia became the ACC's eighth member. Unlike its new conference foes, UVA had decided to leave the Southern after the 1936 season, and had been an Independent ever since. In departing, the schools agreed that it was no longer economically feasible to continue providing support for the smaller colleges. In addition, the size of the Southern Conference created scheduling problems for everyone. With so many schools, it was entirely possible for someone to win the SC without having to play any of the superior teams in the league. The Southern Conference lasts to the present day, and plays solid football in the Division I-AA ranks.

Clemson University (CU) rests on the bottom edge of South Carolina's Blue Ridge Mountains, tucked between Charlotte and Atlanta. Tom Clemson, the son-in-law of former vice president John C. Calhoun, donated the land for the university, and in 1893 the school began accepting students. A military school for its first sixty years, the sleepy town of Clemson comes to life in autumn, when thousands follow the trail of orange Tiger paws on the way to Memorial Stadium. On game days, Clemson becomes one of the most populated towns in the state of South Carolina.

Trinity College became Duke University in 1924, when tobacco mogul James B. Duke donated much of his wealth to the school in remembrance of his father. The Methodist institution had settled in Durham, N.C. three decades earlier. Duke is regarded for its world-class instruction, particularly in the fields of medicine and law, and its campus, which combines Georgian and Gothic architecture. Duke's impressive chapel can be seen for miles around and stands as the official symbol of the school.

The University of Maryland (UM) was founded just outside Washington, D.C. on property owned by Charles Calvert. Calvert was an heir of Lord Baltimore, who had founded the state of Maryland in the seventeenth century. The nickname "Terrapin" came from Harry Clifton "Curley" Byrd, who over several decades worked his way up from Maryland's quarterback to the school's president. When students suggested the idea of changing the school's name from the "Old Liners," Byrd thought of the Terrapin, a turtle native to the area known for its aggression. The stadium on UM's College Park campus is named after Byrd, who helped design and raise funds for the facility.

The University of North Carolina (UNC) lies in Chapel Hill, a small community nestled among the pine trees of the state's Piedmont region. As one of the oldest state universities in the nation, founded in 1789, UNC has long stood for excellence in the liberal arts. There are various accounts for how the nickname "Tar Heels" came into use. Some have said it dates all the way back to Revolutionary times, when tar was dumped into rivers to slow impeding British forces. Others tie it to the Civil War, when a patch of North Carolina troops fighting for the Confederacy fought diligently against Union forces. General Robert E. Lee was said to have uttered the words "There they stand as if they have tar on their heels," and later, "God Bless the Tar Heel Boys."

North Carolina State University (NCSU) lies in the capital city of Raleigh, and was established in 1889 as an agricultural school. Known for its first twenty-five years as the "Aggies," or "Farmers," N.C. State is a national leader in textiles, farming, and engineering. The name "Wolfpack" was derived from an angry spectator in the early 1920s, who claimed that the State fans acted like they were a pack of wolves during games. The nickname was nearly turned over in the 1940s, when the chancellor argued that "Wolfpack" was the name used to describe groups of Nazi submarines. The students outvoted the chancellor, and the moniker has stuck over the ensuing years.

The University of Virginia (UVA) was established and run by some of the most influential men in American history. Thomas Jefferson founded the school in 1819, and two more Virginians who became president of the United States, James Madison and James Monroe, served on the school's Board of Governors. Virginia's football program consistently ranks as one of the nation's elite in both academic performance and graduation rates among its players.

Wake Forest University (WFU) was originally located in the town of Wake Forest, just outside of Raleigh, on a plantation owned by Calvin Jones. In 1956, the Baptist institution was relocated to Winston-Salem, and its Georgian-style buildings give the impression that the school has been there for centuries. Wake Forest, like many of its conference adversaries, has a reputation for solid academics and an elegant layout.

The ACC competed with seven members throughout most of the 1970s and into the 1980s, despite the fact that the Georgia Institute of Technology accepted an invitation into the league in 1978. Georgia Tech (GT) had been playing ACC schools for decades on the gridiron, and had also been a member of both the SIAA and Southern Conference. The Yellow Jackets became an official member of the league on July 1, 1979, and began playing conference games in 1983. Georgia Tech lies in downtown Atlanta, located along Highway I-85. Founded in 1885, Georgia Tech is respected for its work in mechanical and civil engineering. Also known as the "Ramblin' Wreck," Georgia Tech still holds the record for the most lopsided victory in the history of college football, a 222-0 blowout of Tennessee's Cumberland College in 1916.

In 1991, Florida State University (FSU) became the league's ninth school. A power in the sport of football, FSU has brought unparalleled national respect to the Atlantic Coast Conference on the gridiron, claiming a pair of National Collegiate Athletic Association (NCAA) championships and producing the only two players in league history to win the Heisman Trophy, regarded as the most coveted individual honor in all of intercollegiate athletics. John Heisman, the man for which the trophy is named, spent time during his distinguished coaching career at both Georgia Tech and Clemson, and helped both of those schools establish football traditions in the years prior to the founding of the ACC.

Florida State University was founded in 1851 as one of two seminary colleges in the Sunshine State. Originally named the Florida Institute in Tallahassee, FSU was primarily a women's college until the 1940s, when the name was officially changed to Florida State. The nickname "Seminoles" comes from the tribe of Native Americans that inhabited much of the region in and around Tallahassee in pre-

Revolutionary times. From their first season of ACC membership in 1992 to the league's silver anniversary campaign of 2002, Florida State won 116 football games, more than any other Division I-A program with the exception of the University of Nebraska.

Over the years, the ACC has established long-standing ties to two of college football's most prestigious postseason games, Atlanta's Peach Bowl and the Gator Bowl, located in Jacksonville, Florida. In addition, the league sent its annual champion for many years to Orlando's Citrus Bowl, where they met and defeated some of the finest football programs in all of college football, such as Penn State, Nebraska, and Oklahoma. Over the course of the league's first five seasons, the ACC champion went to Miami's Orange Bowl, where they met an opponent from the Big Seven, the precursor to today's Big Twelve. In its first half century, the ACC was represented in every major bowl with the exception of the Rose Bowl, and in 122 total games, the league produced a 60-60-2 record against all opponents.

Over the years, the ACC has bred some of the finest defensive players in the history of modern football. Defensive linemen Stan Jones and Randy White of Maryland, along with linebacker Lawrence Taylor of North Carolina, each went on to Hall of Fame careers in the National Football League, while Duke's Mike Curtis, Clemson's William "The Refrigerator" Perry and Terry Kinard, and North Carolina's Dre' Bly each contributed on teams that won the Super Bowl. White and Taylor were also Super Bowl champions, and both were named to the NFL's Seventy-Fifth Anniversary Team in 1994.

In recent years, the ACC has featured a number of talented players on both sides of the ball, and many have gone on to find success in the professional ranks. With Florida State bringing athletes into the league unparalleled to any other time in history, the conference became a reservoir of talent in the 1990s and into the new century. Florida State has sent a number of its finest players into the pros, including Tamarick Vanover, Marvin Jones, Derrick Brooks, Warrick Dunn, Peter Warrick, Corey Simon, and Chris Weinke. The rest of the league has been forced to improve their own rosters in order to compete with the Seminoles, and as a result, other schools have produced their own standouts. With Virginia's Tiki and Ronde Barber, North Carolina's Julius Peppers, and N.C. State's Torry Holt and Koren Robinson all making significant contributions to professional teams in recent years, it can be expected that the ACC will continue to cultivate players capable of playing football at the highest level well into the future.

More important than the Atlantic Coast Conference's consistent level of excellent play is the integrity of its member schools. No football program in the league has faced major sanctions from the NCAA since the infamous "Death Penalty" ruling administered to Southern Methodist University in 1987. Clemson is the only ACC program that has served probation for major rules violations related specifically to football, but the Tigers have cleaned up their act. Clemson has not faced any major sanctions by the NCAA in the two decades following the school's original investigation in 1982.

With its combination of academic and athletic excellence, the Atlantic Coast Conference has become one of the most respected bodies in all of intercollegiate athletics. Although the ACC is more regarded for basketball than any other sport, the league has enjoyed its share of success on the gridiron. Four different schools have won national championships in football, and the league boasts five NCAA titles as a whole. League members are frequently featured on ESPN and the major networks, and the conference's affiliation with the Bowl Championship Series assures the annual champion a berth in one of the four major postseason games, which brings an annual payout well into the millions.

With expansion on the horizon, the ACC only looks to be getting stronger, and the next fifty years could bring unparalleled growth to a circuit already used to tremendous success from its athletic teams. From Jim Tatum's powerhouse Maryland teams of the early 1950s, to Bobby Bowden's run of excellence at Florida State in the 1990s, the ACC has left an indelible mark on football fans of the Southeastern United States over the last half century. This is an account of the players, coaches, and schools that have created this legacy of football distinction.

1

A New League, a New Champion (1953)

On September 19, 1953, over 30,000 fans braved wind and a dark Columbia sky for the Atlantic Coast Conference's first football game, a contest between Duke and South Carolina. In the first quarter, Duke's Worth Lutz faked a handoff and pitched to Red Smith, who scored the ACC's first touchdown on a 4-yard play. Lutz ran in a sneak and set up another score in the Blue Devils' 20-7 victory over the Gamecocks.

Duke's squad was solid in 1953, but in a pattern that would follow over several years, the Blue Devils were unable to topple Uncle Sam. In a classic confrontation at New York's Polo Grounds, Army knocked off the Blue Devils, 14-13, on a last-second goal line stand. With less than three minutes left and the ball on their own 20-yard line, Lutz handed off to Bob Pascal, who pitched to Smith. Smith was streaking in the opposite direction, and raced 73 yards on the double reverse before being hauled down at the 7. Duke tried four consecutive sneak plays but Army held, corralling Lutz two inches short on fourth down. Following the play, over 2,000 Cadets ran onto the field and carried their comrades off to the locker rooms.

Three weeks later the Blue Devils and Navy played to a scoreless tie, the first of four stalemates between the schools over the next five seasons. On a freezing afternoon in Baltimore, the fans sat through twenty-one punts and very little offense. The loss and tie to the service academies, along with a setback to Georgia Tech, gave Duke no hope of a national championship.

Duke did manage to win all four of its league games, and tied for the first Atlantic Coast Conference football championship with Maryland. Because of scheduling done years earlier, the Blue Devils and

Terrapins were not scheduled to meet on the gridiron until 1957. Most observers, however, were unanimous in agreement that the Blue Devils would have stood little chance against Jim Tatum's mighty Terrapins. Tatum built a football powerhouse at Maryland in the late 1940s and early 1950s with a team bent from his own image. Tatum was an unparalleled worker, often putting in eighteen or twenty-hour days preparing for opponents. Tatum was also intensely devoted to the cause of his teams.

During his playing days at the University of North Carolina, Tatum was once asked to go into a game and take a punch from a hotheaded opposing player, in hopes that the yards gained would spearhead a touchdown drive. Tatum did his job, calling the player an expletive before being decked. When he came to, he was told that the Tar Heels completed a touchdown pass on the play, and the penalty Tatum caused had to be declined!

It was that kind of dedication that marked Tatum's teams at Maryland. Tatum, who never had a losing season in College Park, got the ball rolling in 1947 with seven wins and a 3-0-1 mark in the Southern Conference. The season culminated in a 20-20 tie against Georgia in the Gator Bowl. After winning the Gator Bowl in 1949, Tatum's 1951 team completed an undefeated season with a Sugar Bowl victory over No. 1 Tennessee. The Terrapins would have easily claimed the national championship in the modern era, but in those days the title was awarded before the bowls.

"Jim Tatum was the big man," said Bob Ward, captain of Maryland's 1951 team. "It was just such a pleasure to play at Maryland for such a wonderful coach. He was the best that ever lived. He knew how to handle people, to recruit great players and he had great connections all over the east. We had a lot of big players go through that cycle."

In 1953, the Terrapins put together another strong side. Tackle Stan Jones, a Pennsylvanian with a furious pass rush and instinctive ability to shut down the run, anchored Maryland's defensive line. Jones got help from sophomore Bob Pelligrini and senior Blubber Morgan. Quarterback Bernie Faloney, the first Atlantic Coast Conference Player of the Year, orchestrated Tatum's Split-T offense, which averaged 359.5 yards a game. A stellar offensive line, anchored by John Irvine and Jack Bowersox, gave the backfield all the room they needed to operate. The Terrapin line was so dominating that Faloney threw only 68 times all season, completing 31 for 599 yards and 5 touchdowns.

Equally vital to the Maryland's success was the execution of the special teams. In nearly every game Maryland could count on a big play from the punt or kickoff unit, as explosive runners such as Ron Waller, Ralph Felton, and Dick Nolan provided many a thrill for Terrapin fans. Halfback Chet Hanulak also returned punts, and received the lion's share of the running load. He did not disappoint, averaging 9.78 yards per carry, an ACC record that has stood for half a century.

Hanulak's story was an interesting one, for he was not highly pursued during his days at Hackensack High School in New Jersey. At 160 pounds, Hanulak did not engender much promise for future development. In a coincidental turn of events, a Maryland alumnus met Hackensack's coach while the two were taking summer courses at Columbia University. The conversation between the two men eventually turned to football, and the alumnus, named Santonelli, asked the coach if he knew of any talent. The coach told Santonelli about Hanulak, and before the summer was over, Chet was preparing to report for freshman football at College Park. In 1953, Hanulak emerged into one of the top backs in the country. Thriving in Tatum's Split-T set, "Chet the Jet" ate up huge chunks of yardage both up the middle and to the outside.

In the season opener against Missouri, Hanulak scored on a 61-yard sprint less than two minutes into the game. Breaking through a large hole up the gut, Hanulak broke right and veered down the left sideline, going in untouched. The Terrapins intercepted four Tony Scardino passes, and although they coughed up three fumbles, Maryland cruised to a 20-7 victory.

In their second game, the Terrapins pounded former SC rival Washington and Lee into oblivion. After making a diving interception, Hanulak switched sides and scored on a 12-yard sprint. Later, Waller turned near disaster into another breathtaking score. Receiving a Washington and Lee punt, Waller dropped the ball at the 50-yard line. After fielding the pigskin Waller cut right, and coasted the rest of the way as the Maryland blockers laid out General after General. By the second half Tatum had his starting unit on the sidelines, as his third and fourth-string players finished out the game. The 52-0 shutout was the first of six that the Terrapin defense would register on the season.

Clemson was next to feel Maryland's wrath, and they felt it in the most punishing of ways. The Tigers were not only shut out at home for the first time in eleven years, but they also lost their quarterback to the grips of the Terrapin front. Late in the second quarter, a host of Maryland defenders drilled CU signal caller Don King, wrenching his knee and ending his afternoon. Faloney had already gotten Maryland going with an 88-yard touchdown return on the opening kickoff.

With forty-five seconds left in the half, Nolan found the end zone again for the Terrapins. Catching a Clemson punt at the 10, Nolan broke through a horde of orange tacklers and zipped downfield with five Tigers on his tail. At the Clemson 35, Nolan cut back toward the opposite sideline, and thanks to a crushing block by Dick Shipley, he found daylight and scored. Tatum was worried that his team may overlook Clemson in anticipation of their contest the following week against Georgia. He didn't have to worry, as the UM defense stifled the Tigers, allowing CU to complete only two passes. In the second half Maryland scored a final time on a 65-yard pass from Faloney to Nolan. After hauling in the catch, Nolan was once again the beneficiary of a big block.

Maryland had displayed their big-play capability over the first three games, with individual plays of 61, 65, 88, and 90 yards. Still, there were worries that the Terrapins could not sustain drives and hang onto the football against better opposition. Against Georgia, the Terrapins answered many of their critics. They raced out to an early 14-0 edge, keyed by an offense that kept Georgia and their talented signal-caller, Zeke "The Brat" Bratkowski, off the field. In the first quarter the Bulldogs ran only six offensive plays, and two were punts. In the second quarter the Brat finally got it going, and became one of the few players all season to find success against the vaunted Maryland defense. He led Georgia on back-to-back scoring drives, and it was a 21-13 game at the half.

If there were any doubts as to the game's outcome at halftime, Faloney quickly ended them two minutes into the third quarter. Playing cornerback, Bernie raced in front of Bratkowski's first pass and ran it back to give Maryland a 27-13 advantage. Faloney's touchdown proved to be the turning point of the game, as the Terrapins began unloading on the Brat. Jones and Morgan eventually knocked Bratkowski out of the game, as they consistently beat their respective blockers and met at the quarterback. Finally, after a particularly violent hit, the officials took the Brat out of his misery. Maryland tacked on another pair of scores and left the field with a convincing 40-13 victory. Dominant as the victory was, it was the most points the Terrapins would give up in a game all year.

Maryland headed to Chapel Hill the following week for a showdown of unbeaten teams. The Tar Heels had been impressive in three victories, but the Maryland boys made certain that Tatum's homecoming to North Carolina was not a letdown. The Terps put together scoring drives of 69, 72, 85, and 92 yards, ending much of the doubt about their inability to hold onto the football. Faloney sustained a minor injury in the first quarter, and for the rest of the game he resorted to handing the ball off.

In a game marred by penalties, with 227 yards racked up against the two squads, a pair of 15-yard UNC infractions set up Maryland's first score, a sneak by Faloney. Just before halftime, Maryland scored again on a sneak by backup Charlie Boxhold. The touchdown was set up by a run from Bill Walker, who caught a poorly thrown pitch at his own 35 and was finally brought down at the Carolina 16. Hanulak put the game away in the third quarter when he took a wide pitch, cut upfield, and broke away from three UNC defenders on the way to a 34-yard rumble. After the game, a 26-0 Terrapin victory, a jubilant Tatum was carried off the field. It was Maryland's first victory over UNC in Chapel Hill since 1924. Later, he called it "the greatest win of any team I have ever coached, including the Sugar Bowl."

Maryland's next game was against Miami in the Orange Bowl, a stadium the Terrapins were hoping to return to in January. In an early scoring barrage, Maryland tacked on 27 points in the first twenty minutes. Taking advantage of Miami turnovers, Faloney led the Terrapins to a 14-0 advantage nine minutes in. Hanulak got it going with a 2-yard score, and after Morgan recovered a Miami fumble, Faloney found the end zone on an 8-yard sprint. By the time the shell-shocked Hurricanes recovered, it was a lost cause. Tatum, always the sportsman, ordered his players not to throw any passes or run trick plays in the second half.

The 30-0 victory over Miami set up a showdown with South Carolina in Columbia. The Gamecocks had won four in a row coming into the contest, and figured to pose some problems for UM. It only took twelve minutes for the Terrapins to take control, as Ralph Felton ended a long drive with a smash over the goal line. On their next possession the Gamecocks were forced to punt. Hanulak caught the ball at the 35, plowed over a South Carolina defender, and raced into the clear. Jack Bowersox threw a nasty block to give the Jet all the room he needed to score. The touchdown gave Maryland an insurmountable advantage of 14-0.

Although Maryland didn't prosper offensively for much of the game, they held the Gamecocks to a grand total of 37 yards rushing. South Carolina got a golden opportunity in the second quarter, recovering a fumble on the Maryland 14. In impressive fashion, the Terrapin defense began pushing the Gamecocks backwards, getting back 18 yards of field position in three plays. Although they finally scored on their next possession, South Carolina got no closer. Tatum played his backups generously in the second half, and the Terps cruised to a 24-6 victory.

Ranked No. 2 in the country, the Terrapins next traveled to George

Washington (GW). In the second quarter GW sophomore Lou Donofrio intercepted a Faloney pass and returned it to the Maryland 18. On third-and-8 from the 16, quarterback Bob Sturn tossed the ball to halfback Bill Weaver, who found Richie Gaskell alone in the end zone. The extra point attempt was wide, but George Washington was in the game. The Colonials held Maryland to a single first half score, and went into halftime trailing only 7-6.

George Washington took the second half kick and began moving downfield again, poised to take the lead. With the ball at midfield Gaskell, who scored GW's touchdown, committed a stupid penalty. Gaskell threw a blatant elbow at Walker, taking away a large gain. The penalty stunned the inspired Colonials, and from there the Terrapins took control. Walker, angered by Gaskell's penalty, raced through and partially blocked a punt, which Felton picked up and returned to the George Washington 36. Two plays later, Hanulak ran off right tackle and found a gap, racing his way to a 32-yard score that put the game on ice. Walker set up another Maryland touchdown later with a vicious hit on Weaver, who coughed up the ball. Faloney recovered on the 11, and on fourth down the quarterback sneaked his way over the goal line. A late touchdown made the final score 27-6, as the Terrapin defense once again completely shut down their opponent's running game. Jones, Morgan, John Irvine, and George Palanunik pounded GW's offensive line, and helped hold the Colonials to 33 yards rushing.

Next for Maryland was Mississippi, who had beaten the Terrapins, 21-14, the season before in Oxford to end their nineteen-game winning streak. It was a bitter pill for Maryland to swallow, and with an Orange Bowl berth at stake this time around, revenge was exacted on the Rebels. Despite a slow early start, Maryland jumped out to a 17-0 lead at the half. In the second quarter Felton sprinted 41 yards for a score, keyed by a block from Ron Waller. As the defense pitched its fifth shutout in nine games, the offense pummeled Ole Miss on the ground. The 38-0 win propelled Maryland into another revenge game the following week against Alabama.

Maryland went for its second undefeated regular season in three years under tumultuous skies, as a cloudy haze surrounded Byrd Stadium. The Crimson Tide, like Mississippi, had beaten Maryland in 1952, but on this rain-soaked afternoon, the Terrapins had everything go their way. After forcing an Alabama punt, Maryland needed only two plays to score. From their own 19, the ball was given to Hanulak. After breaking through the Crimson line, the Jet shed a tackler and flew into the clear, trucking 81 yards to the end zone.

Alabama tried to shut down Maryland's powerful running on their next possession by employing an eight-man line. Faloney faked a running play and found Walker streaking down the sideline. Walker hauled in the pass and raced 53 yards for the score. Tatum used many of his second-stringers on defense in the second quarter, and they played nearly as well as the regulars, keeping the Crimson Tide from moving offensively. With a minute left in the first half, a pair of Alabama defenders nailed Faloney after he completed a pass to Hanulak. The impact blew out his knee, and the crowd stood in silence as Maryland's signal caller was carried off. Bernie's day was done, but Boxhold got the Terps another touchdown when he found Walker for his second score of the afternoon. After a scoreless second half, the game ended with Maryland in command of a 21-0 lead.

After the game the crowd remained surprisingly reserved, even after hearing over public address that No. 1 Notre Dame had tied Iowa, 14-14. Although Maryland now stood as the only unbeaten-untied team in the country, Faloney's injury made the victory bittersweet. Faloney would try to make a recovery, but the signal caller reinjured his knee in practice, eliminating any hope of his suiting up on New Year's Day.

Maryland's opponent in the Orange Bowl was the University of Oklahoma (OU), who had posted a regular season mark of 8-1-1. The Sooners nearly upset Notre Dame in their season opener, and tied Pittsburgh 7-7 in their second game. Oklahoma won their final eight contests behind a dominant running attack and a physical defense. Experts predicted a defensive struggle between the two schools, as Faloney's absence created a glaring hole in the Maryland offense.

The Orange Bowl was an intriguing encounter for Tatum, who had spent the 1946 season in Norman as head coach of the Sooners. On his interview for the OU job, Tatum had brought along Bud Wilkinson, an assistant from a team he was coaching in the military. Oklahoma President Dr. George Cross was particularly impressed with Wilkinson, and ordered Tatum to add him to the OU staff upon his acceptance of the head coaching position. Tatum's season in Norman, though successful, was filled with turmoil. Following OU's victory over North Carolina State in the Gator Bowl, President Cross learned that Tatum had paid each of his players a small sum of cash. The two men struggled for power of the program, and in the end, Cross chose to work out a deal that would get his program a new coach.

Cross contacted Maryland President H. C. "Curley" Byrd, and learned that the school was interested in hiring Tatum away. Eager to replace Tatum with Wilkinson, Cross purposely offered a contract that the coach did not accept. Tatum jumped ship to College Park shortly thereafter, and Oklahoma got its guy. The saga did not end there, as the Sooner athletic director was soon fired for his supposed lack of knowledge that Tatum had overspent his budget by more than $100,000. Tatum demanded that Cross issue a statement on behalf of Oklahoma saying he had nothing to do with the situation, but after talking again with Byrd, it was agreed that Tatum would keep the matter quiet.

With all the sidebars leading into the contest, it was easy to forget that two outstanding football teams would play on the field of the Orange Bowl. The game proved to be a brutal struggle, as the Terrapins and Sooners fought bitterly for field position and points. On their second possession, Maryland drove to the Oklahoma 4 behind Boxhold, but the Sooners held out the Terrapins on three consecutive plays. Tatum elected to go for six on fourth down, but Felton was met at the goal line and stopped short.

In all, Maryland drove eight times into Oklahoma territory over the course of the game. They could not find the end zone or the goalposts a single time. Two field goal attempts were missed, and one march was ended by a fumble. Hanulak, Maryland's steadiest performer all season, was manhandled by the Sooners, and held to his lowest output of the year. In the second quarter, Oklahoma drove for the game's only score. From the Terrapin 28, Larry Griggs hauled in an option pitch and rambled through the Maryland defense, which had allowed only 31 points all season. The touchdown was all Oklahoma needed, and the Sooners held on for a 7-0 victory over the stunned Terrapins.

The win, which happened to be the first shutout over a Maryland team in fifty-one contests, propelled Oklahoma into an era of football glory no major college program has enjoyed before or since. Over the next four seasons, the Sooners won forty-seven consecutive games, establishing a standard of excellence that has not been equaled. In an era when college football determined its champion based on regular season play alone, the Terrapins were the NCAA champs before they even stepped onto the field against the Sooners. Maryland was clearly the best team in the country before Bernie Faloney's injury, and although they would never know the outcome of a game against Oklahoma with the starting quarterback under center, UM had a clear case for No. 1.

2

Breaking Ground (1954-1959)

Duke claimed the ACC's second championship in 1954 with a perfect 4-0 mark against league opposition. Although Maryland returned several starters from its national championship squad, the Terrapins were unable to repeat the magic of 1953. Setbacks to UCLA and Miami in a pair of road encounters eliminated UM's hopes of finishing atop the polls again. Although they spent much of the year ranked in the Top Ten, a 13-13 tie at Wake Forest in their third game prevented Maryland from another share of the ACC title. The Terrapins led the league in total offense and total defense, and their 74 points against Missouri in November set a one-game ACC scoring record that would last for nearly three decades.

The Blue Devils were a solid outfit in 1954, led by quarterback Jerry Barger and a host of talented sidekicks. Junior Bob Pascal was a threat from anywhere on the field in Bill Murray's multiple-back offense. Leading the team with 561 rushing yards and 10 touchdowns, Pascal was even called upon to throw the occasional pass. Duke also employed the services of Worth Lutz and Fred Beasley, a pair of versatile backs who could run and catch. Ed Post was Pascal's favorite receiving target, and made a number of important receptions over the course of the year.

Everything went right for Duke against Penn's Quakers up in Philadelphia. As the Blue Devil defense pitched a shutout, the offensive units put up Duke's highest point total in two years in the 52-0 blowout. Following the Penn triumph, the Blue Devils snuck past Tennessee, 7-6, to take their third victory in a row in the series with the Volunteers, and then met Purdue, who featured Len Dawson and the No. 1

passing attack in the nation. Duke jumped out to an early 13-0 lead, but Dawson paced a furious Purdue charge, leading a pair of scoring drives to seal a 13-13 tie.

Hurricane Hazel ripped its way through the North Carolina coast the day before Duke's encounter with Army, and the Devils wound up wishing the game had been postponed indefinitely. The Blue Devils took their first loss mostly as a result of Red Blaik's powerful running game, which became the first all season to put a dent in the Blue Devil defensive armor. With Pete Lash, Mike Zeigler, and Pete Vann all scoring, Army took a 28-14 victory.

North Carolina State came out of the gates strong against Duke in Raleigh, taking the opening kickoff for the game's first touchdown. While the defense shut down State for the remainder of the contest, Pascal scored twice to put the Blue Devils ahead to stay, which included a 51-yard sprint to the goal line. Later, Barger hit Post from 62 yards away to give Duke a 21-7 win. The loss was N.C. State's sixth in a row since joining the ACC, and continued their winless streak at the hands of the Blue Devils that dated back to 1947.

The Georgia Tech game proved to be an inspiration for Duke, as the Blue Devils overcame a 20-0 second half deficit for their fourth victory. The blue and white began their stirring comeback late in the third quarter, and with less than a minute to play, Post hauled in a scoring pass to pull the teams level. Jim Nelson's eleventh consecutive extra point gave Duke a 21-20 victory, as the Blue Devil faithful erupted into what Wilton Garrison of the *Charlotte Observer* later called a "roaring, howling mob."

The Blue Devils were routed by Navy, 40-7, in their next contest, but finished up the regular season with victories against three conference rivals. Barger led the way against Wake Forest, throwing touchdowns to Pascal and Tracy Moon, and taking in a scramble from the 42 to give Duke a three-touchdown advantage. The Deacons came back to make it close, but the Blue Devils held on, 28-21. South Carolina fell victim to a 26-7 score in Durham, as sophomore Buddy Bass had his finest day in a Duke uniform. Bass hauled in a 39-yard pass from Barger to give the Blue Devils the lead, and followed with a passing touchdown to Pascal and a rushing score off left end.

The Blue Devils played their most complete game of the season against North Carolina. The Tar Heels entered the game with a 4-4-1 record, as George Barclay sought to bring Carolina its first winning season since 1949. For a while the Tar Heels hung tough, trailing only 14-6 at the half. However, upon taking the field for the second half,

Duke poured it on their outclassed neighbors to the west. Bryant Aldridge gave Duke a 20-6 advantage with a 20-yard scamper in the opening minutes, and Bill Connor scored another touchdown following a Len Black interception. Lutz and Bill Kirkman added a pair of scores, and in a glaring lack of mercy, Larry Parker ran in from 3 yards away on the game's final play. The 47-12 win gave Duke an invitation to Miami for New Year's Day.

The Blue Devils met Bill Glassford's Nebraska squad in the 1955 Orange Bowl. With a 6-4 record, the University of Nebraska (NU) had been good enough to take second place in the Big Seven Conference, but the disparity between the Huskers and conference champion Oklahoma was evident when the two teams played in Norman in November. The Sooners handed Nebraska a 55-7 trouncing, their worst defeat in nine years. Oklahoma was in a class by itself, having won nineteen consecutive games. Unfortunately for the Sooners, the Big Seven had a policy in place that barred teams from making back-to-back visits to the Orange Bowl. It was a stroke of luck for Duke, for instead of having to gear up to play Bud Wilkinson's punishing running attack, they could prepare for a Nebraska team that proved to be inferior.

The contest was still scoreless as the first quarter came to a close, but the Blue Devils finally made a move on their first possession of the second quarter. Barger passed the Devils into position, and Pascal finished the drive with a 7-yard scoring run. Just before halftime the Devils struck again, as Aldridge intercepted a Don Erway pass and three plays later Barger found Jerry Kocourek in the end zone for a 14-0 edge.

"That intercepted pass gave us that second touchdown and put us on the ice," Murray commented after the game. "Nebraska had a good, tough team. But we got the big break. Nebraska gave us the chance with that pass and we took advantage of it."

Nebraska pulled to within a touchdown early in the third quarter, but that was as close as they would get. Duke took the kickoff following the NU score and began another march against the tiring Husker defense. After a 29-yard run by Pascal, Barger found Sonny Sorrell for a 17-yard touchdown. Nick McKeithan took credit for Duke's fourth goal line crossing, intercepting a pass and then flipping sides to burst through the Cornhusker line from 1 yard out.

With the score 27-7 early in the fourth quarter, many among the Orange Bowl-record crowd of 68,750 began to file their way out of the stadium. Murray emptied his bench in the final minutes, allowing all his players who made the trip to Miami to get some minutes. Duke scored a final time when Sam Eberdt rambled in from 3 yards out, and the ACC had its first taste of postseason glory.

For the second time in three years, Maryland and Duke finished with 4-0 records in conference play in 1955. The fact that the Blue Devils and Terrapins did not meet over this period only intensified the argument as to which team was actually better. Jim Tatum and Bill Murray's programs were clearly the class of the new conference, but the debate would have to carry on for another couple of seasons. Maryland was determined to get back on top of the polls in 1955 after failing to defend the NCAA title in 1954. Leading the way was lineman Bob Pelligrini, who had been recruited to College Park as a quarterback. After packing on some pounds in the weight room Pelligrini was shifted to the trenches, where he became a solid blocker and a defensive standout. For the 1955 season, Pelligrini was moved from guard to center.

Pelligrini flourished in his new position, taking ACC Player of the Year and National Lineman of the Year honors. Pelligrini was not the only Maryland lineman to receive accolades, as guard Jack Davis and tackle Mike Sandusky were both named to the All-ACC team. The Terrapins punished their opposition between the tackles, and led the nation in rushing defense by allowing just 75.9 yards a contest. Bill Walker and Ed Vereb were still around to make plays for the Terrapins offensively, and Frank Tamburello assumed the role of first-string quarterback. Tatum had elected to play Tamburello liberally the year before, and as a result, the quarterback came into the new season ready to perform. One setback for Maryland was the loss of fullback Tom Selep, who was out with a knee injury.

Maryland was a perfect 5-0 against Missouri under Tatum, and a year removed from their record-breaking 74-13 victory over the Tigers in College Park. Things would not be as easy for the Terrapins this time around, for after a Vereb 14-yard run and a pass from Tamburello, which gave Maryland a 13-0 lead, the Missouri defense clamped down. A pair of second half touchdowns gave the Tigers a chance to win, but failed conversion attempts gave the Terps a 13-12 victory that was, by all accounts, too close for comfort.

With the UCLA game being played at Byrd Stadium this time around, Maryland figured to stand a better chance against the favored Californians. Playing on a muddy field, the Bruins made their one and only offensive stand late in the first quarter, moving to the Maryland 3 on passes by Ronnie Knox. In what proved to be the most important defensive play of the game, Pelligrini stripped Doug Peters of the ball on the following play, and UM recovered.

Tamburello passed the Terps into Bruin territory in the third quarter, where they faced a fourth-and-1 from the UCLA 17. Tatum elected to go for the first down, thinking his team could not win with just a field goal. With eight Bruins up the middle ready to stuff the run, Tamburello made an audible at the line of scrimmage and executed a perfect fullback fake, which sucked in the defenders. Tamburello pitched to Vereb from behind, and the halfback was free on a run to the end zone. It proved to be the only points of the contest, and Maryland had their vengeance with a 7-0 victory.

The UCLA triumph propelled the Terrapins to the No. 1 ranking, and they held onto the position for the next several weeks. Baylor fell by a score of 20-6, as Tamburello threw a pair of touchdowns to Jack Healy and Russ Dennis. Wake Forest opened Maryland's ACC schedule, and Pelligrini and the Terrapin front line proved to be an indomitable force. Maryland allowed the Demon Deacons only 9 rushing yards in claiming a 28-7 victory.

North Carolina also found difficulty running the ball against the Terps, compiling only 18 yards. Vereb was the hero for the UM offense, recording a hat trick of touchdowns, along with an interception, to lead the Terrapins to a 25-7 victory. Carolina would have been shut out if not for a freak play, when UNC center Jim Jones ripped the ball away from Tamburello and went 35 yards to the goal. Syracuse was unable to end the Terrapin winning streak on their home field, as Maryland enjoyed its finest scoring output of the year. Touchdowns by Jim Brown and Don Althouse gave Syracuse more points than anyone else against the UM defense, but the Orangemen were on the short end of a 34-13 final.

The Terrapins shut out their next two opponents, wiping away South Carolina, 27-0, and Louisiana State University (LSU), 13-0. The Gamecocks had beaten only Wofford and Furman thus far in the year, and were unable to make any serious threat against the Terrapins. Louisiana State was intercepted four times by the UM defenders, including a costly pick by Phil Perlo in the end zone.

Maryland went to Clemson sporting a perfect 8-0 record, but the Tigers were more than a handful for Tatum's troops. Don King was good to Dalton Rivers to give the Tigers an early lead, and seconds later, running back Joel Wells took a handoff at midfield and broke to the end zone for a 12-0 CU advantage. It was the first time in a long time that Maryland faced real adversity, but the Terrapins were up for the challenge. Second-team quarterback Lynn Beightol threw a pair of touchdowns to Vereb to thrust UM back into the lead, and the defense put the Clemson offense on lockdown. The Tigers mounted only 22 yards in the second half, and another pair of scores led to a 25-12 Terrapin victory, which concluded an unbeaten run through the ACC slate.

George Washington stood in the way of another perfect regular season for the Terrapins, but the Colonials proved to be a minor obstacle. The Maryland defense pitched its fourth shutout of the year, while Vereb scored twice to give him sixteen touchdowns for the season, which tied Lu Gambino for the school record. The 19-0 victory sent Maryland to another Orange Bowl, where they would tangle once again with Oklahoma.

Duke easily won its first four games in 1955, climbing to No. 5 in the polls before running into a Steel City buzz saw. Pittsburgh came to Durham and stifled the Blue Devil attack, shutting down the running game and forcing seven fumbles. Joe Walton caught two touchdown passes as the Panthers knocked off the Devils, 26-7. Duke took the loss to Pitt hard, and it showed in poor performances against Georgia Tech and Navy. Duke salvaged a 7-7 tie with the Midshipmen, but was shut out by the Ramblin' Wreck, 27-0.

Like they had done the year before, Duke finished with dominating performances against their traditional rivals. The Blue Devils buried South Carolina, 41-7, and followed with shutout wins over Wake Forest and North Carolina. Against the Tar Heels, Skitch Rudy raced for a 35-yard score in the second quarter to provide the 6-0 margin of victory. Although Duke won seven games and had no conference losses, there was no justification for the Blue Devils going to the Orange Bowl over Maryland.

Oklahoma's Sooners had rolled over the competition yet again in 1955, claiming an undefeated season and stretching their winning streak to twenty-nine games. Oklahoma went the entire month of November without giving up a point, and came to Miami with the nation's top rushing offense. Maryland had been hoping all year for an Orange Bowl rematch with the Sooners, and engaged in tough practice sessions in the days leading up to the game. With the nation's best rushing defense going up against the nation's best rushing offense, something would have to give.

After thirty minutes of grueling football, the third-ranked Terrapins held the upper hand. As the defense held Oklahoma out of the end zone, Vereb scored on a 15-yard scamper in the second quarter to give the Terrapins a 6-0 lead. Unfazed, Oklahoma started the second half with a fury behind All-Big Seven halfback Tommy McDonald. After returning a punt 33 yards into UM territory, McDonald took an option pass and raced for 19 more. Two plays later, McDonald scored from 4 yards out to tie the game. Billy Pricer nailed the conversion, and Oklahoma took its first lead at 7-6.

With the game up for grabs, Oklahoma's Bud Wilkinson had a trick up his sleeve for his old buddy Tatum. Over the course of the season, Wilkinson had developed a repetitive offensive scheme that was a precursor to the modern-day "no huddle." Dubbed the "Fast break offense," the Sooners tried to get to the line of scrimmage and snap the football before the defense could get in position. Oklahoma frustrated the Terrapins to no end with their speedy attack, and used it for a third quarter score, which came on a sneak from quarterback Jay O'Neal. One time, as Pelligrini was making his defensive play calls, he felt a sudden impact to his back. It was Oklahoma center Bob Harrison, who had already gotten to the ball, snapped it, and charged ahead.

Maryland was still in the game in the fourth quarter, trailing only 14-6, but the brutal practices leading up to the game had taken their toll. The exhausted team could not mount a drive against the OU defense in the latter stages, and their fate was sealed when Carl Todd stepped in front of a Tamburello pass and raced 82 yards for the last points of the game. Aside of denying Maryland bragging rights to the NCAA crown, the 20-6 defeat to the Sooners officially signaled the end of the Terrapin football dynasty. Shortly after the Orange Bowl, Jim Tatum left College Park to accept the head coaching position at his alma mater, the University of North Carolina. As a result, the Terrapins would become a secondary team in the ACC in the coming years.

The autumn of 1956 saw a changing of the guard at the top of the ACC standings. Jim Tatum's return to Chapel Hill paved the way for Tommy Mont at Maryland, who could not duplicate Tatum's success in recruiting or on the field. The Terrapins' football fortunes plummeted under Mont, as losses to North Carolina and South Carolina placed UM fourth in the league with a 2-7-1 overall record. It would be nearly two decades before Maryland again sat at the top of the conference.

Duke's three-year run of ACC dominance was halted in the season opener against South Carolina. Warren Giese, making his debut as Gamecock head coach, brought his nineteen-point underdogs out throwing. An 81-yard drive in the second quarter, climaxed by a 1-yard sneak from Whiz King Dixon, gave USC a 7-0 triumph. It was the school's first win over Duke in twenty-five years, and set off a wild celebration on the field of Carolina Stadium after the contest.

Behind the leadership of eight senior starters, Clemson won Frank Howard his first ACC championship. Howard, a native of tiny Barlow Bend, Alabama, had starred on Wallace Wade's University of Alabama teams of the late 1920s and early 1930s. Dubbed "The Little Giant,"

2||50735

Howard helped lead the Crimson Tide to a 10-0 record and a national championship in 1930, which was culminated by a shutout victory over Washington State in the Rose Bowl.

Blessed, or cursed, depending on who you were talking to, with what Southerners refer to as the "Gift of Gab," Howard left Tuscaloosa soon after the end of his playing career and made the 330-mile journey to the foothills of South Carolina, where he became an assistant on Jess Neely's staff at Clemson. Neely put together some powerful Tiger teams in the late 1930s, winning a Southern Conference championship and combining for a 16-2-1 record in 1938 and 1939. Neely's success at Clemson caught the eye of officials at Rice, where he accepted the head coaching position in time for the 1940 season. When the Clemson Athletic Council met to name a successor to Neely, Professor Sam Rhodes, a council member, nominated Howard to be the new head coach. Howard, who was lounging in the back of the room and was listening on, eagerly replied, "I second the nomination."

Howard's teams were up and down in the old Southern Conference, but in both 1948 and 1950, the balding tactician led Clemson to unbeaten seasons. After struggling in their first two seasons of ACC play, Howard, who had been one of the biggest supporters of the eight-school migration from the Southern Conference, led CU to a 7-3 record in 1955. A loss to Maryland, in which the Tigers led by two touchdowns early in the game, served as their only conference setback.

Running back Joel Wells had earned All-ACC honors after setting a new league record with 782 yards, and returned in 1956 as Clemson's primary offensive threat. Wells went on to justify his being selected to the cover of the NCAA Media Guide by rushing for 803 yards. Wells also returned Clemson's kickoffs and punts, and provided superior coverage in the Tiger secondary. The CU defense was fearsome, holding nine of its eleven opponents to a touchdown or less and shutting out four regular season opponents.

In the opener, the Tigers rolled Presbyterian College, 27-7, taking its thirteenth in a row over the small school from nearby Clinton. Heading to Gainesville for their second contest, Clemson overcame a fierce Florida comeback to salvage a 20-20 tie. After jumping out to a 14-0 advantage, the Tigers watched Florida score three unanswered touchdowns to take the lead late in the game. Wells led the Tigers on a 68-yard march in the final minutes, and CU secured the deadlock with twenty-eight seconds to play.

Clemson went on a four-game winning streak after the Florida encounter, as the defense allowed only 13 points in a month's worth of action. Wells and Charlie Horne each found the end zone against N.C. State, leading Clemson to a 13-7 victory. The Wake Forest game posed an interesting challenge for the Tiger defenders, as they had to contend with Deacon running sensation Bill Barnes. Barnes, moved to fullback by head coach Paul Amen in the preseason, came into his own by running for 177 yards in Wake's 39-0 victory over William and Mary.

Barnes went on to set a new ACC single-season mark with 1,010 rushing yards, earning Player of the Year honors. Barnes also led the ACC in punt return and total yardage, a feat that would not be accomplished again for another four decades. Barnes was held to 73 yards by the Tiger defenders, as the Deacons were held outside the CU 30-yard line for the entire game. Horne scored twice for Clemson on short dives, and backup quarterback Horace Turbeville connected on a 20-yard field goal to give the Tigers a 17-0 win.

The Big Thursday game in Columbia featured a pair of fine defenses, as the Gamecock unit became the first to lead the ACC in all four major categories (total defense, rush defense, pass defense, scoring defense). It was a low-scoring affair as expected, but Clemson took the upper hand following a 39-yard punt return by Jim Coleman. Charlie Bussey's sneak into the end zone gave Clemson its only points. South Carolina had an excellent opportunity to score late in the game, moving deep into Tiger territory, but Don Johnson fumbled in the end zone for a touchback. It was the last offensive stand for USC, and Clemson held on for its second consecutive win in Columbia, 7-0.

Playing at home for the first time in over a month, the Tigers returned to Death Valley and knocked off Virginia Tech, 21-6. The win improved the Tigers to 5-0-1, and gave the team momentum heading into a contest with Maryland. The Terps had lost each of their last five games coming in, although a victory over Wake Forest had them sitting 1-1 in the conference. Although the UM offense played poorly against Clemson's strong defense, Tom Selep reached the end zone to give the Tigers their only blemish in league play. Bob Spooner scored a touchdown for CU, and the game finished a 6-6 tie.

On November 16, the still-unbeaten Tigers headed to the Orange Bowl for a game against Miami. Vice President Richard Nixon was in attendance, and extra protection was arranged for the entering spectators. As the game neared, Clemson's cheerleaders prepared for the pregame ritual of firing the school's cannon. When the Tigers took the field the cannon was ignited, and sent a loud blast throughout the stadium. Nixon and his entourage were not forewarned about Clemson's ritual, and immediately thought the worst. The vice president's security officers jumped on top of Nixon, creating a dramatic scene in the minutes leading up to kickoff. Once order was restored, the Hurricanes took care of the Tigers behind a dominant defensive effort. Miami had the nation's best defense, which had given up only five touchdowns in six games coming into the CU matchup. The 21-0 shutout propelled Andy Gustafson's team to a final ranking of No. 6 in the polls.

The Clemson offense continued to struggle against Virginia, as the unit scored a single touchdown for the third time in five outings. Bussey bowled over on a quarterback keeper, and promptly booted the extra point to give the Tigers a 7-0 lead. Virginia failed to score, and Howard's boys sewed up the conference title. Furman came to Death Valley for Clemson's last regular season game, and played their local rival tough. The Tigers took an early 7-0 lead, but a score by John Edge brought the Paladins even at 7-7. Three unanswered touchdowns, coming from Wells, Spooner, and Dalton Rivers, headed CU to a 28-7 victory.

Clemson represented the ACC in the Orange Bowl against Colorado, which had won seven games for head coach Dal Ward. The Buffaloes were the Big Seven's replacement for Oklahoma, per the rule against repeat appearances in the Orange Bowl. The Sooners were undefeated NCAA champions once again, making the game anticlimactic in regards to the national picture. The Colorado team waiting for Clemson in Miami was better than the Nebraska team that Duke had decisively beaten in 1955, and gave Howard headaches all afternoon.

The first quarter went by scoreless, as Clemson's defenders contained Colorado's potent offense. The second period, however, belonged to the Buffaloes, as they became one of the few teams all season to do whatever they wanted offensively against the Tiger resistance. Colorado broke out of their funk by scoring thrice, with two coming on sustained drives through the heart of the Clemson line. All the while, the Tiger offense stalled due to poor blocking, which allowed the Buffaloes to consistently stuff their running plays at the line of scrimmage.

John "The Beast" Bayuk got the ball rolling with a short plunge to give Colorado a 7-0 lead. The big fullback was a pain in Howard's side all day, finishing with 121 yards. Bob Stransky came up with an interception on CU's next possession, and Boyd Dowler capitalized on the error with another short scoring run for Colorado. The half ended 20-0 when Frank Clarke partially deflected a Tiger punt and Howard Cook ran it in from 26 yards out on the very next play. As the teams broke for the intermission, Howard and Ward crossed paths at midfield. When Ward asked Howard what was the matter with his team, the CU skipper was unable to come up with an explanation.

Howard was highly frustrated with his team at halftime, and let them know about it in the locker room. In a spirited speech, the Clemson coach threatened to resign if his team did not play more inspired football in the second half. The speech struck a chord in the CU players, as the orange and white came out in the third quarter and regained much of the pride that Colorado had so easily taken away from them in the first half.

With Wells leading the way, Clemson surged back by taking control on both sides of the football. The senior back came through when his team needed him most, scoring twice during the Tiger revival. The first came on a 3-yard carry to culminate the team's furious charge out of the locker room, and the second followed a Colorado punt, as Wells took a counter from the 42 and blasted 58 yards through the Colorado defense to make the score 20-14. Wells finished his final Clemson game with a game-high 125 yards.

Now back in the contest, the Tiger defense came up with a big play in the clutch. Pinned deep in their own territory early in the fourth quarter the Buffaloes fumbled, and Tommy Sease recovered it for the Tigers at the 10. With 11:22 remaining, Spooner crashed into the end zone to give Clemson its first lead at 21-20. With the momentum now in Clemson's favor, and with his team already having recovered an onsides kick earlier, Howard was hoping that the Tigers could put Colorado away should they get the ball right back on offense. It did not work out that way, as Colorado fell on a second onsides kick ordered by Howard at their own 47.

With good field position, the Buffs began an eight-play drive that resulted in the go-ahead score from Bayuk. The Buffaloes fumbled yet again on their ensuing possession, and Clemson recovered at the Colorado 26. Needing only a field goal to win, the Tigers gave the game away. Stransky came up with his second interception for Colorado, and the Buffaloes ran out the clock. In a game marred by five turnovers, the Tigers dropped a 27-21 heartbreaker to finish the year with a 7-2-2 mark.

North Carolina State had been a secondary choice for the members of the new Atlantic Coast Conference when the league had come together in 1953. The Wolfpack had finished only two football seasons in history ranked in the polls, and could boast only one postseason appearance, a loss to Oklahoma in the 1947 Gator Bowl. Several schools in the new league doubted the Wolfpack's ability to compete on the gridiron, but the success of NCSU's basketball program was the primary drawing card that resulted in their invitation to the ACC. State was far from a threat in the early years, needing three years and ten games before they finally beat a conference foe.

Earle Edwards, a short, bespectacled man that was highly educated and well versed, took the head coaching position of the Wolfpack in 1954, ending Horace Hendrickson's unsuccessful era in Raleigh. Edwards had been an assistant at Big Ten power Michigan State for a number of years, and was an integral part of the Spartans' 1952 national championship squad. Edwards' first few years at N.C. State were lean, as he worked to build the Wolfpack into a contender from the ground up. With a skimpy budget that included only ten scholarships, in addition to a small stadium that few teams wanted to play in, Edwards had an uphill battle to climb with the NCSU program.

In 1957 Edwards finally had a veteran team, with only one offensive starter gone from the previous season. The key returnee was Dick Christy, who combined field vision with breathtaking speed. Edwards made certain that Christy had plenty of opportunities with the ball. In addition to his running back duties, Christy was the Wolfpack's kickoff and punt returner. Christy had the ability to single-handedly change games with his speed, and led the State offense and special teams all year. Christy would average an impressive 45.4 yards per kick return that season, setting an ACC record that hasn't been challenged in the years since.

The NCSU football team was at a disadvantage from the get-go in the fall of 1957, as the university was serving its first year of NCAA-mandated probation due to misconduct on the part of Everett Case's basketball team. The Wolfpack hoopsters had committed a number of recruiting violations earlier in the decade, invoking a four-year ban of postseason appearances by all of NCSU's athletic teams starting that year and enduring through 1960. Probation was a tough setback for Edwards and the football team, only a year removed from another shady episode of its own doing.

Sanctions had been placed on the 1955 squad after the staff illegally paid for a number of players to come to Raleigh and have personal tryouts for the team. Now, two years later, the NCSU staff was hoping to finally put the past behind them, and move forward in the process of turning N.C. State into a contender on the gridiron. Although the probation ensured that there would be no bowl regardless of their place in the ACC standings, the Wolfpack had a team to be reckoned with. The NCSU defense, led by All-Conference performers Darrell Dess, Dick Hunter, and Bill Rearick, led the league by allowing only 6.7 points an outing. Hunter also served as quarterback and team captain.

Still smarting over their 1956 loss to the Wolfpack in Jim Tatum's first game at UNC, which also happened to be NCSU's first football triumph in the new league, North Carolina marched into Raleigh in the season opener for both teams. In a fierce defensive struggle, the Wolfpack pulled out a 7-0 victory. State set up its lone score on a trick play, when quarterback Frank Cackovic caught a lateral from Wally Prince and raced 52 yards down the sideline. Hunter provided the margin of victory two plays later with a touchdown. Christy put on a show the following week against Maryland, reaching the end zone three times in State's 48-13 blowout. State had not beaten the Terrapins in six years, but John Collar got it going with a 14-yard reception from Hunter. Christy's 96-yard kickoff return and two short runs put State ahead, and scores by Ken Trowbridge and Finley Read put the game on ice.

Christy took the opening kickoff against Clemson and trudged 97 yards through the muddy turf to give State a quick 7-0 advantage. Both teams struggled offensively, and the game turned into a defensive standstill. The Wolfpack broke through in the fourth quarter to take an insurmountable 13-0 lead, as fullback Don Hafer provided the points with a crash from the 1. The Tigers narrowed the gap on a bomb from Bill Barbary to halfback George Usry, and although they outdid State on the ground, Clemson was on the wrong end of a 13-7 final.

A pair of Sunshine State battles with Florida State and Miami resulted in a win and a tie for State. The Wolfpack needed only one play to knock off the Seminoles 7-0 in Tallahassee, as Hunter connected with Christy on a 46-yard halfback toss. The Miami game was a bore, as the teams played sixty minutes on a Friday night without a point being scored. Jim Sciaretti had a chance to give State the victory with a field goal, but the Hurricanes successfully blocked the kick. An interception by Joe Plevil in the fourth quarter gave Miami an opportunity to score, but the Wolfpack defense held on four consecutive plays from within their own 8-yard line.

The following evening in College Park, Tatum made his return to the University of Maryland on a notable occasion. Hoping to see a "typical American sport," Britain's Prince Philip and Queen Elizabeth II made their way to Byrd Stadium for the Maryland-North Carolina contest, as part of their royal tour of the Washington, D.C., area. The Queen later said that the game was the highlight of her visit to the United States, but she was afraid that Maryland governor Theodore R. McKeldin, caught up in the action and sitting nearby, was going to bruise her.

The only bruising was done by the Terrapin defense, which held Carolina to a single touchdown. Two fourth period scores gave Maryland a 21-7 triumph, which Tommy Mont later called the "most won-derful victory of my career." The UM players raised Mont onto their shoulders after the victory, and presented him to the royal entourage.

A week later, the Wolfpack returned to Raleigh for their first home game in six weeks, a highly anticipated showdown with Duke. Both teams came into the game unbeaten, with Duke holding a 5-0 record and NCSU sporting a 4-0-1 mark. The Blue Devils, who had given up only 13 points over their previous four games, had as much luck solving Christy as Maryland and Clemson had. Christy scored both N.C. State touchdowns, hauling in receptions from two different passers. Duke countered with a short scoring burst by Bob Brodhead, and a 53-yard touchdown pass to John Thompson. The game ended in a 14-14 deadlock, and it appeared that the two teams would finish the season tied atop the conference standings.

The Wolfpack came up with a complete effort at home against Wake Forest, muscling out a 19-0 final score. State scored its first points on a fake field goal, as Hunter lined up as the holder and tucked the snap under his arm on his way to the goal line. Christy and Rod Podwika added second half touchdowns for the Wolfpack, while the defense sent the winless Deacons to their third scoreless game of the season.

With a 5-0-2 record, few expected State to have a letdown against 2-5 William and Mary (W&M). Milt Drewer's first W&M team had dropped a number of winnable games, but a victory the week before gave them confidence heading to Raleigh. The Tribe came up with its biggest defensive effort of the year, shutting out State's offensive units. The Wolfpack scored their lone touchdown in the first two minutes of the game, as Hafer broke off a 70-yard sprint on a kick return. Hafer was drilled near the NCSU goal line and coughed up the ball, but Christy was trailing Hafer on his long run, and dove on the pigskin in the end zone for the score. State marched into William and Mary three times in the final thirty minutes, but was unable to cross the goal line again. A halfback pass from Jack Yohe to Dave Edmunds brought W&M close, and another play by Edmonds pushed the Tribe into the end zone. Bob Hardage converted the all-important extra point, and State took their first loss of the year, 7-6.

Hunter was the hero for the Wolfpack against Virginia Tech (VT), as his running and kicking led the way to a 12-0 victory. Backup quarterback Eddie Driscoll threw a touchdown to Bob Pepe to give State their first points, and Hunter broke free on a 58-yard carry in the fourth quarter to add to the final tally. Hunter kept the VT offense at bay with his quick kicks, and had boots of 53, 64, and 80 yards over the

his quick kicks, and had boots of 53, 64, and 80 yards over the course of the game.

The final week of the regular season was at hand, and Duke and State were still tied in first place. Although Georgia Tech ended Duke's unbeaten streak the week after the NCSU game, the Blue Devils knocked off Clemson, 7-6, to improve to 4-0-1 in the ACC. Bill Murray's troops were concluding their schedule at home against North Carolina. Two hundred and fifty miles away, the Wolfpack were in Columbia tangling with the University of South Carolina (USC).

Although it rained all morning, the skies cleared up in time for the all-important contest. For one memorable afternoon, Carolina Stadium became Dick Christy's personal showcase. In his final game as a member of the Wolfpack, Christy put together arguably the finest individual performance by any player in the ACC's first half century. The speedster almost single-handedly kept his team in the contest, as the State defense, which had not allowed two touchdowns in any game all year, proved unable to continue that trend against the feisty Gamecocks. South Carolina took an early lead on a sneak from quarterback Sam Vickers, which was set up by a 40-yard burst by Don Saunders. Christy responded for the Wolfpack with a 53-yard return on the ensuing kickoff, and pulled State level with a run from the 3.

The Gamecocks added to their lead on runs by Stan Spears and Don Johnson, and claimed a 19-6 advantage in the closing moments of the first half. Christy added his second touchdown just before the break, but missed the extra point for a 19-12 score. State took the opening kick of the second half and drove the length of the field, with Christy scoring for a third time and adding the conversion to tie the game. Christy's fourth touchdown early in the fourth quarter gave State its first lead of the game at 26-19, and NCSU held onto the advantage into the final two minutes. South Carolina put together an offensive behind Alex Hawkins, and the multipurpose star connected with Julius Derrick from 16 yards away at the 1:09 mark. The extra point tied the game again at 26-26, but State had time to move. The Wolfpack advanced to the USC 47 in the last minute, where quarterback Tom Katich was forced to make a Hail Mary toss as the final seconds ticked off the clock. Hawkins came up with an interception for South Carolina at the 15. With the crowd in an uproar, Hawkins raced 68 yards before going out of bounds inside NCSU territory.

A tie sealed a winning campaign for South Carolina, and a large group of Gamecock fans took to the field in celebration. Unfortunately for the USC supporters, the festivities were a bit presumptuous. A referee downfield had called pass interference against the Gamecocks, which meant there would have to be one more play. The fans were cleared from the field, and State was awarded the ball on the USC 30 with no time on the clock.

Christy heard it from the Gamecock faithful as he trudged back onto the field for the first field goal attempt of his collegiate career. Hunter took the snap and made a hold, and Christy booted a low, hanging kick that lofted its way through the crossbars for a 29-26 NCSU win. In scoring all 29 of his team's points, the performance helped Christy earn league MVP honors, while Earle Edwards took home his first Coach of the Year trophy.

Duke had scheduled one more league game than State in 1957, and would take the ACC title with a win over the Tar Heels. Things went according to plan for Murray's squad early on, as the Blue Devils raced out to a 13-0 lead. With the title in hand, however, the Duke offense choked, allowing UNC to get back into the contest. Following a second quarter touchdown by Giles Gaca, guard Fred Swearingen recovered a Blue Devil fumble. Tar Heel quarterback Jack Cummings threw a touchdown to Buddy Payne to tie it, and a successful extra point by Phil Blazer put Carolina ahead, 14-13. In the second half John Stallings recovered another fumble for the Tar Heels, and a final touchdown capped a 21-13 upset.

Although NCSU claimed the ACC title with Duke's defeat, the Blue Devils already knew that they were headed to the Orange Bowl. Notre Dame had snapped Oklahoma's impressive winning streak in November, but OU arrived in Miami holding that lone setback. The Blue Devils might have hung with the Sooners back when they were playing better football, but they were playing too poorly late in the season to knock off what was still a superb Oklahoma team.

Oklahoma forced Duke into six critical mistakes, including four in the final quarter, which allowed the Sooners to take control. The first Duke mistake came early in the contest, as Sooner defender David Baker caught a George Harris pass in stride and went 94 yards in the other direction for the game's first score. A high punt snap led to the next Oklahoma touchdown, as Clendon Thomas took the ball to the end zone from the Duke 13. Murray and the boys regained some spirit on a seven-play, 65-yard progression through the Sooner defense to cut the score to 14-7 at halftime.

Following an Oklahoma touchdown the Blue Devil offense went to work again, taking the ball 85 yards to their second goal line crossing. If the Blue Devils could have continued to keep their mistakes at a minimum, pulling off the upset would not have been a stretch. That would not be the case, however, as Duke began handing out gifts like a department store Santa Claus.

Oklahoma gleefully picked up the goodies, and went on a dramatic 27-point surge in the fourth quarter to take a 48-21 triumph. Dennit Morris recovered a pair of Blue Devil fumbles, each leading directly to Sooner scores. Oklahoma's final touchdown came on a masterful 68-yard interception return, as Bennett Watts picked off a pass at his own 32 and threw off to Dick Carpenter, who took the ball the rest of the way from 30 yards out.

The errors allowed the Sooners to turn the game into a commanding victory, OU's third Orange Bowl triumph in five seasons over an Atlantic Coast Conference opponent. The Oklahoma-Duke game wound up being the last of the ACC-Big Seven Orange Bowls, as the game's governing body chose to relieve both conferences of their contractual obligations after the season. The Big Seven relented on its no-repeat clause to the approval of the Orange Bowl people, and continued sending its champion every year to Miami. The ACC went in its own direction, and would not send another team to the game for more than two decades.

Before the 1958 season the NCAA approved a plan that modified the scoring format of college football, the first such change in over forty years. After a touchdown, teams could now run a single offensive play from the 2-yard line. Barring a penalty, any run or pass over the goal on the "conversion" play was good for two points. The change added a new dynamic to the college game, as teams were now able to score eight points on a given possession instead of seven. Over the years, the two-point conversion has provided some of the most memorable moments in college football history.

Paced by a solid defense and the league's best rushing attack, Clemson won five conference games for the school's second ACC title in three years. Harvey White, who had finished the 1957 season among the top twenty in the NCAA in total offense, touchdown passes, and passing yardage, returned as the first-string Tiger quarterback. White went on to earn All-Conference honors as a defensive back, joining end Ray Masneri and center Bill Thomas on the team. The defense allowed just 12.5 points a contest, while the Tiger running backs averaged 225.8 yards a game.

It was an exciting time to be around the town of Clemson, as Tigers fans watched on as Memorial Stadium was modernized to handle the team's new fan base. The stadium was expanded from 20,000 to 38,000 seats that fall, which included the installation of a new scoreboard. For the season opener at the refurbished stadium, the orange-clad Tigers ran down the hill on a large rug donated by a local carpet executive. Virginia, the perennial bottom-feeder of the ACC, came to Death Valley with a revitalized spirit that Saturday. Dick Voris, the new UVA coach, had whipped his players into fine playing condition, as the Cavaliers demonstrated quickness and athleticism not seen in quite a while from a Virginia team.

The Cavaliers gave Clemson quite a battle, taking the lead twice and remaining competitive well into the fourth quarter. The Tigers finally put the game away in the final minutes, as Bill Mathis ended a 95-yard drive by plowing over from the 4. The Mathis touchdown provided CU with a 20-15 verdict. Although Virginia looked solid in the near upset of the Tigers, it proved to be a cruel deception. After beating Duke, 15-12, the following Saturday, the Cavaliers went into a free fall, losing twenty-eight consecutive games over the next three seasons. Voris, who for two short weeks looked to be turning around the Cavalier program, was given an unceremonious ouster following the 1960 season after posting a record of 1-29 in Charlottesville.

The Tigers had to play catch-up again at home the following week against North Carolina, as Jim Tatum brought a fired-up squad to Memorial Stadium. An overflowing crowd of over 40,000 watched on as the Tar Heels took the early edge on a touchdown pass by Sonny Folckomer. The two-point conversion, college football's new novelty in 1958, consumed Tatum and Howard's better judgments on this afternoon. Seven touchdowns were scored, but only once was an extra point kick attempted. Of the six conversion attempts, only two were successful, as Howard and Tatum learned the hard way that conversions fail more often than they succeed. Clemson took an 8-6 lead following a blocked kick, and after the play, a large Tiger located above Memorial Stadium's brand-new scoreboard at the eastern end of the facility wagged its tail for the very first time. Over the ensuing decades, the Tiger always gave its tail a shake of approval following CU touchdowns.

The Tar Heels struck back in the second quarter when Jack Cummings tossed a spiral to Don Kemper, but the Tigers tied it at 14 on the final play of the half. The Tigers struck gold again in the third quarter, but another failed conversion kept the score at 20-14 as the third quarter came to an end. Once again the Tar Heels fought back, tying the game at 20 with an 80-yard drive of its own. This time Tatum played it smart, calling on Phil Blazer to give his team a 21-20 lead.

The Tigers crossed up the UNC defense on their next possession by employing a double-flanker set, and with 2:52 to play, George Usry scored his second short touchdown on a 2-yard plunge. Carolina got a final crack at victory, but Clemson hung on 26-21 for Frank Howard's 100th win as head coach of Clemson. The victory was also Howard's first over Tatum in six head-to-head meetings. It was the first of three ACC losses for the Tar Heels, but proved to be the one that kept UNC out of first place.

Things didn't get any easier for the Tigers in their next contest, played in College Park against Maryland. The first half went by score-less, as neither team was able to make good on their chances. The Ti-gers drove to the Maryland 4 midway through the third quarter, but the Terrapin defense made a fearsome stand. Defensive end Ben Scotti made consecutive great plays for Maryland to hold back the Tiger of-fensive. Maryland couldn't move on their next possession, and promptly kicked the ball back to Clemson.

On first down from the 50, White launched a spiral deep into the Terrapin secondary. Wyatt Cox, who had recovered the fumble on Maryland's opening drive, snagged the pass. After making the catch at the 20, Cox outran a pair of Terrapins to the goal line. Despite eighteen first downs and 332 yards of total offense, the touchdown and a conver-sion proved to be Clemson's only points. Fortunately for the Tigers, the defense held and preserved the 8-0 win.

The cardiac Tigers had kept things interesting in their first three wins, and did it again in Nashville against Vanderbilt. After moving up two spots to No. 8 in the Associated Press (AP) poll, the Tigers found the going rough all over again. Trailing 7-0, the Tigers came awake in the final frame and put together a pair of scoring drives that sealed up victory. After forcing a Vanderbilt punt, the Tigers drove 69 yards for the game-winning score, as White rambled over with nine seconds on the clock. Again the Tigers went for two, and again it failed. Vanderbilt had no time to make a move, and the 12-7 score held.

Although Clemson was unbeaten and ranked among college foot-ball's elite, the Tigers had been skating on thin ice. Three of their victo-ries had come from behind, with the fourth coming against a mediocre team in which the team had only scored one touchdown. With a week off before a Big Thursday showdown with South Carolina, Clemson sought to rest their weary bodies and figure out a way to beat the Gamecocks for the fourth year in a row.

It was not to be for the Tigers this time around, as USC ended Clemson's unbeaten streak with a 26-6 victory at the Fairgrounds. White opened the scoring in the second quarter with a 3-yard sneak, but by game's end the Clemson field general was on the bench, out with a shoulder injury. The Gamecocks, led by ACC Most Valuable Player

Alex Hawkins, riddled Clemson's defense to the tune of 262 rushing yards. The game was still in doubt going into the fourth quarter, with South Carolina holding a 14-6 edge, but scores by Whiz King Dixon and Hawkins sealed the deal.

No longer unbeaten, the Tigers next prepared to meet surprising Wake Forest. Led by their quarterbacking tandem of Norm Snead and Charlie Carpenter, the Deacons suddenly had some offensive punch, and had beaten both Maryland and N.C. State. Wake came into the contest a half game back of the Tigers, with a loss to North Carolina against their record. Snead successfully reached the end zone for the Deacons, but his inability to make a conversion proved to be his team's downfall. White connected with Cox early to give the Tigers an 8-0 advantage, and a sneak gave Clemson their final points. Although Wake scored two touchdowns, and played the Tigers close for much of the game, the failed conversions by the Deacons gave Clemson a narrow 14-12 victory.

Georgia Tech was too much for CU down in Atlanta, as the Yellow Jackets became the only team during the regular season to shut out the Tiger offense. As White and Usry spent the day in a lull, touchdowns by Floyd Faucette and Fred Braselton gave Tech a 13-0 verdict. North Carolina State brought another defensive challenge to the Tigers in Raleigh, but CU hung tough for the victory that clinched the ACC. Late in the third quarter the Tigers began a 51-yard drive, keyed by the carries of Bill Mathis. Usry reached the end zone at the 12:16 mark of the final quarter, and Bobby Morgan scored on a 15-yard scamper a few minutes later for a 13-0 Clemson lead. State scored a desperation touchdown in the final minutes, but ran out of time and dropped a 13-7 final.

"I didn't think we played one of our best games," Howard said after the game. "One thing about me, I can take victory and I can take defeat."

Clemson easily took their final two regular season games, a pair of home encounters against nonconference competition. Boston College (BC) fell 34-12 thanks largely to Charlie Horne, who turned in a pair of touchdowns in the second half. Furman had no chance in the finale, as the Tigers churned out 36 points for their highest total of the year. With the victory in hand, the Tigers were invited to Louisiana for the Holidays. With eight regular season victories and a sustained run in the national polls, the Tigers were a neat fit for the Sugar Bowl.

Clemson's opponent in New Orleans was Louisiana State, who had recently been awarded the No. 1 ranking and national championship on the strength of their 10-0 regular season record. Paul Dietzel's team had struggled in 1957 with a .500 record, and many figured that they would have problems again in 1958 with a squad that included only three seniors. Despite the overall youth of the team, everything fell into place for LSU during a magical run that fall, as the Tiger squad overachieved all season long.

Dietzel employed three rotating units throughout the season, including a defense that became known as the "Chinese Bandits." The Bandits were a fearsome group, failing to yield a touchdown to any opponent over the course of the entire regular season. With fullback Jim Taylor and All-American halfback Billy Cannon leading the charges, LSU was also capable of scoring a lot of points, evident in their 62-0 thrashing of Tulane in their final game leading up to the Sugar Bowl. Although Clemson had nothing to lose by giving LSU their toughest game, there were plenty of obstacles facing Howard's squad.

The game would be played less than a hundred miles from the LSU campus, giving the purple and gold Tigers, for all intents and purposes, the home-field advantage. Louisiana State fans indeed gobbled up most of the tickets, and brought their coolie hats to the Sugar Bowl in full force. The LSU-Clemson showdown was the final Sugar Bowl to be televised in black and white, and in an effort to provide contrast for the nationwide audience, the Tigers elected to wear unique uniforms. As LSU came out in their familiar white shirts and yellow pants, Clemson wore navy blue jerseys with expansive numerals to go along with white pants and their orange headgear.

Although starting quarterback Warren Rabb went out in the first quarter with a fractured hand, the heralded LSU defenders kept Clemson out of the end zone for a full sixty minutes. It was the third shutout of the season for the Louisianans, and the tenth time in eleven games that they held their opponent to seven or fewer points. The Chinese Bandits came up with the game's biggest play in the third quarter, as Duane Leopard recovered a fumbled punt at the Clemson 11.

Three plays later, Cannon took a handoff and dropped back to throw on a halfback option play. The future Heisman Trophy winner spotted Mickey Mangham in the end zone, and Mangham's 9-yard catch gave LSU the only touchdown of the contest. Cannon's extra point gave the Tigers a 7-0 margin of victory, and the school's first perfect season in fifty years. The discouraging loss dropped Clemson to No. 12 in the final Associated Press poll.

"Our center caught a handful of grass, the ball stuck and then slipped out of his hand, hitting one of our backs in the leg," a dejected

Howard said later of the botched kick.

Jim Tatum was hoping to turn the corner with his North Carolina squad in 1959, and finally bring Chapel Hill its first ACC football championship. With an experienced team that included players almost exclusively recruited by his staff at UNC, Tatum's Tar Heels were ranked No. 12 in the preseason. Most experts agreed that the Tar Heels would compete with Clemson for the league's top honors that fall, and were pointing to their season-opening showdown in Chapel Hill as critical in determining the league race.

Tragically, fate had another idea in mind for the Carolina coach. Barely a month before the Tar Heels were scheduled to begin training camp, Tatum was playing a round of golf with a friend when he began feeling under the weather. Upon arriving home, the coach became bed-ridden, falling victim to a sudden, unexplained illness. Within hours, Tatum developed an unnaturally high fever, and became gravely ill. Tatum died in the hospital on July 23, a day prior to his forty-sixth birthday. The cause of death was Rocky Mountain Spotted Fever, a rare infectious disease contracted from ticks.

The Tar Heel community was overcome with grief over the loss of Sunny Jim, who returned to Chapel Hill to bring the same respectability to his alma mater that he had brought to the University of Maryland. In 1956, Tatum took over a UNC team that had endured six consecutive losing seasons. Within a year he brought home a winner. The University of North Carolina would be left with eternal curiosity as to whether Tatum could have turned the school into a football powerhouse.

"He was like a second father to me," said Al Goldstein, an All-American for Carolina in 1958. "It took a lot out of me, losing a man like that. Tatum was probably one of the most inspirational men in my life."

"I went to his funeral that summer, and I recall it resembling a coach's clinic," remembers Woody Durham of the Tar Heel Sports Network. "Bear Bryant, Bud Wilkinson, Frank Howard, all the great coaches of the day, were all there to pay homage. That was a terrible loss to the University of North Carolina. Coach Tatum had star power. When he walked into a room, wearing that big cowboy hat, you knew you were in the presence of somebody important."

Life went on at UNC after Tatum's passing, and the university wasted little time in naming Jim Hickey as the successor. Hickey, who had followed Tatum to Chapel Hill in 1956, was considering another coaching position when Tatum passed away. Hickey did the best he could under the difficult circumstances, and led UNC to a 5-5 regular season record.

"That was an experience I do not want again," Hickey replied years later. "There were no personality problems or anything like that, but the whole thing had such an unsettling effect on the staff, the fans, the players, and everyone else. It's not the type of situation where you go in and become a taskmaster. You've got to pretty much use the staff and the players in the way that Tatum had planned to do it, or you were wrong. That's the way I looked at it, and I wouldn't have done it any differently."

Without Tatum's ample leadership, the Tar Heels were an inconsistent team in the fall of 1959. But on two memorable weekends in November, the squad put everything together in performances that would have made their deceased leader quite proud. The first came against Virginia, as the Tar Heels handed the Cavaliers a 41-0 pounding in Kenan Stadium. In the season finale, the Tar Heels beat Duke, 50-0, for that school's worst defeat in thirty years. The Blue Devils were finishing up a disappointing 4-6 campaign in 1959, as Bill Murray's squad was a year away from getting back to the top of the ACC standings. The crowd at Duke Stadium, in addition to a regional television audience, was stunned at the workmanlike pounding that Carolina administered to its rival.

"All season long, we had made it a point of not mentioning Coach Tatum's name," said quarterback Jack Cummings. "It wouldn't have been fitting. Before Duke it was brought up. We knew we had to get this one for him. I've never heard a more stirring talk than Coach Hickey made to us prior to the game. Hickey told us this was the one for Coach Tatum—this is the one he would want. We also wanted this one for Coach Hickey and ourselves. It was the Gettysburg Address, you might say. Anyone who wasn't moved by it has no feelings. We came out to play a ball game."

Clemson returned most of the starters from their solid 1958 squad, and won the ACC championship for a second straight year. Although they lagged behind other schools in most statistical categories, the Tiger offense led the league with a scoring average of 26.2 points a game. Bill Mathis was tops in scoring with 70 points, while Doug Cline took home the Jacobs Blocking Trophy. Harvey White returned for a third season as leader of the Tiger first-unit offense, and finished his career as the first quarterback in Clemson history to complete more than 50 percent of his passes.

The Tiger defense was one of the finest of the Frank Howard era, leading the ACC in total defense, rushing defense, and scoring defense. Tackle Lou Cordileone, also a star on Clemson's College World Series baseball team, became the first and only Tiger in history to be named an All-American both in the classroom and on the gridiron in the same year. Cordileone was assisted on the Tiger line by All-Conference center Paul Snyder. The Clemson defense shut out five opponents during the season, and went four games without giving up a point during a stretch in October and November.

Jim Hickey had less than two months to regroup the team he inherited from Tatum, and to get their minds back on the patch of Tigers that would invade from the south on September 19. On a perfect fall afternoon, Carolina quickly gave the momentum to Clemson by fumbling away the opening kickoff. The Tigers retrieved the ball at the 44 and drove for the first touchdown, which came on a short sneak by White. Clemson upped its lead to 14-0 in the second quarter by putting together a drive of 42 yards.

North Carolina cut the score to 14-6 before halftime, but Clemson marched relentlessly on the ground in the third quarter, and moved ahead, 20-6, on a 2-yard carry by Mathis. Trailing, 20-12, with less than three minutes remaining, Carolina began another assault at the Clemson goal line. With the ball deep in Tiger real estate, UNC receiver Milan Wall came up with a fine individual effort. Drawing limited coverage from the Clemson secondary, Wall was wide open for a 22-yard reception and a 20-18 score. The Tar Heels decided to throw a short pass in the flats, in hopes that Bob Elliott could power his way over the goal for the critical two-point conversion. Clemson was prepared, however, and as the fullback caught the pass, two Tiger defenders blanketed him. The ball was spotted 2 yards shy of the end zone, and Clemson ran out the clock to escape Kenan Stadium with a 20-18 victory.

After burying Virginia, 47-0, in Charlottesville, the Tigers headed to Atlanta for the twenty-ninth consecutive time to play Georgia Tech, who refused to come north to Clemson to play. Quarterback Fred Braselton scored on a short keeper to give GT a 7-0 lead, but Mathis returned the second half kickoff 99 yards to bring Clemson to within a point. Mathis's return set a new ACC record, but the conversion was unsuccessful. The Yellow Jackets went on to score twice more to swell their lead to 16-6, and held the Tigers off the scoreboard the rest of the way. Clemson began its four-game streak of shutouts against N.C. State, sending the Wolfpack home on the short end of a 23-0 score. Ron Scrudato returned a 60-yard interception to get the Tigers moving, and the CU defense contained heralded NCSU quarterback Roman Gabriel.

Clemson had grown tired of traveling to Columbia each year for the annual Big Thursday showdown with South Carolina. Although Tiger fans had made the trek to the State Fairgrounds to cheer on their boys for decades, the time had come for Clemson to receive more compensation for its contribution to the popular rivalry. It was common knowledge among those close to the programs that the home-standing Gamecocks were benefiting more from the games, taking in an unfair portion of the gate receipts and concession revenue.

The annual USC-Clemson battle at the Fairgrounds was the only college football game played on Thursdays at the time, and had been a Palmetto State tradition since 1896. The state of South Carolina all but shut down on Big Thursday, which highlighted the annual State Fair. Classes at Clemson were often canceled or postponed, and businesses throughout the state closed so fans could make their way to the game. Two years earlier, South Carolina had reluctantly agreed to end Big Thursday after the 1959 contest, and would begin making trips to Clemson starting in 1960.

As the Tiger defenders kept the Gamecocks off the scoreboard, White completed nine-of-ten tosses for 162 yards. The Tiger quarterback ignited the offensive unit, and threw a pair of bombs to Mathis and Gary Barnes in leading his team to a 27-0 victory. After the game, delirious Clemson fans ripped away the steel goalposts, which had been set in a pool of concrete in an effort to thwart any postgame looting. In a gesture that resulted in a classic photograph, Howard bid farewell to Big Thursday by blowing a big kiss in the direction of the field.

The Tigers next made a trip to Texas to take on Rice, and buried the winless Owls with another solid defensive effort. Cordileone and the CU line established early superiority, and an interception return by Snyder headed the Tigers to a 19-0 victory. The Duke game in Death Valley was a nail-biter, as the Tigers struggled mightily against an inspired Blue Devil team. Outland Trophy winner Mike McGee led a Duke line that continuously stifled the Clemson offensive units, and held the Tigers to 236 total yards. Clemson scored its only touchdown in the second quarter, when Ed Bost made an impressive diving reception in the end zone. The 30-yard play was set up by a Duke turnover, when a bad pitch to Joel Arrington was recovered by CU tackle Ronnie Osborne at the Duke 22. The Blue Devils had two excellent scoring opportunities in the fourth quarter, but a fumble and a turnover on downs gave Clemson a rugged 6-0 win.

The Tigers figured to have 2-5 Maryland's number on homecoming, but Tom Nugent's first Terrapin team was primed to pull off an upset. Terrapin quarterback Dale Betty threw a trio of touchdowns, and led a Maryland offense that produced more points against the Tiger defense than their previous six opponents combined. Betty's first touchdown was good to Hank Poniatowski in the first quarter, and gave Maryland an early 7-0 lead. The Tigers fought back with their own passing attack, as White connected with Mathis for a 41-yard play. Clemson scored three touchdowns in the second half, but unwisely chose to go for two after each successful score. All three attempts were nullified by the Terrapin defense, and a pair of touchdowns from Betty to Gary Collins gave UM a 28-25 win.

No less than four schools still had a mathematical chance to win the ACC title on November 21. Wake Forest (WF) was one such team, and could clinch a tie for the conference championship by beating the Tigers. The Demon Deacons struck first, as Bobby Robinson returned a pass in the flats intended for Usry 69 yards for the game's first score. Doug Dagneault countered with a short touchdown for Clemson, but WF quarterback Norman Snead promptly threw to Jerry Ball for a 14-6 Wake lead. Snead, who went on to set new ACC records for touchdown passes and yardage in a season, finished the game with 196 yards. Doug Cline, who scored twice, ended a 71-yard Clemson push, and a pass to Sam Anderson tied the game.

The Deacons continued the up-and-down nature with two scoring marches, as a field goal and Snead touchdown pass gave WF a 24-14 advantage. The Tigers rallied in the third quarter, as Bost caught a 23-yard strike from Lowndes Shingler for his second touchdown in as many weeks. Cline's second touchdown gave Clemson a 27-24 lead, but Johnny Morris piled over in the fourth quarter to give Wake Forest a 31-27 advantage.

Following a fumble recovery, the Demon Deacons had the game in hand, with the ball deep in Clemson territory with just over six minutes on the clock. With a second-and-five on the Tiger 26, Wake elected to throw. Although they had been running the football successfully for most of the contest, the Deacons were trying to put the game away. Usry took in backup quarterback Chuck Reiley's pass and returned it 73 yards to the Wake Forest 10. Usry then concluded Clemson's turn-around with a short burst over the goal line, and the Tigers held on for the dramatic 33-31 victory.

Furman proved to be a much easier opponent than Wake Forest, as the Tigers pounded their local adversary, 56-3. The Paladins surprised most of the spectators by taking an early 3-0 lead, but the Tigers ran seven plays across the goal line. Harry Pavilack added a defensive score on a 26-yard interception return. The victory gave Frank Howard back-to-back eight win seasons for the first time in his Clemson career.

The Tigers next headed to Houston, where they would compete in that city's first annual Bluebonnet Bowl. Texas Christian University (TCU), CU's opponent, came into the contest riding a seven-game winning streak. The No. 7 Horned Frogs featured backs Marvin Lasater and Jack Spikes, and superstar lineman Bob Lilly. The Tigers, who became the first college football team in history to play two bowl games in the same calendar year, were again the underdogs.

Lon Armstrong's field goal pushed Clemson ahead, 3-0, in the opening quarter, but Jack Reding threw a touchdown pass to Harry Moreland to give TCU the lead at halftime. Like they had done three years earlier in the Orange Bowl, the Tigers went on an offensive surge in the second half. Unlike the game with Colorado, however, this time the CU defense held tough. As the Clemson defense held TCU off the scoreboard over the final thirty minutes, the offensive units took control. White and Shingler each threw touchdown passes, one to Barnes and the other to Tommy King. A rushing score later in the contest gave Clemson a 23-7 win, the school's first as a member of the ACC.

3

A Devil of a Dynasty (1960-1962)

Bill Murray, a Rocky Mount native with a friendly smile and a receding hairline, returned to North Carolina in 1951 to become the first former Duke football player to earn the title of head coach at his alma mater. Murray earned his stripes at the University of Delaware, taking over a program in 1940 that had endured five consecutive losing seasons. Murray quickly brought order to the Blue Hens, leading the team to a 5-3 record in his first campaign at the eager age of thirty-one.

Starting in his second season of 1941, Murray brought a winning tradition to the town of Newark that has not been equaled before or since. His 1942 squad went unbeaten at 7-0-1, which was followed the next season by an 8-0 campaign. Delaware's football program took a three-year hiatus as World War II played out, but Murray's team picked up right from where it had left off in 1946. The Blue Hens completed a 10-0 season with a 21-7 demolition of Florida's Rollins College in the Cigar Bowl, which clinched the small college, known more formally at the time as the College Division, national championship.

Murray managed to put together some good squads at Duke in the mid-1950s, but his Blue Devil teams always seemed to be in the shadow of Jim Tatum's squads at Maryland. That all changed in the autumn of 1960, as Duke began its own legacy of Atlantic Coast Conference dominance by claiming the first of three consecutive undisputed league championships. Murray, aside from being a fine coach, was a skilled recruiter, and searched far and wide to bring talent to his team. In the late 1950s and early 1960s, Murray assembled a powerful squad at Duke by consistently beating his local adversaries at recruiting.

By not being so dependent on homegrown talent, Murray was able to lure some excellent players to Durham. Quarterback Walt Rappold came from the same West Virginia high school that had produced NBA standout Jerry West. Pass-catching sensation Tee Moorman was persuaded into coming north from Miami, while standout tackle Art Gregory came from Aiken, South Carolina. Jay Wilkinson, the son of Oklahoma coach Bud Wilkinson, declined becoming a Sooner, and became an All-American instead at Duke.

Although he was not hesitant to go out of state for his players, Murray was also plenty successful recruiting in North Carolina. Duke successfully committed Jack Wilson from Raleigh, a back with lightning quickness, in addition to two-way lineman Jean Berry from Mooresville. Mark Leggett, another fleet-footed runner, came to the Blue Devils from Asheboro. Leggett was the star of Duke's unbeaten 1959 freshman team, which wound up producing several important varsity players in the coming seasons. Don Altman, Duke's starting quarterback in 1960, hailed from Asheville. Altman was the final piece to Murray's offensive puzzle, a stable signal caller with the ability to run Duke's balanced offensive attack.

With his bevy of weapons in place, Murray took the Blue Devils to Columbia for the school's fifth consecutive season opener against South Carolina. Moorman, who had missed nearly two weeks of practice with a virus, stole the show. Catching a variety of short and long passes from Altman and Rappold, Moorman finished the day with a new conference record of eleven receptions. Referred to as the "lonesome end" in Murray's set, Moorman successfully rattled the Gamecock defense. Duke's passing attack spread out the South Carolina defenders, which allowed Leggett and Wilson to pile up yardage on the ground. As a team, Duke finished the game with 322 yards rushing. After failing to score on two tries in the first quarter, the Blue Devils dominated the remainder of the action to take a 31-0 win.

Maryland was prepared to stop Moorman up in College Park, but Duke used the lonesome end primarily as a dummy. After throwing heavily against South Carolina, the Devils went to the air only nine times against the Terrapins. For the second week in a row Duke's second offensive unit displayed its ability to put points on the scoreboard, scoring a pair of touchdowns. The second unit scores were sandwiched around a touchdown by the starters, as the Devils claimed a 20-7 final. Michigan stifled Moorman in Duke's next contest, as the receiver was allowed to make short catches, but was kept from hauling in the longer ones. Michigan's offense got going and handed Duke its first setback, 31-6.

The Blue Devils came back to North Carolina to play N.C. State, and began a month of strong performances. The Wolfpack, behind quarterback Roman Gabriel, had jumped out to a quick 4-0 record. On his way to back-to-back ACC Player of the Year awards, Gabriel had led the nation in completion percentage as a sophomore in 1959, connecting on 60.4 percent of his tosses. Gabriel was running on all cylinders thus far in 1960, scoring four touchdowns against Virginia and driving State to a late come-from-behind victory over Maryland.

Duke overcame another brilliant performance from the junior, winning by what the *Raleigh News and Observer* called a "gnat's eyelash." Following a first quarter field goal, Duke's second offense pushed 58 yards for the game's first touchdown and a 10-0 lead. Gabriel pulled State back into the game before halftime when he found Claude Gibson alone behind the Duke secondary. "Alone" was something of an understatement, as Gibson was at least 20 yards behind every Blue Devil defender. Had Gibson dropped Gabriel's pass, he probably wouldn't have been very welcome on Earle Edwards' bus for the ride back to Raleigh.

State scored again on their opening drive of the second half to take a 13-10 advantage, but Duke finished the scoring late in the third quarter, when Dean Wright bowled over from 9 yards out. Gabriel, who threw for 182 yards in breaking N.C. State's career passing record, tried valiantly to push the Wolfpack back out in front, but his desperation pass from inside the Duke 20 on fourth down was dropped. The Blue Devils ran off the final four minutes to claim their biggest win of the year, 17-13.

Following a 21-6 victory over Clemson in Durham, the Blue Devils prepared to meet Georgia Tech. Tech had been a thorn in the side of ACC schools for years, but on this day Duke got the better of Bobby Dodd's team. As the Blue Devil defenders posted their first shutout of the year, Wright's fourth quarter touchdown gave Murray's boys a 6-0 win.

A group of Duke freshmen brought some added excitement to the Navy game by taking the Midshipmen's famed mascot, Billy the Goat, hostage. The Middies unwisely chose to bring Billy to Durham, and it was not long before he was gone. The Duke students painted a big blue "D" on one of the goat's sides, and decided to present Billy to Navy before the game began. The plan backfired, as the tunnel they attempted to bring the goat out in was filled with over 600 Middies, who were preparing a human tunnel for their own players to run through.

A group of Middies saw Billy being escorted by the Duke people and immediately took off to retrieve him. A scuffle erupted, and several individuals were soon tangled up in a minor brawl. Although the Duke freshman numbered in the fifties, the massive throng of Navy students assembled in the tunnel could have created a nasty scene. Fortunately, order was restored and the game began as scheduled. Duke trailed by 10 points at halftime before Murray and his coaches made an adjustment to neutralize Navy's outside running. The change kept Navy from scoring in the final thirty minutes, and a pair of fumble recoveries paved the way for a 19-10 comeback win.

The Blue Devil offense put it all together in a 34-7 pounding of Wake Forest, which clinched a tie for the league title. A pair of games a week later sealed the fate of the conference standings, as the Blue Devils were in Chapel Hill taking on North Carolina, and State was down in Columbia tussling with USC. The Tar Heels had won only once for Jim Hickey, and did not figure to pose much of a challenge to a Duke team that hadn't lost in six weeks. As the saying goes, you can throw out the records when bitter rivals square off on a football field. That was certainly the case on this blustery afternoon in Chapel Hill.

The teams played a typical Duke-UNC game, physical, aggressive, and defensive. Neither team put any points on the board throughout the first three quarters. Duke had two scoring opportunities before the final period, each coming on field goal attempts. Bill Reynolds' second quarter kick had the distance, but the ball sailed wide. His second attempt, coming in the third quarter, appeared for a split second to be dead-on. Unfortunately for the Blue Devils, the kick fell short of the crossbar. The dark blue finally gained some momentum on a 55-yard punt return by Leggett, which brought them inside Carolina territory. On fourth down from the 2, a good surge by the line helped give Duke a 6-0 lead. Carolina defender Tony Hennessey broke off his block on the extra point and managed to get some fingers on the football, which proved to be the critical defensive play of the contest.

Carolina came back at Duke through the air, as backup quarterback Ray Farris hit halfback Milan Wall for a 38-yard gain. The UNC offense marched all the way down to the 3, where Farris scrambled over to the delight of 42,000 fans. With exactly 2:00 remaining, Bob Elliott converted the vital extra point. The Blue Devils got two more scoring opportunities, but a fumble and interception gave UNC a 7-6 upset. Duke had lost control of its own destiny, but another dose of fate wound up keeping them in first place.

Without Roman Gabriel for most of the game, nursing a leg injury, NCSU spent the day treading water against South Carolina. They were too buoyant with defense to sink, but too empty of offense to move.

After a scoreless first half, the Gamecocks drew first blood in the third quarter, going over in six plays from the State 23. Gabriel, who had been on the sidelines since State's second offensive possession, came back onto the field moments later for his lone shining moment. From his own 41, Gabriel stepped back and found George Vollmar, who caught Gabriel's pass, raced 29 yards, and promptly pitched the ball to end Jim Tapp. Tapp took the lateral at the 30 and went into the end zone untouched. Fullback Jim D' Antonio rammed over behind right tackle for the two-point conversion, and the game ended in an 8-8 deadlock, which awarded Duke the league crown.

With one regular season contest still to be played, the ACC champions headed out to Los Angeles to meet UCLA. The Blue Devil players received star treatment upon their arrival in California, none more so than Don Altman. Altman got a rare chance to meet Elvis Presley, who was in the area working on a film at the time.

"They took the team to 20th-Century Fox for a visit, and Elvis and Millie Perkins were filming a picture—the drama '*Wild in the Country*,'" Altman recalled years later. "I was asked to pose with Elvis, showing him how to throw a football. I was nervous as a kid. I asked if he was going to the game and he said, 'The last time I went to a game, it took 75 cops to get me out.'"

The King was not on hand for the game, but UCLA quarterback Billy Kilmer was. The NCAA leader in total offense, Kilmer frustrated the Blue Devils to no end with his accurate passing. Kilmer, who would lead the Washington Redskins into Super Bowl VII on the same Los Angeles Coliseum field more than a decade later, threw a touchdown to Dan Vena to propel UCLA to a 27-6 victory. Fortunately for Duke, the loss to UCLA had no bearing on their Holiday plans. By virtue of their 7-3 regular season record, along with the ACC championship, the Blue Devils were assured a major bowl berth for the third time in seven years.

Duke rode into Dallas for the Cotton Bowl, where Arkansas greeted the blue and white for the New Year. Frank Broyles and the Razorbacks had dropped a pair of close games in October, but came into the contest as Southwest Conference champions for the second year in a row. With all-purpose superstar Lance Alworth leading the way, Arkansas had won eight regular season games. The fleet-footed Alworth would soon make his mark as one of the showcase performers in the new American Football League, the first serious rival to the established National Football League for supremacy in professional football. In 1960, Alworth led the NCAA in punt return yardage.

Alworth did it all for the Razorbacks, almost single-handedly propelling them to victory with his catching, running, and kicking. The speedster accounted for more than half of his team's total production on offense and special teams, and earned Player of the Game laurels. The teams traded defensive stop after defensive stop in the first thirty minutes, and played to a scoreless tie. With just under three minutes to play in the third quarter, Duke was forced to punt from deep in its own territory. Alworth circled under a high kick and caught it at the Blue Devil 49, and after eluding a couple of would-be tacklers, the Arkansas speedster raced to the end zone, giving Arkansas the first points and a 6-0 lead. Dave Unser came up big for Duke on the ensuing extra point attempt, breaking off his block and sniffing out the kick.

Starting from their own 27 early in the final quarter, Duke began a drive that led to their first and only touchdown of the contest. It took eighteen gritty plays for the Blue Devils to move through Arkansas's defenders, as Altman put forth his most courageous effort of the season. The Blue Devil quarterback completed a pair of fourth down passes on the march, and completed five passes to Moorman who, in a matchup of All-Americans, found a way to shake free of Alworth. With the ball at the Arkansas 9, Altman completed the long march by finding Moorman once again, this time in the end zone. With 2:45 remaining, Art Browning was good on the extra point to give Duke a 7-6 lead.

With Alworth back to return the ensuing kickoff, nothing was set in stone yet for the Blue Devils. Alworth took in the kick and was just getting up to speed when Dave Unser made his second big defensive play. Coming from the outside, Unser leveled Alworth at the 32, forcing a fumble that the Blue Devils recovered. Duke easily ran out the clock for a 7-6 triumph, which proved to be the school's final bowl victory in the ACC's first half century.

With several starters returning to the fold in 1961, the Blue Devils were confident that they could finish at the top of the ACC yet again that fall. Walt Rappold, who had directed Duke's second-string offense to 15 touchdowns in 1960, graduated to the helm of Murray's first unit. Rappold had the luxury of handing off to four talented backs, led by Mark Leggett and Jack Wilson. Gil Garner, a pinpoint passer, took Rappold's spot at the helm of the second team.

Again the Blue Devils opened against South Carolina, and this time the going was much tougher. A 26-yard field goal by Dean Findley gave USC a 3-0 lead in the first quarter, and another successful kick in the fourth quarter appeared to salt away victory for the Gamecocks. With just over five minutes left, Duke got a chance to avert the upset. The Blue Devils had made countless mistakes that helped keep USC out in front, but Dave Burch's 3-yard dive late in the game finally knotted up the score. Bill Reynolds booted the vital extra point, and Duke was victorious, 7-6.

The Blue Devils made things a bit easier on themselves against Virginia, destroying the Cavaliers, 42-0. Virginia had snapped their twenty-eight-game losing streak the week before by beating William and Mary, but the Blue Devils were far less obliging. The Blue Devils scored twenty-eight unanswered points in the second quarter, turning what was a close game into another blowout in the series with UVA. The biggest highlight was turned in by sophomore Jay Wilkinson, who galloped 63 yards through the Virginia resistance on his first play as a varsity player for Duke.

The Blue Devils were not quite as dominant against Wake Forest, but proved good enough to claim their third straight conference victory. Again Duke's defense played spirited football, and for the third straight game, the blue and white defenders held their opponent out of the end zone. A nine-point swing early in the final frame gave Duke its winning margin of 23-3.

Duke's next game, played against Georgia Tech, proved to be a reality check. Four turnovers and a solid effort by the Yellow Jacket defense humbled their efforts. For the first time in two years, Murray's swing-end offense met its match, as Duke was held to only 67 total yards. After marching to the Yellow Jacket 36 on the opening possession, Duke did not earn another first down or complete another pass until the fourth quarter. Three unanswered scores in the second half paved the way to a 21-0 victory for the Ramblin' Wreck.

The Georgia Tech loss chipped away at Duke's confidence, as they dropped a homecoming clash in Durham the following week against Clemson. Jim Parker led the Tigers to two touchdowns and a late field goal in the 17-7 upset. With a steady rain driving down, turnovers again did in the Devils. After Parker ran over from the 1 to give Clemson a 14-7 lead, Duke fumbled on back-to-back possessions. The final turnover gave Lon Armstrong an opportunity to kick a 25-yard field goal for the only points of the final quarter.

North Carolina State provided a welcome reprieve for the Blue Devils, as they got back on track with their fourth win in a row over the Wolfpack. After two weeks of fumbles and missed opportunities, Duke protected the football against State. The Blue Devils coughed it up only on the game's final play, after the issue had long been settled. The hard-fought 17-6 win was exactly what Duke needed to turn their season around. Roman Gabriel was held in check by the Blue Devil secondary, and struggled in completing only nine passes.

For the second consecutive year the Blue Devils traveled to Ann Arbor to play Michigan, and again they were turned away by the Big Ten power. Playing at home for the fifth time in six games, the Wolverines got it going when quarterback Dave Glinka found Bob Brown for a score. The touchdown was followed by a hat trick from Michigan's Bennie McRae, who produced the remainder of the Wolverine points. After hauling in a pass from Glinka for one tally, McRae returned an interception for another touchdown, which came less than a minute after his scoring reception. McRae's final touchdown put Michigan in cruise control, although a pair of touchdowns by Dave Burch pulled the Blue Devils closer. It would not be enough, as Duke dropped a 28-14 verdict.

Going for their second consecutive victory over Navy, Wilkinson raced 77 yards to the end zone on the game's third play. Rappold went 45 yards minutes later for another touchdown, and Bill Reynolds' field goal had the Blue Devils leading, 17-0. Navy finally got on the scoreboard with a pass play, but a dive from Leggett canceled it out. The second half was primarily a lull, as the teams punted back and forth. The downtrodden Middies were unable to chip at Duke's lead aside of a single field goal, and a Jack Wilson interception set up Duke's final score in their 30-9 victory.

The ACC title was up for grabs in Durham on November 18, as Jim Hickey and the Tar Heels came to town. With Duke 4-1 and UNC 3-1 in the conference, a Carolina victory would all but guarantee the school's first ACC championship in football. The game lived up to its billing, as the rivals traded blows for four physical quarters. The Blue Devils got two good early scoring opportunities but kicked themselves in the foot, committing the same kinds of mistakes that had cost them against Georgia Tech and Clemson. On their second possession the Blue Devils mounted a solid drive, but a penalty killed their momentum. Another drive got them back into Carolina territory, but on first down UNC came up with an interception.

A third Duke miscue, a fumble on their 15, set up the game's first score. Bob Elliott kicked a field goal and UNC had a 3-0 lead. The fired-up Blue Devil offense came out gunning in the third quarter, taking their first possession 77 yards to the Carolina 1. After three unsuccessful sneaks, Murray neglected the tie and went for it on fourth down. As they had done all afternoon the Carolina defense held, stuffing Duke a foot short of the line. With only 5:02 remaining, the Blue Devils finally got on the board when Reynolds tied the game with a field goal. In the final minute Carolina had the ball at midfield, and the defensive struggle seemed destined for a 3-3 tie. Then came two of the strangest plays that anyone had ever seen.

With twenty-two seconds left, a long Carolina pass was intercepted by Wright, who returned the ball 41 yards into UNC territory. On the play, the officials called a penalty against the Tar Heels. Although it was later determined that the penalty was for face masking, it was ruled holding on the field. A would-be Carolina tackler had grabbed Wright's mask, and the costly 15-yarder put Duke in Reynolds' range with only six seconds on the clock.

Reynolds received a solid snap and hold, got good leg on it, and watched on triumphantly as the ball sailed through the uprights with only two seconds to play. Carolina received a short kickoff and desperately tried to make something happen, making three laterals. The final one, a toss from Elliott to Ray Farris, sprung a gap. Farris raced downfield for what the briefest of moments looked like a miraculous Carolina touchdown. Unfortunately for UNC, the play had not only been blown dead, but the Tar Heels had been called for another penalty, which Duke would have naturally declined to end the contest. After the game, the opposing head coaches gave their differing opinions on the weird closing moments.

"Holding was the signal on the penalties," said Hickey, referring to the call on the interception return. "How can you be called for holding when you are trying to tackle a man?"

"Two things happened on the final play," Murray added. "There was a penalty against Carolina, and apparently part of Elliott's body touched the ground before he lateraled."

The day after Carolina and Duke's epic struggle, South Carolina forged a 21-14 victory at home over Clemson. The 1961 USC-Clemson contest was not particularly memorable for the actual game, a relatively meaningless encounter between two teams near the bottom of the conference standings. It was what happened on the field before the contest that made this one memorable, and the source of laughter and remembrance for years to come.

Members of South Carolina's Sigma Nu Fraternity, in an effort to humiliate their hated rivals to the west, came up with a brilliant plan for the 1961 game with Clemson. Two years earlier, a group of CU students had made a late-night raid on Columbia's Sumter Street, causing havoc and sabotaging statues of esteemed USC Alumni. In the name of revenge, the fraternity boys decided to pull the ultimate prank; they would come onto the field dressed as the Clemson team, and then proceed to make a mockery of Frank Howard's squad in front of their own fans.

For three weeks the brothers trained as if they were real players. As the "team" did stretches and drills in order to look as authentic as possible, the fifty-large fraternity somehow managed to keep the secret to themselves. As the big day neared, one of the brothers, who had connections to the football team at nearby Orangeburg High, landed a full set of uniforms for the imposters to wear. The uniforms were orange, white, and purple, nearly identical to those worn by the Tigers. To top it all, the Sigma Nus had found an old milk cow that they were going to parade on the field as Clemson's homecoming queen.

Finally, the day of the game arrived. As always when the Gamecocks and Tigers came together on the gridiron, the fans worked themselves into a frenzy in the moments before kickoff. The legions of Tiger fans heckled and cursed at the South Carolina fans, while Gamecock supporters belittled and laughed at the Clemson fans. The respective bands were trying to outdo one another in playing their beloved fight songs. Then, out of the southeast end zone, the imposters began running onto the field. The frat boys had done such a remarkable job of keeping their prank a secret that even the South Carolina fans thought they were the Clemson team. Tiger fans began cheering as the CU cannon fired away, and the band began playing "Hold That Tiger."

The Sigma Nus aligned and began doing push-ups and other exercises. Moments later, a brother dressed as Howard strolled out. He had stuffed a pillow under his shirt in order to give a feasible impression of the Clemson coach. He then began spitting tobacco juice all over the place, and the prank went into action. The punter began kicking the ball backwards behind his head, and the quarterback began deliberately coughing up the ball. As the running back started doing flips and somersaults, a number of the players began making a milking motion with their hands and dancing to music in the background. It was at that moment when the Clemson fans realized that they had been duped. The Tiger supporters began streaming out of the stands and onto the field, and a riot broke out at Carolina Stadium. The frat boys, decked out in shoulder pads and helmets, were ready for the barrage of CU fans. For several minutes, punches were thrown and bodies were slung. The police finally restored order and the game was allowed to proceed.

Today, there are conflicting accounts as to who actually won the onfield melee. Clemson fans will swear that they got the best of the imposters, while Gamecock supporters maintain that they took care of business when the Tiger fans poured out of the stands. Regardless of who won, the riot made newspapers throughout the country, as far away as Detroit and Los Angeles.

With today's multitiered stadiums and increased security, it is safe to say that the ACC may never again see another elaborate scheme such as the one pulled by Sigma Nu that night back in 1961. Ironically, many of the imposters went on to prolific professional success. Among the pranksters were doctors, lawyers, judges, and even the one-day Lt. Governor of South Carolina! Unfortunately, one of the biggest components of the prank never even made it into the stadium that night. Ol' Bessie, the cow that the frat boys had planned to flaunt onto the field as Clemson's Homecoming Queen, died on the way to the game.

Duke had a week off before their final contest, a nonconference encounter with Notre Dame. The Irish were struggling through a trying period in their illustrious history, and no longer invoked the same kind of fear that they did during the days of Frank Leahy. Although the Irish took an early lead on a 54-yard run by Angelo Dabiero, the Blue Devils played a superior game on offense. Three different Duke quarterbacks threw touchdown passes, and the defense allowed only one more Notre Dame score in the 37-13 victory. Although the Devils won seven games for the second year in a row, their midseason collapse kept them from another postseason appearance.

Despite all of his solid teams in recent years at Duke, Murray's 1962 Blue Devils in many ways topped them all. The squad became the first in ACC history to go 6-0 in league play, and along the way captured an unprecedented third consecutive conference title. The Blue Devils led the league in scoring offense and scoring defense, marking the first time since joining the ACC that a Duke team had accomplished that feat. With Mark Leggett, Jay Wilkinson, and Gil Garner all returning for another season, Murray's squad was explosive as ever. Add backs Mike Curtis and Bill Futrell to the mix, and the Blue Devils had all the tools for a powerful team on both sides of the ball.

The Blue Devils flew to California for their season opener against USC, and nearly came up with a victory against the eventual national champions. Playing in front of a nationwide television audience, Duke drew first blood with a 25-yard pass from Garner to Wilkinson. The Trojans came back with a pair of touchdowns by quarterbacks Pete Beathard and Bill Nelson. Beathard connected with Willie Brown, and Nelson completed a pass to Hal Bedsole. The Blue Devils had thrown only nine interceptions in all of 1961, but threw five against USC to kill several threats. Combined with only 55 yards rushing, Duke was unable to overcome USC's 14-7 halftime advantage. The second half went by scoreless for both teams, and the Trojans held on for the slim victory.

South Carolina had their chances against the Blue Devils in the ACC opener, but Duke held the Gamecocks out three separate times from inside the 10-yard line. After a scoreless first half, the Devils finally put points on the board on a 14-yard sweep by Futrell less than five minutes into the third quarter. Duke's final touchdowns each came in the fourth quarter, as the Blue Devils wore down the Gamecocks with drives of eighteen and eleven plays. Leggett reached the end zone from the 6 to make the score 14-0, and Curtis fell over to push the advantage to 21-0. The frustrated Gamecocks finally reached the end zone with thirty seconds to play, but Duke had a 21-8 verdict.

Heading to Jacksonville to meet Florida, the Blue Devils summoned up a courageous second half effort to seize victory from the grasps of defeat. The Gators could do no wrong in the second quarter, jumping out to a 21-0 lead at halftime, but Murray and the Blue Devil coaching staff made a series of key adjustments for the second half. As the Blue Devil secondary tightened up against the Florida passing attack, the Duke offensive unit assumed strategic control. The Devil quarterbacks completed ten consecutive passes to lead three scoring drives, and a second touchdown by Curtis early in the fourth quarter gave the blue and white the lead. Florida continued to struggle against Duke's rejuvenated defenders, and a sack by tackle Chuck Walker at midfield sealed their 28-21 comeback victory.

Marv Levy brought his California team to Wallace Wade Stadium on October 13, and the Bears had no match for Duke's aggressive linemen. Jean Berry and Art Gregory were forces up front for the Devils, helping hold the Bears to only 12 yards rushing and providing enough room for the backs to amass 225 yards on the ground. Curtis scored twice for the second week in a row, and the Blue Devils took the game, 21-7.

The Blue Devil defense had come a long way since the first half debacle against Florida, allowing only one touchdown over their last six quarters. Murray's troops carried that confidence down to Clemson and came back with a 16-0 victory, Duke's first shutout over the Tigers in twenty-six years. Curtis, who by game's end was leading the ACC in scoring, set up Duke's first touchdown with a leaping interception at the 34. Curtis's second pick led to another Duke score, which came on a 4-yard run by Walt Rappold. A 30-yard field goal in the fourth quarter gave the Blue Devils their final margin.

With four consecutive victories under their belt, it seemed elementary that the Blue Devils would wipe out N.C. State on their home field. Without Roman Gabriel in 1962, the Wolfpack had already been shut out twice, and had only one victory against four defeats. State's offensive woes continued against the Blue Devils, as they mounted only 166 yards. Despite their lack of production, the Wolfpack scored two touchdowns to keep the game competitive.

Jimmy Guin caught a 9-yard touchdown from Bill Kriger to put NCSU on the board, and following two Blue Devil scores, Jim Rossi ran over to tie the game at 14. The Wolfpack gave Duke everything they could handle in the fourth quarter, but the Blue Devils finally took control with 1:20 left on the clock. Lonesome end Stan Crisson broke free from his defender and caught a 15-yard touchdown from Rappold, and Reynolds' extra point gave Duke a surprisingly close 21-14 victory.

Georgia Tech quarterback Billy Lothridge enjoyed another fine game against the Blue Devils a week later, completing his first six passes and finishing the game twelve-of-sixteen for 125 yards. Lothridge added 53 rushing yards, and scored 14 of Georgia Tech's 20 points on a touchdown, two field goals, and two extra points. Lothridge's 6-yard run in the first quarter got GT on the board, and his kick late in the half gave the Yellow Jackets a 17-3 lead at intermission. Futrell scored a touchdown in the final quarter to bring Duke closer, but Lothridge's running and cross-field passes led the way to a 20-9 Georgia Tech conquest.

The Blue Devils had only a week to regroup for Maryland, who came to Durham with a 6-1 record. Quarterback Dick Shiner was leading the nation in passing, and had the Terrapins first in the ACC in total offense. The Terrapins also boasted the ACC's top receiver in Tom Brown, who would tie Sonny Randle's league record with forty-seven receptions, and running back Len Chiaverini, who went on to lead the conference with 602 yards rushing. Penn State had snapped Maryland's unbeaten streak the week before the Duke contest, but the Terps came into the game with a perfect ACC record.

In a fierce defensive struggle, Duke scored the first points in the second quarter on a field goal by Reynolds. The kick, which came at the 3:17 mark, gave the Blue Devils a 3-0 lead at the break. It was a frustrating half for Shiner, who threw two interceptions on the Duke goal line. The Blue Devil offense took possession to start the third quarter and moved 58 yards, with Curtis rambling through for a 10-0 advantage. The Terrapins finally scored on their next possession, but were unable to mount any more offensives. The 10-7 victory was Duke's third in a row over Maryland, and all but sealed another ACC title for the Blue Devils. The Terrapins dropped another game to Clemson the following weekend to finish third.

Duke closed out its schedule with road clashes against traditional rivals Wake Forest and North Carolina. The Blue Devils had yet to lose to Wake Forest since the inception of the ACC, and kept their streak intact with an overwhelming performance in Winston-Salem. Behind 342 yards and two defensive touchdowns, Duke sent the Deacons to their ninth consecutive loss with a 50-0 blowout. The wipeout was Duke's biggest margin of victory against any opponent in eight years, and gave the team seven wins for the third year in a row.

For the second year in a row, Reynolds proved to be the hero in the battle against North Carolina. The Blue Devil placekicker was good on two field goals in the opening half, with the first giving the blue and white an early lead. Trailing 7-6 at halftime, Duke finally reached the end zone on a 5-yard carry by Futrell in the third quarter. Duke held its 13-7 advantage into the final quarter, when Junior Edge began passing UNC toward another touchdown. Edge's 39-yard reception to Bob Lacey put the Tar Heels in close, and a diving grab by Lacey at the 8 gave Carolina a 14-13 lead. Duke managed to move into UNC territory as the final minutes ticked away, and put Reynolds in position for his third field goal with forty-nine seconds to play. With the ball spotted in the middle of the field, Reynolds booted a perfect kick through the up-rights for his second consecutive game-winning effort over the Tar Heels.

"It was one of the most exciting games I've ever had anything to do with," Murray said afterwards. "I'm relieved that we won."

Despite an 8-2 record, and a ranking of No. 14 in the Coaches Poll, Duke was again denied a trip to the postseason. Murray's team would have been a good fit for the Bluebonnet Bowl, but Georgia Tech's November victory over the Blue Devils compelled the selection committee to go with the Yellow Jackets instead. It was a bittersweet finish for the Duke seniors, who ended their varsity careers with three Atlantic Coast Conference titles and a record of 16-2 in league play. With the departures of Bill Reynolds, Walt Rappold, Gil Garner, Jean Berry, and Art Gregory after the 1962 season, an era came to an end in Durham. In the four decades since Bill Murray's sixth championship team last took the field, no Duke team has won an outright ACC championship or finished ranked in a national poll.

4

An Era of Change (1963-1968)

The Atlantic Coast Conference went through a great deal of transformation during the turbulent years of the mid-1960s. Duke's reign as the superior team on the gridiron came to an end, while Clemson and North Carolina State assumed new roles as the teams to beat. As the South began to catch up with the rest of the country in terms of educational and athletic equality, African Americans began filling up roster spots throughout the league. One-platoon football gave way to the modern era of unlimited substitution, and new stadiums were dedicated on the campuses of North Carolina State and Wake Forest.

The eight member institutions of the Atlantic Coast Conference began accepting students of color in the late 1950s and early 1960s, as the South gradually rid itself of archaic educational policies that segregated black and white students. It was only a matter of time before the schools began pursuing athletes, and in 1963, the league welcomed its first black football player, Darryl Hill of Maryland. Hill was one of the few bright spots on Tom Nugent's 3-7 Terrapins, and his contributions paved the way for more young men of his race to play football in the ACC.

North Carolina, which won only three times in 1962, rallied behind Jim Hickey to win nine in 1963, the most for a Tar Heel team since the 1948 squad of Choo Choo Justice and Art Weiner. Quarterback Junior Edge and two-way talents Bob Lacey and Chris Hanburger led the way, along with All-Conference halfback Ken Willard. Edge amassed an ACC-best 1,413 all-purpose yards, while Lacey led the league in receiving and starred on a defense that allowed only 84 passing yards a game. Willard finished the year with 648 yards rushing.

Hanburger, a center/linebacker, provided motivation for his teammates in the form of intimidation. As the Tar Heels were driving downfield during one game, Hanburger got in Willard's face and told him, "if you don't get that damn ball down in there this time, you'll have to handle me after the game." Willard wisely punched the ball over the goal line. With Hanburger leading the way on defense, the Tar Heels gave up an average of less than ten points an outing.

Although they played another unbalanced schedule, with seven of their ten regular season contests away from Raleigh, N.C. State won eight games for the first time since joining the ACC. As a result, the Wolfpack tied the Tar Heels atop the standings with a 6-1 record. With Don Montgomery and Joe Scarpati earning All-Conference honors for their second seasons in a row, State's defense led the league by allowing just over nine points a game. Scarpati was also a dangerous offensive weapon, and made a number of big plays on that side of the ball over the course of the year. Quarterback Jim Rossi, who combined speed with an accurate throwing arm, propelled State's offensive charges.

Carolina opened their schedule at home against Virginia, and the Cavaliers surprised the Kenan Stadium faithful with a courageous defensive effort. Virginia held the Tar Heels to a single score in the first half, which came on a field goal attempt that was bobbled but successfully converted. On Carolina's second possession, Edge was knocked senseless after a violent collision with the ground. Backup Gary Black came on to lead the Tar Heel offense, but spent most of the game struggling to find momentum.

The second half began with a bang for Virginia, as Henry Massie took the kickoff and ran it back 99 yards for a touchdown. Just when it seemed that Virginia might escape Chapel Hill with a win for the first time in six years, the Carolina offense came alive. Midway through the final quarter, UNC began a march that resulted in their first and only touchdown of the game. Black connected with backup tight end Joe Robinson three times on the critical march, eating up 43 yards of real estate. With 5:01 left, Willard pounded his way over from the 2 to give Carolina the lead. Going for two, Black found Willard again on a flare pass for an 11-7 score. Virginia, which gained only 80 yards all game against the UNC defenders, was unable to make another comeback.

The Wolfpack played Maryland in a historic season opener, as Hill's appearance officially desegregated the league. The Wolfpack came out like gangbusters in the first twenty minutes, jumping out to a 22-0 lead. Although Dick Shiner led the Terrapins on two scoring marches in the second and fourth quarters, Scarpati's rush and Rossi's second scoring pass completed State's 36-14 victory. Edge returned for a road encounter with Michigan State, but the Carolina quarterback found little success against a formidable Spartan defense. The second half was a nightmare for UNC, as they managed only 27 yards offensively. A pair of fumbles led to two Spartan scores, as quarterbacks Steve Juday and Dick Proebstile each rumbled over from the 1. The sneaks were sandwiched around a solid individual effort by Roger Lopes, who broke free on a 76-yard carry. The scores gave Michigan State a 31-0 triumph.

The Wolfpack had revenge on their minds down in Hattiesburg against defending College Division champion Southern Mississippi. Rossi completed a pair of touchdown tosses, one in each half, to point NCSU in the right direction. Rossi's first pass was to Ray Barlow, giving State a 7-0 lead with thirteen seconds remaining in the first half. Rossi's second touchdown came in the final quarter, and was good for 4 yards to Bob Faircloth. Southern Miss rushed for 205 yards, but was unable to score under the pressure of the Wolfpack defense.

Playing on Saturday night in Winston-Salem, the Tar Heels handed Wake Forest its thirteenth consecutive defeat with a 21-0 victory. Edge got it started in the second quarter with a 1-yard carry over center, and the Carolina defenders held the Deacons to 92 total yards. The Tar Heels put the game on ice on the second play of the second half, when senior halfback Ronnie Jackson ran in a 72-yard touchdown on a pass from Edge. Carolina's second offense scored the final touchdown, as Black connected with end John Atherton in the fourth quarter.

The Wolfpack defense came through again in the Clemson game, as they held their opposition out of the end zone for the second game in a row. The Tigers took a 3-0 lead on a 22-yard field goal by Frank Pearce, but Rossi connected with Barlow on a 77-yard touchdown for NCSU's lone offensive highlight. Despite spending most of the game on their own side of the field, State's defenders secured a 7-3 final through a scoreless second half.

Winless Maryland played the Tar Heels tough in College Park, but a record six interceptions proved to be their undoing. Although Carolina dominated the statistics in the opening half, they went into the locker rooms trailing 7-0. With forty-five seconds remaining in the second quarter, Edge dropped back on a rollout from deep in his own territory, lost control of the football, and Jerry Fishman fell on it in the end zone for a Terrapin score. Carolina tied the game early in the third quarter, and it remained deadlocked until early in the fourth quarter, when UNC took advantage of another Maryland interception. A Lacey touchdown gave Carolina the lead, and Eddie Kesler made a lunging interception in the end zone with only 2:15 remaining to secure the game for the Tar Heels.

South Carolina ended State's scoreless streak in Columbia, but the Wolfpack were too much in a convincing 18-6 victory. South Carolina's lone score came in the final quarter, and ended a run of eleven consecutive touchdown-free quarters by the State defenders. Playing in a heavy drizzle, NCSU dominated the first half by scoring twice and holding USC to only 30 total yards.

The showdown between the Tar Heels and the Wolfpack was at hand on October 19. The rivals were on a collision course, each winning their first three ACC contests behind solid defenses and capable offenses. Despite their successes, only one team would sit in first place at the end of the day. The teams played an even first half, trading field goals and touchdowns to go into halftime tied, 10-10. Taking the opening kickoff of the second half, UNC quickly moved 63 yards in six plays for the go-ahead score. Willard's 6-yard run gave Carolina a 17-10 lead, and they increased it minutes later when Edge connected with Joe Robinson for a 22-yard play. As the Wolfpack offense continued to struggle, Carolina took possession at their 15 and marched to the game's final touchdown. Runs by Willard, Edge, and Kesler ate up 80 yards, and Edge's second scoring pass to Robinson sealed UNC's 31-10 triumph.

"The kids made up their minds they were going to win this one," Hickey said after the contest. "Right after the Maryland game last week, our kids started thinking about this one. They wanted to win it as badly as any we ever played."

Following the loss to Carolina, the Wolfpack regrouped to put a stunner on Duke. The Blue Devils came into the game unbeaten, with each of their four victories coming against ACC competition. Scotty Glacken was flourishing as Duke's new starting quarterback, having set a record with four touchdown passes against Clemson. Unfortunately for the Blue Devil signal caller, his offensive line was not prepared for State's aggressive defense, and he spent the day running for his life. Duke struggled all afternoon to move the football, and the Wolfpack went ahead, 14-0, in the last minute of the first half as Scarpati caught a pass from Rossi and raced 39 yards to the goal line. Although Duke cut the NCSU lead to a touchdown with 9:11 to play, the Wolfpack intercepted three Blue Devil passes in the final quarter. With a 21-7 triumph, the Wolfpack claimed their first victory over the Blue Devils in seventeen years, and ended Duke's thirteen-game winning streak in ACC play.

"Wonderful, wonderful, wonderful," exclaimed Earle Edwards in the locker room. "It's taken a long time coming, but it makes it more enjoyable. It was the hardest we have played this year, an outstanding effort. It is a happy occasion. When you beat Duke, you beat a good football team."

The Tar Heels used the momentum of the N.C. State victory to forge a 7-0 verdict over South Carolina. The first fifty-seven minutes were dominated by the defenses, as UNC mustered little more than two unsuccessful field goal tries. Late in the game South Carolina was backed up at its own 14, where they were faced with a fourth down. South Carolina punter Jack McCathern shanked the kick, and the ball went out of bounds at the Gamecock 34 with 3:38 left on the clock. A couple of plays later, Willard piled over for the first points of the game. The final Gamecock stand was sniffed out by the UNC defense, and the unit could now boast six consecutive quarters without giving up a point.

Carolina continued its inspiring play with a 28-7 home victory over Georgia. An Atlanta writer made controversy before the contest by suggesting that Junior Edge was slow, in a column that wound up on the UNC bulletin board. The Tar Heel quarterback quickly proved the writer wrong by sprinting for 14 yards on the first play from scrimmage. Edge led the Tar Heels on a 57-yard march on their second drive for a 7-0 lead. Edge scored UNC's second touchdown on a 1-yard sneak in the second quarter, and Dave Braine's extra point gave the Heels a 14-7 advantage at the intermission. Edge, who finished the game fifteen-of-twenty for 189 yards passing, found Ronnie Jackson streaking toward the goal line early in the fourth quarter. Edge gave Carolina its final score with an 8-yard scamper later in the period.

N.C. State met Virginia on a blustery day in Norfolk, as a twenty-four-mph wind blew through the stadium for much of the day. The wind kept both teams from making significant strides on offense, and was detrimental to the kicking games. The Wolfpack took control of the game in the second half, scoring a pair of rushing touchdowns to take a 15-7 lead. Virginia scored a safety of its own, but the Cavaliers were on the wrong end of a 15-9 score.

The Wolfpack secondary came up with a formidable effort against Virginia Tech, holding Gobbler quarterback Bob Schweickert to only 12 yards in the air. The State defenders put the game away in the third quarter, falling on a botched VT punt in the end zone for a 13-0 lead. Schweickert's fourth quarter touchdown kept the Gobblers from falling victim to a shutout.

As the Wolfpack were polishing off Virginia Tech in Raleigh, the Tar Heels were having their five-game winning streak snapped by Clemson on their home field. The Tigers came to Chapel Hill and dished out an 11-7 upset that threw Duke and State back into a first place tie with the Tar Heels. The Tigers scored the only points of the first half on a field goal, as Frank Pearce belted a 40-yarder in the second quarter. The Tiger defense neutralized Carolina's explosive offense, allowing them to get no closer than the CU 36 over the course of the opening half.

Carolina came back to take the lead in the third quarter, but the Tigers refused to buckle, starting a drive from their own 12 that resulted in the game-winning touchdown. The Tigers used their running game to put the UNC defenders on their heels, and once they had the Tar Heels thinking run, Frank Howard changed tactics, going to the air on a 34-yard strike from Jim Parker to Johnny Case. Parker snuck over seconds later from the 1, and although there were nearly eight minutes left after a successful two-point conversion, UNC failed to make another first down.

The Tar Heels stayed at home for a third straight week to play Miami, and won 27-16 to avenge three consecutive defeats at the hands of the Hurricanes. Miami drew first blood with a 78-yard march off the kickoff, but UNC tied it on a sneak by Edge in the second quarter. Miami notched a field goal early in the third quarter for a 10-7 lead, but the Heels scored back-to-back touchdowns. Black finished one drive with a 19-yard pass to Ron Tuthill, and Edge threw to Jackson to give UNC a 20-10 lead. George Mira threw a pass to John Bennett to bring the Hurricanes closer, but Willard bowled over in the final minute to conclude a drive that ate off the final half of the fourth quarter.

State met its match in Tallahassee against Florida State, as the Seminoles handed the Wolfpack their second loss of the season, 14-0. The teams played evenly through most of the first half, but a Wolfpack miscue led to FSU's winning score. Following an FSU fumble recovery at the NCSU 31, Larry Brinkley provided the points with a short run. Florida State's final score came in the final two minutes, as backup quarterback Ed Pritchett dived over. The Wolfpack gambled with a fake punt on their own 12, but Rossi's desperation pass to Pete Falzarano was knocked away.

As Friday, November 22, dawned, the ACC race was about to be decided. State and Wake Forest were scheduled to meet that night in Raleigh, while Carolina and Duke were set to play the following day in Durham. That afternoon, word spread throughout the country that

President John F. Kennedy had been assassinated in Dallas. With football suddenly an afterthought, Duke president Douglas Knight and UNC chancellor William Aycock agreed to postpone their game until the following week.

State and Wake Forest chose to play on, and the crowd at Riddick Stadium honored America's fallen leader during the pregame festivities. After the band finished the national anthem, the crowd engaged in an extended moment of silence. North Carolina State chancellor John T. Caldwell addressed the crowd, saying that, "this is a day of deep tragedy for our nation and mankind. Let not the playing of this game diminish our sense of respect for our great President or the office."

"I deeply believe that President Kennedy would have wished the game to go on," Chancellor Caldwell said later that night. "The game would be played now or later, and our sense of respect for the President would not later be diminished. The players wanted to go on with the game, and I took the opportunity to pay respects and pray solemnly for our country."

The Wolfpack exploded for 35 points in the opening half, and set a new school rushing record with 408 yards on their way to a 42-0 blowout. Scarpati, and Rossi each had rushing scores, and Rossi threw to Barlow for another. Ron Skosnik threw a 61-yard touchdown to Shelby Mansfield to complete Wake Forest's annihilation.

Five days after they were originally scheduled to play, the Blue Devils and Tar Heels met on Thanksgiving Day in Durham. The Tar Heels asserted control early, as Willard and Kesler scored on short runs for a 13-0 lead. Duke came back with a vengeance, as Glacken threw a 70-yard touchdown pass to Bill Futrell, and Jay Wilkinson, who went on to earn All-American honors and the ACC Player of the Year award, broke free on a 24-yard touchdown sprint to tie the game. Steve Holloway's extra point gave the Blue Devils a 14-13 lead, and it looked as though Duke would sidestep the Tar Heels yet again. Carolina had other ideas, starting a furious march in the closing moments. The Tar Heels moved deep into Duke territory, and Max Chapman's kick sailed through the posts with thirty-three seconds to play. With a 16-14 win, UNC erased the painful memories of two last-second defeats at the hands of Duke in recent seasons.

North Carolina and N.C. State's impressive regular seasons were appealing to a number of bowls, and both schools received invitations to games. The Tar Heels accepted an invite to the Gator Bowl immediately after beating Duke, while N.C. State agreed to participate in the Liberty Bowl. It was the first time in history that two ACC schools were heading to bowls in the same postseason.

The 1963 Liberty Bowl between the Wolfpack and Mississippi State (MSU) was the last to be played in Philadelphia. With little fanfare, only 8,300 fans came out on a bitterly cold December day to watch the contest. In an interesting side note, protestors lined the sidewalk of Connie Mack Stadium before the game, opposing the decision of the Liberty Bowl Committee to bring two Southern schools without black players to Philadelphia. Mississippi State dominated the first half, scoring first on an 11-yard blocked punt return to the end zone. Following more bad special teams play by NCSU, the Bulldogs drove for a second touchdown to take a 13-0 advantage. The Wolfpack rallied to cut the gap, but the second half was a snapshot of futility, as neither team could mount a touchdown drive in the chilly nineteen-degree weather. With just over two minutes remaining, Rossi finally led NCSU across the goal line, connecting with Barlow to pull his team to within 16-12. After a failed two-point conversion, however, MSU successfully ran out the clock.

The North Carolina staff decided to reward their players for a job well done during the regular season, and put the team up in a posh St. Augustine hotel in the days leading up to the Gator Bowl. In addition, Hickey went with light workouts in hopes of keeping everyone fresh. Ben Martin and the Air Force (AF) staff went with a different approach, housing their players in an Army dormitory outside Orlando, and engaging in boot-camp style sessions in preparation for the Tar Heels. The Tar Heels dominated the Falcons from the outset, taking a 6-0 lead on their second possession. Willard, who led both teams with 94 rushing yards, ran seven times for 50 yards on Carolina's early march. As the Tar Heel defenders continuously stuck the AF offense at the line of scrimmage, Edge snuck over from the 6 and threw to Robinson late in the second quarter for a 20-0 UNC lead at the half.

Air Force, who was expected to give UNC a handful, was a beaten team by the start of the second half. Carolina began its fourth scoring march early in the third quarter, with Kesler finishing the 55-yard push with a dive from the 1. A conversion pass from Edge to Lacey made it 28-0, and Black ended the scoring in the final period with a 5-yard carry. The 35-0 score was the largest winning margin for any Gator Bowl victor in history, and with the win, Carolina entered the final Coaches Poll at No. 19.

In 1964, the one-platoon system of college football, also known by the more contemporary name of "Ironman," gave way to the modern format of unlimited substitution. With only one replacement allowed between plays under the old system, almost every player in the college

game played both an offensive and defensive position. Teams employed first and second offensive units that were in constant rotation,
and injuries were typically the only way that players came off the field
during their shifts. Linemen switched sides after possession changes,
going from a three-point offensive stance to the four-point defensive
look, while backs and receivers faded into the secondary.

The old system had been in place for twelve years, and was all the
Atlantic Coast Conference had ever known. The two-platoon system,
implemented throughout the NCAA before the 1964 season, modernized football at the collegiate level. As separate offensive and defensive
units were formed, players became more specialized. While the basic
concepts of football remained the same after unlimited substitution, the
complexity of the game did not. Teams could now practice their players
to perform on one side of the ball, which allowed the players to become
more skilled in their individual positions.

The autumn of 1964 proved to be a tough one for the ACC, the
first and only season in history in which no league member earned a
winning record. Parity is the word to describe it, as five different
schools finished with 5-5 records, including league champion N.C.
State. The quintet of 5-5 teams included Virginia, which won only once
in the conference but posted victories over all four of its other opponents. It was only the second time since joining the ACC that the Cavaliers finished with as many victories as defeats. Maryland, North Carolina, and Wake Forest were the other teams to post .500 records.

The Wolfpack boasted the ACC's best offensive line, anchored by
All-Conference performers Glenn Sasser and Bennett Williams. State
also found a surprising two-way star in Pete Falzarano. Falzarano had
played sparingly on defense before 1964, but Earle Edwards decided to
use him more on that side of the ball that season to maximize the unit's
speed and athleticism. Falzarano's interceptions and runs proved to be
the difference makers in State's first two victories.

Wake Forest boasted the ACC's top running back in Brian Piccolo,
who was the workhorse of Bill Tate's offense, which tied North Carolina for a league-best 172 points. Piccolo's 1,044 rushing yards that
season led the nation, and replaced another Deacon, Bill Barnes, in the
ACC record books. Piccolo also led the NCAA in points, with 111 tallied on seventeen touchdowns and nine conversions. It was no coincidence that Piccolo was the ACC's Player of the Year and an All-
American.

Piccolo is mostly remembered for his brave struggle with cancer,
which ultimately took his life at the age of twenty-six, and the 1971
made-for-television movie "Brian's Song," which is widely considered

one of the finest sports films in history. The movie starred James Caan and Billy Dee Williams, who portrayed Piccolo and Gale Sayers, the running tandem for the Chicago Bears in the late 1960s who became the first black-white teammates to room together on the road. Today, the Brian Piccolo Award in given annually to the ACC football player that best demonstrates courage on the field of play.

Piccolo was not heavily recruited as a prep player, and the Deacon coaches only learned of him in their efforts to recruit one of his team-mates, tackle Bill Salter. Although Piccolo was a fine high school ath-lete, and was scouted by a handful of professional baseball teams, he was largely overlooked on the gridiron. After committing Salter, the Deacons decided to take a chance and give Piccolo a scholarship as well. In 1961, Piccolo played for the Wake Forest junior varsity squad, helping the team win two out of five games. Averaging over 4 yards a carry, the Baby Deacons never lost yardage when Piccolo took a hand-off. Making the varsity his sophomore season, Piccolo played most of the time at fullback, gaining over 400 yards for the winless Deacons.

Things weren't much better for Wake in 1963, as the team lost its first eight contests to bring the varsity's losing streak to eighteen. In the next-to-last game of the season, the Deacons played South Carolina. In his breakout performance, Piccolo blasted the Gamecocks for 140 yards, and in the game's final minutes, Piccolo led the Deacons to vic-tory by scoring the tying touchdown and then converting the extra point. Tate came aboard for the 1964 season and guided WF to its best record in five years, earning Coach of the Year laurels along the way.

The Wolfpack opened against North Carolina in a showdown be-tween the joint champions of the prior autumn. Carolina was ranked in the preseason polls and favored to win, but State, still bitter about last season's embarrassing defeat to their greatest rival, made their short trip to Chapel Hill a memorable one. The Wolfpack defense came up with the game's first big play early in the second quarter, when end Tony Golmont intercepted a Danny Talbott pass and raced 45 yards to the end zone for a 7-0 lead.

With the game knotted 7-7 early in the fourth quarter, Pete Fal-zarano personally took control of the action. Playing linebacker, Fal-zarano intercepted a deflected pass to give the NCSU offense the ball. Edwards chose to keep him in the game at running back as the Wolf-pack took possession, and on the very next play, the speedster hit a hole and outran everyone to the end zone. Falzarano's interception and scor-ing run on consecutive plays shifted the momentum back to State, and

Harold Deter's extra point gave NCSU a 14-7 advantage with just over twelve minutes remaining.

With only forty-eight seconds on the clock, Talbott lofted a short screen to Ken Willard, who made the catch at the 5 and powered his way over for his second touchdown and a 14-13 score. To the appreciation of the Kenan Stadium crowd, Hickey elected to try for the win. This time Talbott went to the right, but Ron Skosnik spiked the ball to the deck for NCSU. After State nearly gave the game away with a fumbled snap, Talbott was unable to move the Tar Heels in position for a field goal. After the game, Earle Edwards received a ride to the locker room courtesy of his players' shoulders.

"We're just delighted beyond expression," Edwards said amid a joyous celebration in the dressing room. "It was one of our greatest victories—especially under the circumstances. They were pretty mad about the way they played last year. They haven't forgotten that. They just didn't execute. But today, we did those things that we failed to do last year."

The Wolfpack welcomed Clemson for the first game of the season at Riddick Stadium, and the defense again made the difference in a 9-0 shutout. The closest the Tigers came to the end zone was the Wolfpack 32, while State scored on its first two possessions for their only points. The red and white improved to 3-0 the following week by edging Maryland in another close home game. Bo Hickey ran 77 yards for a 7-0 Maryland lead on the first play from scrimmage, and the Terrapins added another score early in the second. Both scores were the result of trickery, as Maryland used unorthodox formations to put the Wolfpack off-balance. The Wolfpack surged late in the third quarter behind Charlie Noggle, who had nearly given away the UNC game with a fumble in the closing minutes. Noggle finished an eleven-play march with a 7-yard keeper, and after a fumble recovery gave NCSU the ball at the Maryland 4, Noggle rolled right and found enough daylight to force his body over the line. Gus Andrews was true on the conversion, and State had a 14-13 win.

The unbeaten Wolfpack next faced the unenviable task of playing Alabama down in Tuscaloosa, where one of Bear Bryant's finest teams was waiting. The Crimson Tide, on their way to the national championship, had dominated their three previous opponents behind a smothering defense and the right arm of Joe Namath. Namath had scouts from both the NFL and AFL drooling, but the NCSU defense dealt a punishing blow to the celebrated quarterback.

With the game still scoreless in the second quarter, Namath rolled out of the pocket and was met by Wolfpack end Bill Hall. The collision wrenched Namath's right knee, forcing him out of the contest. It was one of Namath's first encounters with knee troubles, something that plagued him throughout his football career. The Tide rolled on in Namath's absence, accumulating 171 yards both on the ground and in the air as Steve Sloan led the Crimson to three unanswered scores. State's inability to move the football against Alabama's formidable defense sealed their 21-0 demise.

The Duke veterans had not forgotten about their contest in Raleigh a year earlier, where the Wolfpack had ended their ACC-record winning streak. This time around things would be quite different, as the Blue Devils racked up 319 rushing yards and forced three Wolfpack turnovers. Leading 13-3 going into the fourth quarter, the Devils surged for 22 unanswered points to put the game away. With a 35-3 rout, Duke had its largest margin of victory in the NCSU series in eight seasons.

"I thought we had a good chance to win this game," Edwards said. "It was a real disappointment to all of us. They beat us up front. They out-charged us. It's hard to believe we could play so poorly."

State was still in the thick of the ACC race, but the Duke loss momentarily bumped the Wolfpack into second. With consecutive league games staring them in the face, NCSU pulled it together and got back in position to take the championship. Virginia, riding a surprising three-game winning streak, was first. The Wolfpack offensive line knocked UVA backwards throughout most of the game, and opened up hole after hole for Noggle and Shelby Mansfield. With a dominant effort on the ground, State took command for an important 24-15 triumph.

The Wolfpack returned to Raleigh to play South Carolina, and although USC hadn't won in fourteen contests, they played State tooth-and-nail. Dan Reeves got USC going in the first quarter with a 3-yard run, and after State scored 10 unanswered points, the Gamecock signal caller, who went on to appear in nine Super Bowls as a player and coach, led USC back into the lead with a short scoring burst. With State's championship lives hanging in the balance, Ron Skosnik came through in the clutch. On second down from the NCSU 28, Skosnik took off behind his right tackle and developed some momentum. After crossing the line of scrimmage, Skosnik plowed through a would-be tackler and sailed 72 yards, which thrust State back into the lead, 17-14. The defense got back on track and held out USC the rest of the way for State's fifth, and as it turned out, final win of the season.

Tough road games followed against Virginia Tech and Florida State, and the Wolfpack struggled in both encounters. The NCSU defense came unglued trying to stop VT quarterback Bob Schweickert, who scored twice in leading the Gobblers to a 28-19 verdict. Also that day, Duke rolled into Winston-Salem for a game against Wake Forest. Although they had been unseated as conference champions in 1963, the victory over NCSU had the Blue Devils poised to win yet another ACC crown for Bill Murray. It had been thirteen long years since Wake last tasted victory over their private school rival from Durham.

By game's end, Brian Piccolo had set an ACC record with thirty-six carries, gaining 115 yards and scoring all twenty of Wake Forest's points. Piccolo's first touchdown came in the opening quarter on a plunge from the 1, and he followed with a receiving score and another rushing tally in the second half. Although Piccolo missed his final extra point effort, it was a small consolation for Duke, who gave up its lead in the standings and succumbed to the Deacons, 20-7, to the delight of 17,000 spectators at Bowman Gray Stadium.

"Oh, I have never been so tired in my life," Piccolo said after the game. "But the thrill of winning makes me forget that I'm tired. After playing two years and winning only one game, I would have wondered a long time if somebody had told me in September that we would beat Duke this season."

Florida State outplayed the Wolfpack from the get-go in Tallahassee, using their lethal passing game to score on the game's seventh play. Seminole All-American Fred Biletnikoff had taken part in only one play in FSU's previous game against Houston, but the elusive receiver was back at full strength for the Wolfpack. Biletnikoff scored twice on passes from quarterback Steve Tensi, covering 38 yards and 12 yards, to give the Seminoles a commanding 28-0 cushion. All the while, FSU's "Magnificent Seven" defense stifled the Wolfpack, holding their backs to a paltry total of 6 yards for the entire game. The Seminoles, on their way to nine victories and a Gator Bowl berth, held on for a 28-6 win.

The Wolfpack met Wake Forest on a Friday night in Winston-Salem, and although they had more incentive to win, NCSU didn't play like it. Playing for the final time as a Deacon, Piccolo ran for 115 yards and three touchdowns, each coming on short carries, to lead the Wake Forest charges. As Piccolo wore down State in the second half, the Deacon defense stiffened, shutting out the Wolfpack over the final thirty minutes. Piccolo's second touchdown in the third quarter gave Wake some breathing room at 20-13, and after a penalty on NCSU late in the fourth quarter gave the Deacons the ball at the Wolfpack 8, Piccolo sealed the deal, scoring from the 5 on a sweep. The extra point gave WF a 27-13 victory.

The Wolfpack had lost control of their own destiny, and were forced to cheer for the hated Tar Heels in their contest the following day against Duke. Fortunately for NCSU, Ken Willard and Eddie Kesler unleashed a furious rushing assault on the Blue Devils. Kesler, who was normally reserved as Willard's lead blocker, had a breakout performance, rushing for a school-record 172 yards. Willard added 107 yards in his Chapel Hill curtain call, which included a pair of touchdowns. The 21-15 final gave NCSU the outright conference championship, although their .500 record was not worthy of bowl consideration.

The 1965 season was the first and only in history that the ACC football championship was awarded off the field of play. Duke and South Carolina finished atop the standings with identical 4-2 marks, but the Gamecocks were punished for their inability to monitor the scholastic performance of their players. In a surprising turn of events, Commissioner James Weaver stripped the Gamecocks of what would have been a share of the school's first conference championship at the conclusion of the season.

Weaver claimed that South Carolina had given scholarships to two players and allowed them to participate in games despite the fact that they failed to make the minimum score of 800 on the College Board Exams. As a result, USC forfeited every game in which the ineligible players played. The games included victories over Clemson and N.C. State, which thrust the Tigers and Wolfpack into a tie atop the standings with 5-2 marks. Since Duke had beaten the Gamecocks fair and square, they were offered no additional victories, and had to settle for second place. It was an embarrassing turn of events for the University of South Carolina, and resulted in Marvin Bass not returning for another season as head coach.

It was a down period for the ACC on the gridiron, the second year in a row that no league member won more than six games or appeared in a bowl. Despite their overall mediocrity, the schools fought tooth-and-nail for their places in the standings. All but one team, Wake Forest, won at least four times during the regular season. The Deacons, without its powerful tandem of Brian Piccolo and John Mackovic, scored only 88 points in ten contests.

Frank Howard's Clemson squad finished 5-5 before the USC forfeit, and took a piece of the league title despite getting outscored by their opposition. All-Conference running back Hugh Mauldin led the league with 664 yards, starting a run of three consecutive years in which CU boasted the conference's top ground gainer. Although they didn't know it at the time, Clemson's 21-7 victory at home over NCSU in the season opener would give them unofficial bragging rights to the ACC championship by season's end. The Tigers were an up-and-down team in 1965, for after beating Virginia in an uncharacteristically close 20-14 game, they were blown out in successive road encounters against Georgia Tech and Georgia.

A week later, the Tigers toppled Duke in one of the strangest games of the entire college football season. Bob Foyle blocked a punt through the back of the end zone for a Duke safety, but Frank Pearce kicked a field goal for the Tigers. Clemson won by the "baseball" score of 3-2, and went on to shut out Texas Christian 3-0 in their next contest. Howard's boys broke out of their offensive funk in a 26-13 verdict over Wake Forest, as four Tiger backs found the end zone. Phil Rogers had the highlight of the game, taking a reverse at his own 39 and racing 61 yards to the goal line.

The Tigers fell apart in November, dropping three straight games to close out the year. The passing and kicking of Danny Talbott gave North Carolina a 17-13 win in Chapel Hill, while Maryland's Bob Sullivan came up big in a 6-0 Terrapin upset in Death Valley. Sullivan, who set an ACC single-season record with ten interceptions, made two picks to kill a pair of Tiger drives. Bernardo Bramson kicked a pair of field goals for the Terrapin points.

Clemson could still claim the outright ACC title with a win over South Carolina, and victory was within their reach. Playing in Columbia, the Gamecocks held a 17-10 advantage late in the fourth quarter. Clemson began a desperate march into USC territory, and Rogers scored with under a minute remaining to pull the Tigers to within a point. On the extra point, Clemson's holder shocked the crowd by rising to his feet after taking the snap. The Gamecock secondary quickly responded to the fake pass, and the ball was deflected away for a 17-16 win. Although USC got the glory of on-the-field triumph, Commissioner Weaver's ruling gave Clemson the victory for the record books.

North Carolina State led the ACC in rushing and scoring defense, with linemen Pete Sokalsky and Dennis Byrd leading the charges. Byrd, a sophomore, would become the first defensive lineman in history to earn All-ACC honors three times. State began the year struggling, dropping four of its first five games. Clemson took them out in the opener, and after knocking off Wake Forest, NCSU went into an offensive lull. The Wolfpack scored only twenty points in their next three contests, dropping road games to South Carolina and Florida and losing, 10-7, at home to North Carolina.

Things finally came together for the Wolfpack against Maryland, as the defense set the tone in a 29-7 blowout. Sokalsky deflected a punt in the end zone, and backs Charlie Noggle and Bill Wyland piled over on short touchdown runs. A pass from Page Ashby to Harry Martell put the Wolfpack in domination mode. State's next three opponents were all shut out, as the NCSU defense enjoyed its longest scoreless streak of the Earle Edwards era. State's secondary blanketed Virginia's receivers in a 13-0 victory in Charlottesville, and the unit threw another blank in a 21-0 verdict over Duke.

The Wolfpack played the Blue Devils at the right time, with Duke mired in another late season free fall. For the third year in a row, the Blue Devils were struggling to win games in October and November. Duke started both the 1963 and 1964 seasons 4-0-1, and had dropped four of their last five in 1963 and each of their last five in 1964. The Wolfpack were more than happy to hand the Blue Devils another four-game collapse in the autumn of 1965, as Ashby, Mansfield, and Dan Golden all reached the end zone.

A week later, NCSU took out Florida State, 3-0, in the final game played at Riddick Stadium. Harold Deters was good on a field goal to give State their slim margin. The Wolfpack concluded their season in Iowa against a weak Hawkeye squad, and left town with a 28-20 victory. Although Iowa ended State's defensive shutout streak, the unit came up with seven interceptions. The victory in Iowa City gave State five in a row to finish the year, and with the South Carolina forfeit, the Wolfpack could claim a 7-3 record. For his efforts, Edwards was given Coach of the Year honors for a third time.

Although South Carolina finished only .500 overall, USC won four of its six ACC games before being handed the forfeits. The Gamecocks failed to win back-to-back games all year, and were buried in road contests against Southeastern Conference powers Tennessee, LSU, and Alabama. A loss to Duke got the Gamecocks off on the wrong foot in the conference, but victories over N.C. State and Wake Forest followed. Maryland gave the Gamecocks another league setback, but wins over Virginia and Clemson concluded the slate.

Although the USC forfeits nudged Duke out of the top spot, the Blue Devil offense was the most productive of the Bill Murray era, and one of the finest in school history. The Devils led the ACC with an average of 346.6 yards per contest, the most yardage racked up by an ACC team since Maryland's NCAA title juggernaut of 1953. Running back Jay Calabrese finished second in the conference with 658 yards, and earned All-ACC recognition as a sophomore. Calabrese also scored nine touchdowns, the most for a Blue Devil back in eleven seasons.

Junior quarterback Todd Orvald was good for 850 yards through the air, as Duke averaged a league-best 21 points a contest.

Calabrese was the hero of Duke's road victory over South Carolina, which would have given the Blue Devils a piece of the ACC championship if the Gamecocks hadn't used the ineligible players. Gaining 140 yards on fifteen attempts, Calabrese first reached the end zone on an 11-yard carry up the gut in the first quarter. Fellow sophomore Jake Devonshire added to the Devil lead in the last four minutes of the half, busting over from the 6 to successfully end a 53-yard string of plays. The Gamecocks rallied in the second half, but Calabrese's 67-yard backbreaker in the fourth quarter led the way to a 20-15 Duke victory.

As the Blue Devils endured another downward slide in the fall of 1965, Bill Murray decided the time had come for the program he had built to go in a different direction. Following Duke's 34-7 win over North Carolina to close out the year, Murray was carried to the center of the field as his players sang, "For He's a Jolly Good Fellow." Much of the celebration ended once the Duke team made it to the locker room. After leading his team through its customary postgame prayer, Murray informed the Blue Devil players that he was stepping down as their coach.

For several years leading up to his departure from coaching, Murray had been an important fixture within the American Football Coaches Association. The Blue Devil skipper had served as the president of the coaches since 1962, and had coached in each of the AFCA's first three postseason All-American games, held from 1961 to 1963. The owner of six ACC titles and four Coach of the Year awards, Murray was an opponent of free substitution, and felt that he was better suited in an advisory position than on the field of play.

Soon after his exodus from the Duke football program, Murray left Durham to accept a position as the executive director of the AFCA, a position he held until his retirement in 1982. Although Murray was unsuccessful bringing back an era of football that had lost its time, his contributions make him one of the most storied figures in the history of Duke football. Murray's departure signaled an end to Duke University's presence as an annual contender in the Atlantic Coast Conference football race. The Blue Devils have rarely been competitive in the nearly four decades since Murray's resignation, and have come nowhere near the sustained excellence they enjoyed under his command.

For the third year in a row in 1966, no ACC team earned a berth in a postseason bowl. Although Clemson went 6-1 in the league, the Tigers' three nonconference defeats did not entice any bowls into offering them a game. Clemson played a brutal schedule, with road contests against national powers Georgia Tech, Alabama, and the University of Southern California (USC). The Crimson Tide finished the 1966 season undefeated, while the Trojans went to the Rose Bowl for the first of four consecutive years. Add GT to the mix, a 9-2 team that went on to play in the Orange Bowl, and it was easy to see why Clemson struggled against their outside competition.

The tough early season contests prepared Frank Howard's team for a dramatic home stretch, as the Tigers won four out of their last five games to take Clemson's fourth undisputed ACC championship. Quarterback Jimmy Addison, nicknamed "The Needle" for his pinpoint passing, paced the Tiger offense. Although Buddy Gore and Jacky Jackson were more than competent in the Tiger backfield, it was Addison who led the way, particularly early in the year. The backs were aided up front by tackle Wayne Mass, who became the first CU player in seven seasons to be named All-American. Standing 6'4'' and weighing 240 pounds, Mass was one of the largest players in the ACC at that time, and the junior overwhelmed his opposition on the way to the Jacobs Blocking Trophy and the first of two All-ACC selections.

Clemson had to pull out all the punches to beat Virginia on the first weekend, as UVA quarterback Bob Davis had a career afternoon, setting ACC records for single-game attempts and completions. Davis also tied his own record by accounting for five Virginia touchdowns, with three coming on the ground and two through the air. Behind Davis, the Cavaliers raced out to a 35-18 second half lead on the strength of four unanswered touchdowns. The Tigers did themselves no favors, committing five turnovers to shift the momentum in UVA's favor.

With just over a quarter to play, Addison got Clemson headed back in the right direction with a drive that ate up 73 yards. The march took less than three minutes, and pulled CU to within two scores. The Needle returned to the field minutes later and led another successful rally, hitting Wayne Bell from the 11 to pull CU to within a touchdown. Clemson completed its impressive comeback minutes later, when Addison connected with Jackson from the 25 and the back raced the rest of the way for a 75-yard score, which put the Tigers ahead, 40-35. Davis promptly moved his team 62 yards to the Clemson 14, where he dropped back to throw with 2:06 to play. Phil Marion intercepted the pass, and the Tigers ran out the clock to avoid the upset.

The Tigers took the early lead against Georgia Tech when Addison connected with Bo Ruffner on an 8-yard pass, and it stayed that way until midway through the third quarter, when Tech finally found a way to move against the Tiger resistance. Following a Buddy Gore fumble at the Clemson 31, GT tailback Lenny Snow powered over from the 6. The Tigers used a turnover of their own to get back on top, as Phil Marion caught a bad pass from Yellow Jacket quarterback Kim King for his second interception in as many outings. Eleven plays later, Addison saw Edgar McGee open across the goal line, and the touchdown put the Tigers back ahead, 12-7.

Georgia Tech brought the ensuing kickoff out to the 33, and seconds later Snow took the ball and was off to the races, outrunning the Tiger secondary. Snow's 60-yard touchdown gave GT a 13-12 cushion. Clemson had an opportunity to win in the final two minutes, moving down to the Georgia Tech 10, but the Yellow Jacket defense saved the day, as Bill Eastman stepped in front of an Addison pass with 1:20 to play. Although CU got the ball back seconds later, they were forced to kick an impossible 62-yard field goal against the wind to claim victory. The kick fell woefully short, and the game was lost.

The Alabama defense stifled Addison and the Clemson offense in Tuscaloosa the following Saturday, while southpaw quarterback Kenny Stabler completed seven-of-eight passes, including a pair of touchdowns, to lead the Crimson Tide to a 26-0 shutout victory. It was the second of six scoreless outings that Alabama's defense would register during the season. Frank Liberatore brought the opening kickoff into Crimson Tide territory, but Clemson's best chance to score was snuffed by a missed field goal.

That same afternoon in Raleigh, N.C. State dedicated its new football stadium, a double-decked, open-ended facility adjacent to the State Fairgrounds. The stadium was built at a cost of $3.7 million, and was named in honor of brothers Wilbert James and Harry Clifton Carter. The Carter brothers were NCSU graduates and textile magnates, and had each donated significantly to the stadium project. The Wolfpack had been playing football in antiquated Riddick Stadium since 1907, and an update to the school's football facilities was long overdue. Riddick was too small to effectively accommodate big-time college football, and as a result, N.C. State was forced to consistently schedule a disproportionate amount of their games away from home.

Since 1956, the Wolfpack had been averaging only three home games a season, and the combination of lost revenue and a lack of a home-field advantage necessitated the university to move forward on a stadium project. Earle Edwards was particularly vocal in the need for enhanced facilities at NCSU, citing publicly how unfair it was for his teams to be consistently forced to play on the road. On a perfect afternoon for football, South Carolina came to town and spoiled State's party, taking a 31-21 victory that proved to be USC's only win of the year. South Carolina's victory put a damper on the day for Wolfpack fans, but it would be another ten contests before NCSU lost again at home to a conference opponent.

New Duke coach Tom Harp brought his team to Death Valley and played the Tigers tough, taking a 6-3 lead into the final minutes. With their backs to the wall, the Clemson offense put together its first and only sustained drive. Following a pass interference call against the Blue Devils, Addison dropped back to pass from the 25. Going for it all, Addison lofted a high pass into the end zone. Phil Rogers was on a dead sprint, and caught Addison's pass Willie Mays-style over the shoulder for a Clemson touchdown. Although the extra point failed, the Addison-to-Rogers play gave Clemson a dramatic 9-6 victory.

Southern California was next for Howard's team, and the No. 5 Men of Troy dished out a 30-0 shutout to the Tigers in Los Angeles. Southern Cal was superior to Clemson in every facet of the game, racing out to an 18-0 halftime lead and holding the Tigers to only 126 total yards. The fourth quarter was particularly frustrating for Clemson, as the offense failed to get past its own 10-yard line on three successive offensive possessions.

"I thought we could run and pass on them, but we couldn't block them," a disconsolate Frank Howard said afterwards. "USC has great personnel. Their defense is not complicated, but they have such good personnel at each position. I would like to see them play Alabama."

The late-game heroics continued for the Tigers against Wake Forest, as CU claimed its third consecutive conference victory by virtue of a late game score. Things started out well enough, as Clemson jumped out to a 21-7 halftime lead behind 284 yards of offense. Following a scoreless third quarter, the Deacons began putting on the pressure in the final period. Wake Forest equaled its offensive output for the previous three quarters combined in the final fifteen minutes, and Jimmy Arrington's second touchdown knotted the game at 21. Following an interception by Andy Harper, it appeared as though the Deacons had come back to salvage a tie. With less than a minute remaining, and the ball on the Wake Forest 7, Clemson defenders James Tompkins and Wilson Childers met in the end zone, and their safety gave the Tigers a shaky 23-21 win.

"I'm thankful we won this one," Howard told a group of reporters. "I've lost some close ones in my time and I hear that it evens up after a while. I guess this was one of them days when things got evened up a little."

Clemson had an easier time back at home against North Carolina, using a dominant fourth quarter to seal a 27-3 victory, which was followed by a 14-10 triumph over Maryland in College Park which gave Howard his 150th career victory. The Tiger defense led the way by forcing six turnovers, while Gore and Jackson each ran over in the opening quarter for the CU points. With 1:15 to play in the game, Addison was picked off by the Terrapin secondary, but two plays later, Alan Pastrana coughed up the ball after a hit by Joey Branton. Childers, the hero of the Wake Forest game with his last-second safety, came up with the recovery to seal another Tiger victory.

Clemson was being considered for El Paso's Sun Bowl as they headed north to play N.C. State. The Tigers looked solid in the first half, as Gore and Jackson tallied for a 14-7 halftime lead. However, NCSU dominated the second half, holding the Tiger offense to 39 total yards and only two first downs. As the defense slowed down the Tiger offensive, the State offense exploded, pounding out 169 yards and scoring on four separate possessions. Harold Deters kicked three field goals to give the Wolfpack a 16-14 lead, and Don Dearment iced it with a 53-yard scamper in the closing minutes for a 23-14 final.

South Carolina put up little resistance on the final weekend, as the Tigers took the conference with a 35-10 victory. Jackson got CU going with a 4-yard score in the first quarter, and after the Gamecocks scored twice to take the lead, Clemson tallied the next 28 points. Offensive lineman Harry Olszewski added Clemson's final touchdown in the fourth quarter, alertly retrieving a fumbled exchange from center in midair and running to the goal line. Late in the game, Howard elected to use his time-outs in order to give Gore a chance to take the league's rushing title. On a 30-yard carry, in which he twice recovered his own fumbles, Gore pushed into the lead with 750 yards. The USC victory gave Clemson a 6-4 overall record, making the Tigers the only team in the ACC to finish with a winning record.

In 1967, teams within the ACC fold began seeking different forms of intimidation. Shoe painting became the newest fad, adding spice to one of the most competitive seasons in league history. Although Clemson went through a rough stretch in late September and October, dropping three consecutive games, the Tigers were the premiere team in the league once again. Clemson went perfect through the ACC for the first time in school history, and became the first school since Duke five years earlier to run through the league schedule without a loss or tie.

Offense was the word in Death Valley in 1967, as the Tigers claimed the ACC's top overall unit with an average of over 312 yards a game. It all started up front, where Clemson boasted one of the best offensive lines in the country. Wayne Mass was back for another year in the trenches, and although the big tackle was denied a second season of All-American distinction, guard Harry Olszewski took his place. Olszewski was a dominating force up front, opening gaping holes for Clemson's backs. The Jacobs Blocking Trophy could have gone to either of the stellar CU linemen, but the voters chose to give it to Olszewski.

The tandem of Mass and Olszewski, in addition to Larry Keys, Wayne Mulligan, and Gary Arthur, allowed Buddy Gore to set a Clemson record with an average of 109.1 yards per game. Gore also broke the single-season ACC rushing record with 1,045 yards, surpassing Brian Piccolo's mark by three feet. The mark made Gore the first Tiger back in history to surpass the 1,000-yard plateau in a single season. Jimmy Addison was back as the Tiger quarterback, and the Needle threw for an ACC-best 924 yards. Jacky Jackson, who came up with a number of significant performances, supplemented Gore in the backfield.

North Carolina State boasted one of the finest defensive units in league history in 1967. The Wolfpack gave up just 8.7 points a contest, the fewest by an ACC team in a decade. The unit, led by two All-Americans and three All-Conference performers, gave up no more than 14 points in any game all season, and became known as the "White Shoes Defense" because of an early-season gimmick. The night before their season opener with North Carolina, senior linebacker Chuck Amato decided to try something a little different. Amato thought it might bring the defensive unit together by smearing white polish on their shoes. Defensive coordinator Al Michaels was skeptical, but sure enough, they went out and beat the Tar Heels 13-7 the following day. From there on out, the unit put white polish on their shoes before every game, creating a superstition and a unique bond between the members of the unit.

After touching Howard's Rock on their way down the Memorial Stadium hill for the first time, Clemson went out and manhandled Wake Forest 23-6 behind Jackson and Gore. The rock was a gift to Howard and his team from 1919 Clemson graduate S.C. Jones, who had brought it all the way back from California after visiting the Death Valley desert. The rock sat in Howard's office for years, and was nearly thrown out before a member of IPTAY, the school's athletic council, had it mounted on a pedestal before the 1966 season. Before the Tigers ran down the hill to knock off the Deacons, Howard told his team, "If you're going to give me 110 percent, you can rub that rock. If you're not, keep your filthy hands off it."

Turnovers cost the orange a week later against Georgia, as a pair of interceptions led to two Bulldog touchdowns for an early 17-3 lead. Kirby Moore converted both Bulldog scores, which came after picks by Happy Dicks and Jake Scott. Clemson rallied in the second half behind Gore and Frank Liberatore to knot the game at 17, but Georgia took a 24-17 triumph on a run by Kent Lawrence. The Tigers played poorly against Georgia Tech, dropping a 10-0 final score on a field goal by Tommy Carmichael and a touchdown run by Kim King. Clemson failed to move with any purpose on offense, and took their ninth consecutive loss at the hands of the Yellow Jackets.

State dominated Buffalo and Florida State after the UNC win, but faced a dilemma before their next contest, a tangle against second-ranked Houston. The game would be played inside the spacious Astrodome, which meant that the Wolfpack players would be forced to borrow turf shoes from the Cougars. After some deliberation, the players agreed that they could not break tradition, and decided to go ahead and polish the borrowed shoes. The Cougars took a 6-0 halftime lead on a scoring pass from Dick Woodall to Bob Long, but the White Shoes dominated the second half, holding the nation's top running attack off the scoreboard. Bobby Hall put State in the lead with a pair of smashes over the goal, and Gerald Warren added a field goal to give NCSU a 16-6 verdict.

The Clemson boys played a little better down in Auburn, but dropped another tough game to fall to 1-3. Jimmy Carter got it going for Auburn early, returning a punt 61 yards for a touchdown before the game was two minutes old. Following three Auburn field goals, Addison briefly brought the Tigers back, throwing touchdowns to Phil Rogers and Freddy Kelley. Jackson added a rushing score, and Clemson was back in the game at 26-21. Auburn took control from that point, scoring three unanswered times to take a 43-21 verdict. It was Clemson's twelfth consecutive loss to teams from the Southeastern Conference, a streak that dated back to 1960. After the game, Howard calmly explained the problem.

"The SEC gets dedicated football players. The ACC gets dedicated students," Howard told reporters.

Clemson finally got on the right track in Durham with a 13-7 victory over Duke. Gore led the way, rushing for 97 yards and scoring both Tiger touchdowns. Each of Gore's scoring carries ate up 9 yards, with the first coming in the third quarter and the second in the fourth quarter. Although the Blue Devils ripped Clemson with 327 rushing yards, they were able to penetrate the end zone only once.

The Wolfpack buried Maryland, 31-9, the week before the Wake Forest game, and improved to 6-0 with a 24-7 victory over the Demon Deacons. Members of Wake's offensive line, seeking to steal away some of State's thunder, ran onto the field at Carter Stadium wearing gold shoes. Unfortunately for the Deacons, the magic was reserved for the home team. As the White Shoes overpowered the Deacon offense, kicker Gerald Warren connected on three field goals. Warren, who was named an All-American following the season, set an NCAA record with seventeen converted field goal attempts. Warren also became the first kicker in ACC history to lead the league in scoring.

Things got no easier for Clemson the following week in Death Valley, as powerful Alabama came to town. It was a bad time to be playing the Crimson Tide, as they were coming off a 24-13 loss to Tennessee that had snapped the team's twenty-five-game unbeaten streak. Bear Bryant had yet to lose back-to-back games as Alabama's head coach, and it wouldn't happen on this day. Steve Davis kicked a pair of field goals, and Ed Morgan ran over from a short distance to give the Crimson Tide a 13-10 victory. Gore scored another touchdown for the Tigers, his eighth in six contests, and Steedley Candler notched a field goal for the other CU points. Addison led Clemson on a final rally late in the game, but Eddie Propst snagged a pass to seal victory for Alabama.

Angry and frustrated, the Tigers returned to form in Chapel Hill the following week against North Carolina. Addison threw a touchdown to Billy Michael, and new kicker Art Craig connected on his first field goal. The CU defense added another score when Billy Ware intercepted Jeff Beaver and returned it to the end zone. The 17-0 victory was Clemson's first shutout over Carolina in six years.

Maryland was struggling under new coach Bob Ward in 1967, in the midst of a winless season for the first time since the school's original team of 1892. Clemson's game against the Terrapins was never in doubt, as the Tigers ran their way to a 28-7 final. Paul Fitzpatrick threw a touchdown to help the UM cause, but four different Clemson players found the goal line. Jackson, Rick Medlin, and Charley Tolley all scored on short sneaks, while Gore raced 38 yards for another touchdown.

As Clemson was knocking off Maryland, State was in Happy Valley preparing for a showdown with Penn State (PSU). The Wolfpack had claimed easy victories the previous two weeks over Duke and Virginia, and entered the game with a perfect record of 8-0. State was ranked third in the nation, and with a Sugar Bowl bid and possible national championship on the line, the Wolfpack were favored on the road. The Nittany Lions were an experienced group, but early season losses to Navy and UCLA had put a snag in their championship aspirations. With a defense that hadn't allowed more than one touchdown in any single game, State liked its chances to leave Happy Valley with a win.

The White Shoes had not been scored on in the first quarter all year, but PSU snapped that streak when quarterback Tom Sherman completed passes to Don Abbey and Ted Kwalick. Kwalick's catch gave Penn State the early lead, and it was quickly increased when linebacker Denny Onkotz intercepted a Jim Donnan pass and raced 67 yards the other way for another Lion touchdown. Warren connected on two field goals for the Wolfpack, and the game went into the fourth quarter with the score 13-6 in favor of PSU. With the game entering crunch time, State began a concerted push into Penn State territory. After a holding penalty moved NCSU to the PSU 20, the offense moved to the 9 in three plays. From there, Bobby Hall took a handoff and sprinted to the 3, going out of bounds with fifty-one seconds left. Hall took another carry to the 1, and with forty seconds left and a fourth down play coming, State called time out.

Earle Edwards thought a fast pitch to the outside might surprise the Nittany Lions, but Donnan thought State should go with a dive over the middle. After a few seconds of deliberation, Edwards sided with his quarterback. With the Beaver Stadium crowd watching in nervous anticipation, State retook the field and went in motion. Donnan took the snap, faked a handoff to Settle Dockery, and gave the ball to Tony Barchuk. Barchuk had riddled the Lions throughout the game with his consistent carries across the middle, and it made sense for the Wolfpack to stick with what had worked.

This time, however, Penn State was ready, and their front line jammed the middle. Onkotz and Jim Katz nailed Barchuk at the line of scrimmage, and held him short. Four plays later, PSU punter Tom Cherry intentionally took a safety, making the final score 13-8. Penn State supporters rushed the field after the won contest, and tried to rip the goalposts from their concrete foundations. Others added insult to injury for the NCSU fans by stealing the Confederate flags they had brought with them from North Carolina. For Edwards and the Wolfpack, all that was left was to second-guess their decision to run a dive from the PSU 1-yard line.

"After coaching all these years, I should have been able to come up with a play for just one yard," a dejected Edwards said later. "I was thinking more of a quick pitchout, something to surprise them and get outside. But when the boys really want to do a certain thing they often execute it better than a play you give them."

State had little time to feel sorry for themselves, with only a week to regroup for the ACC championship showdown in Death Valley with Clemson. In a gesture to ensure that the Wolfpack would not show them up on their home field, the Tiger players went to eight different local paint stores in the week leading up to the game. To the delight of the home fans, the entire Tiger squad ran onto the wind-swept Memorial Stadium field wearing bright orange shoes.

The banged-up Wolfpack proved their mettle in the first half, shutting Clemson out and taking a 6-0 lead in the locker rooms. Warren connected on a pair of second quarter field goals, which broke Charlie Gogolak's single-season record for converted kicks. The Tigers got the wind for the second half, and moved powerfully through the White Shoes on their first possession. From the NCSU 28, Addison faded into the pocket and spotted Gore, who made his first catch of the season. Gore raced all the way to the goal line, completing the first scoring reception of his Tiger career. A late score by Jackson gave Clemson its most important victory of the season, 14-6.

To the added dismay of NCSU fans, the Tigers took care of business against South Carolina the following week to claim the ACC title. Gore racked up 189 yards in thirty-one attempts, and his third quarter run of 43 yards set up the Tiger touchdown that put the game out of reach. Following his team's 23-12 victory, Howard praised his star back, and dispelled rumors that he was thinking about retirement.

"That Gore went, didn't he?" Howard said. "I bet he got more than the entire South Carolina team. In spite of what some people think, (Clemson president) Dr. R. C. Edwards told me I'd be around a long time."

With only eight major bowl games in place at the time, Clemson's 6-4 mark was not compelling enough to merit any invitations. The same could not be said for the Wolfpack, who sidestepped the Tigers for a berth in the Liberty Bowl. As a result, NCSU became the first second-place school in ACC history to earn a postseason invite over the league champion when the champion was not on probation. State would also be the first team in four years to represent the conference in a bowl.

Playing in Memphis against the University of Georgia (UGA) was something of a disappointment for Edwards and his team. The heart-breakers to Penn State and Clemson had denied the Wolfpack a trip to New Orleans, and a legitimate chance at the school's first NCAA crown. A pair of one-point losses in November had burst Georgia's championship bubble, but their seven victories were still good enough for second place in their tough league.

The Wolfpack began the game's first successful drive in the second quarter, as Donnan connected with Harry Martell, who eluded his defender and ran in for a touchdown. Georgia did not take long to re-taliate, as Kent Lawrence brought out the kickoff to the 42. Georgia's receiving tandem of Dennis Hughes and Billy Payne began working their way open, and Kirby Moore hit them with deadly accuracy. The Bulldogs used their passing attack to sit the Wolfpack back on its heels, and Ronnie Jenkins ended the march with a short carry to tie the game at 7.

The fourth quarter brought State its second touchdown, when Bar-chuk fell over to conclude a 73-yard drive. With a 14-7 lead, the issue was now left in the hands of the White Shoes. The Bulldogs, frustrated all game by State's superior defensive unit, moved the football when it counted the most. Georgia went 98 yards, from its own 1 to the NCSU 1, on a concerted push through the State defense. Georgia had a first-and-goal, but the Wolfpack held on three consecutive plays. On fourth down, the Bulldogs went to Lawrence on an outside sweep. Billy Mor-row read the play, took out the lead blocker, and brought Lawrence down short of the line.

Georgia got a second chance minutes later by holding State's of-fense and partially blocking the ensuing punt. From the 10, Moore was incomplete on consecutive pass attempts. On third down, Georgia chose to run. The Wolfpack was ready, stuffing the play for only 1 yard. On fourth down the Dogs had no choice but to go for the end zone, but Moore's pass to Payne was batted away. By stopping the Bulldogs on eight separate plays from inside their own 10 in the final minutes, the Wolfpack had truly earned the school's first postseason victory.

Although State lost seventeen starters from their Liberty Bowl championship team, the 1968 squad won six ACC games for Earle Ed-wards' fifth and final conference championship. All-Americans Dennis Byrd and Fred Combs were among the departed from the NCSU de-fense, but the unit proved to be the best in the conference for the third year in a row. Ron Carpenter filled in Byrd's shoes admirably, and be-came the third NCSU defender in as many years to become an All-

American. Mark Capuano was one of only two returning starters from the White Shoes Defense, and he earned All-ACC honors for the second consecutive year.

N.C. State began the year by playing in the first game at newly constructed Groves Stadium, a 32,000-seat facility located adjacent to the Wake Forest campus. Gerald Warren, who had missed only five field goals throughout the entire 1967 season, was off on his first four attempts as the first half went by scoreless. Warren finally connected at the 2:05 mark of the third quarter, and the Wolfpack added to their slim advantage when Jack Klebe piled over from the 1 in the fourth quarter. The officials called pass interference on State at the 1-yard line in the closing seconds, giving WF a single play with no time on the clock. Lee Clymer plowed in, but a two-point effort failed to give NCSU a 10-6 margin of victory.

The Wolfpack took their big guns to Chapel Hill the ensuing week, and spanked the Tar Heels with a complete performance on both sides of the ball. State's speedy secondary settled the issue before the NCSU offense even had to take the field. Early in the first quarter, Gary Yount took a punt from his own 16 and went 84 yards, eluding a number of would-be tacklers along the way. Two plays later, Jack Whitley took a fumble out of the air at the UNC 46 and plowed his way across the field. Impressively, State had a 14-0 lead before many of the Carolina faithful had made it to their seats. State continued to blow away the Tar Heels in the second quarter, driving 80 yards to take a 21-0 advantage. Less than a minute had passed in the quarter when State scored their third touchdown, and the next score came with under a minute remaining. Warren was good on a field goal from the 11, and State had a 24-0 lead after thirty minutes.

Whitley's second big defensive play early in the third quarter ended any hint of a Carolina comeback, as he hauled in Gayle Bomar's toss at the NCSU 38 and returned it inside the Carolina 10. Jimmy Lisk scored his first career touchdown, and the Wolfpack took a 31-0 advantage. It was a tough day for Bomar, who completed only three-of-seventeen passes for 26 yards. Edwards was a good sport in the second half, playing his second units for much of the time. Carolina finally notched a touchdown when Ricky Lanier kept around left end, but State had already scored again on a short run by Jim Hardin. The 38-6 triumph was State's most lopsided in history over the Tar Heels.

Oklahoma brought a serious challenge to the Wolfpack in Norman, and State's inability to capitalize on key opportunities led to a decisive Sooner win. The Wolfpack had the ball at the OU 9 early trailing 6-0, but on fourth down, State was denied by a yard. The offense went 79 yards on their next possession, but Klebe threw one of his four interceptions to kill the rally. Klebe led NCSU on a pair of long scoring drives in the final fifteen minutes, and finished with a game total of 236 yards passing, but State was already behind, 21-0, when Hardin reached the end zone. Oklahoma's talented backfield of Bob Warmack, Steve Owens, and Eddie Hinton kept the Wolfpack defenders busy all day. Owens carried for 164 yards, and Hinton made six catches, including a fantastic grab on a Warmack pass from the 28, to give OU its third score. The Sooners notched their final touchdown following another Klebe interception, and State ended the scoring for a 28-14 final.

Although it meant little in the final standings, the game between North Carolina and South Carolina that same afternoon ranked among the most bizarre in history. The Gamecocks could do little against UNC in the first three quarters, as the Heels bolted out to a 27-3 advantage. Angered over their poor performance against N.C. State, Carolina's offense came alive in a third quarter barrage of 17 unanswered points.

Thinking the game was theirs, the UNC defense came unglued, allowing South Carolina to make a dramatic and historic comeback. South Carolina's offensive trio of Tommy Suggs, Warren Muir, and Fred Zeigler atoned for three quarters of failure in the final frame, leading their team to a 29-point swing and a miraculous 32-27 victory. Zeigler scored USC's first points of the final quarter on an 18-yard reception, and it was followed by consecutive crashes from Muir. With 4:54 to play, Suggs completed South Carolina's resurgence with a dive from the 4. The Tar Heels were too shocked to retake command, and dropped the game to the stunned amazement of the fans in Kenan Stadium.

"I just know that it's the greatest comeback I've ever been associated with," a smiling Paul Dietzel said in the locker room. "It's just a good thing we had a fourth quarter, because we were in a lot of trouble."

The Wolfpack continued their Southwestern romp against a good Southern Methodist team, and left Dallas on the wrong end of a 35-14 score. The Mustangs were led by the passing of Chuck Hixon, who completed twenty-two passes for 323 yards and three touchdowns. Receiver Jerry Levias caught all three scoring passes from Hixon, and spent the day frustrating State's usually top-notch secondary. The NCSU defense was not used to the pass-happy attack employed by Hayden Fry's team, and found themselves out of position on a number of occasions. Klebe did himself no favors, throwing four interceptions to kill NCSU's momentum.

The Wolfpack returned to Carter Stadium for their next four contests, and promptly put together a winning streak. South Carolina was first, as State buried the Gamecocks behind 356 yards on the ground. Scoring on each of its first two possessions, the Wolfpack assumed quick and authoritative control. Charlie Bowers led the way with 128 yards and three scores, with his last coming in the third quarter to give NCSU a commanding 31-12 bulge. Unlike UNC, State refused to yield to a Gamecock comeback, as Carpenter registered a safety with a sack in the end zone, and Warren hit a field goal in the fourth quarter to give State a 36-12 pad. All the while, the defense kept the Gamecocks from scoring any more points.

State continued its upward swing with a 19-0 victory over Virginia, Edward's tenth in a row over the Cavaliers. Bowers again rushed for more than 100 yards, and led an overwhelming Wolfpack running assault. Klebe attempted only two passes, with one setting up Warren for his first field goal. The Wolfpack defenders knew to blanket UVA's dangerous Frank Quayle, who was averaging nearly 10 yards a carry coming into the game. The unit persevered, holding Quayle to only 67 yards on eighteen attempts. A 34-yard interception return by Paul Reid sealed Virginia's demise.

Bowers and the State defense came through again against Maryland, as the Wolfpack took another commanding victory, 31-11. Bowers again ran for over 100 yards, and added another hat trick of touchdowns. Like NCSU, the Terrapins came into the game winners of two straight, and scored first on a field goal by Rick Carlson. Maryland was threatening again when the State defenders began a series of debilitating plays. With the ball on the NCSU 21 early in the second quarter, Whitley intercepted Alan Pastrana's pass in the end zone. Although State couldn't move the ball after the turnover, Klebe completed a 68-yard "quick kick" that put Maryland inside their 10. Two plays later, Pastrana fumbled the exchange from center and NCSU recovered. The Wolfpack scored in three plays, and added two more tallies in the second quarter for a 17-3 lead. Another pair of touchdowns in the final thirty minutes countered a Terrapin score by Billy Lovett.

Clemson came to Raleigh next and ended State's winning streak, taking a 24-19 victory that served as sweet revenge for last season's postseason snub. The Wolfpack headed in the right direction early, as Bobby Hall took the first play from scrimmage 80 yards for a touchdown. The Tigers followed with a big play of their own, as Buddy Gore returned the ensuing kickoff 74 yards that led to the tying score. Clemson twice took the lead at 14-7 and 17-10, but State rallied after each.

Dick Idol completed an NCSU safety with a sack to make the score 17-12, and a late 47-yard pass from Klebe to Lisk gave State a 19-17 advantage.

With only 2:20 to play, the Tigers needed 69 yards in order to score a touchdown. The Wolfpack defense ran onto the field looking for one more stop, but the Clemson offense had other ideas, as quarterback Billy Ammons rapidly drove the Tigers downfield with a series of completed passes. After Charlie Waters made a diving catch to push CU to the NCSU 12, back-to-back carries by Ray Yauger gained 5 yards. On third down Yauger got the call again, and the sophomore cut outside and had a free ride to the end zone. State had only fifty-three seconds to counter, and the Tigers held the Wolfpack to only 7 yards in their final four plays.

Clemson now had the inside track to its fourth league crown in as many years, but State kept the heat on with a 17-15 victory at Duke. The Blue Devils twice moved inside the NCSU 1, but came up short each time. Interceptions by Whitley and Idol added to Duke's problems. Trailing 17-9 late, Blue Devil quarterback Leo Hart sneaked over for the game's final points. Although Hart finished the game as the first quarterback in ACC history to throw for 2,000 yards in a season, State held on for the important victory.

Now finished with its ACC slate, the Wolfpack returned to Raleigh and were drubbed by Florida State 48-7. The Seminoles were on their way to another bowl under Bill Peterson, and all but ended State's postseason aspirations with the dominating victory. State was still in the game at halftime, trailing only 14-7, but four turnovers gave FSU all the advantage they would need. The second half was a nightmare for the Wolfpack, as FSU's Bill Gunter scored three times, quarterback Bill Cappleman threw a pair of touchdowns, and Walt Sumner returned a blocked field goal attempt 58 yards.

For the second year in a row, the ACC title was decided in the annual war between Clemson and South Carolina. Although the Tigers entered the contest with a mediocre 4-4-1 overall record, all of their victories were over conference opposition. The game was decided on special teams, as Clemson's Jack Anderson returned a kickoff 72 yards to set up a field goal and a 3-0 lead. The Gamecocks countered with Tyler Hellams, who caught a punt at his own 27 and raced 73 yards for the winning score and a 7-3 South Carolina verdict. With Clemson's loss, N.C. State jumped back into the top position in the standings.

5

One-Hit Wonders (1969-1970)

In 1969 and 1970, the traditional powers of Atlantic Coast Conference football took a temporary backseat. South Carolina and Wake Forest, a pair of schools with little tradition on the gridiron, stepped to the fore and earned their first and only league championships. With Clemson, Duke, and N.C. State all dropping off the radar screen due to graduations, the door was opened for the Gamecocks and Demon Deacons to make their onetime marks at the helm of the standings. South Carolina had begun its football program way back in 1894, and had yet to win a championship in either the Southern Conference or the ACC. Wake had fared little better, and going into the 1969 season was a decade removed from its last winning season.

Paul Dietzel was in his fourth year at USC in 1969, and had done a great deal over his short time in Columbia to bring respect to the Gamecock program. Dietzel came to South Carolina the year after the 1965 ineligible player scandal, and although his first few teams struggled in mediocrity, the coach's ability to help the university raise funds resulted in a new five-building complex for USC student-athletes, along with a surplus in the athletic department budget. In addition to his political side, Dietzel knew how to win football games. Dietzel had been the architect of the Louisiana State team that won the national championship in 1958, and had beaten Clemson in the Sugar Bowl.

By 1969, Dietzel had enough talent on his team to compete for the ACC title. Fred Ziegler, South Carolina's key offensive target, had asserted himself as the best receiver in the league over the previous two seasons. By the end of his time at USC, Ziegler held every important Gamecock receiving record, and was the leading pass catcher in ACC history. In 1969, Zeigler made 52 catches for 658 yards, both tops in the league. With help from steady regulars like Warren Muir and Rudy

Holloman, South Carolina would enjoy its finest autumn in eleven years. It was the "Year of the Rooster" on the Chinese calendar, a fitting time for the Gamecocks to reign supreme on the ACC gridirons.

The Gamecocks opened against Duke for the second year in a row, and prevailed thanks in large part to a gutsy decision by Dietzel. With the game knotted at 20 and less than five minutes remaining, USC got the ball on its own 25. When the drive stalled on the Duke 4, everyone figured that Dietzel would bring on the reliable Billy DuPre to kick the Gamecocks into the lead. In a surprising move, however, Dietzel and the Gamecocks elected to go for the touchdown. On fourth-and-1, with the Duke defense clamped down, Holloman followed Muir's lead block for the vital first down, and Muir finished the drive on the following play with a crash from the 2. DuPre's extra gave South Carolina a 27-20 victory.

The Gamecocks carried the momentum of the Duke victory into another ACC showdown at home the following week against North Carolina. The Tar Heels dominated the game on the ground, pounding out 251 yards, but failed to make the big plays in the clutch. Leading 6-0 at halftime, the Tar Heels fell victim to a pair of touchdown drives by the Gamecocks. With less than a minute remaining, Dick Harris jumped in front of a pass by UNC quarterback Paul Miller and made an interception at the USC 13. Suggs and the Gamecock offense came back onto the field, got into the victory set, and downed the ball for a 14-6 win.

"Thank the Good Lord for the defense tonight, because we certainly did not have much offense," Dietzel said later. "Bo Davies did some mighty fine things in the secondary and so did Dick Harris. His interception with twenty-two seconds to play was a thing of beauty. Of course, we just jump from the frying pan into the fire against the other Dooley next week."

The "other" Dooley that Dietzel was referring to was Vince, the brother of UNC head coach Bill Dooley. While Bill was still in the early stages of his rebuilding efforts in Chapel Hill, Vince had turned Georgia's football program into a well-oiled machine. Since coming to Athens in 1964, Dooley had won two SEC championships and had led five consecutive winning teams. The Bulldogs, like the Gamecocks, were unbeaten, claiming easy victories over Tulane and Clemson to start the year. Georgia had shut out both opponents, and came into the USC contest ranked in the national polls.

Suggs and the Gamecocks were given a dose of reality by a Bulldog defense that was as opportunistic as it was stifling. Georgia intercepted Suggs four times over the course of the game, while Julian Smiley and Craig Elrod had touchdown runs for the Bulldogs, who coasted to an easy 41-16 victory. The win continued a UGA unbeaten streak against the Gamecocks that dated back to 1959.

The Gamecocks bounced back at home against N.C. State for a 21-16 victory, although things were a little hairy at first. The Wolfpack jumped out 10-0 on a field goal by Mike Charron and a touchdown carry by Leon Mason, but a scoring march and a 72-yard punt return for a touchdown by Jim Mitchell thrust USC into the lead. Muir added an insurance touchdown for USC in the fourth quarter, and although a Wayne Lewis touchdown cut the South Carolina edge to 21-16, the Gamecock defense held State the rest of the way.

Virginia Tech was next, and just as they did against Duke, the Gamecocks had to rely on late-game heroics to preserve victory. The game was close throughout, but VT assumed the advantage with 1:13 remaining when quarterback Gil Schwabe threw a touchdown to Jimmy Quinn, giving Tech a 16-14 lead. With the game on the line, Suggs completed a number of clutch passes, leading South Carolina into VT real estate. The Gamecocks moved to Tech's 30-yard line with nine seconds left, and DuPre came on for a game-winning effort. The kick was perfect, and the Gamecock players celebrated the school's first victory over Virginia Tech since 1936.

Carolina Stadium was rocking with its fourth consecutive sellout crowd when Maryland came to town a week later. The Terrapins were not playing terribly well in 1969, but victories over Duke and Wake Forest had them only a game behind the Gamecocks in the ACC standings. With a chance to solidify their conference lead, the USC defense pitched its first and only shutout of the year. A touchdown pass to Holloman got the Gamecocks going, and a score by Muir put the squad in cruise control. DuPre's field goal completed the 17-0 South Carolina victory, which sent Maryland on a four-game tailspin that resulted in a 3-7 overall record.

After wiping away the Terps, the Gamecocks struggled against Florida State in their worst performance of the season. The Seminoles displayed big-play capability when Paul Magalski scored on a 33-yard play in the first quarter, and Mike Gray followed with a touchdown reception of his own. The Gamecock offense never got on track, managing a single field goal in the first two quarters. South Carolina trailed 20-3 at halftime, and another touchdown by Magalski led Florida State a 34-9 final.

Another difficult encounter awaited South Carolina in Knoxville, where they met No. 3 Tennessee. Doug Dickey's Volunteers were undefeated and on their way to the Southeastern Conference title, but the Gamecocks came to town ready to play. South Carolina controlled the line of scrimmage for most of the first half, and although they trailed 10-7 going into the locker rooms, it was evident that they were capable of winning. Unfortunately for USC, Tennessee successfully converted a field goal in the third quarter to take a 13-7 lead, and assumed command in the final period to take a 29-14 victory.

Playing Wake Forest next, Steve Bowden gave the Demon Deacons an early lead, but Suggs threw three touchdowns. Zeigler made the first score with a 10-yard reception, and Holloman followed with a 13-yard play. The Gamecock defenders successfully shut down Wake Forest after Bowden's score, and kept the Deacons from reaching the scoreboard again. Suggs' scoring passes and a DuPre field goal led to a 24-6 win that clinched the league title. A couple of days later, the Gamecock players and staff learned that they were heading to the Peach Bowl.

Although the conference championship was secured, victory over Clemson was always reason to celebrate within itself for South Carolina. The Tigers were struggling with a young and inexperienced defense in 1969, which gave up more points than any Clemson unit since the school joined the ACC. South Carolina took full advantage, scoring on its first three possessions and rolling up a school-record 517 yards of offense. Holloman started it for the Gamecocks with a 7-yard run, and Muir followed with a scoring carry of 3 yards. Although Ron Yauger posted a pair of touchdowns to bring Clemson closer, Holloman caught a 32-yard pass from Suggs in the third quarter for a 24-13 USC advantage. A late field goal made the Gamecocks 27-13 victors.

The annual USC-Clemson battle would never be quite the same after 1969, for after thirty years as head coach of the Tigers, Frank Howard retired from coaching in December. One of the more memorable figures in collegiate coaching over the years, Howard ended his career with 165 victories, six ACC titles, and four bowl triumphs. A beloved figure in some parts of South Carolina, hated in others, Howard would be long remembered for his witty humor, which reflected his southern roots. Always good for a one-liner, Howard came up with such common phrases as, "Close only counts in horseshoes and hand grenades," and "A tie is like kissing your sister." With his retirement from coaching, Howard shifted his focus on the responsibilities that came with being Clemson's athletic director. Of course, Howard was hesitant to include sports that weren't up his alley.

"We offer no scholarships for rowing," he once said. "Clemson will never subsidize a sport where a man sits on his butt and goes backward."

Over 20,000 South Carolina fans made the trip to Atlanta for the Peach Bowl, where the Gamecocks met West Virginia (WVU). It was USC's first postseason game in twenty-four years, and Dietzel and the Gamecocks were hoping to bring USC its eighth victory for the first time since 1903. The Mountaineers lost only once during the regular season, and quickly asserted its powerful running game on the USC defenders. West Virginia ran the ball a record 79 times over the course of the game, amassing 356 yards. With rain pelting down on Grant Field throughout the game, the Mountaineers attempted only three passes.

Bob Gresham got West Virginia going in the first quarter with a 10-yard scoring run, which gave the Mountaineers a 7-0 advantage. The Gamecocks came back in the second quarter to move into field goal range, and DuPre's kick made the score 7-3 at halftime. West Virginia continued to grind it out in the second half, as Ed Williams rushed for a Peach Bowl record 208 yards. Despite WVU's rushing excellence, the South Carolina defense held strong, keeping the Mountaineers from breaking the game open. With the game winding down, the Gamecocks took a final shot at victory. South Carolina moved to the WVU 7 midway through the fourth quarter, and after three unsuccessful attempts to cross the line, the Gamecocks were stuffed again on fourth down. West Virginia retook possession and drove for the winning touchdown, as Jim Braxton lunged over from the 1 to give the Mountaineers a 14-3 victory.

Like most seasons in the past, Wake Forest was not given much of a shot to compete for the ACC championship in 1970. In fact, the Deacons were picked to finish last by most local observers, including the Raleigh News and Observer. Despite the negative press, Demon Deacon coach Cal Stoll had some reasons to smile. Stoll, a Minnesotan bred out of the Big Ten, had a pair of naturally gifted players in his offensive backfield that perfectly complemented each other's games.

When Stoll came to Wake Forest in 1969, he implemented the "Houston Veer," a unique offensive system created three years earlier by University of Houston head coach Bill Yeoman. The veer, a run-oriented system, employs two running backs, which are split behind the offensive guards. In the veer, the goal is to give the quarterback a multitude of options with the football. In a best-case scenario, the quarterback can expect three options. In a worst-case scenario, the quarterback has no choice but to take off on his own. The term "triple option" comes from the notion that a quarterback can do one of three things;

hand off to his weak-side back on a dive, run outside and pitch to his strong-side back, or take the ball and run himself.

Larry Russell, Wake's first-string quarterback, was the perfect candidate to run Stoll's veer. Agile, elusive, and quick thinking, Russell was capable of making plays from anywhere on the field. Fullback Larry Hopkins, Stoll's other primary weapon, provided bruising yardage reminiscent of former Deacon great Brian Piccolo. The 5'10'' Hopkins, who combined brute strength with a solid burst of speed, arrived in Winston-Salem through the Junior College ranks. With his pair of Larrys in place, Stoll was ready to lead the Demon Deacons to a meteoric rise to the top of the ACC standings.

The Deacons opened in Nebraska's Memorial Stadium, and with 66,103 fans in attendance, the largest crowd a Wake Forest team had ever played in front of, Tracy Lounsbury gave the Deacons an early lead with a field goal. Although Wake played hard for much of the contest, they were no match for one of Nebraska's finest teams. Future Heisman Trophy winner Johnny Rodgers caught a 61-yard touchdown pass from Jerry Tagge in the Cornhuskers' 36-12 romp, which kickstarted their run to the national championship. A last-minute touchdown pass from Jim McMahen to Gary Johnson provided one of the few glitters of hope for Wake.

"This was a great experience for us," Stoll said afterwards. "I didn't like the score, but I thought we grew up a lot today. We hung in there and fought the best we could. We did several things all right. We blocked one punt and an extra point."

Stoll's optimism was stunted the following week when South Carolina buried the Deacons, 43-7, in Columbia. The Gamecocks rolled up 507 yards of offense, and scored on six of their nine possessions in the second half. What was worse for Wake than the lopsided score was the complete ineffectiveness of the veer. The Deacons totaled only 158 yards all day, and had -7 rushing yards aside of a long gain in the first quarter by Hopkins. On the day, Wake entered USC territory only four times. It was a one-sided affair, and anyone that gave the Deacons a realistic chance of winning the ACC title before the game must have been feeling pretty stupid afterwards.

The Deacon offense was revived against Florida State down in Tallahassee, but errors at inopportune times led to Wake's third consecutive defeat. The black and gold led, 14-6, at the half, but were subdued by the Seminole offense in the early moments of the third quarter. Frank Fontes, FSU's barefooted kicker, booted another field goal to make the score 14-9. After a Wake Forest three-and-out, David Snell returned a punt 22 yards to give FSU excellent field position. Seminole quarterback Frank Whigham connected with running back Tommy Bailey, who twisted and turned 47 yards to the WF 2. Arthur Monroe finished the drive with a smashing carry over the goal line to give Florida State a 16-14 advantage. Fonte's fourth field goal was the decider in FSU's 19-14 victory.

Winless and frustrated, the Deacons vowed to keep their mistakes to a minimum against Virginia. The Deacons jumped out to a 20-0 lead in the first half, bullying the Cavaliers into submission with the veer. After a scoreless third quarter, Russell put the game away for Wake Forest in the final period. After two productive carries, Russell rolled right, found a gap, and followed a series of blocks for a touchdown. The Deacon defense, beaten and tattered up to this point, kept the Cavaliers out of the end zone until the final minutes, long after the game was sealed. The 27-7 victory finally put Wake Forest in the win column, and was a harbinger of good times ahead.

Wake's offensive momentum carried into the Virginia Tech game, as Russell became a bona fide offensive force. The junior accounted for all four Wake touchdowns, two on the ground and two in the air, in the Deacons' 28-9 victory. Three unanswered scores sent the game in Wake's direction, as VT's ball-control offense was unable to keep the game competitive.

The Deacons evened their overall record to 3-3 with a convincing 36-20 win over Clemson, their first triumph over the Tigers in nine years. Russell continued his "Two Touchdown October" with another pair of scores, while Hopkins put together a truly impressive performance. Hopkins amassed 230 yards on twenty carries, breaking Frank Quayle's single-game ACC rushing record set a couple of seasons earlier. The Deacons piled up a school-record 444 yards on the ground, as Russell and Hopkins each had carries of 60 or more yards. Wake's defense, which had turned into a formidable unit of late, successfully shut down the Tigers' pass-oriented attack. It was not until the fourth quarter, as the Demon Deacon regulars were cooling their heels on the sidelines, when the Tigers finally scored.

"It was all a team effort," Hopkins modestly replied after his performance. "I was just lucky that I got the call on the plays that went for long yardage. The line did a great job, and deserves the credit."

Next for the Deacons was North Carolina, who limped into Groves Stadium with back-to-back losses after opening the season with four wins. Despite the setbacks, Carolina was still very much in the ACC race, holding a 2-1 conference record. The Tar Heels and Demon Deacons had each lost to South Carolina, but the Gamecocks were in the midst of a five-game losing streak that took them out of contention. The winner of that day's game in Winston-Salem would hold the inside track to the league crown.

The game belonged to Carolina for the first forty-five minutes, as their running game, led by All-American Don McCauley, kept the Deacons at bay. In the third quarter, Paul Miller connected with Tony Blanchard for a 27-yard touchdown, giving UNC a 13-0 edge. The extra point was no good, a mistake that would go down to haunt the Tar Heels. Midway through the final quarter, with a humiliating homecoming defeat looking more and more inevitable, the Deacons finally began penetrating the Carolina defense.

Wake drove 67 yards, and scored on a sneak by Russell to cut the Carolina lead to 13-7. The Tar Heels complained vehemently that Russell helped Hopkins into the end zone by pushing him forward, but the referees made no call. With the game winding down, the Deacons got one final crack at victory. After converting a crucial third down from deep in their own territory, Hopkins sprung free and broke outside for 38 yards, pushing the Deacons into Carolina's side of the field. Wake's most prolific rusher would have scored if not for an open-field tackle by linebacker John Bunting.

With the clock running and the ball on the UNC 3, Hopkins finished the drive seconds later with a plunge across the goal line, tying the game at 13 with twelve seconds to play. Lounsbury converted the extra point, and Groves Stadium went into euphoria. For a program that had played very little significant football games over the years, beating one of their biggest rivals on their home field was a small slice of heaven for Wake Forest supporters.

Wake stepped out of the conference to play Tennessee the following Saturday, and if the Deacons had taken steps forward during their four-game winning streak, the Tennessee game was a giant step backwards. The Volunteers did whatever they wanted offensively, driving for a pair of field goals on their opening two drives of the game. Ranked ninth in the country, Tennessee was on a different level than Wake Forest, and outplayed them in every facet of the game in winning 41-7.

Although the Deacons were only 4-4, and had a trio of humiliating defeats against their record, the ACC championship was still very much in the window of opportunity. If Wake could knock off Duke, who also stood at 4-4, the Deacons would be in perfect position to do something they had been unable to do in seventeen seasons as a member of the conference. Wake headed to Durham for the all-important game, and put together its most complete effort of the season.

The Duke defense was one of the main reasons the Blue Devils stood unbeaten in the league and in first place thus far, but the dark blue had no solution for Wake's veer. The Deacons proved to be the more physical of the two teams, and by game's end, no less than six Blue Devil starters were smarting injuries on the sidelines. With Russell, Ken Garrett, and Hopkins all on their way to 100-yard afternoons, Wake piled up a commanding 14-0 lead at halftime. The Deacons continued to pour it on the Blue Devils in the early stages of the second half, using fifteen plays to score their third touchdown.

Leading 21-6 early in the final stanza, Garrett finished off the Blue Devils with a 9-yard sprint off-tackle. Garrett, who came out of nowhere to gain 141 yards, had a field day taking pitches from Russell in the triple-option set. With a 28-14 victory, Wake Forest ended years of frustration at the hands of Duke. The Blue Devils had won eighteen of their last nineteen contests against the Demon Deacons heading into the 1970 encounter, but this day belonged to the black and gold.

"There was no way we could lose," linebacker Ed Stetz said later. "We all felt that way. Wake Forest hasn't been in a position like this, with a chance to win the championship, I mean. We just couldn't pass up an opportunity like this."

As Wake was polishing off Duke, Don McCauley was making some history in Chapel Hill. The Tar Heel senior, one of the brightest stars in college football throughout the entire 1970 season, ran for 127 yards in Carolina's 62-13 thrashing of the Virginia Military Academy. Scoring twice, McCauley broke UNC's single-season marks for touchdowns and points. He also surpassed Frank Quayle as the ACC's single-season leading rusher with 1,257 yards.

North Carolina State gave Wake a difficult challenge in Winston-Salem, but the gritty Deacons again found a way to win in the closing moments. With NCSU leading 13-10 late in the final period, Garrett completed a nine-play drive with an inspiring touchdown run from the NCSU 10. It appeared that Garrett was stuffed, as a State defender clung to his back and kept him from moving his arms. Despite the resistance, Garrett kept churning his legs, and charged his way into the end zone with only 2:47 remaining. The Deacon defense held off State's final drive, and the 16-13 victory was secured.

With their ACC slate concluded, the Deacons prepared to face off against Houston in their final regular season game. The Cougars had run the veer to great success over the past three seasons, leading the country in total offense every autumn from 1966 to 1968. Since the triple-option was still new, teams were struggling to find ways to defend it.

Before they even stepped on the turf of the Astrodome to play the Cougars, the Wake Forest coaches and players knew that the conference championship was theirs. As the Deacon players were resting up for that night's contest, UNC was administering a humiliating 59-34 defeat to Duke, as McCauley closed out his college career in impressive fashion. The soft-spoken senior rushed for 279 yards, breaking Hopkins' single-game ACC record that was set barely a month earlier.

McCauley added five touchdowns, and stepped off the field holding twenty-three UNC, ACC, and national records, including the all-time NCAA record for rushing yards in a season with 1,720. As McCauley left the field for the final time as a Tar Heel, he was met by thunderous applause, and after the game the Carolina fans flooded the field to mob their hero, who in one afternoon had permanently etched his name in the annals of the college football record books.

"I had trouble sleeping the night before the game," recalls McCauley. "I was scared to death, thinking about this being my last game at home and everything. Going into the game I wasn't even thinking about records. I remember there was a write-up the night before saying this was one game I wasn't to break any. Going into the game I thought the touchdown record was the only one I could break. And I was shooting for 1,500 yards rushing."

"I've said it all season and I will say it again—Don McCauley is the best back in America," said UNC head coach Bill Dooley. "He is unbelievable. This was his biggest day, and he saved it for a fine time."

Although Wake Forest probably couldn't have cared less about McCauley's individual excellence, they were sure glad he chose to have his finest hour against the Blue Devils. The Deacons had a radio connection in their Houston hotel, which allowed them to keep up with the action in Chapel Hill. Although Stoll was preparing for that night's game and wasn't listening, the Wake Forest players brought him the happy news.

"It's great to be champions," Stoll told a small assemblage of reporters in the lobby. "It was a goal we had to work for, and now, we have a ball game to play. Another goal and we have to get ready."

The news of Carolina's win over Duke apparently took the fighting spirit out of the Deacons, as the team played lethargically against Houston. Playing in unfamiliar surroundings, on synthetic grass and in the cavernous atmosphere of the Astrodome, the Deacons were kept out of the end zone for the first time all year. A two-point safety, courtesy of a Pat McHenry blocked punt out of the end zone, was the only scoring

Wake could muster. The safety gave the Deacons an early lead, but mistakes and inconsistency plagued their performance. Penalties and fumbles took away any chance of victory, as the Cougars prevailed 26-2.

As it turned out, 1970 was the only season in the ACC's first half century that Wake Forest claimed a football championship, as three ensuing decades failed to bring another gridiron title to Winston-Salem. With an overall record of 6-5, which included a 1-4 record against non-conference opponents, the Deacons were not invited to a bowl game. The Peach Bowl Committee instead went with North Carolina, who won its final four games after the heartbreaker at Groves.

Carolina met Arizona State (ASU), a team that had enjoyed a dream season under the leadership of Frank Kush. The Sun Devils tore through the regular season unbeaten at 10-0, and came to Atlanta ranked No. 8 in the nation. The Sun Devils were an offensive juggernaut, scoring at least twenty-seven points in each of their first nine games. Arizona State was still several years away from entry into the Pacific Ten Conference at the time, and although they had easily claimed the Western Athletic Conference crown, the Sun Devils were highly underrated. Although they were ranked No. 1 in the NCAA in total offense and No. 3 in total defense, ASU rarely played on television, and were largely unknown to football fans in the South.

The Sun Devils came out with a bang on their opening drive, marching 78 yards for the game's first score. Their running tandem of Monroe Eley and Bob Thomas riddled the Carolina line, breaking through large holes into the secondary. The Sun Devils scored another touchdown early in the second period, culminating another long drive through the frustrated Tar Heel defense. Thomas broke into the clear from the 33, and nobody could catch him once he found daylight.

Carolina drove downfield for a touchdown, but the lightning-fast Sun Devils struck again less than a minute later, as quarterback Joe Spagnola nailed receiver J. D. Hill with a 67-yard strike. After a second touchdown march by the UNC offense, the Sun Devils fumbled the ensuing kickoff. Carolina recovered at the ASU 21, and it took only two carries for McCauley to reach the end zone. The extra point was no good this time, but UNC trailed by a single point. On ASU's second play following another kickoff, Carolina's Lou Angelo stepped in front of a Spagnola pass at the 34 for an interception.

Backup quarterback Mike Mansfield took the reins at quarterback, as Paul Miller had been forced out of the game after taking a late hit on the previous drive. Mansfield led UNC to its fourth touchdown in six minutes, with McCauley rambling in for his third touchdown of the half. The Tar Heels had risen from the dead to take a 26-21 halftime lead, but from there things got ugly.

The first half was played in rugged conditions, as a chilly rain dampened Atlanta. By the start of the second half the rain had become snow, and the field quickly became a blanket of white. It was uncertain as to which team would enjoy the advantage of the conditions, but it quickly became evident that the Sun Devils were less affected by the weather. Carolina was unable to penetrate ASU on their first offensive possession of the second half, and McCauley botched the punt for only 15 yards.

With excellent field position, Arizona State moved through and around the Carolina defense in six plays to take back the lead. The Sun Devils seemed impervious to the falling snow, while the Tar Heels were sluggishly trying to keep their feet. A costly fumble on UNC's next possession gave Arizona State an opportunity to put the game away. Mansfield pitched to Lewis Jolley, but miscommunication resulted in the ball hitting the icy turf. The Sun Devils recovered at the Carolina 14, and scored two plays later to take an insurmountable 34-26 lead. Another pair of touchdowns gave ASU a 48-26 win, which completed their unblemished season at 11-0.

6

Blue Heaven (1971-1972)

When Bill Dooley took the head coaching job at the University of North Carolina in 1966, things could not have been much worse for football in Chapel Hill. The Tar Heels were coming off a 2-8 season, and had enjoyed only three winning seasons over the last seventeen years. Jim Tatum returned to his alma mater to restore Carolina's football tradition in 1956, but his untimely death in the summer of 1959 had left the school in a state of shock. Jim Hickey did his best to replace Tatum, even winning a conference title in 1963, but the UNC program had been on a steady decline ever since.

Dooley brought a solid resume to Chapel Hill, having worked under some of the best football minds of the era. After serving as a graduate assistant at Texas under Darrell Royal, Dooley helped guide Mississippi State to a bowl as the leader of the offensive line. In 1964, Bill went to work for his brother Vince, the head coach at Georgia. As offensive coordinator, Dooley helped lead the Bulldogs to a Southeastern Conference title and a pair of bowl victories. Dooley was praised as an offensive mastermind, and had his choice of three major college jobs in the winter of 1966. He chose UNC, citing the beauty and tradition of the school, in addition to the challenge that it would offer.

"I guess of all things, the program was on the ground, and I was asked to build it up," Dooley said years later.

Dooley brought a Spartan approach to Chapel Hill, which was evident in his first meeting as head coach with his new players. Dooley told the returning Carolina players how much the Georgia teams he coached loved to play UNC, because the Bulldogs always knew they could wear down the Tar Heels in the second half. Dooley quickly got his players into shape with arduous running sessions, and knocked them around during spring football with tough scrimmages.

"It was long, it was grueling," said Gayle Bomar, who shifted from safety to quarterback under Dooley. "It was a tremendous amount of contact every day. I remember one scrimmage on a Saturday in Kenan Stadium. We started about noon, and we could hear the Bell Tower ring every hour. Before it was over, the Bell Tower rang five or six times. It was a long day, a very intense experience. Later, I went into the service and went to boot camp. It was a picnic compared to that first spring practice."

"Coach Dooley was in the process of changing attitudes," said linebacker/guard John Anderson. "It was a boot-camp mentality. We practiced at daybreak until we dropped. We went back at noon until we dropped. Then we went again in the afternoon."

After losing seasons in 1967 and 1968, in which Dooley and his staff weeded out the players that weren't getting it done, Carolina finally turned the corner in 1969. The Tar Heels put together a 5-5 record, which included a four-game winning streak in late October and early November. Don McCauley, a tenacious runner that hit holes like a tank, earned the starting tailback job that spring, and became the first UNC back to surpass the 1,000-yard plateau in a single season.

Dooley had barely a month to attract recruits to Carolina when he first arrived, but successfully signed a small group of talented players, highlighted by the New York-bred McCauley. After that first hectic winter, Dooley installed the same year-round recruiting process at UNC that was commonplace at Georgia and the rest of the Southeastern Conference. As a result, North Carolina became the model for recruiting that other Atlantic Coast Conference schools tried to emulate.

There was reason for optimism in the Tar Heel camp heading into the 1971 season, but tragedy again shook the UNC campus that summer. During a brutal August practice session, defensive reserve Bill Arnold got overheated and collapsed. After an extended period in the hospital, Arnold died from complications created by the onset of heat exhaustion. Dooley came under intense scrutiny about the nature of his sessions after Arnold's passing, and Tar Heel practices in the future included a slew of doctors and athletic trainers. Arnold's death was a tragic eye-opener to everyone involved, and resulted in the advent of an undergraduate Sports Medicine curriculum at the University of North Carolina.

The UNC players came together after Arnold's death, and became a tight-knit, cohesive group. The years of hard work and dedication to Dooley's system paid off in 1971, as the Tar Heels became the best football team Chapel Hill had seen in years. Dooley's first full-fledged batch of recruits were seniors that fall, and their leadership paved the way for a 6-0 mark in conference play.

Running backs Lewis Jolley and Ike Oglesby made up for Don McCauley's graduation to the pros, combining for 1,216 yards and 12 touchdowns. With quarterback Paul Miller leading the ACC in passing, Carolina was first in the league in total offense for the third consecutive year in 1971. The Tar Heel defense, led by linebacker John Bunting and linemen Bill Brafford and Bud Grissom, led the conference in rushing and total defense. It was the second year in a row the Tar Heels were No. 1 on that side of the ball, making North Carolina the first school in ACC history to have the top offense and defense in back-to-back seasons.

For the first time since the league's inaugural season of 1953, the ACC included only seven members in 1971. During the summer, the University of South Carolina, prompted by a vote to raise the academic standards for student-athletes, pulled out of the conference. South Carolina had struggled for years to recruit against their conference rivals, many of which had more renowned academic reputations. By a 5-3 vote, the league members had elected to increase the minimum Grade Point Average for student-athletes from the NCAA-minimum of 1.60 to 1.75. South Carolina was one of the schools that voted against the increase, and although the conference agreed to lower the minimum Scholastic Aptitude Test score to 700, the Gamecocks remained adamantly opposed. The rift created by the GPA increase was the primary reason for South Carolina's exodus from the ACC.

Another, although less important, reason for South Carolina's departure was the lure of independence. Many of the powerhouse football programs of the era were free to make their schedules as they chose. They were not tied into annual meetings against the same opponents. As a result they played more demanding schedules, and were usually invited to better bowls. In leaving the ACC, South Carolina officials may have envisioned Columbia turning into the South Bend or Happy Valley of the South. Things did not turn out that way, as the Gamecocks posted only two winning seasons until Paul Dietzel's ouster before the 1975 season.

Paul Arnold was still fighting for his life in the hospital when Carolina traveled to Richmond for their first game. Whatever emotional baggage the team was carrying was left in the locker room, as the Tar Heels went out and blanked the Spiders behind 350 yards on the ground. Dooley kept it honest, rushing 66 times on a damp Saturday evening. Four different backs scored touchdowns for UNC, as Oglesby finished the game as the leading ground gainer with 126 yards on twenty-nine carries. Scoring once in each quarter, the Tar Heels left town in command of a convincing 28-0 victory.

Illinois alumnus Hugh Hefner was on hand to watch his alma mater face Carolina on September 18, but even the founder of Playboy could not bring the Illini luck against the Tar Heel defenders. Swarming and smothering their Big Ten opposition, Carolina pitched its second straight shutout to begin the year. Oglesby had another big outing, running for 167 yards and scoring twice. The first was a 58-yard strike from Miller, as the Heels caught the Illinois secondary with their collective pants down. The touchdown gave UNC a commanding 17-0 cushion, and the tailback scored his second touchdown later on a 3-yard push, which ended the scoring at 27-0.

Carolina returned home to begin its ACC slate against Maryland, and raced out to a 7-0 lead midway through the first quarter when Jolley carried the ball over from 5 yards out. Jolley also set up Carolina's next score with a fine individual effort, breaking off a 53-yard run to put UNC deep in UM territory. Two plays later Oglesby rambled in from the 9, and Carolina was in command at 14-0. Maryland came back to tie the game at 14 in the second half, taking advantage of UNC turnovers and ending the scoreless streak of the defense, which had reached ten consecutive quarters.

The Terrapins were driving toward a third touchdown when Bunting made a leaping interception of an Al Neville pass and returned it into UNC territory. A quarterback sneak for a touchdown by Miller was a prelude to Jolley, who outran the Terrapin secondary for a 62-yard score with just over eight minutes remaining. The Tar Heels scored a final touchdown when Bunting stepped in front of another pass and lumbered in from 32 yards out. The senior linebacker, who had been a part of Carolina's entire rebuilding process under Dooley, picked a fine time to make a difference. The 35-14 triumph, although ugly at times, was just the kind of victory UNC needed.

"Maryland gave us a real test of character," Dooley commented afterwards. "We've got a lot of character on this club. Some young men, but they are men. I couldn't be prouder of a football team than I am of this ball club."

The Carolina defense was solid again in a victory over N.C. State, shutting out the Wolfpack in the first half and jumping out to a 20-0 lead on the strength of their powerful running game. The teams traded touchdowns in the second half, but a series of big plays by the UNC defense held State at bay. With a 27-7 victory, North Carolina improved to 4-0 for the second autumn in a row.

The Tar Heels figured to have an easy one coming next, playing at home against Tulane. First-year coach Bennie Ellender was struggling with his new team, as the Green Wave brought a 1-3 record to Chapel Hill. The Tulane players were still in the process of learning Ellender's offensive system, a wide-open passing attack that was somewhat unique at that time. The Green Wave were averaging only 9 points a contest, and considering Carolina's defensive excellence, few gave Tulane a realistic chance of knocking off the Tar Heels. As a wise man once said, "that's why they play the game."

Tulane played its finest game of the year, and from the very beginning had the Tar Heels scrambling and out of position. Ellender's unorthodox pass-oriented system finally clicked, as the Green Wave rolled up a 28-11 halftime lead behind the passing of Mike Walker and the receiving of Maxie LeBlanc and Bob Marshall. Walker lit up the UNC secondary like a pinball machine, throwing for 245 yards and four touchdowns. It was a stunning turn of events for the Tar Heels, who gave up more points to the Green Wave than their previous four opponents combined. The Tar Heels rallied in the second half, but were unable to surpass the Tulane uprising from the opening half. The 37-29 loss was a true stunner to all those that witnessed it.

Carolina had no time to reflect on the Tulane setback, as mighty Notre Dame awaited next. Ara Parseghian had built another fine team in South Bend, which had given up only 16 total combined points in a trio of wins over Big Ten opponents. Notre Dame built a 9-0 lead at halftime on the leg of kicker Bob Thomas, who connected from 28, 27, and 24 yards. All-American Tom Gatewood's touchdown provided the winning margin of 16-0, as the Irish defense played another outstanding game. The Tar Heels compiled only 149 total yards on offense, as the Irish ran its scoreless streak to fourteen consecutive quarters.

Tulane and Notre Dame had dashed Carolina's dreams of an undefeated season, but UNC remained unblemished in the conference. They now had to prepare for Wake Forest, who was running the veer to great success once again. The week before the Carolina game, the Deacons had demolished Tulsa, 51-21, running the ball for 528 yards. In earlier contests against Virginia Tech and N.C. State, the Deacons had amassed 354 and 402 rushing yards, respectively. With ACC rushing champion Larry Hopkins leading the way, Wake came to Chapel Hill sporting a solid 4-2 record, and could put themselves in position for their second conference title with a victory.

With Chapel Hill blanketed all afternoon by rain, the field at Kenan Stadium became a mud pit. The conditions were so slippery that the passing games for both teams were virtually nullified. Although neither team could have known it at the time, a Ted Leverenz touchdown for UNC early in the game proved to be the only goal line crossing of the day for either team.

With the game winding down, and the score 7-3 in favor of Carolina, the Deacons made a final push to victory. On third-and-3, with the ball at the UNC 8, Cal Stoll tried to fool Carolina by throwing for only the third time all day. Larry Russell's wounded-duck pass in the direction of Ken Garrett fell harmlessly out of bounds, leaving Wake with a single play to seize victory. The Deacons went to Hopkins for the thirty-sixth time on fourth down, and the back slammed hard into the Carolina front. The Tar Heels made the play at the line of scrimmage, and the ball was spotted inches short of the first down marker. The UNC defense had done its job, and the Tar Heel offense came back onto the field for a single snap and kneel.

"I've never seen a team as fired up as we were for this game," said Bunting, who looked like a giant mudcake. "We didn't even want to rest at the half. We wanted to get back out there and play."

The skies cleared in Chapel Hill for the following week's encounter with William and Mary. The game went back and forth all day, with Carolina matching William and Mary each time they drove downfield and scored. With the score 35-34 after UNC's fifth touchdown, Dooley chose to go for the two-point conversion. With 2:01 on the clock, Miller faded back and threw in the direction of Jolley on a delay pattern. The ball glanced off a W&M defender and into the hands of Jolley, who hauled in the catch to the roar of the Kenan faithful. Rich Stilley secured victory for Carolina moments later with an interception. Despite giving up 478 yards to the upstart Tribe, the Tar Heels had its sixth victory of the season, 36-35.

"I'm just glad it's over," commented Dooley, who watched his team fend off defeat at home for the second week in a row. "But that was a display of character we showed out there today. Five times we came back and scored."

The Tar Heels settled down against Clemson, topping the Tigers for a third consecutive victory over their rivals from Death Valley. After taking a 13-0 lead into halftime, the Carolina defense drove a painful nail in the Tiger coffin early in the third quarter, when Brafford blocked a punt and recovered it in the end zone for a touchdown. Ken Craven tied the ACC single-game record with four field goals, and although Clemson scored on a pair of passes to tight end John McMakin, the damage had been done. The 26-13 victory gave Carolina a 4-0 ACC record, and with their final two games coming against inferior opponents, the Tar Heels were well on their way to the conference title.

After playing three straight weeks in Chapel Hill, the Tar Heels took to the road to play Virginia in Charlottesville. The 2-7 Cavaliers played Carolina tough, coming back from a 13-0 deficit to make a game of it. Unlike Clemson, who also trailed 13-0 to the Tar Heels, Virginia refused to concede. Backup quarterback Harrison Davis riddled the Carolina secondary for 261 yards, and brought the Cavaliers to within 25-20 when he found Dave Sullivan in the end zone. The Heels hung tough on their next possession, going 74 yards in eight plays for the winning points. Miller tossed a touchdown to Jolley, who led the way for UNC with 167 rushing yards, and the extra point gave Carolina a 32-20 final.

Duke had a chance to play the spoiler against the Tar Heels in the regular season finale, just as Carolina had successfully done several times in the past. North Carolina had denied Duke conference championships four times in the last thirteen seasons with season-ending victories, and the Blue Devils would have liked nothing more than to deny Carolina an undefeated ACC championship this time around. Jolley tallied three touchdowns and ran for 159 yards, however, as Carolina rolled to a surprisingly easy 38-0 victory. After going scoreless in the opening quarter, the Tar Heels exploded in the final forty-five minutes. The Blue Devils made one progressive drive into UNC territory in the first half, but an illegal motion penalty ruined their chances of reaching the scoreboard. Carolina broke the game open by scoring twenty-eight unanswered points in the second half, with Leverenz making the final tally on a 27-yard pass from backup Johnny Klise.

With a 9-2 record, the Tar Heels knew they were headed to a post-season game, and were elated to hear that the Gator Bowl wanted them in Jacksonville. The Gator appearance would be North Carolina's first in nine years, and had added significance due to the opposition. The Tar Heels and the University of Georgia would make history, as Bill and Vince Dooley became the first brothers in college football history to square off against one another in a bowl game. The Bulldogs were a solid outfit, starting the season 9-0 before losing a single game in November to Auburn. The UGA defense was even stronger than UNC, going eight consecutive games without giving up any more than a single touchdown.

The "Dooley Bowl" began as a defensive stalemate, as UNC's running game was stunted by the aggressive UGA defense. The Tar Heels were held to only 115 yards on fifty-one attempts. Despite their inability to move the football for most of the game, Carolina remained competitive due to its own defensive success, highlighted by the play of linebacker Jim Webster. Although they ran for twice as much yardage as the Tar Heels, UGA was unable to penetrate far enough to reach the scoreboard in the first half. The teams went to the locker rooms tied at 0.

Carolina finally broke through in the third quarter, moving into field goal range for Craven. Georgia immediately responded to the Tar Heel score, as quarterback Andy Johnson and running back Jimmy Poulos worked through the UNC defenders. Lining up on defense at their own 25, Dooley and the UNC staff chose to run a blitz at the Georgia line, hoping to stuff the Bulldogs for minimal yardage. Poulos took the carry and eased through a gap, and with the Tar Heel linebackers committed to the blitz, Poulos had an easy run to the end zone. The extra point made the score 7-3, and the Bulldog defense held on the rest of the way for the victory.

For several years up until 1972, the NCAA had a policy in place that barred freshmen from competing on varsity teams. The rule was put in place primarily to regulate the NCAA's two biggest revenue sports, basketball and football. Although most freshman players were unable to contribute immediately on major college teams, there were always exceptions. Many talented players over the years had been forced to lose entire seasons of eligibility solely because they were first-year participants.

The Atlantic Coast Conference was one of the leaders in a movement to eliminate the policy, and received help in the cause from the Western Athletic Conference. The two leagues made an official proposal to the NCAA, and the governing body surprisingly voted in its favor. Although most coaches were against the idea of having freshmen compete on varsity teams at the time, the change would have direct causes and effects on the upcoming football season.

North Carolina lost a number of key players between 1971 and 1972, but enough talent returned to Bill Dooley's squad to make another unbeaten tour through the ACC. With Lou Angelo and Jimmy DeRatt returning on defense, the Tar Heels again boasted one of the league's top units. Mike Mansfield took John Bunting's place as the premiere linebacker, and earned a place on the All-ACC team along with linemen Gene Brown and Eric Hyman. The defense was particularly tough in October and November, allowing only 13 points over four games and posting two shutouts.

As was the case with most of Bill Dooley's teams at North Carolina, the 1972 Tar Heels were strong on the ground. The offense churned out 244 yards a contest, tops in the ACC for the third time in four years. Ike Oglesby returned from a leg injury as the featured back, while Nick Vidnovic took over the quarterbacking reins. The Tar Heel strength lied in its offensive line, where a trio of bruising linemen did their thing. Tackle Jerry Sain made the All-Conference team, while guard Ron Rusnak was named first-team All-American. Another future All-American guard, Ken Huff, was in his first season as a Tar Heel starter.

Another opener with Richmond resulted in another Tar Heel victory, although it was a lot closer this time around. The Carolina defense set the tone early, as Greg Ward intercepted a pass and Angelo forced a fumble. The Tar Heels scored following each of the turnovers, as Tommy Bradley and Johnny Klise ran in from short distances. Angelo set up another UNC touchdown with an interception, as Billy Hite, who led the team with 86 yards rushing, scored to give Carolina a 28-6 bulge. The Spiders added two touchdowns in the final quarter, going largely against the backups, to make the final score 28-18.

Over in Raleigh that same day, Maryland and North Carolina State began new chapters in their football histories, as Jerry Claiborne and Lou Holtz made their respective debuts as the head coaches of the Terrapins and Wolfpack. It was the first of many significant encounters between the pair over the next several years. State took a halftime lead on a pair of touchdowns by quarterback Bruce Shaw, but Maryland tied it in the fourth quarter after a controversial pass interference call. The game ended in a 24-24 deadlock.

Maryland's tie with State was a prelude to a home clash with Carolina, and for the second year in a row, UNC jumped all over the Terrapins in the first half. Vidnovic enjoyed his finest performance yet as a Tar Heel, throwing for a touchdown and running for two more. Carolina took a 17-3 lead on Vidnovic's 5-yard scramble, a 24-yard pass to Ted Leverenz, and a 23-yard kick by Ellis Alexander. Just as they had done in Chapel Hill the year before, Maryland put together a spirited comeback in the third quarter. With the score 31-26 late in the game, the Terps began a desperate offensive stand. With under a minute to play, Al Neville spotted Don Ratliff open. The tight end took the ball to the 37, but lost control and fumbled. DeRatt was on it, and the Tar Heels escaped Byrd Stadium with the win.

Although the Maryland battle was spirited, nothing could match the intensity of the game the following week in Chapel Hill between the Tar Heels and N.C. State. State used its powerful running game to roll up a 19-10 halftime lead, but the Tar Heels came roaring back in the second half. Consecutive touchdowns gave UNC a 24-19 advantage, but State retook the lead, 27-24, on a Willie Burden touchdown and ensuing two-point conversion. Carolina tied it with an Alexander field goal in the fourth quarter, and it stayed that way until the final minutes.

With just over a minute remaining, a 27-27 tie seemed imminent as Mark Cassidy lined up to punt from the NCSU 5. In a stunning turn of events, however, the Wolfpack punter misplayed the snap. As Cassidy struggled to recover the ball, the Carolina coverage unit closed in. As the football fluttered across the turf, bodies flew in every direction. DeRatt came up big for the second week in a row, falling on the pigskin at the 1-yard line. Billy Hite scored on a sweep moments later to give UNC a 34-27 lead, and it looked as though Carolina had salted away a freak victory over their archrival.

State got the ball back with fifty seconds remaining, and in four plays, Bruce Shaw marched the Wolfpack 37 yards. With ten seconds on the clock and the ball at the 32, Dave Buckey found Pat Kenney in the end zone. Kenney, who stood only 5'6,'' extended as far as his body would allow him, and made a leaping grab to pull State within a point. The small throng of NCSU supporters, assembled in the corner of the east end zone, went crazy following Kenney's dramatic reception. With only eight seconds remaining, the fate of the game was in the hands of Lou Holtz. The Wolfpack could settle for a tie, but Holtz would have none of it. The State offense returned to the field for a two-point conversion, a play that wound up deciding the conference championship.

With the crowd staring on with a fixed gaze, Buckey dropped back to pass and spotted Burden. Tar Heel defensive back Terry Taylor quickly responded, and tipped the ball just out of the reach of the NCSU tailback. As the ball landed safely on the deck, the home fans let out a spirited cheer, while the Wolfpack fans, after taking a moment to allow the bitter defeat to set in, showered Holtz and his team with a standing ovation. On this day, even the staunchest of Carolina supporters had to respect the winner-take-all attitude of Lou Holtz.

"Carolina has a fine team," a dejected Holtz said afterwards. "We made some mistakes and the ball bounced their way, but they made it bounce. I just feel so damn sick and so do my boys. Everybody feels like they lost the game, but I'm just as proud of this team as I can be."

The unbeaten Tar Heels next headed to Columbus for a game against Ohio State, and the UNC faithful would be wishing back the NCAA's no-freshman policy by the end of the day. The Buckeyes unleashed a surprise rookie sensation in Archie Griffin, who in the coming years would become the first and only player in NCAA history to win the Heisman Trophy twice. Griffin had his coming out party against the Tar Heels, carrying twenty-seven times for 239 yards to break the Ohio State school record in only his second career game. Griffin set up touchdown runs by three different Buckeyes in the second and third quarters, and scored himself on a 9-yarder in the final period, leading the way to a 29-14 Buckeye victory.

After a week off, the Tar Heels got back to their winning ways with a 31-20 verdict over Kentucky in Chapel Hill. Oglesby made his first start of the season and came through with 126 yards, including 99 in the opening half, to pace UNC. Kentucky rallied in the second half to make the game competitive, but the Wildcats were unable to overcome Carolina's rushing onslaught.

With Larry Hopkins, Larry Russell, and Cal Stoll all gone, Wake Forest was searching for a new identity in the fall of 1972. The Deacons had dropped four of their first five games under new coach Tom Harper, and fared little better at home against the Tar Heels. Carolina scored twice in the second quarter and once in the fourth to upend the Deacons 21-0. The only downside for UNC was the departure of Vidnovic, who was nailed on a helmet-to-helmet collision and spent much of the game in a daze on the sidelines.

The Tar Heels got another week off to prepare for Clemson, which gave Vidnovic time to get back into playing form. The quarterback was raring to go against the Tigers, and led a UNC offensive assault that produced 496 yards. After jumping out to a 16-0 halftime lead, the Tar Heel defenders momentarily lost their focus. Utilizing a short passing attack, Clemson quarterback Ken Pengitore led the Tigers to a pair of scores, cutting the Carolina lead to 16-10. Dooley adjusted to the Clemson scheme, bringing out a blitz package to throw off the Tiger signal caller. The ploy worked, as Clemson was held scoreless the remainder of the contest. The Tar Heels put the game away in the second half on an Alexander field goal and an 11-yard run by Dick Oliver, which made the final score 26-10.

The Virginia game was an ugly affair, as the teams combined for six turnovers. A fight broke out on the field during the second quarter, and Tar Heels Ronnie Robinson and Terry Taylor were each ejected. Despite losing the two defensive starters, UNC was relentless against the Cavalier offense. A 25-yard field goal by Alexander and a 9-yard sprint by Vidnovic gave Carolina a comfortable lead at halftime, and in the third quarter, Jimmy Jerome put the game on ice with his second touchdown reception in three games, this one covering 71 yards. The 23-3 victory was all Carolina needed to sew up the ACC title for a second consecutive year.

Duke kept things close a week later, failing to yield against UNC's potent offense. With the game still scoreless in the fourth quarter, a pair of interceptions paved the way for Carolina's eighth victory. With ten minutes remaining, Mark DiCarlo picked off Duke quarterback Mark Johnson and returned the ball to the Blue Devil 23. A Ken Taylor touchdown put Carolina on the board, and Phil Lamm intercepted another Johnson pass minutes later. Taylor scored his second touchdown, and the Tar Heels were on their way to victory. The 14-0 shutout gave Carolina its fifteenth consecutive win in conference play, and the Sun Bowl offered UNC an invitation to their December 30 game in the locker room.

Some in the media thought the Tar Heels would have a letdown against Sonny Randle's 9-1 East Carolina team, as Jerry Sain posted a newspaper clipping in his locker that read, "ECU by a TD." On a cold, dreary day in Chapel Hill, the Tar Heels took care of business by thumping the Pirates, 42-19. Oglesby and Sammy Johnson were too much for the Pirates, combining for 223 yards and four touchdowns. It was a nice breakthrough for Oglesby, who hadn't scored since the N.C. State game a year prior.

The Florida game had no bearing on Carolina's postseason plans, but victory would give the Tar Heels ten regular season victories for the first time since 1914. After taking an early lead, Carolina's defense became vulnerable to the passing of Dave Bowden, who led the Gators on a series of drives to give Florida a 17-14 advantage. Sammy Johnson had another big game in the UNC backfield, and scored his second touchdown in the final quarter to give the Tar Heels back the lead. Florida scored again for a 24-20 margin, setting the stage for some dramatics by Carolina. A third touchdown by Johnson, which came at the 1:41 mark, gave Bowden and the Gators enough time to mount a final drive. They did just that, moving inside the Carolina 10 in the final seconds. The Tar Heel defenders held tough, killing the Florida surge with a series of stops. The Gators failed to score, and UNC had the 28-24 victory.

For only the second time in the ACC's history, two schools were invited to go bowling, and just like in 1963, those schools were North Carolina and N.C. State. As the Tar Heels were making plans for a trip to El Paso, N.C. State was gearing up for a Peach Bowl encounter with West Virginia. Following their tough loss to Carolina back in September, the Wolfpack had dropped another game at Georgia before closing out the season with five wins in six games. Before the bowl, freshman Dave Buckey was thrust into the starting quarterback slot for NCSU, when Bruce Shaw went down in practice with a broken arm.

Buckey, who wouldn't have even been on the NCSU varsity in 1971 with the no-freshman policy, took advantage of his unique opportunity, finding Pat Hovance and his twin brother Don for a pair of touchdowns. After a competitive first half, which State led 14-13, the Wolfpack poured it on the Mountaineers in the final thirty minutes. Behind Willie Burden and Stan Fritts, State scored five unanswered touchdowns to take a 49-13 triumph. Burden rushed for 120 yards, while Fritts crossed the goal line three times. The Wolfpack amassed 337 rushing yards for the game, while holding the WVU to only 91.

The following day, North Carolina pulled out all the punches to beat a tough Texas Tech (TT) team in the Sun Bowl. Carolina led 9-7 at the half, thanks in large part to a controversial call that went in the baby blue's favor. In the second quarter, the Red Raiders blocked a Carolina punt and ran it back for a touchdown. The play was nullified by an unsportsmanlike conduct penalty, as one of the officials spotted a Red Raider coach on the field. The ruling took away what would have been a lethal blow to the Carolina cause. Despite the setback, the Red Raiders began to pull away early in the second half. Carolina's defense, which had been among the best in the country all season, suddenly found itself unable to handle Texas Tech tailback George Smith.

Smith, who torched three teams during the 1972 season for 100-yard games, got the Raiders going with back-to-back touchdown sprints, one covering 65 yards and the other 46. Tech led 21-9, but the Tar Heels were far from done. Vidnovic, who had inspired Carolina fans all season with his aggressive play, put on one final show in a UNC uniform. Vidnovic rallied the Tar Heels to a pair of scores, and a 24-21 lead in the final period. Texas Tech regained possession and Smith scored again, giving the Raiders a 28-24 lead midway through the decisive quarter.

Late in the game, a Phil Lamm punt return put the Tar Heels at the TT 37 yard line. After converting a crucial fourth-and-1, Vidnovic found Leverenz for a touchdown, which thrust Carolina back ahead, 30-28, with less than two minutes to go. After a missed extra point, the Tar Heel defense made a final big play to seal victory. Ronnie Robinson and Bill Chapman eluded their blockers and met at quarterback Joe Barnes, taking him down in the end zone. Carolina easily ran out the clock for an emotional 32-28 victory, which set a UNC single-season school record with eleven wins. The "Cardiac Kids," as they came to be known, had won their four biggest games of the year by a combined 14 points.

"Determination won this one," Dooley commented after the game.

"Determination is the difference between this dressing room and the one across the hall. I said before and I say again, Texas Tech is a fine football team. We just wouldn't let them beat us."

7

Red Tide (1973-1976)

At the end of the 1971 season, Maryland and North Carolina State each decided to make coaching changes. The schools had become the doormats of ACC football in a relatively short period of time, and each were looking for new identities to shake up their programs. Maryland hadn't played in a bowl since the Jim Tatum days, despite the program changing hands five times, while NCSU had fallen into the second division of the league in 1970 for the first time in nearly a decade. The new man in College Park was Jerry Claiborne, a no-nonsense coach from the old school. Claiborne learned the game as a player under Bear Bryant at Kentucky, and had spent more than a decade prowling the sidelines at Virginia Tech, where he turned the Gobblers into a respectable outfit. Claiborne fit the mold of the Southern football coach to a tee—stern, unpredictable, and devoted to his team's success.

"He was a disciplinarian—no sideburns. Your hair could not touch your ears," recalled Frank Burnop, who played on Claiborne's 1970 team at Virginia Tech. "We called him 'The Hawk' because he would stand up in that practice field tower with a bullhorn in his hands. You never wanted to mess up because you knew he was going to blow that horn and holler your name out."

Earle Edwards retired from N.C. State with his program on the decline, and handed the reins over to former assistant Al Michaels in 1971. Michaels was given a single autumn to prove himself as head coach at NCSU, and although his players supported him, he won only three games. After the season, NCSU opted to hire thirty-five-year-old Lou Holtz, who had spent the previous three seasons at William and Mary. Although the Tribe played in a bowl during Holtz's tenure, W&M had failed to produce a winning record. Holtz was largely unknown among the college coaching ranks at the time, and his diminutive, bespectacled appearance made him look more like a math profes-sor than a football coach. At the press conference, in which he was named head coach at NCSU, however, Holtz had an answer for his crit-ics.

"I know how I look and I can't help it," Holtz said. "But I can throw a clipboard as good as any coach who's 6'4'', and I like to win."

Behind a punishing running attack, the Wolfpack cruised to the school's first unbeaten season in league play in 1973. State racked up seven wins in its final eight contests, and finished with the school's highest AP ranking in sixteen years. Behind guard Bill Yoest and a group of talented backs, NCSU overwhelmed their opposition on the ground, setting school records with 2,995 yards and an average of 272.3 yards per contest. Yoest nearly lost his career after a back injury that required surgery to remove part of his vertebrae, but the veteran returned to claim All-American honors that fall.

The Wolfpack came out of the gates strong against East Carolina in the opener, played in front of a record crowd at Carter Stadium. State ran at will against the defending Southern Conference champions, sur-passing the school record for total yardage with 584. Dave Buckey started at quarterback for NCSU and was a perfect six-for-six passing, good for 117 yards. Holtz was generous with playing time, giving min-utes to all sixty-six dressed players as State took a 36-0 lead into half-time. The Wolfpack scored twice more in the final frame to take a 57-8 final, the team's most lopsided victory in forty-five years.

Opening their ACC slate against Virginia, the Wolfpack again found the sailing smooth on offense. State ran up 284 yards on the ground against the Cavaliers, mixing a powerful outside attack with steady dives up the middle. State led, 24-7, in the second quarter, scor-ing on each of their first four possessions. Although Virginia fought to pull within two touchdowns in the second half, State quickly ended any hopes of a comeback with another long drive, covering 62 yards and eating up nearly four minutes from the clock. Burden put NCSU in position with a 28-yard carry, and Charley Young climaxed the 43-23 final with a dive off right tackle.

The victories over ECU and UVA gave the Wolfpack much-needed momentum heading into a showdown with No. 2 Nebraska (NU) in Lincoln. The Cornhuskers had buried a good UCLA team, 40-13, in their opener, and looked forward to showcasing Tony Davis and their high-powered offense in the friendly confines of Memorial Sta-dium. For three quarters, State looked every bit as good as the powerful Huskers, and for the briefest of moments, looked as if they were capable of pulling off one of the biggest nonconference road upsets in ACC history.

The Wolfpack played inspired defensive football for most of the game, and set the early tone in the first quarter by intercepting NU quarterback Steve Runty. Nebraska had marched downfield using a balanced approach, but Wolfpack strong safety Bobby Pilz was ready for a pass across the middle of the end zone, and hauled it in for a touchback. The Wolfpack drew first blood later in the quarter, thanks to an error by the Nebraska special teams. Randy Borg brought back a punt 42 yards for Nebraska, only to fumble it away at the State 24. Three plays later, Fritts broke free on a 59-yard run that sent the red-clad Nebraska crowd into stunned silence. The Cornhuskers were cheating to State's strong side, allowing Fritts easy access on his weak-side jaunt.

NU head coach Tom Osborne brought in Dave Humm in place of Runty at quarterback, and the Cornhuskers quickly responded. Davis began the drive with a 39-yard carry, which was followed by an impressive touchdown grab by Frosty Anderson. State continued to play Nebraska tough in the second half, although the Huskers took a 10-7 lead on their initial possession. State took the football and promptly went through the NU defense on eleven plays, of which ten were rushes. Fritts scored his second touchdown, and State led, 14-10. The Wolfpack lead lasted into the final quarter, when the frustrated Huskers took advantage of an interception and poor punting by the Wolfpack. Scoring 21 unanswered points in the fourth quarter, Nebraska marched their way to a 31-14 triumph. Although the Huskers were victorious, the Nebraska players had nothing but good things to say about the Wolfpack following the game.

"They were twice as good as UCLA," said All-American tackle John Dutton. "Their linemen were bigger, better, and quicker. I don't think I played very well and I don't know why. But they really surprised me. They're a great team."

"It was tough, really tough," commented Daryl White. "North Carolina State would rate with any team in the Big Eight. Their defense was tougher than we thought. They were good and it was hot. It was a tough day."

As the Wolfpack were tangling in Lincoln, Maryland was busy in Chapel Hill ending a number of UNC football streaks. Bill Dooley's Tar Heels had taken fifteen consecutive ACC contests dating back to 1970, and hadn't lost at home in nearly two full seasons. Undaunted, Maryland's aggressive defensive line punished UNC up front, as Carolina was held without a touchdown for the first time since the 1971

Gator Bowl. Louis Carter crossed the line to give Maryland a 7-3 half-time advantage, and quarterback Al Neville completed touchdown passes to Frank Russell and Walter White, which gave Maryland an insurmountable 20-3 lead. With Randy White leading the UM defensive charges with eighteen tackles, the Terrapins ended UNC's reign atop the ACC standings, 23-3.

State remained on the road for another tough contest a week later against Georgia, and once again the special teams proved to be a letdown. Gene Washington, Georgia's lightning-fast freshman, bolted through for an 86-yard return to give the Bulldogs a 7-6 lead early in the game. The Wolfpack were riddled with bad field position all game, thanks to the booming drives of UGA punter Don Golden. Golden averaged 40.6 yards a punt, and combined with the kickoffs and accuracy of placekicker Don Leavitt, State was at a serious disadvantage in this crucial aspect of the game. The Bulldogs scored twice more in the second quarter to take a 21-6 lead, and tacked on a field goal and another touchdown for a 31-12 decision.

Frustrated about their play over the previous two games, the Wolfpack returned to Raleigh the following week to play North Carolina. The Wolfpack were still quite bitter about last season's outcome in Chapel Hill, and didn't care that the Tar Heels were struggling. Carolina had been decimated by graduations, and stood at 1-2 in the midst of a rebuilding season. State took no prisoners early on, jumping out to a 21-3 lead behind a dominant effort on the ground. Their second march ate up 99 yards, as the red and white moved from the UNC 1 to the goal line. Sophomore quarterback Billy Paschall, making his first varsity start for the Tar Heels, finally began to click in the second half, and brought UNC to within 21-11 after a sneak across the line. Following a fumble recovery on the ensuing kickoff, Carolina went into a running frenzy of its own and moved to the NCSU 2, where Paschall executed a perfect play-action pass. An off-tackle fake to Sammy Johnson pinched in the NCSU linebackers, allowing Charles Waddell to streak to the back corner of the end zone and haul in an underthrown ball for a 21-19 game.

The teams traded touchdowns over the next several minutes, and the clock was UNC's greatest enemy as they lined up for an onsides kick with only ninety seconds remaining and the score 28-26 in favor of the Wolfpack. The short kick touched a Carolina defender inside UNC territory, and State had no problems running out the clock. After the game, a relieved Holtz managed to scrape up some sarcasm in discussing his team's punting woes.

"If anybody in the student body can snap on punts, ask them to call 737-2114. That's my phone number. If this is an ad, then bill me for it," he said. "It was an emotion-packed game and the way our players kept coming back was something. It was a typical State-Carolina game."

With UNC now officially off the throne as King of ACC football, the new ruler would be decided the following week in Raleigh, as Maryland came to town. Between their pair of trips to North Carolina, the injury bug had bitten the Terrapins. Al Neville fractured his elbow in the game against Villanova, and backup Bob Avellini was in command as UM blanked Syracuse, 38-0. Neville was not supposed to play, but wound up making a significant contribution following another setback for Claiborne's squad.

Avellini went down on Maryland's first offensive series with an injury, forcing third-string quarterback Ben Kinard into the game. Kinard was unseasoned at best, and had a great deal of trouble receiving the snap from center. The exchange hit the deck on two separate occasions, each in UM territory, and the Wolfpack recovered both fumbles. Kinard fumbled another time on a handoff, and also threw an interception, as the Wolfpack jumped out to a 17-0 lead.

With his team on the verge of getting blown out, Claiborne decided to lift Kinard in favor of the ailing Neville. Neville quickly brought the Terrapins back into contention, leading a touchdown drive to pull UM within 17-6 at halftime. The momentum continued in the second half, as Maryland drove downfield and scored again to make it a game at 17-12. Up to this point, State had taken advantage of Maryland mistakes in order to seize control. With the game now teetering in uncertainty, the Wolfpack put together its first and only sustained offensive drive against the formidable Terrapin defense. Burden ended the march with a run from the 10, giving NCSU a 24-12 advantage heading into the final fifteen minutes.

The Wolfpack felt the sting of Maryland's pressure in the final quarter, failing to make a single first down. After recovering a fumble, the Terrapins went 59 yards, keyed by a fourth down completion from Neville to Frank Russell. The flea-flicker brought UM down to the State 1, where Louis Carter piled in to once again make it a 24-19 contest. After yet another fumble by the Wolfpack, Steve Mike-Mayer was good from 32 yards on a field goal, and once again the Wolfpack would have to hold onto a slim lead down the stretch.

With thirteen seconds remaining, and the score still 24-22 in favor of NCSU, Mike-Mayer took the field again to attempt a 40-yard kick. The snap from center was a bit high, and the ball was not completely on the tee as Mike-Mayer put his foot into it. This forced the quick-kicking

Mike-Mayer to push the ball too far to the left, and wide of the posts. The State players and fans celebrated in typical fashion, taking over the Carter Stadium field and turning it into a sea of red.

"Man, I didn't even see the kick," Holtz said in the locker room. "All I could see was some fans behind the end zone jumping up and down and I just hoped they were for us."

"It was just one of those days," said Claiborne. "I thought we played a tremendous game to get beat."

With their two biggest conference victories behind them, State took to the road for the Clemson contest. Although the Tigers were 2-0 in the ACC coming in, having beaten both Duke and Virginia, they were unable to remain competitive for very long. With the backs on top of their game, State's rushing attack ran on all cylinders, and left Death Valley with a convincing 29-6 win. A week later, NCSU headed back to the Palmetto State to face South Carolina. The Wolfpack turned the Astroturf of Williams-Brice Stadium into their own track surface, as the offense buried USC behind 330 rushing yards. State raced out to a 42-14 advantage in the second half, only to endure a wild fourth quarter onslaught of points. The teams combined for six touchdowns over the final fifteen minutes, and John Gargano's catch of a last-second "rub it in" pass by Buckey gave NCSU a 56-35 verdict.

State had now won four consecutive games since the loss at Georgia, and prepared to go on the road again to play another powerful foe in Penn State. The Lions, behind the stellar running of Heisman Trophy winner John Cappelletti, were a perfect 8-0 coming into the contest, and had just completed a 42-22 dismantling of Maryland in College Park. On a bitterly cold Pennsylvania afternoon, neither team could take the upper hand in the opening quarter. The field had been cleared of a light snowfall before the teams took the field, and flurries came down off and on throughout the first half. With wind swirling through Beaver Stadium as well, and two excellent defenses on display, the game went into halftime with State holding a surprising 14-9 advantage.

Following an 83-yard punt return from Gary Hayman early in the third quarter, which gave PSU a 22-14 lead, Fritts collided over on a fourth down to complete a sustained march through the Lions. Going for the tie, Holtz chose to run a deceptive option pitch. Young hauled in a perfect toss from the left, and went in to knot the game. Following another Penn State score that gave the Lions a 29-22 lead, Young stole the show. On the way to his third consecutive 100-yard performance, Young took a handoff and burst through the line for a 69-yard score, which knocked the breath out of the Happy Valley crowd and proved that Penn State would have to fight to the bitter end in order to claim victory, just like in the 1967 thriller in the same stadium between the same two teams.

With the game tied yet again, Penn State began a gritty 60-yard drive propelled by their superstar. From the NCSU 27, Cappelletti took the ball and headed up the gut of the Wolfpack front. After faking Mike Devine off his feet, Cappelletti went into the end zone standing for his third score of the day. State got two more offensive opportunities, but the Nittany Lions, who held on for the 35-29 win, held each time. Difficult as the loss was for the Wolfpack, they could take solace in being the toughest challenge all season for a team that finished undefeated, claimed victory in the Orange Bowl, and had a justifiable beef for the NCAA title by season's end.

"Today, we beat a great football team," commented PSU coach Joe Paterno. "I thought North Carolina State played a super football game against us. As cold as it was, they ran that veer offense without making any mistakes. Cappelletti is the best player I've ever been around. We had to make the big plays to win, and Gary Hayman certainly made them for us. It was just a great college football game. You'll never see a better one."

State took out some of its frustrations on Duke seven days later, sending the Blue Devils to their eighth loss of the season. Although it was a cool afternoon in Durham, it was tropical compared to the conditions in Happy Valley from the week before. Duke, in the midst of its worst football season in school history to that time, played valiantly, as their defense sought to do what few teams all season had been able to do, shut down the NCSU running game. The Wolfpack spent the first three quarters perplexed by the Blue Devil defenders, managing only a single touchdown on Burden's 1-yard carry in the opening quarter, but a pair of rallies late in the game led to a 21-3 final.

There was still the matter of knocking off Wake Forest in the regular season finale, and Willie Burden turned his final game in Raleigh into a personal showcase. Burden, who would go on to a standout professional career in Canada, staked his claim for ACC Player of the Year honors with 188 yards rushing. By game's end, Burden had amassed 1,014 yards, making him the first North Carolina State back in history to surpass the 1,000-yard mark in a single season. The yardage was just enough to surpass UNC's Sammy Johnson for the conference rushing title.

State eclipsed the school record set earlier in the year against East Carolina with 638 total yards, including 407 on the ground. Shaw threw for 126 yards, moving past Roman Gabriel and into first place in NCSU's all-time passing annals. State made it look easy in the 52-13 triumph, which shattered the NCSU and ACC marks previously held for points in a season (365) and points per game (33.2). Finishing the regular season with an 8-3 record, the Wolfpack were supremely confident heading into their Liberty Bowl encounter with Kansas (KU).

Don Frambrough had turned around a dormant KU program in his three short years in Lawrence, and had the Jayhawks a couple of plays away from a major bowl berth. Although Kansas had won seven games, Frambrough's team was left with a lingering feeling of what might have been. The Jayhawks lost a pair of heartbreaking contests, a 28-27 setback to Tennessee and a 10-9 defeat to Nebraska. Despite those two losses, Kansas came into the game ranked and sporting one of the nation's best quarterbacks in Dave Jaynes.

The Wolfpack and Jayhawks represented the opposite ends of the spectrum offensively. One team was geared toward the run, while the other was content on throwing its way downfield. Each strategy proved effective, as both teams moved the football with relative ease. The All-American Jaynes put forth a fine performance for Kansas, completing twenty-four of thirty-eight passes for 218 yards and a touchdown. The scoring pass, thrown to Bob Miller from the 12, tied the game at 7 in the second quarter. Fritts provided the only points of the first quarter with a dive from the 2. Both teams notched field goals to send the game into halftime tied at 10.

In the second half, State continued to pound Kansas on the ground, going to their backs play after play. Fritts, on his way to Most Valuable Player honors, ran over from the 8 to give NCSU a 17-10 lead. It was the thirteenth touchdown of the year for Fritts, who concluded the game with 83 yards. The Wolfpack added to its lead early in the fourth quarter, as Young concluded a nineteen-play, 80-yard march with a run from the 12. The drive was a microcosm of State's entire season, as they went to the air only once during the steady progression.

"We honestly felt that we could run the ball against Kansas," said Fritts. "We felt all season long we could run against anybody."

Now holding a comfortable 24-10 lead, State could afford to get more aggressive on defense in hopes of making a game-breaking play. It occurred at the 4:03 mark, when freshman defensive tackle Jim Henderson caught a deflected pass by Jaynes and rambled 31 yards to the end zone. Although Jaynes passed KU to another touchdown and conversion in the final minutes, the game belonged to the Wolfpack. The 31-18 victory was N.C. State's second bowl triumph in a row under

Holtz, and their nine victories were good enough for No. 16 in the final AP poll.

"When I had the opportunity to take the N.C. State job in 1972, their program was in a position to take off," Holtz said years later. "It really didn't matter who the coach was going to be. They were going to win. I was just fortunate enough to have the opportunity to be the coach there at that particular time. There were some great people associated with the program at that time."

Eleven days later, Maryland met Georgia in Atlanta's Peach Bowl. Despite the fact that the game was played less than one hundred miles from the UGA campus, and the Bulldogs had soundly beaten N.C. State earlier in the year, the Terrapins were up for the challenge. Claiborne's troops lined up and dominated Georgia offensively, amassing 461 yards. Although the Terps moved into the red zone seven different times over the course of the game, turnovers proved to be their downfall. Maryland turned the ball over four times, allowing the Bulldogs to take command of a game that was tied at 10 at halftime. Mike-Mayer connected on two field goals for the Terps, but Andy Reid scored a touchdown to propel the Bulldogs to a 17-16 victory. Despite the loss, it was evident that Maryland was back on the map as a solid football program.

Maryland's return to gridiron prominence came full circle in 1974, when the Terrapins tore through the ACC unbeaten for the school's first conference title in nineteen years. Behind the passing of Bob Avellini, who set a school record with 1,689 yards, Maryland rolled up forty or more points on four regular season opponents. Tailback Louis Carter and receiver Frank Russell, team leaders during Maryland's resurgent 1973 season, returned for another campaign the following year. Carter led the team with 991 rushing yards, while Russell hauled in 31 passes for 404 yards. Russell finished his career in College Park with 100 catches, setting a career mark for receptions.

Randy White, who set a new standard of excellence for defensive linemen at the collegiate level, led a defense that pitched five shutouts, and held all six of their ACC opponents to 13 or fewer points. Nicknamed the "Manster," for half-man, half-monster, White was an unstoppable force, combining brute strength with the speed of a fullback. Despite constant double-teams by the opposition, White spent much of the season terrorizing ACC quarterbacks and runners. White had 12 sacks, 24 tackles for losses, and was personally responsible for 122 lost yards by the opposition. For his accomplishments, White was awarded the Outland and Lombardi Trophies as major college football's finest defender, and was named ACC Player of the Year.

White got help from linebacker Harry Walters and safety Bob Smith. Walters led the ACC with 173 tackles, while Smith held opposing receivers at bay with his coverage skills. Smith was also the team's punt returner, and ended his career as Maryland's all-time leader in punt returns and yardage. Leroy Hughes and Joe Campbell were also productive as defensive starters.

Despite a solid effort, the Terps were unable to knock off Alabama in the season opener. The highly anticipated game forced Maryland officials to install temporary bleachers in Byrd Stadium's open end, which resulted in a record crowd of over 54,000. The fans were treated to a hard-fought battle, as the Crimson Tide built a big early lead behind Calvin Culliver, who ran for 154 yards in the first half alone. After three field goals by Steve Mike-Mayer, the Terps scored their first touchdown on the second play of the fourth quarter, pulling UM to within five at 21-16. Maryland had the ball late with a chance to win, but Alabama's Ricky Davis came up with an interception of a Ben Kinard pass with less than two minutes remaining.

"I'm sure as heck not happy about losing. I don't care who you're playing," Claiborne said afterwards. "I am not the kind of coach who wants to play a close game. We thought we could win."

Alabama's Bear Bryant was much quicker to heap praise on the Terrapin effort. "We didn't beat anybody," he said. "Maryland deserved a lot more than they got and they are going to go a long way. I am just thankful our team hung in there."

Mistakes killed the Terrapins again the following week against Florida, as the Gators claimed a 17-10 victory in Tampa. A frustrated Claiborne used three quarterbacks in an effort to find some continuity with his offense, and finally found it in Avellini, who came on in place of Ben Kinard and Leon Harris and nearly led UM to the win. In the third quarter Florida took control, starting with an exciting 49-yard field goal by David Posey, which just sailed over the crossbar. The electrified Gator defense came up with a big play after Posey's kick, intercepting a Harris pass and returning it back to the Maryland 28. Five plays later the Gators got their winning score, courtesy of a pass from Jimmy Fisher to Lee McGriff.

The Terps finally got in the win column with a dismantling of North Carolina in College Park, holding the Tar Heels to only 127 yards on the ground. With rain driving through the stadium for much of the afternoon, Louis Carter displayed the promise that put him on many preseason All-America ballots. In the second quarter Carter received a pitch from Avellini and raced 76 yards to the end zone. Carter scored a second touchdown in the third quarter, and his catch and subsequent sideline ramble put the game on ice, giving Maryland a 21-0 advantage. Although the Tar Heels cut into the lead on touchdown passes by Billy Paschall and Chris Kupec, the Terrapins held on for a 24-12 victory.

Starting with a 31-0 pounding of Syracuse in their fourth game, the Terrapins began an October of utter domination. In three successive weeks, Maryland pounded their opposition by a combined score of 119-0. The UM defense set the tone on the game's first offensive play, as Harry Walters took down Tiger quarterback Mike O'Cain for an 8-yard sack. After a 38-yard punt return by Ken Schroy, which advanced the ball to the Clemson 15, three successive runs gave the Terps their first score. The game was less than three minutes old.

With Maryland's special teams consistently placing the Tigers in poor field position, it was impossible for CU to get anything going in the first half. A pair of Mike-Mayer field goals, from distances of 25 and 22 yards, and John Schultz's second touchdown gave Maryland a commanding 20-0 lead at the intermission. Maryland sealed the deal with three fourth quarter touchdowns, the first coming on a 1-yard sneak by Avellini. Despite throwing his first interception of the season, the Hyde Park, N.Y. native was solid once again, with 213 yards on fourteen completions. Both of Maryland's final two scores were tallied by Ken Roy, on carries of 6 and 1 yard. Clemson coach Red Parker, after watching his Tigers lose by its biggest margin in twenty-three overall games against Maryland, echoed the sentiments of his team.

"I have been in coaching for a long time," moaned Parker, "but this was the most helpless that I have ever felt on the sidelines. It was one of the toughest games I have ever been through."

The 41-0 blowout of Clemson was virtually duplicated a week later against Wake Forest, who simply didn't have the personnel to play competitively against the Terrapins. Despite a slow start, losing three fumbles in the first half, Maryland was in command of a 19-0 score after thirty minutes. The Terrapins came out of the gates breathing fire in the second half, breaking the game open by scoring touchdowns on their next four drives. The 47-0 victory was Maryland's third consecutive shutout, and coupled with North Carolina's upset victory over N.C. State, the Terrapins were in sole possession of first place in the ACC, a place they had not been at that point in a season since 1962.

Despite their 33-14 setback to North Carolina, NCSU was a confident group heading to College Park. The Wolfpack had toppled the Terrapins in each of the last two seasons, creating an aura of domination over Maryland that the media referred to as the "State Jinx." Although Lou Holtz truly felt that his team could go up to the nation's capital and bring back a win, the NCSU coach was quick to pay respect to Maryland's superstar defensive lineman.

When asked about Randy White, Holtz joked, "Oh, I guess he's all right, but he probably isn't much better right now than Bob Lilly."

The night before the game, Claiborne had his players watch the film from their painful 24-22 defeat to State from a year earlier, when Mike-Mayer had missed a field goal in the closing seconds that would have propelled Maryland to victory and the ACC title. Several Wolfpack players taunted and shouted at Mike-Mayer after the unsuccessful kick, an act that was not forgotten by the returning Terrapins. Angered by the perceived lack of sportsmanship on the part of the NCSU players, Maryland vowed that this time around the game would not come down to a field goal try.

The Wolfpack ran away from the Manster for most of the afternoon, but the rest of the Terrapin defenders were ready to compensate. The powerful State running game was held to less than three yards per carry, as the Terps swarmed Wolfpack ball carriers play after play. After spotting State an early field goal, Maryland began to take control in the second quarter. Avellini, now firmly entrenched as the starting quarterback, raced 30 yards on a keeper to put the Terrapins ahead 7-3. A chip shot by Mike-Mayer gave Maryland a 10-3 advantage into the locker rooms, and placed the kicker into the ACC record books with his thirty-first successful field goal attempt.

Dave Buckey brought the Wolfpack back in the second half, taking his team 80 yards for the game-tying score. When State got the ball back they promptly began another march, but a costly penalty proved to be their undoing. The penalty forced the Wolfpack into a long field goal attempt, but Sumnuk Vixaysouk's effort went outside the posts. From that point on, the game belonged to the Terrapins. Carter, who had broken Ed Modzelewski's touchdown record earlier in the year, surpassed him on this day as Maryland's all-time leading rusher with a 180-yard output. With a final touchdown, Carter led the way to a 20-10 victory, which put Maryland in the driver's seat of the ACC race.

With an opportunity to prove their mettle in front of a regional television audience and over 60,000 fans, the Terps rolled into Happy Valley a week later for another encounter with Penn State. The well-prepared Nittany Lion defense seemed to be one step ahead of Maryland all afternoon, and scored a pair of touchdowns courtesy of Jeff Hite, normally a substitute for Joe Paterno's squad. Hite's 79-yard interception return and subsequent run of a botched pitch on a kickoff propelled PSU to a 21-7 advantage.

With the score 21-14 at the half, the game had all the makings of a shootout. It was not to be, as the teams traded fourth quarter field goals for the final points. As shadows turned into darkness over Beaver Stadium, the Terps got three separate good opportunities in the final period. The Lions turned them back all but once, when Mike-Mayer connected on a 31-yard kick. Chris Bahr had already put PSU ahead 24-14 with a 44-yarder. The 21-14 defeat was a bitter pill for the Terrapins to swallow, as they dropped another winnable game at the hands of Penn State.

With their first loss in six games behind them, the Terrapins returned to Byrd Stadium and easily took care of Villanova. With twenty-four seniors playing for the final time in College Park, Maryland made quick work of the Wildcats, who had endured a midweek coaching change and were without their starting quarterback. All sixty-three dressed players played for the Terps, as three separate players scored their first collegiate touchdowns. With Clemson knocking off North Carolina, 54-32, on the same afternoon, the Terrapins were assured of at least a tie for the league title. They also learned afterwards that they were headed to the Liberty Bowl, where they would likely play someone from the Southeastern Conference.

Maryland coasted through the first half against Duke, forcing Mike McGee's squad into numerous mistakes. It was 35-0 before Duke finally reached the end zone, and on the second play from scrimmage after the Blue Devil score, Rick Jennings raced 60 yards to give Maryland a 42-7 cushion. The Blue Devils, who came into the game boasting the league's top secondary, were no match for Avellini, who completed ten-of-eleven passes for 191 yards in just over a half of action.

With their opponent hopelessly outgunned, the Terrapins called off the dogs and did not score any more points after Mike Manges led the reserves to another pair of touchdowns to make the score 56-7. For the game the Terps piled on 537 yards, the most ever in an Oyster Bowl, and the best output by a Maryland team since 1957. In addition, their 56 points were the most scored by the Terrapins ever against an ACC opponent. All of this happened without the services of Carter, who had suffered rib injuries against Villanova and was in for only a single play. In the victorious locker room, the Terrapin players boisterously celebrated the school's first ACC title in nearly two decades.

"This game was like over with in the first quarter," said Avellini. "Just think what would have happened if it had been close. We would have torn this place apart."

"This was big for us," said senior lineman Frank Romano. "We've never really won anything. We lost the Peach Bowl last year and three big games this year. We felt denied because we didn't win the ACC last year."

The Virginia game held no real significance for the Terrapins, other than that a loss would keep them from going unbeaten in the ACC. The anticlimactic affair ended 10-0 in Maryland's favor, as Carter came back from his injury to run for 213 yards. Carter's performance was the finest single-game rushing output in school history, breaking a 43-year-old mark. It also gave him a career total of 2,392 yards, which at the time was also a Maryland record.

Less than a month after the UVA triumph, the Terrapins met Tennessee in the Liberty Bowl in a game that featured two of the finest defenses in all of college football. Bill Battle's Volunteers had gone 4-0-1 after an October loss to Alabama, which included a victory over Clemson. Tennessee had been particularly tough down the stretch, holding Memphis and Kentucky to a combined 13 points. As one could expect, the game became a slow, methodical struggle for field position. Carter couldn't get it going for the Terrapins, managing only 65 yards on twenty-two carries. A Mike-Mayer field goal from 28 yards out in the second quarter was the only scoring until the final three minutes of the game.

The Terrapins, desperate to hold on to their slim 3-0 lead, attempted a punt from their own 13. The snapper's nerves got the best of him, and the poor toss was recovered by Tennessee inside the Maryland 10. The Terrapins held momentarily, knocking the Volunteers back to the 11, but with just over two minutes remaining, quarterback Randy Wallace faded back and threw a strike to Larry Seivers for the touchdown and a 7-3 Tennessee lead. Trailing for the first time, Maryland moved steadily downfield on their final drive. From the 20, Avellini threw what for an instant looked like a game-winning touchdown pass. To the disgust of the Maryland faithful, however, the officials ruled the play out of bounds. Minutes later, Tennessee retained possession to hand the Terrapins their ninth consecutive defeat at the hands of Southeastern Conference opposition.

For the third time in history, N.C. State and North Carolina played in postseason games in the same year, and the Liberty Bowl appearance by Maryland gave the ACC three bowl teams for the first time. The Wolfpack had to fight tooth and nail for a tie against Houston in the Bluebonnet Bowl. Leading 17-10 going into the fourth quarter, State gave up 21 unanswered points to the Cougars. After John Housman's second touchdown gave Houston a 31-17 lead, the Cougars were driving downfield again, intent on blowing out the Wolfpack.

With the ball deep in NCSU territory, Houston suddenly fumbled. Clarence Cotton came up with the recovery for State, and seven plays later, Tommy London scored from the 9. Although the two-point effort was no good, State's Louis Alcamo successfully recovered an onsides kick. Don Buckey ended a furious drive with a sneak from the 1, and a conversion to Fritts completed State's inspiring comeback. Although the game ended as a 31-31 stalemate, the courageous reprisal from the Wolfpack was nearly as satisfying as victory.

North Carolina fared worse in the Sun Bowl against Mississippi State, as their powerful offense was unable to produce another El Paso triumph. Things got off on the wrong foot for UNC from the beginning, as MSU running back Terry Vitrano broke off a 55-yard gallop on the game's first play. The Tar Heels came back on the legs of Jim "Boom Boom" Betterson, who scored twice to give Carolina a 21-20 lead going into the fourth quarter. Betterson, along with Mike Voight, had become the first backfield tandem in NCAA history to gain 1,000 yards in the same season. Trailing 24-20 after an Ellis Alexander field goal, Mississippi State began a late drive that ate up over six minutes. Vitrano fell into the end zone from the 2 at the 3:41 mark, and MSU had a 26-24 victory.

Maryland claimed another ACC crown in 1975, going 5-0 in league play to tie North Carolina's record of fifteen consecutive conference victories. Jerry Claiborne was hailed as a defensive wizard before coming to College Park, and this group of Terrapins served their leader well. In 1975, Maryland became the first school in ACC history to lead the league in total defense four consecutive years, and their average of only 8.8 points allowed was the fewest since N.C. State's "White Shoes" unit of 1967.

Villanova was outclassed in the Byrd Stadium opener, as Mark Manges threw a record four touchdown passes to propel a 41-0 Terrapin win. Manges, one of the most renowned high school quarterback prospects in the country two years earlier, assumed the role of starting quarterback with the departure of Bob Avellini. The Terrapins scored on each of their first three possessions, and Manges and the rest of the first offensive unit spent most of the second half on the sidelines. Villanova made few offensive threats, as Maryland won on opening Saturday for the first time in ten years.

Claiborne's boys were geared up for Tennessee, and hoped to avenge their disappointing Liberty Bowl defeat from nine months earlier. With six fumbles over the course of the game, however, the Terps gave themselves no chance of pulling out victory. Manges went down to a shoulder separation in the second quarter, as he attempted to throw a block for one of his backs. Without Manges the Terrapins faltered, managing only two first downs in the opening half. Joe Campbell put two points on the board with a safety, but the offense was able to produce only a single touchdown in the 26-8 setback.

"We started the game off with a fumble and that set the whole tempo," an exasperated Claiborne said later. "Whenever we had a chance to come back, bang, we fumbled and gave them another opportunity. They came up with all the big plays and gave us a good, old-fashioned country licking."

The Terrapins returned to form the following Saturday in Chapel Hill, decking the Tar Heels, 34-7, with a complete team effort. Carolina made a good impression early, scoring their lone touchdown barely a minute into the game on a pass to Charlie Williams. John Schultz returned the ensuing kickoff 92 yards, and Tim Wilson tied it with a 1-yard rumble. Larry Dick, the replacement for Manges at quarterback, led a precise offensive attack. Dick completed nine-of-twelve passes, and led Maryland to five unanswered scores to seal up the contest. Mike Sochko converted a pair of field goals to give UM a 13-7 lead at halftime, and a 49-yard pass to Kim Hoover in the third quarter put the Terps in cruise control. Jamie Franklin and Steve Atkins added final period touchdowns to provide the impressive final tally.

Another Southern battle awaited Maryland in Lexington, as they stayed on the road for the third straight week to play Kentucky. The Wildcats drew first blood, but the Terrapin special teams came through again, as Rick Jennings broke off a 93-yard kick return, and Sochko converted a field goal. With the score 10-7 late in the game, it appeared that Maryland may finally remove the monkey off their backs that was the Southeastern Conference. Unfortunately for the Terrapins, Franklin fumbled at the UM 40 with just over two minutes remaining. Although they struggled all day against the fearsome Terrapin defenders, Kentucky moved into field goal range in the closing moments. With eight seconds to play, John Pierce nailed a 45-yard field goal to deadlock the game at 10.

"This is probably the worst I have ever felt after a game," Leroy Hughes said in the locker room. "Unless we go to a bowl game, I won't get a shot at them again."

Returning home to play Syracuse, the Terrapins made a number of mental miscues, but played well enough defensively to secure a 24-7 win. The teams traded touchdowns from fumble recoveries, as Syracuse's Mike Jones fell on a free ball in the end zone after a carry by Jim Donoghue, and Terrapin lineman Paul Divito plopped on a loose ball that was fumbled by Bob Mitch. Divito's recovery set the stage for freshman Steve Atkins, who scored from 1 yard out for the final points of the game.

North Carolina State and Maryland had become substantial rivals over the past few years, and fuel was added to the fire before their 1975 encounter in College Park. During a closed practice session, Lou Holtz noticed a jogger taking laps around the Wolfpack practice field. Fearing that the jogger may be a Maryland spy, Holtz had the man arrested and brought up on trespassing charges. As it turned out, the man was an NCSU mathematics professor, and red-faced university officials were forced to intervene. All charges were cleared against the professor, and Holtz was scolded for his presumptuous actions.

The Terrapin special teams came out shining again, as Jennings returned a kickoff 96 yards for a touchdown in the first quarter. Jennings' score couldn't have come at a better time for Maryland, as State had just scored a touchdown of their own to take a 7-3 lead. The kick return was a crushing blow to the NCSU momentum, as they were unable to jump back ahead. Atkins pounded over from the 1 for a 17-7 Terrapin advantage, and Hoover, Wilson, and John Schultz added tallies in the second half. By the time Scott Wade scored his second touchdown of the game in the fourth quarter, the Wolfpack were hopelessly behind. The 37-22 victory was Claiborne's second in a row over Holtz, and solidified Maryland's control over the ACC race.

"Coach Claiborne didn't make a big deal out of the spying thing," linebacker Kevin Benson said after the game. "He told us we didn't need a spy to beat them. The whole team just laughed about it."

Wake Forest welcomed the Terrapins to Groves Stadium on October 18, and the Terps jumped out to a 10-0 lead after two quarters. Taking the kickoff for the second half, Maryland drove 56 yards in only four plays, with Jennings doing most of the work. It was a rough day for the Deacon offense, as they struggled to the tune of 150 total yards and only six first downs. With the Terrapin defenders controlling the line of scrimmage, Wake was forced into a number of desperate passes. As a result, the Maryland defenders came up with five interceptions. A 47-yard connection from Dick to Hoover and Sochko's second field goal settled the issue in a 27-0 shutout.

Manges' shoulder was successfully healed in time for the Penn State game, but Claiborne decided to remain with Dick in the beginning. Dick had certainly pulled his weight, leading the Terrapins to a 4-0-1 record under his command. Unfortunately for Dick, it was not his day, as he spent the first half blanketed by the PSU defense. After starting the game zero-for-six passing, and fumbling on Maryland's first two possessions to set up Penn State field goals, Claiborne opted for Manges. The Terrapin offense was revived under their old leader, as the confident sophomore led a scoring rally of 63 yards. Maryland was behind 12-3 when Manges entered the game, but within minutes it was 12-10. That score held into halftime, as Penn State's Chris Bahr was wide on a field goal attempt as the clock expired.

With the game up for grabs in the final minutes, and Penn State in command of a 15-13 score, a freak set of circumstances invoked the ire of Joe Paterno. The clock suddenly stopped at the 1:09 mark, although the Terrapins were unable to call any more time-outs. Paterno claimed that the referees were oblivious to what was going on, while Claiborne contested that a technical error forced the stoppage of play. Regardless of the actual circumstances, Maryland moved to the PSU 25, where in a surprise move, Claiborne opted to kick a field goal on third down. Snapper Marion Koprowski got the ball to the holder low, and instead of throwing it away to set up another attempt, the ball was spotted and Sochko laid into it. With only fifteen seconds to play, Sochko pushed the 42-yard effort wide right, and PSU had earned yet another hard-fought victory over the Terrapins.

Maryland needed victories to secure a berth in another bowl game, and headed to Cincinnati determined to get one. The opportunistic Bearcats nearly pulled off the upset, taking a 19-14 lead into the final minutes. Cincinnati held their lead until the 1:38 mark, when Dick threw to Jamie Franklin for his third touchdown. Franklin had boldly predicted at breakfast that he would score three touchdowns against the Bearcats, and with the 8-yard play, the running back's hat trick was secured. More importantly, the Terrapins had a come-from-behind 21-19 victory to take back to College Park.

The Clemson game in Death Valley was an up-and-down affair, as Tiger quarterback Mike O'Cain scored twice in the first thirty minutes. A pair of Sochko field goals, along with a 92-yard kickoff return by Schultz, provided the Terrapin points in the opening half, and the teams went to the locker rooms with the score 13-12 in favor of the visitors. The teams traded touchdowns in the second half, but Clemson was good on their two-point conversion attempt, while Maryland's failed. Trailing 20-19 with just over six minutes remaining, the Terps summoned up all their strength to rid themselves of the pesky Tigers. Atkins was the catalyst, twice bursting through the line on fourth down to keep the chains moving. With eight seconds to play, Sochko came on for a game-winning kick. Unlike Penn State, this time Sochko had a better opportunity to concentrate and collect himself before the fateful boot. The ball sailed easily through the posts, and the Terps improved to 7-2-1 on the season

The regular season closed with the annual affair against Virginia, and the Terrapins put together a staggering effort on offense. In an impressive display, five Terrapin backs gained at least 100 yards rushing, en route to an ACC-record 802 yards of offense. Virginia scored twice to pull within 14-10, but Maryland scored the next 28 points. The teams traded a pair of touchdowns late in the game, and the Terrapins had a 62-24 victory and another conference title. Duke finished its conference slate with a 3-0-2 record, but was not on the schedule with the Terrapins.

Five weeks later, UM headed to Jacksonville for the Gator Bowl, where they met Florida (UF). The Gators featured running back Jimmy DuBose, who had run for 1,307 yards during the season to set a new SEC record. On top of playing in their home state, Florida had the advantage of the "SEC Curse" over the Terrapins. Maryland had not beaten a member of the Southeastern Conference since 1955, back when they were among the elite programs in all of college football. In order to get back into that upper echelon, Claiborne had to figure out a way to get his team over this particular hurdle.

Like they had done against Virginia, Maryland stuck to the ground against the Gators. The ploy was successful, as the Terrapins rushed for 209 yards. The game's only touchdown was scored in the first quarter, as Dick dropped back from the UF 19 and found Hoover. Sochko was good on a pair of field goals, one in the second quarter and one in the fourth, to lead Maryland to an impressive 13-0 victory. The Terrapin defenders saved their best performance for last, as they stifled the Florida offense with a mixture of blitzes and stunts. The victory gave Maryland nine wins for the first time since the Jim Tatum era, and served as something of a springboard into the following autumn.

Two nights later, N.C. State met West Virginia in the Peach Bowl. The Wolfpack had been solid after the loss to Maryland, claiming victories in four of their final five games, including a 15-14 upset of Penn State in Happy Valley. The game was the curtain call for the Buckey twins, who had begun their NCSU careers on the cover of *Sports Illustrated,* and finished among the all-time greats to wear the Wolfpack Red. Dave finished as NCSU's all-time passing leader, while Don ended as the career leader in receptions and receiving yards.

The game started out in fine fashion for the Wolfpack, as they jumped out to a 10-0 advantage. The Wolfpack came out of the locker room and rolled West Virginia on their first possession of the second half, moving 73 yards to the end zone. State's second score was courtesy of Jay Sherill, who booted a 21-yard field goal in the last minute of the first half. The kick was set up by freshman Ted Brown, who broke free on a 54-yard sprint.

State held onto their lead until the fourth quarter, when West Virginia capitalized on an odd play. Throwing from midfield, quarterback Dan Kendra launched a pass deep down the middle of the Wolfpack secondary. A pair of NCSU defenders made plays on the ball, but it tipped out of their hands. From out of nowhere came Mountaineer receiver Scott McDonald, who made a juggling catch and ran to the end zone for a 13-10 West Virginia lead. The Wolfpack got a final opportunity late in the game, and moved into WVU territory before a sack and illegal procedure penalty killed their momentum. West Virginia held on for the win, which avenged a loss to the Wolfpack in the same game three years earlier. The victory was Bobby Bowden's last at West Virginia, as he would soon be heading to the state capital of Florida to begin a new coaching path.

In 1976, Jerry Claiborne and his coaching staff at Maryland put together one of the finest teams in the ACC's tenure thus far, and the first serious national championship contender in the circuit since Jim Tatum's Terrapin team of 1955. In becoming the second school in league history to win three consecutive conference championships, Maryland held eight opponents to single digits during the regular season, and became the first unit in nearly two decades to lead the conference in rushing, passing, total, and scoring defense. Joe Campbell was back for another year in the trenches, and became the third Terrapin defensive lineman in four years to be named All-American. With Steve Atkins and Mark Manges leading the way on the other side of the ball, the Terrapins also boasted the league's finest offensive unit.

Richmond came to College Park to start off the year, and Milt Ruffin's touchdown gave the Spiders an early 7-0 lead. Manges countered with scoring passes to Dean Richards and Chuck White. Maryland salted the game away in the second half with a dominant ground effort, as Atkins finished with a career-best 169 yards. Brad Carr was the defensive stalwart with twenty-four tackles in the 31-7 Terrapin victory.

Maryland's next opponent was West Virginia, 1-0 under new head coach Frank Cignetti. The Terrapins opened up a 21-3 halftime lead thanks to the efforts of Manges, Atkins, and White. Manges finished the game with 68 rushing yards and 118 passing yards, and scored on a sneak early in the game for a 7-0 lead. Atkins had another promising outing with 133 yards, and reached the end zone on a 15-yard sprint to give UM a 14-3 bulge. White's second touchdown reception in as many games, this one covering 31 yards, gave the Terrapins their final score. It was a 24-3 final after a second half field goal.

Although the defense was roughed up in the third game against Syracuse, Atkins and the Terrapin offense came alive to seal a 42-28 victory. Atkins set a school record with 215 rushing yards, and scored three times, although Syracuse had every reason to think that victory was within their reach until very late. Touchdowns by Bill Hurley and Mike Jones followed a pair of running scores by Bob Avery, and the score was 35-28 in favor of Maryland with just over four minutes to play. Atkins' long run sealed the deal, going 76 yards to put the final points on the scoreboard.

Villanova was Maryland's fourth consecutive nonconference opponent, and with rain tearing through Byrd Stadium for much of the day, the Wildcats took a surprising 9-6 lead after a touchdown by Tony Serge. Claiborne and the Terrapin staff chose a different approach in the second half, in hopes of more effectively moving the football. With their offensive line having already established dominance over Villanova, Maryland decided to run up the middle, staying between the tackles where the backs could get better footing. The plan worked like a charm in the third quarter, as UM picked up a pair of touchdowns to take a 20-9 victory.

"We really had to change our game plan," Chuck White said later. "We had planned on throwing the ball a fair amount because we had thrown for four touchdowns against them last year. But that was impossible."

With four victories already under their belt, the Terps began another defense of the ACC in Raleigh against N.C. State. Lou Holtz had parted ways with NCSU before the season, and new coach Bo Rein was struggling with a young team. Observers expected a showdown between Atkins and NCSU's Ted Brown, two of the most dazzling sophomore backs in the country, but it never materialized. Brown was held to 32 yards by Maryland's hostile defenders, while Atkins spent the day hobbling around with knee troubles. Limited to only seven carries, Atkins was replaced by Tim Wilson, who fumbled twice but scored a touchdown in the second quarter to give the Terrapins an insurmountable 13-6 lead. Sochko added a field goal in the second half to give UM a 16-6 victory, which broke the all-time ACC record for consecutive victories with sixteen.

Atkins was out of commission for the homecoming game with Wake Forest, and the game proved to be a difficult one for UM. Although they had been outscored 134-0 in their previous four games against the Terrapins, the Demon Deacons came to College Park ready to offer a challenge. Although Maryland jumped out to a 17-7 lead in the fourth quarter, WF signal caller Mike McGlamry completed a 29-yard touchdown pass to Bill Milner, and a two-point conversion at the 1:29 mark made it 17-15. Wake got the ball back in the final minute with an opportunity to win, but Campbell came through in the clutch for the Terrapins. On the final play of the game, Campbell made his fourteenth tackle, a sack, to preserve the victory. Although they were happy to get the win, the players realized how close they came to blowing their championship aspirations.

"We got a pretty good shock," said Manges. "Yet we didn't blow everything we have worked so hard for. I'm sure this has affected us. Deep down we know we're a better team than we showed. I say this every week, but we can't afford to do this in Durham."

With a powerful effort on both sides of the ball, the Terps handed Duke a 30-3 whitewashing on the grass of their home field. The UM defense crippled the Blue Devil offense, intercepting three passes, recovering two fumbles, and consistently keeping them pinned on their own side of the field. Manges finished the game with 96 yards passing, and threw to end Bob Raba to give the Terrapins a 20-3 lead at halftime. Larry Dick, the UM starting quarterback for much of the 1975 season, came on in the fourth quarter and completed three-of-five passes, although Maryland kept the ball primarily on the ground to avoid embarrassing Mike McGee's Blue Devils.

Fran Curci's Kentucky (UK) team was struggling in late October, coming off a 31-7 blowout at the hands of Georgia. The Terrapins were not sympathetic, and held the potent UK running game to more than 150 yards below its seasonal average. Although Kentucky scored the first and last touchdowns, Maryland held the upper hand for the vast majority of the contest. Manges got the Terps going with a scoring keeper, and added a conversion on an option run. The 24-14 victory was Claiborne's first over his alma mater since 1967, when he was still coaching at Virginia Tech.

At 8-0, Maryland had asserted itself as one of the top teams in the country. Ranked No. 6, the Terrapins could look forward to a major bowl berth and an outside opportunity to claim the national championship if they remained perfect. Playing like a team under no pressure, the Terrapins were sensational in November, shutting out three consecutive opponents. Cincinnati was first, taking a 21-0 defeat in College Park. Manges led the way again on offense, throwing two touchdowns and running for 72 yards. More important for Maryland was the fact that

Michigan and Notre Dame each lost, dropping upset decisions to Purdue and Georgia Tech, respectively. The losses put only four teams among the unbeaten, and gave Maryland that much more of an opportunity to have something significant to play for on New Year's Day, despite their marginal schedule.

Clemson came to Byrd Stadium the following Saturday and took another defeat from the Terrapins. Tiger coach Red Parker was winless in three tries against Maryland, and with his offense on lockdown, the streak continued. The Terps used some trickery to put Clemson away, as Manges hit Vince Kinney for 33 yards on a perfectly executed fake field goal in the third quarter. Dean Richards had already scored in the first half on a short run, and George Scott did the same in the second half for a 20-0 Terrapin win.

Virginia put up little resistance in the regular season finale in Charlottesville, as Maryland completed their undefeated regular season with a 28-0 victory. The UM defense allowed only 166 total yards, and stifled UVA's two prime scoring opportunities. Richards reached the end zone first for Maryland, and Scott found his way in twice for a 21-0 bulge. The final score was courtesy of a wingback pass, as Donnie Dotter threw to Chuck White. Ten minutes after the final gun, Maryland accepted a bid to the Cotton Bowl, where an opportunity was in place to compete for at least a piece of the national championship. No. 1 Pittsburgh was playing sixth-ranked Georgia in the Sugar Bowl, and a Panther defeat, combined with a Terrapin win, might be enough to thrust UM into the top spot.

While Maryland was polishing off the Cavaliers, North Carolina tailback Mike Voight was making a memorable impression in his final game at Kenan Stadium. Voight, who finished the year with 1,407 yards to claim his second consecutive ACC Player of the Year Award, ran for 261 yards in 41 carries against Duke. Voight also scored four touchdowns, and his two-point conversion with less than a minute remaining gave Carolina a 39-38 win over the Blue Devils, which pushed the Tar Heels to an overall record of 9-2.

Maryland and North Carolina did not schedule each other in 1976, taking away what would have unquestionably been a fine game for the conference title. The Tar Heels lost to N.C. State, 21-13, in October, giving UNC a 4-1 league record and a second-place finish in the standings. On New Year's Eve, Carolina took the field of Atlanta's Fulton-County Stadium for a Peach Bowl encounter with Kentucky. The Wildcats had been impressive since losing to the Terrapins back in October, winning three consecutive games against SEC opposition. Kentucky allowed only 9 combined points in the victories, which came against

Vanderbilt, Florida, and Tennessee.

In a freak accident, Voight suffered a severe ankle injury two days before the Peach Bowl after stepping in a hole, and without their featured back Carolina was unable to muster any kind of sustained offense against the UK defenders. The UNC defense was equally smothering in the opening half, and the score was knotted at 0-0 after thirty minutes. The Wildcats came out with a bang in the second half, as tailback Rod Stewart scored three straight times to propel a 21-0 UK victory. With a throng of nearly 40,000 Kentucky supporters cheering on, the Wildcat defense held UNC to only 108 total yards of offense, forcing five turnovers to seal their demise.

The next day, Claiborne's Terrapins met the University of Houston (UH) in hopes of bringing home the University of Maryland's first undefeated football season since 1951. Bill Yeoman's Cougars had dropped a lopsided decision to Florida early in the year, but won seven of its final eight games to bring a 9-2 record to Dallas. Houston had claimed the Southwestern Conference in its first year as a member of that league, and sought to defend the state of Texas in UH's first New Year's Day bowl in a quarter century.

The first quarter belonged to Houston, as they stunned the Terrapins and the capacity Cotton Bowl crowd with an offensive onslaught. In three successive possessions, the Cougars mounted drives of 80, 38, and 24 yards to take a 21-0 lead. With their chances of victory now painfully slim, Maryland regrouped in the second quarter. As the defense settled down, Manges led a 49-yard drive that resulted in a 6-yard sneak, bringing UM to within 21-7. The score remained that way until the final minute of the half, as Houston solidified their cushion with a breathtaking 97-yard jaunt through the Terrapin defenders. On the seventh play of the march, quarterback Danny Davis threw a touchdown to Don Bass.

The third quarter was dominated by the respective defenses, but Manges and the Maryland offense broke through late to cut the score to 27-14. Following a fumble the Terrapins scored again, bringing them to within striking distance at 27-21. Just when it appeared that the Terps were on their way to a dramatic comeback, Davis made a clutch play for the Cougars. Backed up at his own 11 on third down, the Houston quarterback eluded a Maryland blitz and completed a pass to Robert Lavergne that kept the chains moving.

To the great frustration of Maryland fans all over, the Cougars played a brilliant game of keep away down the stretch, maintaining possession into the final minute. Lennard Coplin booted a field goal with 18 seconds remaining, giving Houston a 30-21 victory that put a serious damper on Maryland's dream season. There would be no NCAA championship in College Park, as Pittsburgh claimed the title following a 27-3 drubbing of Georgia in the Sugar Bowl. Despite the disappointing finish, the Terrapins took home a final ranking of No. 8 in the Associated Press poll.

8

Running Wild (1977-1980)

In the late 1970s and early 1980s, the ACC boasted some of the finest running backs in all of college football. As the league celebrated its first quarter century of gridiron competition, it gained a reputation for having powerful, productive ground gainers, capable of carrying their respective team to victory on any given Saturday. As N.C. State's Ted Brown and North Carolina's Amos Lawrence were rewriting the league's record books, fellow standouts James McDougald, Lester Brown, Tommy Vigorito, Steve Atkins, and Charlie Wysocki were providing fans with countless thrills.

Brown, the first player in ACC history to be named first-team All-Conference in all four years of eligibility, was the ace of the Wolfpack backfield from 1975 to 1978. Lou Holtz, who bolted to the NFL's New York Jets after the running back's freshman year, recruited the High Point, N.C. native to Raleigh. Bo Rein, Holtz's backfield coach at NCSU for three years before going to Arkansas for the 1975 season, returned as State's head coach in 1976, and kept the same veer offense that Holtz used, in which Brown ran for 913 yards and 13 touchdowns in 1975 to earn ACC Rookie of the Year honors.

Although the Wolfpack did not win a conference championship during Brown's career, NCSU remained one of the top teams in the league. After rushing for 1,088 yards in the 1976 season, in which State struggled under their new leadership, Brown dominated the next two years. In 1977 and 1978, Brown led the ACC in rushing and touchdowns, propelling State to seventeen wins and a pair of bowl victories. By the end of his NCSU career, Brown had rushed for 4,602 yards and 51 touchdowns, both league records. Among his finest performances were a 227-yard output against Clemson in 1975 and a 251-yard day against Penn State in 1977. On November 18, 1978, as the Wolfpack knocked off Duke, 24-10, Brown became the first active football player in North Carolina State football history to have his number retired.

"He gets my vote hands down as the best player to come out of N.C. State, and I would go far as to say the best player that's ever come out of the ACC," says Johnny Evans, who punted and played quarterback for the Wolfpack during Brown's tenure. "He was truly what we call a "go-to guy." When we looked around the huddle and needed a play, we always depended on Ted to make that play. Whether it was catching a pass, catching a pitch on a sweep, or running between the tackles. He had an uncanny ability to break tackles and make plays."

McDougald was Wake Forest's premier back from 1976 to 1979, setting school records for yardage, attempts, and touchdowns. McDougald burst onto the scene as a rookie, rushing for 249 yards against Clemson to set a WF record, and setting new Deacon freshman marks with 1,018 yards and 10 touchdowns. In 1977, as the Deacons struggled with a 1-10 record, McDougald paced Wake again with his powerful running, amassing 987 yards. The Deacon sophomore ran for 150 yards against North Carolina that fall, the most any single back gained against the Tar Heels the entire season.

Lester Brown, also known as "The Rubber Duck," helped Clemson move back into the upper echelon of the ACC in the late 1970s. In becoming only the second CU back in history to rush for 1,000 yards in a season, Brown paced a running game that finished fifth in the nation in total production in 1978. Brown was a touchdown-scoring machine, reaching the end zone thirty-two times over the course of his Tiger career. Vigorito starred at Virginia, and led the Cavaliers to a brief return to competitiveness in 1979. In running for more than 100 yards in four out of five outings during a stretch in September and October, Vigorito helped lead UVA to a 6-5 record, the school's first winning campaign in more than a decade. During his Virginia career, Vigorito put together a total of eleven 100-yard rushing games.

Atkins and Wysocki piloted the Maryland backfield throughout the era, and became the most prolific runners in Terrapin history to that time. In 1978, Atkins rushed for at least 100 yards in seven consecutive contests, establishing a new record, and finished the season with 1,261 yards to earn All-ACC honors. Wysocki, a mere sophomore in 1979, replaced Atkins by making a grand entrance, leading the league with 1,140 yards. Wysocki led the ACC in rushing again in 1980, and finished his career ranked fifth in league history with 3,317 yards.

In 1977, Bill Dooley led North Carolina to its third ACC championship under his command. The Tar Heels, behind the spectacular running of the freshman Lawrence, won eight regular season games and finished unbeaten in conference play. Lawrence, nicknamed "Famous Amos" after the popular brand of cookie, took the ACC by storm in his first campaign. Carrying on the torch of UNC running back excellence under Dooley, Lawrence rushed for 100 or more yards six times on his way to 1,211 for the season.

Dooley also had one of the finest defensive units in league history at his disposal, anchored by five All-Conference performers. All-American Dee Hardison led the charges up front, which also included Ken Sheets and Rod Broadway. Leading the nation with an average of 7.4 points allowed, the unit allowed only two regular season opponents to score 14 points against them. In addition, the unit led the ACC in all four major defensive categories, becoming only the third team to ever do so.

The Tar Heels opened in Lexington against Kentucky, in a rare back-to-back football game rematch. The Wildcats had taken some shots since the Peach Bowl victory back in December, as the program was playing its first game under NCAA probation. The governing body had punished Kentucky the previous winter for providing a number of extra perks to the school's fine recruiting classes of the mid-1970s. Although they had been stripped of their Southeastern Conference title and were ineligible for a bowl in 1977, Fran Curci had another solid team waiting for Carolina, led by the multitalented Derrick Ramsey.

Carolina played well enough defensively to win, but a crucial mistake at an inopportune time led to another UK triumph. Just like it had in Atlanta nine months earlier, the Carolina offense struggled to move the football against the Wildcat defense. The unit managed a single score, which came in the fourth quarter on a pass from Matt Kupec to Mike Finn. Kentucky scored first on an opening half field goal, and took a 10-7 victory after recovering a late fumble on a punt. Ramsey provided the winning points for UK, crossing the line on his fourth consecutive attempt from inside the Carolina red zone.

Richmond never had a chance in the Kenan Stadium opener, as Kupec and backup P. J. Gay each threw touchdowns in a 31-0 Carolina rout. The Spiders were stuffed repeatedly by the UNC defenders, leading to their being shut out for the second game in a row. Kupec went to Walker Lee for 35 yards in the third quarter, while Gay nailed Delbert Powell for a score in the fourth. Three field goals by Tom Biddle and the consistent running of Billy Johnson made the difference.

The Tar Heels slaughtered Northwestern in their third game, 41-7, with a complete effort on both sides of the football. Carolina set the tone on their first possession, taking the ball 81 yards from the kickoff to their first score. Lawrence stole the show on UNC's second touchdown with a 53-yard dash. Kupec hit Mel Collins for a 21-0 UNC lead, and Lawrence added a halfback pass for a touchdown to seal Northwestern's embarrassing setback.

Carolina had not played Texas Tech (TT) since the epic Sun Bowl game back in 1972, but the 2-1 Red Raiders came to Chapel Hill intent on reversing history. The Tar Heels took the initial lead on a run by Phil Farris, but TT tied it on a third quarter run by Mark Johnson, who was replacing injured starter Rod Allison. With the UNC offense sluggish once again, Bill Adams kicked a field goal for the Red Raiders in the final period. The Tar Heels could not make an offensive push, and dropped their second 10-7 verdict of the year.

Carolina stayed at home for the ACC premiere against Wake Forest, and the offense continued to sputter, failing to score against a defense that had given up 26 points to Purdue and 41 to N.C. State. Bob Hely kicked a field goal in the first quarter for Wake, and the Demon Deacons took a 3-0 lead into the half. The Carolina defense took the matter into its own hands in the second half, forcing three turnovers in an explosive third quarter surge that resulted in 17 unanswered points. The first came from the Deacon 28, as Bernie Menapace drilled WF ball carrier Ronchie Johnson to force a fumble. The pigskin popped into the air and cornerback Alan Caldwell clutched it for Carolina, racing 72 yards the other way for a 7-3 UNC lead. Bob Paschal scored in the final quarter to give the Heels a 24-3 triumph.

Lawrence made his first collegiate start for the N.C. State game, and the freshman made certain that Dooley would not regret it. Famous Amos ran roughshod over the Wolfpack defenders, who had already pitched two shutouts during the season. State entered the contest with a perfect 5-0 mark, but this day belonged to the baby blue. Lawrence finished with 216 yards, putting the Tar Heels in position to score repeatedly with his steady running. The UNC defense again came up with its own touchdown, as Buddy Curry intercepted a Johnny Evans pass at the NCSU 31 and sprinted to the goal. Evans brought State back momentarily with scoring tosses to Brown and Lin Dawson, but Biddle's three field goals propelled the Tar Heels to a 27-14 win.

Like they did against Wake Forest, UNC struggled to score in the first half against South Carolina. Biddle was good on a career-best 43-yard field goal with under a minute remaining in the half, and the Heels led 3-0 at the intermission. The Gamecocks never mounted a serious threat on offense, amassing only 166 total yards. The Tar Heels put the game away with less than two minutes remaining, as Lawrence scored from the 2 and promptly took a pitch for a successful conversion. The 17-0 shutout was the first victory for UNC over the Gamecocks in six contests dating back to 1964.

An important road clash against Maryland next awaited the Tar Heels. The Terrapins had recovered from a three-game slide in September and early October to bury Wake Forest and Duke, and stood at 3-1 in ACC play. What was more, the Terps had owned the Tar Heels under Jerry Claiborne, winning the last three games in the series decisively. The fact that Carolina and Maryland hadn't played in 1976 only made their contest in College Park that much more significant.

The UNC defense, in the midst of its best stretch in decades, would have posted another shutout if it weren't for Maryland's Lloyd Burress, who intercepted a Kupec pass early in the game at his own 35 and ran it back to the Tar Heel 2. The Terps held a 7-0 advantage until the 11:17 mark of the third quarter, when Carolina made its first drive into Terrapin territory and Kupec located Mel Collins for the game-knotting effort. Biddle's 25-yard field goal on the first play of the final period gave the Heels a 10-7 lead that they would not relinquish. Caldwell and Ricky Barden made interceptions to kill Terrapin drives, and Biddle was good from 30 and 25 yards to give the Tar Heels a 16-7 triumph. It would prove to be Carolina's biggest road victory of the year, and with two losses now in the conference, Maryland's reign as ACC football champion was over.

Clemson's red-hot Tigers, winners of seven straight games, came to Chapel Hill a week later for the ACC's marquee game of the year. The Tar Heels took the early momentum, recovering a botched punt and taking a 3-0 lead. Carolina held its slim lead until the second quarter, when CU began a serious offensive threat. Moving to the UNC 12, Tracy Perry broke free on a carry for the first touchdown of the contest. Minutes later, Lawrence took a pitch from the 41, broke a single tackle and raced alone down the right sideline. The touchdown gave UNC a 10-7 lead, but it would be the final seven-pointer of the game for the Tar Heels. The Tiger defense stifled Carolina the rest of the way, although Lawrence had another solid outing with 150 yards.

Early in the fourth quarter, Lester Brown ran over from the 2 to give the Tigers the lead again at 13-10. Obed Ariri trudged onto the field fully expecting to notch his eighteenth consecutive extra point, but to everyone's surprise, Ariri's kick was off, allowing Carolina to tie the game with a field goal instead of being forced to score a touchdown to win. After stopping Carolina again on offense, the Tigers retook possession and had victory in hand, driving down to the UNC 18 at the 6:12 mark. Steve Fuller took the snap from center and went back to hand off to Brown, but the ball was misplayed and hit the deck. Carolina recovered the loose ball, and began a desperate effort to get back on top.

With Kupec having gone down earlier to an injury, Matt Christensen fulfilled his role admirably, combining accurate passes with handoffs to Lawrence to move the Tar Heels in position. With just over one minute to play, Carolina stalled out at the Clemson 13. Since his team was still undefeated in the ACC, Dooley knew a tie would keep his team ahead of Clemson in the standings. With that in mind, the Tar Heels elected to kick. Biddle came on and was good from 30 yards, which ended the game as a 13-13 stalemate. Afterwards, there was a lingering feeling that Carolina was lucky to have salvaged a tie, and that the Tigers had beaten themselves.

"It won't be the same without the conference," said CU defensive end Jonathan Brooks. "The conference title was everything everybody was playing for. It just won't be the same now. No doubt we'll get back up. It's hard to take, but we've got two more games left."

Famous Amos had been a pleasant surprise for UNC up to now, but his performance at Virginia on November 12 took the entire country by storm. The Cavaliers were vulnerable on defense, dropping a 68-0 debacle to Texas earlier in the season, and giving up 31 points to both Duke and Clemson. Playing for the first time as a collegian in his home state, Lawrence could do no wrong. On the afternoon, Lawrence took thirty-five carries for a UNC and ACC single-game record of 286 yards. The number also established an NCAA record for yardage in a single game by a freshman. Amos had ten carries of at least 12 yards, and scored twice in Carolina's 35-14 wipeout.

Now ranked No. 18, the Tar Heels went to Durham and brought home the league title. Like the Clemson game, Lawrence scored Carolina's only touchdown. The 1-yard carry was the highlight of a 138-yard day for the heralded rookie, while Biddle connected on three field goals to tie a UNC school record with fifteen successful kicks for the season. The final quarter had some drama, as Dee Hardison laid out Duke quarterback Mike Dunn to bring out the ambulance. The 16-3 victory sent Carolina to the Liberty Bowl, where they would meet Nebraska.

Carolina entered the contest ranked No. 14, but was billed as a touchdown underdog to Tom Osborne's No. 12 Cornhuskers. The Tar Heels sought to dispel that notion in the second quarter, scoring two touchdowns to take a 14-7 lead into halftime. Biddle added to the UNC lead on their first possession of the second half, booting a Liberty

Bowl-record 47-yard field goal that struck the crossbar and bounced through.

Leading 17-3 heading into the final quarter, Carolina suddenly fell apart on both sides of the ball, allowing Nebraska to make a dramatic comeback. Frustrated at his team's lack of productivity, Osborne brought on Randy Garcia at quarterback, who brought an instant lift to the Nebraska offense. Garcia paced a series of NU scoring marches, and his pass to Tim Smith at the 3:16 mark gave the Huskers a dramatic 21-17 come-from-behind victory. The loss to Nebraska marked a bitter end to Bill Dooley's successful reign as head coach at North Carolina. Eager to become an athletic director, Dooley left Chapel Hill after the season and headed to Virginia Tech.

Clemson was a team on a mission in 1977, out to prove that they were back as a contender in the ACC. It had been a long time coming for Tiger fans, which had known little more than heartache and under-achievement from their boys since Frank Howard's retirement nearly a decade prior. Charley Pell ascended from defensive coordinator to head coach during the 1976 offseason. Pell, like Jerry Claiborne, was a product of Bear Bryant, and he didn't take long to show that he had the same winning spirit as his storied mentor. Pell and his assistants gener-ated the maximum capabilities of their players during a roller coaster year, in which the Tigers stunned the ACC and college football world by having their finest season in nearly two decades.

Like the 1959 Tigers, the last Clemson team to play in a bowl, the 1977 squad was unable to solve Maryland, who came to Death Valley in the season premiere and won a 21-14 cliffhanger. The Terrapins en-tered the contest holding twenty consecutive conference victories, and although many of their best players had moved on to the pros, UM was still the team to beat, as their seniors had yet to experience defeat to an ACC rival. The Tigers gave the Terrapins their best shot, as Rex Varn returned an interception 93 yards to put CU in position to win. A pair of touchdown passes by Maryland quarterback Larry Dick, however, in addition to a stifling defensive effort, gave the Terps the game.

The Tigers next headed to Athens, where a Clemson team had not won in more than sixty years. Georgia's Sanford Stadium had become a house of horrors for ACC teams, a place where some of the league's best had gone to die over the years. Georgia had won fourteen consecu-tive contests against ACC opponents in Sanford, dating back to 1962. The wins included victories over N.C. State in 1973 and South Carolina in 1969, years in which those schools were the best the ACC had to offer the Bulldogs.

The Tigers came to Sanford confident this time, knowing that victory was within their grasp. In a slow game that crept along like the damp afternoon it was played on, Lester Brown ran over from the 3 to give Clemson a 7-0 lead in the third quarter. The slim lead held until late in the game, when Georgia began a desperation rally in the final minutes. Quarterback Jeff Pyburn was good on his toss to Pay Norris, who reached the end zone with only six seconds on the clock. There would be no deadlock this day, as Bulldogs skipper Vince Dooley elected to go for two. With the game on the line, Georgia went with a pass play. The Tigers brought a furious rush, and the ball fell short of its mark in the end zone. As parties and celebrations broke out back in South Carolina, Pell handed out cigars to his team, starting a new Clemson tradition after victories.

"The next week was much more fun going to class," recalled Steve Fuller. "After two losing seasons and feeling like you had been letting everybody down, it felt good to be able to stick out your chest a little bit. From that point on, there was a connection between the students, the fans, and the players. Everyone knew we were headed in the right direction."

The win over Georgia catapulted the Tigers into a seven-game winning streak, of which four came against conference rivals. The tie in Chapel Hill was Clemson's only blemish in the ACC, and despite a loss to Notre Dame the following week, the orange and white rebounded to take a 31-27 triumph over South Carolina in the final regular season contest. The game went down to the wire, and was a must win for the Tigers if they hoped to play in a bowl game. Trailing with under a minute to play, Jerry Butler used every inch of his being to make a leaping touchdown catch in the front of the end zone, a play which Tiger fans affectionately call "The Catch."

On an overthrown ball, Butler was forced to leap high in the air to snag the pass, and then subsequently fell backwards across the goal line. Butler's play ensured a postseason berth for the Tigers, and many people pointed to the play in later years as a critical turn in the fortunes of the Clemson program. With eight victories, the Tigers received an invitation to the Gator Bowl, where they met the defending national champions from Pittsburgh.

The Panthers were not as dominant as they had been during their undefeated 1976 campaign, but were still solid under first-year coach Jackie Sherrill. Tony Dorsett had moved on to the NFL, but quarterback Matt Cavanaugh was an admirable heir to Pitt's offensive throne. Cavanaugh led Pitt to eight regular season wins, which included a 76-0 massacre over Temple. Narrow losses to Notre Dame and Penn State were the only setbacks keeping Pitt from defending their NCAA crown.

The Tigers were the surprise darlings of the ACC, but the Gator Bowl was a frustrating encounter for Pell and his club. It was Clemson's first bowl berth in eighteen years, and the orange and white played like a team not used to big games. The Tiger secondary spent the game perplexed by Cavanaugh, who set a Gator Bowl record with 387 passing yards on twenty-three completions. Despite the 34-3 loss to the Panthers, Pell's quick turnaround of the CU program was culminated with his being named National Coach of the Year.

Maryland's unprecedented football dominance of the ACC came to an end in October, as N.C. State snapped UM's twenty-one game conference winning streak in Raleigh. Ted Brown ran for 110 yards and two touchdowns, and with 27 seconds remaining, Evans scored on a sneak to provide a 24-20 victory for State. With the additional defeat to UNC, the Terrapins gave up their reign as the league's best with a fourth-place finish in the standings. Despite relinquishing the conference championship, Maryland held tough and beat Minnesota, 17-7, in the first Hall of Fame Classic, as George Scott scored twice to lead the Terrapins to victory.

North Carolina State's presence in the Peach Bowl gave the ACC four postseason berths for the first time in history. The 7-4 Wolfpack met Earle Bruce's Iowa State team, which was making that school's third bowl appearance. State raced out to a 21-0 halftime lead behind Evans and Randy Hall, and withstood a furious Cyclone comeback bid in the second half for a 24-14 triumph.

In 1978, Charley Pell led Clemson to its first ACC football title in eleven years, and along the way picked up his second Coach of the Year Award. As a result, Pell became the first head coach in any ACC sport to take the top coaching honors in each of their first two seasons at the helm. The Tiger offense produced 437 yards a contest, the most by a Clemson team since joining the conference and the third highest total in league history.

Quarterback Steve Fuller returned as starting quarterback, and took league MVP honors for the second year in a row. Lester Brown set a new single-season record with seventeen touchdowns, while inside the trenches, the Bostic brothers, Jeff and Joe, anchored the Tiger offensive line. The Bostics were mainstays on the Clemson front, having each earned starting positions in their respective freshman seasons. The linemen helped the Tiger offense average 297 rushing yards a game, and Joe became the first CU player in over a decade to win the Jacobs Blocking Trophy. In later years, Jeff became a member of the famed

Washington Redskins line nicknamed "The Hogs," and won three Super Bowls in the professional ranks.

Fuller's favorite target was Jerry Butler, who became the first Tiger wide receiver in history to be named first-team All-American. Butler, who arrived at Clemson on a track scholarship, had made catches in twenty-three consecutive games heading into the fall of 1978. Making at least one reception in all twelve contests that season, Butler ran his streak to thirty-five games, enough to set a Clemson school record. Butler finished tenth in the NCAA with 58 receptions, good for 908 yards and three touchdowns.

The Citadel looked quite inferior in the Death Valley premiere, as the Tigers scored every time they took possession in the first half. The Bulldogs managed a field goal, but Clemson took a 37-3 lead into the locker rooms. Fuller connected on all nine of his pass attempts, and threw and ran for a touchdown in less than a half of action. The 58-3 laugher was The Citadel's worst defeat at the hands of the Tigers in twenty-three seasons.

Like they had done the year before, the Tigers rolled into Sanford Stadium for a second-game showdown with Georgia. The Bulldogs hadn't forgotten their surprising defeat at the hands of CU in 1977, and unleashed a fearsome defensive challenge to the Tigers. Georgia forced six Clemson turnovers, and was the only team all year to keep the Tiger offense off the scoreboard. The 12-0 defeat was a wake-up call to Fuller, Butler, Brown, and the rest of the offense, for in the coming weeks, the unit proved to be an unstoppable force.

Brown and Marvin Sims each turned in big games against Villanova, combining for four touchdowns and leading a Tiger running game that amassed 385 yards. The Rubber Duck's 43-yard gallop helped put away the Wildcats in the second half, and the starters gave way to the Tiger backups after the third quarter. Villanova threatened to score once, moving down to the CU 6, but the Tiger defenders miffed their efforts. Obed Ariri kicked a 33-yard field goal in the fourth quarter to make the final score 31-0.

The Tiger defense registered another shutout against Virginia Tech, holding the Gobblers to 182 yards. Fuller pointed the Tigers toward victory on the second play from scrimmage, taking a snap from his own 25 and sprinting 75 yards to the end zone. Ariri added a field goal and Brown a touchdown, and it was 17-0 Clemson at the half. Fuller and Billy Lott finished off the Gobblers with a pair of short runs, giving CU a 38-7 final.

Clemson began a run of six consecutive ACC games with Virginia, and the Tigers claimed a 30-14 verdict in Charlottesville. Brown ran for 178 yards and two touchdowns, including a 59-yard gallop on the first play from scrimmage, while Fuller added 131 yards through the air and a pair of scores. Fuller's first touchdown made the score 23-7 before halftime, and his final scoring run gave CU a 30-7 margin. The Cavaliers, who first reached the end zone on a run by Tommy Vigorito, ended the scoring on a pass from Todd Kirkley to Tim Moon.

In a battle of linebackers, Clemson's Bubba Brown and Randy Scott proved the superior unit against Duke. The tandem headed the Tigers to a 28-8 victory with a number of significant plays. Scott recovered two fumbles and intercepted a pass, with his first recovery setting up CU's second touchdown. The Clemson offense scored a touchdown in each quarter, and successfully ran the ball for the fourth straight game. Brown had a pair of touchdowns yet again, while Fuller scored for the third game in a row. It appeared that the Blue Devils would be shut out, but Cedric Jones caught a 7-yard pass late in the game to provide Duke's only points.

Clemson's greatest defensive challenge of the year awaited in Raleigh, as Ted Brown and the Wolfpack welcomed the Tigers to Carter Stadium. Brown was second in the nation in rushing coming into the contest, and had surpassed the 4,000-yard plateau earlier in the year. North Carolina State looked solid at 5-1, and numerous writers across the region were calling Brown the front-runner for the Heisman Trophy. Annoyed by the amount of attention given to the NCSU star, Clemson simply lined up and shut Brown down. State's featured back was held to only 70 yards on 21 carries, as orange helmets stuck him repeatedly after minimal gains. Meanwhile, the Rubber Duck tore through the Wolfpack defense for 117 yards and another pair of touchdowns, and a pair of scores by the back pushed CU into a 23-3 lead.

The Wolfpack threatened to get back into the game early in the final period, but the Tigers came up with a final defensive blow. Rex Varn intercepted a pass for Clemson at the NCSU 6 and returned it 94 yards down the sidelines for a devastating touchdown. It was a great day to be a Tiger fan, as late in the 33-10 Tiger rout, the Clemson cheerleaders engaged in a chant titled, "Our Brown's better than your Brown." The horde of Clemson fans that made the trip to Raleigh made things particularly difficult on NCSU quarterback Scott Smith, and proved loud enough on one occasion to force Smith to step away from the line of scrimmage and call a time-out.

"This is the greatest team effort I've ever been associated with since I first put on a football uniform in 1958," Pell said after the game. "And that covers a lot of great games and some great players."

The emotional high of beating N.C. State on their home field carried over to another game in North Carolina the following week against Wake Forest. It was 10-0 after Brown's first quarter touchdown and an Ariri field goal, and it only got worse from there for the Demon Deacons. Throwing from the WF 42 early in the second quarter, Fuller connected with freshman Perry Tuttle, who caught the pass and raced free for his first touchdown as a Tiger. Dwight Clark scored later in the quarter, and Clemson outscored Wake, 24-6, in the second half to take a 51-6 laugher.

North Carolina had lost several stars from its great defense from the year before, but the Tar Heels played Clemson through the first forty-five minutes, holding the Tigers out of the end zone and turning the game into a nail-biter. Trailing, 9-6, Clemson finally got going midway through the fourth quarter, moving from their own 20 into Tar Heel territory. Brown and Butler were catalysts on the march, each making individual plays of over 20 yards. A pass interference ruling put the ball at the UNC 1, and the Rubber Duck tumbled over for the go-ahead score. The CU defense held the Tar Heels out for the remainder, and the Tigers withstood the scare for a 13-9 triumph.

The biggest game of the year was at hand, as Pell and his troops trekked north to College Park for a battle with Maryland. The 1978 Terrapins looked every bit as strong as the 1976 team during the first two months of the season, rolling up an 8-0 record and holding six of their opponents to single digits. With Steve Atkins piling on the yardage, UM was averaging 27 points a contest, and came into the Clemson game ranked No. 11. A loss to Penn State the week before had ruined Maryland's undefeated aspirations, but the Terrapins were prepared to defend their home field and reclaim the top position in the conference standings.

The game was a war from the outset, as the Terrapins and Tigers engaged in a physical, hard-hitting conflict. Maryland struck first in the opening quarter, but the Tigers countered in the second quarter. With the score 7-7 late in the half, Maryland brought a furious punt rush, and Neal Olkewicz penetrated far enough to deflect the kick. Mike Carney recovered in the end zone for the Terrapins to the raucous approval of the Byrd Stadium faithful. Clemson remained behind, 14-7, well into the third quarter, when Fuller connected with Butler from the CU 13. In a tremendous effort, Butler beat his defender waltzed and 87 yards to the goal line to knot up the game.

Butler's catch and run momentarily took the wind out of the Terrapin sails, but Atkins quickly blew life back into his team with a big play of his own. With the ball on the UM 2, Atkins took a handoff and burst through a gaping hole. Finding a seam through the Clemson defenders, Atkins turned on the jets and went unmolested for a 98-yard touchdown. Atkins' effort set a new Atlantic Coast Conference record for longest run from scrimmage, and stands as the most productive single play ever executed against a Clemson football team. The spirit was revived in the Terrapin fans, and Ed Loncar's point-after made the score 21-14.

The big plays continued minutes later, when Fuller faded into the pocket on third down from his own 38 and drilled a pass to Clark. Clark hauled in the pass 22 yards downfield, and sprinted the remaining 40 for another tying touchdown. With the game knotted at 21 going into the final quarter, Atkins ran out of magic. Although he finished with a game-high 197 yards, the Terrapin tailback was kept from breaking another long run by the Tiger defenders. On a ten-play, 70-yard march midway through the final frame, the Tigers scored the touchdown that provided their first lead. Brown gained 34 yards on five tough carries, and piled over from the 5 to make the score 27-21. An extra point followed, and the Tigers held on for dear life as the Terrapins mounted a final surge.

With just over four minutes to play, Maryland had the ball at the Clemson 10, poised to tie the game or even take the lead. With the game on the line, the Clemson defense got tough. The front line held on a first down handoff to Atkins, stuffing the Terrapin tailback for a 2-yard loss. After a 5-yard gain on their next play, Maryland decided to try a gimmick on third-and-goal from the 7. Dean Richards prepared to make an option pass, but Bubba Brown came through hard on a blitz and brought Richards down for a loss of 11 yards. It was too risky to make an effort at the end zone from the 18, so Jerry Claiborne opted to kick a field goal. With 1:56 to play, Loncar nailed a 35-yard kick to cut the Clemson lead to 28-24. Maryland unsuccessfully attempted an onsides kick, and the Tigers hung on to preserve a huge road victory, the school's first in College Park in eight seasons.

The Clemson players were spitting nails as they rolled down the hill of Memorial Stadium for the South Carolina game, and unleashed a furious assault on the Gamecocks. The Tiger special teams forced two fumbles, giving Fuller and Brown easy access to the end zone. Fuller got on the board first with a sneak, and Brown added a short touchdown to give the Tigers a 21-0 lead after one quarter of play. The Rubber Duck added a final score in the fourth quarter, which gave the Tigers a commanding 41-17 lead. The home fans enjoyed themselves thoroughly in the final fifteen minutes, watching their boys lay it onto their rivals from Columbia.

North Carolina State and Maryland each appeared in bowls on December 23, with NCSU in the Tangerine Bowl against Pittsburgh, and the Terrapins in the Sun Bowl against Texas. Bo Rein's Wolfpack looked much more prepared for their game than Maryland, handing the Panthers a 30-17 defeat. Ted Brown finished his NCSU career in style, running for 126 yards and a touchdown to take Player of the Game honors. The Wolfpack jumped out to a 17-0 lead early in the game, and the secondary picked off four passes to stall Pitt's comeback bid.

The Sun Bowl was an intriguing matchup, as both Maryland and Texas were in the national championship hunt as late as November. The late-season woes endured by the Terrapins continued against the Longhorns, whose backfield featured three guys by the name of Johnny Jones. Nicknamed "Ham," "Lam," and "Jam," the Joneses ran relentlessly on the Terrapin defenders, combining for 211 yards and four touchdowns. Maryland was shut out for the first time in ninety-five ball games, and the 42-0 final score proved to be Jerry Claiborne's worst setback in all his years at College Park.

Following Clemson's impressive 1978 regular season, Charley Pell was proclaimed as the savior of Tiger football. Almost overnight, Pell had earned the respect and adoration of CU fans all around, which Hootie Ingram and Red Parker would have both agreed was not the easiest thing in the world to accomplish. Less than two weeks after the victory over South Carolina, however, Clemson's love of Pell turned instantly into disgust. Unbeknownst to Clemson supporters and officials, Pell had been communicating with people at the University of Florida for weeks concerning their job opening. On December 5, less than four weeks before the Tigers were scheduled to line up against Ohio State in the Gator Bowl, Pell dropped the bomb in a Gainesville press conference. Pell suggested that Danny Ford would be a worthy successor to Clemson officials before he left town, and the school gave the former assistant the contest in Jacksonville to prove his worth.

The 1978 Gator Bowl between the Tigers and Buckeyes would become one of the most memorable games in college football history, but not because of a great play or a fine display of courage. In one disgraceful act, Ohio State (OSU) head coach Woody Hayes put an indelible scar on himself and on the sport he loved. Hayes was an OSU icon, the owner of thirteen Big Ten championships and three national championships over his twenty-eight seasons as head coach of the Buckeyes.

Despite his success over the years, however, Hayes was notorious throughout Columbus and the rest of the Big Ten for his quick and sometimes violent temper. Hayes often went into vicious tirades during practices and film sessions, and once gave himself a pair of black eyes by punching his own face. Ohio State officials, who cited Hayes' winning tradition and dedication to philanthropy, let most of the incidents regarding his temper slide over the years. The "Old Man," as his former players reverently called him, was a frustrated man in the fall of 1978. With a young team that struggled to keep the pace with Ohio State's lofty standards, Hayes spent much of the season trying to keep it all together. Although the Buckeyes were 7-3-1 coming into the Gator Bowl, they were the first OSU team in seven years that had failed to win the Big Ten. With his blood pressure skyrocketing, many believed that Hayes should not have been on the sidelines that night down in Jacksonville.

The game began innocently enough, as the Buckeyes took a 3-0 lead on a field goal. Fuller and Ohio State quarterback Art Schlicter traded touchdowns in the second quarter, and CU took a 10-9 lead into the intermission following a 47-yard field goal by Ariri. The third quarter belonged to the defenses, as the Tigers swarmed Schlicter and kept him from making any big plays. Clemson added to its lead thanks to freshman Cliff Austin, who spent most of the season fourth on the depth chart at tailback and playing on the junior varsity. Making the most of his Gator Bowl opportunity, Austin piled over from the 1 to give Clemson a 17-9 advantage.

Schlicter's second sneak, coming at the 8:11 mark of the fourth quarter, gave the Buckeyes a chance to tie the game with a successful two-point conversion. The Tigers were ready to stuff the run, and did just that to maintain a 17-15 lead. Ohio State got the ball back minutes later, and was poised to make a game-winning drive. With the game teetering in uncertainty, Tiger noseguard Charlie Bauman made his finest play in a Clemson uniform, and one that would forever link him with the Buckeye coach. Schlicter dropped back and tossed a low screen pass directly into the Tiger line, which was promptly picked off by Bauman. Surprised for an instant, the backup lineman quickly collected himself and took off downfield, finally getting pushed out of bounds along the OSU sideline.

As Bauman was slowing down, Hayes ran over and did the unthinkable, slugging the lineman in the facemask. The Tiger players on the opposite sidelines took off to help their teammate, resulting in an on-field incident that took several minutes to clear up. Shocked by what had happened, many of the viewers watching on ABC were hoping to see a replay of the events. Inexplicably, a replay was not shown. Announcers Keith Jackson and Ara Parseghian made no reference whatsoever to Hayes' tirade, and continued on with the broadcast as if the punches were never thrown. The remainder of the game was anticlimactic, as Fuller successfully ran out the clock to preserve Clemson's 17-15 victory. In the offseason, Danny Ford was given the permanent head coaching position at CU, and he would soon embark on a wildly successful run in Death Valley.

Left with no other choice, Ohio State officials fired Hayes less than twenty-four hours after his mysterious breakdown on the sidelines. The Old Man would never coach again, and died in 1987 without ever apologizing to Clemson or Bauman for his deplorable actions that night. Despite finishing with an 11-1 record and a final ranking of No. 6, Clemson's victory in the Gator Bowl will be forever overshadowed by what happened in the fourth quarter.

North Carolina State returned to the top of the ACC in 1979, but a damaging nonconference run resulted in the Wolfpack not being invited to a bowl. Despite winning five of their six conference games, NCSU became the first league champion since Wake Forest in 1970 to not play in a postseason contest. They would also be the last. With the Bowl Championship Series now in place, it is safe to say that an ACC football champion will never again sit out the annual postseason frenzy.

For the first time in five years, the Wolfpack were without the services of Ted Brown, who had been taken in the first round by the Minnesota Vikings in the previous spring's NFL Draft. The most productive running back in league history would certainly be missed, but Dwight Sullivan was chomping at the bit to show what he could do. Sullivan had largely watched on the previous two seasons as Brown led the way in the State backfield. Sullivan had a grand total of fourteen carries in a Wolfpack uniform before 1979, but with Brown's departure came a chance to assume the lead role. The Wolfpack also retained the services of Jim Ritcher, arguably the finest center to ever play in the conference. The NCSU standout would take a place among the great college blockers of all time by season's end, earning the Outland Trophy as the nation's premier interior lineman.

Of the ACC's three bowl teams, none came as a greater surprise than Wake Forest, who became the Cinderella of the NCAA by toppling three ranked teams for the first time in school history. A year earlier, John Mackovic had returned to his alma mater at a rough time in the road for Wake Forest football. Under Chuck Mills the Deacons had plummeted, hitting rock bottom in 1977 with only one victory. Mackovic began his coaching odyssey immediately after his playing days ended at Wake in 1965, making a number of stops before finally being called home to lead the 1978 team. The Deacons struggled again that fall, losing all ten of their remaining games following a 14-0 shutout of Virginia in the season opener.

Mackovic used the 1978 season to teach a wide-open offensive system to his young players. Although it didn't reflect in the final standings, the Deacons showed improvement over the course of the year, finishing the season with the ACC's top passing offense. It would be the first of four consecutive years in which the Deacons led the league in production through the air. Wake Forest had fallen behind their ACC rivals in the recruiting battles in recent years, but Mills' staff had managed to forge a couple of key commitments.

Mackovic inherited a promising young quarterback in Jay Venuto, who was the driving force of a Deacon offense that would lead the ACC in total yardage in 1979. Venuto had not even lettered in 1978, and the quarterback came from out of nowhere to lead the Demon Deacons on a ride the likes of which their fans haven't experienced before or since. Mills had also signed a talented wide receiver prospect in Wayne Baumgartner. A sophomore in 1979, Baumgartner became only the second receiver in conference history to amass 1,000 yards in a season. With James McDougald back for his senior year, the Deacons had a trio of solid offensive performers. McDougald ended his Deacon career in style, rushing for a career-best 1,177 yards to go along with 11 touchdowns.

State began the year at home against East Carolina, and Sullivan wasted no time showing what he could do. The junior ran for 131 yards on fifteen carries, including a pair of touchdowns, to propel a comeback victory for the Wolfpack. The red and white dominated the third quarter, jumping out to a 27-17 lead following a pair of touchdown runs, and took a 34-20 triumph following a late score by Sullivan.

The following week provided a glimpse of just how wild this season was going to be. As the Wolfpack struggled against a Virginia team that was winless in its last eight ACC contests, Wake Forest shocked the college football world by pulling off its biggest upset in school history. The Cavaliers came to Raleigh a poised team, having buried Richmond 31-0 for their first season-opening victory since 1973. Wake was equally confident going into their showdown with Georgia. The Deacons had disposed of Appalachian State in their first game, and knew that they could move the football against the No. 12 Bulldogs.

The Wolfpack handed it to the Cavaliers early on, but had to hang on for dear life against Dick Bestwick's determined team. After taking a 3-0 lead at the end of the first quarter, State poured on 28 points in a second period surge. Virginia came alive in the second half behind Tommy Vigorito, who finished the day with 192 yards. Following a 47-yard stroll by Vigorito, quarterback Todd Kirtley hit Ted Marchibroda, Jr. for a 34-21 score early in the final frame. Following a recovered fumble Vigorito did it again, breaking free for his second touchdown of the half. The extra point was good, and the Cavaliers were suddenly within four at 31-27. With less than three minutes to play, UVA got the ball back and were in position to drive for the winning score. Marion Gale saved the day for State, however, intercepting a Kirtley pass over the middle in the final minute to preserve the slim victory.

Venuto made few mistakes in leading the Deacons against Georgia, completing twenty passes for 273 yards. On his way to earning national player of the week honors from *Sports Illustrated*, Venuto twice found Baumgartner in the first quarter to give Wake a 13-7 lead. On their way to 570 total yards, Wake continued to surge offensively in the second half. McDougald was a fine compliment to Venuto's passing, leading the Deacon running attack with 189 yards on thirty carries.

McDougald put the Demon Deacons in the lead early in the fourth quarter, catching a pass and taking it over from 9 yards out. Frank Harnisch was good on the critical extra point, and WF led, 22-21. The final ten minutes must have seemed like weeks for the Deacon players, as they sought to maintain their slim advantage. The Bulldogs were unable to make any significant strides on offense, and had to attempt a 58-yard field goal with four seconds left in order to win. The kick was off, and the three-touchdown underdog Deacons celebrated their first victory over an Southeastern Conference opponent in fourteen years. A bevy of Wake Forest supporters trekked to the Raleigh-Durham airport so they could be the first to welcome home their heroes.

"It was a great win and I can't say enough about our people," Mackovic said later. "I'm very proud of this team. We knew once we got the lead we would be okay. The complexion of the game changed when we got the lead and they had to play catch-up."

State went out of the ACC the following weekend for their third game, played at West Virginia. The Wolfpack broke out to a 14-0 lead, but in a complete role reversal of their second half collapse against Virginia, State kept the pressure on this time around. Quarterback Scott Smith scored three times in the final thirty minutes, each coming on short carries over the line, as State left Morgantown in command of a 38-14 score.

Next came the contest that everyone was waiting for, a showdown in Raleigh between the Wolfpack and Wake Forest. The Deacons and Wolfpack had not met in a game that was significant for both teams in years, and although it was still early in the year, both were unbeaten. On a rain-soaked afternoon, the Wolfpack defended their home field admirably in the first half, keeping Wake out of the end zone and taking a 7-0 lead into the locker rooms.

Venuto pulled Wake level early in the third quarter when he strung together a series of conversions. After the Deacons dodged a bullet by recovering their own fumble deep in NCSU territory, Venuto found Baumgartner in the back corner of the end zone to tie the game at 7. The teams traded another pair of scores, and went down the stretch with the game knotted at 14-14. Late in the game, the Deacons advanced to the State 32, when from out of nowhere Wolfpack end Joe Hannah drilled Venuto on a pass attempt and forced him to cough up the ball. State used their good fortune to move into range for a successful field goal try and a 17-14 lead.

The never-say-die Venuto continued to make plays, completing consecutive passes to bring Wake to the State 33. On first down, Venuto saw Baumgartner streaking alone across the middle, and fired a pass through the Wolfpack defense. Unfortunately for Venuto, Baumgartner was unable to haul it in. The Carter-Finley Stadium crowd breathed a collective sigh of relief as the ball hit the deck, as the pass would have put Wake Forest in excellent position to win or at least salvage a tie. The next play sealed Wake's demise, as Venuto fumbled the quarterback exchange and Bubba Green fell on it for NCSU with eighteen seconds on the clock.

Now ranked No. 14 in the nation, State came out sharp against Auburn, breaking out to a 14-0 lead in similar fashion to the early onslaught waged against West Virginia. However, the angry Tigers assumed control from the end of the opening quarter, scoring the next 21 points. The Wolfpack, in the midst of their worst defensive performance all season, were dumbfounded by the Auburn running attack, which rolled up 407 yards. Trailing 44-17 in the second half, State rebounded and made the game respectable in the final fifteen minutes. Despite a pair of late touchdowns, the Wolfpack were humbled, 44-31, by the Tigers.

Wake Forest went to Chapel Hill the ensuing Saturday, where an unbeaten North Carolina team laid waiting. The Tar Heels had rolled to four easy wins over inferior opponents, but the Deacons never trailed, rolling up an early 10-0 lead and holding off a Tar Heel comeback in the final minutes. The Wake Forest defense held Amos Lawrence well under his average, with only 34 yards on twenty-four carries. It was not until the final period, when they were facing almost certain defeat, that the Tar Heels finally responded. Trailing 24-10, quarterback Matt Kupec hit tight end Mike Chatham for a touchdown at the 4:28 mark. Carolina got another opportunity to get back into the game, but the Deacon defense held on for a 24-19 victory, which ran Wake Forest's record to 5-1 for the first time since 1951.

The Wolfpack entertained Maryland at home the same afternoon, and came back with a spirited effort on defense. State shut down heralded Terrapin back Charlie Wysocki, who was held to only 45 yards. On their way to a grand total of 133 yards, Maryland never did solve State's defensive approach. State scored the game's only points in the third quarter, when Sullivan crossed the line from 14 yards out. The 74-yard drive, set up by a penalty for a late hit against the quarterback, was all that State would need, and they held on for a 7-0 triumph. With Carolina's loss to the Demon Deacons, State suddenly found themselves on top of the ACC standings.

The annual rivalry game with Carolina was next for the Wolfpack, and the Tar Heels stepped onto the field at Carter-Finley Stadium and instantly assumed control, going 65 yards for the game's first score. After conceding the Wolfpack a touchdown, the next twenty minutes of the game belonged to the Tar Heels, as they raced out to a 28-7 pad. Bob Paschal replaced the injured Lawrence and was up to the task, running for 117 yards and three touchdowns. Billy Johnson added 71 more from his fullback position, and provided bruising blocking throughout the contest.

The Wolfpack came out for the second half breathing fire, and used the third quarter to get back into the game. As the defense figured out a way to momentarily slow down Carolina, Smith led the Wolfpack on two scoring drives to bring NCSU within a touchdown. With 11:33 remaining in the game, a controversial ruling on the field thrust the momentum back into Carolina's favor dramatically. Hemmed in at his own 8, Smith stepped back into the pocket and was quickly pressured by the hard charge of Lawrence Taylor. Taylor drilled Smith as he let go of the ball, and the referees ruled it a fumble. Television replays revealed that the call might have been blown, as it appeared that Smith's hand was going forward. The Tar Heels quickly capitalized on their good fortune, as Paschal reached the end zone five plays later to give Carolina the game, 35-21, which created a three-way tie atop the league standings.

"I've never in my career felt an official was so wrong as on that call," a tearful Smith said later. "Sure, he might have had a bad angle, I don't know. I just know the ball went forward and I was throwing as I was hit and that you could take that play out and it might have been a different ball game. Like I said, it was a judgment call. But I believe that out of 54,000, the only people that could have ruled that a fumble would have to be a Carolina fan."

Wake Forest faced off against Auburn at home a week later, and the opening half was the very definition of a shootout, as the teams combined for 58 points. With Auburn's running game churning on all cylinders, and Venuto trying to keep pace, the game went into halftime with the Tigers leading, 38-20. Venuto led a pair of possessions that resulted in touchdowns in the third quarter, as Wake cut the Auburn lead to 38-35. McDougald scored each of Wake's third quarter touchdowns, and his fourth score in the final period gave the Deacons a 42-38 advantage in the final quarter. The Deacons twice had to hold off serious late Auburn charges, and with a fumble recovery and interception, the defense completed a second half shutout of the Tigers. The 42-38 score held to the final gun, as Wake triumphed in the first game in Groves Stadium history played between two ranked opponents.

A week later, the Wolfpack headed down to Clemson to meet a fearsome Tiger defense, and managed only 148 yards. Despite their lack of productivity, NCSU pushed to a 13-3 advantage at halftime. Clemson stormed back on a 38-yard field goal and a touchdown from Chuck McSwain, but another field goal propelled NCSU to an important 16-13 victory, which set up a pair of nonconference clashes with South Carolina and Penn State.

George Rogers was the culprit in the USC game for the Wolfpack, as the elusive junior ran for 217 yards. The future Heisman Trophy winner broke off a 25-yard gallop in the second half, which gave South Carolina a 30-14 cushion. State scored twice in the final period to close the gap to 30-28, but interestingly enough, the Wolfpack did not go for a two-point conversion either time. Hoping for a late field goal, NCSU never got close enough to make an attempt.

Bo Rein was still winless at N.C. State against the Nittany Lions, and the streak went to four in the most painful of ways. Herb Menhardt nailed a 54-yard field goal with one second to play, which gave PSU a 9-7 shocker. It was a tough one to take for the Wolfpack supporters, as victory was all but sealed following a touchdown at the 1:18 mark, which gave NCSU a 7-6 lead. Following a sack that left Penn State with a fourth-and-24 on their own 27, quarterback Dayle Tate completed a miraculous 36-yard pass to Terry Rakowski. After two incompletes, Menhardt came on for the clincher.

Duke and Kentucky were playing basketball on November 17, which meant that many of the fans in Wallace Wade Stadium had their eyes on the gridiron and their ears tuned in to the hardwood action on the radio. It was just as well, as State regrouped and demolished the Blue Devils 28-7 to wrap up the school's first and only ACC championship under Coach Rein. With Smith leading four solid marches and scoring twice, NCSU put up their season-high total on offense.

Following their final games, North Carolina and Clemson each received calls from bowl committees. In something of a surprise, the Gator Bowl welcomed the Tar Heels to oppose Michigan, while the Tigers accepted a berth in the Peach Bowl against Baylor. Wake Forest, fresh off its finest season in decades, already knew they were heading to Orlando's Tangerine Bowl. The Wolfpack were hoping to get a ring from either the Fiesta Bowl or Bluebonnet Bowl, but the calls never came. As it turned out, NCSU's lone invitation came from the short-lived Garden State Bowl. Unfortunately for the Wolfpack, exam restrictions kept them at home.

The victory over Duke proved to be the last for Rein at N.C. State. At season's end, Rein decided to become the second ACC championship head coach in as many years to test the waters of the Southeastern Conference. Rein accepted the head coaching position at Louisiana State on November 30, less than two weeks after clinching the ACC title. Tragically, Rein would never coach a game in Baton Rouge. Six weeks later, as he was returning to LSU after a recruiting trip in Shreveport, Rein died in a mysterious plane crash. Flying in inclement weather, the cockpit fell victim to a navigational malfunction, which pulled the plane dramatically off course. After running out of fuel, the doomed Cessna crashed in the Atlantic Ocean off the coast of Virginia, hundreds of miles from its intended destination. Rein's body, along with that of the pilot, was never found.

Rein had been intended to replace Charles McLendon, who announced plans to retire after LSU played Wake Forest in Orlando. It was Wake's first postseason appearance in thirty years, and only the third in school history. The Tigers were a dangerous team for Wake Forest to play, not so much for their talent as for what was at stake. McLendon had been head coach of the Tigers since 1962, and over that time had won 136 games, including a stretch of five years with at least nine victories every season.

The Tiger players were intent on sending their leader out in style, and came out of the gates like a champion thoroughbred, marching for two touchdowns in the first quarter on drives that seemed effortless. The Deacons, so productive offensively throughout the year, succumbed to the jitters of the bowl experience. Wake committed three turnovers in the first half, allowing LSU to rack up a commanding 24-0 lead. The Deacons finally drove on their first possession of the second half, as Venuto connected with Baumgartner for Wake's only touchdown. The final quarter belonged to the Tigers, as they scored ten more points to take a 34-10 victory. WF got two more solid scoring opportunities, but the Tigers, who allowed only 30 yards rushing, stunted both attempts.

Many people, particularly in Raleigh, grumbled about UNC's invitation to the Gator Bowl with a 7-3-1 record, but the Tar Heels proved they belonged against Bo Schembechler's Wolverines. Although they fell behind early, Carolina scored 17 unanswered points in the second and third quarters to take the lead. Michigan had a chance to tie the game after Anthony Carter's second scoring grab, a 30-yard play that made the score 17-15 in the fourth quarter, but their two-point conversion pass fell incomplete to give the Tar Heels the upset. Clemson's 24-18 defeat to Baylor in the Peach Bowl gave the ACC a disappointing record of 9-13-1 in postseason contests throughout the decade of the 1970s.

With two of the finest players in conference history leading his respective offensive and defensive units, Dick Crum led North Carolina to first place in the ACC for the first and only time in 1980, giving the school its fifth taste of life at the top of the gridiron standings. In completing his fourth consecutive 1,000-yard season, becoming only the second running back in NCAA Division I-A history to do so, Amos Lawrence etched his name among the greatest players in the annals of college football. Over the course of his career, Famous Amos rushed for at least 100 yards twenty-five different times, and left UNC second only to Tony Dorsett in all-time rushing yardage among major college backs.

The 1980 season was also the last for Lawrence Taylor in Carolina Blue. "L.T.," as he was called by teammates, played on the defensive front when he first arrived in Chapel Hill, but found a home at outside linebacker in 1979. Capable of taking over games with his combination of speed and instinct, Taylor often had to make plays from the other side of the field, as teams would run away from him as often as possible. With a pass rush from the linebacker position far ahead of its time, Taylor would go on to set a UNC single-season record with sixteen sacks in 1980. The boisterous Taylor soon revolutionized the position of linebacker in the professional game, winning two Super Bowls and the NFL's Most Valuable Player Award in 1986.

The Carolina offense ran on all cylinders against Furman, as the Tar Heels took a 35-13 season-opening victory. Lawrence and Kelvin Bryant were the heroes, accounting for all five UNC scores. Bryant came through again in the Texas Tech game, scoring a touchdown early in the fourth quarter to lead Carolina to a 9-3 triumph. The play, a 58-yard pass from Rod Elkins, broke a 3-3 tie, and gave UNC enough momentum to put away a tough Red Raider team. The Tar Heels kicked themselves in the foot all day, and an interception inside the 20 gave Texas Tech an opportunity to win late. The Carolina defense was up to the challenge, as Taylor drilled Greg Tyler at the 2 to force a fumble. L.T. recovered the ball at the 6:55 mark of the final quarter, and the Tar Heels successfully ran out the clock.

Carolina's mission in the ACC premiere against Maryland was to stop Charlie Wysocki, who came into the game fourth in the NCAA in rushing. The junior had nowhere to go against the Carolina defense, managing only 17 yards on twelve carries. Wysocki fumbled on his first, second, and seventh carries of the game, while as a team, the Terrapins managed only 31 yards on the ground. With the Maryland offense in a lull for most of the day, the Tar Heel offense was able to carefully pick its spots. Carolina took a 10-0 advantage into halftime, and another fumble recovery by L.T. at the Maryland 30 set up UNC's final touchdown, as Bryant muscled his way in from the 6. Dale Castro connected on a field goal for the Terps, but Carolina had the 17-3 win.

"Carolina played well," said Terrapin coach Jerry Claiborne. "You can't lay the ball on the ground five times against a team as good as they are and expect to win."

Dominant as the Carolina defense had been against Maryland, the unit was every bit as good in the Georgia Tech game. The Yellow Jackets, on the way to a 1-9-1 record under first-year coach Bill Curry, had already been blown out by Alabama and Florida as they arrived in Chapel Hill. The Tar Heels were far from sympathetic, as GT signal caller Mike Kelley was consistently ambushed by the aggressive UNC line, and had to be helped off the field on two separate occasions. Lawrence and Bryant each broke the century mark on the ground, and both scored in the second quarter to open up the UNC advantage to 17-0. In racking up over 500 yards of total offense, Carolina scored 16 unanswered points in the third quarter to put the Jackets away, 33-0.

Carolina improved to 5-0 for the first time in thirty-two years with a 27-9 win over Wake Forest in Winston-Salem. Although they struggled to move the ball in the opening quarter, the Tar Heel offense came alive in the second fifteen minutes. Leading 14-3 at the half, Carolina took control in the fourth quarter on a pair of touchdown carries by Lawrence. A pass from Jay Venuto to Kenny Duckett in the final minutes, with Carolina's backup defensive unit on the field, gave the Deacons their only taste of the end zone.

North Carolina State came to Chapel Hill the following week, and the Tar Heel defense continued its string of standout performances. Carolina needed only three big plays to put away the Wolfpack, and the first came midway through the second quarter, when the Tar Heels lined up to punt the ball away. Steve Streater, on the way to leading the ACC in punting, had a trick up his sleeve. With everyone in the stadium looking skyward in anticipation of a punt, Streater tucked the football under his arm and took off toward the Wolfpack goal line. Thanks to a number of key blocks, Streater raced untouched to the end zone for a 7-0 Carolina lead.

"It was one of the biggest plays I've ever had in college football," a smiling Streater said later. "It was also the first time I've been across the goal line since I've been here. I didn't know what to do when I got down there."

Carolina's second big play came less than a minute later, as a pair of All-ACC defenders made their mark. Donnell Thompson drilled NCSU quarterback Tol Avery on the second play after the kickoff, and Darrell Nicholson recovered for UNC on the State 17. Two plays later, Elkins threw Carolina's second touchdown. Another turnover by the Tar Heel defense, an interception by Calvin Daniels, set up an Elkins bootleg for a 21-0 UNC advantage. Elkins threw another touchdown for good measure, and State scored against the backup defense for their only score and a 28-8 final.

With powerful Oklahoma waiting the following weekend in Norman, nobody could have blamed the Tar Heel players if they were looking beyond East Carolina. Whether they were or not, UNC came out with another spirited effort to blow away the Pirates. Lawrence and Bryant combined for 145 yards and three touchdowns, and Elkins threw a touchdown to make the final score 31-3. Playing East Carolina was good practice for the UNC defenders, who would face the same wishbone attack against OU.

The Oklahoma game gave Carolina an opportunity to showcase their talents for a national audience, and victory would put them in prime position to claim a major bowl berth or even the national championship. Despite the press coverage devoted to Oklahoma's excellence, Carolina believed that they had a legitimate shot of winning the game. The Tar Heel defensive starters had yet to give up a touchdown in seven games, and were leading the nation in total defense.

"We've just gotta go and play to our potential," said Taylor. "It's a great opportunity for us as a team to go out there. It's exciting. We've been looking at it in the back of our mind for a long time."

Although the Tar Heel defenders had plenty to say to the Sooners in the tunnel in the moments leading up to kickoff, the unit quickly found itself overmatched by Oklahoma's size and speed. Nonetheless, UNC stayed in the game through a physical first half. Trailing 14-7 late in the second quarter, Carolina had the ball at the OU 9 with an opportunity to tie the game. A dropped pass turned away UNC's aspirations for another touchdown, and a short field goal attempt was off to kill the rally.

Despite their defensive excellence over most of the season, the Tar Heels had faced nothing remotely close to the precision and execution of the Oklahoma offense. Sooner quarterback J. C. Watts was a one-man wrecking crew, scoring three touchdowns and leading a unit that rushed for 495 yards. Oklahoma broke the game open in the third quarter, jumping out to a 34-7 lead. A final score gave the Sooners a 41-7 blowout, one that was particularly memorable to OU coach Barry Switzer for a different reason. When the Tar Heels arrived in Norman, Switzer mistakenly referred to Dick Crum as *Denny* Crum, the head basketball coach at Louisville. All weekend, Switzer made references to Dick as Denny, while the UNC skipper stood by expressionless.

"Then after the game, I went out to midfield to try to say something nice," Switzer said in his 1990 autobiography, *Bootlegger's Boy*. "But before I could get a word out, Crum said, 'Coach, the name is *Dick!*' That was the only thing he said to me in two days, and I felt about two inches high."

The Tar Heels had little time to feel sorry for themselves after the Oklahoma trip, as Clemson was waiting the following week in Death Valley. Although the Tigers were out of the ACC title picture, Carolina had not beaten CU in four years. Playing with spirit and intensity, UNC could do no wrong in the first three quarters, jumping out to a 24-6 lead on the backs of Bryant and Lawrence. Amos raced 58 yards on Carolina's opening drive to set up a touchdown, and Bryant forced his way over from the 1 for a 14-0 UNC lead.

With their backs to the wall, Clemson mounted a furious surge in the waning moments. After scoring twice to make the score 24-19, the

Tigers marched the ball to the UNC 1, where they had a first down with 1:13 left on the clock. With four opportunities to take the game, the Tiger offense prepared for a showdown with L.T. and the Tar Heel defenders. Running on first and second down, CU's Wilbur Bullard was stuffed twice by the hard-charging UNC line. On third down Homer Jordan dropped back to pass, only to be met by the furious rush of Taylor. L.T. drilled Jordan for a 9-yard loss, forcing Clemson into a desperate fourth down pass from the 10. Jordan threw toward Jerry Gaillard, but the ball went wide through the right side of the end zone. With the incompletion, UNC slid out of Death Valley having preserved their unblemished ACC mark.

Carolina completed the regular season 10-1 with dominating performances over Virginia and Duke in Kenan Stadium. Virginia avoided the shutout, but the Bryant-Lawrence running tandem was too much in UNC's 26-3 victory. The Duke game was Lawrence's curtain call in Chapel Hill, and the tailback finished his home career with two touchdowns. Bryant and Billy Johnson combined for three more touchdowns to lead the Tar Heels over the Blue Devils, 44-21.

North Carolina and Maryland each received postseason invites, and the Terrapins kicked it off with an encounter with Florida in the Tangerine Bowl. Playing in the school's seventh bowl in eight seasons under Jerry Claiborne, Maryland took a 3-0 lead after one quarter on a Dale Castro field goal. Florida, piloted by former Clemson nemesis Charley Pell, responded through the air, as Wayne Peace threw to Chris Collinsworth for a 24-yard score. Although Castro booted another pair of threes to give UM back the lead, the Gators tallied again late in the half for a 14-9 intermission edge. Florida continued its offensive surge in the third quarter, notching another pair of touchdowns to build up their lead to 28-20. A final score six minutes into the final frame gave the Gators the game, 35-20.

Playing Texas in the Bluebonnet Bowl eleven days later, Carolina set out to prove that they could beat a power from America's football heartland. The Oklahoma loss had been an embarrassment to Crum and the Tar Heels, but victory over the Longhorns would ensure the second eleven-win season in UNC history. Texas had beaten Oklahoma, 20-13, three weeks before the Carolina game, and had climbed as high as No. 2 in the polls as recently as late October. The Longhorns fell on hard times after the OU upset, dropping four of their last six games to come into the Bluebonnet unranked. Nonetheless, the Tar Heel fans were outnumbered in the stands, where a mass of Texas supporters made the 160-mile trip from Austin.

Lawrence wasted no time establishing Carolina's presence in the Astrodome, taking the fourth play from scrimmage 59 yards for a touchdown. The Longhorns matched Famous Amos' run in the second quarter, when Herkie Walls broke off a 42-yard carry to the UNC 1. Mike Luck pounded it home to tie the game at 7. Bryant scored minutes later on a plunge from the 1, resulting from a recovered Texas fumble. The Tar Heels added to their lead in the second half on another turn-over, as a fumbled punt gave UNC the ball deep in Longhorn territory. Jeff Hayes' field goal completed a 16-7 Carolina triumph, as the UNC defense made a final stamp on what had been an impressive run throughout the season. In holding the Longhorns out of the end zone in the second half, the Tar Heel defense notched its eighth game of the season holding its opposition to single digits.

9

Orange Crush (1981)

Danny Ford had plenty of reasons to feel good about his Clemson football team heading into the 1981 season. At only thirty-three years of age, Ford had fallen into a great situation at Death Valley. Charley Pell's departure after the regular season back in 1978 had opened up the job for the Alabama native, who served as captain of Bear Bryant's 1969 Crimson Tide squad. The third-youngest coach in the NCAA in 1981, Ford had a team that was intent on reaching new heights for Tiger football. All eleven members of the starting offense from 1980 were returning, which meant that Clemson fans could enjoy another season of quarterback Homer Jordan throwing passes to his favorite target, Perry Tuttle.

Tuttle, nicknamed "P.T." by his teammates, had been a bright spot for the Tigers since arriving on campus as a freshman, and had at least one reception in every game he had ever played in for Clemson. Jordan, who Tuttle referred to as a "peanut-butter sandwich eating country boy," was the perfect fit for Clemson's offensive attack. Capable of making quick throws or tucking it up and running, Jordan was the catalyst of a Tiger offense that averaged nearly 29 points a game during the regular season. From the outset, Jordan had an idea of where he wanted to lead his team.

"I don't know if we truly knew it at the time, but our goal was to win the national championship. That's what was instilled in us—to shoot for playing in the Orange Bowl. Coach George Dostal had pictures of oranges in the weight room in the preseason."

Clemson also returned cornerback Terry Kinard and linebacker Jeff Davis, the standouts of CU's defense. Nicknamed "The Judge" for the way in which he seemed to rule the field from his linebacker position, Davis captained a defense that set a single-season record by forcing forty-one turnovers. Tuttle and Davis had each been significant contributors as freshmen on Clemson's 1978 team, which won the ACC title and the Gator Bowl. Their talent and leadership in the autumn of 1981 would prove vital in propelling a dream season in the foothills of South Carolina.

Wofford College trekked into Memorial Stadium for Clemson's season opener. The Terriers were a replacement for Villanova, who had dropped their football program before the season began. Wofford received the kickoff and promptly marched 76 yards against the heavily favored Tigers. Mike Ayers, a former Wofford assistant who ascended to head coach of the Spartanburg-based Terriers in 1988, has a photograph in his office of the scoreboard that day reading "Wofford 3, Clemson 0." From there the Tigers ran roughshod over the helpless Terriers, scoring 45 points and dominating on both sides of the ball. Four Tiger ball carriers had at least 50 yards, while Jordan threw for 177. He got 80 of those yards on one play, when Tuttle split the defense and hauled in a perfectly thrown ball for a touchdown in the second quarter.

Clemson's next opponent was Tulane, and for the second game in a row Clemson gave up a field goal on its opening defensive drive. On Clemson's second offensive possession, freshman punter Dale Hatcher misplayed a snap, and was forced to down the ball in the end zone to give Tulane a 5-0 advantage. With the Tiger offense sputtering, the opportunistic CU defense did everything in its power to secure victory, forcing seven turnovers and holding the Green Wave out of the end zone. Defensive end Joe Glenn recovered a Tulane fumble after the safety, and the Tigers drove 25 yards for the game's only touchdown. Tulane was in a position to score again, but Kinard saved the day with an end zone interception. Bob Paulling was good on a pair of field goals, the second following another interception by the Tigers, to secure a 13-5 victory.

Defending national champion Georgia rode into Death Valley the following week on a fifteen-game winning streak. Their all-everything tailback, sophomore Herschel Walker, had yet to know defeat at the collegiate level. After taking the NCAA by storm as a true freshman, Walker had blistered Tennessee and California for a combined 328 yards in Georgia's first two games in 1981. The No. 4 Bulldogs were again serious national title contenders, and for the No. 16 Tigers, this was their chance to show that they belonged among the nation's elite.

The Tigers got off to a great start on their home field, breaking out to a 10-0 first quarter lead against the startled Bulldogs. Walker got his yardage, churning out 111 on twenty-eight carries, but developed a severe case of the butterfingers. A pair of Walker fumbles led directly to each of the early CU scores, a touchdown pass from Jordan to Tuttle, and a field goal courtesy of Donald Igwebuike. Davis, Jeff Bryant, and freshman William Perry spent the day in the Georgia backfield, and kept the future Heisman Trophy winner from breaking his trademark long-gainer. The Bulldogs made mistake after mistake under the relentless pressure of the Tiger defense, committing nine turnovers. Igwebuike ended the scoring with a second half field goal, and the Tigers had their biggest victory in years by a score of 13-3.

The victory over UGA put Clemson on the radar screen, and Orange Mania continued to grow in the Palmetto State the following week, as a massive throng of Tiger supporters made the trip to Lexington, where Clemson manhandled Kentucky, 21-3. Kevin Mack had an 11-yard touchdown run in the third quarter to help put away the pesky Wildcats, who led 3-0 at halftime. Jordan and Chuck McSwain added touchdowns to seal Kentucky's fate.

Clemson was off to its best start since 1958, when Frank Howard's club had won the school's second ACC championship. While the defense had been the toughest in the country to score against through four games, giving up barely 5 points an outing, the offense had been somewhat average. That all changed on homecoming weekend against Virginia. As the defense dominated again, shutting out the beleaguered Cavaliers, the offensive unit rolled up 426 yards to claim an easy 27-0 final.

In their next outing, CU wasted no time rolling over Duke in Durham. The Tigers took the kickoff and plowed 64 yards in only seven plays, highlighted by a 21-yard blast by Cliff Austin on the first play and a Jordan completion to Frank Magwood for 22. Brendon Crite found the goal line from 4 yards out, and from there the Tigers were in control. Paulling kicked a field goal early in the second quarter, and after a turnover, Clemson scored another touchdown, with Austin taking in a pitch from 15 yards on a sweep. Jordan threw an interception on Clemson's next possession, but Kinard gave the ball right back to the offense when he made his second pick at Clemson's 2-yard line. After moving the ball to the 19, Jordan handed off to Austin. The junior found space up the middle and burst into the clear. Duke's Dennis Tabron caught Austin in a foot race and hauled him in at the 4, but not before he raced 77 yards. Jordan scored on a sneak, and the Tigers led, 24-0.

For the game Clemson amassed 563 yards, with 325 coming in their devastating first half performance. Midway through the third quarter, with Clemson comfortably ahead 31-0, Duke quarterback Ben Bennett found receiver Cedric Jones, who made a diving catch in the end zone. Remarkably, it was only the second touchdown scored against the Clemson defense in six games. The Blue Devils fought bitterly until the end, and were on the brink of touchdowns twice in the fourth quarter. The Tigers held both times, maintaining their streak of not allowing a rushing touchdown.

"At that point in time, we could have just let them in," the Judge said after the game. "But we weren't about to do that. We take a lot of pride in not letting people score. They had scored 10 points, so we had to buckle down."

The Tigers returned to Death Valley the following week to play N.C. State, and although they played lethargically, CU held off the Wolfpack. State was playing its second consecutive game against an unbeaten, ranked opponent. Playing at home against North Carolina the week before, the Wolfpack were on the wrong end of a 21-10 score, which ran Carolina's record to 6-0. State gave the Tigers fits all afternoon, becoming the first team all season to score a rushing touchdown against their defense, a streak that had reached twenty-four consecutive quarters. The score came on State's second possession, following a Tiger fumble. Larmount Lawson's 13-yard sprint to the end zone put an end to Clemson's run.

"We just weren't playing our type of defense," Davis said later. "When we're playing right, we control the pace. But during the first few possessions, they were controlling the flow of the game. That hasn't happened to us often this season."

An Igwebuike field goal cut State's lead to four, and it appeared that it would be that way at halftime before the Tigers scored with thirteen seconds left in the half. The second half belonged to the Tiger defense, as they clamped down against the Wolfpack offense and held them to only four first downs and 21 yards rushing. Although Homer Jordan suffered through one of his worst games in a Tiger uniform, throwing three interceptions, he led the Tigers to a final scoring drive to make the final score 17-7.

After a week of criticism, the Tiger offense came back alive in an 82-24 bombing of Wake Forest. Although the defense gave up more points to the Deacons than their last five opponents combined, it was trivial when compared to the way the Tiger offense lit up the scoreboard. Deacon coach Al Groh had legitimate concerns about his team's chances before the game, and those fears proved to be justified. On their way to setting twenty-one different records, the schools put together the highest-scoring game in the ACC's first five decades of grid-iron competition.

"One of the last things I told one of our coaches coming into the game was I was concerned whether we would be able to stop them," said Groh. "I guess I was correct in that prediction. It was our job to stop them, not their job to stop themselves. I thought they were more than gracious."

The Tigers compiled an astounding 756 total yards against the Deacons, with 536 coming on the ground. Scoring on each of their first seven possessions, Clemson ran up a 49-14 cushion by halftime. Their 82 points broke the ACC single-game scoring record, which had been set by Maryland twenty-seven years prior in a 74-13 demolition of Missouri. Clemson's final score came courtesy of a 72-yard sprint by Craig Crawford, which came on his first carry as a Tiger running back. Tuttle made plays all over the field against Wake, hauling in seven passes for 161 yards and a pair of scores. Tuttle's second touchdown catch, coming from backup Mike Gasque, made the score 63-17, and placed Tuttle ahead of Jerry Butler as Clemson's all-time leading receiver. Austin and McSwain had a field day running through the Wake Forest defense, teaming for 191 yards and five touchdowns.

By game's end, it was apparent that the third-ranked Tigers were for real. After surviving a scare from N.C. State, the Tigers had handed Wake Forest a defeat that only powerhouses can give. With their biggest game of the season at hand, a date in Chapel Hill against North Carolina, the Tigers were finally running on all cylinders. Clemson arrived in Chapel Hill as the nation's second-ranked team, a worthy contender for the national championship with an 8-0 record. The Tar Heels came in solid themselves at 7-1, and were intent on defending their ACC title on the grass of Kenan Stadium.

It was the first time in history that two Atlantic Coast Conference football programs met when each were ranked in the Associated Press Top Ten, making it arguably the most important regular season game in conference history to that time. With the league championship and probable Orange Bowl berth to the victor, the ACC's best of 1981 stood toe-to-toe for sixty minutes of brutal football. The Tar Heels, behind quarterback Rod Elkins and tailback Kelvin Bryant, boasted the ACC's top offense. Bryant, despite missing UNC's last four games with a knee injury, had already scored fifteen touchdowns, including a record six in the season opener against East Carolina. Carolina had scored at least forty points four times, although they had struggled in their last two games without Bryant. Clemson had unquestionably the ACC's best defense, and arguably the most dominant in all of America.

The game began as a defensive standstill, as the first quarter went by scoreless. Bryant was unable to help Carolina's cause for the most part, still struggling with his knee. He gained 31 yards on thirteen attempts. Clemson had a chance to reach the scoreboard first, but Igwebuike missed a 50-yarder midway through the opening frame. Following the failed attempt, Carolina began a successful drive under the leadership of Elkins. Rod completed three consecutive passes to three different receivers, the final one coming on a diving grab by freshman Larry Griffin at the CU 7. With a golden opportunity to take a 7-0 lead, the Tar Heels fell victim, like so many others, to the clutches of the powerful Tiger defenders. On first down, Elkins was taken down by Clemson tackle Dan Benish for a 7-yard loss, and the Tar Heels were unable to get any closer. Brooks Barwick came on for a chip shot, and the kick gave Carolina a 3-0 lead.

Early in the second quarter, Clemson began a drive that resulted in the game's only touchdown. Driving 81 yards against the formidable Tar Heel defense, the Tigers scored on a 7-yard run by Jeff McCall. It stayed that way until the final seconds of the first thirty minutes. Dale Hatcher, Clemson's dependable punter, was back in preparation for a kick that would have been the final significant play of the half.

The Carolina punt unit had other ideas, as a vicious rush thrust linebacker Danny Barlow free. Barlow partially deflected Hatcher's kick, and the ball bounded through the back of the end zone for a safety. Although they trailed 7-5 at the half, North Carolina took the momentum of the special teams play into the locker room. The third quarter, like the two before it, was a struggle between the defenses. The teams traded field goals, with Barwick coming through for UNC in the final minute of the period. It was 10-8 Clemson as the final quarter began. Carolina got a gift at the 10:44 mark, when Dwight Parrish recovered a fumbled punt at the CU 37.

The Tiger defense was running the show at this point, and pushed UNC back 6 yards to force a punt. The final fifteen minutes became a frustrating, desperate struggle for the Tar Heels. Elkins had gone down in the first quarter with an injury, and although he tried to return, it was a brief stint. The reins went to Scott Stankavage, who struggled against Clemson's great defense. The way the Tigers were performing on that side of the ball, the two-point deficit might as well have been twenty. Stankavage led Carolina into CU territory once more, but Hollis Hall deflected away his fourth down toss from the 41.

With under a minute remaining, Carolina got a final opportunity to knock off the Tigers and defend their ACC title. On first down at his own 40-yard line, Stankavage dropped back to throw. The quarterback instantly felt pressure from Clemson's aggressive front, and attempted to throw back to Alan Burrus, but the fullback was unable to come up with the ball. Burrus tried to fall on the pigskin, which was ruled a lateral because it was thrown backwards, but Jeff Bryant was a step quicker. Bryant's recovery sealed victory for the Tigers.

"It was a flare screen," UNC coach Dick Crum said of the fateful play. "Stankavage threw it away from the line of scrimmage, which made it a lateral." Crum struggled to hold back his extreme disappointment on the Carolina sideline as the final seconds ticked away from the clock. Stankavage, who would become one of UNC's most productive signal callers in history in the coming years, was understandably upset over the results of the play.

"This is without a doubt the most disappointing moment of my life," he said. "I'm disappointed that we lost, and I'm very disappointed that the loss might have something to do with a mistake that I made. But there's a lesson in here somewhere. You can't let down. We've still got a great team."

Ford, relieved that his team won, was hesitant to give the Tigers too much credit. "We don't deserve No. 1 because we didn't play well today. We are not ready for No. 1. We still have two more games to play, and we have to get ready."

With one of the most thrilling wins in school history behind them, the Tigers were ripe for a letdown against 3-5-1 Maryland. The Terrapins had owned Clemson for a decade, winning eight of the previous nine games in the series. This day would be different, however, as Jordan led the way for the Tigers, completing twenty passes for 270 yards and three touchdowns. Two went to Tuttle, who closed out his Death Valley career with 151 yards. All three Clemson scores came in the first half, as the Tigers came out and quickly ended any notion that Maryland could win. Tuttle's pair of touchdowns came first, with the last going to Jerry Gaillard in the second quarter. Gaillard was also playing his final game as a Tiger, and had agreed with Tuttle before the game that should he score, they were going to double-spike the pigskin in the end zone. It didn't quite work out that way, for after hauling in the 12-yard pass, Gaillard was mobbed by other teammates.

Once again the Tiger defense was on top of its game, allowing only 44 rushing yards on thirty attempts. The Terrapins would have been shut out if Jordan hadn't fumbled at his own 7 in the fourth quarter. Charlie Wysocki reached the end zone on the ensuing play, but it proved to be Maryland's lone highlight. With the win, Clemson officially locked up the ACC championship, and now needed only to topple the Gamecocks in Columbia to post the school's first unbeaten regular season in thirty-three years.

"We had a lot riding on that South Carolina game," recalled Chuck McSwain. "We used to listen to that old guy—Leonard's Losers. He picked us to lose the game! I remember Coach Ford made a point to tell us, 'you've still got people who don't believe in you.'"

The McSwain brothers proved to be unlikely heroes as the Tigers took South Carolina's best shot. With a chance to knock their hated rival out of the Orange Bowl, USC strapped it on and gave the Tigers all they could handle early on. Taking the ball on their first possession, South Carolina tore through the Tigers for 51 yards in eight plays. Johnnie Wright's tumble into the end zone from the 1 sent a roar through the Williams-Brice Stadium crowd, and gave the Gamecocks temporary momentum. The Tigers stole the show a few minutes later, when Rod McSwain broke through the line and blocked a punt. Johnny Rembert fell on it in the end zone, and although the extra point was no good, the sudden score took some of the wind out of South Carolina's sails.

Paulling added a field goal in the second quarter, which was followed by another big play by the defense. A pass was intercepted and returned to the USC 28, and from there Clemson went on to score its first offensive touchdown. From the 11, Jordan tucked the ball and piled in to give the Tigers a 15-7 advantage at halftime. South Carolina was far from dead, and used the midgame break to regroup. The Gamecocks went on another scoring march after retaking the field. A 10-yard touchdown pass thrown by Gordon Beckham brought USC to within two points of the Tigers, but his pass to tie the game went incomplete.

The Gamecocks lost their composure after the touchdown, and allowed the Tigers to assume control. Chuck McSwain, who had endured an up-and-down career at Clemson, rushed for 110 yards in the second half, propelling the Tigers on two scoring marches that led to victory. The drives were assisted by Gamecock errors, including a costly pass interference ruling and consecutive personal fouls. McSwain powered into the end zone from 1 yard out in the third quarter to push Clemson out in front 22-13, and it stayed that way into the fourth quarter.

On his way to being named ESPN's Amateur of the Week, McSwain continued to punish the Gamecocks. From the USC 23, McSwain finished Clemson's second successful drive of the second half with a spectacular carry. McSwain broke tackle after tackle, finally lumbering over the goal line after seemingly being in the clutches of every Gamecock defender. The inspiring run, which made the final score 29-13, was vindicating for a player who was figured to be Clemson's primary running weapon in 1981, yet had only rushed for 517 yards coming into the contest.

"I've been watching film and I've started running toward people rather than away from them," McSwain commented following his fine performance.

The coronation of Clemson's unbeaten regular season took place during the postgame locker room celebration, when Orange Bowl president Steve Hudson formally invited the Tigers to the game via telephone hookup. Dr. Bill Atchley accepted on behalf of Clemson University, and the ACC was sending one of its teams to Miami for the first time in twenty-four years. A week later the Tigers catapulted to No. 1 when Dan Marino and Pittsburgh were embarrassed on their home field 48-14 by Penn State.

North Carolina successfully fended off Virginia and Duke after the Clemson heartbreaker, and went to the Gator Bowl against Arkansas with nine wins. Lou Holtz's Razorbacks came into the game with eight victories, including a blowout over Texas and a 10-7 November triumph over Texas A&M. Carolina struck first with a field goal, but the Razorbacks answered quickly when quarterback Brad Taylor nailed Derek Holloway for a 66-yard score. The first Tar Heel touchdown came courtesy of Kelvin Bryant, who went over from the 1. An Arkansas field goal sent the game into halftime tied at 10.

Carolina dominated the third quarter, breaking out to a 24-10 lead with a running attack that overwhelmed the Arkansas defense. Ethan Horton and Bryant were a dynamic duo, each carrying the ball twenty-seven times and combining for 292 yards to share Most Valuable Player honors. Horton's contribution was imperative for Carolina to build their lead, as Bryant struggled at times with leg cramps. The Tar Heels had to hold off a furious Arkansas comeback, as Taylor, stifled most of the game by the UNC secondary, finally begin hitting his mark.

Taylor finished the night with 307 yards passing, and after Carolina took a 31-10 lead early in the fourth quarter, the Razorback signal-caller began bringing his team back. Taylor needed only seven plays to move Arkansas 80 yards, and after a successful two-point conversion, the Razorbacks recovered an onsides kick. Taylor's next pass was good to Gary Anderson for 40 yards, bringing Arkansas all the way down to the Tar Heel 3. Carolina dug in their heels and kept the Razorbacks out for three plays, but on fourth down Taylor found Darryl Mason. This time Holtz kicked, and it was suddenly a 31-25 game with 2:44 left.

Carolina took a safety to avoid a fiasco on special teams, and following a nice return on the free kick, Arkansas had a chance to pull off the comeback. An unlikely hero stepped up for Carolina in backup lineman Ronnie Snipes, who broke free of his block on third down and decked Taylor for a 17-yard loss. Taylor was off on his last pass, and the Tar Heels ran out the clock for a 31-27 verdict.

Clemson needed only to knock off Nebraska down in Miami for the school's first national championship in football. It would not be an easy task, as Tom Osborne brought a speedy and talented team east from Lincoln. As always, the Cornhuskers were solid offensively, using the wishbone to great success in averaging just under 35 points a game. With one-day Heisman Trophy winner Mike Rozier and future NFL star Roger Craig leading the way, Nebraska had won nine regular season games, and buried Oklahoma 37-14 in Norman to claim the Big Eight title.

Clemson's quest for college football supremacy began with another defensive gem, as nose tackle William Devane forced Cornhusker quarterback Mark Mauer into a bad pitch on the game's third play. Danny Triplett nailed Craig as he attempted to bring in the ball, and Devane was on it at the Nebraska 29. The Tigers could not mount a touchdown drive, but Igwebuike gave CU a 3-0 lead with a field goal.

Minutes later, Nebraska took a 7-3 advantage by becoming the only team all season to burn Clemson's defense on a single play. The Huskers fooled the Tigers with a perfectly executed halfback pass, as Rozier lured in Kinard and Anthony Rose after taking the ball from Mauer. Anthony Steels worked his way behind the Clemson defenders and took in a halfback pass from Rozier 25 yards to the end zone. The trick play momentarily shook up the Tigers, but it proved to be the only letdown by the defense. The unit forced Nebraska's proud offense into eight three-and-out possessions, and allowed them to cross midfield only four times. After pinning Nebraska deep in their own territory, the Tigers took a punt and moved into field goal range again. Igwebuike's kick was good, and the score was 7-6.

Clemson had no trouble moving against Nebraska for much of the game, and had a chance to take the lead on their following possession by marching to the Husker 10. Jordan found Tuttle open in the end zone, but a Husker defender grappled the ball out of his hands for an interception and touchback. Frustrating as the interception was for Clemson, it proved to be their only turnover. The Tigers took the lead at halftime when the Judge came up with another in a long line of great plays. The ACC's Player of the Year recovered a Nebraska fumble, and Cliff Austin swept into the end zone to thrust the Tigers into the lead, 12-7.

"I will never forget our locker room at halftime," recalled Tiger defensive end Bill Smith. "It was so emotionally high charged. Everyone was excited. We had the lead, we were having fun, and we knew we could win the national championship. There was no tension."

Clemson took control in the third quarter and moved ever so closer to their dream. With the defense continuing to stifle Nebraska, the Tiger offense took a balanced approach to keep the Cornhusker defense honest. Runs by McSwain and Jeff McCall were countered with passes from Jordan to Tuttle, as the Tigers ate up 75 yards in twelve plays. On third-and-goal from the Nebraska 13, Jordan faded into the pocket and hit Tuttle for the touchdown. The image of Tuttle with his hands triumphantly in the air, placed on the cover of the following week's *Sports Illustrated*, is one that Clemson fans will hold dear for years to come.

Now leading 19-7, the Tigers continued to dominate the third quarter by forcing another Cornhusker punt. Billy Davis returned the kick deep into Husker territory, and another field goal gave the Tigers a 22-7 cushion heading into the final quarter. The angry Huskers, completely outplayed by Clemson to this point, summoned up their strength to mount their first productive drive of the second half. Reaching the Tiger 26, Craig broke free for a touchdown run to make the score 22-15 at the 9:15 mark.

From there the Tigers played a fantastic game of keep-away, taking the ball with 7:49 remaining and withering the clock down to the final seconds. As Jordan scrambled all over the Orange Bowl turf, the Tigers maintained possession and kept the seconds coming off. Over the frantic final minutes, Clemson managed to slow down the momentum of Nebraska's quick reprieve. The Cornhuskers got the ball with six seconds left on the clock, but their last-ditch effort failed.

The celebrations back in South Carolina lasted long into the night, as Ford and his team hoisted the Atlantic Coast Conference's second national championship in the sport of football. The 1981 Tigers were a unique group, and stand as one of the great teams in the history of college football. Twenty-two players from the squad went on to play professionally, while others went on to successful careers in other professions. Clemson's meteoric rise to the top of the college football world would be fleeting, however, as Ford and the entire Tiger program would soon face the repercussions that come with scandal.

10

A Two-Team League (1982-1988)

Throughout much of the 1980s, Maryland and Clemson dominated the Atlantic Coast Conference on the gridiron. In the seven-year period from 1982 to 1988, the Tigers and Terrapins won every ACC football title, although Clemson suddenly found itself in hot water as a result of the school's immense recent success in football. During the rejuvenation of Tiger football under Charley Pell and Danny Ford in the late 1970s, Clemson began pushing the limits of fairness in order to stay at the top of the ACC standings. Over a short period of time, many standout high school players had signed letters-of-intent to Clemson, which caught the watchful eye of the NCAA.

In the months following CU's national championship run, the governing body began an extensive inquiry into the Tiger program. After a lengthy investigation, which included the questioning of present and former players, coaches, and institutional members, the NCAA determined that rules had been broken. As a result, Clemson University became the first and only ACC football program in history to receive major sanctions for recruiting violations. As it turned out, Clemson's fine teams of the late 1970s and early 1980s, including their 1981 national championship squad, included a substantial number of players that were illegally recruited. On November 22, 1982, the NCAA summarized its findings and issued a statement from their headquarters in Mission, Kansas. The following are excerpts from that report.

> In December 1980, a former assistant coach offered to provide a prospective student-athlete a substantial sum of cash and an automobile to sign a letter of intent. During the fall of 1978, a representative of the university's athletic interests offered to pay the costs

for the two sisters of a prospective student-athlete to attend the university. In 1978, the university awarded a scholarship to a friend of a prospective student-athlete.

During the 1980-1981 academic year, representatives of the university's athletic interests directly assisted a prospective student-athlete and his family in paying four telephone bills. In December 1980, a representative of the university's athletic interests gave a prospective student-athlete a substantial amount of cash in return for his signature on a letter of intent, as well as several other gifts. In December 1980, a representative of the university's athletic interests arranged for a substantial amount of cash to be given to a prospective student-athlete and provided the young man and his mother other gifts.

On numerous occasions during the 1980-1981 academic year, a representative of the university's athletic interests gave prospective student-athletes cash. In January 1978, a former assistant coach gave a prospective student-athlete's fiancée cash. In the fall of 1981 and again in late February 1982, an assistant football coach telephoned the father of a prospective student-athlete, the remarks on which reasonably could be interpreted as being requests to provide the NCAA false information concerning his son's recruitment by the university.

It was rumored that several of Clemson's best players over the last few seasons were involved in the scandal. In addition, the NCAA claimed the illegal activities had occurred under both Pell and Ford. Although Ford admitted to giving a recruit a car ride, he never admitted to paying any recruits. The sanctions laid down by the NCAA were swift and severe. The Tigers were banned from live television and bowl appearances through 1984, and were stripped of twenty scholarships. It was, at the time, the most scholarships ever taken away from a college football program for NCAA rule violations.

Although Clemson would remain a solid team during their probation years, the Tigers were unable in future years to recruit without the watchful eyes of rival coaches and the NCAA monitoring their every move. Since another violation could constitute the NCAA's "Death

Penalty," it was imperative for CU to clean up its tarnished image. Athletic director Bill McLellan used the sanctions to Clemson's advantage, orchestrating deals with up-and-coming cable stations ESPN and USA to show tape-delayed telecasts of Tiger games. The deal was within the limits of the NCAA restrictions, as the games were not being shown live. More importantly, the deals offered vital airtime to continue selling the Tiger program to prized recruits. As a result, Clemson continued to attract solid talent, and remained near the top of the ACC during their probation, despite the fact that their games did not count in the official standings.

Until the NCAA's ruling, the 1982 season had been another exciting one for Tiger fans. With Homer Jordan, Terry Kinard, William Perry, and Cliff Austin all back in Death Valley that fall, the Tigers were still plenty strong enough to win the ACC, and with a break here or there, possibly win a second straight national championship. An early-season stumble took away the chance for NCAA glory, but the Tigers once again proved superior to their conference rivals.

Ford took his troops into Sanford Stadium for a rare Monday night season opener against Georgia. As the last two NCAA championship schools, the Bulldogs and Tigers were each hoping to propel themselves into another title run. One advantage for Clemson was the fact that Herschel Walker was injured, nursing a fractured thumb on the hand in which he held the ball. The UGA standout wasn't much of a factor, carrying eleven times for 20 yards.

Georgia made up for Walker's lack of presence with a vengeful defensive effort. After giving up first blood to the Tigers in the first quarter, the Bulldogs kept CU off the scoreboard for the remainder of the game. The Clemson touchdown, which came on a draw play from Jordan, was set up by a Perry fumble recovery at the UGA 10. Early in the second quarter, the Tigers were pinned back at their own 10, and faced a punting situation. Georgia defensive end Dale Crowe broke cleanly through the CU line on the snap, and blocked Dale Hatcher's kick. The ball took a high carom off the turf, allowing Bulldog end Stan Dooley to run underneath it and stab it in the end zone. The Bulldogs added a pair of Kevin Butler field goals, and ended Clemson's thirteen-game winning streak with a 13-7 victory.

Stunned at the end of their national championship reign, the Tigers came out strong in the home opener against Boston College (BC). Eagle quarterback Doug Flutie, who came into the game ranked first in the NCAA in total offense, threw interceptions on two of BC's first three possessions. Kinard and Johnny Rembert came up with the passes for Clemson, and the Tiger offense came through to give the Tigers a

14-0 halftime lead. Boston College refused to fold, and after a long drive, Tony Stradford scored on an 11-yard play to cut the CU lead in half. Flutie led another scoring march to tie the game, and following a Clemson fumble, the Eagles took the lead on a field goal. The Tigers woke up after the turnover, and began a long, steady march into BC territory. Staying mostly on the ground, Clemson moved into range for Donald Igwebuike. A 43-yard kick at the 5:40 mark knotted the game up at 17-17, and neither team was able to reach the scoreboard again.

An easy win figured to come Clemson's way when Western Carolina (WCU) came to town, but the game was much more difficult than expected. The Tigers committed four turnovers in the first thirty minutes, allowing the underdog Cats to take a 10-9 lead. Frustrated at his team's offensive problems, Ford made a change at halftime. Mike Eppley, who doubled as the starting point guard on Clemson's basketball team, replaced Jordan at quarterback. Eppley, along with the Tiger defense, provided a much-needed lift, allowing CU to fend off the upset. After sticking WCU deep in its own territory early in the second half, Clemson retained possession and took the lead on a 6-yard run by Chuck McSwain. Minutes later, Rembert intercepted a pass and returned it 25 yards to the Western Carolina 7. Four plays later, McSwain bowled over again to give the Tigers a 21-10 margin of victory.

At 1-1-1, with their lone victory coming against a vastly inferior opponent, it was evident that the Tigers were not going to repeat as national champions. As it turned out, that was the least of Clemson's worries. As the Tigers were preparing to play Kentucky, rumors began swirling about an automobile purchase made recently by CU's most notable player. Homer Jordan had recently purchased a 1982 Chevrolet Monte Carlo, which was cosigned by a local businessman. Although it was unclear whether Jordan had violated any rules in cosigning the loan application, the NCAA's heightening investigation prompted Clemson president Bill Atchley to intervene. In a statement delivered one hour before kickoff against Kentucky, Atchley ordered Jordan to sit out the game.

Eppley started at quarterback in place of Jordan, and led Clemson to a convincing 24-6 triumph. As the defense stuffed UK's ballcarriers to -14 yards rushing, Eppley completed nine-of-thirteen passes for 95 yards. The Tigers rallied for three touchdowns under Eppley, and by the time he gave way to third-stringer Anthony Parete in the fourth quarter, CU was in complete control. Austin scored twice to lead the Tiger assault, and supported Jordan, who would later be cleared of any wrongdoing, in his postgame comments.

"I'm sure Homer feels like any other football player," said Austin. "He feels pressure. He wants to play. And yet here he is, not even injured, and not playing. It's got to hurt him."

Jordan returned to the CU backfield for the Virginia game, which happened to be the first night game in the history of Charlottesville's Scott Stadium. Although they struggled to move on their first two possessions, Clemson dominated the remainder of the first half. As Austin, McSwain, and Jeff McCall all ran up 100-yard games, the Tigers powered to a 34-0 lead. As the CU defenders stifled UVA's weak offensive unit, the offense added another pair of touchdowns to take a 48-0 final.

The Tiger offense continued to shine against Duke, as the unit overshadowed Ben Bennett and the potent Blue Devil attack. Although Duke managed 14 points, they never had a chance against Clemson's lethal running game. Austin, a thorn in the side of the Blue Devils for the second year in a row, ran for a school-record 260 yards, and scored twice to get the Tigers rolling. After building up a 28-14 lead at halftime, the Tigers scored 21 unanswered points to claim a 49-14 blowout. Parete came on at quarterback and threw two touchdowns, the last one good to Frank Magwood for 42 yards.

After taking an early 7-0 lead, N.C. State surrendered three consecutive touchdowns to the surging Tigers in CU's next contest. The Wolfpack revived, however, scoring the next 10 points. Leading 24-16 at halftime, Clemson began to pull away in the second half. Austin ran in from the NCSU 14 to top off a 109-yard performance, and McCall scored for a second time. With a comfortable 38-16 advantage, the Tiger defenders let their guard down late in the contest. State scored back-to-back touchdowns, making the score more competitive in the final reports. Unfortunately for State, their final score came with only nineteen seconds to play, giving them no time to complete the improbable comeback.

Returning home to play North Carolina, the Tigers were expecting another fierce challenge from the Tar Heels. Carolina and Clemson had played a pair of great contests in 1980 and 1981, and with UNC sitting at 5-2 coming into Death Valley this time around, it was clear that another difficult struggle would ensue. The Heels took an early lead on a field goal by Brooks Barwick, but the Tigers countered with a kick from Bob Paulling.

After Barwick nailed another 36-yarder for a 6-3 UNC lead, Clemson reached the end zone on a pass from Eppley to Magwood, and Paulling drilled another kick to give the Tigers a 13-6 halftime advantage. Carolina refused to go easily, marching through the orange pants of the Tiger defenders to tie the game at 13 in the second half. The Tigers roared back, going 49 yards to position Paulling for his third field goal. The kick, good from 46 yards, gave Clemson a 16-13 margin. Like the game in Chapel Hill the year before, the Tar Heels could not break the Tiger defense in the fourth quarter. Holding Kelvin Bryant to only 86 yards, Clemson hung on for the close victory.

A sellout crowd packed into Byrd Stadium for the Maryland-Clemson showdown, which would determine this season's ACC champion. Jerry Claiborne had left College Park after the 1981 season to return to his alma mater, the University of Kentucky. Bobby Ross came aboard and the Terrapins enjoyed a smooth transition. After dropping their first two games, Maryland had reeled off seven consecutive victories, and came into the Clemson contest with a 4-0 record in ACC play. One of the biggest reasons for Maryland's success in 1982 was their ability to hang onto the football. After losing only six fumbles in nine games, the Terrapins came unglued against the fierce pressure of the Tigers.

Maryland put three balls on the deck that the Tigers recovered, and along with two interceptions, Clemson jumped out to a 24-7 lead early in the fourth quarter. With their backs against the wall, Maryland quarterback Boomer Esiason led the Terrapins back into the game. After throwing a 37-yard touchdown to Greg Hill, Esiason led UM downfield for another score to close the gap to 24-22. With the Tiger offense suddenly in a lull, it was left up to the defense to seal victory. The Terrapins got the ball back late, and were content on running the clock down to a last-second field goal attempt. With 3:48 remaining, Maryland was successfully driving toward the winning score. It was then that Terry Kinard showed why he would go on to be named National Defensive Player of the Year by CBS. In a pivotal effort, Kinard drilled John Tice with a vicious hit, forcing the ball loose. Reggie Pleasant came up with the trophy, and the Tigers escaped with the victory.

The week of the South Carolina game provided a number of distractions for the Tigers. Although they were once again the cream of the ACC crop, it was becoming evident that the NCAA was about to impose sanctions on the CU program. The severity of the probation was unknown at the time, but the Clemson players were hopeful that it wouldn't take away from what had been another fine season in Death Valley.

"This team, this year, deserves a bowl game," said Austin. "I know that being a senior, that was one of my goals from the start. But with all the adversity, distractions, and talk of probation, it deserves a bowl even more. It was just one thing after another this year. A slow start, then the probation thing. But I guess the NCAA feels like it has to set an example with someone."

The Tigers put the probation talk far behind them when they took the field against USC, and completed their second consecutive unbeaten season at home with a 24-6 verdict. Clemson stuck to what they did best, running the ball sixty-two times. The Gamecocks put only two field goals on the board, as they were punished all day by the Tiger defenders. Austin scored two touchdowns in his final game at Memorial Stadium, while McSwain added a score and Paulling connected on a field goal for CU's final points.

The day after the NCAA made its ruling, the Clemson players and staff boarded a plane bound for Tokyo, where they would meet Wake Forest in the Mirage Bowl. It was the first football game in league history to be played outside of the United States, and provided the team a temporary break from the rumors and speculation that were swirling throughout the state of South Carolina. Although they were not allowed to play in a postseason game due to ACC sanctions, separate of those laid down by the NCAA, the Tigers could take solace in the fact that victory over Wake ensured another league championship. Considering the Tokyo game their "bowl," the Tigers got off to a fine start with a 16-7 first quarter lead. After Paulling booted a 43-yard field goal to give CU a 19-10 edge going into the fourth quarter, Clemson had to withstand a Demon Deacon comeback bid.

Early in the final frame, WF quarterback Gary Schofield located receiver Tim Ryan, who made the reception 30 yards downfield and broke free along the sidelines. Following Ryan's 84-yard touchdown, the Deacons marched deep into Clemson territory again, forcing CU to clamp down on the goal line. As the Japanese spectators chanted, "Dewhence, Dewhence," the Tiger resistance held tough. Following a reversal of field position, Clemson tacked on its final points with a William Devane sack in the end zone. The Mirage Bowl victory gave Clemson a nine-game winning streak to finish the year, but it was a bittersweet conclusion. With no postseason contest to play in, the Tigers had no choice but to look back on what they did accomplish with pride.

Maryland and North Carolina once again represented the ACC in postseason games, each playing on Christmas Day. The Tar Heels played No. 8 Texas in the Sun Bowl, and for the second time in three years, UNC upset the favored Longhorns. Carolina's strong defense, led by All-American lineman William Fuller, shut down Texas in the second half, allowing the Tar Heels to take the lead and a 26-10 final score.

Maryland spent the Christmas holiday in paradise, taking on Washington in Honolulu's first Aloha Bowl. Esiason threw two touchdown passes to keep the Terrapins in the game, and a run by John Nash gave UM an 18-14 lead in the fourth quarter. Following a two-point conversion that made the score 20-14, Washington began a drive that resulted in the game-winning score. With six seconds to play, Tim Cowan threw his third touchdown pass, hitting Anthony Allen. The ensuing extra point sent the Huskies to a thrilling 21-20 victory.

In 1983, Maryland began a run of ACC supremacy similar to the one they enjoyed in the 1970s under Jerry Claiborne. As Clemson began its two-year probation period, the Terrapins coasted to an 8-4 record, which included six victories in conference play. Norman Esiason, nicknamed "Boomer" by his mother at birth because of his incessant kicking in the womb, led the Terrapins offensively. A nifty Southpaw that combined escape ability with a cannon for a throwing arm, Esiason was the first in a string of top-notch signal callers to line up under center for Bobby Ross at Maryland. Wide receiver Greg Hill and running backs Rick Badanjek and Willie Joyner assisted Esiason in leading the UM offensive charges. Defensively, the Terrapins were paced by linebacker Eric Wilson and defensive back Clarence Baldwin, who were each named to the ACC's first team. Wilson was a fearsome presence throughout the season in Maryland's front seven, while Baldwin led the league in interceptions.

The Terrapins opened with an uninspiring 21-14 verdict over Vanderbilt, coming from behind to seize victory. Following an interception deep in their own territory with 3:24 remaining, the Terrapin offense, frustrated by three fumbles and nearly 100 yards in penalties, returned to the field. On the first play following the turnover, Esiason launched a bomb from the lip of his own goal line. Hill, who was taken down at the Vanderbilt 47, snared the pass with a well-timed jump. Three plays later, Esiason threw a short pass to tight end Bill Rogers, who came back for the pass, spun around his defender, and raced downfield for an electrifying 43-yard touchdown, which proved to be the winning play.

In week two, Maryland ran into a West Virginia brick wall, as the Mountaineers stuffed the Terrapin running game for only 95 yards. Mistakes again plagued UM's performance, as a dropped ball by Hill kept the Terrapins from taking an early 14-0 lead. The inability to capitalize rattled Maryland's confidence, and behind quarterback Jeff Hostetler, the Mountaineers rallied to a 31-21 win.

Maryland returned to form against No. 16 Pittsburgh, stunning the Panthers in Byrd Stadium. Esiason was relegated to the bench, having sprained ligaments in his nonthrowing shoulder. Frank Reich got the starting nod and was effective, throwing for 155 yards. In the second quarter, with UM trailing 7-3, walk-on Doug Cox worked his way through the Pitt punt unit and blocked a kick. Cox caught the fluttering pigskin and raced untouched 32 yards for a touchdown. It was the only goal line crossing of the day for the Terps, as their offense was again largely unproductive. Cox's play, sandwiched between a pair of field goals by Jess Atkinson, was all the Terrapins needed in the 13-7 triumph, as the opportunistic UM defenders recovered three fumbles.

Ross's troops opened up their conference slate against Virginia, and kept things simple in a 23-3 victory. Behind their stacked offensive line, the Terrapins were content to give the ball time and again to their backfield tandem of Badanjek and Joyner. The pair combined for 205 yards on forty-four carries, as the Terrapins pounded the Cavaliers between the tackles and on the outside.

Badanjek injured his foot against the Cavaliers, but the back was back to strength for Syracuse. Although the Orangemen played Maryland tough, and actually were within a touchdown in the fourth quarter, they were unable to capitalize. With a first-and-goal on the Terrapin 9-yard line, the Orangemen were held at bay thanks in large part to a Wilson sack. A field goal attempt was missed, and Syracuse's chances for victory were dashed. The Terrapins moved 80 yards, and Dave D'Addio's touchdown on his fourth consecutive carry from inside the 2 propelled UM to a 34-13 win.

Like they did against Syracuse, the Terps gave Wake Forest every chance to win, giving away three fumbles and playing poorly on defense. Gary Schofield, Wake's strong-armed quarterback, had his third consecutive solid outing against UM, throwing for 365 yards. Trailing 26-14 in the third quarter, the Terrapins began to surge behind Esiason, who had one of his finest games in a Maryland uniform. After throwing a pair of touchdowns to Hill, Esiason found Sean Sullivan for a 30-yard score to put the game on ice. Wake had again taken the lead, this time 33-29, on a 55-yard pass from Schofield to Tim Ryan. The Terrapins got the ball back with just over a minute remaining, and Esiason's pass to Sullivan kept Maryland's championship hopes alive.

With Wake Forest out of the way, the Terrapins settled down and laid the wood to Duke 38-3 back in College Park. Blue Devil quarterback Ben Bennett was frustrated by the pressure of the Maryland front, and was held without a touchdown pass for the first time in eighteen contests. It was also the first time under his command that the Blue Devils were held out of the end zone, a total of twenty-seven games. As the Terrapins pushed Bennett and the Blue Devil offense all over the field, Esiason had another solid performance, throwing for 198 yards and a touchdown. The only negative for Maryland was the loss of the fullback D'Addio, who went down with a separated shoulder. D'Addio was lost for the UNC game and the remainder of the season.

On October 29, the stage was set for the ACC's showcase game of 1983, as North Carolina made the trek to College Park. The No. 3 Tar Heels had overwhelmed their opposition thus far in running up a 7-0 record, averaging over 35 points each time they stepped on the field. With Clemson out of the picture, it was evident that the UNC-UM game would dictate the fate of the conference race. If history were any indicator, the Terrapins would have preferred a few thousand of the 51,200 fans to have stayed home. Maryland had lost their last six home dates when the attendance surpassed 50,000.

With an 18-mph wind swirling through College Park for much of the afternoon, Maryland surged out to a 10-0 first quarter lead. In the second quarter, with the wind now at their own backs, the Tar Heels took control. Scott Stankavage, third in the NCAA in passing efficiency, led Carolina on a 17-point scoring barrage, which gave the Tar Heels a 17-10 lead into the locker rooms. The second half brought the wind advantage back to the Terrapins, and Esiason, playing for the final time at Byrd Stadium, went on a rampage.

Esiason threw a pair of touchdowns, and paced another drive into UNC territory that led to a Jess Atkinson field goal. The swing put Maryland in command of a 28-17 score, but Carolina got the wind back for the decisive fourth quarter, and notched a field goal to cut Maryland's lead to 28-20. With twenty-two seconds to play, UNC scored a dramatic touchdown, cutting Maryland's lead to 28-26 and setting the stage for one of Byrd Stadium's most memorable plays. With Carolina forced to go for two, Stankavage rolled back to pass. Tyrone Anthony was open for an instant, but Stankavage's pass was wide, too much for the lunging Anthony to handle. As the ball settled onto the turf, a sea of Maryland fans poured onto the field.

Although there was still time for the Tar Heels to attempt an onside kick, the field was instantly covered with hundreds of Terrapin supporters, who were worked into a frenzy by their team's supposed victory. Before order could be restored, a large group of fans tore down one of the goalposts, which created an interesting scenario. Since the Terrapins were given a 15-yard penalty after Carolina's failed two-point effort, there was a chance that a new set of goalposts would have to be installed so UNC could attempt a game-winning field goal. It was not to be, however, as Carolina's hands team was ruled offside on the short kick. The loss sent the once-indomitable Tar Heels on a free fall, as they went on to drop three of their last four games, including a heartbreaker at Virginia and a 28-3 whitewashing by Florida State in the Peach Bowl.

Now ranked No. 7 in the country, the Terrapins headed south to play another No. 3 opponent. Pat Dye, Auburn's former Heisman winner and now head coach of the Tigers, had assembled a furious running attack, led by Lionel James, Tommy Agee, and freshman phenom Bo Jackson. Auburn was also 7-1, on their way to the Southeastern Conference championship and victory over Michigan in the Sugar Bowl. The Terrapins played the home-standing Tigers tough, taking the lead in the second half, but they were no match for the powerful Auburn running game. A series of scoring drives, in addition to a late defensive score, gave the home-standing Tigers a 35-23 verdict.

With their hopes of a national championship and New Year's Day bowl eliminated, the Terrapins came out sluggish against Clemson. The sea of orange in Death Valley unquestionably played a factor, as Esiason was forced to halt the game on two separate occasions due to crowd noise. The spirited group created a spectacle before kickoff, releasing more than 350,000 orange balloons into the sky. Another, more decisive factor, was Clemson's punishing running game, which piled up 350 yards. A pair of touchdown passes by Mike Eppley got the Tigers going, and were followed by two scoring runs by Kevin Mack, who finished the day with 186 yards on thirty carries. Hopelessly behind 28-7 at the half, things only got worse for Maryland in the final thirty minutes.

As CU continued to run effortlessly between the tackles, another pair of touchdowns in the third quarter turned the game into an official blowout. Trailing 42-7, and staring one of the worst losses in school history directly in the face, the Terrapins finally got things going offensively. Esiason led the Terps on successive scoring drives, completing each possession with sneaks into the end zone. Clemson continued to pour on the points, and left the field with a convincing 52-24 victory, one in which no honor could be salvaged on the part of the Terrapins.

With North Carolina's surprising loss to Virginia the same afternoon, the dejected Terrapins learned afterwards that they were the "official" ACC champions. Despite a 7-0 mark in league play, which ran Clemson's unofficial conference winning streak to nineteen games, none of their victories counted in the league standings. Although they would be staying home for the Holidays, everyone, from the Tiger fans, chanting "ACC, ACC," to the players and coaches, knew who the real champions were.

"Yeah, we've whipped everybody in the ACC," said Clemson defensive lineman Ray Brown. "Maryland can go away as ACC champs, but after the whipping we gave the Terps, they know we're the real ACC champions."

Esiason agreed. "Who wants a ring with one loss like this in it? Clemson's part of the ACC whether we like it or not, and this loss tarnishes our title."

Tarnished as it may have been, the Terrapins were the recognized champions, and they turned things around in their regular season finale by dismantling N.C. State, 29-6. The Maryland offense clicked like no other time during the season, piling up 490 yards against the Wolfpack. Badanjek and Joyner each had solid games, combining for 260 yards. The scrappy Badanjek, who spent much of the game running with NCSU defenders on his back, put the Terrapins ahead, 18-0, early in the fourth quarter with a 1-yard push over the goal line. The Terrapins put the game away in the final quarter with Atkinson's second field goal and a short run by Tommy Neal.

With Mickey Mouse and Pluto traipsing around the sidelines in the closing moments, it was evident that Maryland was going to get invited to Orlando and the Florida Citrus Bowl. The official word came amid hoots and hollers from the Terrapin players in the locker room, who had overcome adversity and injuries to claim the school's first ACC championship in seven years. Maryland faced Tennessee in the Citrus Bowl, who had finished fourth in the SEC behind Auburn, Georgia, and Florida. The Volunteers had won eight regular season games, their highest win total since 1972. Along the way, Tennessee (UT) had gone a perfect 4-0 in October, and had won seven of their final eight regular season games.

The Terrapins had their opportunities, consistently moving the ball into Volunteer territory. Despite all their chances, the Terps had to settle for three Atkinson field goals in the first half. One of the reasons for Maryland's inability to reach the end zone in the first half was the loss of Esiason, who separated his shoulder in the second quarter. Reggie White, UT's 6-5, 270-pound "Minister of Defense," leveled Boomer on a pass attempt, throwing him to the ground directly onto his throwing shoulder. Although Esiason tried to retake the field moments later, the injury was too much to overcome. As Frank Reich assumed command of the Terrapin offense, Esiason struggled with the news that he could not continue playing, and stood alone for several minutes along the sidelines.

Tennessee scored the only touchdown of the first half on a 12-yard pass from Alan Cockrell to Lenny Taylor, and took a 10-9 lead on a Fuad Reveiz field goal going into the break. Trailing 20-16 heading into the final quarter, the Volunteers owned Maryland in the final fifteen minutes, converting turnovers into 14 unanswered points. Johnnie Jones, who led the way for Tennessee with 154 yards on twenty-nine carries, reached the end zone both times on short carries. Reveiz converted both extras, giving Tennessee a 30-20 advantage. Although Atkinson was good from 26 yards out later in the period, the Terrapins could get no closer. The 30-23 setback was Maryland's fifth consecutive loss to Tennessee dating back to 1952, and the school's fourth bowl defeat in a row.

The Terrapins returned many of the regulars from their resurgent 1983 squad the following year, and won the ACC championship for the second year in a row. Boomer Esiason had moved on to the NFL, but Frank Reich was ready to step in and fill his shoes. Reich had been able to get quite a bit of work in 1983, leading the Terps to victory over Pitt and nearly propelling them to a win in the Citrus Bowl. With Badanjek, Hill, and Tommy Neal all returning offensively, and Eric Wilson and Al Covington coming back on defense, there was no question that the Terrapins were still a potent team.

Things got off on the wrong foot against Syracuse, however, as the Orangemen avenged their loss from 1983 with a surprising upset in College Park. After marching all the way on their opening drive to take a 7-0 lead, the Terrapins stopped Syracuse cold on their first drive. The Terrapins drove to their own 33, where Reich connected with highly touted freshman Azizuddin Abdur-Ra'oof for a 67-yard touchdown. Sadly for Abdur Ra'oof and Maryland, the play was wiped away by a holding penalty. Like they often do, the penalty took the wind out of the sails of the Maryland offense, which turned the ball over on five of six possessions during one disastrous stretch in the second half. The score was tied midway through the third quarter, and by the time the turnover spree was over, Syracuse was leaving Byrd Stadium with a decisive 23-7 triumph.

Things didn't get much better in Maryland's next game, played against Vanderbilt. Although they held onto the football this time, UM was unable to capitalize on their many opportunities against the Commodores. On the second play from scrimmage, the Terrapins recovered a Vanderbilt fumble. With a golden opportunity from the Commodore 21, Reich was sacked for a big loss, one of six he would take on the day, and the Terrapins had no choice but to kick a field goal. A dropped pass near the goal line in the second half took away what would have been the go-ahead score, and the steady passing of Vanderbilt quarter-back Kurt Page held off the Terrapins, 23-14, sending them to a 0-2 record. After the contest, a visibly shaken Ross struggled for an explanation.

"I'm as disappointed as I've ever been in coaching," said Ross, who refused to allow his team to come out of the locker room to answer questions, a first for the Maryland skipper. "I feel like I'd just like to get away from it all, but I know I can't do that. I hate losing; I hate it with a passion. I have to evaluate myself as a coach and professionally."

Some answers came against West Virginia, as the Terrapins simply refused to accept another defeat. Trailing 14-10 late in the third quarter, Reich led the Terps on a 68-yard drive that provided a 17-14 advantage with twelve minutes left. Although the Mountaineers came back to tie it at the 6:53 mark, Reich paced another drive that led to victory. Mixing the run and the pass, Reich took the Terrapins from their own 13 to the doorstep of the West Virginia goal line. From the 16, facing a third-and-7, Reich peeled away from defensive pressure and found Hill, who caught the pass and went down at the 4. Although a touchdown was called back due to illegal motion, Atkinson came on and coolly connected with 21 seconds left to lift Maryland to a 20-17 triumph.

The Terps had to depend largely on backup quarterback Stan Gelbaugh in the ACC opener against Wake Forest, as Reich went down with a separated shoulder. Gelbaugh, who dedicated his performance to his cancer-stricken high school coach, was handed a 24-17 lead by Reich. Gelbaugh came on and was a perfect six-for-six passing, leading UM to another pair of scores to put away the Demon Deacons. The 38-17 win was Maryland's fifth in a row over Wake Forest.

That same afternoon, Georgia Tech shocked No. 13 Clemson, 28-21, in Atlanta. Bill Curry had done a remarkable turnaround of the GT program in four seasons, taking Tech from the bottom of the league to their first 3-0 start since 1970. The Tigers had won twenty consecutive ACC contests, but were stung early and often by the Yellow Jackets. Georgia Tech jumped out to a 21-0 halftime lead behind quarterback John Dewberry, who finished the game with 188 yards passing.

Mike Eppley led Clemson on a furious second half surge, knotting the game at 21 on a 13-yard pass to receiver Terrance Roulhac. Over ten minutes remained when Roulhac found the end zone, and the game remained tied until the closing minutes. Tech began its final drive at their own 46, taking to the ground against the spent Tiger defense. Robert Lavette and reserve Chuck Easley did the damage, alternating for all nine carries on the march. Lavette's 13-yard carry put Tech in position at the Clemson 1, and Easley sealed the deal by scoring with thirty-three seconds left.

Maryland stepped out of the league the following week for a showdown with Penn State, and although the Nittany Lions had toppled the Terps nineteen consecutive times, on this day Maryland gave PSU all they could handle. Unfortunately for Maryland, they lost the game in the most bitter of fashions, as time ran out before they could set up a game-winning kick. Trailing 25-24 with less than ten seconds on the clock, Gelbaugh completed a long pass to Sean Sullivan that brought the ball to the PSU 35. The clock was stopped with four seconds remaining, and the Terrapins were hoping to get to the football, down it, and allow Atkinson to come on for a long field goal attempt.

Someone on the Terrapin sideline yelled for the field goal unit to take the field *then*, before the ball could be snapped and spiked by Gelbaugh. Several of the Terrapin offensive players saw the field goal unit coming onto the field and began trudging off. As a result, the Terrapins had a mixture of offensive and special teams players on the field in those critical moments, and the officials had no choice but to call an illegal procedure penalty against Maryland. In order to keep teams from purposely committing penalties to delay the game in the final minutes, the clock started back once the ball was spotted, and time ran out before a kick could be attempted.

The Terrapins bounced back after the PSU setback, and dealt a punishing blow to N.C. State, scoring 30 points in the first half. Maryland's offensive line worked over the Wolfpack front, allowing the backs to amass a total of 334 yards rushing. Badanjek led the way with 95 yards and three touchdowns, while Gelbaugh put forth his most solid performance yet, throwing for 230 yards and scoring on a short bootleg in the 44-21 win.

Gelbaugh's effort created something of a quarterback controversy in College Park, as the Terrapins entered a bye week before their matchup in Durham against Duke. Gelbaugh, who had ironically asked to be moved to wide receiver after Reich's appointment to starting quarterback, suddenly found himself the toast of the town. Gelbaugh kept his first-string position for the Blue Devil game, and proved his mettle by throwing three touchdown passes in a dazzling first half performance. Neal added 122 yards rushing and a score of his own, as the Terrapins pounded Duke, 43-7.

The Tar Heels were next for Maryland in Chapel Hill, and this time around there would be no need for a wild postgame celebration. Behind the powerful running of Badanjek, the Terrapins made quick work of UNC, completing a four-game sweep of their conference rivals from the state of North Carolina. In the second half, Maryland seized the line of scrimmage, and just as they had done against N.C. State, the Terrapin line began moving UNC's defense off the ball. Badanjek scored four touchdowns, with the final one coming in the fourth quarter, to give the Terps a commanding 34-16 advantage. As the Kenan Stadium faithful began making their way to the exits, Reich came on and helped the Terrapins run out the clock.

Maryland next headed to Miami's Orange Bowl for their final non-conference game of the regular season. Under first-year head coach Jimmy Johnson, Miami was not the same team that had shocked Nebraska for the national championship the previous January. The Hurricanes had dropped early-season contests to Michigan and Florida State, and were no longer in the picture to defend their title. Despite the setbacks, Miami was still a Top Ten team, and were hoping to play in a major bowl again following the regular season.

The Hurricanes were nothing short of spectacular in the first half, jumping out to a 31-0 lead. Sensational was the word to describe Miami quarterback Bernie Kosar, who expertly mixed his targets to the tune of 240 yards and three touchdowns in the first thirty minutes. The frustrated Terrapin defenders could not get to Kosar, failing to sack him even once in the first half. The Hurricane defense was just as productive as the offense, holding Maryland to only 57 total yards. Needless to say, Ross was not happy with his team's performance. He warned his team in the locker room at halftime that a similar effort in the second half would lead to a practice session that night upon returning home to College Park.

Ross also notified Reich that he would be starting the second half under center. Gelbaugh, who had been more than sufficient in propelling Maryland's winning streak, wasn't getting it done against the Hurricanes. It was the perfect opportunity for Reich to reassert himself as Maryland's go-to guy. The Hurricanes returned to the field for the second half an overconfident group, and came out taunting the Terrapins, asking and pleading with them to make it a close game. Reich came out slinging, connecting with Hill in the early moments for a 39-yard touchdown. After the defense forced a Hurricane punt, Reich went to work again, completing a third down pass to Hill that put the Terrapins on the Miami 1. A dive over the line pulled Maryland to within 31-14.

Kosar kept the pressure on Maryland, completing a screen pass to running back Melvin Bratton. Bratton broke into the clear, and looked to be on the way to a long touchdown before Keeta Covington walked him down. The play gained 53 yards, and although nobody could have known it at that time, Covington's tackle may very well have saved the game for the Terrapins. The UM defenders held tough after the long gain by Bratton, and forced the Hurricanes to kick a field goal.

Now trailing 34-14, Maryland continued to fight its way back. Reich, gaining confidence by the second, led his team on a work-manlike 80-yard march, completing long passes to Badanjek and Abdur-Ra'oof. The series ended on a completion from Reich to Alvin Blount, coming on third down from the Miami 1. The third quarter ended with Maryland in much better shape than they had been at half-time, now trailing 34-21.

With their passing game now running on all cylinders, the Terps keyed up Miami on their next possession by moving to the ground. The Hurricanes were off their game by this point, and Maryland found the going easy on the 55-yard drive. From the Miami 14, Neal took a hand-off to the left and raced his way to the goal. The extra point made the score 34-28, and was just the beginning of the nightmare for the Canes. Upon getting the ball back, Reich dropped into the pocket and located Hill. The pass was underthrown, and Miami free safety Darrell Fullington appeared to have an easy interception locked away. Surprisingly, the pass sailed through Fullington's hands and directly into Hill's, who snagged the tipped ball and raced to the end zone from 68 yards away.

It was bedlam on the Terrapin sideline as the extra point split the uprights, giving Maryland its first lead at 35-34. Less than a minute later the Terps scored again, as Badanjek piled over from the 4. The scoring play was set up by a Hurricane fumble on the previous kickoff. In an amazing turn of events, Maryland had outscored Miami 42-3 in the second half to take a 42-34 advantage.

The Hurricanes were not finished, and although Kosar threw an interception with less than three minutes remaining, Miami got a final crack at the Terps. The Hurricane defense forced a punt, and a bad snap provided excellent field position deep in Maryland territory. From the 5, Kosar connected with Eddie Brown to pull Miami to within two at 42-40. With fifty seconds left, the Hurricanes had no choice but to go for two and try to salvage a tie. Kosar faded back and nailed Bratton short of the goal. Covington was on top of the play, and brought the Miami tailback down 2 yards out of the end zone.

The Hurricanes attempted a desperation short kick, but Joe Kraus was on the spot for the Terrapins. In another surprising twist, Kraus ran the ball all the way back to the Miami 1 before going to the ground. The Terps could have tacked on another score for good measure, but Ross ordered Reich to take a knee. As the closing seconds ticked off, the Terrapin skipper was given a victory ride by his jubilant team. Maryland's victorious comeback from 31 points behind was the largest in the history of major college football, surpassing Oregon State's 28-point recovery against Fresno State in 1981.

"This is a game we'll remember for the rest of our lives," Ross said in the locker room, after making sure to tell his players that there would not be practice that night after all. "There were so many things that make this the greatest comeback I've ever been involved in. The 31-0 score, playing in this place before their fans, playing the defending national champions, the team that is No. 6 in the country."

It would not be the final time that Reich staged a miraculous comeback in a backup role. In 1992, as a member of the Buffalo Bills, Reich led an almost identical rally against the Houston Oilers in an AFC Wild Card Playoff game. Playing in place of the injured Jim Kelly, Reich's Bills trailed Houston 35-3 early in the second half. Reich went on to throw four touchdown passes in the third and fourth quarters, leading Buffalo to an improbable 41-38 overtime victory that still stands as the greatest comeback in National Football League history.

The elation of the Miami victory carried over to Maryland's ensuing contest with Clemson, played in Baltimore's Memorial Stadium. The Tigers, in the second and final year of NCAA probation, stood at 7-2 overall, with road defeats against Georgia and Georgia Tech. Although it would not count officially, victory over Maryland would give Clemson bragging rights to another conference championship, which would, at least in theory, make four in a row. The Tiger seniors, who had been freshmen on the national championship team of 1981, had endured a roller coaster college football experience, none more so than William Perry, dubbed "The Refrigerator" by teammates for his girth and voracious appetite.

The lovable lineman, who once spent twenty-two dollars on a single meal at McDonalds, finished his Clemson career as the ACC's Most Valuable Player, joining Randy White and Lawrence Taylor as the only defenders at that time to earn the honor. Perry led the nation in tackles for a loss with twenty-seven, and tied a Clemson school record with ten sacks. A finalist for the Lombardi Award, Perry became the first CU player in history to be named All-American three times. Despite his individual excellence and that of the Tiger teams he played on, the Refrigerator played in only one bowl, and after his sophomore season, never again appeared on live television in a Clemson uniform.

In a matchup of All-Americans, Perry and Terrapin center Kevin Glover went at it all afternoon. With help on double-teams from guards Lenny Lynch and Jeff Harraka, Glover neutralized Perry, and the Terrapin running backs found gaping holes to run through. Using misdirection plays to confuse the Tiger front, Maryland reeled off six drives of 70 or more yards over the course of the game. The 41-23 final was the first November setback for the Tigers in four years, and ensured the Terrapins another ACC title if they could knock off Virginia the following week in Charlottesville.

George Welsh had done an impressive job pumping life into the Virginia program, taking a program with only one winning season in ACC competition and turning it into a contender almost overnight. Unfortunately for UVA, Badanjek took out a personal vendetta, as he enjoyed his finest game yet as a Terrapin. Rushing for 217 yards, Badanjek went on a pair of long runs to give the Terrapins an insurmountable 38-21 advantage, and avenged his not being named to the All-Conference team. Don Majkowski had another productive game for Virginia, throwing for 219 yards and leading five Cavalier drives of 78 or more yards. In the end it was not enough, as Maryland left Charlottesville with a 45-34 win, their sixth in a row since the Penn State heartbreaker. Over the course of the winning streak, the Terrapins had scored no less than 34 points in any single outing.

A rematch with Tennessee was waiting for Maryland in El Paso's Sun Bowl, and this time around things got a little crazy. The week was a wild one for both schools, filled with late-night trips into Mexico, raids by police forces dressed as bandits, and some pregame jawing at a party that nearly led to fisticuffs. Once it was time to play, Tennessee quickly asserted itself as the team to beat. The Volunteers jumped on Maryland big in the early going, scoring three unanswered touchdowns to take a 21-0 halftime lead. The Tennessee defense held the Terrapins to only 55 yards in the first half, as UT did whatever it wanted on both sides of the football. It was complete domination over the first thirty minutes for the orange and white, but the Volunteers should have known to be ready for a Terrapin comeback in the second half.

"I reminded our players that the lead wasn't invincible," Tennessee head coach Johnny Majors said later. "I mentioned the Terps' 42-40 victory over Miami so many times that I didn't think it needed saying again too much. I emphasized I didn't want us to play tight or in fear."

Maryland was a different team in the second half, taking the initiative on their opening possession and going 77 yards to their first score. It was a role-reversal of sorts, as Tennessee's offense suddenly fell apart at the hands of a fired-up Terrapin defense. After giving up 198 yards in the opening half, the Maryland defenders went into lockdown, allowing Tennessee only 82 yards the rest of the way and no points. As the defense stifled UT, Reich and the Terrapin offense finally got on track. Held in check throughout the disastrous first half, Reich began to hit his receivers. The senior led Maryland to another pair of scores in the third quarter, including a 40-yard touchdown to tight end Ferrell Edmunds that gave the Terrapins a 22-21 lead.

Leading, 28-27, late in the contest, Maryland needed a brilliant defensive play to keep Tennessee from claiming victory. With the ball in Maryland territory, Volunteer quarterback Tony Robinson faded back into the pocket, then suddenly took off upfield on a draw play. Robinson juked past Al Covington at the 30, and looked to be off to the races. Then, from out of nowhere came Al's brother Keeta, who had saved the day in Miami a month earlier with an open-field tackle. Keeta drilled Robinson, dislodging the ball and sending it backwards 5 yards. Al got to his feet and fell on the pigskin with 1:12 remaining. The Terrapins easily ran out the clock, and took their first bowl victory since 1977.

A week later, Virginia met Purdue in the Peach Bowl. The Cavaliers would have their hands full in Atlanta trying to stop Boilermaker quarterback Jim Everett. Although Purdue was only 7-4 during the regular season, Everett had enjoyed a stellar campaign, leading the Big Ten in total offense with over 2,400 yards. Virginia was in uncharted waters, playing in a postseason game for the first time in history. They didn't play like it early on, as Howard Petty gave UVA a 7-0 first quarter lead on an 11-yard touchdown run.

Everett had a field day in the first thirty minutes, hitting his mark time after time in leading the Boilers to a 24-14 lead. In the locker room at halftime, Welsh and his assistants devised a strategy for pulling UVA back into the game. First, they would have to apply more pressure on Everett, who had been able to sit back and make decisions with little resistance thus far. Second, they would have to establish the run, which would force Purdue to play more honestly on defense. Both strategies worked like a charm, as Virginia began to relentlessly blitz the Boilermakers. Everett was rushed repeatedly, and was never able to get back on track.

As the Cavalier defense stalled Everett and the Purdue offense, the UVA running attack finally began to pick up some momentum. Using a repertoire of running plays both inside and outside, the Cavaliers mounted nearly 200 yards on the ground in the final half, as Petty finished with a game-high 114 yards to take Player of the Game honors. With the game tied, the final period was a frantic struggle for ball control, as each team sought to get into range for a game-winning field goal.

The Cavaliers got their opportunity first, driving down to the Purdue 1 with less than eight minutes remaining. At the 7:17 mark, a field goal gave Virginia a 27-24 lead. The Boilermakers came winging downfield on the arm of Everett, moving into Cavalier territory until the junior quarterback made a fatal error. Pressured by the UVA front, Everett lofted a dangerous pass into the secondary that was picked off by Ray Daly. With an opportunity to wrap it up, Virginia ran out the clock by stringing together a drive consisting of four consecutive first downs. With the Peach Bowl triumph in hand, Virginia had its first victory in the month of December in twenty-two years.

With nineteen returning seniors, Maryland kept the excitement flowing throughout Byrd Stadium in the autumn of 1985. The Terrapins won four out of five games in College Park, and led the ACC in both total offense and total defense to claim the school's second three-peat of conference championships. Stan Gelbaugh took the full-time reins at the head of the Maryland offense, and led a unit that averaged over 26 points a game. Gelbaugh, like Frank Reich before him, had seen extensive playing time as a backup. The experience gained during the 1984 season was essential for Gelbaugh, as he set a Maryland school record in 1985 with 2,385 yards of total offense.

Penn State was an eternal thorn in the sides of the seventh-ranked Terrapins, but the Terps were favored this time around against the No. 19 Nittany Lions. Things went bad for UM right from the outset, as a rusty Gelbaugh threw two interceptions in the first quarter. After falling behind 17-0, Maryland finally began to surge. As the game went into halftime, it appeared as if Maryland would be okay. They were holding up better in the ninety-four-degree heat than Penn State, as several Nittany Lion players had to be helped off the field with cramps.

The second half brought even more promise to the Terrapin hopes, as Chuck Faucette intercepted a pass on PSU's first offensive possession. Badanjek scored from the 5, and a faked extra point attempt resulted in a two-point conversion, as backup quarterback Dan Henning threw to Chris Knight. The Nittany Lions drove downfield on their next possession, and a field goal gave PSU a 20-18 lead. Although more than twenty-four minutes remained in the game, the brutal heat and physical nature of the contest caught up with the Terrapins. Badanjek was in and out of the lineup for the remainder of the game, and Gelbaugh was unable to find any more continuity. The Terrapins had a final opportunity to move into field goal range, but a fumble by Alvin Blount ended their chances.

Maryland outplayed Boston College for most of their second game, but the Eagles played a frustrating game of catch-up. After taking a 10-0 advantage in the second quarter, the Terrapins gave up a touchdown pass from Shawn Halloran to Kelvin Martin in the final minute of the first half. Maryland put the game away with a dramatic fourth quarter surge, scoring two touchdowns in eleven seconds. After Gelbaugh completed a touchdown pass to Eric Holder, the Eagles fumbled the kickoff. Badanjek's pile gave the Terps a 31-13 verdict.

After a pair of disappointing performances, Gelbaugh came out slinging against West Virginia. Completing fifteen-of-twenty-three passes for 263 yards, Gelbaugh threw to Sean Sullivan and Azizuddin Abdur-Ra'oof for touchdowns. Tommy Neal added two scores himself, and the Terrapin defenders handed WVU their first shutout in three seasons. The 28-0 victory came in front of a sellout crowd in Byrd Stadium, and was West Virginia's only loss in their first six games of the year.

The Terrapins headed to Ann Arbor next for a showdown against a powerful Michigan squad. Everyone was expecting a shootout between Gelbaugh and Michigan quarterback Jim Harbaugh, but the Wolverine signal caller far exceeded his UM counterpart. Gelbaugh had a game to forget, throwing four interceptions amidst the pressure of the Michigan defense. The Wolverines, on their way to a 10-1-1 record and No. 2 ranking in the final polls, were relentless against the Terrapin offense. The 20-0 shutout was the first for a Maryland team since 1979.

The Terrapins continued to struggle against N.C. State, needing a pair of scores in the final 3:27 to seize victory. The defense was the prime reason that Maryland won, as a fumble recovery by Faucette late in the first half allowed the Terrapins to erase a 10-0 deficit. Tied 17-17 late in the game, Blount broke through for a 4-yard touchdown. On the first play following the kickoff, Wolfpack quarterback Erik Kramer fumbled. Gelbaugh ran in a 19-yard sneak, and the Terps were victorious, 31-17.

Ross's troops were dominant in the following three weeks, as Maryland knocked off Wake Forest, Duke, and North Carolina in succession. After a slow start against the Deacons, taking only a 6-3 lead into halftime, the Terrapins exploded for 20 second half points to leave Groves Stadium with a 26-3 victory. Another slow beginning awaited the Terps against Duke, as they scored only one touchdown in the first thirty minutes. Leading only 7-3 against a 2-4 Blue Devil team, boos reigned down on the Maryland players as they sauntered to the locker rooms. Ross was waiting with a verbal tirade, as the normally mild-mannered head coach let his team have it.

"I was pretty damn upset," Ross said in his postgame comments. "We were booed. I'm not going back on that now, but we deserved it."

Although Duke kept the game close throughout much of the third quarter, tying the game 10-10 on a touchdown reception by Doug Green, Maryland suddenly took off. In a wild spree, the Terrapins scored 30 points in the final sixteen minutes. Gelbaugh, on his way to a career-high 314 yards, threw three touchdowns to lead UM to a 40-10 final. Rick Badanjek had always enjoyed playing North Carolina, and the senior enjoyed yet another breakout game against the Tar Heels. Badanjek ran for 88 yards and three touchdowns, leading the Terrapins to a 28-10 victory.

Miami arrived in Baltimore with revenge on their minds, and handed the Terrapins a painful loss. The game was plenty winnable for Maryland, as they took a 20-13 lead early in the second half. Unlike their game in Miami a year earlier, when they scored 42 points in the final thirty minutes, the Terps could not continue their torrid offensive pace. Unable to gain another first down until the final minutes, Maryland allowed Miami to turn the tables. Trailing 22-13, Brett Perriman brought the Canes back into contention with a 74-yard punt return, and Greg Cox kicked a field goal to give his team a 23-22 lead. After retaking possession, Miami ran effortlessly through the worn-out Maryland defenders, and a Melvin Bratton leap gave the Canes a 29-22 margin of victory.

The Terrapins rolled down to Death Valley for a November 16 showdown with Clemson, and needed every ounce of production they could get to squeeze out a win. The Tigers looked solid in the early going, treating the home crowd to a 10-0 lead. Maryland retaliated on the arm of Gelbaugh, who led a pair of drives to give the Terps a 14-10 lead. In an up-and-down affair, Clemson came right back on a run by Kenny Flowers. Leading 24-17 at halftime, Clemson allowed a tying touchdown before assuming a 31-24 advantage on a run by Tracy Johnson.

With 1:18 remaining, Edmunds caught a 3-yard touchdown, which knotted the score at 31. Television replays showed Edmunds bobbling with the football, and it didn't appear that he had control. To the chagrin of the high-fiving Tiger defenders, the officials ruled it a catch. Danny Ford was even angrier that the twenty-five-second play clock had run off before the ball was snapped. Maryland got the ball back with less than a minute remaining, and pulled off an impressive play to put themselves in position to win. Dropping back from his own 49,

Gelbaugh cut loose on a bomb. Edmunds circled under the ball and came up with the play, good for 44 yards, to the CU 7. Dan Plocki nailed a field goal with three seconds remaining, and the emotional 34-31 game belonged to the Terrapins. It wasn't easy for the Tigers to accept defeat, as several of their players, in addition to a few hundred fans, engaged the Terrapin players and coaches near the CU bench. With Ross right in the middle, trying to clear his team from the field, the teams mixed it up for several minutes. Cooler heads finally prevailed, and Maryland returned to College Park with one regular season game to play.

Virginia was guaranteed a winning record with a 6-4 mark coming into the UM game, but the Cavaliers were not the same team in 1985 that they had been a year prior. The Terrapins jumped out to a 23-7 lead behind Badanjek and Blount, and withstood a UVA comeback to take a 33-21 victory. The win ensured a fourth consecutive eight-win season for Maryland, in addition to another game in December. Before Detroit began hosting the Motor City Bowl in 1997, the city briefly hosted a game called the Cherry Bowl. The Cherry lasted only two seasons, and Maryland met a familiar foe in Syracuse in the bowl's final game. It was the first postseason matchup in history between the Orangemen and Terrapins, and marked the fifth consecutive year that the two schools came together for a football game.

Only 30,000 came out to the Silverdome for the contest, and many would be gone before the final gun. The Orangemen took an early 3-0 lead, but the Terrapins dominated most of the opening half. On his way to 223 yards and Most Valuable Player honors, Gelbaugh ran and passed for a touchdown to give UM the advantage. Using a 22-point swing in the second quarter, highlighted by a Scott Tye fumble recovery in the end zone, Maryland took a 28-10 lead at halftime. A final score in the third quarter, combined with a solid defensive effort, gave the Terps a 35-18 victory.

Georgia Tech had its finest regular season thus far as an ACC member in 1985, finishing 5-1 in league play. The Ramblin' Wreck did not play Maryland, taking away their chances of tying for the conference title, but their 8-2-1 record was good enough for an All-American Bowl appearance against Michigan State. Yellow Jacket quarterback John Dewberry led the ACC in passing, while tailback Jerry Mays etched his name among the greatest runners in Tech's storied history. Dewberry was suspended along with three other teammates for the All-American game, but the undermanned Yellow Jackets put up an inspired effort. After falling behind 14-0 to the Spartans, Tech scored 17 unanswered points to take the victory. After Pat Swilling fell on a Lorenzo White fumble for GT, Malcolm King piled over with less than two minutes to play.

Former Duke standout John Gutekunst brought Minnesota into the Independence Bowl against Clemson, who had struggled with a 4-3 record in ACC play. Gutekunst was replacing Lou Holtz at Minnesota, who had departed for Notre Dame after the regular season. Although Kenny Flowers broke Clemson's single-season rushing record with 1,200 yards, the Tigers dropped a 20-13 final. Touchdowns by Mel Anderson and Valdez Baylor were accompanied by two Chip Lohmiller field goals, which overcame Keith Jennings' touchdown reception for the Tigers.

By 1986, Clemson had gone three seasons without winning an ACC title for the first time since the days of Red Parker. The NCAA probation placed on Clemson was now two seasons removed, and could no longer be used as an excuse as to why the team was not talented enough to get back on top. As a result, many had doubts that Danny Ford could win big at Clemson with a clean program. The 1985 Tigers had been particularly mediocre, dropping to third in the conference standings with a 6-6 record. The Tiger seniors were in jeopardy of becoming the first CU football class to leave Death Valley without a conference title in nearly a decade.

Led by a strong defense and a surprise running sensation, the Tigers quieted their critics in 1986, finishing 5-1-1 in the ACC for their first conference title in four years. Running back Kenny Flowers had led the ACC in scoring in 1985, and was billed as a solid Heisman candidate heading into the new year. Anticipation turned to anxiety when Flowers went down with a knee injury in fall practice. Although Flowers would go on to play in the opener, the promising back spent the season riddled with injuries, and failed to put up the numbers that many were expecting him to.

Terrence Flagler, a fifth-year senior who was below Flowers on the preseason depth chart, made good on his chance to become Clemson's go-to guy. Stepping in as the premier back for most of the year, Flagler rushed for over 1,200 yards to earn All-American honors. Flagler also set a Clemson school record for rushing yards per game, averaging 106.9 a contest. With Flagler and Flowers both in the backfield to take handoffs throughout the season, sophomore quarterback Rodney Williams had no problems successfully running Ford's I-formation, Triple-Option set. After a tough 1985 season, in which he was thrown to the wolves as a freshman, Williams became the glue that would hold together the Tiger offense for the next three years.

With eight returning starters on defense, the Tigers gave up the fewest yards in the league for the first time since the national championship team of 1981. Michael Dean Perry had Tiger fans temporarily forgetting about his older brother William, earning All-ACC honors as a junior. Fellow lineman Terence Mack and defensive back Delton Hall joined Perry on the squad.

The Tigers were used to poor Septembers, having dropped four of their last seven games in the ninth month dating back to 1984. It happened again this year, as Virginia Tech came to Death Valley and stole away a 20-14 final. Clemson tied the game at 7 early in the second quarter on a 13-yard run by Flagler, but VT took a 10-7 lead into halftime. The Hokies stretched their lead to 10 points when Erik Chapman hit tight end Steve Johnson from 5 yards out in the third quarter. Flowers cut into the lead with a 1-yard carry late in the third, but the Hokies clung to their slim lead and kept it.

The Tigers did an about-face the following Saturday in Athens, and gave the seniors their first victory over Georgia in Sanford Stadium. The first half was a wild one, as the Tigers and Bulldogs combined for 42 points to take a 21-21 tie into the locker rooms. Rodney Williams gave Clemson a 28-21 lead early in the third quarter, but James Jackson threw a 78-yard touchdown to Fred Lane that brought the teams even again. Williams passed for 149 yards and rushed for 56, and paced Clemson's final drive into Georgia territory. With time for one more play, David Treadwell came on to kick the Tigers to victory. Treadwell had missed a 39-yard effort minutes earlier, but was perfect on the 46-yard attempt as time expired for a 31-28 triumph.

The Tigers began their ACC schedule with Georgia Tech, and completed a Peachtree State sweep for only the third time in school history. Clemson jumped out to an early 14-0 advantage, thanks in large part to Terrence Roulhac. Roulhac returned the opening kickoff 81 yards, preparing Tracy Johnson for a short carry into the end zone. A pair of Treadwell field goals added to the margin. Chris Lancaster scored Clemson's final touchdown on a fourth quarter run, giving the Tigers the game by a score of 27-3.

Following a 24-0 shutout over the Citadel, Clemson buried Virginia and Duke in successive weeks. The Cavaliers were on the wrong end of a 31-17 final score, as the Tigers won for the twenty-sixth consecutive time over their nemesis from Charlottesville. Flagler had quietly become the ace of Clemson's running game, and the senior rambled for 102 yards against the Blue Devils, scoring twice. The Tiger defense was particularly stingy in the first half, making ten tackles for losses. Michael Dean Perry made three sacks, and was named ACC lineman of the week for his efforts. For the game, Duke managed only 67 yards on the ground.

North Carolina State was next on Clemson's schedule, and it proved to be a difficult encounter. The Wolfpack stunned Clemson by beating them at their own game, slipping and sliding for 253 rushing yards on the slick grass of Carter-Finley Stadium. The Tigers did not respond well to the rain, rushing for only 141 yards and playing poorly on defense. State cruised to a surprisingly easy 27-3 victory, one that not only toppled Clemson from the national championship picture, but could have easily denied them another conference title.

The Tigers regrouped after their embarrassing loss to the Wolf-pack, and did not lose again. Staying in North Carolina the following week against Wake Forest, Flagler put together the most dominating performance of his career. The senior carried the ball twenty-two times for 209 yards, and became the third player in Clemson history to score four touchdowns in a single game. Flagler set a school record with 274 all-purpose yards, as he accounted for all of Clemson's points with the exceptions of the extra points. Flagler's scoring runs ate up 88 and 50 yards, while his scoring receptions netted 39 and 21 yards, respectively.

The final moments of the N.C. State-South Carolina game that same day brought back memories of Doug Flutie and his famous "Hail Mary" pass to beat Miami two years earlier. Following a defensive penalty against USC as time expired, Erik Kramer completed a 33-yard touchdown pass to Danny Peebles on the game's final play to give State a miraculous 23-22 victory, which set off a wild celebration in Raleigh.

Clemson athletic director Bobby Robinson suspended three players before the North Carolina game, but it had little effect on the Tigers that did suit up. Flagler and Flowers each scored twice, while the defense made two sacks and forced a pair of interceptions in the 38-10 victory. Midway through the second quarter, with Clemson leading 7-3, the public address announcer revealed that N.C. State had lost 20-16 in Charlottesville to Virginia. The news of an NCSU defeat set well in the minds of the Clemson players, as they went 89 yards to open up their lead to 14-3 at halftime. A barrage of 24 unanswered points in the second half gave Clemson their significant final margin.

With the loss of several key players from their strong teams of recent years, Maryland was a shell of its former self in 1986. With three conference losses, and an overall record of 4-4-1 coming in, it was evident that the Terrapins would not repeat as ACC champions. It was a unique situation on the field of Baltimore's Memorial Stadium, as neither Ford nor Maryland's Bobby Ross were on the sidelines. Ford had verbally abused an official after the Maryland game in Death Valley the year before, while Ross had chased one off the field two weeks earlier following a loss to North Carolina. The two coaches, winners of each of the last five ACC football championships, were relegated to the press box for the duration of the contest.

Maryland gave Clemson all they wanted, twice taking the lead on runs by Tommy Neal. Neal's first carry gave the Terrapins a 7-0 lead in the first quarter, and his second gave UM a 17-14 advantage with just over nine minutes remaining. Late in the game, the Tigers had to drive 92 yards against a surprisingly potent Terrapin defense to wrap up the conference. With two seconds remaining, and the ball on the Maryland 4, Ford elected to go for the sure thing. A tie would give Clemson the outright championship, and although he felt it may damage his team's bowl credibility, Ford sent in the word to kick it. Treadwell, who had missed two long attempts earlier in the game, nailed the short conversion to conclude a 17-17 stalemate.

"I don't blame him (Ford) one bit," Ross said in the locker room. "I would have done the same thing. He did the right thing going for the conference title. I support his decision 100 percent."

Without a bowl to look forward to, South Carolina vented all of their frustrations on the Tigers. Led by Derrick Little's twenty-three tackles, the USC defense held Clemson to 40 yards below their season rushing average. Only three points were scored in the second half, which came on Treadwell's 31-yard kick at the 2:20 mark of the final quarter. After a wild second quarter, in which the teams combined for 24 points, both offenses went cold. The 21-21 final was unsatisfying to most, but good enough to get the Tigers an invitation from the Gator Bowl Committee.

Clemson met Stanford down in Jacksonville, and won the game, 27-21, behind their powerful running game. The Tigers dominated the second quarter, outscoring the Cardinal 20-0 to take a 27-0 lead into the locker room. Treadwell nailed two field goals, and the Williams boys, Rodney and Ray, each notched tallies on the Tiger side of the scoreboard. Stanford adjusted defensively in the second half, and kept Clemson from scoring for the remainder of the game. Behind Brad Muster, the Cardinal began a spirited comeback. After piling over on a 1-yard rush in the third quarter, the Stanford back caught a pair of scoring passes from Greg Innis. Although they cut the Clemson lead to six at 27-21, Stanford ran out of time. The Tigers retained possession and successfully fended off the Cardinal offensive.

North Carolina, led by ACC rushing leader Derrick Fenner, spent Christmas in Hawaii, and met Arizona in the Aloha Bowl. Struggling against Larry Smith's powerful offense, which averaged 29 points a game during the regular season, the Tar Heels fell to the Wildcats 30-21. North Carolina State took on Virginia Tech in the Peach Bowl, and the Hokies held on for the school's fourth consecutive victory over an ACC opponent. Mike Cofer put the Wolfpack ahead 24-22 with a field goal late in the game, but a kick by Chris Kinzer in the final minutes gave VT a thrilling 25-24 final.

After fighting their way back to the top of the ACC standings in 1986, Clemson was on a mission to prove that they were back as the superior team in the league in 1987. Clemson's squad that autumn was arguably the finest collection of talent in the conference since the Tiger team that had gone all the way six years earlier. In winning ten games, including six against ACC foes, the Tigers placed four players on the All-American team. Sophomore Terry Allen replaced Kenny Flowers and Terrence Flagler as the ace of Clemson's backfield, and he didn't disappoint, leading the league with 868 yards. Wes McFadden joined Allen as the other featured back, and his big-play potential kept Tiger fans on the edge of their seats all season.

Michael Dean Perry, who went on to win ACC Player of the Year honors, anchored a defense that was one of the finest in the history of the league. The 1987 Tigers led the ACC in scoring defense and total defense, and their average of allowing only 80 rushing yards a game set a new conference record. Opponents struggled all year to move the football against the CU unit, whose success against the ground was comparable to the 1953 Maryland unit, which had allowed only 83.9 yards an outing on its way to the NCAA title. Perry, a force on the Clemson defensive line since his freshman year, left an indelible mark on the ACC record books. The younger Perry left Clemson as the conference's all-time leader in sacks with 28, and tackles for loss with 61. His brother William previously held both records, and Michael Dean had no problems taking some thunder away from his celebrated sibling.

Guard John Phillips was the leader of Clemson's standout offensive line, which helped the Tigers lead the ACC in rushing for a second consecutive year. Phillips punished opposing defensive lineman, setting a single season record with 103 knockdown blocks, also known as "pancakes." Philips earned the Jacobs Blocking Trophy and was named All-American for the second time. David Treadwell was the next in a long line of celebrated Clemson kickers, leading the league in scoring with 82 points. Treadwell finished his Clemson career fourth in history with 42 converted field goals, and his eighteen successful kicks in 1987 was the third-highest single-season total at that time in the league.

Donnell Woolford was Clemson's standout in the defensive secondary, snagging five interceptions and proving himself as the best coverage defender in the ACC. Woolford also returned punts for the Tigers, and was third in the nation with an average of 15 yards per return. Woolford's touchdown returns against Georgia Tech and Wake Forest were large reasons for his lofty average.

The Western Carolina opener in Death Valley was anticlimactic, as the Tigers annihilated the Catamounts, 43-0. Allen and McFadden each scored twice, and combined for 140 yards rushing. Rodney Williams, the lone returning starter in the CU backfield, came through with 154 yards passing on nine completions. Most of the Tiger regulars sat through the second half, a deserved break after running up a 30-0 halftime lead.

Frank Beamer made his debut at Virginia Tech under rainy skies, and the Tigers made sure that the new Hokie coach left the field disappointed. Treadwell and McFadden were the heroes, doing most of the work to give Clemson a 22-10 victory. Treadwell connected on three field goals, with the first two coming after interceptions by Perry and linebacker Henry Carter. With only 60 yards of total offense, their fewest total in a game in eighteen years, Virginia Tech never had a chance. McFadden scored both of Clemson's touchdowns on long runs, taking one in from 44 yards away, and another from 89. The 89-yard play, coming on a pitch from Williams, gave McFadden 226 yards for the day.

Clemson had not beaten Georgia in back-to-back seasons since 1905 and 1906, and with the Bulldogs also coming in at 2-0, it figured to be a tough endeavor. After tying the game at 3, Clemson's punt unit endured a letdown, as Nathaniel Lewis busted through on a 76-yard return to give UGA a 10-3 edge. The Bulldogs took command early in the final period, marching 74 yards to the go-ahead score. Georgia quarterback James Jackson threw to tight end Kirk Warner for 32 yards, and running backs Lars Tate and Rodney Hampton did the rest.

Trailing 20-16, Clemson took over strategic control following a punt that was downed at the Georgia 1. Two plays later, Jackson rolled to his left and was tackled in the end zone by cornerback James Lott and safety Gene Beasley. With a free kick coming, Clemson had an opportunity to move downfield and set up a game winner. They did just that, pushing 53 yards to set up Treadwell. For the second year in a row, the former walk-on lifted the Tigers over the Bulldogs, booming a kick that split the uprights with two seconds remaining for a dramatic 21-20 Clemson victory, which set off a spirited celebration on the part of the home fans.

Although the offense struggled for most of the way, the Tigers crunched Georgia Tech, 33-12, to get their conference schedule off on the right foot. Perry and linebacker Jesse Hatcher harassed GT quarterback Rick Strom, allowing him to complete only fourteen-of-thirty-four passes. The Tiger special teams settled the issue, returning two kicks for long touchdowns and setting a school record with 227 punt return yards. Woolford took a punt to the house from 78 yards for Clemson's first touchdown, and Joe Henderson brought back a kickoff 95 yards in the fourth quarter.

The Tigers next headed to Charlottesville, where Virginia was holding a three-game winning streak. To nobody's great surprise, the streak ended at the hands of the orange and white. McFadden and Allen were unstoppable, combining for 302 yards on the ground. With massive holes to run through, the Tiger backs as a whole amassed 403 yards. Allen added a pair of touchdowns, the second tying the game at 14 in the second quarter. Although the Cavaliers played the Tigers tough for much of the day, cutting the score to 24-21 midway through the third quarter, Clemson wore UVA down in the second half. Following a 46-yard kickoff return by Henderson, the Tigers moved 54 yards for a touchdown. Late in the game Clemson maintained possession, running down the clock and refusing to give Virginia another chance. With forty-two seconds to play, Henderson piled over from the 3 to complete the 38-21 CU victory.

Duke's Steve Spurrier brought his wide-open offensive attack to Death Valley the following week, and nearly escaped town with a victory. Blue Devil quarterback Anthony Dilweg threw for 305 yards, riddling the Tiger secondary with his accurate bombs. Trailing 3-0 early on, the Tigers reeled off 10 unanswered points in the second quarter on a field goal and touchdown pass from Williams to tight end James Coley. The Blue Devils fought back to tie the game in the third quarter. Although both teams successfully moved the football for most of the day, the score remained tied at 10 well into the final quarter. With McFadden and Allen continuously wrapped up by the Blue Devil defenders, Tracy Johnson stepped up and assumed the role of lead runner for Clemson. The junior fullback finished the game with 93 yards, and guided CU downfield for most of a 97-yard march. With 6:46 to play, Johnson reached the end zone on a 4-yarder, giving CU a 17-10 advantage. Four minutes later, Woolford sealed victory with a diving interception.

Clemson dug themselves too deep a hole in the N.C. State contest, and were dealt a punishing blow at the hands of the Wolfpack for the second straight year. State advanced at will in the first half, piling up 252 yards and building a stunning 30-0 lead at halftime. The Tigers struggled just as much on offense as they did on defense, failing to make a single first down. Surprised and angered by NCSU's dominance, the Clemson players used the time in the locker room to collect themselves, and to regroup for a second half onslaught.

Without enough time to continue on the ground, Ford chose to open up his playbook and run an aerial barrage at the Wolfpack in the final two periods. Williams responded by leading the Tigers to 325 yards, and a 5-yard sneak by the Clemson quarterback made the score 30-8 going into the fourth quarter. A pair of Johnson scores later in the half pulled the Tigers to within 30-20. The Tigers tried two-point rushes after both of Johnson's touchdowns, but the NCSU line held. Clemson added a final touchdown on a pass from Williams to Ricardo Hooper at the 3:56 mark, and the Tigers got the ball back minutes later with a chance to win. Clemson needed only two first downs to set up Treadwell, but the Wolfpack stopped them on downs to take a 30-28 triumph.

Williams injured his knee the Monday before the Wake Forest game, giving backup Chris Morocco a chance to lead the Tiger offense. Although Morrocco struggled, and was replaced by Williams in the third quarter, CU hung tough for a 31-17 victory. Joe Henderson, who had been breaking off big plays all season on special teams for Clemson, did it again this week. Normally the third-string tailback, Henderson reeled off touchdown runs of 31 and 48 yards, and finished the game with a total of 131. After a slow first half, the Tigers ran the football to great success in the second half, amassing over 200 yards on the ground. The Demon Deacons took a surprising 17-10 lead into the locker rooms, coming on a pair of touchdown receptions by Ricky Proehl, but the Tigers outscored WF in the final thirty minutes, 21-0. A 5-yard score by Allen preceded the long carries by Henderson, which put the game on ice.

In a turnover-filled game in Chapel Hill, Clemson improved to 8-1 with a 13-10 victory over North Carolina. The Tigers scored the only points of the first half on a 29-yard pass from Williams to Gary Cooper, and overcame four lost fumbles with the defense. The Clemson defenders stuffed UNC to only 233 total yards, and forced a pair of interceptions. Although Carolina tied the game in the third quarter, and again in the final period, the Tigers had the ball in the closing minutes with a chance to set up Treadwell. Johnson, who led the way with 125 rushing yards, did most of the work, as Clemson went 67 yards in the final three minutes. With thirty-two seconds on the clock, Treadwell calmly trudged onto the field and nailed a 30-yard kick to preserve the game.

"Treadwell did a great job, and it was a great drive there at the end," a relieved Ford said later. "We got the ball on the 20 and were able to drive down and give David a chance to win it for us. David's kicked a lot of them for us. He's just a tremendous football player when the pressure's on, and he did a great job again tonight."

Returning to Death Valley seven days later to play Maryland, the Tigers put together a complete effort to wrap up another conference title. It had been four long years since CU had beaten the Terrapins on the gridiron, but behind 528 yards of offense, the Tigers left little doubt in this one. Although Maryland took an early 7-3 advantage on a 66-yard touchdown pass by Neil O'Donnell, the Tigers owned the remainder of the first half. Williams countered O'Donnell's score with a long pass of his own, hitting Cooper for a 50-yard touchdown. Allen, who finished with a game-high 103 yards, added a pair of short tallies to give Clemson a 24-7 lead. The big plays kept coming for CU in the third quarter, as McFadden broke off a 55-yard run and Cooper caught a 44-yard scoring pass from Williams. The touchdowns gave the Tigers a 38-10 lead, and after the starters were replaced, Morocco came on in the final quarter to give CU yet another score. The 45-16 victory was similar to the blowout in Death Valley from 1983, and all but assured the Tigers a game on New Year's Day.

Despite all their great games in year's past, another one was expected in the 1987 Clemson-South Carolina showdown. The Gamecocks welcomed the Tigers to Columbia sporting a 7-2 record, having shut out each of their previous two opponents. Unlike most years in the past, the CU contest was not the last for South Carolina in the regular season. A matchup with Miami in the Orange Bowl was two weeks away, and USC tuned up for the Hurricanes by manhandling their instate nemesis. For whatever reason, the Tigers played flat against the Gamecocks, for after McFadden scored on a 2-yard carry barely six minutes in, the Clemson offense went into a daze. The proud CU running game netted only 75 yards, as a sea of Gamecock defenders swarmed McFadden, Johnson, and Williams every time they touched the ball.

After allowing USC a pair of field goals in the second quarter, the Clemson defenders succumbed to a big play. From his own 17, Gamecock quarterback Todd Ellis completed a 77-yard pass to receiver Ryan Bethea, which set up a 6-yard run by Harold Green. The 13-7 USC advantage lasted into the final quarter, when safety Brad Edwards salted away victory with a solid individual effort. With 5:37 to play, Edwards stepped in front of a Williams pass and returned it 40 yards for a 20-7 South Carolina victory. The Gamecocks went on to the Gator Bowl, while the Tigers prepared for a Citrus Bowl encounter with Penn State.

With a 7-4 overall record, including a second-place finish in the conference standings, George Welsh led Virginia to an All-American Bowl berth against Lavell Edwards and Brigham Young (BYU). In an up-and-down affair, Scott Secules led UVA to victory with a scoring run and pass. Trailing 16-14 in the second half, Secules completed a touchdown to John Ford, and then executed a fake conversion to give the Cavaliers a 22-16 upset.

Joe Paterno must have liked his team's chances against Clemson in Orlando, having won sixteen consecutive games against ACC foes over the past twelve seasons. Despite losses to Alabama, Syracuse, and Pittsburgh, PSU had knocked off Notre Dame in the final regular season game to finish with an 8-3 record. In preparing for Penn State, Ford and the Clemson staff found an interesting trend. When playing run-oriented teams, such as Clemson, the PSU defenders had a habit of cheating toward the line of scrimmage. With the defensive backs left to single cover wide receivers in most situations, the Tiger coaches felt that Williams could have a field day through the air, much as he had in his second half reprieve against N.C. State.

The prediction held true, as Williams was able to pick his receivers at will throughout much of the contest. Throwing for 214 yards on fifteen-of-twenty-four passing, Williams finished as the game's Most Valuable Player. The quarterback got it going on the first play from scrimmage, hitting Keith Jennings for 24 yards to set up Johnson, who scored from the 7 for a 7-0 CU lead. Penn State took advantage of a Tiger penalty to tie it, but Clemson returned the favor on another Johnson run. The score was set up by a 15-yard diving catch by Cooper, a 31-yard reception by Jennings, and a 22-yard gallop by Allen.

Penn State notched a field goal to cut the Clemson lead to 14-10, but the Tigers scored the next three touchdowns. Midway through the third quarter, CU added to its lead on a third scoring run by Johnson. A 25-yard sprint by Allen and a 4-yard smash by Henderson completed Clemson's 35-10 victory. With the win, Williams tied Homer Jordan atop the all-time career victory list for CU quarterbacks.

Danny Ford entered select company during the 1988 season, joining Duke's Bill Murray and Maryland's Jerry Claiborne and Bobby

Ross as the fourth ACC head coach to lead his schools to three consecutive conference titles. The Tigers had been dominant on the ground throughout their newest dynasty, and the tradition continued in 1988. Averaging 277.6 yards per game, the most since Lester Brown and the 1978 squad, CU ran at will over the majority of its opposition that fall.

Also like Charley Pell's 1978 team, the 1988 Tigers led the conference in scoring offense and scoring defense. Donnell Woolford returned as the star of the CU secondary, and although most teams chose not to throw in his direction, Woolford became an All-American for the second straight year. Terry Allen, Wes McFadden, Tracy Johnson, and Joe Henderson all returned to the Clemson backfield, and each had productive outings against Virginia Tech. As the Tigers buried VT, 40-7, CU racked up 281 yards rushing. All four backs scored touchdowns, with Allen leading the way with 83 yards. New placekicker Chris Gardocki connected on two field goals, and Williams added a second quarter score in becoming the winningest quarterback in Clemson history.

Ranked No. 3 in the nation, Clemson expected another easy one with Furman coming to town. Florida State was looming the following weekend, and many of the Tigers must have had their minds on the Seminoles. In a sluggish effort in the rain, Clemson needed three Gardocki kicks and a pair of short runs by Allen to seal a 23-3 victory. Although the defense was solid, holding the Paladins to 201 total yards and a single score, the Tigers allowed their Division I-AA opponent to keep things competitive.

As was typical in big games at Memorial Stadium, the Tigers ran down the hill wearing orange pants for Florida State. Clemson was 14-1 over the years in their special uniforms, and were hoping that victory over FSU would propel them into a national championship run. To keep pace, the Seminoles wore white pants purchased by none other than former FSU football player Burt Reynolds, who had been a member of the last Seminole team to play a game with all-white uniforms back in the 1950s.

The Tigers struck first, needing only four plays to move 74 yards for a touchdown. From the CU 39, Ford called for a gimmick, an end-around pass. Chip Davis took the ball from Williams and threw to Gary Cooper, who hauled in the toss and went all the way. The Seminoles countered with a long play of their own, as quarterback Chip Ferguson nailed Dexter Carter for 40 yards on a third-and-14. Clemson took a 14-7 lead into the locker room following a methodical 99-yard drive, which took seventeen plays and ate up 7:45 from the clock. Williams did most of the damage, completing passes to Allen and Cooper for big gains. A 7-yard scamper by the Tiger signal caller put the points on the board.

Deion Sanders, FSU's star cornerback and kick returner, provided some magic early in the third quarter to knot up the score. Taking a punt from the Seminole 24, "Prime Time" split the CU coverage unit and turned on his jets to outrun every Tiger in his path. Deion's 76-yard touchdown was just the start of the big plays for the FSU special teams. The Seminoles took their first lead barely three minutes later, as Ferguson completed a 36-yard pass to Bruce LaSane. With the ball at the Clemson 1, Dayne Williams piled over for a 21-14 advantage.

The game remained in Florida State's favor until late in the final quarter, when the Tigers began a last-ditch march. Taking possession at the CU 34, Williams first completed a pass to Ricardo Hooper, then handed off to Allen. Allen rambled for 10 yards, but lost control of the football. Keith Jennings was on the scene for the Tigers, and the drive resumed. From the FSU 19, Johnson took a handoff and broke through the Seminole defense for the score. With just over two minutes to play, Florida State would have to go a long way in a short amount of time in order to win. Bringing the kickoff out to the 15, Ferguson was unable to move the chains. LaSane dropped one pass, and another was nearly intercepted after Otis Moore laid into the intended receiver for the Tigers. On fourth-and-4 from the FSU 21, Clemson had no reason to think that the Seminoles would not punt the ball away, and hope to regain possession following a defensive stop.

Florida State skipper Bobby Bowden, in addition to his offensive coaches, had another idea in mind. Remembering a successful trick play run by Jerry Claiborne during his days at Virginia Tech, Bowden ordered the FSU punt unit to run a "Ruski," or fake punt. Snapper David Whittington faked a high snap to punter Tim Corlew, who leaped high into the air as if to snag the ball. The snap actually went to Dayne Williams, who was playing directly behind the snapper as an extra blocker. Williams laid the ball to the turf, and it was picked up by defensive back Leroy Butler.

Butler waited approximately two seconds before taking off, and ran right by several Clemson players, who were unaware that he had the ball. Butler took off by himself down the far sideline, and would have easily scored if Woolford hadn't spotted him. Woolford sprinted after Butler and knocked him out-of-bounds at the CU 1, after a lengthy footrace and a 78-yard gain. The Seminoles were unable to penetrate the end zone, but kicker Richie Andrews was good on a short field goal to give FSU a 24-21 victory that broke the hearts of the Clemson faithful.

"It was a nice call, it won the game for them," Ford said later. "I don't fault our people for that play. I wish we could have gone back and called a time-out and prepared them for it."

Still in shock over their loss to Florida State, the Tigers allowed Georgia Tech to keep things close in the first half in Atlanta. Johnson and Jennings scored in the first quarter to give Clemson a 14-0 bulge, but GT retaliated on a touchdown catch by Jerry Mays and a field goal by Thomas Palmer. The Yellow Jackets left the field at newly remodeled Bobby Dodd Stadium for halftime confident that victory was within their grasp, down only 17-10.

The Tigers continued to do their thing in the final thirty minutes, and overwhelmed Georgia Tech with a combination of running and passing. The teams went scoreless through the first ten minutes of the third quarter, until the CU defense made a critical play. From the Tiger 36, Tech quarterback Todd Rampley dropped back and located Mays, who had been his primary target all game. Expecting a possible pass to the Yellow Jacket tailback, cornerback James Lott stepped up and made a jolting hit, which popped the pigskin into the air. Tiger Linebacker Doug Brewster snatched the loose ball out of the sky and raced 68 yards for a pivotal touchdown.

Henderson did the rest for Clemson, breaking off a 52-yard run to set up a field goal and plowing through the GT defense for an 11-yard score to give the Tigers a 31-13 triumph. Henderson finished with 118 yards on twenty-one attempts, while Williams ran his streak of pass attempts without an interception to a school-record 96. The win was Clemson's third in as many years against Georgia Tech, marking the first time in the long history of the CU-GT rivalry that the Tigers could claim such a feat.

In a defensive struggle at Charlottesville, Virginia nearly lifted the large and time-tested monkey that was the Clemson winning streak off its collective back. Virginia's talented combo of Shawn and Herman Moore struck hard in the second half, as Shawn lofted a high toss that Herman snagged in the end zone. The touchdown gave Virginia a 7-3 advantage, and the lead held up until the final two minutes. Chip Davis, whose end-around pass had nearly led CU to victory over Florida State, came through big in the clutch. Drawing little resistance from the Cavalier secondary, Davis ran downfield and took in a spiral from Williams, who had called an audible at the line of scrimmage. The point-after gave Clemson a 10-7 victory and a sigh of relief.

The Tigers returned to Death Valley for a showdown against 5-0 Duke, the surprise of the ACC. With Steve Spurrier calling the shots and Anthony Dilweg executing them, the Blue Devils had upset Tennessee in Knoxville, and were hoping to get back to a bowl game for the first time in more than two decades. Clemson was legitimately worried about Dilweg, and spent most of the week leading up to the game specifically preparing for the pass.

As a result, Clemson put together an impressive defensive performance, and sent Duke crashing back to Earth with a 49-17 pounding. The Tigers assumed control from the outset, taking a 21-0 lead on a short rush by Johnson and a pair of receiving touchdowns by Cooper. Cooper's first score was good for 79 yards, and came on a toss by backup DeChane Cameron. The Devils made the score 28-14 at halftime following a 96-yard kickoff return by Quint McCracken and a scoring reception by Clarkston Hines. Clemson dominated the second half, scoring 21 additional points and holding Dilweg, the eventual ACC Player of the Year, to more than 150 yards below his season passing average. The Blue Devils managed only a single field goal over the final two quarters, while Johnson, Allen, and Henderson all reached the end zone for the Tigers.

Ford's troops came out lethargic once again against N.C. State, and dropped their third game in as many seasons to the Wolfpack. Over the previous three years, all championship campaigns for the Tigers, they were unable to solve Dick Sheridan's NCSU squad. Ford could point to a number of key plays that contributed to this defeat, including a delay-of-game penalty deep in Wolfpack territory that forced a field goal, an illegal procedure penalty that put Gardocki out of range for a kick, a turnover-on-downs following a botched pitch in the third quarter, and a bad punt snap, which set up State's winning touchdown. With three turnovers and only 211 total yards, Clemson did themselves no favors.

Playing against a tough NCSU defense, which led the ACC by allowing just 103.6 rushing yards per game, the Tigers were held to their lowest total of the season, and were kept out of the end zone for the first time since their last game in Raleigh played two years earlier. Clemson opened the scoring on a Gardocki field goal, but State ensured a 3-3 tie at the half following a 35-yard boot by Damon Hartman. Taking over at the CU 21 following the poor punt snap, State needed only five plays to score. With 10:04 to play, Chris Williams lumbered across the goal line from the 5. Williams' touchdown was the clincher, as the Wolfpack held on for a 10-3 victory.

The Tigers had justifiable offensive concerns heading to Wake Forest, but the unit returned to form. With Allen running for a season-high 155 yards, Clemson buried the Demon Deacons, 38-21, to get back on the winning track. After going scoreless for only the second time in forty games against N.C. State, CU had no problems crossing the goal line against Wake. It was 17-7 at the half, as Williams ran for one score and threw to Ricardo Hooper for another. Williams scored a second touchdown for a 24-7 Tiger lead, but WF quarterback Mike Elkins threw to Ricky Proehl for a 22-yard tally. The Tiger rushing attack sealed the deal, as Allen ran in from 63 yards out, and McFadden from 19 yards away. Proehl, who became only the third wide receiver in ACC history to amass 1,000 yards in a season, hauled in a 15-yard pass for the game's final points.

With Maryland looming the following week, it could have been easy for Clemson to overlook North Carolina, who came to Death Valley sporting a 1-7 record under new coach Mack Brown. The Tar Heels had shown some promise in recent weeks, knocking off Georgia Tech and nearly beating the Terrapins. Indeed, the game got off slowly for the Tigers. After Gardocki connected on a field goal for Clemson, UNC's Ken Martin, who went on to lead the ACC in rushing, ran free on a 37-yard sprint to give UNC a surprising 7-3 lead. The Tar Heel reprieve was short lived, however, as Clemson scored the next 34 points. Allen was the star once again in the CU backfield, rushing for 167 yards and scoring on a 3-yard carry just before halftime for a 17-7 Tiger cushion. Things went from bad to worse for Carolina in the second half, as Johnson ended a 76-yard CU march with a short plunge, and Gardocki nailed a pair of kicks. Ford called off the dogs and brought on the reserves, but the second-string Clemson offense added another late touchdown.

Although they stood only 5-3 overall, Joe Krivac's Maryland team had beaten four of their five ACC opponents, and could clinch a tie for the league title with a win over Clemson in College Park. With a five-touchdown explosion in the second half, the Tigers made certain that would not be the case. With the rush attack running on all cylinders, churning out 374 yards, CU took a 49-25 win to clinch the conference. Allen had another 100-yard game, and became the first sophomore back in Clemson history to surpass the 1,000-yard plateau.

After Maryland's Ricky Johnson opened the scoring with a 7-yard gallop, Cooper took a reverse for CU and cruised 52 yards to tie the game. Gardocki was good on a kick for a 10-7 score, but UM quarterback Neil O' Donnell threw a 24-yarder to make the score 14-10. Another Gardocki field goal had Maryland ahead by only 14-13 after two quarters of play. Tracy Johnson's short carry preceded Allen's pair of scores, and Cooper ran in on another reverse to give Clemson a 42-17 advantage. Both teams reached the end zone again to provide the final margin.

With another ACC championship wrapped up, Clemson wanted revenge against South Carolina in Death Valley. The Gamecocks were headed to the Liberty Bowl, but were coming off a 59-0 pounding by Florida State just two weeks before the Clemson encounter. Winless at home against South Carolina since 1982, the Tigers were going for their second nine-win regular season in as many years. The CU defenders set the tone, forcing four turnovers and holding USC to only 10 points.

Linebacker Jesse Hatcher had one of his finest performances, with seven tackles, two forced fumbles, and a sack. Gardocki put the first 9 points on the board with a trio of successful kicks, and Allen ran over from the 8 to give Clemson a 16-0 lead. South Carolina made its only goal line crossing on a pass from Todd Ellis to Robert Brooks, but Johnson and Williams each scored in the second half to give the Tigers a 29-7 cushion. The Gamecocks scored the final points, but Clemson had the victory and a berth against Oklahoma (OU) in the Citrus Bowl.

Sooner quarterback Jamelle Holieway had led OU to the 1985 NCAA title as a freshman, but was not quite the same player following a severe knee injury that had ended his 1987 campaign. Although he was a step slower, the elusive Holieway was still productive enough to lead the Sooners into the Citrus with an 8-3 record. Everyone knew that OU was going to run at Clemson, but the Tigers were prepared for Barry Switzer's wishbone. In an inspirational effort, the CU defense held Oklahoma's Holieway, Mike Gaddis, Leon Perry, and Anthony Stafford to a combined total of only 91 total yards. The Sooners were in position early to score a touchdown, but Hatcher brought Holieway down short of the line to force a field goal. The Sooners added another three-ball, but Gardocki kicked two for Clemson to knot the game at 6.

Allen, who took Player of the Game honors with 100 total yards (53 rushing, 47 receiving), won the game for Clemson with a 4-yard blast in the second half. The Tiger defense held OU from crossing the goal line, and the game ended 13-6 in favor of the orange and white. It was only the second time in the decade of the 1980s that Oklahoma was held without a touchdown, and marked the first time in ACC history that one of its football programs knocked off the behemoths from Norman. In addition, the Tigers finished the season ranked No. 9, making Clemson the only school in the entire country from 1986 to 1988 to win both their conference championship and bowl game along with finishing in the Top Twenty.

The night before Clemson's encounter with the Sooners, N.C. State had represented the ACC in the soggy Peach Bowl, where the Wolfpack beat Hayden Fry's Iowa team 28-23. The game nearly turned into an embarrassment for NCSU, as they surrendered an early 28-3 advantage by giving up 20 unanswered points. Chuck Hartlieb threw a pair of touchdowns to bring the Hawkeyes closer, and with eight seconds to play, the Iowa signal caller had a chance for a miraculous finish. With the Wolfpack prepared for a Hail Mary, Hartlieb's final pass fell short of the intended receiver. With the win, State claimed an 8-3-1 final record.

North Carolina State's Dick Christy, who set an ACC record unchallenged since 1957, when he averaged an impressive 45.4 yards per kick return. Against South Carolina, Christy scored every Wolfpack point, including the kicks, in a 29-26 victory that clinched the conference title. (Special Collections, North Carolina State University Libraries)

Maryland's Chet "The Jet" Hanulak of Maryland, who averaged 9.7 yards a carry in 1953 to lead the Terrapins to the NCAA title and a share of the first ACC regular season football championship. (Special Collections, University of Maryland Libraries)

Duke coach Bill Murray, who guided the Blue Devils to six shared or outright ACC football championships between 1953 and 1962. During his tenure in Durham, Murray coached nine All-Americans and three ACC Players of the Year. (Duke University Archives)

Duke's "Lonesome End" Tee Moorman, who earned All-American honors in 1960. Moorman's 9-yard touchdown reception in the fourth quarter of the 1961 Cotton Bowl led the way to a 7-6 Blue Devil victory over Arkansas. (Duke University Archives)

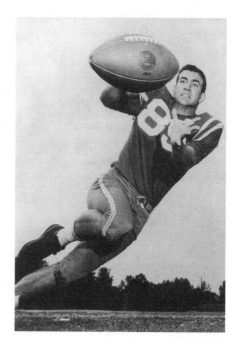

Wake Forest's Brian Piccolo, who led the NCAA with 1,044 rushing yards in 1964. Piccolo's young death in 1971 was the story line for the movie "Brian's Song," and the Brian Piccolo Award is given annually to the ACC football player who best demonstrates courage. (Wake Forest University School of Medicine)

Clemson's Frank Howard, who coached the Tigers to five ACC championships from 1956 to 1967. The field at Memorial Stadium and the rock that Clemson players touch before home games are each named in Howard's honor. (Special Collections, Clemson University Libraries)

Wake Forest's Larry Russell, who quarterbacked the Demon Deacons to their first and only ACC football championship in 1970. Russell scored two touchdowns in three consecutive games in October, leading WFU to victories over Virginia, Virginia Tech, and Clemson. (Wake Forest University School of Medicine)

Don McCauley of North Carolina, who in 1969 became the first Tar Heel running back to gain 1,000 yards in a season. In 1970, McCauley rushed for 1,720 yards to set an NCAA record, and helped usher in a resurgence of UNC football under Bill Dooley. (University of North Carolina Sports Information)

Randy White and Paul Vellano, two standouts on Jerry Claiborne's stellar defensive lines at Maryland in the 1970s. Vellano earned All-American honors for the Terrapins in 1973, while White won the Outland Trophy in 1974. (Special Collections, University of Maryland Libraries)

North Carolina State's Ted Brown, who set an ACC record with 4,602 rushing yards in a career stretching from 1975 to 1978. Brown was the first football player in ACC history to be named All-Conference in each of his four years of eligibility. (Special Collections, North Carolina State University Libraries)

Jeff Davis of Clemson, who earned ACC Player of the Year honors in leading the Tigers to the 1981 national championship. Nicknamed "The Judge" for the way he seemed to rule over the field, Davis anchored a defense that forced 41 turnovers during the title run. (Special Collections, Clemson University Libraries)

Clemson defensive back Terry Kinard, who earned All-American honors in both 1981 and 1982. Kinard was named National Defensive Player of the Year by CBS following the 1982 season, and earned induction into the College Football Hall of Fame two decades later. (Special Collections, Clemson University Libraries)

North Carolina's Lawrence Taylor had 16 sacks in 1980, leading the Tar Heels to an 11-1 record. Taylor went on to a Hall of Fame career in the NFL with the New York Giants, where he helped revolutionize the position of linebacker. (University of North Carolina Sports Information)

Georgia Tech quarterback Shawn Jones, who led the Yellow Jackets to a share of the 1990 national championship. Jones earned Most Valuable Player honors in GT's 1991 Citrus Bowl win over Nebraska, throwing for two touchdowns and accumulating 342 yards of offense. (Georgia Tech Sports Information)

Charlie Ward of Florida State, who became the first player in ACC history to win the coveted Heisman Trophy. After leading the Seminoles to the 1993 national championship in football, Ward went on to play professional basketball with the New York Knicks. (Florida State University Photo Lab)

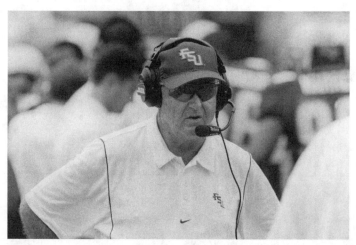

Florida State head coach Bobby Bowden, who guided the Seminoles to nine consecutive ACC championships from 1992 to 2000. Over this period, the Seminoles went 70-2 in league play, won two national championships, and became the first football program in NCAA history to finish ranked the Associated Press Top Five for 14 consecutive years. (Florida State University Photo Lab)

11

Breaking Through (1989)

In 1989, Duke and the University of Virginia ended decades of gridiron futility by jointly putting together two of the finest Blue Devil and Cavalier teams to take the field during the Atlantic Coast Conference era. Throughout most of their history in the conference, the Cavaliers had been the proverbial whipping boys, a team most schools could pencil in for a victory each season. That had also largely been the case with Duke in the years following Bill Murray's retirement following the 1965 season.

Things began to change at Virginia in December of 1981, when George Welsh arrived in Charlottesville. Welsh enjoyed a fine playing career at the Naval Academy, leading the Midshipmen to victory in the Sugar Bowl and finishing third in voting for the Heisman Trophy in 1955. After a decade at Penn State working under Joe Paterno, Welsh went back to Annapolis in 1973. As head coach, Welsh led Navy to three bowls and four successive winning seasons before accepting the Virginia job. Welsh exuded the kind of discipline and steady leadership one would expect from a Navy man, and it was not long before he had the Cavalier ship steered in the right direction.

Welsh and the Cavaliers took their knocks in 1982, winning only twice, but by the next season things were looking up. The Cavaliers went 6-5 in 1983, including conference victories over North Carolina, N.C. State, and Duke. The 1984 Cavaliers completed a strong campaign with a Peach Bowl victory over Purdue, the school's first post-season triumph in history. After a string of successful campaigns in the late 1980s, the Cavaliers were poised to make a serious run in 1989.

The Cavaliers had a couple of guys named Moore in their offensive huddle, and the pair became one of the most productive passing-catching tandems in ACC history. Quarterback Shawn Moore went on to earn league Most Valuable Player honors in 1989, completing 56 percent of his passes for 2,078 yards and 18 touchdowns. Wide receiver Herman Moore had burst onto the scene as a freshman in 1988 with a 175-yard game against Virginia Tech, and set new UVA sophomore records in 1989 with 848 yards and 10 touchdowns. Shawn had another reliable target in tight end Bruce McGonnigal, who led the Cavaliers with 42 receptions and enjoyed two games with 100 or more yards.

Duke's football fortunes began picking up steam in 1987, when Steve Spurrier arrived in Durham. Spurrier had won the Heisman Trophy in 1966 as a quarterback for the University of Florida, and spent a number of seasons playing and coaching in the NFL and USFL. Over the years, Spurrier had developed a wide-open, pass-oriented offense that maximized production and opportunity. Mimicking many professional teams, Spurrier's offense involved speedy wide receivers, excellent pass protection, and a strong-armed quarterback. Spurrier wasted little time turning around the Duke program, beginning his well-deserved reputation for cultivating quarterbacks with his first collegiate project, Steve Slayden. In a breakout campaign, Slayden threw for 2,924 yards and 20 touchdowns in 1987, including a 454-yard performance against N.C. State, in which a record 62 passes were attempted. Although the Devils lost to the Wolfpack, 47-45, a season-ending victory over North Carolina gave the Duke a final record of 5-6 and momentum heading into the offseason.

Anthony Dilweg took the reins as Duke's starting quarterback in 1988, and threw for an ACC-record 3,824 yards. Among his finest performances was a 475-yard passing game against Wake Forest, and completing 34 passes against Maryland and 33 against N.C. State. The Blue Devils passed for more than 350 yards a game, also a new conference record, and won seven games for the first time in more than two decades. Surprisingly, given their quick turnaround, Duke was not invited to a bowl.

The Blue Devil offense was even better in 1989, setting a new Atlantic Coast Conference record by averaging 501.7 yards per outing. Duke also topped the conference by averaging 323 yards passing and 32.4 points a contest. It was the third consecutive season that Duke boasted the ACC's best offense, and was even more proof of Spurrier's offensive genius. When considering that most of his standout players at Duke were recruited from the previous regime, it made it even easier to laud Spurrier's leadership and coaching ability.

Dave Brown and Clarkston Hines were the primary stars of the Blue Devil offense in 1989, with Brown leading the ACC in passing and Hines leading the league in scoring. Hines, who scored seventeen touchdowns to earn All-American honors, left Duke as the ACC's all-time leading receiver, wrapping up his career with 189 receptions for 3,318 yards and 38 tallies.

With All-ACC offensive lineman Chris Port and Carey Metts providing ample time to throw, Brown threw for 1,479 yards in limited work, which included two games of more than 400 yards. The Blue Devils got additional help from Randy Cuthbert and Billy Ray. Cuthbert came on at midseason and was a fearsome presence in the Duke backfield, while Ray spent much of the season as starting quarterback, and flourished early in Spurrier's productive offensive sets.

Notre Dame's defending national champions met the Cavaliers in the Kickoff Classic, and the Irish picked up from where they had left off in 1988. With the majority of their star players back for another season, Lou Holtz's Irish dominated Virginia, 36-13, by scoring on each of their first six possessions. Notre Dame pounded the ball on the ground to great success, as running backs Rodney Culver, Anthony Johnson, and Ricky Watters all reached the end zone. Quarterback Tony Rice also scored a rushing touchdown, and connected with receiver Raghib "Rocket" Ismail for 121 of his 147 total yards passing. Moore threw a pair of touchdowns for UVA, but the Cavaliers were unable to keep pace with one of college football's most powerful teams.

Ray began the year as the starting quarterback at Duke, and threw for 341 yards in the opener against South Carolina. Despite their offensive success, the Blue Devils were burned badly by turnovers and lapses in the kicking game. A pair of costly interceptions, combined by a blocked punt that directly resulted in a USC touchdown, shifted the momentum away from the Blue Devils. Although Hines caught two touchdowns to set a new ACC record with twenty-three scoring receptions, South Carolina won the game, 27-21.

Duke returned home to meet Northwestern a week later, and in a matchup of schools known more for their brains than their brawn, the Blue Devils won their fifth in a row over the Wildcats, 41-31. Tailback Roger Boone eased through the NU defenders for 201 yards, becoming the first Duke runner since Steve Jones to eclipse the 200-yard barrier in a single game. Although the Devils didn't play much defense, allowing 512 yards and 30 first downs, Ray's 295 yards and four touchdowns were more than enough for Duke to salt away the Wildcats.

Although they had lost five of their last six games, Penn State was ranked No. 12 as the Cavaliers headed north to Happy Valley. The Moore-to-Moore combination came through in fine style in the first half, as Shawn hit Herman twice for scores. Taking a 14-0 lead into halftime, the Cavaliers momentarily allowed PSU to gain some momentum. The Lions converted a pair of field goals in the third quarter to cut the lead to 14-6 as the final period loomed. Nonetheless, Virginia hung tough on Penn State's final offensive possession, knocking away a desperate fourth down pass with less than thirty seconds remaining to preserve victory.

Georgia Tech knew that the Moores would be looking to connect, but the Cavaliers were a step ahead in the ACC opener. McGonnigal became Shawn's favorite target, and the big tight end came through with six catches for 157 yards. McGonnigal hauled in two long passes that led directly to UVA scores, helping the Cavaliers take the Yellow Jackets, 17-10. Terry Kirby's 3-yard touchdown broke a 7-7 tie, and McGonnigal's 42-yard reception in the third quarter led to a field goal by Jake McInerney. Scott Sisson nailed a field goal of his own in the second half for Tech, but they were unable to come up with another touchdown.

That same evening, Duke faced off against Tennessee in Knoxville. Johnny Majors' Volunteers, on their way to eleven victories and the SEC Championship, put forth a determined defensive effort against the Blue Devils. The UT defense became the only unit all season to hold the Duke offense to single digits, stifling Spurrier's passing game by often dropping eight men into pass coverage. The Blue Devils were held to only two field goals, and with Volunteer running back Reggie Cobb enjoying a fine game, including a 61-yard scoring gallop in the final quarter, UT took the game by a 28-6 score.

The Duke-UVA encounter was at hand, and although it was still September, many pointed to this game as the one that would dictate the league standings. Playing like a team on a mission on their home field, the Cavaliers executed to near perfection, scoring more points against the Blue Devils than they had in their previous three games combined. Moore completed a school-record thirteen consecutive passes, riddling the Blue Devil secondary with his accurate tosses. Finishing the game fourteen-of-fifteen passing, Moore led UVA to three touchdowns in the second quarter for a 21-10 lead.

The Cavaliers sealed victory with an eleven-play, 63-yard scoring drive to begin the second half, as they jumped out to a 28-10 cushion. Brown threw three touchdowns for Duke to make the score closer, but UVA took a 49-28 final with another trio of end zone crossings. Virginia's dominating performance gave Cavalier fans bragging rights that would last through the winter. Taking on William and Mary in their fifth game, the Cavaliers again displayed precision on offense and stubbornness on defense, piling up 392 rushing yards in a 24-12 victory over their ranked I-AA opposition.

Duke rebounded from their decisive setback at the hands of the Cavaliers, and beat Clemson at home for the first time since 1975. Playing on a rain-soaked field, the No. 7 Tigers broke out to a 14-0 bulge, but in a stunning reversal of fortunes, Duke held Clemson to only 95 total yards in the final thirty minutes, shutting down their prized rushing assault to only 46 yards. The Blue Devils came back to tie the game at 14 by the end of the third quarter, and although Chris Gardocki put CU back into the lead briefly with a field goal, Ray connected with fullback Chris Brown at the 3:18 mark of the final quarter to give the Devils a 21-17 advantage. Clemson immediately went on the attack, as quarterback Chris Morocco completed a 25-yard pass to Wes McFadden, and Terry Allen broke off an 11-yard run. With their backs to the wall at the 16, the Blue Devil defenders held out CU in four consecutive plays to preserve the victory.

Clemson had no plans to give up their ACC championship lying down, and blew out Virginia, 34-20, the following week for their twenty-ninth victory in a row over the Cavaliers. Matt Blundin made his first career start at quarterback in place of the injured Shawn Moore, and threw a pair of touchdowns to keep UVA close. The Cavs trailed by only 7 points at halftime, but Chris Morocco's run and 43-yard touchdown pass gave the Tigers an insurmountable lead. One of the few bright spots for Virginia in the second half was a 75-yard scoring play by Herman Moore. The receiver beat his defender and hauled in a perfect spiral from Blundin, who had put the Clemson defense off-guard by faking a reverse. With the victory, Clemson joined Virginia at the top of the standings, and maintained their chances of an unprecedented fourth consecutive league title.

The Blue Devils played good football for three quarters against Army, but nearly gave away the game thanks to a fourth quarter letdown. With Hines catching three touchdown passes from Ray, and new running sensation Randy Cuthbert adding 147 yards and another pair of scores, Duke ran up a 35-10 lead going into the final period. Two Blue Devil fumbles, combined with solid execution of the Army wishbone, resulted in three unanswered scores for the Cadets, resulting in a 35-29 final. Although Duke held on to take the win, the game had an unsettling effect on Blue Devil fans.

Shawn Moore took advantage of his week off, and was back at full strength for the North Carolina game. Although the Tar Heels came out of the gates strong with a 71-yard touchdown drive, the Cavaliers dominated with 513 yards of offense. Virginia turned three Carolina turnovers into scores in the first half, and went into halftime in command of a 24-10 score. Moore finished the game with 207 yards passing, with 116 going to Herman. Virginia's pass-catching sensation netted nearly half the yardage on a single play early in the second half, taking in a 53-yard pass for a 31-10 advantage. Following a Carolina safety, Virginia tacked on 17 more points to build up a 50-10 lead five minutes into the final quarter. Although the Tar Heels scored a late touchdown, the Cavaliers had already equaled a school record for points scored in a conference game. With Georgia Tech's 30-14 upset of Clemson in Death Valley that same day, UVA was now sitting alone in first place.

McGonnigal was Moore's main target in the Wake Forest game, as the tight end came through with eight catches for 137 yards and two touchdowns. Both of McGonnigal's scores came in the second half, as Moore read a pair of Wake Forest blitzes and delivered the ball over the middle. Moore finished with 357 total yards, coming on 280 passing and 77 rushing, to lead UVA to a 47-28 victory. Although Wake enjoyed its highest point total thus far in the season, Virginia's 601 yards of offense was too much to overcome.

After a week off, Duke returned to the fold for a game against Maryland in College Park. It proved to be a good time for a bye, as the Blue Devils came out fresh and relaxed against the Terps. Making only his second career start, Cuthbert was a force in the Duke backfield, running for 161 yards in thirty-eight carries, and hauling in six catches for 84 more. Ray again riddled the opposing secondary, throwing for 308 yards and three touchdowns. Building a 22-3 lead at halftime, the Devils continued to pour it on the Terrapins in the second half, taking a 46-25 final. It was the first victorious trip to College Park for Duke since the 1960 ACC championship team, and the Blue Devils wanted something to remember it by. In a gesture that rubbed some people the wrong way, the Duke players and coaches commemorated the event by huddling for a team photo on the Byrd Stadium field after the game.

Stepping out of the ACC to play Louisville the ensuing week, Virginia nearly fell victim to the dreaded letdown. Despite giving up 369 yards to the UVA offense, Louisville allowed the Cavaliers only one touchdown, which came in the second quarter on a 4-yard Moore-to-Moore completion. The scrappy Cardinals trailed only 13-9 at halftime, and a pair of second half field goals by Klaus Wilmsmeyer put them in position to win. Wilmsmeyer's kick at the 3:26 mark of the fourth quarter was his third successful conversion, and gave Louisville a 15-13 lead. Moore passed his way through the Cardinal secondary, as the Cavaliers moved to the Louisville 20 in the final seconds. With the clock running out, McInerney was good from 37 yards to push UVA ahead to stay 16-15.

Cuthbert continued to dazzle Blue Devil supporters in the Georgia Tech game, setting a new school record with 234 rushing yards. Spurrier fooled the Yellow Jacket defensive coaches by taking to the ground, disdaining Duke's successful "Airball" style with a more conventional attack. Cuthbert's three touchdowns, combined with a defensive effort that held GT to only three first downs in the opening half, propelled the Devils to a 30-19 victory. The Yellow Jackets rallied in the final thirty minutes, cutting the Duke lead to 24-17 at one point, but a 59-yard gallop by Cuthbert broke their backs.

The ACC lead was up for grabs in Raleigh on November 4, as the Cavaliers met N.C. State. The 7-1 Wolfpack boasted the conference's best scoring defense, but had yet to play either Virginia or Duke. With both the Cavaliers and Wolfpack sporting 4-1 conference records, the game would make the winner and break the loser. The Wolfpack took a 6-0 lead on two field goals by Damon Hartman, but UVA countered with a McInerney boot and a defensive touchdown courtesy of cornerback Jason Wallace, who intercepted a pass and rambled 40 yards down the sideline for a 10-6 Cavalier lead. McInerney added another field goal in the third quarter, and the Moore combination was good for 32 yards to give the Cavaliers a 20-9 margin. Although they outdid Virginia offensively, State was unable to mount a comeback, and watched their ACC·title hopes fade away on the turf of their home field.

Another high-scoring affair awaited Spurrier's team in Winston-Salem, as Wake Forest and Duke combined for 87 points. Dave Brown took full advantage of his opportunity to start over the injured Ray, hooking up with Hines for a 76-yard scoring play on the first play from scrimmage. Hines finished with 251 yards, which included a 97-yard sprint for another Blue Devil score. The Duke passing attack accounted for 444 yards, while the running backs added 165 to complete a 600+ yard offensive performance. Scoring 31 points in the opening half, Duke added another trio of scores in the final thirty minutes for a 52-35 triumph.

The Cavaliers were nothing short of sensational in the first half against Virginia Tech, rolling out to a 24-0 lead behind 254 yards of offense. Durwin Greggs reached the end zone first for the Cavaliers with a 4-yard run, and Shawn Moore added to the lead with an 11-yard scamper. The Hokies came back in the third quarter with 16 points, but a 22-yard run by Greggs gave the Cavaliers enough points to withstand the VT charge. With the 32-25 victory, Virginia claimed nine victories in a regular season for the first time in the twentieth century. It had been a mere ninety-four years prior, 1895 to be exact, since Thomas Jefferson's University had last toasted a nine-victory football team.

The annual N.C. State-Duke game was the very definition of a shootout, as both teams threw caution to the wind with their passing attacks. State's Shane Montgomery set a new NCAA record with 73 pass attempts, and although he threw for 535 yards, five of the quarterback's passes were intercepted. Brown was just as productive in the opening half, throwing for 282 yards to give Duke a 28-10 lead. Held off the scoreboard over the final two quarters, Brown and the Duke offense were stuffed to only 164 yards. Their only touchdown came courtesy of the defense, as sophomore cornerback Wyatt Smith jumped in front of an ill-advised Montgomery pass and raced 64 yards for a 35-20 score. Montgomery completed a 65-yard play in the fourth quarter to flanker Reggie Lawrence, but a missed conversion made the final score 35-26 in favor of Duke.

Virginia's junior quarterback put together one of his finest performances in the regular season finale against Maryland, which clinched the Cavaliers at least a share of their first ACC championship in thirty-six seasons of league competition. In an explosive opening half, Maryland hung tough by scoring two touchdowns in the first twenty minutes. The Cavaliers countered by scoring three touchdowns of their own in the final 10:05 of the first half, with the last coming on a 36-yard bomb from Shawn to Herman on the final play. The Moore-to-Moore touchdown gave UVA a 28-14 lead at the half, and it increased late in the third quarter on a pass to Tim Finkelston. Moore finished the game nine-of-eighteen with 161 yards passing, and ran for 121 more as the Cavaliers wiped away the Terrapins, 48-21.

"They had higher aspirations than I did," George Welsh said of his team. "I wasn't thinking about ten wins or an ACC title. We had great leadership, a solid group of kids. Whatever they had to do, they went out and did."

Few days are as satisfying for football fans as those when you dominate your age-old rival, and in doing it to clinch a share of the ACC championship with Virginia; Duke's 41-0 obliteration of North Carolina in Chapel Hill ranks among the finest days in the history of Blue Devil football. Brown played at the highest level, completing 33-of-54 passes for 479 yards and three scores. All three touchdowns went to Hines, who surpassed 1,000 receiving yards for the third year in a row. By game's end, Hines had surpassed his own ACC yardage mark for a single season, and edged out New Mexico's Terrance Mathis as the NCAA's all-time leader in receiving touchdowns.

The game was never in doubt, as Duke drove for two early touchdowns and took a 17-0 lead after only fifteen minutes of play. Cuthbert, who also went past the 1,000-yard mark during the contest, scored from 2 yards away for Duke's second score. By halftime, the Devils had stretched their lead out to 27-0, as the defense neutralized Carolina's young offense. Duke scored its final points early in the final quarter, although the offense attempted a couple of plays late in the game that some may have considered cheeky. With a 41-0 advantage, Duke not only attempted a field goal, but also continued completing passes up until the next-to-last play of the game. Following the contest, the Blue Devils assembled beneath the opposing scoreboard for another photo.

By virtue of their victory over the Blue Devils, Virginia made plans to spend New Year's Day in Orlando, while Duke prepared for an encounter with Texas Tech in Birmingham's All-American Bowl. Clemson and N.C. State also earned postseason berths, the Wolfpack in the Copper Bowl against Arizona, and the Tigers in the Gator Bowl against West Virginia. It was only the second time in history that four ACC teams received bowl invitations, and considering the rapid additions of bowl games across the country in the coming years, it was now safe to say that virtually every first-division ACC school in the future could look forward to a phone call from a bowl committee following their final regular season game.

Duke was the first to play their bowl, ending a streak of nearly three decades without a postseason contest for the Durham school. A Blue Devil team had not won nine games since 1941, when Wallace Wade, the namesake of the school's stadium, had guided the Blue Devils to the Rose Bowl. It was not to be this year either, as Texas Tech opened the game with a formidable offensive surge. Behind running back James Gray, who set an All-American Bowl record with three touchdowns in the first half, the Red Raiders jumped out to a 28-0 advantage.

Brown, on his way to 268 yards through the air, completed a pair of scoring strikes to cut the TT lead in half, but the Red Raiders wrapped up the game in the third quarter, scoring another pair of touchdowns to take a commanding 42-14 lead. Although the competitive phase of the game was over, Dave Colonna caught his second touchdown pass from Brown, covering 16 yards, to bring Duke to within 42-21. Just for good measure, Gray did it again, busting free on a 32-yard scoring run to complete the scoring at 49-21. Although

Duke's seven-game winning streak came to an end with the defeat to Texas Tech, everyone associated with the Blue Devil program was proud of the vast improvement of the team under Spurrier.

Now one of the hottest commodities in coaching, few people expected Spurrier to stay at Duke very long. Indeed, it only took three days for Spurrier to make his move, accepting the job at his alma mater, the University of Florida, on New Year's Eve. Florida was still searching for the school's first Southeastern Conference Championship when Spurrier arrived, but under the former quarterback, the Gators would soon begin to thrive. Utilizing the same offensive strategy at UF that he used at Duke, Spurrier would soon have Florida among the elite programs in all of college football.

North Carolina State's offense came unglued in Tucson, as the Wildcats enjoyed nothing short of a home game in the Copper Bowl. The Arizona defense, led by twins Chris and Kevin Singleton, neutralized the NCSU line late, keeping State from making a dent into their 17-10 advantage. The Wildcats took the lead on an 85-yard interception return by Scott Geyer, and held on for the single-touchdown victory.

Clemson renewed ACC pride with victory over West Virginia in Jacksonville, giving the Tiger seniors a perfect 4-0 record in bowl games. Although James Jett got the Mountaineers on the scoreboard first with a 12-yard reception, CU scored the next 27 points in succession. The Tiger defense held WVU to 237 total yards, and added a touchdown of its own in the final quarter to put the game on ice. Leading 17-7, lineman Chester McGlockton recovered a fumble in the end zone, giving Clemson their final touchdown. Gardocki's final field goal cemented a 27-7 victory for the Tigers, which ended Danny Ford's run in Death Valley.

Following the 1989 season, more rumors surfaced about possible NCAA violations on the part of the Clemson football program. Although the school did not face any sanctions, the speculation was enough to create a major stir, and land Ford on the hot seat. With a rift between Ford and CU's athletic administration evident, the Tiger head coach was soon out of work. Ford resigned at Clemson less than three weeks after the Gator Bowl triumph, ending one of the most successful coaching careers in the history of the league.

Ford left Death Valley tied for first in career victories (96) and second in winning percentage (76 percent) among Atlantic Coast Conference head football coaches. The Tiger skipper had earned the adoration of fans with his down-home charm and successful coaching prowess, and many CU supporters expressed anger and frustration at his resignation, which was not a voluntary decision. Ford laid low for a couple of years, but would be back on the sidelines at the University of Arkansas by the early 1990s.

Virginia had the distinction of being the only ACC member to play on New Year's Day in 1990, meeting Illinois in the Citrus Bowl. Illinois took the upper hand behind Jeff George, who threw for 321 yards on his way to being named the first overall selection of the upcoming NFL Draft. George threw 15 yards to Steven Williams for the first Illini touchdown, and followed with strikes to Dan Donovan and Mike Bellamy. Virginia tried to hang tough, as Shawn Moore accounted for 225 total yards. Although Moore connected with Finkleston for a 30-yard score in the first half, UVA trailed 17-7 into the locker rooms. Wilson scored another touchdown for the Cavaliers in the third quarter, but not before Howard Griffith had piled over for the Illini. Bellamy's 24-yard reception from George gave Illinois a commanding late bulge, and although Shawn found Herman for a final score, Virginia dropped the contest, 31-21.

Despite the loss to Illinois, Virginia had every reason to believe that the following season would bring even more success to Charlottesville. Both Moores were returning to the Cavalier offense, in addition to Bruce McGonnigal, Terry Kirby, and defensive standout Chris Slade. Following the 1989 season, many experts predicted that Virginia would be in the hunt for the NCAA title the following year. Although the experts were correct in thinking that the ACC could produce a national championship-caliber team in 1990, most picked the wrong school.

12

Wrecking Crew (1990)

Georgia Tech was hoping to have a solid football team heading into the 1990 season, but nobody could have prepared Bobby Ross and his Yellow Jackets for what was to come. Exceeding all expectations, Tech claimed the school's first unbeaten season since 1952, and ascended to the No. 1 ranking in the Coaches Poll following their Citrus Bowl victory over Nebraska. Ross, who became the first head coach in history to lead two different schools to Atlantic Coast Conference championships, was rewarded by being named National Coach of the Year.

Ross entered a different situation at Georgia Tech than he had at Maryland, where he replaced Jerry Claiborne following the 1981 season. Ross stepped into a solid foundation at College Park, as the Terrapins were loaded with talented players recruited by the old staff. Instead of rebuilding the Terrapin program, Ross was left with the task of continuing to steer the ship in the right direction. After five years and three ACC championships at Maryland, Ross was ready for a new challenge by the end of the 1986 season.

Over that same period of time, Georgia Tech had established itself as the eighth member of the ACC. Although Bill Curry led the Yellow Jackets to a bowl game in 1985, things were looking bleak in Atlanta by the time Ross arrived in town. Stars such as Robert Lavette and Pat Swilling were gone, and Curry's staff had struggled to recruit equally talented players. By the time Ross arrived at Georgia Tech, the cupboard was bare.

Ross struggled in his first two seasons at Tech, posting a 2-9 record in 1987 and a 3-8 record in 1988. Although the Yellow Jackets were winless against their ACC rivals during these rebuilding seasons, the recruiting battles were a different story. Ross and his staff quickly reloaded the GT program with a number of skilled players, particularly on the defensive side of the ball.

In the offseasons of their rebuilding campaigns, the Georgia Tech staff reeled in a pair of prized recruits in Marco Coleman and Ken Swilling. Swilling, a defensive back, and Coleman, a defensive end, combined speed with outstanding defensive awareness, and the pair served as catalysts on the 1990 Yellow Jacket defense. Coleman and Swilling got help from Willie Clay and Calvin Tiggle, and the quartet all made the All-ACC defensive team. Ross's staff was also successful recruiting on offense, bringing in multitalented quarterback Shawn Jones and running back William Bell. Blessed with speed and throwing accuracy, Jones was exactly what Ross and offensive coordinator Ralph Friedgen were looking for to run their offense. Bell was a solid addition to the GT backfield, posting four 100-yard rushing games in 1990, and finishing the season with 1,050 total yards.

"I don't think there could be a more skilled athlete at his position in college football than Shawn," Ross once said of his quarterback. "There may be some guys who have a stronger arm, but I don't think they have a more accurate one."

Although the Georgia Tech players and staff were excited about the possibility of having a great season in 1990, the rest of the college football world had its doubts. As the preseason polls were released, Georgia Tech did not find itself ranked in the Top Twenty Five. With 1989 ACC rushing leader Jerry Mays gone, the media was skeptical that Tech had someone capable of taking his place. As it turned out, Bell and Jeff Wright filled the large shoes of Mays admirably, combining for 1,286 yards on the ground. With a defense that played above and beyond its supposed ability all year, and a kicker that combined accuracy with steely nerves, Atlanta became the site of one of the surprise stories in the history of college football in the fall of 1990.

The Jackets took the field on an oppressively hot summer afternoon for the opener against N.C. State. The first play from scrimmage was a bad omen for Tech, as miscommunication between Jones and Bell resulted in a fumble. Minutes later, Damon Hartman booted a field goal for a 3-0 NCSU lead. Following another fumble, this one from Stefen Scotton at the Wolfpack 11, Fernandus Vinson came up with the ball and ran over for a 10-0 State advantage. Trailing 13-7 going into the fourth quarter, the Jackets finally took control behind Jones, who expertly piloted their option attack through the Wolfpack for a pair of critical touchdowns. The first went to Bell on a pass play, and the other went to Wright on a short run. The GT defense held strong, and the home team took the game by a score of 21-13.

The Yellow Jackets carried the momentum of their spirited second half effort against NCSU into the team's second contest, played in Atlanta against Tennessee-Chattanooga. Tech forced seven turnovers from the Moccasins, while Jones hooked up with Bell for a 78-yard touchdown to give the Jackets a 10-3 advantage. Leading 17-9, the Ramblin' Wreck broke the game open in the second half by scoring 27 unanswered points. Scotton avenged his fumble against N.C. State with a touchdown, and Derek Goshay added another late tally for a 44-9 final.

South Carolina came to Atlanta favored and ranked No. 25, led by a strong offense. With an opportunity to prove itself against solid opposition, Tech's defense established superiority from the beginning. South Carolina was held to only 40 rushing yards, as Yellow Jackets swarmed the Gamecock ballcarriers play after play. Georgia Tech racked up 346 yards with their offensive unit, and took the lead on a sneak by Jones in the second quarter. The teams traded field goals for a 10-3 score at the intermission. Runs by Scotton and Wright gave the Yellow Jackets a 24-6 advantage at the end of three quarters, and a Scott Sisson field goal in the final frame made the score at the end 27-6 in favor of Tech.

Ross had yet to win a game for Georgia Tech at his old stomping grounds, but his overwhelming defensive unit was ready to make another statement against Maryland in College Park. T. J. Edwards replaced the injured Bell in the Yellow Jacket backfield, and rushed for 97 yards. The defensive unit dominated Maryland's offensive front, sacking Terrapin quarterbacks Scott Zolak and Jim Sandwisch eleven times. Marco Coleman completed five of the sacks all by himself, as the Jackets ran their streak without allowing an offensive touchdown to fourteen consecutive quarters.

Jones put together another solid performance, throwing for a career-high 271 yards on fifteen-of-twenty-four passing. Scoring in every quarter, the Jackets ran up a 17-3 halftime lead, and put the game out of reach early in the third quarter on a 40-yard scoring toss from Jones to Greg Lester. On first-and-10, Jones changed the play at the line. He checked off and found Lester along the left sideline. Lester beat UM cornerback Michael Hollis, caught the ball at the 5-yard line, and dived into the end zone for a score. Another touchdown in the final period gave the Jackets an easy 31-3 win.

Clemson had already dropped a league game to Virginia, and could not afford to lose another if they hoped to finish among the ACC's top teams when they arrived in Atlanta on October 13. The Jackets welcomed their nemesis with a fast start, as they built up a 14-0 lead on touchdown passes to Lester and Emmett Merchant. The Georgia Tech offense was stifled the next two quarters, as Clemson's defensive unit kept them in the game. Edwards, who again led GT in rushing, wound up injuring his ankle, leaving most of the offensive burden on Jones. After his early success, things got ugly for the sophomore signal caller. Jones threw three incompletes and an interception in the second half, and was unable to move the Ramblin' Wreck back into position for a touchdown.

Following a scoreless second quarter, Clemson kicker Chris Gardocki nailed a couple of field goals to make the score 14-9 heading into the final fifteen minutes. The Tiger offense got the ball back after an interception, and moved into range once again for Gardocki, who made his fourth kick to make the score 14-12. Stagnant on offense now for nearly forty minutes, Georgia Tech finally got the break it needed on the ensuing kickoff. Returner Kevin Tisdel found a seam and sprinted 87 yards to the Tiger 13, and three plays later, Edwards rambled over for a 21-12 Georgia Tech advantage.

Clemson wasn't finished, and promptly put an end to GT's defensive touchdown streak by moving 41 yards in seven plays. DeChane Cameron cut the Yellow Jacket lead to 21-19, and the Tigers got the ball back late in the game with a chance to prevail. After easing slightly into GT territory, Gardocki trudged out for another effort, this one from 60 yards. With fifty-nine seconds on the clock, Gardocki lined up and booted the game-winning try. With the odds stacked significantly against him, the kick fell short and wide right. Tech ran out the clock, and improved to 5-0 for the first time in twenty-four years.

Now holding the longest winning streak in Division I-A at nine games, Georgia Tech next headed to Chapel Hill to play North Carolina. The UNC defense was up to the challenge, and forced a pair of turnovers that resulted in field goals. The Tech defenders also played well, holding UNC to 151 yards and only nine first downs. Nonetheless, Carolina took an early 3-0 lead. The slim UNC advantage vanished in the second period, as Jones broke off a 26-yard scamper to the end zone for the only touchdown of the half. Sisson added a field goal three minutes later to make the score 10-3 at halftime. As the defense held the Jackets off the scoreboard throughout the third quarter, Tar Heel kicker Clint Gwaltney boomed his second field goal to make the score 10-6.

Another mistake by Tech, this one on a punt return, set up a go-ahead score for Carolina. The normally sure-handed Willie Clay let one slip, and the dropped punt was secured by UNC's Reggie Clark. With the ball on the GT 5, Natrone Means bulled his way across the goal line, and suddenly the Yellow Jackets were staring a major upset in the face. Jones got the Georgia Tech offense moving again, charging 85 yards to the brink of victory. With the ball on the 1, the Yellow Jacket offensive stalled out. Carolina came up with a courageous goal line stand, stuffing Scotton on fourth down to reclaim possession. Realizing that victory was slipping away, Ross finally elected to take what he could get. With 1:01 remaining, Sisson came on and kicked his second field goal, and the teams left the field deadlocked at 13. Although it was a bitter end to what had been a poorly played game by his team, Ross could take solace in the fact that the Yellow Jackets were still unbeaten.

Duke had won three consecutive games against the Yellow Jackets, and came to Atlanta geared up for another tough encounter. Without Ken Swilling for the second game in a row, GT's defense gave up 31 points to the Blue Devils, the most it had given up to anyone thus far in the year. Fortunately for the Yellow Jackets, the offense thrived against Duke's poor defensive unit. With Jones and Scotton each running for two scores, and Bell rushing for a career-high 166 yards and a score of his own, it was smooth sailing on that side of the ball. With 2:08 to play in the third quarter, Kevin Tisdel broke off an 85-yard return, which drove a painful nail into Duke's hopes for victory. The play couldn't have come at a better time for the walk-on, who was awarded a scholarship following the game.

Tech's 48-31 victory over the Blue Devils served as a tune-up for one of the biggest games of the entire college football season. On November 4, the Yellow Jackets rolled into Charlottesville for a showdown with Virginia. Both teams were unbeaten, with the winner holding an inside track to a New Year's Day game and a shot at the NCAA title. It had been a magical autumn thus far in Charlottesville, as Virginia had ascended to the No. 1 ranking in the country for the first time in school history. Behind the offensive production of Shawn and Herman Moore, Virginia had rolled up seven easy victories to begin the season.

Shawn Moore was leading the nation in passing efficiency, and had led the Cavaliers to a 59-0 shellacking of Duke, a 56-14 pounding of Navy, and a 49-14 dumping of Wake Forest. In addition, the Cavaliers had dumped Clemson 20-7 back in September, ending Virginia's twenty-nine year losing streak at the hands of the Tigers. One bad note for UVA was the fact that pass-catching threat Bruce McGonnigal had been lost before the victory over Wake Forest, after suffering a freak accident while chasing a dog outside his girlfriend's apartment. The tight end would be sorely missed, but despite McGonnigal's absence, UVA got an extra week to prepare for the invading Yellow Jackets.

An electric atmosphere surrounded Charlottesville throughout the week, as the normally subdued community prepared for its biggest football game in history. In a featured game on CBS that included a pair of Top Ten teams, it ironically took some quick thinking on the part of UVA officials to ensure that the game would even be played on schedule. In the early morning hours the night before the contest, an unknown individual entered Scott Stadium and burned a hole in a large section of the Astroturf. Upon learning of the vandalized field, stadium workers toiled throughout the night, installing a new section on the burned spot using remnants of the turf used to cover the Cavalier baseball field. After allowing the glue to dry, officials from both Georgia Tech and Virginia, in addition to ACC Commissioner Gene Corrigan, inspected the field and agreed that it was acceptable to play on.

On an unusually humid November afternoon in Charlottesville, Virginia's offense gave the overflowing home crowd plenty to cheer about early on, driving for a touchdown and leading marches that resulted in two Jake McInerney field goals. Trailing 13-0, it was imperative that Georgia Tech go downfield and score, and they did just that. With the ball on the UVA 23, Jones dropped back to throw and found nobody open. Cutting his way from the middle of the field to the sideline, Jones quieted the capacity crowd by scampering to the end zone, bringing the Jackets to within six. The second quarter was a shootout, as Shawn Moore dove in twice and Jones threw a scoring pass to make the score 28-14 after two quarters.

In the second half, linebacker Calvin Tiggle became a vacuum for Georgia Tech, helping the Yellow Jackets climb their way back into the game. Tiggle's first big play came in the third quarter, as he recovered a Virginia fumble. Jerry Gilchrist took the ball on a flanker reverse, and galloped the distance for a 28-21 score. After the Yellow Jacket defense stopped the Cavaliers again, Jones tossed to a leaping Merchant from 26 yards away to tie the game at 28.

Virginia needed a big play, and got it courtesy of its All-American tandem. From the GT 37, Shawn dropped into the pocket and drilled Herman, who raced through the resistance for a 63-yard touchdown and a 35-28 Cavalier lead. Virginia got the ball back minutes later, but Tiggle came up with another important defensive effort. Stepping in front of a Moore pass and making an interception, Tiggle gave the Yellow Jackets yet another chance to remain close. Although Tech couldn't score on their ensuing possession, it was becoming more and more evident as darkness fell over Charlottesville that Georgia Tech was not going to fold.

William Bell ran over with the third quarter winding down to tie the game at 35, and GT took its first lead early in the final quarter, as Sisson booted a field goal for a 38-35 advantage. Virginia quickly went on the move, driving deep into Yellow Jacket territory. In an unfortunate lack of execution, however, the orange-shirted Cavaliers could not cross the goal line on six separate opportunities from inside the Georgia Tech 6-yard line. Virginia was penalized twice for illegal procedure, the second nullifying a touchdown pass to Aaron Mundy. Instead of taking a four-point lead, Virginia settled for McInerney's 23-yard field goal, which tied the score at 38 with 2:34 remaining.

With uncanny coolness for a sophomore, Jones ran and passed the Jackets into field goal range in the closing moments, and with seven seconds on the clock, Sisson came on for a 37-yard kick. When the ball passed through the uprights, the small horde of Ramblin' Wreck fans assembled in Scott Stadium, about 1,000 strong, went into a golden frenzy. On a day when four of the top five teams in the nation were beaten, the 41-38 victory made a significant stride in helping Georgia Tech enter the national picture. The loss was a demoralizing one for Virginia, as they lost two of their final three regular season games to drop from the school's first and only taste of life as college football's No. 1 team.

"This is something you can't describe," said Scott Aldredge, who held for Sisson's winning boot. "On the sidelines, I got him ready. He kicked into the net a few times, and I patted him on the head and told him, 'Just stroke it.'"

Prevailing over Virginia had proven quite difficult for the Yellow Jackets, and the following week's encounter with Virginia Tech proved to be just as much of a challenge. In a reversal of fortunes from the contest in Charlottesville, the Jacket offense played its worst game of the year, unable to move effectively against VT's wide-tackle defensive approach. After forty-five minutes of football, the game was still scoreless. Virginia Tech finally reached the scoreboard in the final period, as Mickey Thomas came on and gave the Hokies a 3-0 advantage.

Georgia Tech countered with a drive of its own, and Sisson nailed a kick to knot up the game. Another Yellow Jacket defender, Chris Simmons, came up with a big play in the final minutes, falling on a muffed handoff to give the Jackets the ball in position to win. With eight seconds on the clock, Sisson was called upon once again to lift his team to victory. Kicking into the wind, Sisson got plenty of leg on the pigskin, and it sailed through the posts to kick-start another gleeful celebration for Yellow Jacket fans.

After blowing out Wake Forest 42-7 in Winston-Salem to claim the ACC title, Tech entered its annual dogfight with Georgia. With an opportunity to play for the national championship, the Yellow Jackets could not afford to let down against UGA, who they knew would give them their best shot. Sure enough, Georgia outplayed their instate nemesis early, taking a 9-0 lead on a run by Doobie Hearst and a kick by John Kasay. With Jones leading the way, the Georgia Tech offense clicked in the second quarter unlike it did at any other time over the course of the season. Completing twelve consecutive passes at one point, Jones led the Jackets to 23 points in the second frame, and took an eleven-point lead into the locker rooms.

Georgia made a change at quarterback for the second half, going with Greg Talley in place of freshman Joe Dupree, who had made his first collegiate start under center. Although the backup threw a touchdown to Andre Hastings, Jones and Bell continued to assault the Bulldog defense. Jones finished with a quartet of scoring passes, while Bell added 128 yards. When it was over, the scoreboard read 40-23 in favor of the Yellow Jackets. It was UGA's worst defeat at home since 1951, when Jim Tatum's Maryland squad had run over the Bulldogs, 43-7.

With the school's first ACC football championship in hand, in addition to a 10-0-1 overall record, Georgia Tech stood at No. 2 in the country. Victory in the Citrus Bowl over Nebraska would ensure at least consideration for the national championship for the Yellow Jackets, although the ideal scenario would have Notre Dame beating Colorado in the Orange Bowl. Should the Irish prevail, and Tech take care of business in their game, all signals pointed to the Ramblin' Wreck being named the undisputed champions. Before the Citrus Bowl was to be played, three other ACC schools had postseason games to look forward to, with Virginia playing in the Sugar Bowl on New Year's evening following Georgia Tech's afternoon contest in Orlando.

Maryland played its only bowl of the Joe Krivac era on December 15, tying Louisiana Tech (LT) 34-34 in Shreveport's Independence Bowl. The Terrapins and LT played an up-and-down game, with Maryland taking an early 14-0 advantage and Louisiana Tech later going ahead, 31-21. Maryland came back to take the lead, but Louisiana Tech placekicker Chris Boniol nailed a field goal at the final gun to officially knot up the contest.

North Carolina State earned a berth against Southern Mississippi in the All-American Bowl, despite the fact that the Wolfpack had a losing record of 3-4 in conference play. State's secondary struggled against Southern Miss quarterback Brett Favre, who threw three touchdowns, but the Wolfpack hung tough. After scoring 17 points in the opening half to take the lead, State stretched out its advantage on a Bobby Jurgens touchdown catch and a score by Greg Manior. Favre threw another scoring pass late in the game, but NCSU held on for a 31-27 verdict.

Clemson was hoping to have more luck on New Year's Day against Illinois in Tampa's Hall of Fame Bowl than Virginia had the year before in the Citrus Bowl. Although Jeff George had moved on to the NFL, the Illini were still a potent offensive team, led by running back Howard Griffith. The Tigers were hardly intimidated by Griffith, however, and made quick work of Illinois. The CU defense played its finest game of the season, holding Griffith to 59 yards. With Griffith neutralized, the Clemson offense passed its way through the Illini secondary. DeChane Cameron threw a pair of touchdowns, and Arlington Nunn returned an intercepted pass the length of the field for another CU score. Chris Gardocki added a hat trick of field goals, as the Tigers overwhelmed the Illini, 30-0. With the game, the Tiger seniors became the most victorious class in the history of the Atlantic Coast Conference, with forty triumphs in four seasons.

On New Year's afternoon, the chance to prove itself as No. 1 came calling for Georgia Tech against Nebraska's Cornhuskers. Jones and the Jacket offense wasted little time on their opening possession, as the quarterback broke free for a 46-yard scamper on the fourth play from scrimmage. Scotton scored from the 2 seconds later, and the fired-up Yellow Jackets had a 7-0 advantage. With the defense shutting down the Nebraska running game throughout the first twenty-five minutes, the Georgia Tech offense added to its lead on their second possession of the second quarter. From the 22, Jones stepped into the pocket and located Merchant, who had beaten his defender and was on a tear to the goal line. Merchant's over-the-shoulder grab gave Georgia Tech a stunning 14-0 bulge.

Jones continued to have the game of his life midway through the second quarter, as he riddled the Nebraska secondary with his steady passing. After completing long passes to Bell and Brent Goolsby, Jones went back to Bell for the 2-yard scoring completion. Now trailing by 21 points, the Nebraska offense finally found some life. With the Yellow Jacket defense holding the nation's second-ranked rushing offense to only 126 yards, the Cornhuskers had no choice but to throw. Desperately needing big plays, Nebraska got them courtesy of quarterback Tom Haase, who completed a pair of passes to Johnny Mitchell. The second was good for 30 yards and a touchdown, and the Cornhuskers had reason to hope.

Nebraska's hope was turned into glee minutes later, when Derek Brown gave Husker fans their only shining glimpse of the running game that they took so much pride in. Taking a handoff from midfield, Brown found a seam and raced 50 yards to the end zone. Tech's defenders were caught with their pants down, fully expecting Nebraska to continue trying to throw. With plenty of gaps in the spaced-out Yellow Jacket defense, Brown sprinted the distance.

It was suddenly a ball game, and although Sisson came on late in the half to give Georgia Tech a 24-14 lead, the momentum had clearly shifted to the Cornhuskers. Nebraska carried their momentum into their opening drive of the third quarter, as the red and white moved into field goal range for Gregg Barrios. With a chance to cut the lead to just a touchdown, Tech defender Keith Holmes made one of the biggest plays of the game. In an effort that changed the course of the contest, Holmes deflected Barrios' kick, and the Yellow Jackets took control at their own 22.

Jones, on his way to earning Most Valuable Player honors, continued his torrid pace, hitting Bell for 30 yards and Jerry Gilchrist for 23 more. Pushing the ball inside the Nebraska 1, Jones sealed the deal with a lunge across the line. Nebraska threw another long touchdown to make the score 31-21, but the fourth quarter belonged to the Yellow Jackets. Bell's second touchdown, which concluded a drive on which he did much of the work, gave Georgia Tech a commanding 38-21 cushion, and with the GT defense stifling the Cornhuskers throughout the decisive period, the Jacket offense made a final series of plays to make its case for the NCAA crown.

After completing a pass to Merchant for 16 yards, which put the ball at the Georgia Tech 43, Jones handed off to Bell. Behind textbook blocking, Bell sprung into the clear, and raced 57 yards for the touchdown that ended the competitive phase of the game. As the final minutes played out of Tech's 45-21 blowout, the debate as to which team was No. 1 officially began. As Bobby Ross was carried to the center of the Citrus Bowl field, the scoreboard in the far end zone spelled out, "Georgia Tech National Champions."

The Yellow Jackets had done all they could do, and the only thing left now was to watch on that evening and see if Notre Dame could beat Colorado in the Orange Bowl. The Yellow Jacket players and coaches could all but taste the national championship following Raghib "Rocket" Ismail's 91-yard punt return in the final minutes for Notre

Dame, but a controversial clipping penalty took away the score. Colorado held on for the controversial 10-9 victory, and the issue was left up to the pollsters to settle.

Tennessee was the opponent for Virginia in the Sugar Bowl, as the Cavaliers made the Atlantic Coast Conference's first New Orleans postseason football appearance since Frank Howard's 1958 Clemson squad. The Cavaliers dominated early, taking a 16-0 lead behind the play of Shawn Moore and the defense. Although they looked to be in control, UVA ran out of gas against the steady pressure applied by Tennessee's offense. The Volunteers slowly but surely cracked at the Virginia advantage, as Greg Burke kicked a field goal and Tony Thompson ran over for another score. A third score pulled Tennessee to within two points at 19-17.

Virginia, desperate to hold its slim advantage, got some insurance following a field goal by McInerney. Tennessee had to score a touchdown for victory, and with the game on the line the Volunteers did just that. Volunteer quarterback Andy Kelly completed a clutch last-minute pass to Alvin Harper to put Tennessee in position. Following a running play that brought the ball down to the 1, Thompson scored for the second time. With only thirty-one seconds remaining on the clock following Thompson's score, UVA did not have enough time to erase the 23-22 deficit.

Although they were left as the nation's only unbeaten team, Georgia Tech was forced to share the NCAA title with Colorado. The Buffaloes took the top spot in the Associated Press poll, while the Yellow Jackets were voted No. 1 in the Coaches Poll. Without a clear-cut way to determine a national champion in football, the Georgia Tech-Colorado debate would only intensify in the coming seasons, as the NCAA tried to figure out a definitive way to determine the best college football team in the land.

13

A New Arrival (1991-2000)

The notion of a football powerhouse at Florida State University seemed outrageous in the mid-1970s, when Bobby Bowden returned to Tallahassee to become head coach. The Seminole program had fallen into complete disarray by 1975, winning only four games in three years. After a winless campaign in 1973, Darrell Mudra came to FSU intent on repeating the successes he enjoyed at North Dakota State and Arizona. Although Mudra did well later at smaller schools, his tenure at FSU was marred by a lack of discipline. Many of his players quit going to class, and there was a noticeable slip in the team's academic performance. Combined with a glaring lack of execution on the field, the Florida State boosters were up in arms for a new coach following the 1975 season.

Several men were rumored to be in the running for the Florida State job, but Athletic Director John Bridgers had only Bowden in mind. A former Seminole assistant, Bowden left Tallahassee in 1966 to become offensive coordinator at West Virginia. After four years as an assistant, Bowden became head coach of the Mountaineers in 1970. West Virginia, solid on both sides of the ball during Bowden's tenure, won 42 games in six seasons. Despite the team's success, however, Bobby could not win over the locals.

In the midst of a 4-7 season in 1974, Bowden was hung in effigy by angry fans. Bobby and his family had to endure humiliating signs that hung throughout Morgantown, saying such things as "Bye Bye, Bobby," and "Leave Town Bowden." One day, upon returning home from work, Bobby found a "For Sale" sign in his yard. Bowden overcame these attacks on his coaching ability, but never forgot the way in which the Mountaineer faithful turned on him. In 1975, Bowden led

WVU to seven wins and the Peach Bowl, where they beat Lou Holtz's N.C. State squad, 13-10.

After meeting Bowden at a Pensacola golf tournament in 1974, Bridgers decided that if he ever had the opportunity to lure the charismatic coach back to Tallahassee, he would take advantage. By November of 1975, Bowden was getting frequent phone calls from Seminole alumni and boosters, despite the fact that Mudra was still officially the head coach. A few weeks later, the boosters helped buy out Mudra's contract, and on January 12, 1976, Bowden accepted the Florida State job. In his first team meeting as head coach of the Seminoles, Bowden set the tone for the glorious future of the FSU program. He set clear guidelines for his team to follow, and instructed the players that they could leave if they did not like them.

"In the past three years, your Florida State football team has won only four games, and in the meantime, lost 29. Y'all have tried it your way. And where did it get you? Nowhere," Bowden told his new team. "Now, I think I know how to win. And from now on at Florida State, we are going to do things my way. If you don't like it, then hit the door. Go somewhere else. Because if winning doesn't mean something to you, we don't need you here."

Bowden's first Seminole team started the season 2-6, but began to pick up steam after a victory against Southern Mississippi, as FSU overcame a seventeen-point fourth quarter deficit to knock off the Golden Eagles, 30-27. The Seminoles won their final two games to finish with a 5-6 record, which turned out to be Bowden's only losing season in Tallahassee. The Bowden Era at Florida State began in earnest in 1977, as the Seminoles won ten games, including the school's first victory over archrival Florida in a decade. After dominating Texas Tech, 40-17, in the Citrus Bowl, it was evident to everyone following the FSU program that good times were ahead.

"I just love to coach," Bowden once said about himself. "That may sound simple, but I have always gotten my greatest pleasure of breaking down film, learning about opponents and yourself, then implementing a game plan to take advantage of your strengths and their weaknesses. I love to take a group of young men in the late summer and mold them into a team."

Bowden had an opportunity to leave Tallahassee in 1979, but after seriously considering the job at LSU that was eventually taken by the late Bo Rein, he elected to stay at Florida State. It turned out to be a wise decision, as the 1980s brought great promise to FSU's football fortunes. Starting in 1985, with their Gator Bowl victory over Oklahoma State, the Seminoles won eleven consecutive postseason games. In 1987 and 1988, the Seminoles lost only twice, each time to Miami. The losses prevented Bowden from claiming his first NCAA title.

Throughout these formative years, Florida State was a school without a conference. Like fellow powers Miami, Penn State, and Notre Dame, Florida State was a Division 1-A Independent. The annual FSU schedule was littered with SEC and ACC opponents, along with the obligatory games against the Hurricanes and Gators. By the late 1980s, however, the school was ready to begin reaping the benefits of membership in a major conference. The success of the Florida State football program would have been a nice addition to either the Southeastern Conference or the Atlantic Coast Conference, but over time it became clear that the SEC was not going to have a spot for the Seminoles. The conference was already larger than the ACC, with ten members to eight, and two more schools, Arkansas and South Carolina, were entering the league in 1992.

On July 1, 1991, the member institutions of the Atlantic Coast Conference unanimously voted to accept Florida State University as the league's ninth school, to begin competing for conference championships in all sports in 1992. With the Seminoles a cut above every other football program in the league, every school would have to step up their efforts in order to remain competitive. As it turned out, few teams in the conference were able to do so in FSU's first seasons of membership.

Clemson was able to enjoy one more season as the top dog of the ACC in 1991, finishing 6-0-1 to claim the school's thirteenth conference championship. The Tigers were used to being the big bullies of the league, but with Florida State preparing to invade, CU took one final crack as the team to beat. The landscape at Clemson had changed dramatically since the end of the 1989 season, when Danny Ford was pushed out as head coach. More rumors had surfaced about shady activities that may have taken place in the mid-1980s, allegations of improprieties on the part of Tiger boosters, players, and officials. A couple of players were accused of accepting small amounts of money from boosters and from each other, and the CU staff was blamed for giving impermissible car rides and clothes.

Although the NCAA did not lay down any penalties on the Clemson program, the accusations were enough to force Ford into resigning from his post as head coach of the Tigers. Despite the many questions about the integrity of his program, nobody could deny Ford's success on the field. He left Death Valley with five ACC championships, six bowl victories in eight appearances, and a legacy that proved to be too much for his successor to overcome. Three days after Ford's resignation, Clemson brought on Kan Hatfield as the school's new coach, a move that, at least in theory, appeared to be perfect for both parties.

Hatfield had proven himself a winner at the University of Arkansas, running a similar option-style offense to the one that Ford had used to such great success. Despite his familiarity with Ford's approach to football, Hatfield was different from his predecessor in many ways, some of which were difficult for Tiger fans to accept. Hatfield was strictly business most of the time, and rubbed many people the wrong way in his manner of handling things. Coming to a program used to tremendous football success, all Hatfield really needed to do was keep winning to ensure a legacy of his own at Clemson.

Led by future NFL stars Levon Kirkland and Chester McGlockton, the Tigers led the NCAA in rushing defense and finished second in the ACC in points allowed in 1991. The Tigers were also strong on the offensive side of the ball, averaging 26.4 points per outing over the course of twelve contests. Appalachian State came to Death Valley for an early warm-up, and the Tigers ran at will against their nemesis from Boone. Three different CU runners reached the goal line, making the score 24-0 after two quarters of play. With the defense looking sharp throughout, holding the Mountaineers scoreless, Nelson Welch nailed a field goal and Richard Moncrief threw a touchdown to complete a 34-0 blowout.

The Temple (TU) game was almost as easy for the Tigers, although the Owls were able to find the scoreboard against the Clemson defenders. A pass from Trent Thompson to Bryant Garvin gave TU an early lead, but the Tigers tied it on an end-around by Larry Ryans. From there the CU offense scored 30 unanswered points, with Dwayne Bryant and Rudy Harris each crossing into the end zone. In control after Temple's early score, Clemson's defense neutralized the line of scrimmage and took a 37-7 final.

Playing for the third straight time in Death Valley, the Tigers welcomed defending national champion Georgia Tech to town. Shawn Jones got GT going early, sneaking over the line for a 7-0 advantage. In a staunch defensive battle, Clemson was able to muster only a single field goal attempt in the first thirty minutes, and Welch booted it through to make the score 7-3 at the half. The game remained that way throughout the entire third quarter and into the final period, as a pair of excellent defenses exchanged blows to the respective offensive units. With the game waning into the final three minutes, Tech was hoping to hang on and escape Death Valley with the win. Robert O' Neal ensured that it wouldn't happen, as the CU punt returner brought a kick deep into Yellow Jacket territory. With 2:06 to play, the Tigers scored a touchdown to claim a dramatic 9-6 victory.

At 3-0, Clemson was looking solid, particularly on the defensive side of the ball. The unit had allowed only fourteen points in twelve quarters of play, and was hoping to carry that momentum to Sanford Stadium for an encounter with Georgia. In another defensive struggle, Welch and Kamon Parkman exchanged field goals for a 3-3 tie late in the first half, but UGA quarterback Eric Zeier completed a pair of long bombs to receivers Art Marshall and Andre Hastings. Marshall and Hastings each scored, and Georgia took a 17-3 advantage. The Tigers moved into range for another field goal, but Zeier threw another scoring pass to Hastings. Still unable to reach the end zone, the Tigers added another pair of kicks, but Garrison Hearst finished off CU with a late touchdown run. Unable to do any more, the Tigers took their first defeat of the year, 27-12.

Virginia began a three-game home stand for Clemson, and although the Tigers played a solid game, they were unable to knock off the Cavaliers. Matt Blundin, who went on to take league MVP honors, threw an early touchdown to Aaron Mundy, and led a drive that resulted in a Mike Husted field goal. Trailing 10-0, the Tigers came back to tie it, only to watch Virginia retake a ten-point advantage at 20-10. Clemson refused to fold, again reeling off ten unanswered points to knot up the game at 20. The Cavaliers moved into range for Husted with the game on the line, but Virginia was unable to claim their second consecutive victory over the Tigers. Clemson linebacker Wayne Simmons made the play of the game, deflecting the kick to the turf to preserve the 20-20 score. Although the Tigers were now winless in consecutive games for the first time since 1986, the tie to UVA proved to be their only ACC setback.

After two lackluster performances, Hatfield and his staff decided to try something different before the N.C. State game. For the first time in decades, the Tigers stepped onto the field wearing purple jerseys. The Tigers responded in their new apparel, toppling NCSU from the ranks of the unbeaten, 29-19. Welch, who became the fifth different Clemson placekicker in twelve seasons to be named All-ACC, tied a school record with five field goals, and although the Wolfpack kept the game close throughout, the CU defense made its presence felt. Kirkland and noseguard Rob Bodine wreaked havoc on State ballcarriers, combining for eighteen tackles. A pair of second half touchdowns gave Clemson their winning margin.

Wake Forest made six home games for Clemson out of seven total contests, and the Tigers made it a perfect 6-0 on the friendly grass of Memorial Stadium. Rodney Blunt scored a pair of touchdowns to lead the Tiger cause, while Doug Bolin added a score as well. Clemson dominated the opening two quarters, and took a 28-0 lead into halftime. Hatfield relented somewhat in the second half, and the Tigers did not score any more points. Wake reached the scoreboard on a Todd Dixon score and Mike Green field goal, but was on the wrong end of a 28-10 final.

With heavy rainfall pouring through Kenan Stadium for much of the game with North Carolina, Clemson struggled offensively. The game remained 7-6 until the final fifteen minutes, when the Tigers finally put away the Tar Heels. Staying largely on the ground, CU reeled off consecutive touchdown drives, while the defense continued to keep UNC at bay. The 21-6 victory over Carolina set up Hatfield for his first ACC title, which would become a reality should his team find a way to knock off Maryland. Although the Terrapins took an early lead on a 56-yard touchdown pass from Jim Sandwisch to Jason Kremus, the Tigers dominated the game from that point on. Clemson overwhelmed the Terps with 40 unanswered points, including an 89-yard punt return for a touchdown by freshman Darnell Stephens.

The annual showdown with South Carolina resulted in a 41-24 Tiger victory, making the group of 1991 seniors the first to go undefeated against USC since the class from 1983. The victory gave Hatfield ninety-nine for his career, and he would have to go halfway around the world to reach the century mark. For the second time in school history, Clemson flew to Japan for a season finale, meeting Duke in Tokyo at the Coca-Cola Classic.

The Blue Devils, who were struggling at 4-5-1 in the second year after the departure of Steve Spurrier, responded favorably to the strange surroundings, and took a 14-7 lead into the final quarter. Dave Brown completed a pair of tosses to Brad Breedlove for the Blue Devil points. Although Chris Brown briefly gave Duke a 21-7 cushion, Clemson suddenly went on the attack. In a similar performance to the Temple, Wake Forest, and Maryland contests, the CU offense became unstoppable over a short period of time, scoring 26 unanswered points. The flurry gave Clemson a come-from-behind 33-21 victory, and for their accomplishments, the Tigers were invited to Orlando for a Citrus Bowl matchup with the University of California.

Georgia Tech, which finished the regular season 7-5 and 5-2 in the ACC, opened the league's bowl festivities on Christmas Day by meeting Stanford in the Aloha Bowl. Although they were unable to defend their national championship, the Yellow Jackets finished off the year in fine fashion, claiming an 18-17 win. The score was 17-10 in favor of the Cardinal at halftime, and it remained that way until the final minute of the game. Shawn Jones, who again led a dramatic late-game surge by the GT offense, piled into the end zone with fourteen seconds on the clock. Bobby Ross didn't come to Hawaii to tie, and left his offense on the field to either win it or lose it. Jimy Lincoln took the ball on a handoff and sprinted across the goal to give Georgia Tech the two points they needed. Although Stanford got the ball back for an instant, the Jackets held on to take the victory.

Virginia and N.C. State proved far less successful in their respective bowls. The Cavaliers met a vastly superior opponent in Oklahoma, while the Wolfpack defense came unraveled trying to stop East Carolina. Sooner signal caller Cale Gundy threw a pair of touchdowns in the Gator Bowl, and broke an Oklahoma school record by throwing for 329 yards. The Sooners, always known for their powerful running attacks under Barry Switzer, had changed to a pass-happy style under Gary Gibbs, and the scheme proved equally effective. Matt Blundin, who had set an NCAA record by throwing 224 consecutive passes during the year without an interception, was finally picked off by Oklahoma's Darrell Walker. With Mike Gaddis recording a hat trick of scores, and the OU defense keeping the Virginia offense from matching, the Sooners cruised to a 48-14 verdict.

North Carolina State met East Carolina in the final Peach Bowl at Atlanta's Fulton-County Stadium, and the teams wound up playing a nip-and-tuck affair. Under Bill Lewis, who would soon join the ACC ranks at Georgia Tech, the Pirates had enjoyed a breakthrough season, finishing 10-1 and entering the national polls for only the second time since becoming a member of Division I-A. Quarterback Jeff Blake was a thorn in the side of the Wolfpack all day, throwing four touchdowns to tie a Peach Bowl record and rushing for a fifth score. Although NCSU trailed 17-14 at the half, the offense surged to a 34-17 lead on the strength of twenty unanswered points.

Trailing by seventeen points with less than a quarter to play, Blake went into action. In a gutsy performance, which brought national football recognition to the Greenville, N.C. school for one of the first times in history, Blake led the Pirates on three scoring marches over the final fifteen minutes. After running over one touchdown, Blake tossed to Dion Johnson and Luke Fisher for another pair of scores. Fisher's diving score gave the Pirates a 37-34 advantage with less than three minutes to play, and ECU was forced to withhold one final Wolfpack stand. State moved into range for a tying field goal effort, but the ball went wide, sending the purple and gold into the Top Ten for the first time in school history.

The Tigers were outclassed in the Citrus Bowl by an underrated California team, which dominated Clemson from the get-go. Trickery got the Golden Bears on the scoreboard first, as quarterback Mike Pawlawski began a flea-flicker by pitching to Russell White. After White tossed to Sean Dawkins, the ball went back to Pawlawski. With the Clemson defenders woefully out of position, White hauled in Pawlawski's catch and raced downfield. Two plays later, the Bears took a 7-0 lead. California added more points on a field goal and a 72-yard punt return by Brian Treggs. Although Clemson scored the next ten points to get back into the game, the Bears cemented victory with their passing attack. Staying largely off the ground against the NCAA's best defenders against the run, the Bears pounded CU up top, throwing passes on 29 of their first 35 offensive plays. With the Tiger offense unable to score any additional points, California added another pair of touchdowns and a field goal for a decisive 37-13 triumph.

The Atlantic Coast Conference did not renew its contract with the Florida Citrus Bowl after the New Year's Day game in 1992, which meant that the league champion would begin going elsewhere in the coming years. The conference had proven its worth in the Orlando game, with Clemson and Georgia Tech knocking off Penn State and Big Eight powers Oklahoma and Nebraska in three successive seasons. As it turned out, the ACC leadership had bigger and better plans for its annual champion, and the coming years would provide more notorious and lucrative opportunities for the league's best teams.

Football fields would never be the same again around the Atlantic Coast Conference after the fall of 1992, when Florida State University made its celebrated introduction into the league. The Seminoles brought instant national credibility to the ACC on the gridiron, even more so than the legacies already wrought by Georgia Tech, Maryland, and Clemson. Unlike their new conference rivals, however, Florida State was still without that one shining jewel that marks a great program, a national championship. Already in the midst of its finest football era in history, the early 1990s brought added fortune to Bobby Bowden's team. Year after year, the Seminoles were pursuing and signing some of the top high school players in the country, scouring the rich recruiting grounds of Florida and the entire Southeast for talent. With added credibility due to its new conference membership, the future at FSU would only get brighter.

In that first season, and in the coming years, it was obvious to observers that the Seminoles simply had better athletes than their new conference adversaries. Florida State's combination of athleticism and depth was too overwhelming for anyone in the league to compete against for a full sixty minutes, and served as an indication that every program in the ACC would have to improve if anyone else wanted another opportunity to seize the conference championship. That would not be the case in the beginning, as the Seminoles came, saw, and conquered from the outset.

In addition to Florida State's arrival as the newest member of the league, college football as a whole took part in a new innovation in 1992, largely the brainchild of ACC commissioner Gene Corrigan and his associate commissioner, Tom Mickle. While sketching out brainstorms on the back of a napkin, Mickle came up with a concept for realigning the big money bowls, which would result in a new "Coalition" of games for the champions of the major conferences. Mickle's plan guaranteed the annual ACC football champion an annual berth in either the Orange, Cotton, Fiesta, or Sugar Bowl, in addition to the champions of the other major conferences with the exception of the Big Ten and Pacific Ten, which maintained their relationship with the Rose Bowl.

With Corrigan's influence, the idea was refined and passed on to the NCAA, where it was adopted into place for the 1992 season. Mickle and Corrigan's proposal was a significant factor in Florida State's eagerness to become a member of the Atlantic Coast Conference. Since they could now be ensured of a big money bowl game every year should they win the ACC, joining the league at this time had nothing but positive benefits. Although all of FSU's athletic teams were a part of the entry in the conference, football was by far the biggest motivating factor.

The Seminoles were rusty in their first league game against Duke, committing five turnovers. The Blue Devils were unable to take advantage, and gave the ball back to FSU four times themselves. The Devils moved into Seminole territory early in the game, but Leon Fowler picked off a pass at the FSU 6 and went 94 yards in the other direction for the first touchdown. Things only got worse for Duke, as a brutal hit by FSU linebacker Marvin Jones knocked their starting quarterback out of the game. Although he threw four interceptions, Charlie Ward accounted for five Seminole touchdowns, including two scoring tosses to Kez McCorvey and a 68-yard bullet to Matt Frier. Although FSU took an easy 48-21 victory, Ward was not exactly pleased with his performance.

"Those interceptions have to go," he said. "I have to concentrate a little more on not throwing so much. It was the adrenaline."

Tragedy befell the Florida State team before their second contest, played in Clemson against the Tigers. The night before the game, freshman tight end Michael Hendricks was killed in his hometown of Baytown, Texas. Injured and unable to play, Hendricks was not on the traveling squad for the showdown in Death Valley. After an evening of hanging out with friends, Hendricks was climbing a utility tower when he touched a live wire and was electrocuted. The news came as a shock to the FSU players and coaches, and it reflected in their performance against the Tigers.

The Clemson game was something of a rubicon, a turning point from which there would be no return. The Tigers had won four of the last six ACC championships, with Ken Hatfield boasting a 13-0-1 record in Memorial Stadium. The Seminoles were the new bullies on the street, intent on taking away CU's title as the premier program in the conference and seizing it for themselves. In the first night game played at Death Valley in 36 years, the Tigers fought hard to keep their place as the elite team in the league. Although the Seminole defense was fearsome throughout, the Tigers trailed only 10-3 at halftime.

Clemson remained focused, and a pair of turnovers by Ward allowed the Tigers to take a 13-10 lead early in the second half. Defensive back James Trapp made the biggest play, catching a poorly thrown ball by Ward at the 39 and returning it all the way for six points. Although Ward led a quick scoring drive to retake the lead for FSU, Tiger quarterback Richard Moncrief threw a 35-yard touchdown to Terry Smith, which gave Clemson a 20-17 advantage. The game remained that way until Florida State's final drive, when Ward, plagued all night by inaccuracy, began hitting his mark. The junior completed all five of his attempts on FSU's late march, which ate up 64 yards and resulted in a touchdown pass to Kevin Knox. Clemson got one last chance, but an interception at the 1:25 mark ensured a 24-20 victory for the visitors.

Although Ward was leading the ACC in total offense going into the N.C. State game, the Seminoles were not overly impressed with their first two performances. After going scoreless in the opening quarter, FSU finally tacked on a pair of touchdowns to take a 14-3 lead into the locker rooms. Catching NCSU on blitzes, Ward threw to Tamarack Vanover for 60 yards and Shannon Baker for 32. Baker added a touchdown in the third quarter, and the Seminoles put ten more points on the board in the final quarter for a 34-13 triumph.

Vanover's touchdown against NCSU was the first big play for the freshman in the garnet and gold, and it only got better the following week against Wake Forest. With the game tied 7-7 in the first quarter, Vanover caught a kickoff and sprinted 96 yards to put the Seminoles ahead to stay. Ward played his first game without an interception, and threw for 240 yards in less than three quarters before giving way to backup Danny Kanell. With two minutes to play in the third quarter Sean Jackson broke off an 88-yard run, the third longest in FSU history. The long play gave FSU a 35-7 cushion, and the margin held through the final fifteen minutes.

After their decisive victory over Wake, it appeared that the Seminoles were ready for an Orange Bowl encounter with Miami. Everyone knew how difficult the game would be, with the No. 2 Hurricanes holding a forty-eight-game winning streak at home. However, Miami was not as dominant as they had been in recent years. Arizona had nearly beaten them a week before in the Orange Bowl, as a wide field goal in the closing moments had been the only thing keeping the Wildcats from victory. The near-defeat dropped Miami out of the top ranking in the polls, and set the stage for another thriller in the Sunshine State rivalry.

The Seminole defenders gave Miami quarterback Gino Torretta fits, rushing and slamming him to the turf numerous times over the course of the contest. In the third quarter, FSU did not allow Miami a single first down. Dan Mowrey kicked his third field goal to give FSU a 16-10 lead with 9:05 to play, but Torretta, who went on to win the Heisman Trophy, came through when the Hurricanes needed him most. Leading a surgical assault through the Seminole secondary, Torretta keyed a 58-yard drive, which ended on a 33-yard pass to Lamar Thomas for a touchdown.

Although they trailed 17-16, FSU was still in a position to seize victory. The defense clamped down, and forced a Miami punt with just over three minutes remaining. Corey Sawyer hauled in the Hurricane punt at his own 1, but was pulled across the goal line by his own momentum. Instead of kneeling on the football, Sawyer mistakenly thought that he had to leave the end zone. Sawyer threw an illegal forward pass, which resulted in a safety for Miami. Tying the game at 19 was still within the realm of possibility for FSU, and the offense got into position for Mowrey, who came on for an attempt at his fourth field goal. With eight seconds to play, Mowrey's kick sailed wide right. For the second year in a row, Florida State was denied against Miami because of a missed kick, and sadness loomed in Tallahassee, as another shot at the national championship was gone by the wayside.

The Seminoles were addled after their gut-wrenching defeat in Coral Gables, and fought among themselves in their ensuing game against North Carolina. Although FSU turned the ball over four times, the defense held Carolina to 223 yards. The Tar Heels could produce only three points out of the FSU mistakes, and runs by Ward, Vanover, and William Floyd gave the Seminoles a 36-13 victory. Danny Kanell played extensively, as Bowden continued to be concerned about Ward's continued mistakes.

The tension of a potential quarterback controversy carried over to the Georgia Tech game for Florida State, as Ward was benched after throwing his second interception. Kanell came on for one series, which was designed to give Ward a wake-up call. Bowden's plan worked, as Ward returned to lead the Seminoles to a courageous comeback. The Yellow Jackets gave the Seminoles their toughest ACC game all year, scoring more points than anyone else against the FSU defense. William Bell and Shawn Jones paced a series of Tech scoring drives, resulting in four Scott Sisson field goals. The Jackets scored a pair of touchdowns in the third quarter, but were unsuccessful on two-point conversions after each effort.

As the game entered the final period, Florida State was all but beaten. Held in check by a formidable defensive effort by GT, the Seminoles trailed 21-7 following Sisson's third kick. Now in something of a desperation mode, the Seminoles went into a no-huddle, fast break offensive scheme. Throwing the ball on almost every play, and quickly reassembling at the line of scrimmage for the next snap, Ward took control and led Florida State back into contention.

In one of his most significant performances, one that gave him and his teammates supreme confidence in his abilities, Ward directed three touchdown marches over the final fourteen minutes. The first was good for 80 yards, with Floyd going over to make the score 21-14. Georgia Tech rallied to another field goal, but the Seminoles went 80 yards again to cut the lead to 24-21. With only 3:16 to play, Bowden decided to take a gamble. With his defense struggling to stop the Yellow Jackets, he opted for an onsides kick. The short boot fluttered along the turf, and Sawyer came up with the critical recovery. Six plays and 45 yards later, Ward completed a pass to McCorvey in the end zone, which set off a spirited celebration on the field and on the Seminole sidelines. Less than a minute after McCorvey's third touchdown reception, FSU forced Jones out of the back of the end zone, completing a safety and a 29-24 Seminole triumph.

The Virginia game remained scoreless until the second quarter, when Mike Husted kicked the Cavaliers to a 3-0 lead. The FSU defenders shut down UVA after the score, holding quarterback Bobby Goodman to one completion and the Cavalier offense to only two first downs for the remainder of the half. Midway into the period, Ward finally made a scoring connection, hitting Vanover on a 27-yard strike for a 7-3 advantage. Ward provided the winning margin for the Seminoles in the third quarter, taking off on a scramble and beating the Cavalier secondary to the goal line. After eluding two would-be tacklers, Ward reached the end zone to give FSU a 13-3 victory and the school's first Atlantic Coast Conference title.

The Seminoles exploded offensively in their next two games, dominating Maryland and Tulane in preparation for the showdown against Florida. A number of significant ACC records were shattered against the Terrapins, as FSU ran up 858 yards and 40 first downs in a 69-21 spanking. After scoring twenty points in the third quarter to take a 62-14 advantage, Bowden called off the dogs. Tulane met a similar fate a week later, as Ward again threw four scoring passes. Clifton Abraham added a pair of defensive touchdowns, one on a blocked punt and another on an interception, as the Seminoles took a 70-7 victory.

The Seminoles went with all-garnet uniforms for Florida, and continued their torrid offensive pace. Going almost exclusively with the no-huddle, FSU scored 38 points during an overwhelming first half performance. Vanover added kickoff returns of 80 and 76 yards, and the Seminoles were on their way to an easy victory. With the 45-24 win, Florida State completed the regular season 10-1. The Seminoles were ranked No. 3, trailing only Miami and Alabama in the polls. As one could expect, Bowden asked Steve Spurrier to "Beat Bama" in the following week's SEC Championship game.

"We're the No. 1 team in the nation, no question," Marvin Jones said afterwards. "This was supposed to be No. 6, and, let's face it, we could've done anything we wanted today."

With a 5-6 record in 1992, Clemson failed to reach a bowl for the first time since the end of their NCAA probation back in 1984. It was a dramatic drop for one of the nation's most successful football programs, and had plenty of people in South Carolina wishing Danny Ford back onto the CU sidelines. The Tigers were replaced in the postseason by North Carolina, N.C. State, and Wake Forest, which represented the ACC in the Peach, Gator, and Independence Bowls.

The Tar Heels were making their first postseason appearance under Mack Brown, and turned in a thrilling performance against Mississippi State. After falling behind to the Bulldogs, Natrone Means led an offensive flurry and a 21-17 UNC victory. The Wolfpack fared worse against Florida in the Gator Bowl, as NCSU was unable to control UF's high-powered passing attack. With Spurrier claiming his first bowl championship at his alma mater, NCSU took a 27-10 defeat. Bill Dooley brought Wake Forest to its first bowl since 1979, and beat Oregon 39-35 for the school's first taste of postseason glory since joining the ACC.

Although the Gators easily handled N.C. State, they had been unable to come through for Florida State, dropping a 28-21 decision in the SEC Championship game to the eventual national champions from Alabama. Although FSU would not get their rematch with Miami, an intriguing showdown with Nebraska was awaiting them in the Orange Bowl. The Cornhuskers were solid as always in 1992, finishing 9-2 and winning their second consecutive Big Eight title. The Seminoles could finish No. 2 with the victory, and playing in the familiar surroundings of the Orange Bowl gave them all the advantages.

The defense set the tone early, stopping Nebraska on a fourth-and-1 to give the ball and momentum to Ward. The junior quickly responded, leading a drive that consumed 51 yards. From the 25, Ward found Vanover open for a 7-0 lead. After kicking a field goal early in the second quarter, another big play by the Seminole defense led to a 17-0 bulge, as Dan Footman recovered a fumble by NU quarterback Tommy Frazier inside the 2. Three plays later, Ward and McCorvey connected for a score.

Although the Huskers finally reached the end zone on a 41-yard bomb from Frazier to Corey Dixon, the Seminoles were in control. The FSU offense added another field goal late in the first half, and Sean Jackson's 11-yard scoring jaunt in the third quarter pushed the advantage to 27-7. Nebraska scored a late touchdown, but the game went to the Seminoles, 27-14. The victory indeed catapulted Florida State to the No. 2 ranking in both the Associated Press and Coaches Polls, and with most of their talented players remaining on campus for another run in 1993, Seminole fans were eager for August to arrive.

The start of football season in Tallahassee was always something to look forward to, but 1993 was a particularly good year to be rooting for the Seminoles. With the majority of their stars returning from 1992, almost everyone expected FSU to finally finish No. 1. It would not be easy, with a road game against Notre Dame to go along with the annual wars with Miami and Florida. If anyone could run through such a demanding schedule, it was this team. With Derrick Brooks, Corey Sawyer, Tamarick Vanover, and William Floyd all headed to the professional ranks in the coming years, Bowden's cupboard was as stocked as it had ever been.

The Seminoles had been denied opportunities to play for the national championship both in 1991 and 1992 due to missed field goals against Miami, and plenty of writers and analysts felt that Bowden, despite all his success at Florida State, was unable to win the "Big One." As the FSU staff prepared for the 1993 season, priorities were made to bring in not only a first-rate running back, capable of producing immediately, but a kicker that would make the big conversions under pressure. The Seminoles beat out LSU for Baton Rouge's Warrick Dunn, a speedy, elusive back that was able to contribute as a true freshman. Dunn was an inspiring addition to the Seminole family, the son of a police officer mother that was killed in the line of fire during his senior year of high school.

Dunn helped raise his siblings before and after his mother's passing, and his dedication would rub off on his teammates. The Seminoles also signed placekicker Scott Bentley from Colorado, who was considered the finest prep kicker in the country in 1992. Bentley spurned Notre Dame, his father's alma mater, to attend Florida State, and like Dunn, was able to make an immediate contribution. Bentley made a splash before he had attempted a single kick at FSU, appearing on the cover of *Sports Illustrated* for the magazine's college football preview.

In the fall of 1993, Florida State completed the most dominant run through the Atlantic Coast Conference schedule by any school in history, beating their eight conference opponents by an average score of 48-6, and holding all but two teams to seven or fewer points. The Seminoles placed nine players on the All-ACC first team, and another three on the Consensus All-American squad. Charlie Ward was the executor of offensive coordinator Brad Scott's "fast break" attack, a no-huddle system that capitalized on speed and a lack of response time on the part of opposing defenses. As a scrambler, Ward brought a difficult challenge to defensive coordinators throughout the ACC. Teams had to respect FSU's horde of gifted receivers, but also had to be prepared to respond if Ward tucked the ball up and ran from out of the pocket.

With cool efficiency, the Seminoles easily handled Kansas in the August 28 premiere at the Meadowlands in New Jersey. Sean Jackson scored the first points of the year on a 4-yard carry, and Abraham recovered a blocked punt in the end zone for a 14-0 lead after one quarter of play. The Seminole defense put together an inspirational goal line stand, and Jackson, Floyd, and Marquette Smith all ran over. Backup quarterback Jon Stark threw a 21-yard pass to Rhodney Williams to complete FSU's 42-0 blowout of the Jayhawks.

Duke and Clemson took heavy losses at the hands of the powerful Seminole offense, which racked up a combined 102 points in the two contests. Florida State ran off twenty-two in a row in the second quarter to put away the Blue Devils, as Brooks returned an interception 32 yards, and Jackson and Ward both broke off scoring runs. Ward threw two touchdown passes, and added 41 yards on the ground. Duke finally reached the end zone in the fourth quarter to make the final score 45-7, but were allowed only 147 yards.

Although they were angry about being listed as a twenty-three-point underdog to Florida State, Clemson did nothing on the field to make its case. If anything, the Tigers made the Vegas oddsmakers look conservative. The Seminoles dished out a 57-0 lashing to the Tigers, CU's worst defeat since a 44-0 defeat at the hands of Tennessee way back in 1931. Ward threw for 317 yards and four touchdowns, and Danny Kanell added a pair himself. Brooks notched his second defensive touchdown in as many games, picking up a loose ball at the FSU 17 and running it back 83 yards. The stalwart linebacker also blocked a punt, which was recovered in the end zone by Abraham for seven more Seminole points.

The fans in Kenan Stadium were pumped up momentarily after North Carolina took a 7-0 lead over the Seminoles, but FSU quickly took control. Dunn scored his first rushing touchdown as a collegiate player to tie the game, and a second quarter field goal ensured a 10-3 halftime lead. Brooks put the game away late in the third quarter, completing a hat trick of defensive scores for the Seminole unit with a 49-yard interception return. Floyd added a late tally, and FSU left town victorious, 33-7.

Returning home for the first of four consecutive games at Doak-Campbell Stadium, the Seminoles were determined to not struggle for a second year in a row against Georgia Tech. Although Ward threw four touchdowns once again, Dunn, in his breakout performance, scored three times. In a fine tune-up for Miami, Florida State blasted the Jackets, 51-0, for Georgia Tech's worst shutout defeat in 86 years.

Miami headed north to Tallahassee ranked No. 3, having already beaten a ranked team, Colorado, on the road. The Florida State seniors were winless in three tries against Miami, and were not about to finish their FSU careers without a victory over the Hurricanes. With an opportunity to finally remove the green and orange monkey from their backs, the Seminoles vowed that this time around, there would be no wide right. The teams traded touchdowns early before Ward came up with the first of what would be a number of big plays. Taking a snap from the shotgun at his own 28, Ward rolled right and threw a lofting pass down the sideline in the direction of Matt Frier. Frier had beaten his Miami defender, and with nobody in front of him to impede his running, the receiver galloped 72 yards for a 14-7 Seminole lead.

With the defense putting Miami on lockdown, the Frier touchdown provided an advantage that would not be relinquished. Ward's second long touchdown connection went to Sean Jackson, and FSU took a 21-7 cushion into the locker rooms. The Florida State defense, intent on avoiding the same Hurricane magic that had taken them out in previous years, refused to relent. The Miami offense produced just 119 yards in the second half, and only 14 in the decisive fourth quarter. With the realization setting in that this would indeed be their day, the Seminole defense made a final play to seal victory. Sophomore Devin Bush ran in front of a Frank Costa pass and sprinted down the sidelines for a 28-10 final score. Many among the Florida State players, including senior William Floyd, could not bring themselves to leave the field following the impressive victory. The fullback leaned back on his helmet at the 25-yard line, and sat with a fixed gaze on the scoreboard.

"I'm going to stay here all night," he said. "I told them to get my sleeping bag. I might pitch a tent, too. It took us four years to do it, and I was here for every one. I'm going to stay here and look at that score-board."

Although Virginia was the opponent the following week, delirious Seminole fans were still beside themselves after having finally toppled Miami. In another performance that solidified his status as the Heisman front-runner, Ward torched UVA for 360 total yards in a 40-14 wipe-out. During the intermission, with the garnet and gold leading 30-0, the Seminole band could not help but toot their collective horns about the victory over the Hurricanes. During their performance, the band spelled out, "28-10."

Wake Forest concluded Florida State's October home stand, and the Deacons became the next to take another lopsided loss from the home team. Although Ward left in the first half, he stepped off the field with FSU leading 34-0. Abraham scored his third defensive touchdown of the year with a 29-yard interception return, while Ward broke off a 33-yard scoring run. Midway through the final quarter, the Demon Deacons had a lone shot to get on the scoreboard, but when Bill Hollows' kick went wide, the shutout was inevitable. The Seminole back-ups played out the 54-0 verdict.

Although FSU clinched its second consecutive ACC title by beating Maryland, their effort was anything but dominant. In their worst conference performance of the year, the FSU defense allowed twenty points to the Terrapins, including thirteen in the second quarter alone. Although Kanell, playing in place of the injured Ward, had already thrown four touchdowns, the score was 28-20 early in the third quarter. Maryland may have possibly pulled off the upset had their defense clamped down, but the Seminoles quickly assumed momentum. Kevin Knox caught a 33-yard pass from Kanell to make the score 35-20, and Vanover and Jackson scored later to make the final 49-20. Although Florida State set a new ACC record with their sixteenth consecutive overall victory, Bowden was in no mood to celebrate afterwards.

"If Maryland can get 20 points on us—which they did, and they earned them all—then Notre Dame will get 40," Bowden said. "Our mood and attitude had better change by next week, or we'll get laced pretty good. I don't know what they were thinking out there."

As Florida State and Notre Dame prepared for their No. 1-No. 2 showdown in South Bend, the media hyped the contest as college football's newest "Game of the Century." Although the Irish were unbeaten, and had toppled national powers Michigan, USC, and BYU, the storied program had never beaten a top-ranked team on the grass of Notre Dame Stadium. The game began as expected for Florida State, as Ward led a ten-play, 89-yard march for a 7-0 lead.

The Fighting Irish promptly returned the favor, going 80 yards through the Seminole defense. Ray Zellars provided momentum with an 18-yard burst up the gut on the opening play, and seconds later Adrian Jarrell took a handoff at the 32 and broke free to tie the game, much to the delight of the capacity crowd. The Notre Dame defense played inspired football in the second quarter, shutting down Ward and putting their own unit in position for another score and a 14-7 advantage. The Seminoles would have been happy to take that score into the locker room, but a rare error in judgment by Ward gave Notre Dame another chance to get on the board before halftime. On one of the only bad throws he made all year, Ward put a pass in the hands of Irish safety John Covington, and with 7:48 to play in the half, Jeff Burris ran across the goal line. In a surprising turn of events, the Seminoles had given up three rushing touchdowns in the first thirty minutes, and went into the intermission trailing, 21-7.

The Irish continued to outplay the Seminoles in the third quarter, as Kevin Pendergrast connected on a 47-yard field goal. Staring at a 24-7 deficit, the angry Florida State offense finally got on track. In only their second successful drive thus far in the game, the Seminoles fast-breaked their way downfield. It took eleven plays for FSU to go 80 yards, as Ward mixed passes with his own running. From the 6, Ward handed off to Dunn, and the rookie broke through the pile to make the score 24-14. Although it took nine minutes for the Seminole offense to score again, Bentley's 24-yard field goal in the fourth quarter cut the Notre Dame lead to a touchdown.

On a nine-play possession, which ate up 80 yards and nearly four minutes, Notre Dame drove a painful nail in the Seminole coffin. Continuing to run the ball at will, Burris scored his second touchdown on a carry from 11 yards out. Now trailing 31-17 with only 6:53 to play, Ward threw in the direction of McCorvey at the 20. McCorvey caught the pass, which was first tipped by Notre Dame's Brian Mageec, and raced to the end zone. Again trailing by a touchdown, Ward got a final chance to win the game in the final minute. Without any time-outs to work with, Ward pushed the Seminoles to the Notre Dame 14, where on the game's final play, with three precious ticks on the clock, Ward's final desperation toss was spiked to the ground by Irish safety Shawn Woodson. The second after Woodson's play, a massive throng of Irish supporters took to the field in celebration.

Although Florida State dropped from the No. 1 spot in the polls after the draining Notre Dame defeat, it proved to be a short descent. The Seminoles entered the ACC finale against N.C. State ranked second, and with Notre Dame having lost in a shocking upset to Boston College earlier in the day, an opportunity was in place for FSU to get right back where they had been a week earlier. Playing in front of the Tallahassee faithful for the final time, Ward went out like a champion. Throwing for 278 yards on twenty-seven of thirty-six passing, Ward was responsible for five Florida State touchdowns in just over a half of action. As No. 17 left the game for good in the third quarter, the chants of "Charlie, Charlie, Charlie," could be heard throughout Doak-Campbell Stadium. In beating the Wolfpack, 62-3, FSU erased some of the doubts that were in place after their failed comeback bid against the Fighting Irish.

"We were so emotionally drained after that game, it was like, 'Wow, we got to go out and play these guys.' That's when we made up our mind that we had to go out and just crush North Carolina State," Abraham said. "After groups of us gathered together in different dorm rooms and saw Notre Dame lose the way that they did, it was hugs and kisses everywhere."

Florida was the only thing standing in FSU's way of a berth in the Orange Bowl, and the Seminoles came into Gainesville coolly confident. After dominating the opening fifteen minutes, and taking a 7-0 lead on a 5-yard pass from Ward to Vanover, Bentley nailed a pair of field goals for a 13-0 Seminole advantage. Florida cut the score to 13-7 following a pass from Danny Wuerffel to Willie Jackson, but the Seminoles scored twice in the third quarter to take control. Staring at a 27-7 deficit on their home field, Florida finally began to play the Seminoles tough. Terry Dean came on at quarterback in place of Wuerffel, and led a pair of scoring marches. Florida's receiving tandem of Jacksons, Willie and Jack, lit up the FSU secondary, and each caught touchdowns to make the score 27-21.

The Seminoles were not about to blow the game, and Ward made one final play that all but secured him the Heisman Trophy. With Florida's fans creating a deafening roar, Ward's first two passes were batted down. On third down at the FSU 21, the quarterback escaped pressure and found Dunn just behind linebacker Ed Robinson. Ward lofted a perfect pass to Dunn, and the freshman outran everybody to the end zone. Dunn's touchdown proved to be the final points of the contest, and the Seminoles had a 33-21 victory to finish with an 11-1 regular season mark.

"People saw us play. We were on television enough times this year," Bowden said, when asked about his team's chances of playing for the national championship. "I don't have to say anything. I'll let them vote whatever they think."

By beating Florida decisively on their home field, the Seminoles had set up a rematch with Nebraska in the Orange Bowl, only this time around it would be for the national championship. Notre Dame's last-second loss to Boston College relegated them to the Cotton Bowl, where they were given a slim chance of finishing No. 1. The showdown in Miami would ensure that either Bowden or Nebraska's Tom Osborne would finally claim his first NCAA title. The pair had become coaching icons over the past two decades, but despite all their successes at their respective schools, neither had tasted life at the top of the final polls.

Despite nearly losing to both UCLA and Kansas, beating each team by a single point, Nebraska managed to complete the regular season undefeated, and were ranked No. 1 coming into the big game. Osborne had been denied the national championship twice before on the cruel turf of the Orange Bowl, and although they were heavy underdogs against FSU, Nebraska believed this was the time their luck in Miami would finally change. Florida State had proven vulnerable against the Notre Dame running attack, and if anyone could keep up with Ward and the Seminole scoring machine, it was Tommy Frazier and the

Husker offense. With Frazier and Lawrence Phillips doing most of the damage, Nebraska had again been an offensive force in 1993, scoring at least 40 points on six separate occasions.

Before the Orange Bowl, Charlie Ward traveled to New York City for the Heisman Trophy presentation at the Downtown Athletic Club. Several ACC players had been mentioned for the award in the past, but no player from the league had ever heard his name called on the big day. After setting nineteen Florida State and seven ACC records, in addition to earning Player of the Year honors, Charlie's name was indeed called, as he beat out Tennessee quarterback Heath Shuler by 1,622 points, the second-widest margin in history. Remembering his roots, Ward gave the Heisman to the public library in his hometown of Thomasville, Georgia.

In addition to the Seminoles, who were preparing for their game in Miami, four other ACC schools earned bowl berths, with all the games being played in a span of two days. It was a tough postseason for the conference, as North Carolina, N.C. State, and Virginia were all on the receiving end of decisive defeats by their opposition. Only Clemson, who beat Kentucky, 14-13, in the Peach Bowl, spared the ACC from four consecutive bowl losses before the Seminoles played the Cornhuskers. Tommy West took over as head coach of Clemson for the game in Atlanta after Ken Hatfield unexpectedly stepped down less than three weeks prior to the contest. The Tigers won the game in the final minute, as Terry Smith threw a touchdown to Patrick Sapp.

North Carolina, coming off one of its best regular seasons since the days of Dick Crum, struggled to move the ball against Alabama in the Gator Bowl. The Crimson Tide had been unseated as NCAA champions, but they once again had an excellent team, and handed UNC a 24-10 setback. Although Alabama would be forced to forfeit nine of their victories from the 1993 season in the coming years for using an ineligible player during the regular season, the victory over Carolina was preserved for the ages. North Carolina State had no chance against Michigan in the Hall of Fame Bowl, as Wolverine running back Tyrone Wheatley enjoyed a banner day. Running for 124 yards on eighteen carries to take Most Valuable Player honors, Wheatley scored twice to lead Michigan to a 42-7 blowout. That same day, Boston College handled Virginia, 31-13, giving the Cavaliers four consecutive defeats in postseason contests.

Despite the presence of two great offenses at the Orange Bowl, Nebraska and Florida State were equally stacked on the defensive side, and at the end of the opening quarter, the game was still scoreless. Florida State got on the board first in the second quarter, marching 63 yards and into range for Bentley. Bentley was good from 34 yards out, and the Seminoles led, 3-0. Nebraska countered the Florida State score by taking to the air. The garnet and gold had proven quite successful in shutting down Nebraska's vaunted running game, but they completely missed the target when Frazier dropped back and threw in the direction of Reggie Baul. Devin Bush got in front of the pass and tipped it, but the ball landed in Baul's hands. Baul outran the other Seminoles for a 34-yard touchdown, much to the delight of the sea of red covering one side of the Orange Bowl. The Seminoles could not mount a touchdown march against the Huskers in the second quarter, and a second field goal by Bentley made the score 7-6 at halftime.

Nebraska had plenty of reasons to think that the game was theirs during the intermission, but the garnet and gold quickly dispelled that notion on their opening drive of the second half, as Ward drilled Knox between the numbers for a 41-yard gain to set up Floyd. The big fullback was money from the 1, and Florida State led for the second time. Ward and the offense stayed on the field for a conversion effort, but the pass was incomplete to keep the score at 12-7. After stifling the Huskers on their next possession, FSU got the ball back at their own 12. On first down Ward handed off to Floyd, who burst through the Huskers for a 34-yard gain, the longest of his Seminole career. There were no more big plays on this drive, although Florida State moved to the 22. Bentley connected on his third field goal, and the Seminoles led by eight at 15-7.

Nebraska controlled the football for the remainder of the third quarter, and Phillips broke through for a 12-yard score on the first play of the final period. The Huskers could tie it with a two-pointer, but Frazier was forced out-of-bounds by the Seminoles at the 1 to preserve FSU's slim lead. Upon retaking possession Nebraska mounted another march, moving into Florida State real estate and running down much of the final quarter. The game was beginning to turn in Nebraska's favor before Richard Coes came up with a huge play for the Seminoles. Coes stepped in front of a Frazier pass and picked it off at the FSU 9 with only 4:39 remaining.

Florida State had a chance to run out the clock, but the Husker defense again came up with a stand. The Seminoles had no choice but to punt, and Nebraska went on the offensive. With momentum and time to stay on the ground, Nebraska marched 76 yards through the tiring FSU defense to put themselves in position to win. Phillips got things started with a 17-yard gainer on the first play of the drive, while Frazier tucked an option keeper for 32 more. With the ball on the 4 and time running out, the Seminoles held strong. Florida State's down linemen, bullied on the last two drives by Nebraska's strong offensive line, dug in their heels and began to win back the line of scrimmage. The Huskers attempted three consecutive runs, but FSU pushed them back 5 yards. With only 1:16 remaining, Byron Bennett came on and nailed a clutch kick, pushing Nebraska ahead, 16-15.

With the game up for grabs, the Cornhuskers made a series of critical errors. Following a 21-yard pickup by Dunn, a Nebraska defender ran in and hit him late. The penalty tacked 15 yards onto the play, and a pass interference call a few seconds later put FSU in close. With 21 seconds on the clock, and the ball on the Nebraska 5, Bentley came on for the biggest kick of his young life. An opportunity was in place to justify his *Sports Illustrated* appearance from back in August, and the freshman came through in fine fashion.

With ice water pumping through his veins, Bentley put tears in the eyes of the Cornhusker State by connecting on the 22-yard kick. Now trailing, 18-16, Nebraska had time for little more than a desperation rally. With the title hanging in the balance, Frazier faded into the pocket and found Trumane Bell open across the middle. Bell caught the ball and raced 29 yards to the FSU 28, where he was brought to the ground. The Seminole players thought time had run out, and several raced onto the field while Bowden was doused with Gatorade.

The celebration was short lived, as the officials ruled that Nebraska had called time out with one second remaining on the clock. It would allow Bennett to attempt a 45-yard field goal for the victory. The field was cleared, and although Nebraska protested, there was no penalty assessed to the Seminoles for their preliminary celebration. Bennett received a solid snap and hold, but his kick sailed far left and never had a chance of going through. As the Huskers lamented another Orange Bowl setback, the Seminoles officially began their celebration, storming the field and turning the city of Miami into Tallahassee II.

In ironic fashion, Florida State's victory made them the third Atlantic Coast Conference member in thirteen seasons to claim the NCAA championship by virtue of a victory over the University of Nebraska. By insuring the first twelve-win season in Florida State history, the Orange Bowl triumph completed Bobby Bowden's remarkable work in rebuilding the Seminole football program. There was some debate across the nation that the title should be shared, given Notre Dame's 24-21 win over Texas A&M in Dallas, but the pollsters did not believe the Irish had beaten the Aggies convincingly enough. The Seminoles were voted No. 1 in both the Associated Press and Coaches Polls, giving the ACC its second NCAA title on the gridiron in four years. Unfortunately, like Clemson had a decade earlier after winning their NCAA crown, Florida State would soon make headlines that had nothing to do with their performance on the gridiron.

In the months following FSU's championship run, it was reported that several team members had spent $6,000 at a Tallahassee Foot Locker retail store with money given to them by an agent, a direct violation of NCAA code. The incident resulted in a *Sports Illustrated* cover piece, along with the nickname "Free Shoes University," which Steve Spurrier first used at Florida to label the Seminoles. The episode included a number of FSU's most important players, and like the investigation into the Clemson program in 1982 following their national championship run, the incident was an embarrassment to all those associated with Seminole football. Although Florida State would avoid major sanctions from the NCAA, the negative image created by the scandal would not go away any time soon.

Although the defending champions cruised through their conference schedule once again in 1994, Florida State was unable to defend its NCAA title. With Charlie Ward having dribbled his way to the NBA's New York Knicks, the quarterback position in Tallahassee was left to Danny Kanell. Kanell had been a worthy backup to Ward for two seasons, and easily stepped into the starting role. With Derrick Brooks and Clifton Abraham returning for another year to patrol the FSU defense, the Seminoles were again vastly superior to their conference opposition.

Brooks broke the mold of the stereotypical college football player, a student-athlete in the truest sense. Brooks was named an Academic All-American at FSU to go along with his laurels on the football field. Finishing another season with 77 tackles, Brooks had four tackles for loss and three quarterback sacks in 1994. Following his graduation, the linebacker was awarded an NCAA postgraduate scholarship. An All-Pro in the National Football League, Brooks was named to the Board of Trustees at Florida State in the spring of 2003. Abraham became the fifth consecutive FSU cornerback to become a consensus All-American under Bobby Bowden, joining such notable names as Deion Sanders, Leroy Butler, and Terrell Buckley. As a senior in 1994, Abraham ended his career with four blocked punts for touchdowns, which established a new school record. Abraham also left Tallahassee with eight interceptions, 160 tackles, and wound up a finalist for the Jim Thorpe Award, given to the nation's top defensive back.

Virginia came to Tallahassee intent on shutting down the FSU rushing attack, which had trampled them for 205 yards the year before.

Although the ploy was successful, holding FSU to only 34 in the first half, the Seminoles simply went to the air. Although they were outscored in the first quarter and trailed 3-0 to the Cavaliers, Kanell threw three touchdown passes in the second quarter to put the Seminoles in cruise control. Rock Preston and Zack Crockett added short runs in the third quarter, and Kez McCorvey's second touchdown gave the Seminoles their final points. Jermaine Crowell caught two scoring passes for Virginia, but the Cavaliers were on the short end of a 41-17 score.

It was evident in the early going that the Seminoles were a bit overconfident against Maryland, as quarterback Scott Milanovich threw touchdowns to two different receivers and led another pair of drives that resulted in field goals. To everyone's surprise, the Terrapins took a 20-17 lead into the locker rooms. In the second half, Florida State used its overwhelming depth to take control. Going 80 yards in twelve plays, Preston put FSU ahead for good early in the third quarter with a 6-yard sprint. Preston's run opened the floodgates for a Florida State offensive barrage, as the unit accounted for 28 more points to win the game going away, 52-20.

Derrick Brooks returned to the Seminole fold for the Wake Forest game, having served a two-game suspension for his role in the Foot Locker debacle. Brooks wasted little time making his presence felt, blocking a punt into the end zone that was snagged by Abraham, which gave FSU a 21-0 lead in the opening quarter. E. G. Green and Crockett had already scored for the Seminoles, and three more touchdowns in the second quarter gave the garnet and gold a 42-0 lead at halftime. The Demon Deacons scored two touchdowns in the final period against FSU's reserves, but the Seminoles matched both tallies to take a 56-14 victory, the largest point total ever put up by a team in Groves Stadium.

The Seminoles took their fourth consecutive ACC victory, 31-18, over North Carolina, although it was much more difficult than the score indicated. Just when it appeared that Florida State was going to run away with it, Carolina scored eleven consecutive points midway through the second half, turning what was a 31-7 deficit into a competitive contest. The Tar Heels had a pair of opportunities to cut even deeper into the Florida State lead, but turnovers proved to be their undoing.

Following a Kanell fumble, Carolina had the ball on the FSU 6, poised to pull to within a single touchdown. Quarterback Jason Stanicek lofted a high pass in the direction of Octavius Barnes, who lost the ball before coming down to his feet. Inexplicably, the referees ruled the play a fumble instead of an incompletion. Tar Heel coach Mack Brown vented his frustrations on the sidelines, but the arguments fell on deaf ears. Although the Seminoles did not score in the final quarter, another fumble ended Carolina's last chance to come back.

The Seminoles returned to the site of their greatest triumph for another showdown with Miami, but this game was far different from the last one they played on the turf of the Orange Bowl. On a muggy Saturday night in Coral Gables, the Hurricanes outplayed FSU in a game marred by mistakes on both sides. Kanell struggled with three interceptions, allowing Miami to take control in the second half. Trailing 14-7, the Hurricanes dominated the final forty minutes to take a 34-20 victory, Bowden's fifth consecutive defeat to Miami in the Orange Bowl.

The Seminoles returned home following the Miami fiasco, and knocked off Clemson, 17-0, for their first shutout of the year. The FSU defenders left a lasting impression on the Tigers, who produced only 149 total yards and were not allowed past midfield until their final possession of the third quarter. Warrick Dunn scored both Florida State touchdowns in the second quarter, and with 141 yards on the ground, nearly outgunned Clemson by himself. Despite FSU's defensive excellence, the team's offensive woes continued to give Bowden fits. The Seminoles moved inside the Clemson 20 six times over the course of the game, but were only able to come up with points on three of those possessions.

Next for the Seminoles was an encounter with Duke, the surprise story of college football. Under first-year head coach Fred Goldsmith, the Blue Devils had come together for a magical early-season run. Behind a strong defense and the running of Robert Baldwin, who became only the third Duke back in history to gain 1,000 yards, the Devils reeled off seven consecutive victories to start the season. The victories included four ACC opponents, and an upset over FSU would put the Blue Devils in position to miraculously win the conference championship.

Despite their early success, few gave Duke a realistic chance of toppling the Seminoles on their home field, and the garnet and gold quickly took care of business. With a 32-point scoring barrage in the second quarter, Florida State wiped away Duke's chances for victory, and turned the game into a laugher. Duke scored its only points of the first half on a fumble recovery, but by the end of the half, the score was 38-6 in favor of the Seminoles. Florida State continued to pour it on in the third quarter, taking a 52-13 lead after a Kanell pass and another Crockett run. Thad Busby's short carry in the fourth quarter made the final margin 59-20. If Duke was the second-best team in the ACC, it

was evident that the entire league had a lot of catching up to do if anyone ever planned on beating Florida State.

After blowing out Georgia Tech, 41-10, in Atlanta, the Seminoles
prepared for a rematch with Notre Dame in Orlando. The Irish had two
weeks to prepare for FSU, and spent a great deal of time in practice
preparing for three-wide and four-wide receiver sets from the Seminoles. Bowden and his staff crossed up defensive coordinator Bob
Davie by going to the ground, running fifty-six times over the course of
the game. Notre Dame briefly took a 10-9 edge in the third quarter, but
did so before the FSU running attack swung into high gear. With Dunn
and Preston each running for more than 160 yards, the Seminoles ran
seamlessly through the Irish defenders all afternoon. Preston put Florida State ahead for good on a 28-yard sprint, and Dunn followed with a
5-yard scoring carry of his own. Ron Powlus threw a touchdown to
help the Irish's cause, but FSU's offense, which accounted for 517
yards, was enough to take a 23-16 revenge victory.

Having already broken Maryland's ACC record for consecutive
conference victories with the win over Duke, the Seminoles blasted
N.C. State to finish another unbeaten run through the league. Dunn,
who finished with 122 yards, thrust Florida State ahead, 7-3, on the
first play of the second quarter, and Kanell needed only five plays on
FSU's next possession to provide a 14-3 advantage. Leading 21-3 at the
half, the Seminoles finished off NCSU with a pair of methodical drives
early in the third quarter. Preston capped a 61-yard drive with a rush
from the 5, and Kanell hit Andre Cooper with a 25-yard scoring strike
to give the Seminoles a 34-3 win. It was a dominating performance for
Bowden's boys, and considering that their closest league games were
by winning margins of 13 and 17 points, it was easy to place Florida
State in a class by themselves.

Victory over Florida in the season finale, coupled by a Miami loss
to Boston College, would ensure a rematch with Nebraska in the Orange Bowl for the Seminoles. The Cornhuskers would finish the regular
season unbeaten once again, and staked claim to the No. 1 ranking in
the polls. Florida spent much of the earlier part of the year ranked No.
1, but a midseason loss at home to Auburn knocked them out of the
ranks of the unbeaten.

The first three quarters belonged to Steve Spurrier's Gators, as the
orange and blue rolled into Doak-Campbell Stadium and embarrassed
their bitter rivals to the west. Sophomore quarterback Danny Wuerffel
threw a pair of touchdowns to Jack Jackson and one to Aubrey Hill,
completing an impressive offensive display that resulted in a 24-3 halftime deficit for the Seminoles. Considering that the FSU defense had

not allowed 24 points in any entire game, much less a half, most of the home fans, in addition to a nationwide television audience watching on ABC, were in shock at the way Wuerffel and the UF receivers had successfully attacked the Florida State secondary.

Florida added another touchdown in the third quarter, and took a 31-3 lead into the final fifteen minutes. It had been a decisive effort by the Gators thus far, and staring a humiliating defeat directly in the face, the Seminoles had nothing to lose by going for broke. Going almost exclusively in the no-huddle, FSU went 84 yards in barely four minutes. Kanell survived a fourth down disaster by throwing to McCorvey at the UF 6, and Crockett got in seconds later. Without enough time to grind out another possession, the Seminoles gave up on their running game, which struggled to move for most of the contest. Staying up top, Kanell completed three quick passes, the last to Cooper from the 6, to make the score 31-17. Now back in the game, the fired-up Seminole defenders forced a Gator punt. Kanell piled in a couple of minutes later, and suddenly Florida State was in real striking distance, down only 31-24 with plenty of time remaining.

The Gators continued to struggle against the Seminole defense, which looked like an entirely different unit than the one from the first half. Kanell and the offense took the field ready to shine again, and quickly went on the move. Dunn took in a short toss on the first play and found a bit of daylight. The sophomore trudged 37 yards to the UF 23, to the great delight of the now invigorated Doak-Campbell crowd. Six plays later, Preston powered across the goal line from the 4, making the score 31-30. Bowden and his staff disagreed on what to do next. With momentum on their side, the coordinators wanted to go for the win. Bowden, hesitant to lose the game after such an inspiring comeback, elected to go for the tie. With 1:45 on the clock, Mowrey drove the extra point through the uprights for a 31-31 deadlock.

"I did not want to lose after coming back like that," Bowden said. "The staff has nine votes and I have ten. Florida ridiculed us all week, and came up here and whipped us in our backyard. I got on them at halftime. I asked them, 'What are you going to do? Fight back or let them whip you in your own back yard?' The kids really showed what they were made of."

For the second year in a row, more than half of the ACC's membership was invited to bowls. North Carolina, with only losses to FSU and Clemson against its conference record, headed to El Paso, the site of one of the school's greatest football triumphs, to play Texas in the Sun Bowl. Although the memory of the 1972 classic against Texas

Tech had faded from most minds, the game was another opportunity for UNC to show that they could go into Texas and beat the Lone Star State's best teams in their own state. The last three bowl trips to Texas had resulted in victories for Carolina, and for most of this game, it looked like it was going to happen again.

After a pair of big plays early in the fourth quarter, the Tar Heels owned a 31-21 lead. Marcus Wall broke free on an 82-yard punt return less than two minutes into the final frame, and after retaining possession, Octavius Barnes took in a 50-yard catch from midfield. There was still over nine minutes for the Longhorns to make a push, and after marching 57 yards to the UNC 9, Priest Holmes busted into the end zone for his third score. The Texas defense did its job, and gave possession back to the offense with an opportunity to win. The final series was all Holmes, as he caught an 11-yard pass and rushed six times for 32 yards. From the UNC 4, Holmes took the pigskin and soared over the defensive line, falling into the end zone. With 161 yards Holmes earned MVP honors, and catapulted Texas to a 35-31 triumph.

Duke made its first and only bowl appearance of the 1990s on January 2, meeting Wisconsin in Tampa's Hall of Fame Game. The Blue Devils struggled late in the year, but their impressive early start ensured the school's first January encounter since the days of Bill Murray and Tee Moorman. Unfortunately for Duke, this game would not turn out like that Cotton Bowl thriller back in 1961. Wisconsin's powerful running game, the envy of many within the Big Ten, pounded out the yardage all day between the Blue Devil defensive front. Terrell Fletcher set a new Hall of Fame Game record with 241 yards, with 190 of those coming in a dominant second half performance. Although Duke cut the score to 27-20 late in the game, and had the Badgers facing a critical third-and-1 in the final minutes, Fletcher raced for a 49-yard score to break the Devils' backs, 34-20.

Virginia and N.C. State, a pair of teams that spent most of the season among the middle tier of the ACC, went on to win their bowls. NCSU was the underdog against Mississippi State in the Peach Bowl, which came to Atlanta with an 8-3 record and victories over Tennessee and archrival Mississippi. Although MSU moved the football effectively, the Wolfpack held on in the fourth quarter and took a 28-24 victory.

Virginia met Texas Christian in Shreveport, and beat the overmatched Horned Frogs, 20-10, in the Independence Bowl. The win gave George Welsh and the Cavaliers nine victories in consecutive seasons for the first time in school history. With a number of their stars returning in 1995, the offseason allowed those associated with the Virginia football program a chance to envision a team capable of beating Florida State.

Without another chance to play for all the marbles, the Seminoles accepted a unique opportunity to settle the score once and for all with Florida. It was fitting that the Seminoles and Gators had a chance to go at it again in the Sugar Bowl, as their showdown in Tallahassee five weeks earlier had been nothing short of a classic. Dubbed the "Fifth Quarter in the French Quarter," the game in New Orleans would write 1994's final chapter of a saga between two schools in which hatred is not too strong a word to describe their animosities toward one another.

After trading field goals in the early going, the Seminole defense forced a turnover that changed the complexion of the game. Todd Rembol stripped Gator tailback Fred Taylor of the ball, and Sean Hamlet was on it at the FSU 27. Bowden decided to take a gamble, opting to run a halfback pass. Bowden knew that the Gator secondary was keyed on Dunn, and would probably bite if he were to take the ball on a wide pitchout. Dunn, a quarterback in high school, had yet to complete a pass for the Seminoles, but when his number was called he came up in a big way. Taking the ball, Dunn faded back and located Omar Ellison, who outran the Gator secondary and took the pass in from 73 yards out. It was momentarily the longest pass play in Sugar Bowl history, and gave Florida State a 10-3 lead.

Kanell connected with McCorvey on a 16-yard touchdown that gave FSU a 17-3 pad midway through the second period, but Florida retaliated when Danny Wuerffel calmly went into the pocket and found Ike Hilliard, who weaved through the FSU defensive backs and into the end zone. The 82-yard touchdown marked the third time during the first half that the Sugar Bowl record for longest pass play had been eclipsed. More importantly for Florida, they were back in the game at 17-10. Another fumble recovery by Hamlet set up Mowrey's second field goal, which sent the game into halftime, 20-10, in favor of FSU.

Things went from good to great for Florida State on the second half kickoff, as Preston found a seam and raced 62 yards before going down at the Florida 30. Although they could not get a first down, Mowrey was good from 45 yards to give the Seminoles a commanding 23-10 advantage. It would prove to be the final points of the game for FSU, but the defense continued to clamp down on Wuerffel and the Florida passing attack. The remainder of the third quarter was a defensive stalemate, as the teams traded punts and field position.

Hoping to perform their own magical comeback this time around, Florida pushed 80 yards in seventeen plays on a frantic fourth quarter march, with Wuerffel sneaking in from the 1 at the 3:47 mark to bring the Gators to within 23-17. Following an unsuccessful onsides kick Florida held on defense, giving the offense another opportunity to seize victory. It was not to be, as Brooks stepped in front of a Wuerffel pass in the final minute to secure victory for the Seminoles, a triumph that required eight quarters of game action to complete.

The Sugar Bowl victory was the tenth postseason win in a row for Florida State, establishing a new NCAA record. It was also the school's thirteenth consecutive bowl appearance without a defeat, going all the way back to 1982. With their tenth victory of the season, the Seminoles moved up to No. 4 in the final Associated Press poll and No. 5 in the final Coaches Poll, making FSU the first school in NCAA history to finish in the Top Five of both polls for eight consecutive seasons.

Warrick Dunn and Danny Kanell returned to the head of the Seminole offense for the 1995 season, and with its finest offensive line in years, led by All-ACC selections Clay Shiver, Jesus Hernandez, and Lewis Tyre, the unit had all the makings of a juggernaut. Unfortunately for Bobby Bowden, his defense was another story. Although the unit boasted two of the league's best pass rushers in Reinard Wilson and Andre Wadsworth, the departures of Derrick Brooks, Derrick Alexander, and Clifton Abraham left some serious holes for the FSU coaching staff to fill. The team clearly had potential to remain the class of the ACC, but it remained to be seen if the reign over their conference rivals would continue for a fourth season in a row.

Virginia, widely considered to be the second-best team in the ACC heading into the new season, took a heartbreaking loss to Michigan in the Pigskin Classic to kick off the year. The Cavaliers played the Wolverines tough on the storied grass of Michigan Stadium, shutting out the maize and blue for three full quarters. Leading 17-0 two minutes into the final period, Virginia's secondary suddenly fell apart defending Wolverine quarterback Scott Dreisbach and his favorite target, Mercury Hayes.

Dreisbach, the first freshman to start under center for Michigan in eighteen years, completed twelve passes for 236 yards in the final thirteen minutes of the contest, and throws to Hayes set up a pair of touchdowns, the second a 31-yard bullet that made the score 17-12. With eight seconds left and time for a final play, Dreisbach took the snap and threw to Hayes again, who was sprinting to the corner of the end zone. Hayes caught the pass with one foot in bounds, completing a seven-catch, 179-yard game. Time was expired, and Michigan had its biggest fourth quarter comeback in school history, 18-17.

Duke didn't have a prayer in the opener against the Seminoles, which the Blue Devils shifted to Orlando for a price tag of $800,000. The Seminoles scored on seven of its first eight possessions, and took a 54-12 lead into the locker rooms. Florida State followed its 70-26 victory over Duke by manhandling Clemson in Death Valley. It was the first time in history that the Tigers faced the No. 1 team in the nation at home, and the contest quickly got out of CU's control. Dunn followed excellent blocking on the way to 180 yards on twelve carries, as the Seminoles needed barely nine minutes to accumulate all of their points. Although the 45-26 defeat matched the most points ever allowed by a Clemson team in Death Valley, the Tiger running game pounded out 321 yards, the most against an FSU defense since 1990.

The Seminoles could have played even more poorly on defense against N.C. State, but it really wouldn't have mattered. On a scorching day in Tallahassee, everything went right for the FSU offense. With Kanell and Thad Busby combining for 466 yards through the air, and Dunn again averaging more than 10 yards a carry, it was smooth sailing all afternoon. Leading 42-14 at halftime, Bowden was able to unleash his tremendous depth on the Wolfpack. Playing mostly their second teams in the final quarters, FSU added another quintet of touchdowns to complete a 77-17 demolition.

As FSU was polishing off the Wolfpack, Virginia was dishing out a decisive 41-14 defeat at home to Georgia Tech. Cavalier fans were unsure what team would step onto the field at Scott Stadium that afternoon, for after blowing out William and Mary after the Michigan heartbreaker, the Cavaliers had been forced to come from behind to edge NCSU, 29-24. The UVA offensive linemen manhandled the GT defensive front, and had the Yellow Jackets bickering with one other before the game was through. Combining bursts up the middle with bounces to the outside, Tiki Barber knifed his way through the Georgia Tech defense for four touchdowns. A long jumper on the Virginia track team, Barber would go on to set UVA records with 1,906 all-purpose yards and 1,397 rushing yards in 1995.

After dominating Central Florida, 46-14, the Seminoles welcomed Miami to Doak-Campbell Stadium for their annual Sunshine State battle. This was clearly not the same Hurricane team that had knocked off FSU in 1994, as Miami limped into the game unranked for the first time in eleven years. Losses at UCLA and Virginia Tech had shaken Miami's confidence, and with a secondary unable to keep up with Florida State's speedy receivers one-on-one, first-year coach Butch Davis decided to employ a slow, methodical offensive scheme, hoping to keep the Seminole offense off the field. With redshirt freshman Ryan Clement making his first start at quarterback, Miami was content on running up the middle and making safe passes to the outside.

The prevent strategy failed miserably, as the Seminoles jumped out to a 24-7 halftime lead. Miami's only points came on a blocked punt, which briefly tied the game at 7. Andre Cooper did most of the work to give FSU their large halftime bulge, making a pair of touchdown receptions. Whatever chance the Hurricanes had of coming back were quickly wiped away in the opening minutes of the third quarter, as Dunn single-handedly moved the Seminoles in position for a rout. Taking three handoffs for 56 yards, Warrick rambled across from the 1 for a 31-7 score. The teams traded touchdowns in the remaining thirty minutes, and with another field goal to boot, Florida State had its highest point total in history against the hated Hurricanes, 41-17.

As Florida State was busy demolishing their in-state nemesis, Virginia was in Chapel Hill taking on the Tar Heels. Carolina crossed up Virginia with a number of gimmicks in the first half, including a half-back-option pass from Leon Johnson to Marcus Wall that gave the Tar Heels a 13-0 lead in the second quarter. The Cavaliers came back on a touchdown from Mike Groh to Jermaine Crowell, but Carolina's defense continued to play tough. Trailing 17-16 midway through the fourth quarter, UNC coach Mack Brown made a difficult decision. With a fourth-and-1 deep in UVA territory, Brown elected to try for the first down instead of a go-ahead field goal. The decision paid off handsomely, as Johnson broke off a 19-yard sprint to push the Tar Heels inside the 10. Johnson scored from the 6 minutes later, and Carolina had its first victory over a Top Ten team in thirteen years.

The FSU offensive machine surged again in victory over Wake Forest, as the unit put together its third 70-point outing. The Demon Deacons were hopelessly overmatched, and trailed 20-0 before their offense could get a first down. Kanell threw for 323 yards and five touchdowns, while Dunn added 112 yards on the ground. After leading the Seminoles to six touchdowns and nearly 500 yards in total offense, Kanell gave way after the opening series of the second half. The Seminoles shifted to their running game in hopes of keeping the score down, but the hapless Deacons were unable to stop the FSU train. Three different Florida State players ran in touchdowns in the final two quarters, with backup Khalid Abdullah scoring twice and Dee Feaster adding a 55-yard touchdown sprint.

Georgia Tech was FSU's fifth consecutive home opponent, and like those that came before them, the Yellow Jackets met stiff resistance. In setting a school record with forty-one completions, Kanell threw touchdowns to Cooper and E. G. Green, giving FSU a 21-10 lead. Preston added another rushing score late in the half, and the rout was on. The third quarter came and went without any points for either side, but Florida State still had some work to do. Green caught his second touchdown pass early in the final period, and Cooper made another scoring grab following a GT fumble to make the final score 42-10.

With a 7-0 record and twenty-nine consecutive ACC victories to their credit, the Seminoles rolled into Charlottesville for a Thursday night game against UVA. Although they had dropped to No. 2 in the polls, it was evident that this was Bowden's best offensive team thus far at Florida State. Bowden's offense was averaging 56 points a game as they headed north, and had scored no fewer than 41 points against any single opponent. The Seminole defense had also dramatically improved in recent weeks, holding each of their last five opponents to under twenty points.

Although the cold weather and home field would play into Virginia's favor, there was no question that their work was cut out for them. The Cavaliers were still ranked, but few actually believed they could remain competitive against the Seminoles for very long. Virginia enjoyed a bye week before the contest, offering additional time to prepare their game plan for Florida State. Dr. Jerry Punch of ESPN was working the sidelines for that night's game.

"Gary Danielson, Brad Nessler and myself arrived in Charlottesville on Tuesday, and we went to Virginia's practice," he recalls. "Rick Lantz, UVA's defensive coordinator, decided to try something different against Florida State. The Seminoles had a great offensive line that year, and the Cavaliers wanted to free up more linebackers. They were practicing a 3-4 alignment, with safety Anthony Poindexter playing as the extra linebacker. Poindexter was an excellent athlete, and Virginia chose to use him in their strategy to neutralize Warrick Dunn. Poindexter's job was to mirror Dunn, follow him wherever he went on the field. When asked what to do if Dunn had to go to the bathroom, Lantz told Poindexter that they wanted him to lift the lid for Warrick."

After recovering a UVA fumble in the early minutes, Florida State needed only two plays to score, which came on a 35-yard completion from Kanell to Philip Riley. On Virginia's next possession, quarterback Mike Groh read a Seminole blitz and promptly called an audible at the line. Instead of falling back into the pocket, Groh tossed to Tiki Barber, who outran the charging Seminole front and raced 64 yards for the tying score. Another Virginia turnover set up FSU's second touchdown, as Kanell spotted Dunn, who eluded the UVA defenders to the right and danced untouched into the end zone. Barber went on to score again when Virginia got the ball back, and the game was tied at 14.

The UVA special teams came through big moments later, blocking an FSU punt. The pigskin was scooped up by Brian Owen, and Raphael Garcia made a field goal to give the Cavaliers their first lead. The game remained 17-14 until late in the first half, when Virginia was forced into a third-and-12 from their own 28. Groh found wide receiver Demetrius Allen running a post route to his left. Allen made an over-the-shoulder catch, and worked his way around a pair of Seminole defenders that had collided into one another. Allen raced untouched down the sideline for a 72-yard touchdown. Although Green caught a 38-yard pass from Kanell to make the score 24-21, a late Garcia field goal gave Virginia a 27-21 halftime lead.

"When the Florida State team got into the locker room, Bobby Bowden climbed on top of a bunch of duffel bags assembled in the middle of the floor," recalls Dr. Punch, who was allowed access into the visitor's dressing room during the intermission. "Bowden told his team flat out that they were going to lose the ball game if they did not start playing better football. He referred to the Florida game from the year before, and told them that they would need that kind of effort to knock off this Virginia team. If they didn't get it, he told them not to be surprised to go home disappointed. That's the thing you have to respect about Bowden. He doesn't paint floral pictures. He is very honest with his football team."

In the third quarter, the game became a battle of defense and field position. Garcia blasted another field goal, this one from 40 yards, to give Virginia a 30-21 edge. With the Cavalier defense playing outside of themselves, and Poindexter effectively neutralizing Dunn, Virginia held their lead into the final quarter. With 6:53 to play Garcia was good again, giving UVA a 33-21 advantage. With the horde assembled in Scott Stadium ready to explode, and a nationwide television audience looking on in shock at what was being played out in front of them, Florida State finally came together. Realizing that it was now or never, Kanell led FSU's first sustained march through the Virginia defense in nearly two full quarters of play. On a first-and-goal from the 8, Dunn dove into the end zone for his second touchdown of the game, and in less than a minute, the Seminoles had cut the score to 33-28.

The Cavaliers took possession following Dunn's touchdown intent on running down the clock, but Barber was stuffed on a critical third down to force a punt. Florida State had more than three minutes to work with, and after converting a single first down, Kanell made his second critical error of the game. Hurried to make a pass, Kanell was intercepted by Virginia's Percy Ellsworth. It was Ellsworth's second pick of the night, and appeared to salt away victory for the Cavaliers.

With a little more than two minutes to play, all Virginia had to do was string together a couple of first downs and the game was theirs. The Seminoles were ready again for Barber on the first play, and brought the UVA tailback down for a 4-yard loss. Barber gained 6 on his next carry, and on third down, Welsh decided to throw a pass. It was not a wise decision, as a poor shotgun snap resulted in a fumble. Although the Cavaliers recovered, they were forced to punt the ball back to FSU. With 1:37 on the clock, Florida State retained possession at their own 20.

Kanell could not afford to throw another interception, but the FSU quarterback held nothing back on first down. On a long heave through the UVA secondary, Kanell connected with Riley, who brought in the catch for a large gain. Virginia protested that the ball hit the turf, and after consulting for a moment, the officials concurred that the pass indeed hit the deck. Undaunted, Kanell threw to Riley again on second down, who ran 14 yards for a first down. The chains moved again following the next play, as Kanell tossed to Cooper for 12 yards to the 46. After an incompletion, in which the FSU receiver was shoved out-of-bounds, Kanell went to Cooper again for another 12 yards.

Although they were now in Virginia territory, time was becoming a serious factor. With the clock running under thirty seconds, a pass was dropped along the sidelines. Cooper made another catch on second down, although he was unable to gain first down yardage. Florida State had to hurry up to the football, and Kanell found Dunn alone across the middle. Dunn outran the Cavaliers to the 13, where he was brought down with nine seconds to play. As the clock stopped for the chains to be realigned, the FSU quarterback had time to assemble his team at the line and spike the ball. Virginia, dazed at what was taking place, was caught out of position on the play. With twelve men on the field, the officials gave Florida State half-distance yardage, placing the ball down at the 6.

The Seminoles had time for two plays, and with the capacity crowd on its feet, Kanell overthrew a pass in the end zone. Although four seconds remained on the clock, a slew of Cavalier fans ran onto the field. The game was clearly not over, and the UVA public address announcer pleaded for the spectators to leave the field, lest the Cavaliers be dealt another penalty. The game hinged on one play, and the Seminoles went with a surprise. Instead of lining up for another pass play, the ball was snapped directly to Dunn on a shotgun draw.

Dunn sprinted down to the 2, where he lunged toward the goal line. The ESPN commentators originally signaled touchdown, but the people directly responsible for making that call, the officials, never did. Poindexter and Adrian Burnim met the FSU tailback inches shy of the line, holding him out by a matter of inches. As Bowden stood by in shock, speaking to his coaches on his headset, Scott Stadium erupted. In what many consider the most thrilling finish in the history of the Atlantic Coast Conference, Virginia became the first league member to topple the giants from Tallahassee.

"As soon as the game ended, we took off in the direction of George Welsh," recalls Dr. Punch. "We finally got to him, after having a couple of cameras trampled and one of our crew members run over. We wanted to get away from the fans, so we found a place at the edge of the stadium, where there was a brick wall and a little bit of protection. As I was talking to Welsh, students were diving from the stands onto us! It was quite a memorable scene."

Although the national championship now looked to be a stretch, the Seminoles could still clinch a tie for the conference. With Virginia also holding one league defeat, FSU would have to win both games, against North Carolina and Maryland, if they wanted to guarantee themselves a berth in the new Bowl Alliance, which had replaced the Bowl Coalition at the start of the season. The Bowl Alliance, similar in design to the Bowl Coalition, took away conference tie-ins for the Sugar, Fiesta, and Orange Bowls, and was another step in the NCAA's efforts to produce a true Division I-A football champion without giving up its lucrative bowl system.

The Seminole defense took care of things quickly against the Tar Heels, as freshman Mario Edwards blocked a punt and ran 24 yards for the game's first touchdown. Minutes later, on the first Seminole offensive play of the game, Dunn took a handoff and broke 43 yards to the goal line. It looked as though FSU was headed towards another 70-point outing, but the Carolina defense came together. Although the Seminoles scored two more touchdowns, coming on a short run by Dunn and a six-yard reception by Cooper, UNC kept the game competitive. The Tar Heels scored twice, but the Seminoles held on for a 28-12 verdict in the rain.

As FSU was putting the finishing touches on their victory in Chapel Hill, Virginia was completing its improbable run toward a split of the conference championship. With Barber rushing for 116 yards to set a new single-season UVA record, the Cavaliers snuck by Maryland, 21-18, in College Park. Although they trailed 11-0 early, Virginia began a courageous comeback, spearheaded by the running of Barber.

Garcia connected on a pair of field goals for the first UVA points, and
Barber and fellow running back Kevin Brooks added scores to help the
Cavalier cause.

Although UVA had no qualms in beating Maryland, the Cavaliers
were compelled to jump on the Terrapin bandwagon the following
week, as they headed to Tallahassee to play the Seminoles. It was a
memorable afternoon for Kanell, as the senior finished his home career
as the ACC's all-time leader in touchdown passes. With scoring tosses
to Green and Cooper, Kanell upped his touchdown total to 56, which
surpassed Ben Bennett of Duke and Shawn Moore of Virginia. Kanell
added 346 yards on twenty-four-of-thirty-four passing, and led Florida
State to a 59-17 victory.

The Fiesta Bowl Committee, which was scheduled to host the national championship game on January 2, was clearly hoping to have
two unbeaten teams play in its game. The only way that would happen
was if Florida could beat Florida State in Gainesville and go on to win
the SEC Championship Game. Nebraska was undoubtedly headed to
Tempe as the nation's No. 1 team, and would likely play the winner of
the showdown in "The Swamp." For the Seminoles, an opportunity was
in place not only to beat their archrival in a significant game, but to go
after the school's second NCAA title in three years.

On a cool, damp afternoon in Gainesville, the Gators went for the
school's first 11-0 regular season in history. The Seminoles would have
liked nothing more than to burst the UF bubble, and at least in the first
quarter, it looked as though it might happen. After Florida receiver Ike
Hilliard fumbled on the first play of the game, Cooper caught a pair of
passes to move FSU into field goal range. Scott Bentley was good from
40 yards away, and the Seminoles led, 3-0. After UF quarterback
Danny Wuerffel threw to Jacquez Green for a 22-yard touchdown,
Bentley converted another kick.

The score remained 7-6 into the second quarter, when Florida took
advantage not only of the home crowd, but also an uncharacteristically
bad stretch for the Florida State offense. Kanell was unable to stay on
track in the second quarter, allowing UF to take over strategic control
of the game. Terry Jackson started up the Florida engine with a 1-yard
rush, making the score 14-6 in favor of the Gators. Nine minutes later,
after making several defensive stops against the Seminoles, Florida
scored again, courtesy of a 42-yard bomb from Wuerffel to Hilliard.
With less than a minute remaining in the half, the Gators struck again,
as receiver Chris Doering made three consecutive catches, including a
20-yard touchdown, to send Florida into the locker rooms leading 28-6.

After going an entire half without scoring a touchdown for the first time all season, the Seminoles regained some confidence midway through the third quarter when Dunn crossed the line for a 28-12 score. Following a two-point conversion, FSU was suddenly within two touchdowns of a tie. Although an uneasy feeling crept into the minds of the Gator faithful following the quick Florida State score, Wuerffel quickly shifted the momentum back to the orange and blue. On the first play after the kickoff, Wuerffel found Hilliard deep, who had beaten FSU defender Harold Battles. Hilliard brought in the catch and raced 74 yards for a devastating touchdown.

Trailing by eleven points heading into the final fifteen minutes, Florida State was out of magic. The Florida defense kept FSU from making any significant strides in the fourth quarter, and won the game, 35-24, to put themselves in position for the national championship. Although the Gators went on to get embarrassed by Nebraska in the Fiesta Bowl, they earned the right to play in the game by virtue of their victory over FSU. Despite the loss, the Seminoles got another invitation to a major bowl, as the Orange Bowl matched them up with Notre Dame for the third consecutive season.

Prior to the 1995 season, the ACC had negotiated a contract with the Carquest Bowl Committee, agreeing to send its fourth-place school to Miami's Joe Robbie Stadium for a game against a school from the Southeastern Conference. The league sent North Carolina, who finished the regular season with a 6-5 record. Their opponent was Arkansas, fresh off getting blown out by Florida in the SEC Championship Game. Although Arkansas, led by former Tar Heel nemesis Danny Ford, was heavily favored, the Tar Heels played a physical contest. With All-American Marcus Jones and the Carolina defense neutralizing the Razorback running game, the Tar Heels produced enough offense to mount a 20-10 victory.

Clemson welcomed in the New Year with a Gator Bowl appearance against Syracuse, and the game quickly got out of hand for the Tigers. Unable to control Syracuse's passing combination of Donovan McNabb and Marvin Harrison, Clemson took its worst bowl defeat as a member of the ACC. McNabb torched the CU secondary, completing thirteen passes for 309 yards and three touchdowns. Harrison was on the receiving end on several of McNabb's tosses, and with the score 20-0 still in the first quarter, it became evident very early that it was not Clemson's day. With the Tiger offense mounting only 94 yards the entire game, the Orangemen completely dominated the action. Adding another trio of scores later in the game, Syracuse claimed a 41-0 final.

Virginia met Georgia in the Peach Bowl, and for the seventh time over the course of the season, the Cavaliers played a game that went down to the wire. The Cavaliers jumped out to a 24-6 advantage late in the second quarter following an 82-yard scoring catch and run by Demetrius Allen, but Georgia mounted a late rally to send the game into halftime 24-14. Although UVA allowed another Georgia field goal, the game headed into the final minutes with the Cavaliers ahead, 27-20. With possession of the ball and less than two minutes to play, Virginia made a crucial error. Pinned back deep in their own territory, UVA was trying to run out the clock when the ball hit the deck. Georgia defensive tackle Jason Ferguson picked up the loose pigskin at the 10, and rambled across the line to the delight of the throng of Bulldog supporters assembled in the Georgia Dome. With the extra point, the game was suddenly tied at 27.

The officials ruled that Georgia celebrated excessively after their miraculous touchdown, and forced the Bulldogs to kick off from their own 20. As the UVA kickoff unit ran onto the field, Cavalier fans must have been shocked at what had just transpired. With the game suddenly up for grabs, their anxiety would soon turn into ecstasy. The kick was caught by Allen at the 17, and the receiver took off in the direction of the Bulldog coverage. Reaching full speed and finding a gap, Allen broke into the clear. In a stunning turn of events, Allen ran all the way to the end zone for a dramatic touchdown. With only 57 seconds remaining following Allen's 83-yard play, the Bulldogs were out of miracles. In a heartbreaking end to the Ray Goff era at Georgia, the Cavaliers held on for a 34-27 triumph.

"I had said all season that I was going to return a kickoff for a touchdown," Allen said after the game. "But, at that moment, I wasn't even thinking about what I had said. All I could see was the goal line."

In the final Orange Bowl game played at the old stadium, the Irish outplayed FSU in the opening quarter, as Derrick Mayes took in a 39-yard pass from Tom Krug to give Lou Holtz's team an early lead. Although Cooper caught a 15-yard pass to tie the contest at 7, a field goal gave Notre Dame a 10-7 advantage after fifteen minutes. Late in the period, the FSU offense worked itself back into the lead when Cooper hauled in his second scoring grab. The touchdown, the thirtieth of the year for the All-American Kanell, gave the garnet and gold a 14-10 lead at the intermission.

The momentum shifted back to the Irish in the third quarter, as Mayes caught another long touchdown pass from Krug. Following a safety, in which Kanell was forced to step out-of-bounds in the end zone, Notre Dame scored again on Krug's third touchdown pass. With a little less than twelve minutes to play, the Seminoles found themselves trailing, 26-14. The FSU offense covered 73 yards in less than two minutes, however, and Kanell hit Green between the numbers to make the score 26-21. The revitalized Seminole defense shut down Notre Dame on its next possession, and gave the ball back to its streaking offense. This time it took only six plays for the Seminoles to score, as Kanell connected with Cooper for the go-ahead touchdown. Florida State stuck with what had been working all game on the conversion attempt, and Kanell tossed to Cooper again for a 29-26 advantage.

Notre Dame still had over six minutes to make a push, but each of their final possessions resulted in failure. A fumble on the first drive stunted the Irish momentum, and in their last gasp, Krug was pressured by the Seminole front and forced to intentionally ground the ball in the end zone. The officials awarded a safety to Florida State, and Bobby Bowden claimed his third Orange Bowl title in four years by a score of 31-26.

Throughout their years of domination in the ACC, Florida State always seemed to have one particular strength over another. In 1992, it had been the play of linebackers Marvin Jones and Derrick Brooks. The following year, it was the Heisman-winning performance of quarterback Charlie Ward. In 1995, it was the play of the entire offense, which averaged over 50 points a game for most of the season. In 1996, FSU's strength unquestionably lied in its defensive line, where three of the best down linemen in the country wreaked havoc on opposing quarterbacks and ballcarriers. With All-Americans Peter Boulware and Reinard Wilson playing on the ends, and Andre Wadsworth up the middle, the Seminole front was the most powerful in all of college football.

The Seminole defenders specialized in getting off the football before opposing offensive linemen, and disrupting the backfield before plays could even develop. With impeccable speed, the FSU line was the driving force of a defense that led the nation against the run, and finished third in the NCAA in total yardage allowed. Boulware and Wilson were unstoppable forces, combining for 32.5 sacks. Wilson finished his career as the Seminole career leader in sacks with 35.5, and led FSU in tackles in 1996 with 105.

A converted linebacker, Boulware was simply too fast for most linemen to keep him in front. As a result, Boulware was capable of single-handedly hindering the running games of his opposition, and even when he wasn't making sacks, he was constantly putting pressure on the quarterback. Opposing coaches were forced to adjust their passing schemes specifically for Boulware's fearsome pass rush, and it was no surprise that he was named National Defensive Player of the Year at the end of the season. The big lineman went on to set a new FSU single-season record with nineteen sacks, which also led the nation. As a whole, the garnet and gold defenders held nine of their twelve opponents to seventeen or fewer points.

With Danny Kanell's graduation following the 1995 campaign, the stage was set for the reign of Thad Busby as the starting quarterback of the Seminoles. Like Kanell and Ward before him, Busby was eased into the top slot, having paid his dues for two seasons as a backup. With Warrick Dunn and E. G. Green returning to the Seminole fold, in addition to All-ACC linemen Chad Bates, Walter Jones, and Todd Fordham, there was no question that FSU would again be in the thick of the national championship hunt at the end of the year.

Another premiere with Duke resulted in another FSU wipeout, although the Blue Devils held it together a little better this time than they had in 1995. Both Seminole lines overwhelmed the white shirts of Duke, moving the ball with ease on offense and dominating on the other side of the ball. Boulware and Wilson plugged the outside, and terrorized three different quarterbacks in helping the defense set up 24 FSU points. Six different Seminoles scored touchdowns, and the reserves played out a 44-7 final.

The FSU athletic department had compelled Wake Forest and Maryland before the season into moving their home games to Orlando and Miami for money, which meant that the Seminoles would only have to leave the Sunshine State twice during the regular season. The first out-of-state trip sent the Seminoles to Raleigh, where they met Mike O'Cain's Wolfpack. Busby led an assault that accumulated 271 yards in the opening half, and coupled with a defensive effort that held State to under 100 yards, the Seminoles were cruising 24-0 after two quarters of play. It never did get any better for the Wolfpack, as Cooper caught a 29-yard missile six minutes into the third quarter for a 31-3 FSU advantage. Although State finally reached the end zone later in the contest, the Seminoles tacked on twenty more points for a 51-17 final. The North Carolina coast had been ravaged by Hurricane Fran days earlier, and now NCSU was left with the task of picking up the pieces of their battered team.

The nation's best two defenses were on display in Tallahassee the following week, as Mack Brown's Tar Heels strolled into town. North Carolina came into the contest looking good at 3-0, and boasting its finest defensive unit since the days of Lawrence Taylor. Carolina had recently shut out both Clemson and Georgia Tech, the former a 45-0 pounding that had the orange section in Kenan Stadium booing and shouting insults at Tiger coaches. North Carolina had also beat a good Syracuse team on the road, holding Donovan McNabb and the Orangemen offense to only ten points. It was North Carolina's best chance to beat the Seminoles since FSU had joined the ACC four years earlier, and was Mack Brown's first big opportunity to lead a major program to a conference title.

In the rain and mud, Carolina was only able to muster 187 yards of offense, and wound up being held off the scoreboard. A blocked field goal attempt led to a successfully converted kick for Florida State, and Dunn went in from 10 yards away after a Tar Heel fumble. Unable to mount any kind of offensive surge, Carolina opted to play a strictly defensive game, hoping their unit could pull off a play of their own and give the team a chance to score. The Seminoles mounted only 213 yards offensively, but field position played a factor throughout the contest. Stuck primarily on their own side of the field, and unable to move the ball effectively, the Tar Heels could not get close enough to even attempt a field goal, much less reach the end zone. Against one of the better defensive teams they would face all season, Bowden and the Seminoles were happy to just get dry somewhere after their 13-0 victory.

Busby looked sharp against Clemson, throwing three scores and locating his receivers to the tune of 259 yards in the first half. The Tigers managed to reach the scoreboard with a field goal, for their first points against the Seminoles in Tallahassee since the garnet and gold joined the ACC, but it was their lone bright spot, as they dropped the game handily, 34-3. The Seminoles next met Miami, and although they were vastly superior on paper this season, there was always something daunting about playing the Hurricanes in the Orange Bowl. Florida State had not won a game against Miami in Coral Gables since 1984, and was without consecutive victories over the Hurricanes since the days of Howard Schnellenberger.

Florida State settled the issue in the first eleven minutes, taking advantage of two Hurricane errors to build a 17-0 lead by the end of the first quarter. With an opportunity to exorcise past demons against the Hurricanes, Dunn made one of his finest plays in the garnet and gold, sprinting through the Miami linebackers and outrunning the secondary to the end zone for an 80-yard score. After cutting the lead to 27-16, UM made a march into Seminole territory again, where Reinard Wilson made the defining play of the contest. In pushing the Hurricanes out of field goal range with a sack, Wilson forced Miami to attempt a desperate fourth down conversion, which was not to be. Busby added a late 1-

yard sneak, and Florida State took a 34-16 triumph. It was FSU's most decisive victory in Coral Gables since 1970, and gave Bobby Bowden plenty of reasons to smile afterwards.

"Wilson was unbelievable," said Bowden, who once declared his epitaph would read: He Couldn't Beat Miami. "The way it is going now, I may not even die," he added.

The Seminoles had more to prove the following week in Tallahassee, as 5-1 Virginia rolled into town. No final score would be enough to equate the 1995 disaster in Charlottesville, and with an opportunity to solidify their No. 3 national ranking against a fourteenth-ranked opponent, FSU quickly took the offensive. Dunn made the first big play, breaking through a seam in the UVA defense and racing 65 yards for the game's first touchdown. Virginia countered with Tiki Barber, who broke off a 48-yard carry seconds later to knot the game at 7. In earning league MVP honors, Barber entered select company in 1996, becoming the first ACC player since Wake Forest's Bill Barnes back in 1956 to lead the conference in rushing, total yards, and punt return yardage.

The big plays continued in the second quarter, as Busby lofted a clean toss over the shoulder of Wayne Messam, who caught the bomb at the edge of the goal line for a 48-yard score. Although the Cavaliers trailed 14-7, they were far from finished, as following a Busby fumble, Aaron Brooks snuck over to tie the game again. Rafael Garcia connected on a field goal minutes later, and Virginia led 17-14 after two quarters of play. Busby got back on track in the third quarter, completing a 21-yard pass to Green to give the Seminoles a 21-17 advantage. Bentley added to the lead early in the fourth quarter, and Rock Preston pointed FSU in the direction of victory with a 24-yard sprint at the 9:06 mark. Now trailing 31-17, Virginia gave one last go at a comeback. Although Tim Sherman tossed a strike to Germaine Crowell to make the score 31-24, there would be no magical finish this year. The Seminoles successfully ran down the clock, and all but ensured another undisputed ACC championship.

The following two weeks provided a relative break for the Seminoles, as Georgia Tech and Wake Forest came calling. Although they took an early 3-0 advantage, Tech soon found itself at the mercy of the Seminole defense. A 56-yard interception return by Lamont Green was a prelude to a series of outstanding individual efforts by Boulware, who bullied and intimidated Georgia Tech all game. After sacking Yellow Jacket signal caller Joe Hamilton for a big loss, Boulware forced a Yellow Jacket fumble, which led to another Seminole touchdown. With FSU now leading 14-3, Boulware officially put the game in rout mode when he broke free and blocked a punt at the GT 13. Shevin Smith fell on the loose ball in the end zone, and FSU took an eighteen-point advantage. The Seminoles added a quartet of touchdowns against an outclassed Georgia Tech defense, and left Atlanta on the positive end of a 49-3 blowout.

Dan Kendra made his celebrated first start at quarterback for FSU against the Demon Deacons, as Busby rested a hairline fracture on his nonthrowing wrist. The redshirt freshman looked strong, completing twenty passes for 281 yards and three touchdowns in leading FSU to a 44-7 victory. As the Seminoles went out of the conference the following week to play Southern Mississippi, North Carolina and Virginia tangled in a key conference matchup in Scott Stadium. The Tar Heels arrived in Charlottesville with an 8-1 mark, the loss to FSU back in September providing their lone setback. North Carolina had not won at Virginia since 1981, and needed the game desperately in order to claim an at-large berth in the Bowl Alliance, thereby guaranteeing UNC's first major postseason berth since the 1950 Cotton Bowl.

After the teams traded field goals in the first half for a 3-3 deadlock, UNC dominated the third quarter. Quarterback Chris Keldorf threw a 4-yard score to Octavius Barnes, which gave more momentum to an already spirited Carolina defense. Barely a minute after the Barnes touchdown, freshman cornerback Dre' Bly turned in another big play in what had been a breakthrough season. Bly took the conference by storm in 1996, becoming the first ACC rookie and only the fifth first-year player in NCAA history to earn consensus first-team All-American honors. Opponents were unaware of Bly's instinctive abilities during his first season, and made the mistake of steadily throwing in his direction. As a result, Bly led the nation with eleven interceptions during the regular season, and his 51-yard scamper after catching an errant Aaron Brooks pass gave UNC a 17-3 edge over the Cavaliers.

The Tar Heels were driving again, poised to take a 20-3 lead with a little more than ten minutes remaining when Keldorf made a costly error, putting a pass directly in the outstretched arms of Virginia cornerback Antwone Harris. The freshman ran 95 yards in the opposite direction, and instead of UNC leading by three scores, they found themselves up by only a touchdown. Tim Sherman replaced Brooks at quarterback and led UVA 58 yards through the Carolina defense, and with 3:07 to play, ran across to make the score 17-16. Garcia was money on the crucial extra point, and the game was tied.

North Carolina was unable to move the football yet again, and Virginia took possession with a chance to seize victory. The Tar Heels, who entered the game with the No. 2 defense in the NCAA, were unable to put any pressure on Sherman. Fading back into the pocket, Sherman threw to Germaine Crowell, who caught the pass and ran 41 yards to set up Garcia for a game-winning kick. To the disbelief of North Carolina fans, who watched their team completely unravel over the final ten minutes, Garcia booted a 32-yard field goal with thirty-nine seconds to play. Taking a 20-17 defeat, the disappointed Tar Heels were out of the picture for a berth in the Alliance.

Florida State easily handled Southern Mississippi, as Dunn enjoyed one of his finest games in the garnet and gold. Scoring three times, Dunn set a new FSU record with 47 career touchdowns, and added five receptions for 137 yards. Although the Eagles briefly led 7-0 following a Busby interception, the Seminole quarterback threw for 302 yards, and led his team to a commanding 54-14 win. With an opportunity to move to No. 2 in the polls, the Seminoles buried Maryland behind 24 first half points. For the second week in a row, Florida State gave up the first touchdown, but Green and freshman Peter Warrick countered with long scoring receptions. Dunn added a second quarter tally, and Bentley kicked two field goals. With Kendra in place of Busby late in the game, after the starter went down with a mild knee sprain, FSU scored another pair of touchdowns to take a 48-10 verdict.

The Florida game was at hand for the Seminoles, and none in the storied history of the two rivals had been any more significant than this one. Both teams came into the contest undefeated, with Florida ranked No. 1 and FSU ranked No. 2. The Gators sported a 10-0 record, and came to Tallahassee averaging 49.3 points a contest. With eventual Heisman Trophy winner Danny Wuerffel and a host of talented receivers, in addition to running back Fred Taylor and one of the country's finest defenses, Florida was a worthy adversary to the Seminole juggernaut. However, Florida State would have the advantage of playing in Doak-Campbell Stadium, where 80,000 fans would be cheering and war-chanting their hearts out for the home team.

"There's never been a bigger Florida State game than this one," Bowden mentioned in the days leading up to the contest. "For the first time in a long time, the Florida-Florida State game has national implications. People in Hawaii are going to be interested in it."

The game looked to be a mismatch in the first fifteen minutes, as the Seminoles bullied Florida thoroughly on both sides of the football. Bentley put FSU on the board with a 26-yard field goal, and Boulware followed by deflecting a punt at the UF 3-yard line. Pooh Bear Williams ran over from there, and it was a 10-0 game. Following more excellent defense by the Seminoles, Warrick hauled in a 38-yard reception from Busby, putting the ball at the UF 1. Melvin Pearsall was FSU's man at the goal line, and the touchdown completed a first quarter of complete domination by Florida State.

Trailing by seventeen points, and facing the prospect of an embarrassing defeat on the turf of their greatest nemesis, Wuerffel hit Reidel Anthony with a 50-yard bomb, which put Florida on the FSU 1. Jacquez Green was on the receiving end of Wuerffel's next pass, and UF was within ten. Seminole penalties aided Florida again on their next offensive possession, as the officials cited two different FSU defenders for personal foul and roughing the passer. After Wuerffel found Taylor alone across the middle for 38 yards on a screen pass, the UF quarterback threw another touchdown to Green. With new life, the Gators ran confidently off the field after the second quarter, down only 17-14. The third quarter was dominated by the defenses, with neither team able to score any points. The nation's best two teams now had fifteen minutes to prove their respective mettle.

The Gators drove into FSU territory early in the final period, but a missed field goal took away an opportunity to tie the game. Warrick began the next FSU drive with a 29-yard reception, and Dunn followed with a 15-yard sprint through the heart of the Gator defense. On his way to a game high of 185 yards, Dunn took another carry 17 yards to the UF 2, and Williams scored three plays later to give FSU a 24-14 cushion. Florida made another scoring march in the final four minutes, as Wuerffel threw his third touchdown pass, to make the score 24-21 heading into crunch time.

Florida State got the ball back with an opportunity to run out the clock, and with a chance to play for the national championship at stake, there was no question as to who the Seminoles were going to go with. Even the Gators knew than Warrick Dunn was getting the ball, but there was nothing they could do about it. The senior tailback galloped 14 yards for the critical first down, which allowed the offense to kneel on the ball and tick off the final seconds. With a 24-21 victory in hand, Florida State was headed to the Sugar Bowl for the second time in three years.

"Warrick came into the huddle on that last possession and said, 'Whatever you got left in your heart, give it. One more first down and we're in the Sugar Bowl,'" guard Todd Fordham said later.

Florida rebounded from their gut-wrenching defeat in Tallahassee, and buried Alabama 45-30 in the SEC Championship to earn a rematch with the Seminoles in New Orleans. The Sugar Bowl would be the fifth UF-FSU matchup in the last three seasons, and would guarantee the winner at least a piece of the national championship. Bruce Snyder's

Arizona State team joined Florida State as the nation's only other unde-feated team, and if they could knock off Ohio State in the Rose Bowl, many expected the title to be split.

Virginia began the ACC's annual bowl extravaganza by meeting Miami in the Carquest Bowl, and it became clear in the early going that the Cavaliers were not going to be able to hold up. The Hurricanes dominated from the outset, as Ryan Clement threw a 70-yard scoring pass to Yatil Green to make the score 7-0 barely two minutes into the contest. The remainder of the game belonged to Miami defender Tre-main Mack, who almost single-handedly propelled the Hurricanes to victory. Mack scored twice, sprinting 79 yards with a recovered fumble and 42 yards with an interception, and also blocked a kick to seal UVA's fate. Unable to make any significant strides against their 24-7 halftime deficit, the Cavaliers dropped the game by a score of 31-21.

Although the Peach Bowl went by relatively slowly, the opposing Tiger teams played down to the wire. Clemson scored the first touch-down in the first quarter, as quarterback Nealon Green piled over from 5 yards away for a 7-0 lead. Louisiana State put all their points on the board in the second quarter, as Kevin Faulk ran over from the 3, and kicker Wade Richey pushed a 22-yarder through the uprights. The score remained that way until the very end, when Clemson got a chance to tie the game with a 52-yard field goal with 1:10 to go. Matt Padgett appeared to have put good leg on the football, but LSU's Aaron Adams broke through to deflect it. The blocked field goal was Clemson's final opportunity to score, and sealed a 10-7 LSU verdict.

North Carolina was forced to settle for the Gator Bowl with their 9-2 record, where they met West Virginia. Tar Heel backup signal caller Oscar Davenport completed eleven of his first fourteen passes, and Carolina opened up a 17-3 lead at halftime. West Virginia closed to within a touchdown in the second half, but mistakes did them in. A fumble, combined with a pair of penalties levied against the WVU de-fense, allowed Carolina to fend off the Mountaineer surge. Josh McGee kicked a second field goal, and the UNC defense endured for a 20-13 victory. With the win, North Carolina moved into the final Associated Press Top Ten for the first time since the end of the 1981 season.

On the evening of January 2, 1997, the national championship of college football was decided between two of the most bitter rivals in all of sports. With Arizona State's 20-17 defeat at the hands of Ohio State the day before in Pasadena, either Florida State or Florida would be hoisting the championship trophy by night's end. It was no secret that Bobby Bowden and Steve Spurrier did not like one another, and the coaches exchanged barbs in the days leading up to the contest. In addition, it was reported that Seminole and Gator players got into shouting matches on Bourbon Street, and on more than one instance, fights nearly broke out among members of the opposing teams.

Between the two showdowns, Spurrier developed a simple but effective plan to neutralize Florida State's pass rush, which had sacked Danny Wuerffel six times back in November. The Gator quarterback was knocked to the turf on countless occasions by oncoming FSU defenders, and spent much of the contest eluding would-be tacklers. By placing Wuerffel in the shotgun, Spurrier allowed his signal caller an extra second or two of pocket time, a valuable number considering the speed and precision of the Florida wide receivers. Keeping his plan top secret until game time, Spurrier and the Gators unleashed a furious assault on the Seminoles under the roof and the bright lights of the Louisiana Superdome.

Utilizing their new style from the very beginning, Florida went 77 yards early in the first quarter to take a 7-0 lead. With plenty of time to find his receivers, Wuerffel sat back and justified his selection for the Heisman Trophy, completing passes to a number of receivers. With the ball on the FSU 9, Wuerffel threw to Ike Hilliard for the points. The Seminoles narrowed the gap on their ensuing possession with a Scott Bentley field goal, but the nightmare was just beginning for the garnet and gold.

After a field goal gave the Gators a 10-3 lead at the end of the opening quarter, the UF offense tore through the Seminoles for 73 yards on only four plays. Fred Taylor's 2-yard score gave Florida a 17-3 lead, and began what turned out to be a roller coaster of a quarter. The Gators and Seminoles combined for 28 points in the second fifteen minutes, with Busby throwing to Green from 29 yards away for one score, and Dunn racing around end for a 12-yard score just before halftime. Florida added a 31-yard missile from Wuerffel to Hilliard, and took a 24-17 lead into the locker rooms.

Following Bentley's second field goal, which cut the UF lead to 24-20 four minutes into the third quarter, the game appeared to be up for grabs. Unfortunately for Florida State, they would soon be without their leader. Dunn, hampered all evening by symptoms of the flu, had to leave early in the second half. It was a bitter end to Dunn's impressive four-year run at FSU, as he compiled only 28 yards on nine carries. Dunn's absence did more than simply leave the Seminoles without their featured running back. The senior had been the heart and soul of the FSU offense all year, the man who had stepped into the huddle and willed his team to victory over the Gators five weeks earlier. From the moment Dunn left the field to the final gun, the game belonged to Florida.

In a second half outburst, Florida tallied 28 points over the final two quarters of the contest, and turned the game into a blowout. Hilliard caught his third scoring reception to make the score 31-20, and Wuerffel added a rare rushing touchdown from 16 yards out to end the third quarter, 38-20. With Wuerffel completing eighteen-of-thirty-one passes from the shotgun for 306 yards and three touchdowns, there was little for FSU to do but to watch on bitterly as their national championship dreams slithered away. Terry Jackson sealed the game in the fourth quarter with a pair of runs, the first from 42 yards and the second from the 1. Steve Spurrier, never one to go easy on an opponent, continued to pile on the points well into the final quarter, and gave his alma mater its first NCAA football championship with a 52-20 victory. With the loss, Florida State slipped to No. 3 in the final polls, and were left for a second season in a row to blame the Gators for their inability to finish at the top of the college football world.

For the first time since Florida State had entered the league, it appeared that there was a team capable of knocking them off the top position in the ACC standings in 1997. With a first-rate defensive unit, in addition to a solid pair of quarterbacks, Mack Brown and his North Carolina team received quite a bit of attention in the preseason. The Tar Heel defense featured several players that would move on to the NFL in the coming years, and many were pointing to the FSU-UNC showdown in Chapel Hill on November 8 as a game with national championship implications. Although Warrick Dunn, Reinard Wilson, and Peter Boulware were all departed from the garnet and gold, there was still plenty of talent in Tallahassee that autumn. Along with quarterback Thad Busby, a new group of Seminoles were ready to take their place among the Florida State stars of the past.

Most schools around the country used the term "rebuilding" to talk about a team full of new starters, but at Florida State under Bobby Bowden, the better word to use was "reloading." With a powerhouse football program to go along with a warm climate, it has never been terribly difficult for Bowden to attract some of the nation's finest high school football players to Tallahassee. With a steady group of nationally regarded signing classes coming in each August throughout the 1990s, the Florida State coaching staff was afforded the luxury of picking their starting teams from among a wealth of skilled players at virtually every position.

This was the case again in 1997, as the Seminoles put together another potent set of offensive and defensive units. True freshman Travis Minor grabbed Warrick Dunn's tailback position midway through the season, and would keep it over the next four years. A young group of receivers, led by Peter Warrick and Laveranues Coles, helped Busby shine all season. The next in a long line of signal callers to thrive in the FSU offensive system, Busby threw for a school record 3,317 yards, and added 25 touchdowns against only ten interceptions.

Andre Wadsworth returned to anchor the defensive line, and became Florida State's highest NFL draft pick in history the following spring when the Baltimore Ravens took him with the third overall pick. Boulware came to Tallahassee as a walk-on in 1993, and left town as the ACC Defensive Player of the Year. Without the speedy tandem of Wilson and Boulware on the outside in 1997, the FSU coaches elected to move Wadsworth from noseguard to end. Andre thrived in his new position, recording sixteen sacks and dominating the post in similar fashion to his celebrated predecessors to earn Consensus All-American honors.

The Seminoles flew to Los Angeles for FSU's first game in history against Southern California on September 6. Wadsworth and Sam Cowart did the job for the defense, and helped hold USC to only seven points. Cowart, playing for the first time since having reconstructive knee surgery, had a career high with eighteen tackles, which included twelve on solos. Wadsworth added eight tackles and two sacks, as Florida State stifled the Trojans to only 25 rushing yards. In a tough battle, Dan Kendra snuck over from the 2 and Dee Feaster added a touchdown to give the Seminoles a 14-7 victory.

Florida State was dominant in the ACC opener against Maryland, scoring 30 points in the first two quarters and overwhelming the Terrapin offensive line. Busby threw for 308 yards in a half of action, and backups Dan Kendra and Chris Weinke flourished as well. Kendra hit Warrick twice for touchdowns in the third quarter, and Weinke added a 9-yard scoring toss in the fourth. With the Terrapins producing only 105 yards of total offense, the Seminoles coasted to a 50-7 triumph.

Clemson welcomed Florida State to Death Valley with their confidence brimming after two season-opening victories, and gave the garnet and gold its best shot. The Tigers got the home crowd going early with an 80-yard march, highlighted by quarterback Brandon Streeter's 32-yard keeper for a touchdown. Although the Tigers recovered an FSU fumble minutes later, the Seminole defense returned the favor when Daryl Bush intercepted a pass and brought it to midfield. Bill Gramatica's field goal made the score 7-3, and helped shift the momentum to the visiting sidelines. The Seminoles caught another break late in the first quarter, as a bad shotgun snap was recovered by Cowart in the end zone. Although they failed to post an offensive touchdown in the opening thirty minutes, the Seminoles led 10-7.

The second half belonged to Warrick, as the sophomore dazzled the Death Valley crowd with his catching and running. On his way to a school-record performance of 372 total yards, Warrick leaped over a defender to haul in a 48-yard touchdown grab midway through the third quarter. The play gave FSU a 21-14 advantage, and although they kept the game close, Clemson was unable to retake the lead. Warrick scored the next Florida State touchdown on a punt return, bringing in a catch at the 10 and racing 90 yards for a 28-17 score. Peter's final scoring play settled the issue, following another Clemson tally that had cut the lead to 28-25. Bringing in the ball at the 34, Warrick weaved his way to the end zone, and the game ended with FSU ahead, 35-28.

The annual game with Miami was nowhere near as much of a concern as it had been in years past for the Seminoles. The Hurricanes were severely down, having lost three of their first four contests. Without the depth and talent that was a staple of past Miami teams, the game became just another blowout for the garnet and gold. It was never competitive, as Florida State handed the Hurricanes its worst defeat since World War II, and posted the first shutout over its nemesis to the south in 33 years. In holding Miami to negative rushing yardage and allowing only 131 total yards for the whole contest, the FSU defenders enjoyed one of their finest days. With five different Seminoles scoring touchdowns, Miami was taken behind the woodshed, 47-0.

After burying Duke in Durham, 51-27, to improve to 5-0, the Seminoles returned home to meet Georgia Tech. Although they couldn't move the ball for much of the contest, the Ramblin' Wreck gave Florida State its toughest challenge yet during the year, allowing only seven points in the first half on an 18-yard pass from Busby to Damian Hartrell. Mixing the run and the pass expertly on a drive midway through the third quarter, Busby moved the Seminoles to the GT 27, where Minor bolted free and scored to give Florida State a 14-0 advantage. The Minor touchdown unleashed a furious garnet and gold offensive over the final twenty minutes, as Busby added three scoring passes to go along with his 399 yards in the air in the 38-0 shutout.

Minor and Cowart were the heroes in the Virginia game, as the pair earned ACC Player of the Week honors. Making his debut as the Seminole starter, Minor ran the first play from scrimmage 87 yards for a touchdown. With additional scoring runs of 6 and 42 yards, it was evident that Bowden had found himself a new tailback. Cowart dominated on his end, leading a defensive effort that held the Cavaliers to -9 yards rushing. The senior linebacker had fourteen tackles and a pair of sacks, and by game's end FSU was leading the NCAA in rushing defense. With the 47-21 verdict over UVA, Florida State was 7-0 for the third time in the last four seasons.

The N.C. State contest was a roller coaster of emotions for the Seminoles, for after jumping out to a large early cushion, the defense allowed itself to lapse in the second half. As a result, NCSU put up more points against Florida State than any other previous ACC opponent. The opening quarter was a breeze, as the Seminoles pummeled the Wolfpack on the way to building up a 27-0 lead. Although FSU finished with 48 points, the second half belonged to N.C. State wide receiver Torry Holt. In a thrilling performance, which placed Holt's name among the all-time greats of ACC pass catchers, the junior caught a record five touchdowns, and accounted for all of his team's points with exception of the extra points. With 168 yards on twelve receptions, the FSU defense without question knew who Torry Holt was by game's end.

With the unsettling 48-35 victory over the Wolfpack completed, the Seminoles prepared to head into its biggest game of the year thus far, and the first legitimate threat of toppling their five-year reign at the top of the ACC standings. Mack Brown had brought respect to the North Carolina football program unseen since Dick Crum's teams of the early 1980s, and had done did it much the same way that Crum had. By recruiting speed at all positions, Brown had his Tar Heels sitting at 8-0, and in position to compete for UNC's first national championship in football. It would take a complete effort, but should Carolina find a way to knock off the Seminoles, they were looking at a berth in the Orange Bowl.

The ESPN College Gameday crew made its way to Chapel Hill for the morning of November 8, as college football fans throughout the nation prepared for a day that would play a large role in shaping the national championship race. The weekend was dubbed "Judgment Saturday," as fellow unbeatens Michigan and Penn State were also meeting in Happy Valley. The winners of the two games, in addition to Nebraska, held the keys that would unlock the doors to the NCAA title.

With Florida State ranked No. 3 and North Carolina ranked No. 5, many argued that it was the biggest game in the ACC's gridiron history, right up there with the UNC-Clemson classic in 1981 and the Georgia Tech-Virginia showdown in 1990. It was without question the outcome that ACC officials had hoped for at the beginning of the year, a pair of undefeated Top Five teams meeting on national television. For a town used to national recognition for basketball, Chapel Hill gladly accepted its brief status as a college football hotbed.

An overflowing crowd entered Kenan Stadium for the night contest, as students stormed the gates and scaled fences in order to fill the seats in their respective session. With alumnus Burt Reynolds on the sidelines for inspiration, FSU came out ready to play. In a dominating defensive performance, the Seminoles held UNC to only nine yards of total offense in the entire first half. Oscar Davenport was harassed by the speedy Seminole front, which overwhelmed the Carolina offensive line and sacked him seven times on the evening. After going down with an ankle injury, Davenport was replaced by Chris Keldorf, who went down twice for an FSU school-record total of nine quarterback drops.

The Seminole offense did not thrive against the Tar Heels like they had against most opponents, but proved strong enough to get the job done. E. G. Green and Melvin Pearsall made scoring receptions in the first thirty minutes, and kicker Sebastian Janikowski added a field goal for a 17-0 lead at the intermission. The second half was anticlimactic, as Carolina continued to struggle offensively and the Seminoles followed suit. The teams traded field goals over the final two quarters, but with the FSU defense coming up as big as it ever had on the road, the Seminoles were able to chop up some of the Kenan Stadium soil and bring it back to Tallahassee, symbolic of a significant victory on the road. With the 20-3 victory in hand, FSU was two games away from another trip to Miami.

The Wake Forest game served as a tune-up for Florida, and the Seminoles played like something was at stake. In a smothering offensive performance similar to the one against N.C. State two weeks earlier, Florida State built up a 28-0 lead after fifteen minutes of play. With an additional thirty points over the final three quarters, it was smooth sailing for the garnet and gold. Busby finished with 390 yards, and led an assault that built up a 38-0 halftime bulge. Florida State tacked on another touchdown and field goal in the final period, and improved to 10-0 with the 58-7 demolition.

Over the past several years, the showdowns between Florida and Florida State had shaped not only the national championship picture, but also the layout of the major bowls. This encounter was no different, as the Seminoles could complete the school's first undefeated regular season in history with the win, and move on to the Orange Bowl for another NCAA title showdown with Nebraska. Although Florida was not in the hunt for the title, with losses to LSU and Georgia against their record, an opportunity was in place to shake up everything.

In the week prior to the contest, Steve Spurrier came up with another ploy to put the Florida State defense on its heels. By rotating quarterbacks Doug Johnson and Noah Brindise after almost every play, the Gator skipper hoped to keep the Seminole secondary guessing and out of position. The plan worked on UF's opening drive, as the home team marched 82 yards for the game's first score. The Seminole defense atoned for its early failure later in the quarter, as Sam Cowart picked up a fumble and coasted 15 yards to the end zone. Scooping up the loose ball at the 15, Cowart coasted the rest of the way. A Seminole field goal made the score 10-6 after fifteen minutes of play.

Busby did most of the damage early in the second quarter, passing FSU to a 17-6 advantage. The Gators got on track after the second Seminole touchdown, and rallied to take the lead going into the locker rooms. Sticking with their quarterback shuttle, UF went 80 yards midway through the period. A 49-yard bomb from Brindise to Travis McGriff came after a 21-yard strike to Jacquez Green, and McGriff came through again from the 6 for a score. Green continued to shine on Florida's third touchdown drive, which he set up with a punt return. After making an excellent lunging catch to keep the drive moving along, the receiver coaxed a pass interference penalty against the Seminoles, which put the Gators at the FSU 4. Fred Taylor scored on his second burst through the line, and UF took an 18-17 lead.

The game continued its up-and-down pace in the third quarter, as the lead changed hands three different times. Taylor, who enjoyed one of the finest games by an opposing running back against Florida State in years, raced to the goal line on a long carry to give UF a 25-20 edge. Minor added to the running circus minutes later, taking the ball at the 23 and racing to the end zone to put FSU back ahead, 26-25. It stayed that way well into the final period, when Janikowski came back onto the field and sailed another kick through the uprights at the 2:38 mark. The Gators would now need a touchdown to win, and with the sea of blue and orange at the Swamp getting restless, the FSU defense dug in its heels, hoping for the stop that would send them to the Orange Bowl.

Taking the ball at the 20 after a touchback, Johnson faded back into the pocket to pass. The Seminoles were expecting Florida to take to the air, but no adequate defense could stop the throw and subsequent catch by Green. The strike gained 63 yards, and Florida, thought for dead moments earlier, was suddenly in position to win. From the FSU 18, Taylor took the ball on a draw play. With the Seminoles out of sorts, Taylor rambled 17 yards to the edge of the goal line. There would be no stand for Florida State, as Taylor plowed over on the next play for his third touchdown. Spurrier and the Gators had challenged the FSU defenders by running the ball, and Taylor responded with 161 yards against a unit that allowed barely 40 yards a contest coming in.

Gator fans celebrated their 32-29 victory well into the night, while the Seminoles were left to lament how they could have shut down so thoroughly on defense on Florida's final scoring march. It was a bitter time in Tallahassee, as the Seminoles watched another chance at a national championship slip away. Although FSU still had a big game to look forward to, a Sugar Bowl encounter with Ohio State, this particular defeat to Florida would take quite awhile to overcome.

The ACC was well represented once again in the postseason, and only Clemson, which fell, 21-17, to Auburn in the Peach Bowl, failed to take victory. With four schools winning at least seven games, and Florida State and North Carolina each claiming eleven, the 1997 season was one of the most successful in league history. Playing in its first bowl under George O'Leary on December 29, Georgia Tech met West Virginia in the Micron PC game. Joe Hamilton led the way for the Yellow Jackets, quarterbacking his team to a 35-30 victory over the Mountaineers.

Mack Brown was not around to coach the Gator Bowl for North Carolina, as he accepted the open position at Texas in the weeks prior to the game. Brown was a hot commodity in college coaching, and although he expressed desire to stay where he was, there was more money at Texas, in addition to a fertile recruiting base and a loyal group of followers. Defensive coordinator Carl Torbush stepped in for the game against Virginia Tech, and his unit made a final stamp on what had been an impressive season. Carolina could have won the game with their defensive points alone, as Dre' Bly returned a fumble 6 yards for one score, and Greg Ellis fell on a loose ball in the end zone for another Tar Heel touchdown. Chris Keldorf threw three touchdowns, and Jonathon Linton, the next in a long line of UNC backs to rush for 1,000 yards in a season, drove over from 1 yard out. Torbush's performance in his debut was enough to earn the permanent head coaching position, as the Tar Heels waxed the Hokies, 42-3.

The Seminoles got off to a decent early start against the Buckeyes, as Busby threw 27 yards to Green on the final play of the first quarter for a 7-3 lead. Florida State tacked on a pair of touchdowns in the second quarter to take a 21-3 cushion into halftime, and although the Buckeyes got closer in the third on a field goal and forced safety, the game was in hand. Four-year starter E.G. Green, who finished his

Seminole career as the Sugar Bowl's Most Valuable Player, hauled in seven catches for 176 yards and a touchdown. Although the game remained close throughout much of the fourth quarter, with FSU holding a 24-14 lead, William McCray's touchdown in the final minute sealed victory for the Seminoles. With the school's twelfth postseason win in thirteen games, Florida State guaranteed itself another Top Five finish.

The 1998 season brought a new era of quarterbacking excellence to the campus of Florida State. Throughout the 1990s, standouts such as Ward, Kanell, and Busby had flourished in the Seminole offensive system, and had etched their names among the finest signal callers in ACC history. With Busby gone after the 1997 campaign, it was time for another FSU quarterback to step up and make his presence felt. Most observers believed that the position would go to Dan Kendra, who had been groomed as the next great Florida State quarterback ever since his high school days back in Bethlehem, Pennsylvania.

The 1998 spring football season was business as usual for the Seminoles until the Garnet and Gold game, the annual conclusion of the seasonal workouts. On a freak play, Kendra had his leg caught up in a pile, and subsequently blew out his knee. It was a somber moment for the entire FSU football family, as the promise of Kendra's quarterback career came to a sudden halt. Although Kendra returned to the fold and would play admirably at fullback in the coming years, he was never quite the same player after his injury.

A year removed from what had turned out to be an unsuccessful professional baseball career, Chris Weinke was suddenly the oldest starting quarterback in the history of the Atlantic Coast Conference. It had been a long time coming for the Minnesota native, who spent most of the Florida State glory years traveling on the buses of minor league baseball teams. After quarterbacking his high school team to a state championship as a junior, Weinke was arguably the finest prep athlete in America during his senior year of 1988-1989.

A star in three sports, Chris threw passes in the fall, captained his school's hockey team during the winter, and was the star of the Cretin-Derham baseball team in the spring. By the time of his final prep baseball season, Chris had already signed a letter of intent to Florida State for football after a recruitment that included more than seventy Division I-A programs. A power-hitting first baseman on the diamond, he was also drawing big attention from major league scouts, and was taken in the second round of the 1990 amateur draft by the Toronto Blue Jays.

After spending four days on the FSU campus that August, Chris began his odyssey in the Toronto farm system. Weinke had some pop in the minor leagues, but hit only .248 over the course of six seasons. As the Blue Jay management began entertaining thoughts to moving him from first baseman to catcher, it became more and more clear that the major leagues were in distant view for Weinke. A few weeks after leaving Tallahassee back in 1990, Chris had received a personal note from Bobby Bowden, stating that he was welcome to come back to Florida State if or when baseball didn't work out. Weinke kept the note in his bedroom throughout his stint in the minors, and after hanging up his glove and spikes, gave the coach a call in hopes of following a new dream.

Weinke, who would be twenty-six years old by the start of the 1998 season, inherited Kendra's position following the freak injury. Possessing maturity and a solid grip of the FSU scheme, Weinke was a natural fit at the helm of the Seminole offense. As with his predecessors, Weinke had plenty of explosive weapons at his disposal. Along with the ACC's most dominant offensive line, the Seminoles had a seasoned running back and a potent set of wideouts. Peter Warrick was back for his junior year, and was ranked among the finest wide receivers in the country coming into the new season. Warrick would team with Weinke to complete another magical touchdown connection for the Seminoles over the next two seasons. Travis Minor returned for his second year as the featured tailback, and with All-American defensive lineman Corey Simon and kicker Sebastian Janikowski ready to make plays, FSU was geared up for yet another national championship run.

Playing an early game on August 26, Florida State had more to fear than just Texas A&M. As the Aggies played tough, taking a 14-10 lead into halftime, the collective gasps of the Seminole faithful could almost be heard all the way up in New Jersey from down in Florida when Warrick went down hard, appearing to have badly sprained his ankle. To the relief of FSU supporters, No. 9 limped his way off the field and ultimately led his team to victory, catching a 9-yard pass from Weinke and returning a punt that set up another touchdown. With the defense holding A&M to 20 yards in the second half, the Seminoles took the game, 23-14.

Opening the ACC schedule against N.C. State, nothing figured to be out of the ordinary for the Seminoles. The Wolfpack had been outscored by an average of 51-15 in their six previous ACC contests against Florida State, and virtually nobody, save the NCSU players and staff, gave them a chance to win the game. Picked to finish seventh in the conference by the media, State had needed a blocked punt to beat lowly Ohio University, 34-31, just a week earlier. Although they lacked significantly compared to the Seminoles in overall personnel, NCSU head coach Mike O'Cain had wide receiver Torry Holt, who could play with anyone on the Florida State side.

In 1998, Holt became the most prolific receiver in ACC history, setting records for yardage, receptions per game, and yardage per game. Along the way, Holt became the first NCSU receiver in history to be named ACC Player of the Year. The Seminoles already knew of Holt's excellence, after unsuccessfully trying to stop him the year before on their home field. With a regional audience watching on ABC, Holt put forth one of his finest performances, and led the Wolfpack to the unthinkable.

Anyone betting on the twenty-five-point Florida State spread must have been happy in the early minutes, as Weinke connected with Warrick for a seemingly effortless 74-yard touchdown. Warrick had so decisively beaten his defender that he caught the pass in stride, and could have walked into the end zone. Although Florida State had begun many of their blowout victories in previous years with similar big plays, something was different this time around. The NCSU defense suddenly came together, and forced Weinke into the worst game of his college career. Still getting used to the intricacies of the FSU offensive system, Weinke struggled all day to complete passes. Finishing nine-of-thirty-two for only 243 yards, Weinke went on to throw six interceptions.

Later in the opening quarter, NCSU quarterback Jamie Barnette came up with a big play of his own, finding Eric Leak for a 31-yard touchdown to tie the game. As the Wolfpack defense forced a punt, Holt dropped back to return a punt at his own 32. Holt caught the football, made a couple of moves, and found a seam in the Seminole coverage unit. In an electrifying effort, Holt zipped downfield for a touchdown and 13-7 NCSU advantage. Everyone expected that Florida State would quickly counter, but it simply never happened. By consistently killing Seminole momentum with turnovers, State's defenders did something that few teams had ever done against a team coached by Bobby Bowden; control the flow of the game. For the first time since getting shut out by Miami in 1988, Florida State went three consecutive quarters without scoring.

With FSU unable to reach the end zone for the remainder of the contest, State continued to add to its lead. After a scoreless second quarter, NCSU notched a field goal in the third to take a 16-7 advantage. Although there was plenty of time for the Seminoles to come back, they continued to be mired in their own poor play. After taking back possession in the fourth quarter, the Wolfpack drove a final nail in the FSU coffin. Throwing from the NCSU 37, Barnette dropped back and connected with Holt, who made his second catch and run of more than 60 yards. With nine receptions for 135 yards, in addition to his excellence on special teams, Holt proved to be a worthy adversary to a team used to snagging most of the headlines.

In the final minutes of the contest, as it became evident that there would be no magical Florida State comeback, thousands of Wolfpack fans lined the outer reaches of the end zones in preparation to storm the field. When the game ended, in favor of NCSU by a score of 24-7, the turf of Carter-Finley Stadium was quickly consumed in a sea of red. As the Seminoles lamented how they could have played so poorly, the goalposts were ripped from their foundations and walked onto the North Carolina State campus by delirious students.

The Seminoles were glad to have Duke for their following game, as few things can heal the sting of defeat better than a decisive victory. The fans at Doak-Campbell were unsettled following an early Duke touchdown, but 24 points in the second quarter pointed the way to a Seminole victory. Warrick hauled in a pair of scoring grabs from Weinke, while Laveranues Coles broke off a 97-yard kickoff return. Unable to remain competitive, the Blue Devils surrendered 38 points in the second half, and took an embarrassing 62-13 defeat back to Durham.

Following a 30-10 victory over Southern Cal, the Seminoles headed to College Park for a game against Maryland. Although Weinke and the offense drove 69 yards on their opening drive for a 7-0 lead, the unit went the final three quarters without a touchdown for the second time in four outings. Leading 13-0 after one quarter of play, Florida State momentarily lapsed on defense, allowing Maryland to score ten unanswered points. With the game up for grabs, Janikowski did his part to keep FSU out in front. The Polish immigrant converted five field goals, and with a third quarter safety added to the mix, FSU took an uncharacteristically difficult 24-10 final.

Although the Maryland game proved to be a struggle, it was the third consecutive contest in which Weinke did not throw an interception. With the disaster against N.C. State becoming more and more of a memory by the day, Weinke was rapidly becoming the player Bowden hoped he would become. In his first 300-yard performance, Weinke tossed for 316 against Miami, and became only the second FSU signal caller in the last fourteen seasons to lead a Seminole victory in Coral Gables. With Warrick enjoying one of his finest games, making seven catches for 190 yards and a touchdown, the Seminoles dominated the second and third quarters, outscoring the Hurricanes, 17-0. Warrick was particularly ready for the Miami contest, as his defensive counterpart, Hurricane cornerback Leonard Myers, had publicly trash-talked him in the days leading up to the contest. Following the 26-14 victory, Warrick had an answer for anyone that may have doubted his abilities.

"Talk is cheap," he said. "There's a difference between talking about us and going out and doing it. I know he was trying to get himself motivated, but what he didn't know was that he was actually motivating me."

The Clemson game got out of hand quickly, as Weinke took advantage of a Tiger turnover and threw a 40-yard strike to Coles. Warrick and Ron Dugans also caught scoring passes from in the opening half, as the Seminoles took a 24-0 lead. With the defense shutting out Clemson, FSU added 24 more points in the second half for a 48-0 whitewashing.

Georgia Tech was hoping to continue its breakthrough season with victory over the Seminoles. After dropping their season opener to Boston College, the Jackets had breezed through New Mexico State and four consecutive ACC opponents. With Joe Hamilton at the reins of the GT offense, the unit had scored at least forty points in all five of their victories, and was among the most productive in the nation. The Ramblin' Wreck came into the game first in the ACC standings, and stood in position to claim the outright conference title should they beat FSU.

Much like the North Carolina game the year before, the Seminoles took care of business in hostile territory, outplaying the Yellow Jackets on the turf of Bobby Dodd Stadium. With Hamilton's receivers blanketed by the FSU secondary, the quarterback was unable to put up nearly the same numbers he was used to putting up. Hamilton eventually gave way to backup George Godsey after injuring his hip, and although the Jackets trailed only 10-7 when he entered, Godsey was unable to make a solid contribution. With the Yellow Jackets on lockdown throughout the second half, Florida State eventually broke the game open. A pass to Warrick with 13:41 remaining made the score 17-7, and was only the beginning of the nightmare for Georgia Tech. After Janikowski booted another field goal, the FSU defense forced a fumble, which led to another Warrick touchdown. The game ended on another big play, as Coles raced 60 yards for the final score of the contest. With the 34-7 victory, the Seminoles not only created a three-way tie atop the ACC standings, but solidified their rise back into the NCAA title picture.

After dominating North Carolina, 39-13, Florida State welcomed Virginia to Doak-Campbell. The Cavaliers had been ranked as high as No. 7 earlier in the year, when they gave up a three-touchdown lead to

Georgia Tech on the way to a 41-38 defeat on the road. The loss stood as UVA's only setback, and they arrived in Florida tied for the conference lead with a 5-1 record. The game had added significance for FSU, as No. 1 Ohio State had been beaten earlier in the day by Michigan State.

With an opportunity to get closer to the Fiesta Bowl, the Seminoles turned out the lights on the Cavaliers in the third and fourth quarters. The Seminoles dominated the second half, shutting out Virginia and moving with cool precision on offense. The unit notched three rushing touchdowns, and moved into range for Janikowski for another score. With the 45-14 game in hand, Florida State now had eight consecutive victories, and were back in the hunt to land another berth in the NCAA championship game.

The win over Virginia was bittersweet for the Seminoles, as Weinke went down with a neck injury. The FSU leader was lost for the year, and the offense was forced to rally around backup Marcus Outzen for the remaining three contests. The quarterback struggled early in the game at Wake Forest, misfiring on eight of his first thirteen passes. With the Seminoles committing fourteen penalties and coughing up four turnovers, the Demon Deacons were able to remain competitive. Florida State took a 10-0 lead at halftime, but the Deacons briefly cut the score to 10-7 on a 56-yard toss by Brian Kuklick. With the game surprisingly in doubt, Minor took control. The sophomore ran over twice in the final twenty minutes, including a 22-yard blast early in the final quarter. The Minor scores gave the Seminoles a 24-7 victory and a share of the league title.

Wake Forest headed down to Atlanta a week later, where they again faced a team bent on claiming a piece of the ACC championship. This one proved far less competitive than FSU, as Georgia Tech came out and instantly assumed dominance. The Jackets scored on each of their first three possessions, and had a 21-0 lead barely eight minutes into the contest. Tech continued to pour on the points, scoring two touchdowns in each of the final three quarters to finish with 63 for the game. It was the most scoring done by a Ramblin' Wreck team since 1921, when Bill Alexander's team had disposed of Davidson and Furman on consecutive weekends by scores of 70-0 and 69-0. The final count was 63-35, and George O'Leary's team celebrated the Institute's second taste of life at the top of the ACC standings.

College football was undertaking a new national championship system during the 1998 season, the Bowl Championship Series (BCS). The BCS, like the Bowl Coalition and Bowl Alliance before it, sought to utilize the four major bowl games (Rose, Sugar, Orange, and Fiesta Bowls) in an effort to create a definitive national championship game. Using a sophisticated computer system, which included strength of schedule and margin of victory into a formula that included conference affiliation and won/loss records, the BCS graded the NCAA's finest teams on a point system. Following the regular season, the two schools with the lowest overall point totals would earn the right to play for the title.

By beating Georgia Tech decisively in their head-to-head matchup, Florida State was assured of a berth in one of the four Bowl Championship Series games. Which bowl remained to be seen, for victory over Florida could possibly set up a showdown in the national championship game against either Tennessee, Kansas State, or UCLA. Florida had not won in Tallahassee since 1986, but without Weinke to worry about, many in the media felt that this would be their time to win in Doak-Campbell Stadium. The Gators were as powerful as they had ever been, with a 20-17 loss to No. 1 Tennessee the only thing keeping them from being undefeated. Although they knew they were out of the NCAA title hunt, Florida had an opportunity to burst FSU's bubble for the fourth year in a row.

Before the game could even begin, the bitter rivals engaged in a heated altercation at midfield. During warm-up drills, UF defensive back Tony George took a shot at FSU assistant Odell Haggins, which set off a small skirmish around the painted head of Chief Osceola. The officials ejected George, along with a pair of Seminoles that were not expected to be big contributors. The loss of George was a big one for the Gator secondary, and Outzen took full advantage. In a silent but steady performance, the sophomore completed thirteen-of-twenty-two passes for 167 yards.

Florida took a 12-6 lead after a physical opening half, but Outzen hit Warrick for a 32-yard score early in the third quarter for a 13-12 FSU advantage. The Seminoles never trailed again, as the defense put forth one of its finest efforts in years. Playing against an offense that had rolled up more than 1,100 yards passing in their last three outings, FSU held the Gators without a point over the final thirty minutes. Warrick, who finished the game with eight receptions and 119 yards, put the game on ice early in the fourth quarter. Taking the football on a reverse handoff, Warrick tossed to a wide-open Dugans, who went 46 yards for the touchdown that made the score 20-12. A Janikowski field goal made the final score 23-12, which Bowden said later was his most satisfying victory in a decade.

In impressive fashion, the Seminoles had recovered to win ten consecutive games, and snuck their way into the Fiesta Bowl with the No. 2 ranking in the BCS standings. Unlike 1997, when their lone regular season defeat came in the season finale, it had paid off to lose earlier in the year in 1998. With a drop in the polls imminent after the UF setback twelve months prior, there was not enough time to move back among the top two teams. The loss to N.C. State back in September had given the Seminoles enough time to watch other teams in the hunt, such as Kansas State, fall to the wayside. The Wildcats were geared up for a trip to Tempe after an unbeaten regular season, but dropped a heartbreaker to Texas A&M in the Big 12 Championship Game, which all but guaranteed Florida State a spot in the title showdown.

North Carolina began the bowl season for everyone by meeting San Diego State (SDSU) in the Las Vegas Bowl, and the game belonged to freshman quarterback Ronald Curry. Heralded as the future of the UNC program, Curry accounted for 96 of Carolina's 196 total yards of offense, and broke off a 48-yard touchdown sprint in the first quarter. The Tar Heels added to their lead in the second period, as Quinton Savage blocked his second punt in as many bowl games. Brian Schmitz had pinned the Aztecs deep with a long kick, and Savage's deflection was recovered in the end zone by David Bomar for a Carolina touchdown. Josh McGee added a pair of field goals, and although SDSU kept the game competitive, Keith Newman's late interception preserved a 20-13 UNC victory.

Ten days later, N.C. State met Miami in the Micron PC bowl. The emotional levels of the two teams were on decidedly different paths, as the Wolfpack had just endured a gut-wrenching overtime defeat to North Carolina, which punched UNC's ticket to Las Vegas. The Hurricanes' last game was an emotional thriller, in which running back Edgerrin James posted a school-record 299 yards to lead Miami to a 49-45 win over previously undefeated UCLA. The victory over the Bruins was a huge favor to the hated Seminoles, helping them to sneak back into the Fiesta Bowl picture.

After three years of NCAA sanctions, and a resulting drop in its football success, the Hurricanes overwhelmed the Wolfpack to prove that they were back among college football's elite. With quarterback Scott Covington throwing for 320 yards and two touchdowns, and the running back combination of Edgerrin James and James Jackson adding four more tallies, NCSU struggled to remain competitive. With workmanlike precision, Miami gained 594 yards of offense to take a 46-23 triumph. In his final collegiate game before moving on to the NFL, James raced for 156 yards, his seventh consecutive 100-yard outing.

With Virginia dropping a 35-33 verdict to Georgia in the Peach Bowl, it was left up to Georgia Tech to ensure that the ACC did not take a 1-3 record into the National Championship game. In the school's first New Year's Day contest since the Citrus Bowl domination of Nebraska back in 1991, Hamilton got Tech going early, running over from 5 yards away for a 7-0 lead. Notre Dame countered with its own rushing attack, as Autry Denson piled across the line from the 9 to tie it up. The second fifteen minutes belonged to the white-shirted Yellow Jackets, as they seized the momentum and tallied consecutive touchdowns.

The Irish came out recharged in the third quarter, as Denson scored for the second time on a 1-yard smash and quarterback Jarious Jackson followed with a sneak of his own. Although the touchdowns shifted the momentum back to Notre Dame, a missed extra point conversion allowed Tech to maintain a slim 21-20 advantage. With the game teetering in uncertainty, Dez White stepped to the fore. Playing in his hometown of Jacksonville, the Yellow Jacket wide receiver came through in fine fashion in the final two quarters, hauling in a pair of long scoring catches to point his team in the direction of victory. White's first touchdown came late in the third quarter, as he caught a pass from Hamilton and sprinted 44 yards to the goal line. White's second touchdown was the clincher, as the Yellow Jacket defense held Notre Dame scoreless down the stretch. With the 35-28 victory, Georgia Tech claimed ten victories in a season for the seventh time in its history.

Although many debated whether or not the Seminoles should have had the chance to play for the national championship, their opponent faced none of those concerns. Tennessee had earned its trip to Tempe, bringing a 12-0 record to the contest following a victory over Mississippi State in the SEC Championship game. The Volunteers had also toppled Florida, Georgia, and Alabama during the regular season, and were hoping to bring home the school's first NCAA title since 1951.

Stopping Peter Warrick was a priority in UT's preparation for the Fiesta Bowl, and No. 9 found himself double-covered throughout the game. With Outzen making only his third collegiate start, the Volunteers were also planning on applying plenty of pressure on the FSU signal caller. Dugans was Outzen's favorite target for much of the game, and although he had six receptions for 135 yards, he was unable to score. The job was left to the FSU defense to shut down the Volunteer offense, and although it did an admirable job, a series of big plays resulted in a frustrating evening for the garnet and gold.

With two of the finest defenses in the country clashing on the field of Sun Devil Stadium, there was no great surprise that the first quarter ended scoreless. The scoreboard finally lit up early in the second quarter, as Tennessee quarterback Tee Martin threw a 4-yard touchdown pass to Shawn Bryson. The large contingent of orange-clad spectators had plenty more to cheer about moments later, as just twenty-five seconds after the scoring pass, cornerback Dwayne Goodrich walked in front of an Outzen pass at the UT 44. Catching the ball on the run, Goodrich raced down the sideline for a 14-0 Volunteer lead.

The game remained that way until later in the second period, when FSU's Derrick Gibson intercepted Martin at the Tennessee 46 and rambled 43 yards to the 3. William McCray reached the end zone three plays later, and Janikowski added a field goal to make the score 14-9 at halftime. The third quarter was a microcosm of the first, as neither team was able to add to their total. The Tennessee defense continued to stifle the inexperienced Outzen, who finished the game nine-of-twenty-two passing for only 145 yards.

With a little more than nine minutes to play, the Volunteers came up with the biggest play of the game. In possession of the ball at their own 21, Tennessee decided to take a gamble. The Volunteer offensive coaches were hoping that wide receiver Peerless Price could beat FSU cornerback Mario Edwards in single coverage, and haul in a bomb by Martin. As the UT quarterback dropped back to throw, Price raced down the right sideline on a fly pattern. The receiver outraced Edwards to the pass, and ran 79 yards for a devastating Tennessee touchdown. Adding a field goal at the 6:01 mark, the Volunteers held a 23-9 lead, and had all but secured victory.

Neutralized by the UT coverage for only one catch, Warrick instead became a spirited cheerleader down the stretch, cajoling his teammates and keeping up the spirits on the FSU sidelines. The Seminoles responded, going 29 yards in a desperate effort to salvage the game. From the 7, Outzen scampered into the end zone, and with 3:42 to play, the Seminoles were within a touchdown at 23-16. The Volunteers, hoping to run down the clock after an unsuccessful onsides kick, moved to the Seminole 10 before fumbling the ball away. Although FSU had another chance to score, Outzen threw an interception on the very next play. Tennessee's offense retook the field to take their victory set, and for the second time in three years, Florida State lost a game that would have brought Tallahassee another NCAA title.

The loss to Tennessee in the Fiesta Bowl had the returning Florida State players seething throughout the winter, and the Seminoles did all the necessary preparations to get ready for another title run in 1999. The offseason gave Chris Weinke time to heal his ailing neck, and he was back at 100 percent for August workouts. Florida State also got a favor from its best athlete, who gave up the instant riches of the pros for a final chance at college football's greatest prize. Peter Warrick could have left Florida State after his junior season to be one of the first players taken in the 1998 NFL Draft. However, with the Fiesta Bowl still stinging in his recent memory, Warrick decided to give it one more go with the Seminoles. Hauling in passes once again from Weinke, Warrick left Tallahassee as the ACC's all-time leading receiver with 3,517 yards. With Weinke, Minor, and Janikowski all returning, FSU was ranked preseason No. 1 by the Associated Press.

Starting first and finishing first are two entirely different things, something that many of the finest teams in college football history have learned over the years. Since 1950, the first year that the Associated Press began ranking teams before and after the season, no team had ever won the national championship when ranked No. 1 prior to their first game. In order for it to happen this time around, the Seminoles would have to win in Gainesville, something they had failed to do since the last time they hoisted the trophy in 1993.

They would also have to win at Clemson, where history would be made on October 23. That evening, Bobby and Tommy Bowden would become the first father-son tandem in history to make up the opposing coaches in a major college football game. The younger Bowden, fresh off leading Tulane to an undefeated season in 1998, had become the third new Tiger head coach in ten seasons. With threatening home encounters against Georgia Tech and Miami to boot, the Seminoles would have to fight for everything they got.

Florida State was supposed to play Auburn in the Tallahassee premiere, but the Tigers bought out of the game, knowing full well what would have been in store for them. Louisiana Tech jumped aboard, and it took awhile for the Seminoles to get going. After playing lethargically for the first twenty-nine minutes, Warrick made a play that energized his team. Taking a handoff from Weinke, Warrick raced in one direction, then changed field and began running in the other. In running laterally across the field, Peter sidestepped numerous Bulldogs, and went in for a 20-yard score and a 14-7 FSU lead. Warrick's play ignited the Seminole offense, which scored 34 points in the second half to take an easy 41-7 verdict.

Everyone expected a shoot-out when Georgia Tech made the trek south to Tallahassee, and nobody was disappointed. The opposing defenses were burned to a crisp in the second quarter, as the teams com-

bined for 35 points. Kendra thrust FSU into the lead when he slid unde-
tected into the end zone from the 3, but Joe Hamilton sprinted across
for GT to tie it at 14. Leading 28-21, Warrick made a scoring grab in
the third quarter to give Florida State some breathing room, but Georgia Tech was not about to give up. Kerry Watkins concluded an 80-play
march by becoming the third different receiver to haul in a touchdown
catch from Hamilton. After GT recorded a "stop" of sorts, holding the
Seminoles out of the end zone, Janikowski made the score 38-28 by
converting a field goal.

Janikowski belted another long kick to push the lead to 41-28, and
although the game appeared lost for the gold and white, Hamilton went
down slinging. In a spirited performance, completing twenty-two-of-
twenty-five passes for 387 yards and four touchdowns, the Yellow
Jacket quarterback connected with Kelly Campbell for a 22-yard tally.
There was time for an onsides kick but the Seminoles recovered, and
FSU Nation let out a big exhale as the final seconds ticked off the
clock.

After successfully leaping their first major hurdle, the Seminoles
returned to dominance in their next three games, all coming against
opposition from North Carolina. N.C. State caught the wrath of the
angry FSU defenders, who had spent most of the Georgia Tech game
getting abused. The unit scored twice, on a recovered fumble in the end
zone, and a 47-yard interception return. Weinke exorcised the demons
of his performance against NCSU in 1998, completing twenty-three
passes for 229 yards. Although he threw another pair of interceptions,
the FSU quarterback helped put Janikowski in position for five field
goals. When it was over, the Seminoles had revenge and a 43-11 win.

The game in Chapel Hill was out of hand before many even got to
their seats. In a stunning performance, the Seminoles scored 28 unanswered points in the first seven minutes of the game, and had many
North Carolina fans heading to the exits early. After Minor scored
twice for an early 14-0 FSU lead, Carolina quarterback Ronald Curry
threw a strike directly into the arms of cornerback Sean Key, who ran
25 yards for a 21-0 Florida State advantage. The Tar Heels again struggled to move the ball, and Warrick positioned himself underneath a
punt at his own 25. With a quick burst of speed and a couple of side-
steps, Warrick broke into the clear and raced 75 yards to the end zone.
With a rush by Marcus Outzen and a scoring pass from Weinke late in
the first half thrown into the mix, the Seminoles cruised, 42-10.

Duke moved their home game from Durham to Jacksonville, and
got the same result that likely would have occurred at Wallace Wade

Stadium. Warrick had a hat trick before the game was fifteen minutes old, hauling in touchdown receptions of 3, 39, and 2 yards. Trailing by 21 points after one quarter of play, it only got worse for the Blue Devils. The Seminoles scored 23 more in the second quarter, as Janikowski nailed a trio of kicks, and Laveranues Coles and Kendra hauled in scoring passes in the 51-23 blowout.

With the Miami game looming on the horizon, one would have expected the Florida State players to be on their best behavior in the week leading up to the showdown in Tallahassee. That did not turn out to be the case however, as Peter Warrick and Laveranues Coles became the next in a long line of Seminole players to have a brush with the law. Charged with grand theft, stemming from their underpayment of hundreds of dollar's worth of clothing from a local Dillard's department store, Bowden had no choice but to suspend the receivers indefinitely. Although Warrick would have a chance to return to the Seminole fold before the end of the season, Coles was not so lucky. Having already faced legal trouble in the past, the Dillard's episode was the fatal blow to Coles' collegiate career. Warrick stood on the sidelines throughout the heated Miami encounter, which was stirred up before kickoff when a Hurricane player shouted something to an FSU player near midfield. The teams gathered near the center of the gridiron, each forming a large circle. The players from both teams began jumping up and down in unison, and looked to be on the verge of a rumble before the coaches cleared everyone out.

Miami played hard in the first half, matching the Seminole offensive with its own passing attack. Hurricane quarterback Kenny Kelly threw three touchdowns in the opening two quarters to cancel out two scoring tosses by Weinke and a rushing tally by Jeff Chaney. With the game tied at 21 heading into halftime, the game looked to be heading toward the stratosphere. The momentum of the first thirty minutes was altered dramatically in the second half, as the Seminole defense took control. Kelly was unable to lead Miami back to the end zone, as FSU's linemen began applying added pressure. Although they managed only a field goal in the third quarter, a 2-yard run by Minor in the final frame gave Florida State some breathing room. The defenders held on for a 31-21 victory, FSU's fifth in a row over the Hurricanes.

Weinke put together his finest performance thus far as a Seminole a week later against Wake Forest. With Atrews Bell providing a worthy set of hands, the FSU offensive machine clicked as always. Bell hauled in a pair of touchdowns in the third quarter, allowing the Seminoles to break open a game that was only 9-3 at halftime. A final score in the fourth period provided the 33-10 margin of victory.

After a two-week hiatus, Warrick returned to the Seminoles for the first annual "Bowden Bowl" against Clemson. The Dillard's matter was resolved the day before the contest, as Warrick entered a guilty plea and received probation. With Ann Bowden, Bobby's wife and Tommy's mother, wearing a half-Florida State/half-Clemson sweater, the elder Bowden went for his 300th career victory. As the Tiger defense kept the Seminole offense from gaining momentum in a spirited first half effort, Clemson's offense scored a pair of touchdowns to take a surprising 14-3 lead into halftime.

With the crowd at Death Valley ready to explode in celebration of the school's first home victory over a No.1-ranked team, Florida State crept back into the contest. Although he failed to score, Warrick brought a lift to the FSU attack, catching eleven balls for 121 yards. The Seminole offense rallied for 11 unanswered points, as Janikowski slid a kick through the uprights to tie the game at 14. The game remained tied until the 5:26 mark of the final quarter, when Janikowski trudged back onto the field for another kick. The momentum of the game had dramatically shifted in Florida State's favor over the course of the second half, and by the time Sebastian's 39-yard kick sailed through, the Tigers were as good as dead. Although they had a chance to tie it, and actually moved into range for a field goal, Clemson's last chance was nixed by a Tay Cody deflection. Bobby embraced his son warmly following his team's 17-14 victory, which proved to be the toughest of their eight ACC contests.

"Momma's happy, I know that," Bobby said after the game. "Momma wanted a close win because I had more riding on it, and she wanted her boy to look good."

With the league championship all but secured barring a disaster, the Seminoles clipped Virginia and Maryland in succession. Weinke shook off three interceptions against UVA, and got his act together with a flawless third quarter performance. The junior signal caller nailed Marvin Minnis and Minor with a pair of touchdown tosses, Marvin's covering 20 and Minor's going for 66, to give FSU the lead. After a slow forty-five minutes, Warrick got into the act in the final period, taking in a catch from the 50 to give the Seminoles a 28-10 advantage. Outzen came on to run out the clock, and his sneak made the final score 35-10.

Maryland put up considerably less resistance than Virginia, and struggled all game to contain the FSU offense. Weinke, who went on to throw six touchdowns, already had four by halftime. Warrick's second touchdown, which ate up 28 yards, allowed Weinke to tie the Florida

State school record for touchdown passes in a season. Maryland scored late, but the 49-10 win put the Seminoles at 10-0 for the Florida game.

The Gators came into the contest at 9-1, and were still in position to play for the national championship should they beat both the Seminoles and their opponent in the SEC Championship Game. The opening quarter began slowly, but FSU took the early advantage following a 4-yard carry by Warrick. The 7-0 score held into the second period, when Janikowski kicked a 22-yard field goal on the first play. Jeff Chandler kicked a pair of field goals in the session stanza for Florida, and Janikowski countered with one conversion as the game went into half-time with Florida State leading 13-6.

Florida took control in the first eight minutes of the third quarter, and gave the sea of blue and orange assembled in the Swamp something to cheer about. After Chandler kicked his third field goal, Bennie Alexander stepped in front of a poorly thrown ball by Weinke at the FSU 43 and scored to give UF a 16-13 lead. The sudden play had 85,000 fans thinking victory over the garnet and gold was imminent once again. Although the crowd may have thought the issue was settled, the Seminoles kept their composure. The FSU offense promptly moved into range for Janikowski again, and his field goal knotted up the game at 16. Tommy Polley came through moments later for the Seminoles with a blocked kick, which was recovered at the UF 21. Five plays later Chaney scurried across the line for a 23-16 Seminole lead.

Florida continued to struggle offensively, and a 73-yard bomb from Weinke to Marvin Minnis had Seminole fans thinking they were on Easy Street. With the game slipping away, UF began another scoring march to cut the score to 30-23, but the home-standing Gators were unable to complete a comeback. Florida State successfully withheld Florida's final surge, and completed an 11-0 regular season. With the victory, Florida State took the No. 1 ranking in the Bowl Championship Series into the school's fourth Sugar Bowl in six seasons, where they would once again play for the NCAA title.

In an unfortunate turn of events, an outbreak of food poisoning struck the Arizona State (ASU) team the morning of their Aloha Bowl encounter with 6-5 Wake Forest. With several major contributors, including three starters, unable to play, ASU was at a disadvantage to the Demon Deacons before the teams even stepped onto the field. Quarterback Ben Sankey took care of the rest, throwing a touchdown and leading four additional Wake Forest drives that resulted in points. With the defense shutting down a solid offensive team, Morgan Kane's late touchdown gave Wake a commanding 23-3 victory.

Virginia and Clemson each played on December 30, the Cavaliers in the Micron PC Bowl against Illinois, and the Tigers in the Peach Bowl against Mississippi State. Both teams met stiff resistance, and went down to decisive defeats at the hands of their opposition. Illinois quarterback Kurt Kittner ate up the UVA secondary in the first thirty minutes, accounting for a record four touchdowns and scoring in three different ways. Playing in a bowl for the first time since 1994, the Illini amassed 611 yards of total offense, and took a 42-7 lead into the locker rooms. With the Virginia defenders unable to slow down their devastating charge, Illinois added another trio of touchdowns to take a 63-21 final score.

Although Clemson played Mississippi State tougher than Virginia had played Illinois, the result was the same. A first half had never gone scoreless in the Peach, but that was the case in this encounter. Facing the nation's No. 1 defense, which had the Bulldogs sitting at 8-0 at one point during the year, the Tigers never got on track offensively. With five interceptions to its credit, the Bulldog defense could take much of the credit for the 17-7 victory, Jackie Sherill's first bowl conquest as head coach at Mississippi State.

Two days later, Georgia Tech went into its second consecutive Gator Bowl. The Gator was the curtain call on Joe Hamilton's stellar career at Georgia Tech. In finishing second in voting for the Heisman Trophy in 1999, Hamilton had set eighteen school records and led an offense that scored at least 30 points in all but one of its regular season games. Despite receiving the short end of the media attention in the days leading up to the contest, Miami was undaunted at the prospect of playing the nation's No. 1 offense. For the first time in fourteen games, Hamilton was held without a scoring pass, and although Tech moved the football well for most of the contest, the Yellow Jacket offense was unable to capitalize on the scoreboard. Tech scored a season-low 13 points, and despite his 17-yard scamper for a touchdown, Hamilton spent the game running for his life. The senior was sacked three times and threw a pair of interceptions, spending much of the game throwing off his back foot due to pressure. With Kenny Kelly leading a pair of UM scoring drives, the white-shirted Hurricanes prevailed, 28-13.

In forty years of coaching, Bobby Bowden had yet to lead any school to an undefeated season. That could change on the evening of January 4, 2000, as he brought his Seminoles into the Louisiana Superdome once again to meet Virginia Tech. The Hokies had been the darlings of college football in 1999, riding a solid defense and the left arm of redshirt freshman Michael Vick into their own 11-0 campaign. Although VT was the underdog, the Seminoles were aware of Vick's individual excellence, and knew they would have their hands full slowing down the slippery scrambler.

Warrick saved his best performance as a Seminole for his final game, astonishing 79,000 fans in the Superdome and a nationwide television audience with his athletic gifts. Warrick's first score came in the opening period, as he took in a dart from Weinke and outraced the VT secondary down the middle of the field to the end zone. Less than a minute later, the Seminole defense made a statement by blocking a punt. Tommy Polley was the FSU player with the deflection, and Jeff Chaney scooped it up at the 6 and ran in for a 14-0 advantage.

Now trailing by two scores, Vick quickly regrouped his team on the ensuing possession, heaving a bomb downfield in the direction of Andre Davis. Davis hauled in the catch, good for 49 yards, to bring the Hokies back to within seven. It was a quick moment of glory for Virginia Tech, as FSU dominated the second quarter. Immediately following a 73-yard strike from Weinke to Ron Dugans, Warrick took a punt return and sped free, giving the garnet and gold a 28-7 bulge. It appeared as if Virginia Tech was going to get dominated, but Vick suddenly took over.

In a performance that mesmerized those that witnessed it, and made an entire nation aware of his unlimited potential, Vick led the Hokies to 22 unanswered points over a period of fourteen minutes. The first score came late in the opening half, as Vick wrestled across the goal line to make the score 28-14 at the intermission. The Hokie defenders finally played as advertised in the third period, holding the Seminoles scoreless and consistently giving their offense decent field position. Vick took advantage, throwing a 26-yard completion to set up Shayne Graham for a 23-yard field goal and a 28-17 score.

After the Hokie defense forced FSU into a punt, Ike Carlton repaid the favor to the Seminoles for Warrick's special teams play, bringing the kick back 46 yards. Moments later, Vick deceived the Seminoles by handing off to Andre Kendrick. From the 29, Kendrick took the ball and was gone, piercing through the FSU resistance to make the score 28-23. The Seminoles went back to their big play strategy, but VT cornerback Anthony Midget came through with an interception. The Hokie offense continued to surge, as Vick threw for 23 yards to Cullen Hawkins and danced for 22 more to the 6. Kendrick tallied from there, and Virginia Tech was suddenly leading by a score of 29-28.

With fifteen minutes of football to play, one could only wonder if the Big One would slip through Florida State's hands once again. The Seminoles were winless in their last two national championship game appearances, and with their opposition peaked with momentum, many among the Seminole faithful were biting their fingernails. Weinke quickly got the garnet and gold back out in front, throwing to Dugans for 15 yards at the 12:59 mark. Warrick was good on a conversion, and the Seminoles were up by a touchdown at 36-29.

Throughout the second and third quarters, the running of Vick had been a thorn in the sides of the FSU defenders. Despite his success, it was clear that Vick was being dangerous in the way in which he was holding the ball. With superior escape ability, Vick was able to make rapid body shifts and leave opponents throughout his collegiate career flailing at air. However, by holding the football with a single hand out in front of his body, it was only a matter of time before the pigskin squirted free.

It happened at the most opportune of times for Florida State, as linebacker Bobby Rhodes' helmet jarred the ball loose from Vick on VT's ensuing possession. Sean Key made the vital recovery at the 34, and a kick by Janikowski gave FSU some breathing room with a ten-point advantage. After getting the ball back, an opportunity was in place for the Seminoles to rid themselves of the pesky Hokies, and Weinke and Warrick made a memorable final connection. On a pass route that was destined for the end zone, Warrick was harassed by Virginia Tech cornerback Roynell Whitaker. Weinke cut loose on a bomb in the direction of Warrick, and the senior made his finest play in a Seminole uniform. In a tremendous individual effort, Warrick dove for the ball with Whitaker hanging over him, and brought in the catch at the lip of the end zone for a 43-yard score.

Warrick's touchdown was the lethal blow to VT's hopes for victory, and the Seminoles ran out the closing minutes to complete their undefeated masterpiece 46-29. Warrick's performance, which had produced a Sugar Bowl record 20 points, was good enough to earn the receiver Most Valuable Player honors in his final game as a Seminole. As Bobby Bowden accepted the Sears Trophy to deafening roars from FSU supporters in the Sugar Bowl, the Seminoles began the celebration of the school's second national championship in seven years.

In spending only five weeks out of the Top Ten throughout the 1990s, and finishing the decade with a .890 winning percentage, Florida State had proven itself as one of the truly elite major college football programs in the United States. With a record of 109-13-1 in the 1990s, the only blemish on FSU's unmatched football resume was the elusive perfect season. With the Sugar Bowl game and 12-0 record for

1999 secured, Florida State University enjoyed an extended period of time as the undisputed King of college football.

There was still plenty of talent in the FSU camp in August of 2000, enough for the Seminole coaches to put together two outstanding units on each side of the football. Although Peter Warrick had moved on to the NFL, Chris Weinke still had a number of fine receiving targets to throw to. Weinke closed out his Seminole career as the most productive signal caller in ACC history, the all-time leader in passing yards, touchdown passes, and 300-yard games. Marvin "Snoop" Minnis, who had stepped in admirably for Warrick during his suspension in 1999, came on and became the team's leading receiver. With Ron Dugans and four-year starting tailback Travis Minor also returning to the FSU fold, the unit was just as powerful as it had ever been.

The Seminole secondary was particularly imposing, with Tay Cody, Derrick Gibson, Clevan Thomas, and Chris Hope all capable of making big plays. The foursome were all named All-Conference, and with the FSU defensive line providing intense pressure to imposing quarterbacks, the secondary was able to sit back and deflect whatever came its way. Jamal Reynolds added to Florida State's legacy of stellar defensive linemen, becoming the second Seminole in history to win the Lombardi Award. Reynolds was a consistent playmaker, with twelve sacks to go along with four forced fumbles and two safeties.

Florida State began the defense of its national championship with another August game, played in Jacksonville against BYU. The Seminoles wasted little time, scoring on its opening possession and taking less than three minutes to do it. After Atrews Bell scored another touchdown and Reynolds forced a safety for a 15-0 FSU lead, Weinke took off on a 22-yard scamper, which set up a 6-yard scoring run by Bell. With a 22-0 deficit less than twenty minutes in, it was apparent that BYU was overmatched. Although the Cougars scored on a third quarter field goal, which allowed them to maintain their NCAA-record scoring streak, Minor added a late run to give the Seminoles a 29-3 triumph.

Georgia Tech came calling next in Atlanta, and FSU struck in a variety of ways in the opening quarter to take a 12-0 lead. Without Joe Hamilton to rely on for offensive production, Georgia Tech went with an unorthodox approach in the second half, rotating quarterbacks George Godsey and Jermaine Crenshaw. The Yellow Jackets had already scored on a long interception return, and with 3:17 left in the third quarter, Joe Burns smashed into the end zone, giving GT a 13-12 advantage. Following a two-point conversion, Tech not only had a three-point lead, but the spirit of an invigorated home crowd cheering them on.

Weinke wasted little time giving the advantage back to Florida State, hooking up with Robert Morgan for a 30-yard touchdown strike early in the fourth quarter. With 7:45 remaining, William McCray ran in from the 1 to give the Seminoles a 26-15 advantage. The contest looked to be getting away from the home team, but the Yellow Jackets continued to fight. Three minutes after the Morgan score, Jon Muyres took in a 27-yard toss from Godsey to cut the Seminole lead to 26-21. Although they would get another chance, the Florida State defenders foiled Tech's last gasp, holding them on downs near midfield.

Things got a little easier for FSU the following week against North Carolina, as they returned to Tallahassee for their home opener. McCray delivered the first Seminole points on a 1-yard carry less than five minutes in, and Weinke followed with a 35-yard strike to Bell. Following a field goal by Chance Gwaltney, Chris Hope recovered a fumble and raced 12 yards to give FSU a 23-7 lead. Later in the period, Jeff Chaney provided one of the most entertaining runs by a Seminole back in years, breaking several tackles and eluding a number of UNC defenders on his way to a 39-yard score. Weinke and Minnis hooked up for the period's final touchdown, and the Seminoles took a 36-7 lead into halftime. By the time Greg Jones ran in from the 1 to make the final score 63-14, no less than ten different Seminoles had reached the end zone. As his offense put forth a record performance against the outclassed Tar Heels, FSU offensive coordinator Mark Richt could be seen casually munching on popcorn in the coaches' booth during the anticlimactic second half.

Although the Seminole offense wasn't nearly as potent the following week against Louisville, it didn't have to be. With the FSU defenders holding the Cardinals to only 3 rushing yards and ten first downs, the garnet and gold could have won with a single score. As it turned out, the Seminoles scored liberally in the first three quarters, taking a 31-0 advantage into the final period. Bowden allowed the backups to complete a scoreless fourth quarter. A week later, the Seminoles buried Maryland on a Thursday night. Before leaving with a sprained ankle, Weinke threw three touchdowns. The first went to Morgan for 58 yards, while Bell caught the next two. By the time Weinke left the contest, the Seminoles were in command of a 45-7 score. With most of the stadium empty by the fourth quarter, FSU added another pair of scores to take a 59-7 final.

Over the past few seasons, Steve Spurrier and Florida had taken Miami's place as Florida State's chief nemesis in the Sunshine State. Although the Hurricanes remained an important game each year, the Seminoles did not hinge their national championship hopes in the mid-to-late 1990s nearly as much on beating Miami as they did on toppling the Gators. Hurricanes had fallen off the radar screen since 1995, when Butch Davis arrived in Coral Gables to replace Dennis Erickson. A protégé of Jimmy Johnson, Davis slowly rebuilt the Miami football machine, and along the way brought respect to a program notorious for scandalous activity. By 2000, Davis had the Hurricanes ready to once again compete against Florida State. The struggles with Miami in the early 1990s had become a distant memory to Seminole fans by the turn of the century, with FSU claiming victories in six of their last seven contests against the Hurricanes. With an opportunity to solidify their No. 1 ranking on the turf of the Orange Bowl, the Seminole players took to the field a confident group.

To the surprise of the visitors, the first thirty minutes belonged to the orange-clad home team, as the Hurricane defense put forth an inspiring effort. Quarterback Ken Dorsey outplayed Weinke, who was wearing a plastic brace to protect his tender ankle, throughout the first two periods. The Hurricane quarterback threw a 22-yard strike to Najeh Davenport, and led another pair of drives that resulted in points. In commanding fashion, Miami took a 17-0 lead into the locker rooms.

After being shut out in the first half for the first time in twelve years, FSU had something to prove in the third quarter. Weinke got his act together, leading two marches that had the score 17-10 within seven minutes. After the Hurricanes increased their lead to 20-10 with a field goal, Weinke took control again. In throwing for 496 yards to set a career high, Weinke led a furious Seminole rally, which resulted in a pair of touchdowns. The second, a 29-yard missile to Bell, gave FSU a 24-20 advantage with less than two minutes to play.

In a clutch performance, the sophomore Dorsey completed six passes down the stretch, taking only 51 seconds to move the Hurricanes 68 yards. His final completion to Jeremy Shockey, good for a touchdown, forced Weinke into making another last-second charge. Florida State went down fighting, moving the ball to the 32 in the closing seconds. With enough time for a final kick, Matt Munyon stepped onto the field with the task of maintaining the Seminole winning streak. Munyon got good leg on the ball, but the kick faded to the right, and outside of the posts. Miami celebrated the conclusion of FSU's seventeen-game winning streak, and string of twenty-six consecutive regular season games with a victory.

For the second time in three years, the Seminoles met Duke at home coming off a defeat. Weinke threw for another new record of 536 yards, and already had four touchdowns by halftime as the Seminoles led 42-0. Weinke's 48-yard bomb to Atrews Bell in the second half gave the senior 66 career touchdown passes, which broke Joe Hamilton's league record. Furthermore, the 63-14 victory was Bobby Bowden's sixty-sixth in ACC history, which tied him with Clemson's Frank Howard for second on the all-time list.

Bowden easily surpassed the Clemson legend the following week, as the Seminoles dominated Virginia, 37-3. The Cavaliers were unable to progress against a smothering effort by the FSU defense. The unit sacked UVA quarterbacks five different times, and also forced a quintet of turnovers. Weinke and Minnis ate up the UVA secondary, as the pair came together four times for 131 yards. Minnis hauled in scoring receptions of 58 and 30 yards, and with the Cavaliers mired in poor play throughout most of the first half, FSU built up a 27-0 cushion. With its seventh straight 500-yard offensive performance, the Seminoles clawed closer to the national championship picture.

After blowing out N.C. State, 58-14, in Raleigh, the Seminoles returned home to play Clemson. The Tigers were dominant early in the year, building up an 8-0 record and entering the Top Ten. The week before playing FSU, Clemson entertained Georgia Tech in home. In a classic finish, the Yellow Jackets had snatched away a 31-28 verdict in Death Valley. Clemson seemed to lose its spirit after the Georgia Tech game, and the Seminoles made the Tigers pay for every lapse.

In an overwhelming performance, the Florida State offense piled up a record 771 yards against the Tigers, and took another lopsided final score over the orange and white. After kicking a field goal for the early 3-0 lead, Weinke and Minnis came together for another impressive play. Following a 74-yard punt that pinned FSU back to the 2, Weinke faded back on a play-action pass. The fake left the quarterback standing in the middle of the end zone, and Weinke threw a dart to Minnis, who had worked his way free from his defensive counterpart. Snoop hauled in the catch 20 yards downfield, and sped all the way across the field for a 98-yard touchdown. The play set a new school record for longest scoring pass, and put the Seminoles on a collision course with another ACC title.

With the score 40-7, the garnet and gold continued to make big plays. Weinke, who surpassed Thad Busby in career passing yardage over the course of the contest, threw to Chaney for 42 yards. Four minutes later, backup running back Davy Ford broke off an 82-yard sprint to the end zone. With Tommy Bowden in shock, kneeling on the sidelines with his heads in his hands, the Seminole faithful chanted, "Who's your daddy? Who's your daddy?"

The 54-7 verdict over Clemson prepared FSU for a road encounter with Wake Forest. The Seminoles needed a decisive victory to prove they belonged at No. 2 in the Bowl Championship Series standings, and although they took a 35-6 final, most of the Florida State players were upset with their performance. With three tailbacks going down to injuries, things could have gone much better for the visitors.

"It's gotten to be that the expectations are so high with this team, that if we don't win by 50 we didn't do a good job," Weinke said afterwards. "Winning by 29 is still nice, but we know it's probably going to cost us."

In the week between the Wake Forest game and the regular season finale with Florida, the Seminoles dropped to No. 3 in the polls. Beating the Gators at home would bode well for FSU's chances of another championship appearance, as the annual FSU-UF winner had gone on to play for the title in four of the last six seasons. The game was surprisingly easy for Florida State, as they outplayed the Gators for their fifty-second consecutive victory in the friendly confines of Doak-Campbell Stadium. Holding a 14-7 lead at the half, the Seminoles took control in the third period thanks to Weinke's passing and Florida's penalties. A pair of interference calls against the Gator secondary put FSU in position for a score, and a 51-yard strike to Minnis made the score 27-7. Weinke, who finished the game ahead of Ben Bennett in the ACC career passing annals, made a strong case for the Heisman Trophy with 353 yards and a trio of scoring passes. A final field goal made the score 30-7, and gave FSU supporters optimism for a third consecutive chance at the NCAA crown.

"That computer better not betray me," Bowden said later, "I'd rather have the computer decide who plays for the national championship than a person who may have some biases."

Two weeks later, the final Bowl Championship Series poll was released. The decisive victory over Florida was indeed enough to help the Florida State cause, as the Seminoles claimed the computer's No. 2 ranking. Although their defeat in October to Miami gave plenty of people reason to argue against it, FSU would go on to meet Oklahoma in the Orange Bowl, where they hoped to defend their crown. The Sooners, under former Florida assistant Bob Stoops, completed an undefeated regular season with a Big Twelve Championship triumph over Kansas State. With a strong defense and running game, OU figured to be a tough challenge for the Seminoles. However, few doubted FSU's excellence, and the garnet and gold entered the game as double-digit favorites.

With thirty-three touchdown passes to go along with ACC records for career passing and per-game yardage, Chris Weinke had flourished in his final collegiate season. In leading the Seminoles to a stellar 32-2 record as starting quarterback over three years, Weinke had become the first quarterback in major college history to lead a school to three consecutive NCAA championship games. The Heisman Trophy Committee measured Weinke's production with his team's success, and honored him as the recipient of their 2000 award. In joining Charlie Ward as the second ACC player to win the Heisman, Weinke hoped to do something the former Seminole quarterback hadn't done, bring back-to-back national championships to Tallahassee.

Virginia's Oahu Bowl encounter with Georgia opened the bowl season for the ACC. The Cavaliers and Bulldogs were familiar postseason foes, as their showdown in Hawaii would be the third meeting in six seasons between the two schools. The Bulldog defense set the tone, and helped their team build up a 17-0 lead after only one quarter of play. After Terrence Edwards broke off a 40-yard scoring run on a reverse, safety Kentrell Curry recovered a fumble in the end zone for another UGA tally. Georgia had picked up fourteen points in less than thirty seconds, and although Virginia scored a touchdown on their own fumble recovery in the third quarter, the Dawgs tacked on 13 points in the final period to claim a 37-14 victory.

Chuck Amato, the former N.C. State linebacker who had urged his defensive teammates to paint their shoes white back in the fall of 1967, put the Wolfpack back into the bowl picture in 2000 as the team's rookie head coach. State was led by freshman quarterback Philip Rivers, who set ACC first-year records with 3,054 yards and twenty-five touchdowns. The son of an Alabama high school football coach, Rivers was the prize recruit of Amato's first class at State, and would have the Wolfpack in the thick of the conference race for years to come.

Rivers couldn't find the handle early on against Minnesota, and an interception fifty seconds into the contest gave the Gophers momentum that would last throughout the first half. Staying heavily on the ground, the Gophers ate up the front line of the Wolfpack defense. With running back Tellis Redmon reaching the end zone twice, after two quarters of play the Wolfpack trailed, 24-8. State regrouped during the intermission, and in a play that changed the course of the game, Brian Williams deflected a punt to put the Wolfpack in position deep in Gopher territory. From the 19, wide receiver Koren Robinson took the ball on a reverse and sped to the goal line. Robinson's score, coupled with a two-point conversion, made the score 24-16, and a field goal by Kent Passingham cut the Gopher advantage to 24-19.

Ray Robinson tacked on another NCSU score to give the Wolfpack its first lead at 25-24, and although Minnesota retook the lead on a field goal early in the fourth quarter, Rivers threw a touchdown at the 11:01 mark to push State back into the lead at 31-27. Minnesota again kicked a field goal, but the Gophers committed a crucial error late in the contest. With only 3:16 to play, quarterback Travis Cole lost control of the football deep in his own territory. Needing only 8 yards, Ray Robinson wrapped up the game for State with a blast across the goal. With the 38-30 victory in hand, Amato became the first NCSU skipper since Lou Holtz to win a bowl game in his first season as head coach.

The following evening, Georgia Tech went into its Peach Bowl matchup with LSU as heavy favorites. With former offensive coordinator Ralph Friedgen having left for Maryland after the final regular season game, however, the Yellow Jackets were at a serious disadvantage. Friedgen watched the game from a luxury box, but was little help to a GT offense that struggled in his absence. Under Friedgen, the Ramblin' Wreck had committed a total of twelve turnovers throughout the regular season. In the Peach Bowl, the Jackets gave the ball away half that amount. Despite their errors, the game relied on field position, and Tech got close enough to run over twice in the first two quarters. Joe Burns hit a hole and pounded 32 yards for a 7-3 lead, and a 9-yard run by Jermaine Hatch made it 14-3 at halftime. Rohan Davey came on in the second half and led a Tiger resurgence, completing seventeen-of-twenty-five passes and leading three strikes that killed Georgia Tech's spirit. With the Yellow Jacket offense in a standstill in the second half, LSU won its fourth consecutive bowl, 28-14.

New Year's Day welcomed Clemson for the eleventh time in 2001, as the Tigers met Virginia Tech in Jacksonville. Like he had done against the Seminoles a year earlier, Michael Vick had a rude awakening in store for the Clemson defense. The elusive quarterback threw for 205 yards, and handed off to Lee Suggs for a trio of touchdowns. Although they moved the ball fairly well, Clemson's offense self-destructed when they were in position to score. Unable to keep up with VT's powerful offense, the Tigers took another Gator Bowl pounding, 41-20.

Florida State was dealt a serious blow in the days leading up to the Orange Bowl, as Minnis was declared academically ineligible for the game. With a career in the National Football League in the near future for the All-American, classes became an afterthought for Minnis. As a result, the receiver missed out on an opportunity to play for all the marbles. In addition to the absence of Minnis, the FSU offense faced another major distraction. With offensive coordinator Mark Richt having accepted the head coaching position at Georgia following the final regular season game, preparing for Oklahoma became a more trying endeavor. Although Richt agreed to stick around at FSU for the Orange Bowl, the coach clearly had his mind in two places, and was unable to give his undivided attention to preparing the Seminole offense for Oklahoma.

The first half was void of almost any offense, as a Tim Duncan field goal for Oklahoma provided the only points. In a team effort, the OU defenders went on to hold the Seminoles to a staggering 248 yards below their seasonal average. Duncan connected on another kick in the third quarter, and with the Seminoles locked down offensively, the Sooners charged to victory early in the final period. With 8:30 to play, sophomore running back Quentin Griffin rambled 10 yards to give OU a 13-0 advantage. Florida State had time for a comeback, but the Seminole offense continued to struggle. Weinke had a miserable final outing in the garnet and gold, and was unable to lead his team to the end zone a single time.

It appeared that OU was heading toward a shutout victory until the closing moments, when the Seminoles recorded a meaningless safety. The two points were little more than a slap in the face for FSU, as they avoided going scoreless, but lost another NCAA title game by the score of 13-2. Before the game, there was a great deal of speculation on whether or not the national championship would be shared by Miami and the Seminoles. Oklahoma decisively ended that talk, claiming Norman's first national championship since the days of Barry Switzer.

Ever since 1987, when the Seminoles of Danny McManus and Deion Sanders had finished 11-1 and ranked second in the country, Florida State had concluded every season ranked in the Top Five and with at least ten victories. No college football program had ever accomplished either feat, establishing a code of excellence in Tallahassee that was unmatched by any other college football program in America. With 20-point victories over opponents now considered "bad" games, Seminole Nation was going to eat quite a bit of humble pie once the team began its decline, however large or small it may be.

14

A Half Century Comes to an End (2001-2002)

As the 2001 season dawned around ACC football fields, one thing was certain; Florida State was not going to be the same team they had been in years past. With Chris Weinke, Marvin Minnis, Tay Cody, Jamal Reynolds, and Tommy Polley all gone from the previous year's Orange Bowl squad, there was no doubt that the Seminoles were facing a rare rebuilding year. Florida State went into the season at a serious disadvantage on offense, as wide receivers Anquan Boldin and Robert Morgan had each gone down with season-ending injuries during the offseason. In addition, the Seminoles had faced another tragedy during spring workouts, as freshman linebacker Devaughn Darling died after collapsing during a morning run. Darling was expected to start during the 2001 season, and his untimely passing left the team in a state of shock.

Just how far the garnet and gold fell depended largely on freshman Chris Rix, the most inexperienced quarterback to ever lead a Florida State offense coached by Bobby Bowden. In addition to Rix, Bowden was working with a young defense and an unseasoned offensive line. An opportunity was in place for someone to topple the Seminoles off their lofty perch, and a team that nobody expected to have a chance turned out to be the one that did it.

Before the new season, four ACC schools hired new head coaches, dramatically changing the landscape throughout the league. Three of the new coaches returned to their alma maters, while the other brought a reputation for rebuilding dormant programs. In the end, it was Ralph Friedgen and Maryland, a team picked among the bottom three schools in almost every preseason publication, which earned the league championship and ensuing berth in the Bowl Championship Series.

North Carolina reportedly went after a number of high-profile coaching figures after letting Carl Torbush go following the 2000 season, but ultimately elected to go with one of its own. After spending a number of seasons as an assistant coach in the NFL, John Bunting returned to Chapel Hill for his self-proclaimed "dream job." Bunting, who had been a standout at linebacker for North Carolina in the early 1970s and had started in Super Bowl XV for the Philadelphia Eagles in 1981, brought a more intense style that his predecessor.

George Welsh ended his impressive run at Virginia after the 2000 season, where he had quietly won 134 games, more than any other coach in the history of the Atlantic Coast Conference. Alumnus Al Groh, fresh off leading the New York Jets to the AFC playoffs, was given Welsh's large shoes to fill. Having already spent time in the conference at Wake Forest, Groh set out to improve on his 26-40 overall mark as a head coach in the league.

Jim Grobe came to Wake Forest from the University of Ohio, where he had turned around one of the worst Division I-A football programs in America. When Grobe arrived in Athens in 1995, the Bobcats had won only seventeen games in ten years. Although Ohio struggled in Grobe's first season, the Bobcats showed promise in 1996, finishing with a .500 record. For taking OU from 0-11 to 6-6 in only two seasons, Grobe was awarded the Mid-America Conference Coach of the Year award. The Bobcats posted a pair of winning seasons in 1997 and 2000, making Grobe a popular choice for the Demon Deacons, who had struggled throughout their football history to produce more wins than losses.

"Quite honestly, its time for a new challenge," Grobe said at his hiring for the WF job. "We'll see if we can get another program jump-started."

Ralph Friedgen got the call he had been waiting decades for when Maryland separated its ties with Ron Vanderlinden after the 2000 campaign. Friedgen, an understudy of Bobby Ross and George O' Leary at Maryland and Georgia Tech, had spent nearly two decades in the ACC as an assistant coach and offensive coordinator. With the Yellow Jackets, Friedgen helped devise an offensive scheme that was as unpredictable as it was successful. Opponents rarely found a way to stop the Yellow Jacket offense in the late 1990s, as Joe Hamilton put up some of the finest numbers by any quarterback in league history.

Despite his success as an offensive coordinator, Friedgen continued to get snubbed for several head coaching positions, including the one he wanted the most. A 1969 graduate of UM, Friedgen wanted nothing more than to someday return to College Park as head coach. The university could have had Friedgen on two prior occasions, but elected both times to hire outsiders. Mark Duffner and Vanderlinden were brought on in 1992 and 1997, respectively, and the pair combined to win 35 games in nine years, an average of less than four a season. With the Terrapin players imploring management to consider "that guy from Georgia Tech," the school finally gave Friedgen his chance.

"It was so unfortunate to see one of the smartest, most well-deserved coordinators in the college game not get a head coaching job because he couldn't pass the eye test," says Dr. Jerry Punch. "Friedgen began taking George O' Leary's phone calls, press conferences, and interviews at Georgia Tech specifically to help build up his skills. People knew he could coach, and he proved it when he got to Maryland."

As Friedgen soon found out, the Vanderlinden staff left him with a number of talented players on both sides of the ball. Guilian Gary, the team's leading receiver in each of the previous two seasons, returned for another year. As quarterback Shaun Hill's primary pass catcher in 2001, Gary hauled in forty-nine catches for 727 yards and six touchdowns. Sophomore Bruce Perry, who turned in the most surprising season of all the Terrapins, handled the running load for Friedgen's offense. Perry galloped for 1,242 yards to lead the conference, and added forty receptions for 359 yards. With linebacker E. J. Henderson and his 150 tackles, in addition to Tony Jackson's six interceptions, UM was also solid on the defensive side.

Friedgen and Bunting began their respective ACC coaching careers with a face-off, as the Tar Heels traveled to College Park for the season opener. It looked like a long day was ahead for the Terrapins after the first play from scrimmage, as UNC tailback Willie Parker ran 77 yards for a touchdown. The Maryland defense clamped down after the big play, and kept the Tar Heels from scoring for the remainder of the game. A 20-yard scoring pass by Hill tied it up, and the Maryland defense notched the only points of the second quarter. Having pinned UNC deep in its own territory, safety Tyrone Stewart tackled Parker in the end zone to make the score 9-7.

The score remained that way until the final period, when the Terrapin offense started running over the tiring Carolina defenders. Following Jackson's first interception of the year, Maryland drove 65 yards, with Hill nailing Scooter Monroe between the numbers to make the score 16-7. Perry dominated UM's final scoring drive, eating up 33 yards on two separate carries and setting up a 1-yard blast by Marc Riley. Perry finished the game with 116 yards, and the Terrapin fans saluted their team after the 23-7 upset over the favored Tar Heels.

Eastern Michigan was outclassed in Maryland's second game, as the Terrapins scored six rushing touchdowns. Perry was again the standout, posting 133 yards on sixteen attempts and notching three of the six-pointers. Henderson and the UM defenders isolated the EMU running game, holding it to a meager 24 yards. The Eagles finally reached the scoreboard with a fourth quarter field goal, but a 2-yard run by Jason Crawford gave Maryland a 50-3 verdict.

Off to a 2-0 start, Maryland was eagerly anticipating a third consecutive home game, as West Virginia was preparing to invade on September 15. Like the rest of the country, the week began with the same routine, but on Tuesday, September 11, the focus went elsewhere. The terrorist attacks committed in Pennsylvania, New York City, and Washington, D.C., that morning put a temporary hold on sports in the United States, and forced Maryland to make some changes to its schedule. The Terrapins were supposed to play West Virginia that Saturday, but the game was postponed two weeks. Troy State was supposed to visit Byrd Stadium on the September 29, but the Trojans were pushed back to November 3, a weekend that UM originally had idle.

A pair of surprise unbeatens met in Winston-Salem after the week off, as the Terrapins made the trek to Wake Forest. Again it was Perry who led the Maryland charges, with touchdown sprints of 80 and 50 yards to his credit. Perry finished the game with 276 yards, and found himself leading the NCAA in rushing by the end of the day. The Terps owned a 17-3 lead midway through the third quarter, but the Demon Deacons refused to fold. An 11-yard run by Terrence Williams, who like Perry enjoyed his third consecutive 100-yard performance, made the score 17-10 heading into the final fifteen minutes. The teams traded field goals in the early stages of the period, which set up Perry's 50-yard gallop. Jason Anderson pulled Wake Forest close with a leaping 42-yard touchdown catch, but the Terrapins took the game, 27-20.

As the Terrapins were playing in Winston-Salem, Florida State was also in North Carolina, meeting the Tar Heels in Chapel Hill. With easy victories over Duke and Alabama-Birmingham already under its belt, the Seminoles looked to be on track for another standout season. The FSU offense had been productive in both victories, and although the competition figured to be stiffer in Kenan Stadium, Florida State had never lost to UNC on the gridiron. With the Tar Heels coming into the game 0-3, there were no indications that this game would be any different.

The Seminoles trudged onto the contest holding a 71-2 all-time record in ACC play, but Carolina was far from intimidated. The Tar

Heels had already played three difficult opponents in Oklahoma, Maryland, and Texas, and the experience wrought from those encounters was more significant than the effortless victories posted thus far by FSU. With a more talented team than Florida State for the first time in anyone's recollection, the Tar Heels took out their frustrations on the Seminoles, and stunned a capacity crowd and regional audience watching on ABC.

After scoring the first touchdown in the opening quarter, Carolina surrendered 9 unanswered points to the Seminoles, which came on a safety and a scoring pass to Talman Gardner. Although UNC trailed 9-7 going into halftime, there was an odd sense that something was different about this game. Coming out of the locker room in a rage, Carolina dominated the third quarter, taking a 20-9 lead behind the defense and the passing of freshman Darian Durant. Durant put UNC in the lead with a 52-yard toss to Chesley Borders, and led another pair of drives that resulted in field goals. By the early moments of the fourth quarter, the delirious Carolina fans seized a rare opportunity to mock their beaten opposition. Thousands of blue-clad spectators began mocking FSU's tomahawk chant, waving their arms and yelling in similar fashion as the Seminole supporters had done countless times over the years.

With the Carolina defense humiliating the Seminole offense, the game was a complete role reversal of the previous two UNC-FSU contests. Scoring three unanswered touchdowns in the final frame, Carolina turned a close game into a decisive blowout. With a 41-9 victory, North Carolina took its first gridiron win in history ever over a Top Five opponent, and many around the country thought the media had accidentally switched the scores when the final score was displayed on television.

Despite a sore hamstring, Perry was back in the fold for West Virginia, and rushed for 153 yards and a score in helping UM build up a 13-0 advantage. After the Mountaineers came back to tie the score at 13, UM took the lead for good thanks to a big defensive play. With just over two minutes to play in the half, linebacker Mike Whaley scooped up a WVU fumble at his own 44 and raced 56 yards for a 19-13 Maryland advantage. With the ball on the West Virginia 29 late in the third quarter, Hill stepped into the pocket and hit Gary, who had decisively beaten his defender. The celebration after Gary's 71-yard score was short lived, as Mountaineer kick returner Shawn Terry went 100 yards on the ensuing kickoff. Like they had done against North Carolina, the Terrapins wore down WVU in the final quarter, as Hill snuck over from the 1 to complete a 32-20 knockout for Maryland.

After opening the Virginia game scoreless for a period, Maryland exploded offensively in the second fifteen minutes. Hill sprinted across to start the scoring, and Nick Novak added a field goal for a 10-0 lead. Al Groh replaced starting quarterback Bryan Spinner with Matt Schaub, and the backup drilled receiver Billy McMullen with a 63-yard strike. Hill matched Schaub's bomb with his own 53-yard pass, hitting Gary downfield for a 17-7 cushion. The Terrapins added another late score through the special teams, as Curtis Williams blocked a punt that was recovered by Leroy Ambush in the end zone. Virginia cut into the UM advantage in the third quarter, as Schaub ran and passed for scores to make the game 24-21. Maryland pulled away from there, as Hill found Jafar Williams in the right corner of the end zone, and following an interception, Perry scored from the 6. A late field goal made the final 41-21.

The Terps had less than a week to prepare for Georgia Tech, who they met on a Thursday night down in Atlanta. The Yellow Jacket defense was solid against the rush, and became the first opposing unit all season to hold Perry under 100 yards. Struggling for yardage all night, Perry managed 49 yards on eighteen attempts. Maryland caught a couple of breaks in the first two quarters, and although GT played them almost even, the Terps led 14-0 at halftime. The Yellow Jackets evened the score in the second half, using similar plays from the ones that Maryland had used to take their advantage.

Georgia Tech placekicker Luke Manget connected on a field goal at the 6:33 mark of the final period, which made the score 17-14. With the Yellow Jackets hoping to reenter the ACC championship picture, the stage was set for a thrilling finish. Desperate to make strides on offense, Hill led the Terrapins downfield in the late moments. With time running down in regulation, UM was in position for a kick of its own. The ball was placed at the GT 29, where Nick Novak would seek to avenge what had been a tough season thus far for the Maryland placekicker. Terrapin supporters were holding their breath as Novak took the field, for no matter how hopeful they were that he could convert, he had not exactly won over their confidence. The kicker had already missed a 32-yard attempt against the Yellow Jackets, and stood only four-for-eleven on the year. With an opportunity to send the game to overtime, however, Novak's pressure-packed kick was true.

The Terrapins got the ball first in the overtime session, but the inspired Tech defenders were ready. The Yellow Jackets held UM from scoring a touchdown, and Novak was called back onto the field for another important kick. This time from 26 yards, Novak coolly booted the ball through the uprights. With the score 20-17, Georgia Tech had an opportunity to win with a touchdown, but running back Joe Burns committed a fatal error. The GT tailback dropped the ball, and line-backer Randall Jones secured it to bring an abrupt end to the contest. As the small contingent of Terrapin supporters went crazy, the golden mob at Bobby Dodd Stadium sat in a collective state of shock.

The emotional victory over Georgia Tech carried over to the Duke game, as Maryland overwhelmed their inferior opposition. Friedgen reminded his players of the 1999 homecoming fiasco against the Blue Devils, and the Terrapins made sure it wouldn't happen again. With 34 first downs and 697 yards of total offense, UM moved effortlessly through the Duke resistance, and took a 42-10 lead into halftime. The Terrapin backups got some work in the second half, and the offense continued to thrash the Blue Devils for a 59-17 final. With Duke out of the way, Maryland now prepared for their most significant encounter thus far. The loss to North Carolina had been an embarrassment for Florida State, but the Seminoles recovered to take decisive conference victories over Wake Forest and Virginia. An opportunity was still in place for FSU to share the league title with Maryland, and with the game being played in Tallahassee, the cards were stacked against Friedgen's boys.

The Terrapins held the upper hand early on, as fullback James Lynch took the ball up the middle and galloped 65 yards less than two minutes in. Controlling the field position throughout the opening half, UM was able to move into range again, and midway through the second quarter, Riley fell over to make the score 14-0 in favor of the Terrapins. Florida State dominated the remainder of the first half, as Chris Rix threw twice to Talman Gardner for touchdowns. Although Perry and Hill ran into the end zone in the third quarter to keep Maryland close, FSU's second quarter surge had awakened the entire Seminole team. After Xavier Beitia connected on a field goal to tie the game at 24, the Seminoles took advantage after a fumbled kickoff to score again.

The game headed into the final quarter tied at 31, but it was evident to those watching that Florida State was in command. Rix went to Gardner again early in the fourth quarter, nailing the receiver for a 28-yard play to make the score 38-31. The Terrapins were hoping to run their way downfield once again, but Perry fumbled deep in his own territory. The error was a costly one for Maryland, as Rix promptly threw his fourth touchdown, a 22-yard missile to Javon Walker. The quick scores spelled an end to UM's chances of victory, and another long scoring pass to Atrews Bell gave Rix a quintet of passing touchdowns. Another late touchdown made the final score 52-31, and put

FSU in position to claim another share of the ACC title should they win out.

The Terps rebounded from the FSU disaster by dominating Troy State, 47-14, scoring the first 44 points and holding the Trojans to -1 yards rushing. A week later, Maryland decisively outplayed Clemson, building a 31-7 advantage early in the fourth quarter. With the defense shutting down CU's running game, Gary and Perry each caught scoring passes from Hill. Clemson tallied a pair of touchdowns in the final period, including a 100-yard kickoff return, but Maryland's early advantage was too much to overtake. The 37-20 victory was significant in and of itself for the Terrapins, as it ensured nine wins and a berth in a major bowl. As it turned out, the victory would have added significance as it related to what was going on down in Tallahassee.

With former FSU assistant Chuck Amato reading his every move, Bobby Bowden was in a dogfight with N.C. State. In his first return to Doak-Campbell Stadium since taking the NCSU job, Amato guided a spirited effort by the red and white. The Wolfpack offense accumulated 463 total yards, and took a 31-21 lead early in the fourth quarter on a 24-yard run by Ray Robinson. Robinson, who finished the game with 106 yards and a pair of goal line crossings, spun through a would-be tackler on the way to the points.

Barely a minute later, Florida State scored on a short dive by Rix, making the score 31-28 with more than ten minutes to play. State immediately went into a stall, eating up time and yardage with a steady downfield march. Eight minutes and seventeen plays later, Adam Kiker booted a 32-yard field goal, giving the Wolfpack a 34-28 advantage at the 2:11 mark. The Seminoles took possession at their own 22, and Rix, who had already thrown three touchdowns, began working his receivers. Florida State moved down to the NCSU 14 in the final seconds, where Rix got two opportunities to propel his team to victory. In a courageous stand, State was able to deflect both passes, with Brian Williams knocking the ball away from Gardner in the corner of the end zone on the game's final play. With the victory, N.C. State became the first ACC team to win a game on Florida State's home field, and also became the only school in the conference to knock off the Seminoles twice.

"All we needed was one of them and we win," a dejected Bowden said later. "They made one more catch than we did. We had a chance."

"To see the emotion of Chuck Amato, crying on the sidelines during the National Anthem, made me realize how much he wanted to win that particular ball game," recalls Dr. Jerry Punch. "After all those years as an assistant at Florida State, to go back down there for the first time as a head coach and win, was really awesome to watch."

Now holding two conference losses and three total defeats, it was evident that Florida State was not going to be hoisting a national championship trophy this January. Even worse for FSU was the fact that a Maryland victory over NCSU the following Saturday night would knock the Seminoles out of at least a tie of the ACC championship for the first time since the school had entered the league. As tension mounted in Tallahassee, the Terrapins prepared to invade Raleigh.

Adam Kiker, whose kick in the waning moments of the game in Tallahassee had helped lead NCSU to victory, was at it again in the Maryland contest. As the Wolfpack offense struggled to reach the end zone, Kiker kicked four field goals in the first three quarters, and accounted for all 12 of State's points. With the Terrapins also unable to mount a great deal of offense, the game went into halftime with State leading 9-3. An uncharacteristically irate Friedgen went into a tirade in the locker room, throwing chairs and yelling in an effort to fire up his team.

Maryland responded to Friedgen's outburst, taking the second half kickoff and driving 70 yards in more than six minutes. From the Wolfpack 5, Hill connected with Gary for the game's first touchdown. Maryland briefly held a 10-9 advantage, but Kiker's fourth successful kick gave NCSU a 12-10 lead heading into crunch time. The Terrapins successfully mounted another offensive, needing only four minutes to move into position. Hill threw again to Gary for 22 yards, and the UM quarterback scrambled over from the 6 for the points. With a 16-12 lead, Friedgen elected to go for two, but Hill's pass was unsuccessful.

In a march similar to the one executed by the Terrapins to start the second half, N.C. State went on a dedicated move midway through the fourth quarter. With Philip Rivers at the helm, the Wolfpack plowed 80 yards in thirteen plays, which included a fourth down conversion at the UM 7. With the ball on the 1 and less than four minutes to play, Rivers faded into the pocket and located Cotra Jackson, who hauled in the pass for an 18-16 NCSU advantage. Kiker's kick gave State a three-point cushion.

The next few minutes were a wild roller coaster of emotions for both teams, as the Terrapins and Wolfpack each watched victory slip in and out of their grasp. Maryland struck first, as Hill connected with Rich Parson on a long pass play. Parson broke into the clear, and was gone for a game-winning touchdown before disaster struck. In a shocking turn of events, Parson lost control of the football after Wolfpack defender Lamont Reid corralled him by the back of his jersey. The fumble took place just outside the end zone, and with the touchback, State appeared to have the game salted away.

The Maryland defense had other ideas, and forced the Wolfpack into a quick three-and-out. With the game, and the ACC title, hanging on one possession, Hill and the Terrapin offense retook the field. Mixing passes and runs through the NCSU defenders, Maryland worked itself back into enemy real estate. With under a minute remaining UM found itself at the Wolfpack 8, and Hill ended the progression with a scoring pass to Gary. Maryland's final possession was a microcosm of their entire season, a well-developed march put together by a group of unheralded players that would not allow themselves to lose. State was out of miracles, and the Terrapin contingent at Carter-Finley Stadium began pelting the turf with oranges following the 23-19 victory.

"It's a tribute to our players," Friedgen said later. "I couldn't be prouder of them. They'll always have a special place in my heart because they wouldn't quit. They just refuse to lose. They're a special football team and I feel very privileged to have a chance to coach them."

The accolades for Friedgen came pouring in after the regular season, as the Terrapin coach was lauded nationwide for one of the most impressive one-year turnarounds by any program in major college football history. The previous August, Friedgen had inherited a program that posted only two winning seasons and a single bowl appearance in eleven years. In only one autumn at the helm, Friedgen had the Terrapins going to the Orange Bowl for the first time since January of 1956.

Friedgen was not the only ACC participant to receive postseason accolades, as North Carolina's Julius Peppers earned the Bednarik Award, given annually to the finest defensive player in all of college football. After leading the nation in sacks in 2000, Peppers was a human highlight film during the 2001 season, using athleticism and uncanny speed for a defensive end to earn unanimous All-American honors. Among his finest plays included an interception return for a touchdown against Oklahoma, in which he spiked down and caught an errant pass at the line of scrimmage, and a lunging interception against Florida State, in which Peppers jumped to deflect a ball and then dove to haul it in before it hit the ground. Peppers was also an important contributor to UNC's basketball team during his time in Chapel Hill, and became only the sixth player in conference history to be taken with the second pick in the NFL Draft.

After routinely sending four or five of its schools to bowls throughout the 1990s, the 2001 postseason ushered in a new era of enhanced participation for the ACC. With extra bowl games being added on an almost yearly basis, the NCAA was now sending nearly half of its Division 1-A programs to a postseason contest. The lure of hosting a college football game in late December or early January appeals to several American cities, which can expect thousands of tourists to come into their area for several days. This influx of tourism and television money has resulted in an almost endless supply of entries for schools that can post at least six victories during the regular season. For the first time, the ACC sent six schools to bowl games following the 2001 season. Duke, Virginia, and Wake Forest, the three schools with the worst overall football winning percentages in ACC history, proved to be the only schools that could not produce the necessary victories.

North Carolina State began the show with a Tangerine Bowl clash against Pittsburgh. Pitt overwhelmed the Wolfpack secondary, as All-American wide receiver Antonio Bryant played through an ankle injury. Quarterback David Priestley threw to Bryant for touchdowns twice in the first half, and led an offensive assault that was too much for Philip Rivers to overcome. Trailing 17-3, Rivers and the NCSU offense scored twice to make the game competitive, but Pitt's offense countered each time. In a frustrating evening for NCSU fans, the Panthers took a convincing 34-19 final score.

In the week between N.C. State's Tangerine Bowl appearance and Georgia Tech's game in the Seattle Bowl, the Yellow Jacket program became an integral part of one of the most interesting stories to hit college football in decades. As former Ramblin' Wreck coach George O' Leary endured a self-induced hell, integrity among coaching figures was brought to the forefront of the media. Before the Jackets were scheduled to meet Stanford in Seattle, O' Leary had accepted the vacant opening at Notre Dame, where he was hoping to turn around the storied program that had fallen on recent hardships. Few people were surprised at O' Leary's decision to leave Atlanta for South Bend, where he would assume arguably the most prestigious coaching position in all of collegiate sports. In a shocking turn of events, however, a New Hampshire newspaper reporter began uncovering discrepancies in O' Leary's past a few days after his acceptance of the Notre Dame job.

On his resume, O' Leary claimed that he lettered in football three times at the University of New Hampshire (UNH) in the late 1960s. According to the reporter's sources, which were confirmed by officials at the school, O' Leary had never played in a game at UNH. Furthermore, the coach had written on a resume submitted to Syracuse University in 1980 that he had received a master's degree from New York University in 1972. That also proved to be false, as NYU officials con-

According to the reporter's sources, which were confirmed by officials at the school, O' Leary had never played in a game at UNH. Furthermore, the coach had written on a resume submitted to Syracuse University in 1980 that he had received a master's degree from New York University in 1972. That also proved to be false, as NYU officials confirmed that although O' Leary attended school there, he did not complete his studies. Unable to continue his relationship with Notre Dame after this initial breach of trust, O' Leary had no choice but to resign from his dream job only five days after accepting it.

"Many years ago, as a young married father, I sought to pursue my dream as a football coach," he said. "In seeking employment, I prepared a resume that contained inaccuracies regarding my completion of course work for a master's degree, and also my level of participation in football at my alma mater. These misstatements were never stricken from my resume or my biographical sketch in later years."

Georgia Tech was caught right in the middle of the uproar in South Bend, as offensive line coach Mac McWhorter was given the interim post for the bowl game. The O' Leary fiasco had many wondering how the same discrepancies could have been missed by the hiring committee at Georgia Tech and other places where O' Leary had coached. With everything that was taking place off the field, one could have easily seen how the Seattle Bowl could become a golden nightmare for Tech.

In impressive fashion, the Yellow Jacket players left all the distractions in the locker room, and came together to outplay Stanford. The game itself was particularly unique, played in the middle of a baseball diamond with the opposing teams sharing one large sideline. In the first football game played at the Emerald City's Safeco Field, Tech put together a momentum-shifting goal line stand on Stanford's opening possession. The Cardinal had three chances from the 1, but GT held strong each time. Stanford went for it again on fourth down, but Daryl Smith dropped Kerry Carter for a 2-yard loss.

With quarterback George Godsey throwing effectively, Tech built up a 17-3 halftime lead. Stanford rallied to pull within 17-14 early in the final quarter, but the Yellow Jackets held on for a 24-14 final. It was McWhorter's only taste of glory at the helm of the Ramblin' Wreck, and although his players chanted his name afterwards, GT officials were already actively pursuing a permanent coach. With a heavy recruiting period only weeks away, Georgia Tech wanted to get someone in place quickly. Although they denied it in the days leading up to the Seattle game, GT was actively negotiating with former Dallas Cowboys head coach Chan Gailey. A coach that could handle the lime-

enjoy Tommy Bowden's first successful postseason encounter at Clemson. With Woodrow Dantzler enjoying a final curtain call to his CU career, tying a school record with four touchdown tosses, the Tigers cruised to a 49-14 victory. Later that night, North Carolina toppled Auburn, 16-10, in the Peach Bowl to give the Tar Heels four consecutive bowl triumphs.

Although it hadn't been the best of years for Florida State, the Seminoles made it four consecutive bowl verdicts for the ACC with a decisive victory over Virginia Tech in the Gator Bowl. Denied a major bowl berth for the first time since joining the league, the garnet and gold outplayed the Hokies for a 30-17 win. In tying his idol, Bear Bryant, with his 323rd career victory, Bobby Bowden also claimed his seventh bowl championship as an ACC coach, surpassing Clemson's Danny Ford for first place in that category.

Maryland's inspirational regular season was curtailed in the Orange Bowl, as Florida overwhelmed the Terrapins on both sides of the football. In what turned out to be Steve Spurrier's final game at UF, the Gators used a one-two punch at quarterback to great success. Brock Berlin replaced Heisman runner-up Rex Grossman early in the game, and completed eleven-of-nineteen passes for 196 yards. Grossman came on midway through the second quarter, and added 248 yards and four touchdowns to seal Maryland's fate. The Terrapin secondary, so effective throughout most of the season, was unable to contain Florida's receiving tandem of Taylor Jacobs and Jabar Gaffney. Jacobs hauled in ten catches for 170 yards and two touchdowns, while Gaffney added seven grabs for 118 yards. With tailback Earnest Graham running for 151 yards and two scores as well, the Gators were able to do whatever they wanted offensively. In a startling departure from their defensive dominance during the regular season, the Terps allowed Florida to run up 659 yards, and take a 56-23 victory.

Florida State returned to a familiar place in 2002, the fiftieth anniversary season of the Atlantic Coast Conference. Although FSU was not ready to reenter the national championship picture, the Seminoles disposed of seven of its eight league opponents to claim the school's tenth ACC championship in eleven seasons, and eighth outright. Chris Rix returned to the head of the FSU offense, and along with backup Adrian McPherson, Bobby Bowden figured to have a solid group of signal callers in town for the next few years. Unfortunately, the ghosts of past problems with off-the-field behavior resurfaced, and by the end of the regular season, both quarterbacks were off the team.

Bowden spent the spring and summer months tied with Bear Bryant for second place on the all-time college football victory list. The

Seminole skipper wanted nothing more than to surpass the Bear in the season opener against Iowa State (ISU), and although it proved to be more difficult than expected, the Old Man got his wish. Florida State looked solid early on, jumping out to a 24-0 lead behind a pair of Rix touchdown tosses and a rush by Nick Maddox. The Cyclones finally got on track in the second quarter following a 56-yard kickoff return by Lance Young, as Hiawatha Rutland scored from 36 yards away to make the score 24-7. The Seminoles and Cyclones traded touchdowns before halftime, and the game went into the intermission, 31-14.

From there, Iowa State quarterback Seneca Wallace took control. Wallace, who went on to throw for 313 yards, scrambled over to make the score 31-24. Rix threw his third touchdown five minutes later for a 38-24 score, but Wallace threw 39 yards to Jamaul Montgomery to pull his team within a touchdown yet again. The final minutes proved to be hellacious for Seminole fans, as the FSU defense endured a final Iowa State rally. With under a minute remaining, Wallace passed the Cyclones into Seminole territory. From the 21, Wallace rambled down to the 1, where ISU had the ball with only four seconds to play. The partisan-ISU crowd assembled in Kansas City's Arrowhead Stadium rose to its collective feet, hopeful to see the Cyclones score a touchdown. On the game's final play, Wallace rolled to his right, reaching the 1-foot line before being corralled by FSU's Kendyll Pope and Jerel Hudson. The play was eerily familiar to the one that had bitten Florida State against Virginia back in 1995, but this time around, the Seminoles were the ones that were smiling.

The Seminoles recovered the following week to hand Virginia a decisive 40-19 defeat down in Tallahassee. With tailback Greg Jones rushing for 173 yards, FSU went away from its normal pass-happy approach in favor of a conservative strategy. It paid off handsomely in the first half, as the garnet and gold built up a 23-0 lead. The Seminoles continued to dominate in the third quarter, building up a 33-0 lead behind Jones' second touchdown and a field goal by Xavier Beitia. Matt Schaub threw three touchdowns to three different receivers, but the Virginia scores merely kept the game from appearing like a complete washout.

Florida State headed to College Park two weeks later, and were looking forward to handing out some revenge to Ralph Friedgen's Maryland team. Although the Seminoles had yet to experience defeat to the Terrapins since joining the ACC, UM's surprise conference championship in 2001 had rubbed plenty of people the wrong way down in Florida. Intent on proving its superiority, the Seminole offense exploded in the first thirty minutes, scoring 30 points. All the while, the FSU defenders were dominating the Terrapin offense, holding the unit scoreless for the first forty minutes of the contest. Although Maryland finally got on the scoreboard, a final touchdown gave the Seminoles a handy 37-10 triumph.

Rix went down to an elbow injury in the UM game, and spent much of the second half of the ensuing week's encounter with Duke on the bench. As with most FSU-Duke showdowns, the game eventually got out of hand for the Blue Devils, although they were tied as late as the second quarter. With the Seminole offense once again highly productive, FSU went on to take a 48-17 final. The game provided some comic relief for Florida State haters, as Blue Devil tight end Calen Powell rambled into the Seminole sidelines and ran over Bowden. After jumping to his feet, Bowden displayed his trademark grin.

At 4-0, Florida State was looking every bit as strong as they had looked in season's past, although it remained to be seen if the Seminoles had truly been tested yet. With difficult games to come against Clemson, Miami, and Notre Dame, it was easy for Florida State to forget about Louisville, who welcomed the Seminoles to town with open arms. With the remnants of Tropical Storm Isidore hovering over the area, the teams engaged in a soggy defensive clash.

After trading field goals in the opening quarter, Rix thrust the Seminoles into the lead by finding Talman Gardner from 23 yards out in the second period. Another pair of kicks sent the game into the locker rooms with FSU leading 13-6. Although the Cardinals had more first downs than penalties in the opening half, quarterback Dave Ragone kept his team in the game, throwing a 30-yard strike to Joshua Tinch to knot up the contest. Rix returned the favor, tossing his second touchdown to Gardner to send the game into the final period with FSU on top, 20-13.

Louisville tied the game again early in the fourth quarter, as Ragone threw his second touchdown. The final eleven minutes of regulation proved futile for both squads, as neither could get in position to claim victory. Louisville claimed the all-important coin toss for overtime, and like most teams do, they elected to play defense first. Florida State decided to waste no time, electing to throw downfield in hopes of scoring a quick touchdown. Unfortunately for the Seminoles, Rix's pass on first down was intercepted by Louisville's Anthony Floyd at the edge of the goal line.

The Cardinals needed only a field goal to win, but with the Seminoles deflated after Rix's interception, the game was theirs for the taking. On the first play after the turnover, running back Henry Miller split a gap and raced 25 yards for the game-winning score. As Miller reached the end zone, thousands of fans poured onto the field at Papa John's Cardinal Stadium. Within minutes, the horde had ripped away both goalposts.

"They were better than we were," Bowden said later. "Before the season, I was very concerned about this game because they were playing as good as anybody last season."

Although they were far from dominant, the Seminoles recovered at home a week later to beat Clemson in another Thursday night battle. Although the defense allowed 441 yards, only 18 of those were accumulated in the final quarter, as FSU opened up its 38-31 lead. In all, Florida State recovered three botched Clemson punts or kicks, which resulted directly to 17 points. When combined with a 50-yard kickoff return by Gardner and a 97-yard scoring sprint by Leon Washington, the Seminoles scored 31 points on special teams alone. Florida State put the game away in the final period, using Tiger errors to add 10 points to their total and claim a 48-31 final score.

Throughout all of its years of service to college and professional football, the Orange Bowl had never held a crowd larger than the one that sauntered in for the annual FSU-Miami war in 2002. With 81,927 fans in attendance, the Seminoles and Hurricanes played yet another classic. Miami was the defending national champions, and entered the contest with twenty-seven consecutive victories. Although the victory over Clemson had brought some confidence back to the FSU camp, they were decided underdogs against Larry Coker's Hurricanes this time around.

After Willis McGahee raced for a 4-yard touchdown midway through the first quarter, Florida State dominated the remainder of the first half. Taking on the nation's No. 1 team without an ounce of fear, the Seminoles tallied 17 points in the second quarter, as Maddox raced 30 yards, Beitia kicked a field goal, and Gardner caught a 10-yard pass from Rix. Miami quarterback Ken Dorsey threw his own scoring strike in the final minute of the half to send the game into the intermission, 17-14.

The third quarter was run by the defenses, as the Seminole defenders shut down one of the country's most potent offensive attacks. Beitia added his second field goal at the 3:25 mark, and FSU went into the fourth quarter leading, 20-14. It only got better for Bowden's troops in the final frame, as Greg Jones broke off an 11-yard sprint to make the score 27-14 with less than twelve minutes to play. With 189 yards,

Jones was a constant thorn in Miami's side, and his touchdown looked to have the garnet and gold heading in the direction of victory.

Dorsey, in an effort to motivate his offense, collected the group and gave a quick motivational talk after the Jones score. After struggling through most of the contest, Dorsey elevated his own performance, and led the Hurricanes to a pair of scores in less than three minutes. After leading a steady progression through the white-shirted Seminoles, Dorsey connected with Kevin Beard to make the score 27-21. Minutes later, after retaking possession, Dorsey threw to McGahee on a screen pass. The elusive Hurricane back made a move and took off upfield, galloping 67 yards. McGahee's fine individual effort placed the ball on the FSU 11, and on the following play, Jason Geathers scored to tie up the contest at 27. Todd Sievers was money on the critical extra point, and the Hurricanes led, 28-27.

There was still more than five minutes on the clock after the Geathers touchdown, and the Florida State offense drove into position to win. With enough time for a single play, the ball was spotted at the Miami 26. Xavier Beitia, who was two-for-two in this game and thirteen-for-fifteen over the course of the season, ran onto the field with a chance to give the Seminoles victory. Bowden had been in this very situation plenty of times before as the FSU skipper, and was hoping that this time around, the winds of destiny would blow his way. Beitia lined up and put solid leg on the kick, but as the final seconds ticked off the Orange Bowl clock, the ball sailed wide to the left. As the Hurricane fans displayed a mixture of relief and ecstasy in the stands, Coker offered his condolences to Bowden in the middle of the field. In a game that Florida State deserved to win, another cruel dose of fate resulted in a classic dubbed, "Wide Left II."

The dejection of the Miami encounter carried over into the following week's game against Notre Dame, as signal caller Carlyle Holiday threw a 65-yard touchdown pass through the FSU secondary on the first play from scrimmage. The teams traded field goals before FSU matched Notre Dame's touchdown in the second period, as Washington rambled over from the 1 to tie the game at 10. Taking advantage of Florida State errors, Notre Dame scored 17 unanswered points in the third quarter, sending the capacity crowd at Doak-Campbell Stadium into stunned silence.

Trailing 27-10 as the fourth quarter began, the hole only got deeper for FSU, as a 31-yard scoring run gave Notre Dame a 34-10 lead. The Irish advantage held into the final minutes, as the Seminoles were unable to make a dent. Finally, in the final three minutes, the FSU offense went into attack mode. With backup Adrian McPherson at the helm, the offense drove into Notre Dame territory, and with only 1:12 on the clock, the quarterback threw to Maddox for a score. Florida State promptly recovered an onsides kick, and McPherson quickly struck Anquan Boldin for a 29-yard touchdown.

Only twelve seconds remained after Boldin's score, but the game was now within reach at 34-27. Incredibly, the Seminoles recovered another onsides kick, and had possession with a chance to miraculously tie the game. Although the Doak-Campbell crowd finally had something to stand for, FSU's late reprieve served as little more than a tease. McPherson's desperate final toss fell incomplete, and the Seminole bid for 21 points in just over a minute was derailed.

The Notre Dame defeat was only the fifth setback for Florida State in its last ninety-one games at Doak-Campbell Stadium, and even worse, the Seminoles had now lost three out of four games for the first time since 1981. Wake Forest provided a much-needed break from the pressure of Miami and Notre Dame, and although it wasn't a decisive performance, FSU got an important victory. With a national championship now completely out of view, Bowden and his team were forced to make less lofty goals, notably to remain on top of the ACC standings. Despite the three defeats, the Seminoles were still perfect in conference play, and improved to 5-0 with a 34-21 verdict over the Demon Deacons.

As was tradition in Florida State-Georgia Tech encounters in Atlanta, the Seminoles came out in their all-garnet apparel. McPherson took control as the starting quarterback for FSU, and responded with a pair of long scoring passes. The first was good to Craphonso Thorpe from 72 yards out in the second quarter, and the second was good to Boldin from the 32 in the third period. Combined with an 82-yard interception return by Stanford Samuels, which had first gotten FSU on the board, and Bowden's troops had enough for a 21-13 victory.

After getting revenge with a 40-14 domination of North Carolina, which clinched a tie for the conference title, the Seminoles prepared for another clash with Chuck Amato's Wolfpack. Playing a weak schedule early in the year, NCSU had raced out to a 9-0 record to start the season. State fans were briefly thinking national championship, but the team was on a three-game skid in the month of November, which included a pair of tough defeats to Georgia Tech and Maryland.

The tone of the game was set on Florida State's opening possession, after McPherson had worked his team to the NCSU 16. Following consecutive sacks by the State defense, punter Chance Gwaltney had a kick blocked. The Wolfpack took possession and drove into field goal range, and Adam Kiker made the score 3-0. The Wolfpack drove into position for another kick minutes later, which served as a prelude to one of the strangest plays in the history of Carter-Finley Stadium. On a fourth-and-7 deep in Seminole territory, the Wolfpack lined up for a field goal. Amato had another thought coming, and elected to run a fake. Holder Chris Young took the snap and burst through the FSU line, only to be stripped of the football by defender Allen Augustin. Michael Boulware picked up the loose pigskin for Florida State and ran 84 yards to the end zone, briefly quieting the electrified crowd.

The N.C. State defense played its finest game of the year, shutting out the garnet and gold offense. Although they led 7-3, it was only a matter of time before the Seminole defense caved in against Philip Rivers and the NCSU passing attack. In an unusual formation, with Rivers lined up as a wide receiver, the ball was snapped directly to running back Josh Brown. With Rivers throwing an important block to spring him free, Brown raced 60 yards to the FSU 1. On the very next play, freshman T. A. McLendon scored to give the Wolfpack a 10-7 advantage.

The second half was largely unproductive, as the Wolfpack defense held FSU at bay and kept them from retaking the advantage. State put the game away in the final period, as Rivers put together a nearly flawless drive. Rivers drove State all the way down to the FSU 1, where the Wolfpack were held out by a fierce goal line stand. Nonetheless, the field position gained by the march paid huge dividends seconds later. The Seminoles retook possession at the 1, but on the first play, NCSU applied enough pressure on McPherson to force a safety. Now leading, 12-7, the Wolfpack took the free kick and moved back into field goal range. Kiker converted his second kick, and NCSU held a 15-7 spread. Florida State still had an opportunity to win, but continued to stall against the red-shirted defenders, as their ensuing drive was stuffed by another sack. Gwaltney was forced to punt, and the Wolfpack came through with a block. Freshman Manny Lawson was the culprit, and the ball bounded out of the end zone for a safety. It wasn't pretty, but NCSU had done enough to claim a 17-7 victory.

Although the Wolfpack fans were able to celebrate another sweet triumph on their home field over the Seminoles, the defeat had little bearing on FSU's postseason hopes. Despite four losses, and a gradual progression out of the Top Ten over the course of the regular season, Maryland's defeat at the hands of Virginia the same day guaranteed the garnet and gold another undisputed ACC championship, and a berth in the Bowl Championship Series.

The week of the Florida game provided a number of distractions for Florida State, as McPherson was arrested, and subsequently kicked off the team, for allegations of felony grand theft. Rix, who had been supplanted as starting quarterback by McPherson a month earlier, got another chance at the head of the FSU offense. Although the game wouldn't affect the national championship picture, the Seminoles played their finest game of the year, and defended Doak-Campbell Stadium once again in the face of a Gator sighting.

Florida had its chances early on, twice moving inside the FSU 20, but was forced each time to kick a field goal. The momentum shifted over to Rix, who took advantage of his new opportunity by leading a pair of surgical strikes through the UF secondary. The sophomore threw a pair of touchdowns in the second quarter, each covering 22 yards, to propel the garnet and gold to a 17-6 advantage. The game continued to get out of hand for Florida in the third quarter, as Kendyll Pope jumped up to snag a tipped Rex Grossman pass. Pope took in the ball at the 13, and raced to the end zone to give FSU a 24-6 cushion five minutes into the half. Grossman promptly led UF to a touchdown, but the Seminoles tallied the game's final points. With Rix and Boldin doing the damage, FSU went 80 yards, and a 19-yard score by Boldin completed the 31-14 triumph. In a dirty ball game, which included several cheap shots by linemen and a verbal warning from the officials, the Seminoles left the field with the school's fourth consecutive home verdict over the Gators.

The lucrative slice of the annual bowl pie got even fatter for the ACC in 2002, as seven of the league's nine members earned at least a .500 record. In setting a new NCAA record by sending 78 percent of its teams to postseason games, only Duke and North Carolina were left out of the festivities. Clemson opened with a Tangerine Bowl appearance against Texas Tech, and although the Tigers were favored, they quickly found themselves overmatched. The Red Raiders featured quarterback Kliff Kingsbury, who by game's end became only the third signal caller in Division I-A history to surpass 5,000 passing yards in a single season. Kingsbury embarrassed the CU defenders, hitting five different receivers for touchdowns and throwing for 375 yards. The game got out of hand quickly for the orange and white, as Texas Tech handed out a 55-15 whitewashing.

Five days later, Virginia met West Virginia in the first Continental Tire Bowl, played in Charlotte's Ericcson Stadium. In an interesting coincidence, the opposing tailbacks, WVU's Avon Cobourne and UVA's Wali Lundy, had attended the same high school. Cobourne, four years Lundy's senior, had become the Big East's all-time leading rusher during his tenure in Morgantown. Although he was just a freshman, Lundy was ready to show that he could get the job done as well. Lundy was the catalyst of an offensive explosion for UVA, as the Cavaliers broke a four-game postseason skid by burying the Mountaineers. Lundy scored four touchdowns, and hauled in scoring passes from both Marques Hagans and Matt Schaub. In a game that signaled the return of the Virginia football program as a major player, the Cavaliers beat the sloppy West Virginians, 48-22.

For only the fourth time since joining the ACC, Wake Forest also entered the bowl picture. It had been a breakthrough season for Jim Grobe's Demon Deacons, with a record-setting blowout over North Carolina and an upset triumph on the road over Georgia Tech. For the first time in years, Wake had been competitive in each of their conference games, and proved a difficult opponent for everyone they played. For the second time in the school's last three bowl appearances, the Deacons met Oregon, this time on the field of the Seattle Bowl.

After staying on the ground for most of the season, Wake took to the skies against the Ducks. Oregon's pass defense was one of the weakest in Pacific Ten, and quarterback James McPherson took full advantage. In his best performance of the season, McPherson threw for 241 yards, running for one touchdown and tossing two more. Taking a 21-10 lead into halftime, Wake added another series of scores in the final thirty minutes for a 38-17 triumph. The victory was Wake Forest's third in a row over Pacific Ten opposition, dating back to the 1992 victory over Oregon in the Independence Bowl.

If Wake Forest's victory over Oregon was considered an upset, Georgia Tech's performance in the Silicon Valley Classic game had to be considered just as much of a surprise. Tech's opponent, Fresno State, was making its third consecutive trip to San Jose, and a throng of Bulldog fans made the 150-mile western journey to cheer on their team. Although Fresno was missing seven players due to grade issues, the weather conditions were an obstacle that the Yellow Jackets struggled to overcome. Playing on a muddy field, which quickly dirtied Tech's sparkling white jerseys and gold pants, the Bulldogs took the early advantage. The Yellow Jackets rallied in the second half behind backup signal caller Damarius Bilbo, but the running of Fresno tailback Rodney Davis made the difference. After a field goal gave Fresno a late 23-21 advantage, Davis sprinted free on a 28-yard run. Davis finished with 153 yards and a pair of tallies, and his late score gave the Bulldogs the game, 30-21.

As 2002 turned into 2003, Maryland and N.C. State made decisive statements that they were back among the nation's strongest programs. The Terrapins and Wolfpack upset Tennessee and Notre Dame, respectively, a pair of schools that have traditionally overwhelmed ACC competition. With a dominating performance on defense, including a 54-yard interception return for a score by Curmoe Cox, the Terrapins ensured that the Volunteers were out of contention very early. Maryland quarterback Scott McBrien ran over twice, and Nick Novak kicked three field goals to hand Tennessee its worst margin of defeat ever in a bowl game, 30-3. Terrapin linebacker E. J. Henderson culminated the year by earning the Bednarik Award, joining North Carolina's Julius Peppers as the second consecutive ACC player to be named national defender of the year.

The Wolfpack were just as dominant the following afternoon against the Irish, as Amato opened up his bag of tricks much like he had done five weeks earlier against Florida State. With the defense recording its second consecutive touchdown-free game, Philip Rivers did the rest. Using a fumblerooski and a flea-flicker against the bewildered Irish defenders, Rivers led a surge of three NCSU touchdowns in the second quarter. Completing thirteen consecutive passes at one point, Rivers finished with a bang for the second season in a row. In impressive fashion, N.C. State capped its most successful football season in history with a 28-6 triumph.

The Sugar Bowl would be another tough encounter for Florida State, as Bobby Bowden was again forced to face an opponent that knew his every move. Former FSU offensive coordinator Mark Richt had quickly turned Georgia into a national contender, as a 20-13 loss to Florida back in November was the only thing keeping the Bulldogs from an undefeated record. In an error of poor judgment, FSU signal caller Chris Rix had failed to attend any of his final examinations, and was deemed ineligible for the game. As a result, the Seminoles had to go with Fabian Walker under center, a quarterback with an injured arm and only eighteen snaps of game action under his belt.

With a fearsome UGA defense ready to blitz away at Walker, things went bad for FSU from the very beginning. Walker was responsible for three turnovers, including a pass that was returned for a touchdown by the Georgia defense. Anquan Boldin took over the reins at quarterback for the Seminoles permanently in the second half, but was unable to overcome Georgia's 17-7 halftime lead. The Bulldogs laid claim to the No. 3 ranking in the final rankings with a 26-13 verdict, which evened the ACC's all-time bowl record in the final game of the league's first half century.

15

The Future of Atlantic Coast Conference Football

A new century has ushered in a new era of overall strength to Atlantic Coast Conference football programs, which figures to only increase in coming years. Unlike the 1990s, when their stranglehold on the league was evident to everyone, Florida State is no longer the clear-cut favorite every year to win the conference championship. Although the Seminoles stand to remain one of college football's elite programs over the next several years, the aura of invincibility that surrounded the FSU program in the 1990s among their league rivals has largely evaporated. The mere presence of the garnet and gold does not intimidate opponents like it once did, and the Seminoles realize now more than ever that they must play every game at full strength in order to maintain their place as the superior program in the conference.

Every school in the ACC has been doing a better job of recruiting talented athletes in recent years, which has made the league, from top to bottom, as solid on the gridiron as anytime in past history. With seven of the ACC's nine members appearing in bowls following the 2002 season and six more making games in 2003, the league's stock is unquestionably on the rise. With a 5-1 bowl record in 2003, the ACC posted the best postseason winning percentage of any major conference. In addition, nearly half of the league's coaches are serving at their respective alma maters, putting the loyalty and intensity of these programs at an all-time high.

At an age when most men are enjoying their retirement years, Bobby Bowden is writing the final chapters of his storybook coaching career at Florida State. Although he claims to still be in good health, and is always in great spirits, Bowden's coaching career is undoubtedly winding down. A significant transition will take place in Tallahassee when Bowden steps away, as FSU endures the struggle of maintaining its excellence following the retirement of a legendary coach. There are a number of worthy candidates to replace him, including Mark Richt of Georgia, longtime Seminole defensive coordinator Mickey Andrews, and Chuck Amato of N.C. State. In addition to filling Bowden's large shoes, the next Florida State skipper will have to continue luring many of America's finest high school gridiron talents to Tallahassee to enjoy even a whiff of the old man's success.

"It's so difficult to be the 'guy after the guy,' so to speak," comments Dr. Jerry Punch. "The coaches that replaced Bear Bryant, Shug Jordan, and John Robinson all were unable to succeed largely because they were under the cloud of their predecessor. It's much easier to replace the legend's replacement, to be the second guy after a Bryant or Bowden, than to fall immediately after them. With the task of maintaining the school's football dynasty, in addition to the added pressure of measuring up to his excellence, Coach Bowden has indicated that he does not want one of his sons to replace him at Florida State."

There are other issues at FSU aside from the looming retirement of their longtime leader. In past years, an undeniable lack of control over the Seminole players has existed among the administration and coaching staff, and although the university has avoided NCAA violations by isolating itself from the activities of the players off the field, the problem is clearly not going away. The "Big Man on Campus" complex is common at most Division I-A schools when it comes to high-profile athletes, but in the case of Florida State, the complex is reaching a dangerous turning point, from unfair to downright criminal.

Throughout their years in the ACC, FSU football players have been arrested for numerous serious offenses, ranging a large spectrum of criminal activity. Seminoles have been busted for drug possession, theft, assault and battery, and solicitation of sex. Although every major college football program can expect a bad seed or two from time to time, it is evident that Florida State deals with such cases far and away more than its league adversaries. Bowden's punishments are usually mild, from one-game suspensions to temporary leaves from the team.

Bowden rarely kicks players off his team permanently, and only does so following multiple offenses or extreme offenses, such as quarterback Adrian McPherson's stealing and forging of a check from a Tallahassee business during the 2002 season. The McPherson saga continued in 2003, as the former signal-caller was brought to trial on allegations of widespread gambling, including bets made on FSU contests.

Bowden himself was brought in to testify in the McPherson trial, and although the Seminole coach contributed to the prosecution's argument that McPherson could have played poorly to affect Florida State's ability to win, the jury was unable to reach a verdict. Nonetheless, McPherson has lost his opportunity to suit up for the garnet and gold again in the future.

To his credit, new Florida State president T. K. Wetherell has decided to intervene. In June 2003, Wetherell ordered an expansive overhaul of the Seminole sports infrastructure, citing a glaring separation between the athletic department and the university as a whole. In the future, components of the FSU athletic department, such as compliance, sports information, and student services, will report directly to the university. In addition, Wetherell has pledged to find ways to punish coaches and school officials that are complacent about rules violations, or who allow rules to be broken without acknowledging the school. Wetherell, a former player on Bill Peterson's Seminole teams of the mid-1960s, has vowed to clean up the image of his tarnished alma mater, although only time will tell if the president's proposal will create positive results.

Heading into the autumn of 2003, Bobby's son Tommy had not lived up to the high expectations placed on him at Clemson after leaving Tulane following the Green Wave's unblemished 1998 season. Clemson won only one of four bowls coached by the younger Bowden from 1999 to 2002, and had failed to seriously compete for an ACC championship during his tenure. The Tiger skipper appeared to be on the chopping block until November, when Clemson knocked off Florida State for the first time as a member of the ACC, and followed it up with impressive victories over South Carolina and Tennessee in the Peach Bowl. Bowden was rewarded after the South Carolina triumph with a three-year contract extension and his second recognition as ACC Coach of the Year. With Clemson's newfound stability, and Bowden in the driver's seat for the foreseeable future, the Tiger faithful expects their team to continue making postseason appearances and finishing among the upper echelon of the league standings.

Former linebacker Chuck Amato breathed new life into the North Carolina State program during his first four seasons in Raleigh, bringing a spirit and enthusiasm to the school's football supporters unseen in years. The school's convincing victory in the 2003 Gator Bowl completed NCSU's first eleven-win season in history, and their final ranking of No. 12 in the polls is the schools' best since the days of Lou Holtz. The city of Raleigh rewarded the team following their triumph in Jacksonville with a downtown celebration.

Amato, a protégé of Holtz and Bowden, is finally receiving long-deserved credit for his individual coaching skills. N.C. State is the first ACC program thus far to catch up with Florida State on the gridiron, becoming the first team to beat the Seminoles in consecutive seasons. Combined with their victory over FSU in 1998, N.C. State handed Florida State three of their first five losses in Atlantic Coast Conference competition. Aside of his in-depth knowledge of the FSU system from his many years spent in Tallahassee as an assistant, Amato has been a successful recruiter, bringing talent to N.C. State that is beginning to mirror that of the Seminoles in both speed and athleticism. Although the Wolfpack will sorely miss Philip Rivers, who broke every significant ACC passing record during his four-year run in Raleigh, Wolfpack fans are hopeful to see their team continue making bowls and appearing in the national polls in the coming years.

Duke finally broke its school-record twenty-three-game losing streak in 2002, but with only ten winning seasons over forty years, the Durham school has earned a dismal national reputation for football. The midseason firing of Carl Franks in 2003 brought an end to one of the most unsuccessful coaching reigns in the history of the ACC, as the Blue Devils posted a record of 7-45 under his command. Although Ted Roof came aboard and led Duke to victories over Georgia Tech and North Carolina, the school's first conference triumphs in four seasons, the team finished with a losing record for the ninth consecutive year. Duke's community of fans and alumni seem content with their current status as one of the elite basketball programs in the country, and combined with Duke's stellar academics, the football team's inability to win seems trivial to most Blue Devil supporters.

Although steps are being made to enhance the facilities in Durham with the addition of a new football center, money is not the primary issue. Duke's most important battle lies in recruiting. Blue Chip gridiron recruits are intimidated by the stuffy academic climate at Duke, and combined with the sustained ineptness of the team, it has proven difficult for the Blue Devils to acquire players that allow them to compete against their ACC foes. Until they can figure out a way to attract student-athletes in the same manner as the Duke basketball program, namely by sustained winning, the Blue Devil football program can expect to remain stagnant.

Like Duke, the University of North Carolina is a school rich in basketball tradition with a shaky football legacy. Although UNC boasts more 1,000-yard running backs than any other program in major college football history, the school has struggled to maintain the right formula for long-term gridiron success. Mack Brown revived the Tar Heel program in the 1990s, but a larger contract and the lure of better recruits shuffled him off to the University of Texas following Carolina's final regular season game in 1997. With Roy Williams now back in town to re-identify the UNC hoops legacy, John Bunting faces the same problem that has faced virtually every North Carolina football coach since the start of the school's national hardwood notoriety in the late-1950s. Winning football games is the only thing that will endear Bunting to Tar Heel fans, and in bringing in a highly-rated freshman class in 2003, the coach hopes to put UNC back on the level their fans were used to seeing their teams at under Brown.

Al Groh, like many of his conference adversaries, seems happy with the decision to return to his alma mater. Groh has unquestionably matured as a coach since his previous stint in the ACC, when he disappointed at Wake Forest. Bringing expertise and savvy that one can only acquire from the NFL, Groh has injected a new confidence into the Virginia program, evident by the solid recruiting classes he has brought to Charlottesville. The Cavalier star is rising, and Groh has put the pieces in place to thrust UVA back among the upper echelon of the ACC, where they stood for much of the 1990s under George Welsh. The Cavaliers won nine games in 2002 against one of the toughest schedules in the nation, and did so with one of the youngest teams in the country. In all, twenty-two true or redshirt freshmen saw playing time for UVA in 2002, and that experience could lead to big things in the future.

Ralph Friedgen has taken no time to rebuild the program at Maryland, and appears to be on the final stop of his long coaching trail. In only three seasons under Friedgen, the Terrapins have gone from a perennial doormat into one of the most feared teams in the conference. Friedgen, long overlooked for a head coaching position, is finally getting his just due at the place where it all started for him, College Park. Friedgen's offense is as unpredictable and productive today as it was when he was first fine-tuning it under Bobby Ross, and along with a renewed defensive presence, Maryland has become a Top Twenty-caliber program virtually overnight. With a bevy of recruiting options available in the Baltimore/Washington, D.C. area, in addition to a rejuvenated program, Maryland should have no problem attracting talented players to College Park in the coming years.

"Without question, the balance of power in the ACC is shifting to the north," says Dr. Punch. "I think Virginia is really going to surprise some people in the coming years. Also, you just can't say enough about what Ralph Friedgen has done at Maryland."

In 2001 and 2002, Jim Grobe led Wake Forest to consecutive winning seasons for the first time since the late 1980s, and appears to have found a winning formula in Winston-Salem by doing things a little differently than the majority of his rivals. The ACC has turned into a passing conference over the past several years, due to a number of talented signal callers, such as N.C. State's Philip Rivers and Virginia's Matt Schaub, entering the league. Grobe has bucked the trend, and has old-time Deacon fans remembering the days of Russell and Hopkins by sticking almost exclusively to the ground. The Demon Deacons led the ACC by amassing 241 yards a game on the ground in 2002, more than 40 above their nearest competitor. In addition, five different Wake Forest backs rushed for at least 300 yards. Although the Deacons are a few years away from competing for the league championship, Grobe has successfully passed the first test in his effort to revive the Wake Forest program.

Like Al Groh and John Bunting, Georgia Tech's Chan Gailey has arrived in the ACC from the professional ranks. As the former head coach of the Dallas Cowboys, one of the more high-profile positions in all of sports, Gailey is clearly equipped to handle the weight that comes with leading a team that expects to win. With the success of George O' Leary's Yellow Jackets fresh in the minds of GT fans and administrators, Gailey faces much of the same pressure to win in Atlanta that he did in Dallas, without the microscope of the Cowboy management breathing down his neck. Gailey, regarded for being a great teacher of the game, is also being asked to bring back some of the credibility that Georgia Tech lost after O' Leary's hiring and subsequent resignation from Notre Dame.

In discussing the long-term future of the Atlantic Coast Conference, many have indicated the need for the league to react to the changing landscape of major intercollegiate athletics over the past two decades. Television revenue has turned college football into a major cash engine for Division I-A schools, and in an effort to stabilize athletic departments from a financial standpoint, schools across the country have taken new steps to ensure their respective stake in the lucrative pool of revenue. In the 1990s, two of college football's most well-respected conferences, the Southeastern Conference and the Big Eight, expanded their memberships to include twelve schools. As a result, these conferences earned the right to host a conference championship football game by the NCAA.

The SEC and Big Twelve, as it came to be known after its expansion, have earned millions through television contracts for their championship games, and have brought prestige to their leagues unsurpassed in years past. Widely considered among the strongest football conferences in the nation, the SEC and Big Twelve consistently find several of its members ranked in the national polls, and since 1998, when the Bowl Championship Series was formed, the two conferences have been among the NCAA's most well-represented leagues. The SEC sent two of its members to the BCS following the 1998, 1999, and 2001 seasons, while the Big Twelve sent two schools in 2001 and 2003.

For the 2002-2003 academic year, the Southeastern Conference distributed a record $101.9 million to its twelve member institutions, with more than half of the staggering revenue—$52 million—coming from television. In coordinating television contracts with the networks, the conferences naturally include each of its members into the negotiations, not just the ones that have traditionally been more successful in certain sports. As a result, schools that rarely have a chance of competing in a conference championship game earn a sizable payout regardless of whether or not they ever actually participate in such a contest.

Although the ACC received the nation's highest per-school television payout during the 2002-2003 academic year, due largely to lucrative basketball contracts negotiated with FOX Sports and Raycom/Jefferson Pilot Sports, the powers that be saw an opportunity to draw even more revenue. Going largely by the models established by the SEC and Big Twelve, the Atlantic Coast Conference decided to make its own push for a conference championship football game in the spring of 2003 by expanding its membership by three schools. The presidents and chancellors of the nine standing members initially went after the University of Miami, Boston College, and Syracuse University, a trio of private schools from the Big East Conference that fit into the league's vision of institutions that combined superior academics with top-notch athletic programs.

At the time, Atlantic Coast Conference bylaws stated that seven of the league's nine members must vote favorably in order for the league to progress on an expansion project. Six schools, Clemson, Florida State, Georgia Tech, Maryland, North Carolina State, and Wake Forest, were in agreement that expansion was the way to go. None of these six institutions faced side issues or outside influence, which may have forced them away from their intended goal. Florida State was particularly eager to expand, and rumors flew that the Seminoles were entertaining thoughts of leaving the ACC should the league not include the University of Miami.

The sextet was unable to persuade Duke and the University of North Carolina from seeing it the same way. A pair of schools known more for their hardwood excellence than their prowess on the gridiron, Duke and UNC were major components of the ACC's basketball contract, and with that money already in place, those schools saw expansion as a needless dilution of their own power and influence. North Carolina chancellor James Moeser, facing staunch opposition from his own faculty against expansion, cited the move as an unnecessary evil, which would increase traveling for student-athletes, thereby keeping them out of the classroom even more than the status quo. Both schools ultimately voted against expansion, and with the league still a vote away from being able to move forward, the University of Virginia's vote suddenly became paramount to the entire process.

In the state of Virginia, where animosities between the state's two largest institutions, the University of Virginia and Virginia Tech, run rampant, the Cavalier athletic department was placed in a difficult position. According to several reputable news sources, it was evident that significant players in Virginia government, including Governor Mark Warner, were placing intense political pressure on the University of Virginia to expand the ACC if and only if Virginia Tech, another member of the Big East, was included. By leaving the Hokies out in the cold, the Virginia politicians felt that the state would be losing considerable amounts of revenue should the VT program no longer be involved in a major football conference. It is naive to think that the University of Virginia truly wanted its longtime nemesis to join the ACC, which will result in an even greater struggle over time between the two rivals to secure Virginia's finest gridiron recruits, but in the end, UVA was left with little choice. If the university wanted to expand, it would have to bring Virginia Tech along.

As ACC commissioner John Swofford and the heads of the nine league members endured tedious negotiations through conference calls, Moeser offered something of a compromise. The UNC chancellor proposed to increase the ACC's membership by one, offering only Miami a formal invitation. Although this scenario complied with UNC's long-term vision for the league, it did little to improve the ACC's chances of getting a conference championship football game, the primary goal of the expansion. In the end, those presidents and chancellors in favor of expansion had no choice but to modify their original vision for the future of the league.

On July 1, 2003, in the city where it all began, Greensboro, N.C., the Atlantic Coast Conference formally announced the expansion of two new schools, the Virginia Polytechnic Institute, more commonly known as Virginia Tech, and the University of Miami. It was the first time in history that the ACC was expanding by more than one school at a time, and was only the third time in fifty years that the league was opening its ranks to new members. Although many in the media criticized the expansion, comparing the ACC's raid of the Big East to a corporate takeover, few can deny the positive impacts it will have for the league. Already regarded among the strongest in the NCAA in the sport of basketball, expanding Virginia Tech and Miami will significantly help the ACC's efforts to solidify its future as a football power. The Hurricanes and Hokies will begin competing for Atlantic Coast Conference championships beginning in the 2004-2005 academic year, twelve months earlier than originally anticipated. With animosities between the Big East and the ACC running at an all-time high, everyone involved agreed that the expansion should take place sooner rather than later.

With five national championships over its history on the gridiron, the addition of the University of Miami is a crowning achievement in the ACC's efforts to become a major national player in football, which began with the invitation of Florida State back in 1991. With both the Seminoles and Hurricanes now serving as conference members, the ACC boasts two bona fide college football heavyweights, a pair of schools that are used to playing on the sport's biggest stages. From 1998 to 2002, either Florida State or Miami appeared in all five Bowl Championship Series national championship games, and the schools combined for two NCAA titles over this period of time.

The University of Miami was founded in 1925, and its sports teams were given the nickname "Hurricanes" to idolize the powerful tropical masses that have affected Florida's coastal landscape for centuries. The schools' predominant colors, orange and green, symbolize the orange trees that have been such a major part of South Florida's agricultural stability over the years. Since the late 1930s, Miami's football teams have played in the Orange Bowl, one of America's most recognized sporting facilities. In addition to hosting its namesake game, the Orange Bowl, from 1938 to 1996, the stadium has hosted five Super Bowls, and was the home for both the Hurricanes and the NFL's Miami Dolphins throughout the 1960s, 1970s, and into the 1980s.

After two decades as a lower-rung program, the University of Miami entered the major college football scene in 1945, and was competitive from the start. Jack Harding led the Hurricanes to 9-1 and 8-2 records in 1945 and 1946, while Andy Gustafson led the program to four Top Fifteen finishes from 1950 to 1956. Under coaches Howard Schnellenberger, Jimmy Johnson, and Craig Erickson, the Miami program launched itself into the college football stratosphere in the 1980s, earning three national championships and posting an overall record of 74-11 from 1983 to 1989. The Hurricanes continued to flourish in the early 1990s, claiming a share of a fourth NCAA title in 1991 and winning five of the first six Big East Conference championships.

Although the program lost much of its luster following an NCAA investigation and subsequent probation in 1995, Miami began to pick up steam once again in the late 1990s under the leadership of former Johnson assistant Butch Davis. Davis left the Hurricane program for the NFL's Cleveland Browns in 2001, but new head coach Larry Coker has put Miami back among the nation's elite. In 2001, Coker became the first rookie head coach in fifty-three years to win the NCAA title, and nearly duplicated the feat the following year, as his Hurricanes lost an overtime thriller to Ohio State in the 2003 Fiesta Bowl, which awarded the Buckeyes the national championship.

The annual showdown between Florida State and Miami, regarded as one of the most eagerly anticipated college football games each season, now takes its place alongside the annual Duke-North Carolina basketball rivalry as one of the most bitterly contested in all of collegiate athletics. Although FSU and Miami would have remained rivals regardless of the schools' respective conference affiliations, the fact that they now play in the same league only intensifies the struggle for supremacy between the two Sunshine State behemoths. More importantly for the ACC, sending two schools to the Bowl Championship Series is now a very realistic possibility, and the revenue from those appearances will make every conference member stronger in the long run.

The invitation to join the Atlantic Coast Conference is the culmination of a five-decade quest for Virginia Tech to gain membership to a league that, from a regional standpoint, is a perfect fit for that school. The term "Hokie," for which the school's teams are known by, represents no physical entity, and can be attributed to a fight song that was coined out of the blue by a fan in the late nineteenth century. The school employs a bird of prey, strongly resembling a turkey, as its mascot, and features maroon and burnt orange as its primary colors. Founded in Blacksburg, a small community neatly positioned in the southwestern portion of the state, Virginia Tech opened its doors in 1872 as a land-grant college. Known originally as the "Virginia Agricultural and Mechanical College," VT, like its new conference rivals in Atlanta and Raleigh, features a solid engineering program, and produces nearly half of all the Ph.D.'s in the state of Virginia.

Virginia Tech's football program played its first game in 1892, the same year that Georgia Tech, North Carolina State, and the University of Maryland also fielded their first teams. It was only four years after the historic round-robin series of games between Duke (then Trinity), Wake Forest, and the University of North Carolina, and was several decades before the advent of the programs at Miami and Florida State. From the very beginning, when the charter members chose to leave the Southern Conference in the spring of 1953, Virginia Tech was hoping to be a part of the Atlantic Coast Conference. Much like in recent times, the school received support from the University of Virginia, but in the end, VT was held out of the original exodus of the Southern.

Virginia Tech remained in the Southern Conference for another decade before finally leaving following the 1964 season. Over the next quarter century VT played football as an Independent, maintaining its rivalries with Virginia and other ACC members such as Wake Forest, Clemson, and North Carolina State. All the while, the school held out optimistic hope that one day the conference would again open up its ranks. Another opportunity arose in the late 1970s, as the league sought to fill the void left by the University of South Carolina's departure. Once again VT was snubbed, this time for Georgia Tech. Georgia Tech brought more to the table at the time, providing a larger television market in addition to a more prestigious gridiron reputation.

In 1990, Virginia Tech hooked up with seven other football-playing Independents, including the University of Miami, to create the Big East football conference. The Big East had been in place for basketball for more than a decade, although each of its new members had been playing football as Independents for years. During its tenure in the Big East, the Hokies went from an up-and-down football program to a perennial Top Ten team and national contender. Under the leadership of alumnus Frank Beamer, Virginia Tech won three Big East titles from 1995 to 1999, and played for the national championship following the 1999 season. The Hokies competed in eleven consecutive bowl games through 2003, which included a pair of visits to the Sugar Bowl and an appearance in the Orange Bowl, and won seventy-six games between 1995 and 2002, more than any other school in the Big East, including Miami.

Excited with the prospect of two new members, but unsatisfied with the conclusion of the original deal, the ACC formally petitioned the NCAA to host a conference championship football game during the summer of 2003 with eleven members. Although the official ruling wasn't to be laid down until 2004, in September the governing body gave an overwhelming recommendation against the petition. Shut out of the postseason sweepstakes with their present setup, the ACC began making alternate plans. Notre Dame was thrown around as a potential candidate to become a twelfth member, but the Irish were unwilling to relent their Independent status, along with their lucrative television contract with NBC, in order to join the conference.

Still needing a school in order to successfully petition for a championship football game, the ACC again went after Boston College, which had been lured back into the Big East after the decimation of the prior deal. Boston's media market, in addition to the renowned academic reputation of the school itself, made Boston College a neat fit into the ACC's plans once the league was forced into securing another member. League officials had fulfilled the requirement of touring the BC campus during the spring months, and on October 12, 2003, the school received a unanimous vote for acceptance. In accepting the ACC's invitation on behalf of Boston College, President Rev. William Leahy echoed the sentiments of those that have been in favor of expansion from the beginning.

"The ACC is a strong, stable conference," said Leahy. "The move to the ACC will generate greater revenues in the future."

Founded in 1863 in the direct vicinity of metropolitan Boston, BC stands as one of the oldest Jesuit Catholic institutions in the country. By the turn of the twentieth century the school had outgrown its urban location, and in 1909, ground was broken on a farm in then-rural Chestnut Hill, where the main campus lies today. Boston College fielded its first football team in 1893, and remained an Independent for nearly a full century before joining the Big East in 1990. Boston College first gained gridiron notoriety in 1940, when future Notre Dame legend Frank Leahy led the Eagles to an 11-0 record and a Top Five ranking. Two years later, Denny Myers led BC back into the Top Ten with an 8-2 mark. The school again became prominent in the 1980s, when Heisman Trophy winner Doug Flutie propelled the Eagles to a 19-5 overall record in 1983 and 1984.

With Boston College now in place, the visionary expansion process set forth by the Atlantic Coast Conference's leadership has culminated. BC will remain in the Big East for one final autumn in 2004, but will officially join the ACC as the league's twelfth member starting with the 2005 football season. Disallowed to host a title game with eleven members in 2004, the Atlantic Coast Conference anticipates hosting its first championship football contest in December of 2005. With professional stadiums stretching throughout the new ACC region in cities such as Atlanta, Baltimore, Charlotte, Jacksonville, Miami, Philadelphia, Tampa, and Washington, D.C., the league should never have a problem finding a site to host its game.

In the months following the conclusion of the expansion, the ACC negotiated a new television contract with ABC and ESPN. The deal, stretching through the 2010 season, nearly doubles the league's prior contract, and will guarantee each member of the conference more than $3 million per season over the life of the agreement. This amount does not include the current agreement with Jefferson Pilot, which will also be renegotiated in the coming years. The ACC will have six appearances on ESPN's Thursday Night Football telecasts over the next seven seasons, doubling the prior amount, and the new conference championship game will be valued at approximately $5 million per year.

In addition to a league championship football game in the coming years, the ACC will continue sending its best teams to some of the finest postseason bowls in the country well into the future. With long-standing ties to the Gator and Peach Bowls, in addition to an annual berth in a Bowl Championship Series contest, the conference will continue to be well represented in late December and on New Year's Day. The league has negotiated contracts in recent years with bowl committees in Boise, Charlotte, and Orlando, and is guaranteed to send six of its schools to postseason contests on an annual basis should that many schools finish with six victories or better.

With the prospect of increased revenue and national prominence, the next fifty years figure to bring even more promise to the members of the Atlantic Coast Conference, both new and old. The league will soon boast twelve of the finest athletic programs in the country, which combine academic integrity with a large and diverse fan base. The pieces are now in place for the ACC to become just as prominent on the gridiron as it has been for decades on the hardwood. With that in mind, the administrators, students, alumni, and fans of each Atlantic Coast Conference member institution can take pride in being part of an athletic body that should rival any in the country in the coming decades.

Appendix A: Coaching Records

Clemson

Coach	Seasons	Games	W	L	T
Frank Howard	1953-1969	172	96	71	5
Hootie Ingram	1970-1972	33	12	21	0
Red Parker	1973-1976	44	17	25	2
Charley Pell	1977-1978	23	18	4	1
Danny Ford	1978-1989	129	96	29	4
Ken Hatfield	1990-1993	46	32	13	1
Tommy West	1993-1998	59	31	28	0
Tommy Bowden	1999-2002	49	29	20	0
Totals	**50**	**555**	**331**	**211**	**13**

Duke

Coach	Seasons	Games	W	L	T
Bill Murray	1953-1965	133	80	45	8
Tom Harp	1966-1970	51	22	28	1
Mike McGee	1971-1978	88	37	47	4
Red Wilson	1979-1982	44	16	27	1
Steve Sloan	1983-1986	44	13	31	0
Steve Spurrier	1987-1989	34	20	13	1
Barry Wilson	1990-1993	44	13	30	1
Fred Goldsmith	1994-1998	56	17	39	0
Carl Franks	1999-2002	45	5	40	0
Totals	**50**	**539**	**223**	**300**	**16**

Florida State

Coach	Seasons	Games	W	L	T
Bobby Bowden	1992-2002	137	116	20	1
Totals	**11**	**137**	**116**	**20**	**1**

Georgia Tech

Coach	Seasons	Games	W	L	T
Bill Curry	1983-1986	45	23	19	3
Bobby Ross	1987-1991	58	31	26	1
Bill Lewis	1992-1994	30	11	19	0
George O'Leary	1994-2001	85	52	33	0
Mac McWorter	2001	1	1	0	0
Chan Gailey	2002	13	7	6	0
Totals	**22**	**232**	**125**	**103**	**4**

Maryland

Coach	Seasons	Games	W	L	T
Jim Tatum	1953-1955	32	27	4	1
Tommy Mont	1956-1958	30	11	18	1
Thomas Nugent	1959-1965	70	36	34	0
Lou Saban	1966	10	4	6	0
Bob Ward	1967-1968	19	2	17	0
Roy Lester	1969-1971	32	7	25	0
Jerry Claiborne	1972-1981	117	77	37	3
Bobby Ross	1982-1986	59	39	19	1
Joe Krivac	1987-1991	56	20	34	2
Mark Duffner	1992-1996	55	20	35	0
Ron Vanderlinden	1997-2000	44	15	29	0
Ralph Friedgen	2001-2002	26	21	5	0
Totals	**50**	**550**	**279**	**263**	**8**

North Carolina

Coach	Seasons	Games	W	L	T
George Barclay	1953-1955	30	11	18	1

Jim Tatum	1956-1958	30	14	15	1
Jim Hickey	1959-1966	81	36	45	0
Bill Dooley	1967-1977	124	69	53	2
Dick Crum	1978-1987	116	72	41	3
Mack Brown	1988-1997	116	69	46	1
Carl Torbush	1997-2000	35	17	18	0
John Bunting	2001-2002	25	11	14	0
Totals	**50**	**557**	**299**	**250**	**8**

North Carolina State

Coach	Seasons	Games	W	L	T
Horace Hendrickson	1953	10	1	9	0
Earle Edwards	1954-1970	173	77	88	8
Al Michaels	1971	11	3	8	0
Lou Holtz	1972-1975	48	33	12	3
Bo Rein	1976-1979	46	27	18	1
Monte Kiffin	1980-1982	33	16	17	0
Thomas Reed	1983-1985	33	9	24	0
Dick Sheridan	1986-1992	84	52	29	3
Mike O'Cain	1993-1999	81	41	40	0
Chuck Amato	2000-2002	38	26	12	0
Totals	**50**	**557**	**285**	**257**	**15**

South Carolina

Coach	Seasons	Games	W	L	T
Rex Enright	1953-1955	29	16	13	0
Warren Giese	1956-1960	50	28	21	1
Marvin Bass	1961-1965	50	17	29	4
Paul Dietzel	1966-1970	53	21	31	1
Totals	**18**	**182**	**82**	**94**	**6**

Virginia

Coach	Seasons	Games	W	L	T
Ned McDonald	1954-1955	19	4	15	0
Ben Martin	1956-1957	20	6	13	1
Dick Voris	1958-1960	30	1	29	0

Bill Elias	1961-1964	40	16	23	1
George Blackburn	1965-1970	61	28	33	0
Don Lawrence	1971-1973	33	11	22	0
Sonny Randle	1974-1975	22	5	17	0
Dick Bestwick	1976-1981	66	16	49	1
George Welsh	1982-2000	223	134	86	3
Al Groh	2001-2002	26	14	12	0
Totals	**49**	**540**	**235**	**299**	**6**

Wake Forest

Coach	Seasons	Games	W	L	T
Tom Rogers	1953-1955	30	10	17	3
Paul Amen	1956-1959	40	11	26	3
Bill Hildebrand	1960-1963	40	7	33	0
Bill Tate	1964-1968	50	17	32	1
Cal Stoll	1969-1971	32	15	17	0
Tom Harper	1972	11	2	9	0
Chuck Mills	1973-1977	55	11	43	1
John Mackovic	1978-1980	34	14	20	0
Al Groh	1981-1986	66	26	40	0
Bill Dooley	1987-1992	67	29	36	2
Jim Caldwell	1993-2000	89	26	63	0
Jim Grobe	2001-2002	24	13	11	0
Totals	**50**	**538**	**181**	**347**	**10**

Appendix B: Season Records

NOTE: This appendix indicates the full season records for each school, NOT the individual Atlantic Coast Conference standings.

BOLD print indicates recognized Atlantic Coast Conference regular season champion (ties indicated by **two bold** names).

W	Wins
L	Losses
T	Ties
PS	Points Scored
PA	Points Allowed
*	Serving ACC or NCAA Probation
**	Forfeited ACC Victories
***	NCAA Champions (Associated Press or Coaches)

1953

Team	W	L	T	PS	PA
***Maryland	10	1	0	298	38
Duke	7	2	1	217	81
South Carolina	7	3	0	198	97
North Carolina	4	6	0	173	187
Wake Forest	3	6	1	123	157
Clemson	3	5	1	139	172
N.C. State	1	9	0	80	263
Virginia	1	8	0	75	242

-Virginia did not officially begin ACC play until 1954

1954

Team	W	L	T	PS	PA
Duke	**8**	**2**	**1**	**270**	**161**
Maryland	7	2	1	280	67
South Carolina	6	4	0	172	153
Clemson	5	5	0	193	121
North Carolina	4	5	1	140	222
Virginia	3	6	0	113	162
Wake Forest	2	7	1	129	165
N.C. State	2	8	0	104	193

1955

Team	W	L	T	PS	PA
Maryland	**10**	**1**	**0**	**217**	**77**
Duke	**7**	**2**	**1**	**280**	**67**
Clemson	7	3	0	206	144
North Carolina	3	7	0	117	208
Wake Forest	5	4	1	131	157
South Carolina	3	6	0	120	209
* N.C. State	4	5	1	206	193
Virginia	1	9	0	96	201

1956

Team	W	L	T	PS	PA
Clemson	**7**	**2**	**2**	**167**	**101**
South Carolina	7	3	0	126	67
Duke	5	4	1	184	100
N.C. State	3	7	0	94	169
Virginia	3	7	0	92	167
Wake Forest	2	5	3	91	102
Maryland	2	7	1	68	168
North Carolina	2	7	1	99	183

1957

Team	W	L	T	PS	PA
* N.C. State	7	1	2	155	67
Clemson	7	3	0	216	79
Duke	6	3	2	182	135
North Carolina	6	4	0	142	129
Maryland	5	5	0	119	144
South Carolina	5	5	0	202	167
Virginia	3	6	1	117	164
Wake Forest	0	10	0	64	225

1958

Team	W	L	T	PS	PA
Clemson	8	3	0	169	138
South Carolina	7	3	0	168	116
North Carolina	6	4	0	195	109
Duke	5	5	0	128	131
Maryland	4	6	0	132	175
Wake Forest	3	7	0	124	163
* N.C. State	2	7	1	120	160
Virginia	1	9	0	89	301

1959

Team	W	L	T	PS	PA
Clemson	9	2	0	285	103
South Carolina	6	4	0	170	169
Wake Forest	6	4	0	218	178
Maryland	5	5	0	184	188
North Carolina	5	5	0	198	142
Duke	4	6	0	104	159
* N.C. State	1	9	0	117	201
Virginia	0	10	0	80	393

1960

Team	W	L	T	PS	PA
Duke	8	3	0	173	114
* N.C. State	6	3	1	148	113
Clemson	6	4	0	197	124
Maryland	6	4	0	171	164
South Carolina	3	6	1	117	186
North Carolina	3	7	0	117	161
Wake Forest	2	8	0	119	215
Virginia	0	10	0	103	332

1961

Team	W	L	T	PS	PA
Duke	7	3	0	183	106
Maryland	7	3	0	156	141
Clemson	5	5	0	199	126
North Carolina	5	5	0	121	141
N.C. State	4	6	0	129	149
South Carolina	4	6	0	128	187
Virginia	4	6	0	123	190
Wake Forest	4	6	0	103	159

1962

Team	W	L	T	PS	PA
Duke	8	2	0	199	105
Clemson	6	4	0	168	130
Maryland	6	4	0	170	128
Virginia	5	5	0	194	167
South Carolina	4	5	1	187	148
N.C. State	3	6	1	108	139
North Carolina	3	7	0	112	206
Wake Forest	0	10	0	66	278

1963

Team	W	L	T	PS	PA
North Carolina	**9**	**2**	**0**	**197**	**103**
N.C. State	**8**	**3**	**0**	**188**	**107**
Clemson	5	4	1	181	140
Duke	5	4	1	230	198
Maryland	3	7	0	148	201
Virginia	2	7	1	76	169
South Carolina	1	8	1	104	170
Wake Forest	1	9	0	37	318

1964

Team	W	L	T	PS	PA
N.C. State	**5**	**5**	**0**	**119**	**194**
Maryland	5	5	0	164	126
North Carolina	5	5	0	172	178
Virginia	5	5	0	163	214
Wake Forest	5	5	0	172	178
Duke	4	5	1	148	135
South Carolina	3	5	2	95	176
Clemson	3	7	0	105	135

1965

Team	W	L	T	PS	PA
Duke	6	4	0	216	157
N.C. State	**6**	**4**	**0**	**134**	**110**
Clemson	**5**	**5**	**0**	**117**	**137**
** South Carolina	5	5	0	151	167
Maryland	4	6	0	132	164
North Carolina	4	6	0	146	195
Virginia	4	6	0	170	189
Wake Forest	3	7	0	88	204

1966

Team	W	L	T	PS	PA
Clemson	**6**	**4**	**0**	**174**	**177**
Duke	5	5	0	164	237
N.C. State	5	5	0	191	168
Maryland	4	6	0	180	204
Virginia	4	6	0	214	235
Wake Forest	3	7	0	90	162
North Carolina	2	8	0	90	196
South Carolina	1	9	0	95	216

1967

Team	W	L	T	PS	PA
N.C. State	9	2	0	214	94
Clemson	**6**	**4**	**0**	**166**	**128**
South Carolina	5	5	0	159	156
Virginia	5	5	0	172	169
Duke	4	6	0	143	153
Wake Forest	4	6	0	175	256
North Carolina	2	8	0	104	182
Maryland	0	9	0	46	231

1968

Team	W	L	T	PS	PA
Virginia	7	3	0	329	222
N.C. State	**6**	**4**	**0**	**205**	**185**
Clemson	4	5	1	184	179
Duke	4	6	0	214	287
South Carolina	4	6	0	204	226
North Carolina	3	7	0	178	272
Wake Forest	2	7	1	212	228
Maryland	2	8	0	171	299

1969

Team	W	L	T	PS	PA
South Carolina	**7**	**4**	**0**	**189**	**195**
North Carolina	5	5	0	200	164
Clemson	4	6	0	178	250
Duke	3	6	1	161	224
N.C. State	3	6	1	183	201
Maryland	3	7	0	100	249
Virginia	3	7	0	115	270
Wake Forest	3	7	0	125	279

1970

Team	W	L	T	PS	PA
North Carolina	8	4	0	372	227
Duke	6	5	0	229	252
Wake Forest	**6**	**5**	**0**	**191**	**241**
South Carolina	4	6	1	285	253
Virginia	5	6	0	240	187
N.C. State	3	7	1	90	179
Clemson	3	8	0	164	313
Maryland	2	9	0	112	241

1971

Team	W	L	T	PS	PA
North Carolina	**9**	**3**	**0**	**288**	**152**
Duke	6	5	0	170	149
Wake Forest	6	5	0	218	178
Clemson	5	6	0	155	202
N.C. State	3	8	0	147	274
Virginia	3	8	0	134	272
Maryland	2	9	0	224	283

-South Carolina left the ACC before the 1971 season began

1972

Team	W	L	T	PS	PA
North Carolina	**11**	**1**	**0**	**324**	**210**
N.C. State	8	3	1	409	240
Maryland	5	5	1	243	217
Duke	5	6	0	132	156
Clemson	4	7	0	143	245
Virginia	4	7	0	199	276
Wake Forest	2	9	0	88	339

1973

Team	W	L	T	PS	PA
N.C. State	**9**	**3**	**0**	**396**	**251**
Maryland	8	4	0	335	141
Clemson	5	6	0	231	263
North Carolina	4	7	0	242	266
Virginia	4	7	0	199	300
Duke	2	8	1	132	204
Wake Forest	1	9	1	73	326

1974

Team	W	L	T	PS	PA
N.C. State	9	2	1	317	241
Maryland	**8**	**4**	**0**	**312**	**150**
Clemson	7	4	0	246	250
North Carolina	7	5	0	364	279
Duke	6	5	0	201	208
Virginia	4	7	0	207	239
Wake Forest	1	10	0	74	348

1975

Team	W	L	T	PS	PA
Maryland	**9**	**2**	**1**	**312**	**150**
N.C. State	7	4	1	260	210
Duke	4	5	2	197	212
North Carolina	3	7	1	207	272

Wake Forest	3	8	0	221	264
Clemson	2	9	0	177	381
Virginia	1	10	0	175	428

1976

Team	W	L	T	PS	PA
Maryland	**11**	**1**	**0**	**294**	**115**
North Carolina	9	3	0	243	220
Duke	5	5	1	234	245
Wake Forest	5	6	0	177	206
Clemson	3	6	2	172	237
N.C. State	3	7	1	205	258
Virginia	2	9	0	106	266

1977

Team	W	L	T	PS	PA
Clemson	8	3	1	228	163
North Carolina	**8**	**3**	**1**	**251**	**102**
Maryland	8	4	0	254	179
N.C. State	8	4	0	259	181
Duke	5	6	0	231	221
Virginia	1	9	1	56	280
Wake Forest	1	10	0	113	270

1978

Team	W	L	T	PS	PA
Clemson	**11**	**1**	**0**	**368**	**131**
Maryland	9	3	0	261	167
N.C. State	9	3	0	280	208
North Carolina	5	6	0	199	216
Duke	4	7	0	108	247
Virginia	2	9	0	139	236
Wake Forest	1	10	0	104	274

1979

Team	W	L	T	PS	PA
North Carolina	8	3	1	290	167
Clemson	8	4	0	205	116
Wake Forest	8	4	0	240	283
Maryland	7	4	0	198	135
N.C. State	**7**	**4**	**0**	**258**	**213**
Virginia	6	5	0	258	134
Georgia Tech	4	6	1	152	190
Duke	2	8	1	152	264

-Georgia Tech did not officially begin ACC play until 1983

1980

Team	W	L	T	PS	PA
North Carolina	**11**	**1**	**0**	**297**	**130**
Maryland	8	4	0	211	165
Clemson	6	5	0	217	222
N.C. State	6	5	0	222	212
Wake Forest	5	6	0	251	213
Virginia	4	7	0	144	259
Duke	2	9	0	214	296
Georgia Tech	1	9	1	113	260

1981

Team	W	L	T	PS	PA
***Clemson	**12**	**0**	**0**	**338**	**105**
North Carolina	10	2	0	375	140
Duke	6	5	0	210	230
Maryland	4	6	1	232	294
N.C. State	4	7	0	182	223
Wake Forest	4	7	0	217	365
Georgia Tech	1	10	0	124	308
Virginia	1	10	0	127	261

1982

Team	W	L	T	PS	PA
Clemson	**9**	**1**	**1**	**289**	**147**
Maryland	8	4	0	373	220
North Carolina	8	4	0	348	149
Duke	6	5	0	307	290
Georgia Tech	6	5	0	239	286
N.C. State	6	5	0	206	255
Wake Forest	3	8	0	200	286
Virginia	2	9	0	208	320

-Clemson was ineligible for a bowl following the 1982 regular season

1983

Team	W	L	T	PS	PA
* Clemson	9	1	1	338	200
Maryland	**8**	**4**	**0**	**316**	**253**
North Carolina	8	4	0	337	216
Virginia	6	5	0	252	280
Wake Forest	4	7	0	257	281
Duke	3	8	0	246	350
Georgia Tech	3	8	0	222	313
N.C. State	3	8	0	236	246

1984

Team	W	L	T	PS	PA
Maryland	**9**	**3**	**0**	**380**	**280**
Virginia	8	2	2	337	216
* Clemson	7	4	0	346	215
Georgia Tech	6	4	1	296	201
Wake Forest	6	5	0	205	232
North Carolina	5	5	1	234	274
N.C. State	3	8	0	263	311
Duke	2	9	0	128	301

1985

Team	W	L	T	PS	PA
Georgia Tech	9	2	1	252	132
Maryland	**9**	**3**	**0**	**326**	**192**
Virginia	6	5	0	262	317
Clemson	6	6	0	244	222
North Carolina	5	6	0	224	223
Duke	4	7	0	193	252
Wake Forest	4	7	0	212	249
N.C. State	3	8	0	186	305

1986

Team	W	L	T	PS	PA
Clemson	**8**	**2**	**2**	**296**	**187**
N.C. State	8	3	1	328	274
North Carolina	7	5	0	305	279
Georgia Tech	5	5	1	282	211
Maryland	5	5	1	262	211
Wake Forest	5	6	0	325	295
Duke	4	7	0	200	284
Virginia	3	8	0	198	315

1987

Team	W	L	T	PS	PA
Clemson	**10**	**2**	**0**	**333**	**176**
Virginia	8	4	0	292	276
Wake Forest	7	4	0	201	185
Duke	5	6	0	301	243
North Carolina	5	6	0	214	207
Maryland	4	7	0	194	301
N.C. State	4	7	0	212	302
Georgia Tech	2	9	0	199	275

1988

Team	W	L	T	PS	PA
Clemson	**10**	**2**	**0**	**342**	**157**
N.C. State	8	3	1	312	175
Duke	7	3	1	324	324
Virginia	7	4	0	251	244
Wake Forest	6	4	1	282	238
Maryland	5	6	0	260	304
Georgia Tech	3	8	0	200	194
North Carolina	1	10	0	217	391

1989

Team	W	L	T	PS	PA
Clemson	**10**	**2**	**0**	**368**	**138**
Virginia	10	3	0	371	272
Duke	8	4	0	377	335
Georgia Tech	7	4	0	265	213
N.C. State	7	5	0	290	230
Maryland	3	7	1	215	238
Wake Forest	2	8	1	194	319
North Carolina	1	10	0	138	297

1990

Team	W	L	T	PS	PA
*** Georgia Tech	**11**	**0**	**1**	**379**	**186**
Clemson	10	2	0	333	109
Virginia	8	4	0	464	227
N.C. State	7	5	0	298	189
North Carolina	6	4	1	227	186
Maryland	6	5	1	237	284
Duke	4	7	0	240	295
Wake Forest	3	8	0	247	351

1991

Team	W	L	T	PS	PA
Florida State	11	2	0	449	188
Clemson	**9**	**2**	**1**	**317**	**181**
N.C. State	9	3	0	304	322
Virginia	8	3	1	327	167
Georgia Tech	8	5	0	283	214
North Carolina	7	4	0	282	199
Duke	4	6	1	231	280
Wake Forest	3	8	0	195	300
Maryland	2	9	0	138	302

-Florida State did not officially begin ACC play until 1992

1992

Team	W	L	T	PS	PA
Florida State	**11**	**1**	**0**	**446**	**186**
North Carolina	9	3	0	289	233
N.C. State	9	3	1	335	211
Wake Forest	8	4	0	266	260
Virginia	7	4	0	341	229
Clemson	5	6	0	261	213
Georgia Tech	5	6	0	237	286
Maryland	3	8	0	292	365
Duke	2	9	0	265	343

1993

Team	W	L	T	PS	PA
***Florida State	12	1	0	536	129
North Carolina	10	3	0	431	253
Clemson	9	3	0	198	192
N.C. State	7	5	0	278	327
Virginia	7	5	0	317	217
Georgia Tech	5	6	0	260	286
Duke	3	8	0	214	349
Maryland	2	9	0	243	479
Wake Forest	2	9	0	199	318

1994

Team	W	L	T	PS	PA
Florida State	**10**	**1**	**1**	**428**	**200**
N.C. State	9	3	0	305	275
Virginia	9	3	0	370	195
Duke	8	4	0	380	241
North Carolina	8	4	0	374	267
Clemson	5	6	0	164	188
Maryland	4	7	0	270	326
Wake Forest	3	8	0	143	373
Georgia Tech	1	10	0	185	319

1995

Team	W	L	T	PS	PA
Florida State	**10**	**2**	**0**	**563**	**246**
Virginia	**9**	**4**	**0**	**378**	**270**
Clemson	8	4	0	303	219
North Carolina	7	5	0	284	220
Georgia Tech	6	5	0	260	243
Maryland	6	5	0	210	251
Duke	3	8	0	282	386
N.C. State	3	8	0	260	354
Wake Forest	1	10	0	190	360

1996

Team	W	L	T	PS	PA
Florida State	**11**	**1**	**0**	**446**	**174**
North Carolina	10	2	0	357	123
Clemson	7	5	0	245	241
Virginia	7	5	0	341	203
Georgia Tech	5	6	0	220	236
Maryland	5	6	0	187	239
N.C. State	3	8	0	268	401
Wake Forest	3	8	0	144	374
Duke	0	11	0	162	379

1997

Team	W	L	T	PS	PA
Florida State	**11**	**1**	**0**	**468**	**181**
North Carolina	11	1	0	348	146
Virginia	7	4	0	277	242
Clemson	7	5	0	292	319
Georgia Tech	7	5	0	314	296
N.C. State	6	5	0	325	268
Wake Forest	5	6	0	245	288
Duke	2	9	0	223	341
Maryland	2	9	0	161	355

1998

Team	W	L	T	PS	PA
Florida State	11	2	0	401	161
Georgia Tech	10	2	0	426	295
Virginia	9	3	0	358	247
North Carolina	7	5	0	288	283
N.C. State	7	5	0	366	352
Duke	4	7	0	229	319
Clemson	3	8	0	218	272
Maryland	3	8	0	202	290
Wake Forest	3	8	0	235	335

1999

Team	W	L	T	PS	PA
***Florida State**	12	0	0	458	203
Georgia Tech	8	4	0	461	361
Virginia	7	5	0	345	365
Wake Forest	7	5	0	266	209
Clemson	6	6	0	322	253
N.C. State	6	6	0	244	302
Maryland	5	6	0	292	260
Duke	3	8	0	217	363
North Carolina	3	8	0	186	272

2000

Team	W	L	T	PS	PA
Florida State	**11**	**2**	**0**	**511**	**136**
Clemson	9	3	0	416	253
Georgia Tech	9	3	0	386	237
N.C. State	8	4	0	379	338
North Carolina	6	5	0	269	284
Virginia	6	6	0	242	292
Maryland	5	6	0	247	284
Wake Forest	2	9	0	181	362
Duke	0	11	0	155	430

2001

Team	W	L	T	PS	PA
Maryland	**10**	**2**	**0**	**413**	**266**
Florida State	8	4	0	403	304
Georgia Tech	8	5	0	405	281
North Carolina	8	5	0	337	271
Clemson	7	5	0	369	339
N.C. State	7	5	0	319	257
Wake Forest	6	5	0	292	311
Virginia	5	7	0	249	331
Duke	0	11	0	212	491

2002

Team	W	L	T	PS	PA
Maryland	11	3	0	451	228
N.C. State	11	3	0	460	238
Florida State	**9**	**5**	**0**	**428**	**301**
Virginia	9	5	0	402	348
Clemson	7	6	0	330	349
Georgia Tech	7	6	0	280	267
Wake Forest	7	6	0	356	327
North Carolina	3	9	0	223	421
Duke	2	10	0	227	353

Bibliography

NOTE: All Web site citations include the last date accessed in parentheses ( ).

"About Bobby Bowden." Florida State Seminoles Official Athletic Site. 2003. seminoles.ocsn.com/sports/m-footbl/mtt/fsumfootbl sbowden.html (23 March 2003).

"About the AFCA—Past Executive Directors." American Football Coaches Association. 2000. www.afca.com/lev3.cfm/343 (17 July 2003).

"ACC Decade in Review—1990s." Lindy Sports, D.M.D. Publications. 2000. www.lindyssports.com/features/acc_decade_review.html (3 May 2003).

"ACC 50th Anniversary Football Team." Official Athletic Coast Conference Web Site. 2002. theacc.ocsn.com/sports/m-footbl/specrel/072302aag.html (9 January 2003).

"ACC has 12 to Stage Title Football Game." ESPN Internet Ventures. 2003. http://espn.go.com/ncaa/news/2003/1012/1636467.html (15 October 2003).

"ACC Statistics 2002." ESPN Internet Ventures. 2003. sports.espn.go.com/ncf/statistics?group=1 (16 January 2003).

"ACC Welcomes Virginia Tech and Miami." Techsideline.com, Maroon Pride, LLC. 2003. www.techsideline.com/news/2003/2003 0702news.htm (3 July 2003).

"Ageless Wonder—Weinke Takes Long Way to College Football Stardom." CNN/Sports Illustrated, an AOL/Time Warner Company. 2001.sportsillustrated.cnn.com/football/college/2000/heismannews /2000/12/07/heisman_weinke_ap/ (23 April 2003).

"Aloha Bowl 1999. www.geocities.com/CollegePark/Quad/6028/alohabowl.html (15 May 2003).

Apple, Charles. "The 1978 Gator Bowl." Chuck's Football Page. 2002. capple.mybravenet.com/gatorbowl.html (9 January 2003).

Asheville Citizen-Times, 15 August 2002.

Athens (GA) Banner-Herald, 31 August 2002.

Atlanta Journal and Constitution, 9 September 1990-2 January 2003.

"A Whole Different Landscape." CNN/Sports Illustrated, an AOL/ Time Warner Company. 2001. sportsillustrated.cnn.com/football/ college/2001/bowls/news/2001/12/26/thisweek_acc/ (2 May 2003).

"Big East Conference." ELibrary, a service of Alacritude LLC. 2003. www.infoplease.com/ipsa/A0758349.html (24 April 2003).

"Bluebonnet Bowl 1980." Mack Brown Texas Football. 1998-2003. www.mackbrowntexasfootball.com/pages/winningtrads/bowl games/80blue.html (2 March 2003).

"Boston College: A History From the Ground Up." Marketing Communications and the Trustees of Boston College. 2002. http:// www.bc.edu/about/history/ (15 October 2003).

Brewer, Rick. "Tar Heels Get Wild Gator Bowl Win." TarHeelBlue. com. 2003. tarheelblue.ocsn.com/sports/m-footbl/spec-rel/010303 aaa.html (17 January 2003).

"Buff Bowl No. 3-1957 Orange Bowl." The Official Athletic Site of the University of Colorado Buffaloes. 2003. cubuffs.ocsn.com/sports/ m-footbl/spec-rel/122302aaa.html (20 February 2003).

"Carquest Bowl 1996." University of Virginia Football. 2002. Virginia sports.ocsn.com/sports/m-footbl/archive/va-m-footbl96carquest .html (9 May 2003).

Charleston News and Courier, 25 September 1966-3 January 1989.

"Clemson Football All-Americans." clemson_football.tripod.com/Clem sonfootball/id2.html (27 February 2003).

"Clemson Perfect in Championship Game." Orange Bowl Committee. 2003. www.orangebowl.org/OB.php?sec=years&year=1982 (17 January 2003).

"Clemson Wins in 1978!" Gator Bowl Gazette. 2002. www.gatorbowl. com/34th.htm (9 January 2003).

"Clemson Wins in 1986!" Gator Bowl Gazette. 2002. www.gatorbowl. com/42nd.htm (9 January 2003).

"Clemson Wins in 1989!" Gator Bowl Gazette. 2002. www.gatorbowl. com/45th.htm (9 January 2003).

"Clemson's 25 Greatest Players of the 20th Century." The Tiger Online Edition. 2003. clemsontigers.ocsn.com/genrel/102299aaa.html (9 January 2003).

Clemson University Football Media Guide, 2003.

"Coach Hayes." Ohio State Archive. 2003. www.bucknuts.com/osu history/coachhayes.htm (17 April 2003).

College Football Data Warehouse. 2001-2003. www.cfbdatawarehouse. com (5 October 2003).

"Colorado Holds Off Incredible Clemson Comeback." Orange Bowl Committee. 2003. www.orangebowl.org/OB.php?sec=years&year =1957 (9 January 2003).

"Continental Tire Bowl 2002." ESPN Internet Ventures. 2003. sports. espn.go.com/ncf/bowls02/bowl?game=continental (15 May 2003).

"Danny Ford." Tiger Tales. 2003. www.geocities.com/clemsontiger tales/ford.htm (17 April 2003).

Decatur (AL) Daily, 26 June 2003.

"Dishing Out the Discipline." Microsoft Corporation. 2003. espn.go. com/ncf/s/2001/1126/1284797.html (17 April 2003).

Doughty, Doug. "Sorry to Say, Ducharme Injury Reminiscent of McGonnigal." Virginia Insider Online. 1999. www.roanoke.com/ uvainsider/0114dd.html (18 April 2003).

"Duke Turns Nebraska Blue." Orange Bowl Committee. 2003. www. orangebowl.org/OB.php?sec=years&year=1955 (9 January 2003).

Duke University Football Media Guide, 2001, 2003.

Durham Herald-Sun, 24 April 2003.

Finney, Peter. "The Fighting Tigers II: LSU Football, 1893-1980." Baton Rouge, La.: Louisiana State University Press, 1980.

"Florida Citrus Bowl 1983." Official Web Site of the University of Tennessee Volunteers. 2003. utsports.ocsn.com/genrel/121401aaa. html (9 January 2003).

"Florida State at Virginia, November 2, 1995." ESPN Productions. 1995. (Aired on ESPN Classic, 24 November 2002).

Florida State University Football Media Guide, 2000, 2001, 2003.

"Frank Howard, the Legend." Tigernet. 2003. www.thetigernet.com/ football/history/howard.jsp (17 July 2003).

Freeman, Criswell (compiler and editor). *The Book of Football Wisdom.* Nashville, Tenn.: Walnut Grove Press, 1996.

"Gator Bowl 1999." CNN/Sports Illustrated, a Time Warner Company. 1999. sportsillustrated.cnn.com/football/college/1998/bowls/gator/ news/1999/01/01/gator_bowl/ (14 May 2003).

"Gator Bowl 2000." CNN/Sports Illustrated, an AOL/Time Warner Company. 2000. sportsillustrated.cnn.com/football/college/1999/ bowls/gator/news/2000/01/02/gator_follow_ap/ (15 May 2003).

"Gator Bowl 2001." Techsideline.com, Maroon Pride LLC. 2001. www.techsideline.com/football/2000/games/clemsonrecap.htm (15 May 2003).

"Gator Bowl 2002." ESPN Internet Ventures. 2003. espn.go.com/ncf/bowls01/gator.html (15 May 2003).

"Gator Bowl 2003." ESPN Internet Ventures. 2003. sports.espn.go.com/ncf/bowls03/bowl?game=gator (15 May 2003).

Georgia Institute of Technology Football Media Guide, 2001, 2003.

"Georgia Tech at Virginia, November 3, 1990." CBS Productions. 1990. (Aired on ESPN Classic, 7 August 2003).

"Georgia Wins in 1971!" Gator Bowl Gazette. 2002. www.gatorbowl.com/27th.htm (9 January 2003).

"Hall of Fame Bowl 1977." Official Web Site for the University of Minnesota Athletics. 2002. www.gophersports.com/history/mfball/1977HallOfFameasp?sport_id=mfball (9 January 2003).

Hassell, Lou. "Bluebonnet Bowl." The Handbook of Texas Online. 2002. www.tsha.utexas.edu/handbook/online/articles/view/BB/xxb1.html (9 January 2003).

Haynes, Tony. "Behind the Scenes with Tony Haynes: N.C. State and the 50th Anniversary Team." The Official Athletics Web Site of North Carolina State University. Student Advantage, Inc. 2003. gopack.ocsn.com/genrel/070102aaa.html (17 July 2003).

Heath, Frank. "Frank's Football Faves—Favorite Moments from Tar Heel Football History." TarHeelDaily.com. 2002. tarheeldaily.com/article.html?aid=1547 (4 April 2003).

Heath, Frank. "Frank's Football Faves II—Favorite Moments from Tar Heel Football History." TarHeelDaily.com. 2002. tarheeldaily.com/article.html?aid=1585 (30 March 2003).

Heath, Frank. "Images in the Snow—Remembering the 1970 Peach Bowl." TarheelDaily.com. 2002. www.tarheeldaily.com/article.html?aid=1139 (9 January 2003).

"Herman's College Career Notes." The Herman Moore Unofficial Homepage. 2003. www.geocities.com/Colosseum/Track/6059/collegenotes.html (18 April 2003).

Hudson, Don. "The Season in Review." Georgia Tech Alumni Association. 1991. gtalumni.org/StayInformed/techtopics/spr91/review.html (29 March 2003).

"Humanitarian Bowl 2001." CNN/Sports Illustrated, an AOL/Time Warner Company. 2002. sportsillustrated.cnn.com/football/college/2001/bowls/humanitarian/ (15 May 2003).

"Independence Bowl 1985." Official Web Site for the University of Minnesota Athletics. 2002. www.gophersports.com/history/mfball/1985Independence.asp?sport_id=mfball (9 April 2003).

Independent Florida Alligator, 21 November 1996.

"Jim Grobe Profile." Wake Forest Demon Deacons Official Athletic Web Site. 2003. wakeforestsports.ocsn.com/sports/m-footbl/mtt/ grobe_jim00.html (13 April 2003).

Kallestad, Brent. "Florida State Hit with NCAA Penalties." Kernel Press, Inc. 1996. www.kernel.uky.edu/1996/spring/0320/s3f.html (16 January 2003).

Kallestad, Brent. "Florida State Reorganizes Athletic Department." *Associated Press* (17 July 2003).

"Ken Hatfield." Tiger Tales. 2003. www.geocities.com/clemsontiger tales/hatfield.htm (17 April 2003).

Kohn, Theodore. "A Firsthand Account of the 1961 Sigma Nu Prank." GamecockInsider.com. 2002. southcarolina.theinsiders.com/2/765 14.html (9 January 2003).

Lancaster, Mark. "1967 Liberty Bowl Brought Future Together." Athens Daily News. 1998. www.onlineathens.com/1997/09139709 13.liberty.html (9 January 2003).

Lubbock Avalanche-Journal, 29 December 2000.

Major College Football Results—1957 to 1981. Kinston, N.C.: OPUS Associates, Inc., 1982.

"Maryland Wins in 1975!" Gator Bowl Gazette. 2002. www.gatorbowl. com/31st.htm (12 January 2003).

McGrew, David. "1977: The Drought Ends." The Official Athletic Site of Clemson University. 2002. clemsontigers.ocsn.com/sports/m footbl/spec-rel/101002aaa.html (10 October 2002).

"Miami Football History." The Official Athletic Site of the University of Miami. Student Advantage, Inc. 2003. hurricanesports.ocsn.com /sports/m-footbl/archive/043002aaa.html (25 September 2003).

"Micron PC Bowl 1999." CNN/Sports Illustrated, an AOL/Time Warner Company. 2000. sportsillustrated.cnn.com/football/college/re caps/1999/12/30/vvb_iic/ (15 May 2003).

Miller, Jeff. *Sunshine Shootouts.* Marietta, Ga. Longstreet Press, Inc., 1992.

Milwaukee Journal-Sentinel, 2 January 1995-29 December 1998.

Mitchell, Daniel. "Seminoles Start Season Armed with Unity, Pride." Florida State Times. 1995.www.fsu.edu/~fstime/FSTimes/Volume 1/Issue3/Seminoles.html (17 April 2003).

"More Memorable Clemson Performances in Bowl Games Over the Years." The Official Athletic Site of Clemson University. 2003. clemsontigers.ocsn.com/sports/m-footbl/spec-rel/122499aaa.html (20 February 2003).

Morris, Jeannie. *Brian Piccolo: A Short Season.* Chicago: Bonus Books, 1995.

Munson, Don. "Orange Memories—The Terps." InsideTiger
    Sports.com. 2003. www.insidetigersports.com/InsideTigerSports
    2001/articles/orangememories/memories_111102.htm (27 March
    2003).
New York Daily News, 24 April 2003
New York Herald Tribune, 9 May 1953.
New York Times, 11 October 2003.
"No. 1 Maryland Stopped by Tough Sooner Defense." Orange Bowl
    Committee. 2003. www.orangebowl.org/OB.php?sec=years&year
    =1954 (9 January 2003).
North Carolina State University Football Media Guide, 2003.
"North Carolina Wins in 1963!"   Gator Bowl Gazette. 2002.
    www.gator bowl.com/19th.htm (9 January 2003).
"North Carolina Wins in 1979!" Gator Bowl Gazette. 2002. www.gator
    bowl.com/35th.htm (9 January 2003).
"North Carolina Wins in 1981!" Gator Bowl Gazette. 2002. www.gator
    bowl.com/37th.htm (9 January 2003).
"Oahu Bowl 2000." ESPN Internet Ventures. 2000. espn.go.com/ncf/
    bowls00/oahu.html (15 May 2003).
"Oklahoma Flurry Breaks Open Game." Orange Bowl Committee.
    2003.   www.orangebowl.org/OB.php?sec=years&year=1958   (9
    January 2003).
"Oklahoma Keeps Streak(ing)." Orange Bowl Committee. 2003. www.
    orangebowl.org/OB.php?sec=years&year=1956 (9 January 2003).
"Oklahoma Wins in 1991!" Gator Bowl Gazette. 2002. www.gator
    bowl.com/47th.htm (9 January 2003).
Pace, Lee. "John Bunting: The Carolina Years, Part III." Official Site
    of Tar Heel Athletics. 2003. tarheelblue.ocsn.com/sports/extra
    points/spec-rel/040901aaa.html (6 February 2003).
"Peach Bowl 1976." University of Kentucky Athletics Association On-
    line. 2003. ukathletics.ocsn.com/sports/m-footbl/archive/071802
    aaf.html (6 March 2003).
"Peach Bowl 1995." University of Virginia Football. 2002. virginia
    sports.ocsn.com/sports/m-footbl/archive/va-m-footbl-95peach.html
    (3 May 2003).
"Peach Bowl 1999." The Official Athletic Site of Clemson University.
    2003.   clemsontigers.ocsn.com/sports/m-footbl/recaps/123099aaa.
    html (15 May 2003).
"Peach Bowl 2000." CBS Sportsline. 2003. www.sportsline.com/coll
    egefootball (15 May 2003).

"Peach Bowl 2001." CNN/Sports Illustrated, an AOL/Time Warner Company. 2002. sportsillustrated.cnn.com/football/college/2001/bowls/peach/ (15 May 2003).

"Peach Bowl 2002." Morris Digital Works. 2003. govols.fanaticzone.com/data/football/stories/recap_244057.shtml (15 May 2003).

"Peach Bowl 2002." ESPN Internet Ventures. 2003. sports.espn.go.com/ncf/bowls02/bowl?game=peach (15 May 2003).

Perrin, Tom. *Atlantic Coast Conference Football: A History Through 1991.* Jefferson, N.C.. McFarland and Company, Inc., 1992.

"Pro Football Player and Philanthropist Warrick Dunn." Teen Ink. 2003. www.teenink.com/Past/2002/September/Heroes/ProFootball Dunn.html (23 March 2003).

Raleigh News and Observer, 26 September. 1954—2 January. 1990.

Rappoport, Ken. *Tar Heel: North Carolina Football.* Huntsville, AL.: The Strode Publishers, Inc. 1976.

Rappoport, Ken. *The Nittany Lions: A Story of Penn State Football.* Tomball, Tx.: The Strode Publishers, Inc., 1987.

"Rexlamation Point! 2002 Orange Bowl." Orange Bowl Committee. 2003. www.orangebowl.org/OB.php?sec=years&year=2002 (15 May 2003).

"Rodney Williams: 2000 Clemson Hall of Fame Inductee." The Official Athletic Web Site of Clemson University. 2003. clemsontigers.ocsn.com/genrel/061900aaa.html (17 April 2003).

"Ross Eyes 1991 Season." Georgia Tech Alumni Association. 1991. gtalumni.org/StayInformed/techtopics/fall91/ross.html (3 April 2003).

"Royal Remembrances: Celebrating the Fortieth Anniversary of the Queen's Game." University of Maryland Libraries. 2002. lib.umd.edu/ARCV/univarch/exhibits/queen/ (17 April 2003).

"SBC Cotton Bowl Classic Hall of Fame—The Players—Lance Alworth." SBC Cotton Bowl Committee. 2002. www.cottonbowl.com/hof_players.asp#alworth (9 January 2003).

"Seattle Bowl 2001." CNN/Sports Illustrated, an AOL/Time Warner Company. 2001. sportsillustrated.cnn.com/football/college/2001/bowls/seattle/ (15 May 2003).

"Seattle Bowl 2002." ESPN Internet Ventures. 2003. sports.espn.go.com/ncf/bowls02/bowl?game=seattle (15 May 2003).

"Seminole's Bentley Hopes to Add Another National Title to Career." Sports Server Archive. 1996. archive.sportserver.com/newsroom/ap/fbo/1996/col/acc/feat/archive/123096/acc69279.html (23 March 2003).

"Short Tenure—O'Leary Out at Notre Dame After One Week." CNN/ Sports Illustrated, an AOL/Time Warner Company. 2001. sportsill ustrated.cnn.com/football/college/news/2001/12/14/oleary_notreda me/ (16 May 2003).

Sikes, Phillip. "Clemson Great Has Gone From 'The Judge' to 'Mister.'" The Official Athletic Site of Clemson University. 2003. clemsontigers.ocsn.com/sports/m-footbl/spec-rel/090302aad.html (3 Sept. 2002).

"Silicon Valley Football Classic 2002." ESPN Internet Ventures. 2003. sports.espn.go.com/ncf/bowls02/bowlgamesilicon (15 May 2003).

Southwestern Bell Cotton Bowl Classic Media Guide, 2002.

Stewart, Cricket. "1981 Revisited." The Official Athletic Site of Clemson University. 2003. clemsontigers.ocsn.com/genrel/1981-revisited-stewart.html (15 January 2003).

Mississippi State University Football Media Guide, 2002.

"Sugar Bowl 2003." ESPN Internet Ventures. 2003. sports.espn.go.com /ncf/bowls02/bowl?game=sugar (15 May 2003).

"Sun Bowl 1978." Mack Brown Texas Football. 1998-2003. www. mackbrowntexasfootball.com/pages/winningtrads/bowlgames/78 sun.html (2 April 2003).

"Sun Bowl 1994." Mack Brown Texas Football, 1998-2003. www. mackbrown-texasfootball.com/pages/winningtrads/bowlgames/94 sun.html (1 May 2003).

Switzer, Barry. *Bootlegger's Boy.* New York: William Morrow and Company, Inc., 1990.

Tallahassee Democrat, 27 November 2002.

"Tangerine Bowl 1979." Wake Forest Demon Deacons Official Athletic Site. 2003. wakeforestsports.ocsn.com/sports/m-footbl/archiv e/history/wake-m-footbl-bowlgames.html (9 January 2003).

"Tangerine Bowl 2000." CNN/Sports Illustrated, an AOL/Time Warner Company. 2003. sportsillustrated.cnn.com/football/college /2001/bowls/tangerine/ (15 May 2003).

"Tangerine Bowl 2002." ESPN Internet Ventures. 2003. sports.espn.go. com/ncf/bowls02/bowl?game=tangerine (15 May 2003).

"Tiger Timeline." Tigernet.com. 1995-2002. www.tigernet2.com/foot ball/history/timeline.jsp (9 January 2003).

"The Catch to Dual Firings-Ranking the Games." The State Online. 2003. www.thestateonline.com/rivalry100/rankings.htm (11 January 2003).

The Chronicle (Duke Independent Newspaper), 12 October 2003.

"The Rivers Report." The Official Athletic Web Site of North Carolina State University. 2002. gopack.ocsn.com/sports/m-footbl/spec-rel/102902aad.html (29 October 2002).

The Roanoke Times, 25 September 2000.

"The Space Cowboy—A Tribute to Michael Ray Voight." CarolinaFan. com. 2000. www.carolinafan.com/f/tributes/voight/mike_voight. html (14 January 2003).

"The Way Things Used To Be." The Tiger Online Edition. 2003. www. thetigernews.com/vnews/display.v/ART/2002/11/22/3dddadee521a (9 January 2003).

"Torry Holt's College Records." Deridden Web Operations. 1999. www.angelfire.com/biz3/deridden/collegerecords.html (27 April 2003).

Two Cousins College Football Emporium. 2003. 2cuz.com/teams/teams.html (25 September 2003).

"Unforgettable Moments." The Tiger Online Edition. 2003. www. thetigernews.com/vnews/display.v/ART/2002/11/22/3dddaeb9180 4 (9 January 2003).

University of Maryland Football Media Guide, 2001, 2003.

University of North Carolina Football Media Guide, 2001, 2003.

University of Virginia Football Media Guide, 2002.

USA Today, 22 April 2003-10 February 2004.

Vancil, Mark (editor). *ABC Sports College Football All-Time All-American Team.* New York: Hyperion Books., 2000.

"Vidnovik is Triple Threat in Win at Maryland." TarHeelBlue.com. 2003. tarheelblue.ocsn.com/genrel/092501aaa.html (17 January 2003).

"Virginia Bowl Games—1984 Peach Bowl." University of Virginia Cavaliers Official Athletic Web Site. 2002. virginiasports.ocsn.com/ sports/m-footbl/archive/va-m-footbl-84peach.html (28 January 2003).

"Virginia Bowl Games—1990 Citrus Bowl." University of Virginia Cavaliers Official Athletic Web Site. 2002. virginiasports.ocsn.com/ sports/m-footbl/archive/va-m-footbl-90citrus.html (18 April 2003).

"Virginia Tech First to Jump into the ACC." ESPN Internet Ventures. 2003. msn.espn.go.com/ncaa/news/2003/0627/1573771.html (25 September 2003).

"Wake Forest Football All-Americans." Wake Forest Demon Deacons Official Athletic Web Site. 2003. wakeforestsports.ocsn.com/sport s/m-footbl/archive/history/wake-m-footbl-allameric.html (9 January 2003).

Wake Forest University Football Media Guide, 2001, 2003.
"Wake Forest Wins Thriller." Raleigh News and Observer Online.
    2002. sports.newsobserver.com/sports/college/wfu/story/1855778
    p1851671c.html (13 January 2003).
Washington Post, 20 September 1953-3 January 2002.
"What's a Hokie?" The Official Site of the Virginia Tech Hokies. 2003.
    www.hokiesports.com/whatsahokie.html (25 September 2003).

Index

Abbey, Don, 75
Abdullah, Khalid, 273
Abdur-Ra'oof, Azizuddin, 187,
    191, 196
Abraham, Clifton, 253, 255-257,
    259, 264-265, 271
Adams, Aaron, 288
Adams, Bill, 138
Addison, Jimmy (The Needle),
    68-74, 76
Agee, Tommie, 185
Alcamo, Louis, 123
Aldredge, Scott, 235
Aldridge, Bryant, 11
Alexander, Bennie, 311
Alexander, Bill, 302
Alexander, Derrick, 271
Alexander, Ellis, 103-105, 123
All-American Bowl (Birmingham,
    Ala.), 143, 198, 208, 225, 236
Allen, Anthony, 182
Allen, Demetrius, 275, 280
Allen, Terry, 203-210, 212-214,
    221
Allison, Rod, 138
Aloha Bowl (Honolulu, Hawaii),
    182, 203, 247, 311
Althouse, Don, 13
Altman, Don, 38, 41-42
Alworth, Lance, 41-42
Amato, Chuck, 72, 321-322, 330,
    340-341, 344, 348-350, 363

Ambush, Leroy, 328
Amen, Paul, 17, 364
American Broadcasting Corporation
    (ABC), 150, 268, 299, 327
American Football Coaches
    Association (AFCA), 67
American Football Conference
    (AFC), 192, 324
American Football League (AFL),
    41
Ammons, Billy, 81
Anderson, Frosty, 111
Anderson, Gary, 171
Anderson, Jack, 81
Anderson, Jason, 326
Anderson, John, 96
Anderson, Mel, 199
Anderson, Sam, 34
Andrews, Gus, 61
Andrews, Mickey, 348
Andrews, Richie, 210
Angelo, Lou, 93, 102
Anthony, Reidel, 287
Anthony, Tyrone, 184
Appalachian State University (ASU),
    151, 244
Ariri, Obed, 139, 144, 146, 149
Arizona State University (ASU), 93-
    94, 288, 311
Armstrong, Lon, 35, 43
Arnold, Bill, 96-97
Arrington, Jimmy, 70

Arrington, Joel, 33
Arrowhead Stadium (Kansas City,
  Miss.), 336
Arthur, Gary, 72
Ashby, Page, 66
Associated Press (AP) Poll, 27, 29,
  110, 117, 133, 167, 239, 254,
  263, 271, 288, 307
Astrodome (Houston, Tex.), 73, 92,
  162
Atchley, Dr. Bill, 171, 178
Atherton, John, 53
Atkins, Steve, 124-125, 128-129,
  135-136, 146-147
Atkinson, Jess, 183-184, 186-189
Auburn University, 73, 101, 153,
  155, 185-186, 267, 296, 307,
  335
Augustin, Allen, 341
Austin, Cliff, 149, 165, 167, 172,
  177-181
Avellini, Bob, 113, 117-123
Avery, Bob, 129
Avery, Tol, 159
Aycock, William, 57
Ayers, Mike, 164

Badanjek, Rick, 182-183, 186-187,
  189-191, 193, 195-198
Bahr, Chris, 121, 126
Bailey, Tommy, 89
Baker, David, 24
Baker, Shannon, 250
Baldwin, Clarence, 182
Baldwin, Robert, 266
Ball, Jerry, 34
Baltimore Ravens, 291
Barbary, Bill, 21
Barber, Ronde, xix
Barber, Tiki, xix, 272, 274-278, 284
Barchuk, Tony, 75, 77
Barclay, George, 10, 362
Barden, Ricky, 139
Barger, Jerry, 9-11
Barlow, Danny, 168
Barlow, Ray, 53, 57-58

Barnes, Bill, 17, 59, 284
Barnes, Gary, 33, 35
Barnes, Joe, 107
Barnes, Octavius, 265, 269, 285
Barnette, Jamie, 299
Barrios, Gregg, 238
Barwick, Brooks, 168, 179
Bass, Buddy, 10
Bass, Don, 132
Bass, Marvin, 64, 363
Bates, Chad, 282
Battle, Bill, 122
Battles, Harold, 279
Baul, Reggie, 262
Bauman, Charlie, 149-150
Baumgartner, Wayne, 151-153, 157
Baylor University, 13, 156-157
Baylor, Valdez, 199
Bayuk, John (The Beast), 18-19
Beamer, Frank, 204, 357
Beard, Kevin, 339
Beasley, Fred, 9
Beasley, Gene, 204
Beathard, Pete, 47
Beaver Stadium (University Park,
  Pa.), 75, 114
Beaver, Jeff, 74
Beckham, Gordon, 170
Bednarik Award, 332, 344
Bedsole, Hal, 47
Beightol, Lynn, 13
Beitia, Xavier, 329, 336, 338-339
Bell, Atrews, 309, 315-318, 329
Bell, Trumane, 263
Bell, Wayne, 68
Bell, William, 230-231, 233, 235-
  238, 252
Bellamy, Mike, 227
Benish, Dan, 168
Bennett, Ben, 166, 179, 183, 278,
  319
Bennett, Byron, 263
Bennett, John, 56
Benson, Kevin, 125
Bentley, Scott, 255, 260, 262-263,
  278, 286, 289

Berlin, Brock, 335
Berry, Jean, 38, 48, 50
Bestwick, Dick, 152, 364
Bethea, Ryan, 207
Betterson, Jim (Boom Boom), 123
Betty, Dale, 33-34
Biddle, Tom, 137-140
Big East Conference, 343, 353-358
Big Eight Conference, 111, 172, 248,
     254, 352
Big Seven Conference, xix, 11, 14,
     18, 25
Big Ten Conference, 20, 44, 87, 98-
     99, 149, 194, 249, 269
Big Thursday, 17, 27, 33
Big Twelve Conference, xix, 319,
     352-353
Bilbo, Damarius, 343
Biletnikoff, Fred, 63
Billy Goat (Navy Mascot), 39
Black, Gary, 52-53, 56, 58
Black, Len, 11
Blackburn, George, 363
Blaik, Red, 10
Blake, Jeff, 247
Blanchard, Tony, 90
Blazer, Phil, 24, 26
Blount, Alvin, 191, 195-196, 198
Bluebonnet Bowl (Houston, Tex.),
     35, 50, 122, 156, 161
Blundin, Matt, 221, 247
Blunt, Rodney, 246
Bly, Dre', xix, 285, 296
Bobby Dodd Stadium (Atlanta, Ga.),
     211, 301, 329
Bodine, Rob, 245
Boldin, Anquan, 323, 340, 342, 344
Bolin, Doug, 246
Bomar, David, 304
Bomar, Gayle, 78, 96
Bowers, Charlie, 80
Boniol, Chris, 236
Boone, Roger, 219
Bootlegger's Boy, 160
Borders, Chesley, 327
Borg, Randy, 111

Bost, Ed, 33-34
Bostic, Jeff, 143
Bostic, Joe, 143
Boston College (BC), 28, 177-178,
     196, 259-261, 267, 301, 353,
     358
Boulware, Michael, 341
Boulware, Peter, 281-282, 284, 286,
     290-291
Bourbon Street (New Orleans, La.),
     289
Bowden Bowl, 310
Bowden, Ann, 310
Bowden, Bobby, xi, xx, 128, 210,
     241-243, 252-253, 255, 258,
     260, 263-264, 266-268, 270-
     271, 274-275, 277, 281, 283-
     284, 286, 288, 290, 293, 298-
     300, 303, 307, 309-310, 312,
     314, 316, 318, 323, 330, 335,
     337-340, 344, 347-350, 362
Bowden, Dave, 106
Bowden, Steve, 86
Bowden, Tommy, 307, 310, 319,
     335, 349, 361
Bowersox, Jack, 2, 5
Bowl Alliance, 277, 285-286, 302
Bowl Championship Series (BCS),
     xx, 150, 302-304, 311, 319,
     323, 341, 353, 355-356, 359
Bowl Coalition, 249, 277, 302
Bowman Gray Stadium
     (Winston-Salem, N.C.), 63
Boxhold, Charlie, 5, 7-8
Bradley, Tommy, 103
Brafford, Bill, 97, 100
Braine, Dave, 55
Bramson, Bernardo, 65
Branton, Joey, 71
Braselton, Fred, 28, 32
Bratkowski, Zeke (The Brat), 4
Bratton, Melvin, 190-191, 197
Braxton, Jim, 87
Breedlove, Brad, 246
Brewster, Doug, 211
Brian Piccolo Award, 60

Brian's Song, 59
Bridgers, John, 241-242
Brigham Young University (BYU),
    208, 258, 315
Brindise, Noah, 295
Brinkley, Larry, 56
Broadway, Rod, 137
Brodhead, Bob, 22
Brooks, Aaron, 284-285
Brooks, Derrick, xix, 254, 256, 264-
    265, 271, 281
Brooks, Jonathan, 140
Brooks, Kevin, 278
Brooks, Robert, 214
Brown, Bob, 44
Brown, Bubba, 145, 147
Brown, Chris, 221, 246
Brown, Dave, 218-220, 223-225, 246
Brown, Derek, 238
Brown, Eddie, 191
Brown, Gene, 102
Brown, Jim, 13
Brown, Josh, 341
Brown, Lester (The Rubber Duck),
    135-136, 139-140, 142-148, 209
Brown, Mack, 213, 253, 265, 273,
    282-283, 290, 293, 296, 351,
    363
Brown, Ray, 186
Brown, Ted, 128-129, 135-136, 138,
    143, 145, 148, 150
Brown, Tom, 49
Brown, Willie, 47
Browning, Art, 42
Broyles, Frank, 41
Bruce, Earle, 143
Bryant, Antonio, 333
Bryant, Dwayne, 244
Bryant, Jeff, 165, 169,
Bryant, Kelvin, 158-162, 167-168,
    171, 180
Bryant, Paul (Bear), 30, 61, 74, 109,
    118, 141, 163, 335, 348
Bryson, Shawn, 306
Buckey, Dave, 104, 106-107, 110,
    114, 120, 127

Buckey, Don, 107, 123, 127
Buckley, Terrell, 264
Buffalo Bills, 192
Bullard, Wilbur, 161
Bunting, John, 90, 97-98, 100, 102,
    325, 351-352, 363
Burch, Dave, 43-44
Burden, Willie, 103-104, 107, 110,
    113, 115
Burke, Greg, 239
Burnim, Adrian, 277
Burnop, Frank, 109
Burns, Joe, 315, 321, 329
Burress, Lloyd, 139
Burris, Jeff, 258-259
Burrus, Alan, 169
Busby, Thad, 266, 272, 282-287,
    289-292, 294-297, 318
Bush, Daryl, 291
Bush, Devin, 257, 262
Bussey, Charlie, 17-18
Butler, Jerry, 142, 144, 146-147, 167
Butler, Kevin, 177
Butler, Leroy, 210, 264
Byrd, Dennis, 65, 77
Byrd, Harry Clifton (Curley), xvii, 7-
    8
Byrd Stadium (College Park, Md.),
    6, 12, 21, 103, 118, 121, 123 ,
    129, 131, 146, 180, 182, 184,
    187, 196, 326

Caan, James, 60
Cackovic, Frank, 21
Calabrese, Jay, 66-67
Caldwell, Alan, 138-139
Caldwell, Jim, 364
Caldwell, John T., 57
Calhoun, John C., xvi
Calvert, Charles, xvii
Cameron, DeChane, 212, 232, 237
Campbell, Joe, 118, 124, 128, 130
Campbell, Kelly, 308
Candler, Steedley, 74
Cannon, Billy, 29
Cappelletti, John, 114-115

Cappleman, Bill, 81
Capuano, Mark, 77
Cardiac Kids, 107
Carlson, Rick, 80
Carlton, Ike, 313
Carmichael, Tommy, 73
Carney, Mike, 146
Carolina Stadium (Columbia, S.C.).
    See Williams-Brice Stadium.
Carpenter, Charlie, 28,
Carpenter, Dick, 25
Carpenter, Ron, 77, 80
Carquest Bowl (Miami, Fla.), 279,
    288
Carr, Brad, 128
Carter, Anthony, 157
Carter, Dexter, 209
Carter, Harry Clifton, 69
Carter, Henry, 204
Carter, Jimmy, 73
Carter, Kerry, 334
Carter, Louis, 112-113, 117-118,
    120-122
Carter, Wilbert James, 69
Carter-Finley Stadium (Raleigh,
    N.C.), 69, 74, 80, 110, 114, 145,
    153-154, 201, 300, 332, 341
Case, Everett, 20
Case, Johnny, 56
Cassidy, Mark, 104
Castro, Dale, 158, 161
Cavanaugh, Matt, 142-143
Chandler, Jeff, 311
Chaney, Jeff, 309, 311, 313, 316,
    318
Chapman, Bill, 107
Chapman, Erik, 200
Chapman, Max, 57
Charlotte Observer, 10
Charron, Mike, 85
Chatham, Mike, 154
Cherry Bowl (Pontiac, Mich.), 198
Cherry, Tom, 75
Chesley, Castleman D., xii
Chiaverini, Len, 49
Chicago Bears, 60

Chief Osceola, 303
Childers, Wilson, 70-71
Chinese Bandits, 29
Christenson, Matt, 140
Christy, Dick, 20-24
Cigar Bowl (Tampa, Fla.), 37
Cignetti, Frank, 128
Citrus Bowl (Orlando, Fla.), xix,
    186-187, 208, 214, 227, 229,
    236, 238, 242, 246, 248, 305
Civil War, xv, xvii
Claiborne, Jerry, xi, 103, 109, 113-
    114, 117-118, 120, 123-130,
    132, 139, 141, 147-148, 158,
    180, 182, 210, 229, 362
Clark, Dwight, 146-147
Clark, Reggie, 233
Clarke, Frank, 18
Clay, Willie, 230, 232
Clement, Ryan, 273, 288
Clemson, Tom, xvi
Clemson University (CU), xi-xii,
    xvi, xviii, xx, 3-4, 13, 15-19,
    21-23, 25-35, 39, 43-49, 51, 53-
    54, 56, 61, 64-74, 76-77, 80-81,
    83-84, 86, 89, 100-101, 105,
    114, 119, 121-122, 126, 131,
    135-136, 139-150, 155-157,
    160-161, 163-173, 175-182,
    185-186, 188-189, 192-193,
    197-215, 221-222, 225-226,
    231-233, 237, 239, 239, 243-
    246, 248, 250, 253, 256, 261,
    264, 266, 268, 272, 279, 282-
    283, 288, 291, 293, 296, 301,
    307, 310, 312, 318-319, 321,
    330, 334-335, 337-338, 342,
    349, 353, 357, 361, 365-381
Cleveland Browns, 356
Cline, Doug, 31, 34
Clymer, Lee, 78
Coaches Poll, 50, 58, 229, 239, 254,
    263, 271
Cobb, Reggie, 220
Cobourne, Avon, 342
Coca-Cola Classic (Tokyo), 246

Cockrell, Alan, 187
Cody, Tay, 310, 315, 323
Coes, Richard, 262
Cofer, Mike, 203
Coker, Larry, 338-339, 356
Cole, Travis, 321
Coleman, Jim, 17
Coleman, Marco, 230-231,
Coles, Laveranues, 291, 300-301,
    309
Coley, James, 205
Collar, John, 21
College Board, 64
College Division, 37, 53
College Football Hall of Fame, xi
College of William and Mary
    (W&M), 17, 22, 43, 100, 109,
    220, 272
College World Series, 31
Collins, Gary, 34
Collins, Mel, 138-139
Collinsworth, Chris, 161
Colonna, Dave, 225
CBS (Columbia Broadcasting
    System), 180, 234
Columbia University, 3
Combs, Fred, 77
Connie Mack Stadium (Philadelphia,
    Pa.), 58
Connor, Bill, 11
Continental Tire Bowl (Charlotte,
    N.C.), 342
Cook, Howard, 18
Cooper, Andre, 267-268, 273-274,
    276-278, 280-282
Cooper, Gary, 206-209, 212-214
Copper Bowl (Tucson, Ariz.), 225-
    226
Coplin, Lennard, 132
Cordileone, Lou, 31, 33
Corlew, Tim, 210
Corrigan, Gene, 234, 249
Costa, Frank, 257
Cotton Bowl (Dallas, Tex.), 41, 131-
    132, 249, 260, 269, 285
Cotton, Clarence, 123

Covington, Al, 187, 194
Covington, John, 258
Covington, Keeta, 190-191, 194
Covington, Scott, 304
Cowan, Tim, 182
Cowart, Sam, 291-293, 295
Cox, Curmoe, 344
Cox, Doug, 183
Cox, Greg, 197
Cox, Wyatt, 27-28
Craig, Art, 74
Craig, Roger, 172
Craven, Ken, 100, 102
Crawford, Craig, 167
Crawford, Jason, 326
Crenshaw, Jermaine, 315
Crisson, Stan, 49
Crite, Brendon, 165
Crockett, Zack, 265-266, 268
Cross, Dr. George, 7-8
Crowe, Dale, 177
Crowell, Jermaine, 265, 273, 284,
    286
Crum, Denny, 160
Crum, Dick, 157, 160-161, 169, 261,
    363
Culliver, Calvin, 118
Culver, Rodney, 219
Cumberland College, xviii
Cummings, Jack, 24, 26, 31
Curci, Fran, 130, 137
Curry, Bill, 158, 188, 229, 362
Curry, Buddy, 138
Curry, Kentrell, 320
Curry, Ronald, 304, 308
Curtis, Mike, xix, 47-49
Cuthbert, Randy, 219, 221-223, 225

D' Antonio, Jim, 41
D' Addio, Dave, 183-184
Dabiero, Angelo, 47
Dagneault, Doug, 34
Dallas Cowboys, 334, 352
Daly, Ray, 195
Daniels, Calvin, 159
Danielson, Gary, 274

Dantzler, Woodrow, 335
Darling, Devaughn, 323
Davenport, Najeh, 317
Davenport, Oscar, 288, 294
Davey, Rohan, 321
Davidson College, 302
Davie, Bob, 267
Davies, Bo, 84
Davis, Andre, 313
Davis, Billy, 173
Davis, Bob, 68
Davis, Butch, 272, 317, 356
Davis, Chip, 209, 211
Davis, Danny, 132
Davis, Harrison, 101
Davis, Jack, 12
Davis, Jeff (The Judge), 163-166, 172
Davis, Ricky, 118
Davis, Rodney, 343
Davis, Steve, 74
Davis, Tony, 110-111
Dawkins, Sean, 248
Dawson, Len, 9-10
Dawson, Lin, 138
Dean, Terry, 260
Dearment, Don, 71
Dennis, Russ, 13
Denson, Autry, 305
DeRatt, Jimmy, 102-104
Derrick, Julius, 23
Dess, Darrell, 20
Deters, Harold, 61, 66, 71
Devane, William, 172, 181
Devine, Mike, 115
Devonshire, Jake, 67
Dewberry, John, 188, 198
DiCarlo, Mark, 106
Dick, Larry, 124-127, 130, 141
Dickey, Doug, 85
Dicks, Happy, 73
Dietzel, Paul, xii, 29, 79, 83-84, 87, 97, 363
Dillard's Department Store, 309-310
Dilweg, Anthony, 205, 212, 218
Divito, Paul, 124-125

Dixon, Corey, 254
Dixon, King (Whiz), 15, 28
Dixon, Todd, 246
Doak-Campbell Stadium (Tallahassee, Fla.), 256, 259, 267-268, 272, 286, 300-301, 303, 330, 339-340, 342
Dockery, Settle, 75
Dodd, Bobby, 39
Doering, Chris, 278
Donnan, Jim, 75, 77
Donofrio, Lou, 6
Donoghue, Jim, 124
Donovan, Dan, 227
Dooley, Bill, xi, 84, 92, 95-96, 98, 100-102, 105, 108, 111, 136-138, 141, 254, 363-364
Dooley, Stan, 177
Dooley, Vince, 84, 95, 101, 142
Dorsett, Tony, 142, 157
Dorsey, Ken, 317, 338-339
Dostal, George, 163
Dotter, Donnie, 131
Dowler, Boyd, 18
Downtown Athletic Club (New York, N.Y.), 261
Dreisbach, Scott, 271
Drewer, Milt, 22
Driscoll, Eddie, 22
DuBose, Jimmy, 127
Duckett, Kenny, 159
Duffner, Mark, 325, 362
Dugans, Ron, 301, 303, 305, 313-315,
Duke, James B., xvii
Duke Stadium. See Wallace-Wade Stadium
Duke University, xi, xv-xvii, 1, 9-12, 14-15, 18, 22-26, 31, 33, 37-45, 47-51, 54-57, 62-67, 70-71, 73-74, 81, 83-85, 90-92, 101, 106, 114-115, 121, 127, 130, 136, 139-140, 145, 156, 161, 165-166, 171, 179, 183, 189, 196-197, 199-201, 205, 212, 217-226, 233, 246, 249, 256, 266-

267, 269, 272, 282, 292, 300,
308-309, 318, 326, 329, 333,
337, 342, 350, 353-354, 356-
357, 361, 365-381
Duncan, Tim, 322
Dunn, Mike, 140
Dunn, Warrick, xix, 255-256, 259-
260, 263, 266-268, 270-277,
279, 282-284, 286-287, 289-291
DuPre, Billy, 84-87
Dupree, Joe, 236
Durant, Darian, 327
Durham, Woody, xiii, 30
Dutton, John, 111
Dye, Pat, 185

Easley, Chuck, 189-190
East Carolina University (ECU),
106, 110, 115, 151, 159, 167,
247
Eastern Michigan University, 326
Eastman, Bill, 69
Eberdt, Sam, 11
Edge, John, 18
Edge, Junior, 50-53-56, 58
Edmunds, Dave, 22
Edmunds, Ferrell, 194, 197-198
Edwards, Brad, 208
Edwards, Dr. R. C., 76
Edwards, Earle, 20, 24, 39, 55, 60-
62, 66, 69, 75-78, 80, 109, 363
Edwards, Lavell, 208
Edwards, Mario, 277, 306
Edwards, T.J., 231-232
Edwards, Terrence, 320
Eley, Monroe, 93
Elias, Bill, 363
Elkins, Mike, 213
Elkins, Rod, 158-159, 167-168
Ellender, Bennie, 99
Elliott, Bob, 32, 40, 44-45,
Ellis, Greg, 296
Ellis, Todd, 207, 214
Ellison, Omar, 270
Ellsworth, Percy, 276
Elrod, Craig, 85

Enright, Rex, 363
Eppley, Mike, 178-179, 185, 188
Ericcson Stadium (Charlotte, N.C.),
342
Erickson, Dennis, 317, 355
Erway, Don, 11
Esiason, Norman (Boomer), 180,
182-187
ESPN, xx, 170, 177, 274, 277, 293
Evans, Johnny, 136, 138, 143
Everett, Jim, 194-195

Faircloth, Bob, 53
Faloney, Bernie, 2, 4-8
Falzarano, Pete, 56, 59-60
Farris, Phil, 138
Farris, Ray, 40, 45
Fast Break Offense, 15
Faucette, Chuck, 195-196
Faucette, Floyd, 28,
Faulk, Kevin, 288
Favre, Brett, 237
Feaster, Dee, 273, 291
Felton, Ralph, 3, 5-6, 8
Fenner, Derrick, 203
Ferguson, Chip, 209-210
Ferguson, Jason, 280
Fiesta Bowl (Tempe, Ariz.), 156,
249, 277-279, 302-305, 307,
356
Findley, Dean, 42
Finkelston, Tim, 224, 227
Finn, Mike, 137
Fisher, Jimmy, 118
Fisher, Luke, 247
Fishman, Jerry, 53
Fitzpatrick, Paul, 74
Flagler, Terrence, 199-201, 203,
Fletcher, Terrell, 269
Florida Institute in Tallahassee, xviii
Florida State University (FSU), xi-
xiii, xviii-xx, 21, 56, 63, 66, 73,
81, 85, 88-89, 185, 190, 209-
211, 241-243, 248-268, 270-
323, 326-327, 329-332, 335-

342, 344, 347-350, 353, 355-
357, 362, 378-381
Flowers, Kenny, 197, 199, 201, 203
Floyd, Anthony, 337
Floyd, William, 252, 254-257, 262
Flutie, Doug, 177-178, 201, 358
Folckomer, Sonny, 26
Fontes, Frank, 88-89
Foot Locker, 264-265
Footman, Dan, 254
Ford, Danny, xii, 148, 150, 163, 169-
170, 173, 175-176, 178, 197,
199, 202, 206-209, 211-213,
226-227, 243-244, 253, 279,
335, 361
Ford, Davy, 318
Ford, John, 208
Fordham, Todd, 282, 287
Fowler, Leon, 249
FOX Sports, 353
Foyle, Bob, 65
Frambrough, Don, 116
Franklin, Jamie, 124, 126
Franks, Carl, 350, 361
Frazier, Tommy, 254, 260-263
Fresno State University, 192, 343
Friedgen, Ralph, 230, 321, 323-325,
329, 331-332, 336, 351, 362
Frier, Matt, 249, 257
Fritts, Stan, 107, 111, 114, 116, 123
Fry, Hayden, 79, 215
Fuller, Steve, 139, 142-147, 149-150
Fuller, William, 181
Fullington, Darrell, 191
Fulton County Stadium (Atlanta,
Ga.), 131, 247
Furman University, 13, 18, 28, 34,
158, 209, 302
Futrell, Bill, 47-50, 57

Gabriel, Roman, 32, 39-41, 44, 48,
116
Gaca, Giles, 24
Gaddis, Mike, 214, 247
Gaffney, Jabar, 335
Gailey, Chan, 334, 352, 362

Gaillard, Jerry, 161, 169
Gale, Marion, 152
Gambino, Lu, 14
Garcia, Randy, 141
Garcia, Raphael, 275, 277, 284-286
Garden State Bowl (E. Rutherford,
N.J.), 156
Gardner, Talman, 327, 329-330, 337-
338
Gardocki, Chris, 209, 212-214, 221,
226, 232, 237
Gargano, John, 114
Garner, Gil, 42, 47, 50
Garrett, Ken, 91, 100
Garrison, Wilton, 10
Garvin, Bryan, 244
Gary, Guilian, 325, 327-328, 330-
332
Gaskell, Richie, 6
Gasque, Mike, 167
Gatewood, Tom, 99
Gator Bowl (Jacksonville, Fla.), xix,
2, 7, 19, 57-58, 63, 101, 112,
127, 142-143, 148-150, 156-
157, 164, 171, 202, 208, 225-
226, 242, 247, 253, 261, 279,
288, 296, 312, 321, 335, 349,
359
Gay, P. J., 137
Geathers, Jason, 339
Gelbaugh, Stan, 188-190, 195-198
George, Jeff, 227, 237
George, Tony, 303
George Washington University
(GW), xv, 6, 14
Georgia Dome, 280
Georgia Institute of Technology
(GT). See Georgia Tech
Georgia Tech (GT), xi, xiii, xviii, 1,
10, 14, 23, 28, 32, 39, 43-44,
49-50, 65, 68-69, 73, 131, 158,
188-189, 192, 198-200,
204-205, 211, 213, 220, 222-
223, 229-239, 244-248, 252,
256, 267, 272-273, 274, 282,
284-285, 292-293, 296, 301-

303, 305, 307-308, 312, 315-316, 318, 321, 324-325, 328-329, 333-334, 340, 343, 350, 352-353, 356-357, 362, 374-381
Geyer, Scott, 226
Giants Stadium (E. Rutherford, N.J.), 255
Gibbs, Gary, 247
Gibson, Claude, 39
Gibson, Derrick, 306, 315
Giese, Warren, 15, 363
Gilchrist, Jerry, 234, 238
Glacken, Scotty, 54, 57
Glassford, Bill, 11
Glenn, Joe, 164
Glinka, Dave, 44
Glover, Kevin, 193
Godsey, George, 301, 315-316, 334
Goff, Ray, 280
Gogolak, Charlie, 76
Golden, Dan, 66
Golden, Don, 112
Goldsmith, Fred, 266, 361
Goldstein, Al, 30
Golmont, Tony, 60
Goodman, Bobby, 253
Goodrich, Dwayne, 306
Goolsby, Brent, 237
Gore, Buddy, 68-69, 71-74, 76, 80
Goshay, Derek, 231
Graham, Earnest, 335
Graham, Shayne, 313
Gramatica, Bill, 291
Grant Field (Atlanta, Ga.), 87
Gray, James, 225
Gray, Mike, 85
Green, Bubba, 153
Green, Doug, 197
Green, E. G., 265, 274, 278, 281-282, 284, 286, 289, 294, 296-297
Green, Harold, 207
Green, Jacquez, 278, 287, 295
Green, Lamont, 284
Green, Mike, 246
Green, Nealon, 288

Green, Yatil, 288
Greggs, Durwin, 223-224
Gregory, Art, 38, 48, 50
Gresham, Bob, 87
Griffin, Archie, 104-105
Griffin, Larry, 168
Griffin, Quentin, 322
Griffith, Howard, 227, 237
Griggs, Larry, 8
Grissom, Bud, 97
Grobe, Jim, 324, 343, 352, 364
Groh, Al, xi, 166-167, 324, 328, 351-352, 364
Groh, Mike, 273, 274
Grossman, Rex, 335, 342
Groves Stadium (Winston-Salem, N.C.), 78, 89-90, 93, 125, 196, 265
Guin, Jimmy, 49
Gundy, Cale, 247
Gunter, Bill, 81
Gustafson, Andy, 18, 355
Gutekunst, John, 199
Gwaltney, Chance, 316, 340-341
Gwaltney, Clint, 232

Haase, Tom, 237
Hackensack High School (N.J.), 3
Hafer, Don, 21-22
Hagans, Marques, 343
Haggins, Odell, 303
Hall of Fame Bowl (Tampa, Fla.), 237, 261, 269
Hall of Fame Classic (Birmingham, Ala.). See All-American Bowl
Hall, Bill, 61
Hall, Bobby, 73, 75, 80
Hall, Delton, 200
Hall, Hollis, 168
Hall, Randy, 143
Halloran, Shawn, 196
Hamilton, Joe, 284, 296, 301, 305, 308, 315, 318, 324
Hamlet, Sean, 270
Hampton, Rodney, 204
Hanburger, Chris, 51-52

Hannah, Joe, 153
Hanulak, Chet (The Jet), 3, 5-8
Harbaugh, Jim, 196
Hardage, Bob, 22
Hardin, Jim, 78-79
Harding, Jack, 355
Hardison, Dee, 137, 140
Harnisch, Frank, 152
Harp, Tom, 70, 361
Harper, Alvin, 239
Harper, Andy, 70
Harper, Tom, 105, 364
Harraka, Jeff, 193
Harris, Antwone, 285
Harris, Dick, 84
Harris, George, 24
Harris, Leon, 118
Harris, Rudy, 244
Harrison, Bob, 15
Harrison, Marvin, 279
Hart, Leo, 81
Hartlieb, Chuck, 215
Hartman, Damon, 212, 223, 230
Hartrell, Damian, 292
Hastings, Andre, 236, 245
Hatch, Jermaine, 321
Hatcher, Dale, 164, 168, 177
Hatcher, Jesse, 205, 214
Hatfield, Ken, 244-246, 250, 261, 361
Hawkins, Alex, 23, 28,
Hawkins, Cullin, 313
Hayes, Jeff, 162
Hayes, Mercury, 271
Hayes, Woody, 148-150
Hayman, Gary, 114-115
Healy, Jack, 13
Hearst, Doobie, 236
Hearst, Garrison, 245
Hefner, Hugh, 98
Heisman Trophy, xii, xviii, 29, 88, 105, 114, 145, 155, 165, 172, 185, 199, 217-218, 251, 257, 260-261, 281, 286, 289, 312, 319-320, 335, 358
Heisman, John, xviii

Hellams, Tyler, 81
Hely, Bob, 138
Henderson, E. J., 325, 344
Henderson, Jim, 116
Henderson, Joe, 205-206, 208-209, 211-212
Hendricks, Michael, 250
Hendrickson, Horace, 20, 363
Hennessey, Tony, 40
Henning, Dan, 195
Hernandez, Jesus, 271
Hickey, Bo, 61
Hickey, Jim, 30-32, 40, 44-45, 51, 54, 58, 61, 95, 363
Hildebrand, Bill, 364
Hill, Aubrey, 267
Hill, Darryl, xii, 51-52
Hill, Greg, 180, 182-183, 187-188, 190-191
Hill, J. D., 93
Hill, Shawn, 325, 327-332
Hilliard, Ike, 270, 278-279, 289-290
Hines, Clarkston, 212, 218-219, 221, 223-225
Hinton, Eddie, 79
Hite, Billy, 103-104
Hite, Jeff, 120
Hixon, Chuck, 79
Holder, Eric, 196
Holiday, Carlyle, 339
Holieway, Jamelle, 214
Hollis, Michael, 231
Holloman, Rudy, 83-86
Holloway, Derek, 171
Holloway, Steve, 57
Hollows, Bill, 257
Holmes, Keith, 238
Holmes, Priest, 269
Holt, Torry, xix, 293, 299-300
Holtz, Lou, 103-104, 109-110, 112, 114, 117, 119-120, 125, 129, 135, 171, 199, 219, 242, 280, 321, 349-350, 363
Hooper, Ricardo, 206, 210, 213
Hoover, Kim, 124-125, 127
Hope, Chris, 315-316

Hopkins, Larry, 88-91, 99-100, 105, 352
Horne, Charlie, 17, 28
Horton, Ethan, 171
Hostetler, Jeff, 182
Housman, John, 122
Houston Oilers, 192
Houston Veer, 87
Hovance, Pat, 107
Howard, Frank (The Little Giant, The Baron), xi, 15-16, 18-19, 26-27, 30-31, 33-34, 46, 56, 64-65, 68, 70-71, 73, 76, 86, 141, 239, 318, 361
Howard's Rock, 72-73
Hudson, Jerel, 336
Hudson, Steve, 171
Huff, Ken, 103
Hughes, Dennis, 77
Hughes, Leroy, 118, 124
Humanitarian Bowl (Boise, Idaho), 334
Humm, Dave, 111
Hunter, Dick, 20-24
Hurley, Bill, 129
Hurricane Fran, 282
Hurricane Hazel, 10
Husted, Mike, 245, 253
Hyman, Eric, 102

Idol, Dick, 81
Igwebuike, Donald, 165-166, 168, 172, 178
Independence Bowl (Shreveport, La.), 199, 236, 253, 269, 343
Ingram, Hootie, 148, 361
Innis, Greg, 202
Iowa State University (ISU), 143, 336
IPTAY, 72
Ironman Football. See One-Platoon Football
Irvine, John, 2, 6
Ismail, Raghib (Rocket), 219, 238

Jackson, Bo, 185

Jackson, Cotra, 331
Jackson, Jack, 260, 267
Jackson, Jacky, 68, 71-74, 76,
Jackson, James (Georgia), 200, 204
Jackson, James (Miami), 304
Jackson, Jarious, 305
Jackson, Keith, 150
Jackson, Ronnie, 53, 55-56
Jackson, Sean, 251, 254-258
Jackson, Terry, 278, 290
Jackson, Tony, 325
Jackson, Willie, 260
Jacobs Blocking Trophy, 31, 68, 72, 143, 203
Jacobs, Taylor, 335
James, Edgerrin, 304-305
James, Lionel, 185
Janikowski, Sebastian, 294-295, 298, 300-303, 306-311, 314
Jarrell, Adrian, 258
Jaynes, Dave, 116
Jefferson, Thomas, xvii, 224
Jenkins, Ronnie, 77
Jennings, Keith, 199, 208, 210-211
Jennings, Rick, 121, 124-125
Jerome, Jimmy, 105
Jett, James, 226
Jim Thorpe Award, 264
Joe Robbie Stadium (Miami, Fla.), 279
Johnson, Andy, 102
Johnson, Anthony, 219
Johnson, Billy, 137, 154, 161
Johnson, Dion, 247
Johnson, Don, 17, 23
Johnson, Doug, 295
Johnson, Gary, 88
Johnson, Jimmy, 190, 317, 355
Johnson, Leon, 273
Johnson, Mark (Duke), 106
Johnson, Mark (Texas Tech), 138
Johnson, Ricky, 213
Johnson, Ronchie, 138
Johnson, Sammy, 106, 112, 115
Johnson, Steve, 200
Johnson, Tracy, 197, 200, 205-214

Jolley, Lewis, 94, 97-98, 100-101
Jones, Calvin, xviii
Jones, Cedric, 145, 166
Jones, Greg, 316, 336, 338-339
Jones, Jim, 13
Jones, Johnnie, 187
Jones, Johnny (Ham), 148
Jones, Johnny (Jam), 148
Jones, Johnny (Lam), 148
Jones, Marcus, 279
Jones, Marvin, xix, 249, 253, 281
Jones, Mike, 124, 129
Jones, Randall, 329
Jones, S. C., 72
Jones, Shawn, 230-238, 244, 247, 252
Jones, Stan, xix, 2, 4, 6
Jones, Steve, 219
Jones, Walter, 282
Jordan, Homer, 161, 163-166, 169-170, 172-173, 177-179, 208
Jordan, Shug, 348
Joyner, Willie, 182-183, 186
Juday, Steve, 53
Jurgens, Bobby, 237
Justice, Charlie (Choo Choo), 51

Kane, Morgan, 311
Kanell, Danny, 251-252, 256, 258, 264-268, 270-276, 278, 280-282, 297
Kansas State University, 303-304, 319
Kasay, John, 236
Katich, Tom, 23
Katz, Jim, 75
Keldorf, Chris, 285, 294, 296
Kelley, Freddy, 73
Kelley, Mike, 158
Kelly, Andy, 239
Kelly, Jim, 192
Kelly, Kenny, 309, 312
Kemper, Don, 26
Kenan Stadium (Chapel Hill, N.C.), 31-32, 52, 61, 96, 99-100, 131,
137, 161, 167, 190, 246, 256, 283, 294, 326
Kendra, Dan (Florida State), 285-286, 291, 297-298, 308-309
Kendra, Dan (West Virginia), 128
Kendrick, Andre, 313
Kennedy, John F., 57
Kenney, Pat, 104
Kesler, Eddie, 53-54, 57-58, 64
Key, Sean, 308, 314
Keys, Larry, 72
Kiffin, Monte, 363
Kiker, Adam, 330-331, 341
Kilmer, Billy, 41
Kinard, Ben, 113, 118
Kinard, Terry, xix, 163-165, 172, 177, 180,
King, Don, 3, 13
King, Kim, 69, 73
King, Malcolm, 199
King, Tommy, 35
Kingsbury, Kliff, 342
Kinney, Vince, 131
Kinzer, Chris, 203
Kirby, Terry, 220, 227
Kirkland, Levon, 244-245
Kirkman, Bill, 11
Kirtley, Todd, 145, 152
Kittner, Kurt, 312
Klebe, Jack, 78-81
Klise, Johnny, 101, 103
Knight, Chris, 195
Knight, Douglas, 57
Knox, Kevin, 250, 258, 262
Knox, Ronnie, 12
Kocourek, Jerry, 11
Koprowski, Marion, 126
Kosar, Bernie, 190
Kramer, Erik, 196, 201
Kraus, Joe, 191
Kremus, Jason, 246
Kriger, Bill, 49
Krivac, Joe, 213, 236, 362
Krug, Tom, 280-281
Kuklick, Brian, 302
Kupec, Chris, 119

Kupec, Matt, 137-140, 154
Kush, Frank, 93
Kwalick, Ted, 75

Lacey, Bob, 50-51, 53, 58
Lamm, Phil, 106-107
Lancaster, Chris, 200
Lane, Fred, 200
Lanier, Ricky, 78
Lantz, Rick, 274
Las Vegas Bowl (Las Vegas, Nev.),
	304
LaSane, Bruce, 210
Lasater, Marvin, 35
Lash, Pete, 10
Lavergne, Robert, 132
Lavette, Robert, 188-189, 229
Lawrence, Amos (Famous Amos),
	135, 137-140, 154, 157-162
Lawrence, Don, 364
Lawrence, Kent, 73, 77
Lawrence, Reggie, 224
Lawson, Larmount, 166
Lawson, Manny, 341
Leahy, Frank, 47, 358
Leahy, Rev. William, 358
Leak, Eric, 299
Leavitt, Don, 112
LeBlanc, Maxie, 99
Lee, Robert E., xvii
Lee, Walker, 137
Leggett, Mark, 38, 40, 42, 44, 47-48
Leonard's Losers, 170
Leopard, Duane, 29
Lester, Greg, 231-232
Lester, Roy, 362
Leverenz, Ted, 100-101, 103, 107
Levias, Jerry, 79
Levy, Marv, 48
Lewis, Bill, 247, 362
Lewis, Nathaniel, 204
Lewis, Wayne, 85
Liberatore, Frank, 69, 73
Liberty Bowl (Memphis, Tenn.), 57-
	58, 76-77, 116, 121-123, 140-
	141

Lilly, Bob, 35, 120
Lincoln, Jimy, 247
Linton, Jonathon, 296
Lisk, Jimmy, 78, 81
Little, Derrick, 202
Lohmiller, Chip, 199
Lombardi Trophy, 117, 192, 315
Loncar, Ed, 147
London, Tommy, 123
Long, Bob, 73
Lopes, Roger, 53
Lord Baltimore, xvii
Los Angeles Memorial Coliseum, 41
Lothridge, Billy, 49
Lott, Billy, 144
Lott, James, 204, 211
Louisiana State University (LSU),
	13, 28-29, 66, 83, 156-157, 242,
	255, 288, 295, 321
Louisiana Superdome, 289, 312-313
Louisiana Tech University, 236, 282,
	307, 334
Lounsbury, Tracy, 88, 90
Lovett, Billy, 80
Luck, Mike, 162
Lundy, Wali, 342-343
Lutz, Worth, 1, 9, 11
Lynch, James, 329
Lynch, Lenny, 193

Mack, Kevin, 165, 185
Mack, Terence, 200
Mack, Tremain, 288
Mackovic, John, 64, 150-152, 364
Maddox, Nick, 336, 338, 340
Madison, James, xviii
Magalski, Paul, 85
Mageec, Brian, 259
Magnificent Seven Defense, 63
Magwood, Frank, 165, 179
Majkowski, Don, 193
Majors, Johnny, 193, 220
Manges, Mike, 123-126, 128, 130-
	132
Manget, Luke, 328
Mangham, Mickey, 29

Manior, Greg, 237
Mansfield, Mike, 93-94, 102
Mansfield, Shelby, 57, 62, 66
Marchibroda, Ted Jr., 152
Marino, Dan, 171
Marion, Phil, 68-69
Marshall, Art, 245
Marshall, Bob, 99
Martell, Harry, 66, 77
Martin, Ben, 58, 363
Martin, Kelvin, 196
Martin, Ken, 213
Martin, Tee, 306
Masneri, Ray, 25
Mason, Darryl, 171
Mason-Dixon Line, xv
Mason, Leon, 85
Mass, Wayne, 68, 72
Massie, Henry, 52
Mathis, Bill, 26, 28, 31-34
Mathis, Terrance, 225
Mauer, Mark, 172
Mauldin, Hugh, 64
Mayes, Derrick, 280
Mays, Jerry, 198, 211, 230
McBrien, Scott, 344
McCall, Jeff, 168, 173, 179
McCathern, Jack, 55
McCauley, Don, 90-94, 96-97
McCorvey, Kez, 249, 252, 254, 259,
    265, 268, 270
McCracken, Quint, 212
McCray, William, 297, 306, 316
McDonald, Ned, 363
McDonald, Scott, 128
McDonald, Tommy, 14
McDougald, James, 135-136, 151-
    152, 155
McFadden, Wes, 203-205, 207, 209,
    213, 221
McGahee, Willis, 338-339
McGee, Edgar, 69
McGee, Josh, 288, 304
McGee, Mike, 33, 121, 130, 361
McGlamry, Mike, 130
McGlockton, Chester, 226, 244

McGonnigal, Bruce, 218, 220, 222,
    227, 233-234,
McGriff, Lee, 118
McGriff, Travis, 295
McGuire, Frank, xii
McHenry, Pat, 92
McInerney, Jake, 220, 223, 234-235,
    239
McKeithan, Nick, 11
McKeldin, Gov. Theodore R., 21
McLellan, Bill, 177
McLendon, Charles, 156
McLendon, T. A., 341
McMahen, Jim, 88
McMakin, John, 100
McManus, Danny, 322
McMullen, Billy, 328
McNabb, Donovan, 279, 283
McPherson, Adrian, 335, 339-342,
    348-349
McPherson, James, 343
McRae, Bennie, 44
McSwain, Chuck, 155, 165, 167,
    170-171, 173, 178-179, 181
McSwain, Rod, 170
McWhorter, Mac, 334, 362
Means, Natrone, 233, 253
Medlin, Rick, 74
Memorial Stadiium (Lincoln, Neb.),
    88, 110
Memorial Stadium (Baltimore, Md.),
    192, 201
Memorial Stadium (Clemson, S.C.),
    xvi, 25-26, 147, 164, 209, 246,
    250
Memphis State University (MSU),
    72, 76, 122
Menapace, Bernie, 138
Menhardt, Herb, 155-156
Merchant, Emmett, 232, 234, 237-
    238
Messam, Wayne, 284
Metts, Carey, 219
Miami Dolphins, 355
Michael, Billy, 74
Michaels, Al, 72, 109, 363

Michigan Stadium (Ann Arbor,
    Mich.), 271
Michigan State University (MSU),
    20, 53, 198-199, 271
Mickey Mouse, 186
Mickle, Tom, 249
Micron PC Bowl (Miami, Fla.), 296,
    304, 312
Mid-America Conference, 324
Midget, Anthony, 313
Mike-Mayer, Steve, 113, 117-122
Milanovich, Scott, 265
Miller, Bob, 116
Miller, Henry, 337-338
Miller, Paul, 84, 90, 93, 97-98,
    100-101
Mills, Chuck, 151, 364
Milner, Bill, 130
Minnesota Vikings, 150
Minnis, Marvin (Snoop), 310-311,
    315-316, 318-319, 321-323
Minor, Travis, 291-292, 295, 298,
    302, 307-310, 315,
Mira, George, 56
Mirage Bowl (Tokyo), 181
Mississippi State University (MSU),
    58, 95, 123, 253, 269, 305, 312
Mitch, Bob, 125
Mitchell, Jim, 85
Mitchell, Johnny, 237
Modzelewski, Ed, 120
Moeser, James, 354
Moncrief, Richard, 244, 250
Monroe, Arthur, 89
Monroe, James, xviii
Monroe, Scooter, 325
Mont, Tommy , 15, 22, 362
Montgomery, Don, 52
Montgomery, Jamaul, 336
Montgomery, Shane, 224
Moon, Tim, 145
Moon, Tracy, 10
Moore, Herman, 211, 218-224, 227,
    233-234
Moore, Kirby, 73, 77
Moore, Otis, 210

Moore, Shawn, 211, 217, 219-224,
    227, 233-234, 239, 278
Moorman, Claude (Tee), 38, 42, 269
Moreland, Harry, 35
Morgan, Bob (Blubber), 2, 4-
Morgan, Bobby, 28,
Morgan, Ed, 74
Morgan, Robert, 316, 323
Morocco, Chris, 206, 221
Morris, Dennit, 25
Morris, Johnny, 34
Morrow, Billy, 77
Motor City Bowl (Pontiac, Mich.),
    198
Mowrey, Dan, 251, 268, 270
Mudra, Darrell, 241-242
Muir, Warren, 79, 83-86
Mulligan, Wayne, 72
Mundy, Aaron, 235, 245
Munyon, Matt, 317
Murray, Bill, xi, 9, 11-12, 23-24, 31,
    37, 39-40, 43-45, 47-48, 50, 63,
    66-67, 208, 217, 269, 361
Muster, Brad, 202
Muyres, Jon, 316
Myers, Denny, 358
Myers, Leonard, 301

Namath, Joe, 61-62
Nash, John, 182
National Basketball Association
    (NBA), 38, 264
National Broadcasting Corp. (NBC),
    358
National Collegiate Athletic
    Organization (NCAA), xii,
    xviii-xx, 8, 12, 15, 18, 20, 25,
    41, 59, 66, 74, 77, 92-93, 97,
    102, 104, 115, 133, 137, 140,
    143-144, 150, 163-164, 175-
    178, 180-181, 184, 199, 203,
    214, 224-227, 233, 238-239,
    243-244, 247-249, 253, 260-
    261, 263, 271, 277-278, 281,
    285, 290, 293-294, 301-306,
    311, 315, 319-320, 322, 326,

333, 342, 348, 352-353, 355-356, 358
National Football League (NFL), xix, 41, 61, 135, 150, 158, 172, 187, 192, 218, 227, 237, 244, 264, 290-291, 307, 315, 321, 324, 332, 351, 355-356
Neal, Tommy, 186-187, 189, 191, 196, 202
Nelson, Bill, 47
Nelson, Jim, 10
Nessler, Brad, 274
Neville, Al, 98, 103, 112-113
New Mexico State University, 301
New York Jets, 135, 324
New York Knicks, 264
New York University (NYU), 333
Newman, Keith, 304
Nicholson, Darrell, 159
Nixon, Richard, 17
Noggle, Charlie, 61-62, 66
Nolan, Dick, 3-4
Norris, Pay, 142
North Carolina Intercollegiate Football Association (NCIFA), xv
North Carolina State University (NCSU), xi, xvi-xvii, xix, 10, 17, 20-24, 28, 32, 39-41, 43, 48-49, 51-66, 69-81, 83, 85, 91, 98-99, 103-104, 106-107, 109-117, 119-120, 122-123, 125, 127, 129, 131, 135-136, 138, 141, 143, 145-146, 148, 150-156, 159, 166-167, 179, 186, 189-190, 196, 201, 203, 206, 212-213, 215, 217-218, 223-226, 230, 236-237, 242, 245, 247-248, 250-251, 253-254, 259, 261, 267, 269, 272, 282, 293-294, 298-300, 304, 308, 318, 320-321, 330-333, 340-341, 344, 348-350, 353, 356, 363, 365-381
Northwestern University, 137-138, 219

Notre Dame Stadium (South Bend, Ind.), 258
Novak, Nick, 328, 344
Nugent, Tom, xii, 33, 51, 362
Nunn, Arlington, 237

O' Cain, Mike, 119, 126, 282, 299, 363
O' Donnell, Neil, 207, 213
O' Leary, George, 296, 302, 324-325, 333-334, 352, 362
O' Neal, Jay, 15
O' Neal, Robert, 244
Oahu Bowl (Honolulu, Hawaii), 320
Oglesby, Ike, 97-98, 103, 105-106
Ohio State University (OSU), 104-105, 148-150, 288, 296, 302, 356
Ohio University, 298, 324
Oklahoma State University, 242-243
Oliver, Dick, 105
Olkewicz, Neal, 146
Olszewski, Harry, 71-72
One-Platoon Football, 51, 58-59
Onkotz, Denny, 75
Orange Bowl (Miami, Fla.), xii, xix, 5-8, 11, 14-15, 17-18, 24-25, 35, 68, 115, 163, 167, 170-171, 173, 190, 207, 236, 238, 249, 251, 254, 259, 260-263, 266-267, 277, 280, 283, 279, 293-295, 303, 317, 319, 321, 323, 332, 335, 338-339, 355, 357,
Orangeburg High School (SC), 46
Oregon State University (OSU), 192
Orvald, Todd, 67
Osborne, Ronnie, 33
Osborne, Tom, 111, 141, 172, 260
Outland Trophy, 33, 117, 150
Outzen, Marcus, 302-303, 305-306, 308, 310
Owen, Brian, 275
Owens, Steve, 79
Oyster Bowl (Norfolk, Va.), 121

Pacific Ten Conference, 93, 249, 343

Padgett, Matt, 288
Page, Kurt, 188
Palanunik, George, 6
Palmer, Thomas, 211
Papa John's Cardinal Stadium
    (Louisville, Ky.), 338
Parete, Anthony, 178-179
Parker, Jim, 43, 56
Parker, Larry, 11
Parker, Red, 119, 131, 148, 199, 361
Parker, Willie, 325
Parkman, Kamon, 245
Parrish, Dwight, 168
Parseghian, Ara, 99, 150
Parson, Rich, 331
Pascal, Bob, 1, 9-11
Paschal, Bob, 138, 154
Paschall, Billy, 112, 119
Passingham, Kent, 321
Pastrana, Alan, 71, 80
Paterno, Joe, 115, 120, 126, 208, 217
Paulling, Bob, 163-164, 170, 179-
    181
Pavilack, Harry, 34
Pawlawski, Mike, 248
Payne, Billy, 77
Payne, Buddy, 24
Peace, Wayne, 161
Peach Bowl (Atlanta, Ga.), xix, 86-
    87, 93, 106, 117, 121, 127, 131,
    137, 143, 156-157, 185, 194-
    195, 203, 215, 217, 242, 247,
    253, 261, 269, 280, 288, 296,
    305, 312, 321, 335, 349, 359
Pearce, Frank, 53, 56, 65
Pearsall, Melvin, 287, 294
Peebles, Danny, 201
Pell, Charley, 141-143, 146, 148,
    161, 163, 175-176, 209, 361
Pelligrini, Bob, 2, 12-13, 15
Pendergrast, Kevin, 258
Pengitore, Ken, 105
Pennsylvania State University
    (PSU), xii, xix, 49, 74-75, 77,
    114-115, 120-121, 125-127,
    135, 143, 146, 155, 171, 189,

    193, 195, 208, 217, 219-220,
    243, 248, 293
Pepe, Bob, 22
Peppers, Julius, xix, 332, 344
Perkins, Millie, 41
Perlo, Phil, 13
Perriman, Brett, 197
Perry, Bruce, 325-330
Perry, Leon, 214
Perry, Michael Dean, 200-201, 203-
    205
Perry, Tracy, 139
Perry, William (The Refrigerator),
    xix, 165, 177, 192-193, 200,
    203
Peters, Doug, 12
Peterson, Bill, 81, 349
Petty, Howard, 194
Philadelphia Eagles, 324
Phillips, John, 203
Phillips, Lawrence, 261-262
Piccolo, Brian, 59-60, 63, 72, 88
Pierce, John, 124
Pilz, Bobby, 111
Playboy Magazine, 98
Pleasant, Reggie, 180
Plevil, Joe, 21
Plocki, Dan, 198
Pluto the Dog, 186
Podwika, Rod, 22
Poindexter, Anthony, 274-275, 277
Polley, Tommy, 311, 313, 323
Polo Grounds (New York, N.Y.), 1
Poniatowski, Hank, 34
Pope, Kendyll, 336, 342
Port, Chris, 219
Posey, David, 118
Post, Ed, 9-10
Poulos, Jimmy, 102
Powell, Calen, 337
Powell, Delbert, 137
Powell, K. Adam, xiii
Powlus, Ron, 267
Presbyterian College, 16
Presley, Elvis, 41
Preston, Rock, 265, 267-268, 270,

274, 284
Price, Peerless, 306
Pricer, Billy, 15
Priestley, David, 333
Prince Philip (Great Britain), 21
Prince, Wally, 21
Pritchett, Ed, 56
Proebstile, Dick, 53
Proehl, Ricky, 206, 213
Propst, Eddie, 75
Punch, Dr. Jerry, 274-275, 277, 325,
    330, 348, 351,
Purdue University, 9-10, 131, 138,
    194-195, 217
Pyburn, Jeff, 142

Quayle, Frank, 80, 91
Queen Elizabeth II, 21
Quinn, Jimmy, 85

Raba, Bob, 130
Rabb, Warren, 29
Ragone, Dave, 337
Rakowski, Terry, 156
Raleigh News and Observer, 39, 87
Rampley, Todd, 211
Ramsey, Derrick, 137
Randle, Sonny, 49, 364
Rappold, Walt, 37-38, 42, 44, 48-50
Ratliff, Don, 103
Ray, Billy, 219, 221-223
Raycom/Jefferson Pilot Sports, 353
Read, Finley, 21
Rearick, Bill, 20
Reconstruction, xv
Reding, Jack, 35
Redmon, Tellis, 320
Reeves, Dan, 62
Reich, Frank, 183, 186-188, 190-
    192, 194-195
Reid, Andy, 117
Reid, Lamont, 331
Reid, Paul, 80
Reed, Thomas, 363
Reiley, Chuck, 34
Rein, Bo, 129, 135, 148, 155-156,

242, 363
Rembert, Johnny, 170, 177-178
Rembol, Todd, 270
Reveiz, Fuad, 187
Reynolds, Bill, 40, 43-45, 49-50
Reynolds, Burt, 209, 294
Reynolds, Jamal, 315, 323
Rhodes, Bobby, 314
Rhodes, Prof. Sam, 16
Rice University, 16, 33
Rice, Tony, 219
Richards, Dean, 128, 131, 147
Richey, Wade, 288
Richt, Mark, 316, 322, 344, 348
Riddick Stadium (Raleigh, N.C.), 57,
    61, 66, 69
Riley, Marc, 325, 329
Riley, Philip, 274, 276
Ritcher, Jim, 150
Rivers, Dalton, 13, 18
Rivers, Philip, 320-321, 331, 333,
    341, 344, 350, 352
Rix, Chris, 323, 330, 335-338, 342,
    344
Robinson, Bobby (Clemson), 201
Robinson, Bobby (Wake Forest), 34
Robinson, Ed, 260
Robinson, Joe, 52, 54, 58
Robinson, John, 348
Robinson, Koren, xix, 320-321
Robinson, Ray, 321, 330
Robinson, Ronnie, 105, 107
Robinson, Tony, 194
Rocky Mountain Spotted Fever, 30
Rodgers, Johnny, 88
Rogers, Bill, 182
Rogers, George, 155
Rogers, Phil, 65, 70, 73
Rogers, Tom, 364
Rollins College, 37
Romano, Frank, 121
Roof, Ted, 350
Rose Bowl (Pasadena, Calif.), xviii,
    16, 68, 225, 249, 288, 303
Rose, Anthony, 172
Ross, Bobby, xi, 180, 182-183, 188,

190-192, 196-198, 202, 209,
229-231, 233, 238, 247, 324,
351, 362
Rossi, Jim, 49, 52-54, 56-58,
Roulhac, Terrence, 188, 200
Roy, Ken, 119
Royal, Darrell, 95
Rozier, Mike, 172
Rudy, Skitch, 14
Ruffin, Milt, 128
Ruffner, Bo, 68
Runty, Steve, 111
Rusnak, Ron, 103
Russell, Frank, 112-113, 117
Russell, Larry, 88-91, 100, 105, 352
Rutland, Hiawatha, 336
Ryan, Tim, 181, 183
Ryans, Larry, 244

Saban, Lou, 362
Safeco Field (Seattle, Wash.), 334
Sain, Jerry, 103, 106
Salter, Bill, 60
Samuels, Stanford, 340
San Diego State University (SDSU),
304
Sanders, Deion (Prime Time), 210,
264, 322
Sandusky, Mike, 12
Sandwisch, Jim, 231, 246
Sanford Stadium (Athens, Ga.), 141,
144, 177, 200, 245
Sankey, Ben, 311
Sapp, Patrick, 261
Sasser, Glenn, 59
Saunders, Don, 23
Savage, Quinton, 304
Sawyer, Corey, 251-252
Sayers, Gale, 60
Scardino, Tony, 3
Scarpati, Joe, 52, 54, 57
Schaub, Matt, 328, 336, 343, 352
Schembechler, Bo, 157
Schlicter, Art, 149
Schmitz, Brian, 304
Schnellenberger, Howard, 283, 355

Schofield, Gary, 181, 183
Scholastic Aptitude Test, xii, 97
Schroy, Ken, 119
Schultz, John, 119, 124-126
Schwabe, Gil, 85
Schweickert, Bob, 55, 62
Sciaretti, Jim, 21
Scott Stadium (Charlottesville, Va.),
179, 234-235, 272, 275, 277,
285
Scott, Brad, 255
Scott, George, 131, 143
Scott, Jake, 73
Scott, Randy, 145
Scotti, Ben, 27
Scotton, Steffen, 230-231, 233, 237
Scrudato, Ron, 32
Sears Trophy, 314
Sease, Tommy, 19
Seattle Bowl, 333-334, 343
Secules, Scott, 208
Sedgfield Inn (Greensboro, N.C.),
xvi
Seivers, Larry, 122
Selep, Tom, 12, 17
Seminole Tribe, xviii
Serge, Tony, 129
Shaw, Bruce, 103-104, 107, 115
Sheets, Ken, 137
Sheridan, Dick, 212, 363
Sherill, Jackie, 142, 312
Sherill, Jay, 128
Sherman, Tim, 284-286
Sherman, Tom, 75
Shiner, Dick, 49, 52
Shingler, Lowndes, 34-35
Shipley, Dick, 4
Shiver, Clay, 271
Shuler, Heath, 261
Shockey, Jeremy, 317
Sievers, Todd, 339
Sigma Nu Fraternity, 45-47
Silicon Valley Classic (San Jose,
Calif.), 343
Silverdome (Pontiac, Mich.), 198
Simmons, Chris, 235

Simmons, Wayne, 245
Simon, Corey, xix, 298
Sims, Marvin, 144
Singleton, Chris, 226
Singleton, Kevin, 226
Sisson, Scott, 220, 231-233, 235, 238, 252
Skosnik, Ron, 57, 61-62
Slade, Chris, 227
Slayden, Steve, 218
Sloan, Steve, 62, 361
Smiley, Julian, 85
Smith, Bill, 173
Smith, Bob, 118
Smith, Daryl, 334
Smith, George, 107
Smith, Larry, 203
Smith, Marquette, 255
Smith, Red, 1
Smith, Scott, 145, 152, 154-156
Smith, Shevin, 285
Smith, Terry, 250, 261
Smith, Tim, 141
Smith, Wyatt, 224
Snead, Norman, 28, 34,
Snell, David, 88
Snipes, Ronnie, 172
Snow, Lenny, 69
Snyder, Bruce, 287
Snyder, Paul, 32-33
Sochko, Mike, 124-127, 129
Sokalsky, Pete, 65
Sorrell, Sonny, 11
Southeastern Conference (SEC), xv, 73, 84, 86, 95-96, 121-122, 124, 127, 131, 137, 152, 156, 185-186, 220, 226, 243, 253-254, 278-279, 287, 305, 311, 352-353
Southern Conference (SC), xv-xvi, xviii, 2-3, 16, 83, 110, 357
Southern Intercollegiate Athletic Association (SIAA), xv, xviii
Southern Methodist University (SMU), xx, 79
Southwestern Conference (SWC), 41, 132
Spagnola, Joe, 93
Spears, Stan, 23
Spikes, Jack, 35
Split-T Offense, 2-3
Spinner, Bryan, 328
Spooner, Bob, 17-19
Sports Illustrated, 127, 152, 173, 255, 264
Spurrier, Steve, 205, 212, 218-220, 226, 246, 253-254, 288-290, 295, 317, 335, 361
Stabler, Kenny, 69
Stafford, Anthony, 214
Stallings, John, 24
Stanford University, 202, 247, 333-334
Stanicek, Jason, 265
Stankavage, Scott, 168-169, 184
Stark, Jon, 256
Steels, Anthony, 172
Stephens, Darnell, 246
Stetz, Ed, 91
Stewart, Rod, 132
Stewart, Tyrone, 325
Stilley, Rich, 100
Stoll, Cal, 87-88, 92, 100, 105, 364
Stoops, Bob, 319
Stradford, Tony, 178
Stransky, Bob, 18-19
Streater, Steve, 159
Streeter, Brandon, 291
Strom, Rick, 205
Sturn, Bob, 6
Sugar Bowl (New Orleans, La.), 2, 5, 28-29, 75, 83, 131, 133, 185, 217, 236, 239, 249, 270-271, 277, 287, 296, 303, 311, 314, 344, 357
Suggs, Lee, 321
Suggs, Tommy, 79, 85-86
Sullivan, Bob, 65
Sullivan, Dave, 101
Sullivan, Dwight, 150-151, 154,
Sullivan, Sean, 183, 189, 196
Summers, Freddie, xii

Sumner, Walt, 81
Sun Bowl (El Paso, Tex.), 106-107,
     123, 138, 148, 181, 193, 268
Sun Devil Stadium (Tempe, Ariz.),
     306
Super Bowl, xix, 41, 62, 144, 158,
     324, 355
Swearingen, Fred, 24
Swilling, Ken, 230, 233
Swilling, Pat, 199, 229
Switzer, Barry, 160, 214, 247, 322
Swofford, John, 354
Syracuse University, 13, 113, 119,
     124, 129, 183, 187, 198, 208,
     279, 283, 333, 353

Tabron, Dennis, 165
Tagge, Jerry, 88
Talbott, Danny, 60-61, 65
Talley, Greg, 236
Tamburello, Frank, 12-13, 15
Tangerine Bowl (Orlando, Fla.), 148,
     156, 161, 333, 342
Tapp, Jim, 41
Tar Heel Sports Network, xiii, 30
Tate, Bill, xii, 59-60, 364
Tate, Dayle, 156
Tate, Lars, 204
Tatum, James (Sunny Jim), xi, xx, 2-
     5, 7-8, 12-13, 15, 21, 26-27, 30-
     32, 37, 95, 109, 127, 128, 236,
     362
Taylor, Brad, 171-172
Taylor, Fred, 270, 286-287, 289,
     295-296
Taylor, Jim, 29
Taylor, Ken, 106
Taylor, Lawrence (L.T.), xix, 154,
     157-158, 160-161, 192
Taylor, Lenny, 187
Taylor, Terry, 104-105
Temple University (TU), 143, 244,
     246
Tensi, Steve, 63
Terry, Shawn, 327
Texas A&M University, 171, 263,

298, 304
Texas Christian University (TCU),
     35, 65, 269
Texas Tech University (TT), 107-
     108, 138, 158, 225-226, 242,
     268-269, 342
The Citadel, 144, 200
Thomas, Bill, 25
Thomas, Bob (Arizona State), 93
Thomas, Bob (Notre Dame), 99
Thomas, Clendon, 24, 315
Thomas, Clevan, 315
Thomas, Lamar, 251
Thomas, Mickey, 235
Thompson, Donnell, 159
Thompson, John, 22
Thompson, Tony, 239
Thompson, Trent, 244
Thorpe, Craphonso, 340
Tice, John, 180
Tiggle, Calvin, 230, 234
Tinch, Joshua, 337
Tisdel, Kevin, 232-233
Todd, Carl, 15
Tolley, Charley, 74
Tompkins, James, 70
Torbush, Carl, 296, 324, 363
Toretta, Gino, 251
Toronto Blue Jays, 297-298
Trapp, James, 250
Treadwell, David, 200, 202-204,
     206-207
Treggs, Brian, 248
Trinity College. *See* Duke University
Triplett, Danny, 172
Tropical Storm Isidore, 337
Trowbridge, Ken, 21
Troy State University, 326, 330
Tulane University (TU), 29, 84, 99,
     164, 253, 307, 349
Turbeville, Horace, 17
Tuthill, Ron, 56
Tuttle, Perry (P. T.), 146, 163-165,
     167, 169, 172-173
Two-Platoon Football, 59
Tye, Scott, 198

Tyler, Greg, 158
Tyre, Lewis, 271

United States Air Force Academy
    (AF), 58
United States Football League
    (USFL), 218
United States Military Academy
    (Army), 1, 10, 221
United States Naval Academy
    (Navy), 1, 10, 14, 39-40, 44, 75,
    217, 233
University of Alabama (UA), 6-7,
    15-16, 61-62, 66, 68-70, 74,
    118, 122, 158, 163, 208, 253,
    261, 287, 305
University of Alabama-Birmingham
    (UAB), 326
University of Arizona, 203, 226, 251
University of Arkansas, 41-42, 135,
    171, 227, 243-244, 279
University of Buffalo, 73
University of California (Cal), 48,
    164, 246, 248
University of California-Los Angeles
    (UCLA), 9, 12-13, 41, 75, 110-
    111, 260, 272, 303-304
University of Central Florida, 272
University of Cincinnati, 126, 130
University of Colorado (CU), 18-19,
    35, 236, 238-239, 256
University of Delaware, 37
University of Florida (UF), 16, 48,
    65, 106, 118, 127, 132, 148,
    158, 161, 186, 218, 226, 242,
    253-254, 259-260, 267-268,
    270-271, 275, 278-279, 286-
    290, 294-295, 303-305, 311,
    317, 319, 335, 341, 344
University of Georgia (UGA), xii, 2,
    4, 55, 65, 73, 77, 84-85, 95-96,
    101-102, 106, 112, 114, 117,
    130-131, 133, 141-142, 144,
    151-152, 164-165, 177, 186,
    192, 200, 204, 236, 245, 280,
    295, 305, 320, 322, 344, 348

University of Houston (UH), 73, 87,
    91-93, 122, 132-133
University of Illinois (IU), xii, 98,
    227, 237, 312
University of Iowa, 7, 66, 215
University of Kansas (KU), 116,
    255-256, 260
University of Kentucky (UK), 105,
    109, 122, 124, 130-132, 137,
    156, 165, 178, 180, 261
University of Louisville (UL), 160,
    222-223, 316, 337
University of Maryland (UM), xi-xii,
    xvi-xvii, xx, 1-9, 12-17, 21-22,
    27, 30, 33-34, 37-39, 49, 51-54,
    59, 65-66, 71, 74, 80, 85, 98,
    103, 109, 111-114, 117-133,
    136, 139, 141, 143, 146-148,
    154, 158, 161, 167, 169, 175,
    180, 182-198, 201-203, 207-
    208, 213, 218, 222, 229, 231,
    236, 246, 248, 253, 258, 265,
    267, 277-278, 282, 291, 300,
    310-311, 321, 323-332, 335-
    337, 340-341, 344, 351, 353,
    357, 362, 365-381
University of Miami (UM), 5, 9, 17-
    18, 21, 56,
    190-192, 197, 201, 207, 243,
    251, 253-257, 266-267, 272-
    273, 283-284, 288, 292, 299-
    301, 304, 307, 312, 317, 319,
    322, 337-340, 353-357
University of Michigan, 38, 44, 131,
    156-157, 185, 190, 196, 258,
    261, 271-272, 293, 302, 309
University of Minnesota, 143, 199,
    320-321
University of Mississippi (Ole Miss),
    6, 269
University of Missouri (UM), 3, 9,
    12, 167
University of Nebraska (NU), xii,
    xix, 11, 18, 88, 110-111, 116,
    140-141, 172-173, 190, 229,

236-238, 248, 254, 260-263, 267, 278-279, 293-294, 305
University of New Hampshire (UNH), 333
University of New Mexico, 225
University of North Carolina (UNC), xi-xii, xv-xvii, xix, 2, 4-5, 10, 13-15, 21-24, 26-28, 30, 32, 40, 44-45, 50, 51-60, 65, 67, 71-74, 78-79, 84, 89-90, 92-107, 111-113, 118-119, 121-124, 131-132, 135-141, 143, 146, 153-162, 166-169, 171-172, 179-181, 184-185, 189-190, 196-197, 201-203, 206, 213, 217-218, 221-222, 224-225, 232-233, 246, 252-254, 256, 261, 265-266, 268-269, 273, 277, 279, 282-283, 285-286, 288, 290, 293-294, 296, 301, 308, 316, 324-327, 329, 332, 335, 340, 342-344, 350-351, 353-354, 356-357, 362, 365-381
University of Notre Dame (ND), 7, 24, 47, 99, 131, 142-143, 199, 208, 219, 236, 238-239, 243, 254-255, 258-260, 263, 267, 279-281, 305, 333-334, 337, 339-340, 344, 352
University of Oklahoma (OU), xix, 7-8, 11, 14-15, 18-19, 24-25, 78-79, 159-161, 172, 214-215, 247-248, 319, 322, 327, 332
University of Oregon, 254, 343
University of Pennsylvania (Penn), 9
University of Pittsburgh (Pitt), xii, 7, 14, 131, 133, 142-143, 148, 171, 182-183, 187, 208, 333
University of Richmond, 103, 128, 137, 151
University of South Carolina (USC), xi-xiii, xvi, 1, 5, 10, 13-15, 17, 23-24, 27-28, 33, 38, 40-43, 45-46, 48, 54-55, 60, 62, 64-67, 69-71, 76, 79-80, 83-89, 97, 138-139, 141-142, 147-148,

155, 170, 180-181, 201-202, 207, 214, 219, 231, 243, 246, 349, 357, 363, 365-371
University of Southern California (USC), 47, 68, 70, 258, 291, 300
University of Southern Mississippi (USM), 53, 236-237, 242, 285-286
University of Tennessee (UT), 2, 9, 66, 74, 86, 90, 116, 122-123, 132, 164, 186-187, 193-194, 212, 220, 239, 256, 261, 269, 303, 305-306, 344, 349
University of Tennessee-Chattanooga, 231
University of Texas, 95, 140, 148, 161-162, 171, 181, 268-269, 296, 327, 351
University of Tulsa, 99
University of Virginia (UVA), xi, xvi-xvii, xix, 18, 26, 31, 32, 39, 43, 52, 55, 59, 62, 65-66, 68, 75, 80, 89, 101, 105, 110, 114, 122, 127, 131, 136, 140, 145, 151-152, 161, 165, 171, 179, 183, 185, 193-195, 198, 200-201, 205, 208, 211, 217-225, 227, 231, 233-237, 239, 245, 247, 253, 257, 261, 264-265, 269, 271, 273-277, 280, 284-286, 288, 292-293, 301-302, 305, 310, 311, 318, 320, 324, 328-329, 333, 336, 341-343, 351, 354, 357, 363, 365-381
University of Washington, 182
University of Wisconsin, 269
Unser, Dave, 42
USA Cable Network, 177
Usry, George, 21, 26, 28, 34

Vanderbilt University (Vandy), 27, 132, 182, 187-188
Vanderlinden, Ron, 324-325, 362
Vann, Pete, 10
Vanover, Tamarick, xix, 250-254,

258, 260
Varn, Rex, 141, 145
Vena, Dan, 41
Venuto, Jay, 151-153, 155, 157, 159
Vereb, Ed, 12-14
Vick, Michael, 312-314, 321
Vickers, Sam, 23
Vidnovik, Nick, 103, 105, 107
Vigorito, Tommy, 135-136, 145, 152
Villanova University, 113, 121, 123, 129, 144, 164
Vinson, Fernando, 230
Virginia Military Institute (VMI), 91
Virginia Polytechnic Institute (VT). *See* Virginia Tech
Virginia Tech (VT), xi, 17, 22-23, 55-56, 63, 85, 89, 99, 109, 130, 141, 144, 200, 203-204, 209-210, 218, 223-224, 235, 272, 296, 312-314, 321, 335, 354-357
Vitrano, Terry, 123
Vixaysouk, Sumnuk, 120
Voight, Mike, 123, 131-132
Vollmar, George, 41
Voris, Dick, 26, 363

Waddell, Charles, 112
Wade, Scott, 125
Wade, Wallace, 15, 225
Wadsworth, Andre, 271, 281, 291
Wake Forest University (WF), xi-xii, xv-xvi, xviii, 9-10, 13-14, 17, 22, 28, 34, 40, 43, 50-51, 53, 56-57, 59-60, 63-66, 70-74, 78, 83, 85-93, 99-100, 105, 115, 119, 125, 129-130, 138-139, 146, 150-157, 159, 166-167, 181, 183, 188, 196, 201, 206, 204, 213, 218, 222-223, 233-234, 236, 246, 251, 253-254, 257, 273, 282, 284-285, 294, 302, 309, 311, 319, 324, 326, 329, 333, 340, 343, 351-353, 357, 364-381
Walker, Bill, 5-7, 12

Walker, Chuck, 48
Walker, Darrell, 247
Walker, Fabian, 344
Walker, Herschel, 164-165, 177
Walker, Javon, 329
Walker, Mike, 99
Wall, Marcus, 269, 273
Wall, Milan, 32, 40,
Wallace Wade Stadium (Durham, N.C.), 31, 48, 156, 308
Wallace, Jason, 223
Wallace, Randy, 122
Wallace, Senneca, 336
Waller, Ron, 3, 6
Walls, Herkie, 162
Walters, Harry, 118-119
Walton, Joe, 14
Ward, Bob, 2, 74, 362
Ward, Charlie, xii, 249-262, 264, 281-282, 297, 320
Ward, Dal, 18
Ward, Greg, 103
Ware, Billy, 74
Warmack, Bob, 79
Warner, Gov. Mark, 354
Warner, Kirk, 204
Warren, Gerald, 73-76, 78, 80
Warrick, Peter, xix, 286-287, 291-292, 298-301, 303, 305-311, 313-315
Washington Redskins, 41, 144
Washington and Lee College (W&L), 3
Washington State University (WSU), 16
Washington, Gene, 112
Washington, Leon, 338-339
Waters, Charlie, 81
Watkins, Kerry, 308
Watters, Ricky, 219
Watts, Bennett, 25
Watts, J. C., 160
Weaver, Bill, 6
Weaver, James, 64-65
Webster, Jim, 102
Weiner, Art, 51

Weinke, Chris, xii, xix, 291, 297-302, 307-311, 313-320, 322-323
Welch, Nelson, 244-245
Wells, Joel, 13, 16-19
Welsh, George, 193, 208, 217, 224, 269, 276-277, 324, 351, 364
West, Jerry, 38
West, Tommy, 261, 361
West Virginia University (WVU), xv, 87, 106, 127-128, 153, 182, 188, 196, 225-226, 241-242, 288, 296, 326-327, 342-343
Western Athletic Conference, 93, 102
Western Carolina University (WCU), 178, 204
Wetherell, T. K., 349
Whaley, Mike, 327
Wheatley, Tyrone, 261
Whigham, Frank, 89
Whitaker, Roynell, 314
White Shoes Defense, 72-78, 123
White, Chuck, 128-129, 131
White, Daryl, 111
White, Dez, 305
White, Harvey, 25, 27-28, 31-35
White, Lorenzo, 199
White, Randy, xix, 112, 117-118, 120, 192
White, Reggie, 186
White, Russell, 248
White, Walter, 112
Whitley, Jack, 78, 80-81
Whittington, David, 210
Wild in the Country, 41
Wilkinson, Bud, 7, 11, 15, 30, 38
Wilkinson, Jay, 38, 43-44, 47, 57
Willard, Ken, 51-52, 54-58, 61, 64
Williams, Bennett, 59
Williams, Billy Dee, 60
Williams, Brian, 320, 330
Williams, Charlie, 124
Williams, Chris, 212
Williams, Curtis, 328
Williams, Dayne, 210

Williams, Ed, 87
Williams, Jafar, 328
Williams, Pooh Bear, 286-287
Williams, Ray, 202
Williams, Rhodney, 256
Williams, Rodney, 199-200, 202, 204-211, 213-214
Williams, Roy, 351
Williams, Steven, 227
Williams, Terrence, 326
Williams-Brice Stadium (Columbia, S.C.), 15, 23, 46, 85, 114, 170
Wilmsmeyer, Klaus, 222
Wilson, Barry, 361
Wilson, Eric, 182-183, 187
Wilson, Jack, 38, 42, 44
Wilson, Red, 361
Wilson, Reinard, 271, 281-284, 290-291
Wilson, Tim, 124-125, 129
Wofford College, 13, 164
Woodall, Dick, 73
Woodson, Shawn, 259
Woolford, Donnell, 204-205, 209-210,
World War II, 37
Wright, Dean, 39, 45
Wright, Jeff, 230-231
Wright, Johnnie, 170
Wuerffel, Danny, 260, 267-268, 270-271, 278-279, 286-287, 289-290
Wyland, Bill, 66
Wysocki, Charlie, 135-136, 154, 158, 169

Yauger, Ray, 81, 86
Yeoman, Bill, 87, 132
Yoest, Bill, 110
Yohe, Jack, 22
Young, Charley, 110, 114, 116
Young, Chris, 341
Young, Lance, 336
Yount, Gary, 78

Zeier, Eric, 245
Zeigler, Fred, 79, 83, 86

Zeigler, Mike, 10   Zolak, Scott, 231
Zellars, Ray, 258

K. Ada fifty years of Atlantic *order Wars*
represen   University
of North   WITHDRAWN   a freelance
writer a   ans include
writing **10–04**   **ML** d investing
in real es......